Discovering AutoCAD Release 13 for Windows®

MARK DIX and PAUL RILEY

CAD Support Associates

Prentice Hall
Upper Saddle River, New Jersey 07458

Library of Congress Cataloging-in-Publication Data

Dix, Mark
    Discovering AutoCAD, release 13 for Windows / Mark Dix & Paul Riley.
      p.   cm.
    Includes bibliographical references and index.
    ISBN 0-13-739491-8
    1. Computer graphics.   2. AutoCAD for Windows.   I. Riley, Paul.
II. Title.
T385.D6323   1998
620'.0042'02855369--dc21   97-7749
                                                                  CIP

Editor-in-chief: *Marcia Horton*
Acquisitions editor: *Eric Svendsen*
Managing editor: *Bayani Mendoza De Leon*
Production editor: *Irwin Zucker*
Director of production and manufacturing: *David W. Riccardi*
Copy editor: *Cheryl Smith*
Cover director: *Jayne Conte*
Cover designer: *Bruce Kenselaar*
Manufacturing buyer: *Julia Meehan*
Editorial assistant: *Andrea Au*

© 1998 Prentice-Hall, Inc.
Simon & Schuster / A Viacom Company
Upper Saddle River, New Jersey 07458

All rights reserved. No part of this book may be
reproduced, in any form or by any means,
without permission in writing from the publisher.

The author and publisher of this book have used their best efforts in preparing this book. These efforts include the development, research, and testing of the theories and programs to determine their effectiveness. The author and publisher make no warranty of any kind, expressed or implied, with regard to these programs or the documentation contained in this book. The author and publisher shall not be liable in any event for incidental or consequential damages in connection with, or arising out of, the furnishing, performance, or use of these programs.

Printed in the United States of America

10 9 8 7 6 5 4 3 2 1

ISBN 0-13-739491-8

Prentice-Hall International (UK) Limited, *London*
Prentice-Hall of Australia Pty. Limited, *Sydney*
Prentice-Hall Canada Inc., *Toronto*
Prentice-Hall Hispanoamericana, S.A., *Mexico*
Prentice-Hall of India Private Limited, *New Delhi*
Prentice-Hall of Japan, *Tokyo*
Simon & Schuster Asia Pte. Ltd., *Singapore*
Editora Prentice-Hall do Brasil, Ltda., *Rio de Janeiro*

AutoCAD, AutoLISP, and 3D Studio are registered trademarks of Autodesk, Inc. dBase III is a registered trademark of Ashton-Tate. DMP-61, DMP-29, and Houston Instrument are trademarks of Amtek, Inc. IBM is a registered trademark of International Business Machines Corporation. LaserJet II is a trademark of Hewlett-Packard. LOTUS 1-2-3 is a trademark of Lotus Development Corporation. MultiSync is a registered trademark of NEC Information Systems, Inc. MS-DOS and Windows are trademarks of Microsoft Corporation. Summagraphics is a registered trademark of Summagraphics Corporation. Zenith is a trademark of Zenith Data Systems, Inc.

The AutoCAD Primary Screen Menu Hierarchy and Pull Down Menus are reprinted with the permission of Autodesk, Inc. The AutoCAD Table Menu, Screen menu, and Pull-Down Menu are reprinted for the AutoCAD Reference Manual with permission from Autodesk, Inc.

Drawing credits: Hearth Drawing courtesy of Thomas Casey: Double Bearing Assembly compliments of David Sumner, King Philip Technical Drawing; Isometric Drawing Flanged Coupling courtesy of Richard F. Ross; Isometric Drawing of Garage courtesy of Thomas Casey.

For
Katelyn, Jesse,
Kathleen, and Michael

Contents

Preface   *xi*

Introduction to Release 13 for Windows®   *xiii*

Road Map   *xv*

PART I
Basic Two-Dimensional Entities   1

Chapter 1   1

Commands:	END, LINE, NEW, REDO, REDRAW, SAVE, SAVEAS, U, UCSICON 1
Task 1:	Beginning a New Drawing 2
Task 2:	Exploring the Drawing Editor 3
Task 3:	Drawing a LINE 10
Task 4:	Review 18
Task 5:	Drawing and REDRAWing a Square 18
Task 6:	Saving Your Drawings 19
Drawing 1–1:	GRATE 22
Drawing 1–2:	DESIGN 24
Drawing 1–3:	SHIM 26

Chapter 2   28

Commands:	CIRCLE, DDRMODES, DIST, ERASE, GRID, OOPS, SNAP, UNITS 28

Task 1:	Changing the Snap 29	
Task 2:	Changing the Grid 31	
Task 3:	Changing Units 32	
Task 4:	Drawing Circles Giving Center Point and Radius 34	
Task 5:	Drawing Circles Giving Center Point and Diameter 34	
Task 6:	Using the ERASE Command 37	
Task 7:	Using the DIST Command 44	
Task 8:	Printing or Plotting a Drawing 45	
Drawing 2–1:	APERTURE WHEEL 48	
Drawing 2–2:	ROLLER 50	
Drawing 2–3:	FAN BEZEL 52	
Drawing 2–4:	SWITCH PLATE 54	

Chapter 3   56

Commands:	CHAMFER, DDLMODES, FILLET, LAYER, LTSCALE, PAN, REGEN, VPORTS, ZOOM 56
Task 1:	Creating New Layers 57
Task 2:	Assigning Colors to Layers 59
Task 3:	Assigning Linetypes 60
Task 4:	Changing the Current Layer 62
Task 5:	The Screen Menu 64
Task 6:	Editing Corners Using FILLET 65
Task 7:	Editing Corners with CHAMFER 68
Task 8:	ZOOMing Window, Previous, and All 70
Task 9:	Moving the Display Area with PAN 72
Task 10:	Creating Multiple Viewports in 2D (Optional) 74
Task 11:	Using Plot Preview 77
Drawing 3–1:	MOUNTING PLATE 80
Drawing 3–2:	STEPPED SHAFT 82
Drawing 3–3:	BASE PLATE 84
Drawing 3–4:	BUSHING 86
Drawing 3–5:	HALF BLOCK 88

Chapter 4   90

Commands:	ARRAY (rectangular), COPY, LIMITS, MOVE, Prototype drawings 90
Task 1:	Setting LIMITS 91
Task 2:	Creating a Prototype 93
Task 3:	Selecting a Prototype Drawing 94
Task 4:	Using the MOVE Command 95
Task 5:	Using the COPY Command 99
Task 6:	Using the ARRAY Command—Rectangular Arrays 102
Task 7:	Changing Plot Configuration Parameters 105
Drawing 4–1:	PATTERN 110
Drawing 4–2:	GRILL 112
Drawing 4–3:	WEAVE 114
Drawing 4–4:	TEST BRACKET 116
Drawing 4–5:	FLOOR FRAMING 118

Contents vii

Chapter 5   120

Commands:	ARC, ARRAY (polar), MIRROR, ROTATE	120
Task 1:	Creating Polar Arrays	121
Task 2:	Drawing Arcs	124
Task 3:	Using the ROTATE Command	129
Task 4:	Creating Mirror Images of Objects on the Screen	132
Task 5:	Changing Paper Size, Orientation, Plot Scale, Rotation, and Origin	136
Drawing 5–1:	FLANGED BUSHING	140
Drawing 5–2:	GUIDE	142
Drawing 5–3:	DIALS	144
Drawing 5–4:	ALIGNMENT WHEEL	146
Drawing 5–5:	HEARTH	148

Chapter 6   150

Commands:	BREAK, EXTEND, OSNAP, STRETCH, TRIM	150
Task 1:	Selecting Points with Object Snap (Single-Point Override)	151
Task 2:	Selecting Points with OSNAP (Running Mode)	154
Task 3:	BREAKing Previously Drawn Objects	157
Task 4:	Using the TRIM Command	161
Task 5:	Using the EXTEND Command	163
Task 6:	Using the STRETCH Command	165
Task 7:	Plotting from Multiple Viewports in Paper Space	168
Drawing 6–1:	BIKE TIRE	176
Drawing 6–2:	ARCHIMEDES SPIRAL	178
Drawing 6–3:	SPIRAL DESIGNS	180
Drawing 6–4:	GROOVED HUB	182
Drawing 6–5:	CAP IRON	184
Drawing 6–6:	DECK FRAMING	186

PART II
Text, Dimensions, and Other Complex Entities   188

Chapter 7   188

Commands:	CHANGE, CHPROP, DDCHPROP, DDEDIT, DDEMODES, DDMODIFY, DTEXT, MTEXT, SCALE, SPELL, STYLE, TEXT	188
Task 1:	Entering Left-Justified Text Using DTEXT	189
Task 2:	Using Other Text Justification Options	192
Task 3:	Entering Text on an Angle and Text Using Character Codes	196
Task 4:	Entering Paragraph Text Using MTEXT	197
Task 5:	Editing Text with DDEDIT	199
Task 6:	Modifying Text with DDMODIFY	201
Task 7:	Using the SPELL command	205
Task 8:	Changing Fonts and styles	206
Task 9:	Changing Previously Drawn Text with CHANGE	211

Task 10:	Using Change Points with Other Entities 213	
Task 11:	SCALEing Previously Drawn Entities 214	
Drawing 7–1:	TITLE BLOCK 218	
Drawing 7–2:	GAUGES 220	
Drawing 7–3:	STAMPING 222	
Drawing 7–4:	CONTROL PANEL 224	

Chapter 8   226

Commands:	BHATCH, BPOLY, DDIM, DIMALIGNED, DIMANGULAR, DIMBASELINE, DIMCONTINUE, DIMEDIT, DIMLINEAR, DIMOVERRIDE, DIMSTYLE, DIMTEDIT, LEADER 226
Task 1:	Creating and Saving a Dimension Style 227
Task 2:	Drawing Linear Dimensions 230
Task 3:	Drawing Multiple Linear Dimensions—Baseline and Continue 234
Task 4:	Drawing Angular Dimensions 236
Task 5:	Dimensioning Arcs and Circles 239
Task 6:	Dimensioning with Leaders 243
Task 7:	Draw Ordinate Dimensions 245
Task 8:	Changing and Overriding Dimension Variables 247
Task 9:	Changing Dimension Text with DIMEDIT 251
Task 10:	Using the BHATCH Command 252
Task 11:	Scaling Dimensions Between Paper Space and Model Space 257
Drawing 8–1:	TOOL BLOCK 264
Drawing 8–2:	FLANGED WHEEL 266
Drawing 8–3:	SHOWER HEAD 268
Drawing 8–4:	NOSE ADAPTOR 270
Drawing 8–5:	PLOT PLAN 272
Drawing 8–6:	PANEL 274

Chapter 9   276

Commands:	DONUT, FILL, MLEDIT, MLINE, MSTYLE, MSLIDE, FFSET, PEDIT, PLINE, POINT, POLYGON, SKETCH, SOLID, VSLIDE 276
Task 1:	Drawing POLYGONs 277
Task 2:	Drawing "DONUTs" 279
Task 3:	Using the FILL Command 280
Task 4:	Drawing Straight Polyline Segments 281
Task 5:	Drawing Polyline Arc Segments 284
Task 6:	Editing Polylines with PEDIT 286
Task 7:	Creating Parallel Objects with OFFSET 287
Task 8:	Drawing "SOLIDs" 289
Task 9:	Making and Viewing Slides 291
Task 10:	Drawing and Editing Multilines 292
Task 11:	Drawing "POINTs" (Optional) 299
Task 12:	Using the SKETCH Command (Optional) 300
Drawing 9–1:	BACKGAMMON BOARD 302
Drawing 9–2:	DART BOARD 304
Drawing 9–3:	PRINTED CIRCUIT BOARD 306
Drawing 9–4:	CARBIDE TIP SAW BLADE 308
Drawing 9–5:	GAZEBO 310

Contents ix

Chapter 10 — 312

Commands:	ATTDEF, ATTDISP, ATTEDIT, ATTEXT, BLOCK, COPYCLIP, DDATTE, DDATTDEF, GROUP, INSERT, WBLOCK, XBIND, XREF 312
Task 1:	Creating GROUPs 313
Task 2:	Creating BLOCKs 315
Task 3:	INSERTing Previously Defined Blocks 317
Task 4:	Using the Windows Clipboard 321
Task 5:	Defining Attributes with DDATTDEF 323
Task 6:	Editing Attributes with DDATTE and ATTEDIT 326
Task 7:	EXPLODEing Blocks 331
Drawing 10–1:	CAD ROOM 334
Drawing 10–2:	BASE ASSEMBLY 336
Drawing 10–3:	DOUBLE BEARING ASSEMBLY 338
Drawing 10–4:	SCOOTER ASSEMBLY 338

Chapter 11 — 342

Commands:	ELLIPSE, ISOPLANE, SNAP (isometric), VIEW, ZOOM (dynamic) 342
Task 1:	Using Isometric SNAP 343
Task 2:	Switching Isometric Planes 344
Task 3:	Using COPY and Other Edit Commands 345
Task 4:	Drawing Isometric Circles with ELLIPSE 348
Task 5:	Drawing Ellipses in Orthographic Views 350
Task 6:	Saving and Restoring Displays with VIEW 353
Task 7:	Using Dynamic ZOOM 355
Drawing 11–1:	MOUNTING BRACKET 358
Drawing 11–2:	RADIO 360
Drawing 11–3:	FIXTURE ASSEMBLY 362
Drawing 11–4:	FLANGED COUPLING 364
Drawing 11–5:	GARAGE FRAMING 366

PART III
Three-Dimensional Modeling 368

Chapter 12 — 368

Commands:	DDVPOINT, RULESURF, UCS, UCSICON, VPOINT 368
Task 1:	Creating and Viewing a 3D Wireframe Box 369
Task 2:	Defining and Saving User Coordinate Systems 375
Task 3:	Using Draw and Edit Commands in a UCS 379
Task 4:	Working on an Angled Surface 383
Task 5:	Using RULESURF to Create 3D Fillets 385
Task 6:	Other Methods of Using the VPOINT Command (Optional) 388
Drawing 12–1:	CLAMP 392
Drawing 12–2:	GUIDE BLOCK 394
Drawing 12–3:	SLIDE MOUNT 396
Drawing 12–4:	STAIR LAYOUT 398

Chapter 13   400

Commands:	3DFACE, 3DMESH, DVIEW, EDGESURF, HIDE, MVSETUP, REDRAWALL, REGENALL, REVSURF, RULESURF, TABSURF, VPORTS 400
Task 1:	Using Multiple Tiled Viewports 401
Task 2:	Creating Surfaces with 3DFACE 403
Task 3:	Removing Hidden Lines with HIDE 406
Task 4:	Using 3D Polygon Mesh Commands 407
Task 5:	Creating Surface Models Using the "3D Objects" AutoLISP Routines 415
Task 6:	Creating Approximated Surfaces Using PEDIT (Optional) 418
Task 7:	Using the MVSETUP Program 424
Task 8:	Creating Perspective and Clipped 3D Views with DVIEW 428
Drawing 13–1:	REVSURF DESIGNS 436
Drawing 13–2:	PICNIC TABLE 438
Drawing 13–3:	GLOBE 440
Drawing 13–4:	NOZZLE 442

Chapter 14   444

Commands:	BOX, CYLINDER, EXTRUDE, INTERSECT, LIGHT, MATLIB, RENDER, REVOLVE, RMAT, SCENE, SECTION, SHADE, SLICE, SPHERE, SUBTRACT, UNION, WEDGE 444
Task 1:	Creating Solid BOXes and WEDGEs 445
Task 2:	Creating the UNION of Two Solids 448
Task 3:	Working Above the XY Plane Using Elevation 450
Task 4:	Creating Composite Solids with SUBTRACT 451
Task 5:	Creating Chamfers and Fillets on Solid Objects 455
Task 6:	Creating Solid Objects With EXTRUDE 459
Task 7:	Creating 2D Region Entities 461
Task 8:	Creating Solids by Revolving 2D Entities Using REVOLVE 462
Task 9:	Creating Solid Cutaway Views with SLICE 464
Task 10:	Creating Sections with SECTION 465
Task 11:	SHADEing Solid models 466
Task 12:	RENDERing Solid Models 468
Drawing 14–1:	BUSHING MOUNT 481
Drawing 14–2:	LINK MOUNT 483
Drawing 14–3:	3D ASSEMBLY 484
Drawing 14–4:	TAPERED BUSHING 485
Drawing 14–5:	PIVOT MOUNT 486

Appendices

A	Drawing Projects 487
B	Menus and Macros 505
C	Additional AutoCAD Commands 511

Index   515

Preface

Drawing on a CAD system is a skill that can be learned only through many hours of practice. Like driving a car or playing a musical instrument, it cannot be learned by reading about it or watching someone else do it.

Accordingly, this book takes a very active approach to teaching AutoCAD. It is designed as a teaching tool and a self-study guide and assumes that readers will have access to a CAD workstation. It is organized around drawing exercises or tasks that offer the reader a demonstration of the commands and techniques being taught at every point, with illustrations that show exactly what to expect on the computer screen when steps are correctly completed. While the focus is on the beginning AutoCAD user, we have found over the years that experienced CAD operators also look to our books for tips, suggestions, and clear explanations of AutoCAD commands and principles.

The AutoCAD world is full of books, many of which do little more than duplicate the function of the AutoCAD Command Reference. In this text we strive to present an optimal learning sequence. Topics are carefully grouped so that readers will progress logically through the AutoCAD command set. Explanations are straightforward and focus on what is relevant to actual drawing procedures. Most important, drawing exercises are included at the end of every chapter so that newly learned techniques are applied to practical drawing situations immediately. The level of difficulty increases steadily as skills are acquired through experience and practice.

All figures and working drawings have been prepared using AutoCAD. Drawing exercises at the end of all chapters are reproduced in a large, clearly dimensioned format on each right-hand page with accompanying tips and suggestions on the left-hand page. Drawing suggestions offer time-saving tips and explanations on how to use new techniques in actual applications. The book is not a drafting manual, yet the drawings include a wide range of applications. While the focus is on mechanical drawings, there are also architectural drawings in many chapters, and anyone completing all the drawings will be well equipped to move on to more advanced and specialized applications.

We would like to thank the many people who have helped us in the preparation of this book. To begin with, thanks to Eric Svendsen, our editor at Prentice Hall, for his encouragement and support, and to Irwin Zucker, for his work in production editing.

We are grateful to a number of people at Autodesk, Inc., for the use of software and support. Thanks to Houston Instruments for the use of plotters and to Summagraphics for the use of digitizers.

We are grateful to Mike Pillarella for technical advice and support; and to John Williams and John Warren at Mount Ida College, for their interest in this project and commitment to CAD education.

Thanks to Lauri O'Brien and Don Chapman at DTI Technologies for their expert advice and support. Finally thanks to Mike Major, Eric White, Tony Marzullo, Peter Golaszewski, Nate Pond, and Andy Eckard for classroom testing this manuscript.

Mark Dix and Paul Riley

Introduction to Release 13 for Windows

Release 13 offers major enhancements in the areas of text and dimensioning. In addition, solid modeling, which was previously available through the add-on AME program, is now fully integrated. Rendering is also fully integrated. The Windows version of Release 13 makes full use of toolbars and other features that will be familiar to Windows users.

Using This Book with Release 13 for DOS

With Release 13, AutoCAD has clearly moved toward greater similarity between DOS and Windows versions. The biggest difference is the importance of toolbars in the Windows version. In Windows and DOS you will find all of the same commands and dialogue boxes. The differences will be minor and you will quickly get the feel for where to find things. Once you know where to find commands, you will find that there is virtually no difference in basic drawing and editing procedures, so that everything learned in one version will translate quickly to the other.

Varieties of CAD

This book will take you through a broad range of essential AutoCAD drawing techniques. In Part I (Chapters 1–6) you will learn 2D drawing and editing procedures using lines, arcs, and circles, with multiple layers, linetypes, and colors. In Part II (Chapters 7–11) you will add text and dimensions to your drawings and work with blocks, polylines, and other complex 2D entities. Part III (Chapters 12–14) will lead you into the exciting world of 3D, including wireframe, surface, and solid modeling.

AutoCAD has become the industry standard software for computer-aided drafting and design. It is widely used for the preparation of all types of drawings that previously would have been created on a drafting board. Its "open architecture" allows companies and third-party developers to customize it for specific applications, so that productivity is further enhanced.

AutoCAD is a full 3D package capable of a tremendous range of both 2D and 3D applications. As you learn, it will be useful to begin to think in terms of a hierarchy of complexity in the use of CAD.

On the first level is 2D drafting. This is the world for which AutoCAD was originally developed. Two-dimensional drawings in AutoCAD can be stored, edited, and plotted to any scale or paper size. The windowing, layering, and multiple viewport capabilities of AutoCAD allow a single drawing to produce a variety of different plots, depending on the type of information required. Through the process of attribute extraction, 2D drawings also can be used in conjunction with database programs to produce numerical data for cost estimates and bills of materials (see Chapter 10). 2D drawing techniques are the subject of Chapters 1–11. However, everything you learn in the 2D chapters will be useful when you get to 3D, and nothing will need to be relearned.

The second level in this hierarchy is 3D wireframe modeling. This is the focus of Chapter 12. Wireframe models share with 2D drawings an emphasis on precise dimensioning, which can be used in communicating design specifications for manufacturing, as well as for cost estimates and bills of materials. There is no attempt in either 2D drafting or wireframe modeling to represent the physical qualities of the object being drawn. Rather, the emphasis is on a precise mathematical description of outlines, boundaries, and edges. A wireframe model may be viewed from any angle and can be used to produce 2D orthographic projections, which may be plotted simultaneously.

Surface modeling is the third level. A surface model not only shows the outline of objects; it also attempts to fill in between the lines. Surface models are explored in Chapter 13. One of the primary uses of surface modeling is to produce realistic shaded renderings that simulate the effect of light and shadow on real surfaces. AutoCAD Release 13 includes full rendering capabilities, which are introduced in Chapter 14.

Finally, solid modeling is the fourth level of CAD. Solid models can be constructed by combining and subtracting basic solid shapes. In some applications, the goal of solid modeling is to represent not only the shapes but also interior characteristics of solid objects. Solid modeling is used by engineering firms to perform finite element analysis (FEA). FEA allows designers and engineers to simulate and predict the behavior of 3D objects based on mathematical representations of their interior physical properties. In Chapter 14 we offer a substantial introduction to Release 13 solid modeling and rendering.

Road Map

You will notice that all the chapters in this book follow the same layout. We have included this road map to help you s find your way around. Following is a description of each of the major sections of the chapter format along with sample entries.

COMMANDS (sample)

HELP	**MODIFY**
HELP	ERASE
	MOVE
	ROTATE

The COMMANDS section lists the commands and topics that are introduced in the chapter. Headings are taken from the AutoCAD standard menu and may refer to pull down menu headings or toolbars. For example, you will see HELP under its own heading because there is a Help pull down menu. ERASE, MOVE, and ROTATE appear under Modify, referring to the Modify toolbar.

OVERVIEW

Each chapter begins with a brief overview, providing an idea of what you will be able to do with the new commands in that chapter.

TASKS (sample)

1. Read about introductory tasks.
2. Read about drawing projects.
3. Begin Chapter 1.

All the tasks that make up a chapter are listed at the beginning of the chapter. This tells you at a glance exactly what you will be required to do to complete the chapter.

Each chapter consists of two types of tasks. The body of the text includes fully illustrated, step-by-step exercises in which new commands and techniques are introduced. Then, at the end of the chapter, you will find drawing projects, which require the use of the new commands and techniques. By completing the exercises in the chapter you will learn the skills needed to complete the drawings at the end of the chapter.

Task 1: Introductory tasks

Procedure (sample)

1. Select "Help" from the pull down menu bar.
2. Select "Search for Help On..." from the Help menu.
3. Type a command name or use the scroll bar and pick from the list of commands for which help is available.
4. Click on "Go To".

A procedure list is placed at the beginning of many of the introductory exercises. It is intended as a reference and a quick overview of the command sequence you will be learning. The instructions in the list are general and are not sufficient to give the specific results that are required to complete the task. The procedure list is not the exercise itself, and we do not recommend that you try to learn the command by following the list. The actual instructions in the Discussion section are much more specific. All instructions that require an action on your part are preceded by an arrow ">".

Discussion. The Discussion section includes specific instructions along with explanations, illustrations, and feedback about what will happen on your computer screen when you carry out the instructions. Typically, there will be an instruction followed by AutoCAD's response and any information we feel is necessary or helpful.

The HELP command

The following sample instructions show how to use AutoCAD's HELP command. It is included here for reference and as an example and is not intended for actual execution at this time. The HELP feature is useful, however, and you are encouraged to consult it frequently as you progress through the book.

(sample instructions)

> Select "Help" from the pull down menu bar at the top of the drawing editor.

This will cause a menu to drop down below the word Help. You can also enter HELP from the Standard toolbar or the command line, but the results will be different from what is described here.

> Select "Search for Help On..." from the Help menu.

This will call up the AutoCAD Help Search dialogue box shown in Figure 1.

To move quickly through the list you can click in the edit box, type the name of a command, and press Enter. Alternatively, you can move the cursor arrow over the scroll bar arrow and scroll down until you find the item you are looking for. Then move the cursor over the item and press the pick button twice to highlight it and the "Go To" box. Let's try it.

> Type "line".

Notice that AutoCAD responds to each keystroke so that you may not have to type the whole word.

> Press Enter.

"LINE Command" will be shown as the selected topic in the lower box.

> Press Enter or click on Go To to call up information on the selected command or topic, in this case the LINE command.

This will call up information on the LINE command as shown in Figure 2.

> Click on File and then "Exit" to exit the HELP command.

(end of sample)

Notice that all instructions are highlighted with an arrow (>). This will make it easy for you to know exactly what you are expected to do. The comments that accompany instructions are important for your understanding of what is happening and will help you to avoid confusion.

Task 2: Drawing projects

There are three to six drawing projects at the end of each chapter. These are progressive, making use of previously learned commands as well as new ones. You will find the drawing itself on the right-hand page and drawing suggestions on the left-hand page.

Remember that any drawing may be executed in a number of ways. Our suggestions are not written in stone. Unlike the instructions in the introductory exercises, drawing instructions will not take you through the complete project.

Besides the suggestions themselves, there is information on the drawing page that may assist you. In earlier chapters, this includes a list of commands you will need to use, a list of function keys and their functions, and, of course, the dimensions of the drawing itself. Later on you will see only the drawing and its dimensions.

Task 3: Chapter 1

You are now ready to begin Chapter 1.

PART I
Basic Two-Dimensional Entities

CHAPTER 1

COMMANDS

DRAW	EDIT	FILE	OPTIONS	VIEW
LINE	REDO	END	UCSICON	REDRAW
U		NEW		
		SAVE		
		SAVEAS		

OVERVIEW

This chapter will introduce you to some of the tools you will use whenever you draw in AutoCAD. You will begin to find your way around the Release 13 for Windows menus and toolbars, and you will learn to control basic elements of the drawing editor. You will produce drawings involving straight lines and learn to undo your last command with the U command. Your drawings will be saved, if you wish, using the END, SAVE, QSAVE, or SAVEAS commands.

Look over the following tasks to get an idea of where we are going, and then begin Task 1.

TASKS

1. Begin a new drawing.
2. Explore the drawing editor.
3. Draw a line. Undo it, using the U command.
4. Review.

5. Draw a square. Use REDRAW to remove blips.
6. Save a drawing.
7. Do Drawing 1–1 ("Grate").
8. Do Drawing 1–2 ("Design").
9. Do Drawing 1–3 ("Shim").

Task 1: Beginning a New Drawing

Discussion. When you load Release 13 for Windows you will find yourself in the drawing editor, which is where you do most of your work with AutoCAD. You can begin drawing immediately and name your drawing file later, or you can open a new or previously saved file. In this task you will begin a new drawing and ensure that your drawing editor shows the "No Prototype" default settings we have used in preparing this chapter.

> From the Windows Program Manager, click on the AutoCAD Release 13 group.
> In the Release 13 group box, click on the AutoCAD Release 13 icon.
> Wait....

You will see the Release 13 for Windows drawing editor, as shown in *Figure 1-1*. If other people have been using the computer you are using, it is quite possible that your screen will show other toolbar arrangements than the one shown here. We will take care of this shortly. If you are using an earlier version of AutoCAD, the screen will certainly be different. But in all cases, when you see the "Command:" prompt at the bottom of the screen you are ready to continue.

At this point you could begin drawing. However, for our purposes it will be a good idea to use the NEW command to ensure that your drawing editor shows the same settings as are used in this chapter.

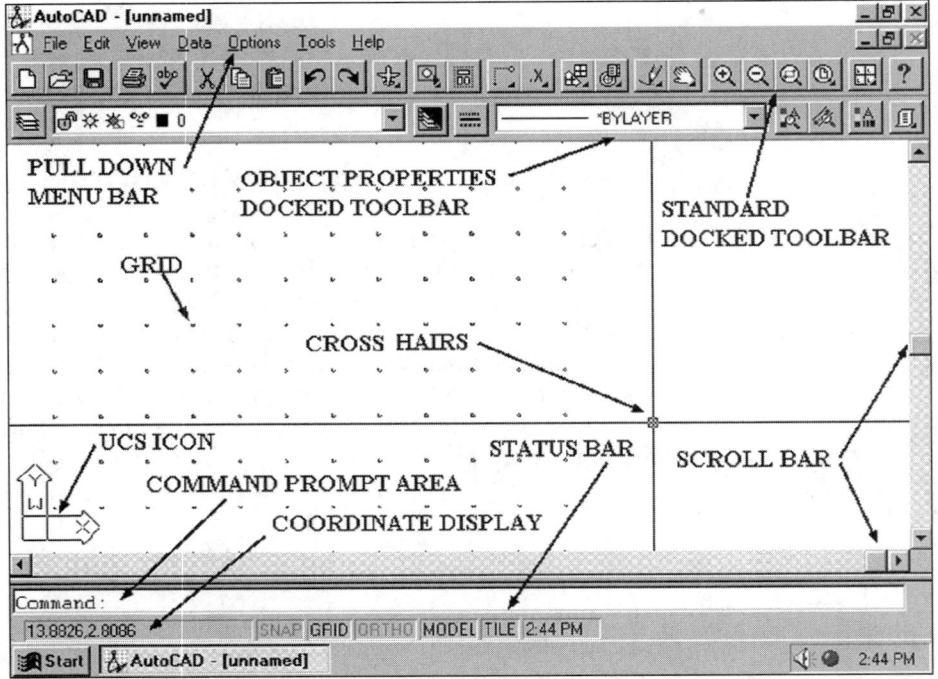

Figure 1-1

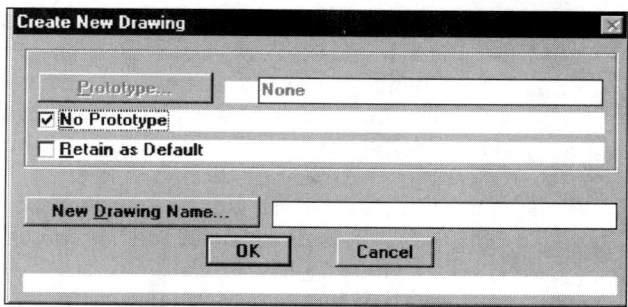

Figure 1-2

> Type "new" and press Enter.

A dialogue box will appear, as shown in *Figure 1-2*. Dialogue boxes are used extensively in Release 13 and are discussed throughout this book. For now, simply notice the flashing vertical line in the rectangle at the bottom right. This indicates that AutoCAD is ready to accept typed input.

You will also see your cursor arrow somewhere on the screen. If you do not see it, move your pointing device to the middle of your drawing area or digitizer. When you see the arrow, you are ready to proceed.

If the box labelled "No Prototype" has an ✓ in it, you can skip the next step. If it is blank, you will need to select it as follows:

> Move your pointing device until the arrow is in the box labelled "No Prototype" and press the pick button.

An ✓ will appear in the box and "No Prototype" will be surrounded by dotted lines, indicating that this option has been selected.

> Move the arrow down to "OK" and click there. Typing <enter> will also work.

The dialogue box will disappear and your screen should resemble *Figure 1-1* again. You are now ready to proceed to Task 2.

Task 2: Exploring the Drawing Editor

Discussion. You are looking at the AutoCAD drawing editor. There are many ways that you can alter it to suit a particular drawing application. To begin with, there are a number of features that can be turned on and off using your mouse or the function keys (F-keys) on your keyboard. Note that the six function keys and their functions are listed at the bottom of every drawing through Chapter 8 of this book, so it is not necessary to memorize them now. You will learn them best through repeated use. Also note that if you are using something other than an IBM-style keyboard, these important functions may be assigned to different keys. If you need more information, refer to the *AutoCAD Installation Guide for Windows*.

The Screen

At the top of the screen you will see the title bar, including the word "AutoCAD" followed by the name of the current drawing. Since your drawing is unnamed you will see "[UNNAMED]". This line also includes the standard windows close button on the left and the maximize and minimize buttons on the right. The close button will take you out of AutoCAD back to the program manager. The maximize and minimize buttons are used to switch between open applications and should be left alone while you are drawing in AutoCAD.

Below the title bar you will see the pull-down menu bar, including the titles for the File, Edit, View, Data, Options, Tools, and Help pull-down menus. Pull down menus are discussed later in this task.

The next line down is probably the standard toolbar. This toolbar is one of many toolbars that can be displayed on the Release 13 Windows screen. The use of toolbars will also be discussed later in this chapter and in Chapter 3.

Typically, there will be one more line before you reach the drawing area. This is the Object Properties toolbar, which displays the current layer and linetype. It also includes tools for changing other object properties. Layers and linetypes are discussed in Chapter 4. If you do not see this bar don't worry, we are about to turn it off anyway.

Below these toolbars is the drawing area. You may also have one or more floating toolbars in the drawing area. These will be discussed later.

Continuing down the screen, below the drawing area and along the right side of the screen you will see scroll bars. These work the same as the scroll bars in any other Windows application. Clicking on the arrows or clicking and dragging the square sliders will move your drawing to the left or right, up or down within the drawing area. You should have no immediate need for this function.

Beneath the scroll bar you will see the command prompt area. Typed commands are one of the basic ways of working in AutoCAD. The command line can be moved, resized, and reshaped like a toolbar. This is not recommended at this point.

At the bottom of the screen is the status bar, with the coordinate display on the left along with five mode indicators and the time display. The coordinate display and mode indicators are discussed shortly.

Switching Screens

> Press F2

What you see now is the AutoCAD text window. AutoCAD uses this text window to display text that will not fit in the command area. You can switch back and forth between text and graphics using F2, the flip screen key.

> Press F2 again.

This brings back the graphics screen. Any text that does not fit in the command area is not visible.

NOTE: Sometimes AutoCAD switches to the text screen automatically when there is not enough room in the command area for prompts or messages. If this happens, use F2 when you are ready to return to the graphics screen.

Cross Hairs and Pickbox

You should see two lines at right angles horizontally and vertically, intersecting somewhere in the display area of your screen. If there are no cross hairs on your screen, move your pointing device until they appear. These are the cross hairs, or screen cursor, that tell you where your pointing device (puck, mouse, cursor, stylus, whatever) is located on your digitizer or mouse pad.

At the intersection of the cross hairs you will also see a small box. This is called the "pickbox", used to select objects for editing. You will learn more about the pickbox later.

Move the pointer and see how the cross hairs move in coordination with your hand movements.

> Move the pointer so that the cross hairs move to the top of the screen.

When you leave the drawing area, your cross hairs will be left behind and you will see an arrow pointing up and to the left. The arrow will be used as in other Windows applications to select tools and to pull down menus from the menu bar. Pull-down menus are discussed at the beginning of Task 3.

NOTE: Here and throughout this book we show the Release 13 Windows 95 versions of AutoCAD screens in our illustrations. If you are working with another version, your screen may show significant variations.

> Move the cursor back into the drawing area and the selection arrow will disappear.

Toolbars and Pull-Down Menus

There are 50 toolbars available in the standard AutoCAD Release 13 for Windows package. Toolbars can be created and modified. They can be moved, resized, and reshaped. They are a convenience, but they can also make your work and your drawing area overly cluttered. For our purposes you will not need more than a few of the available toolbars.

Before going on we will simplify your screen and ensure uniformity by turning off all toolbars and then turning on only the Standard and Draw toolbars.

> Move the selection arrow up to the word "Tools" in the pull-down menu bar.
> Click the pick button (usually the button on the left) on your cursor.

This will open up the Tools menu as shown in *Figure 1-3*.

> Move the arrow down the menu to "Toolbars" and click.

The small black triangle to the right of "Toolbars" indicates that this selection calls a submenu. Clicking on it will open up the Toolbars submenu as shown in the figure. All of the toolbars you will need to use in this book are on this submenu and can be opened by selection.

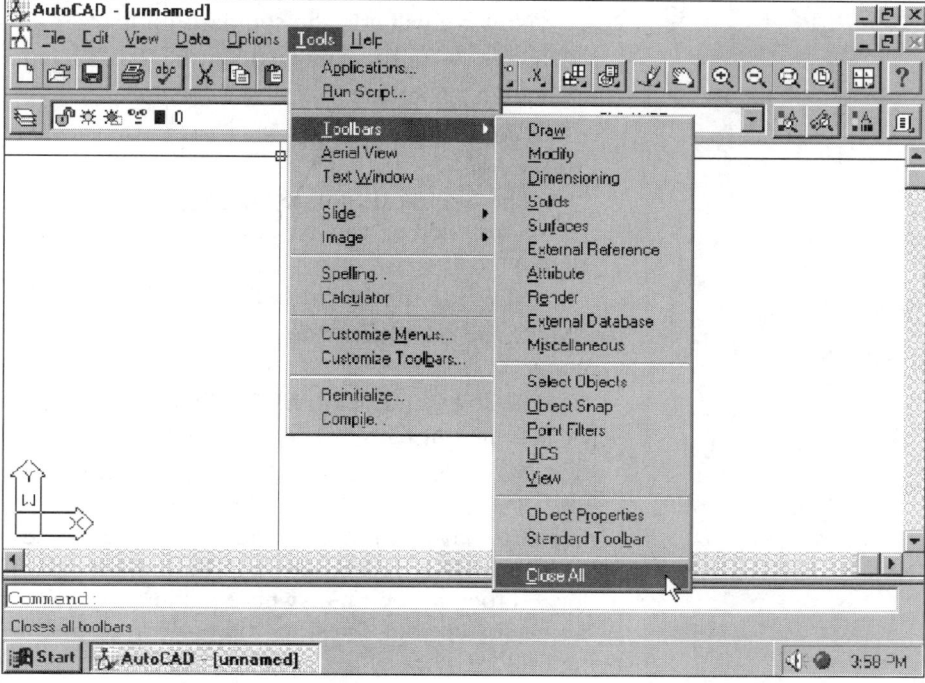

Figure 1-3

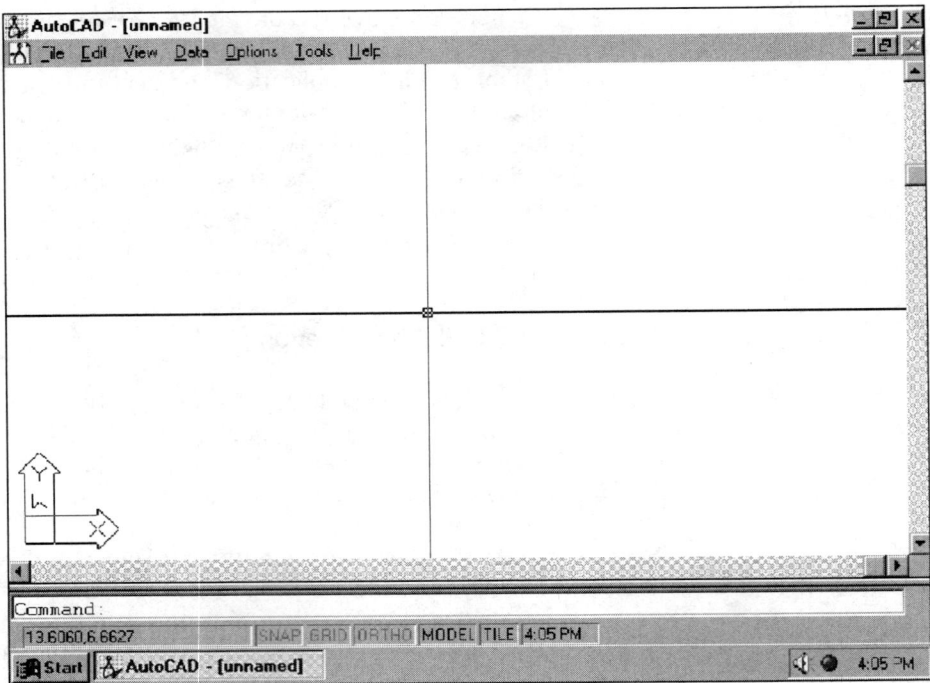

Figure 1-4

> Move the arrow all the way down the Toolbars submenu, and click on "Close All".

The menus will disappear, along with any toolbars, and your screen will resemble *Figure 1-4*. This is the basic Release 13 for Windows drawing screen in its simplest form, with no toolbars or screen menu.

Now we will add the standard toolbar.

> Click on "Tools" again to open the Tools menu.
> Click on "Toolbars".
> Click on "Standard Toolbar" near the bottom of the menu, just above "Close All".

The Standard toolbar will be added to your screen as shown in *Figure 1-5*. This toolbar can be left on in your drawing area, as you will use it frequently.

Now add the Draw toolbar.

> Move the select arrow to the menu bar again and open the Tools pull-down menu.
> Move down and open the Toolbars submenu.
> Click on "Draw".

The Draw toolbar will be added and your screen will resemble *Figure 1-6*. The Draw toolbar in the illustration is shown in a floating position, meaning that it is not attached to the side of the screen. Yours will probably appear in a docked position on the left side of the screen. To detach a docked toolbar, point anywhere in the gray area around the icons, hold down the cursor button, and drag the toolbar across the screen. To dock a floating toolbar, click in the gray area and drag it to any edge of the screen.

Chap. 1

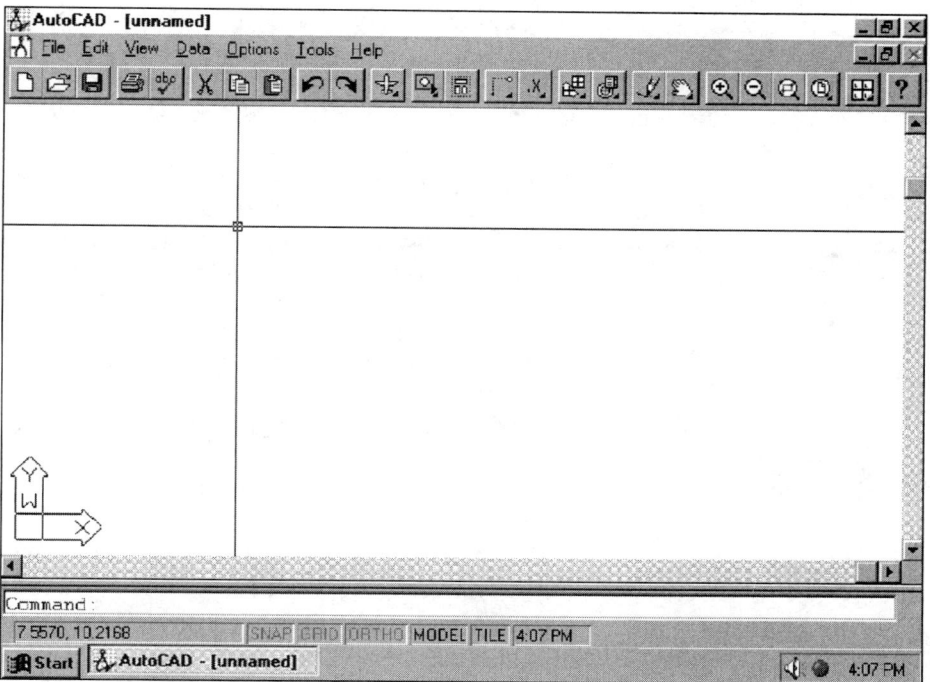

Figure 1-5

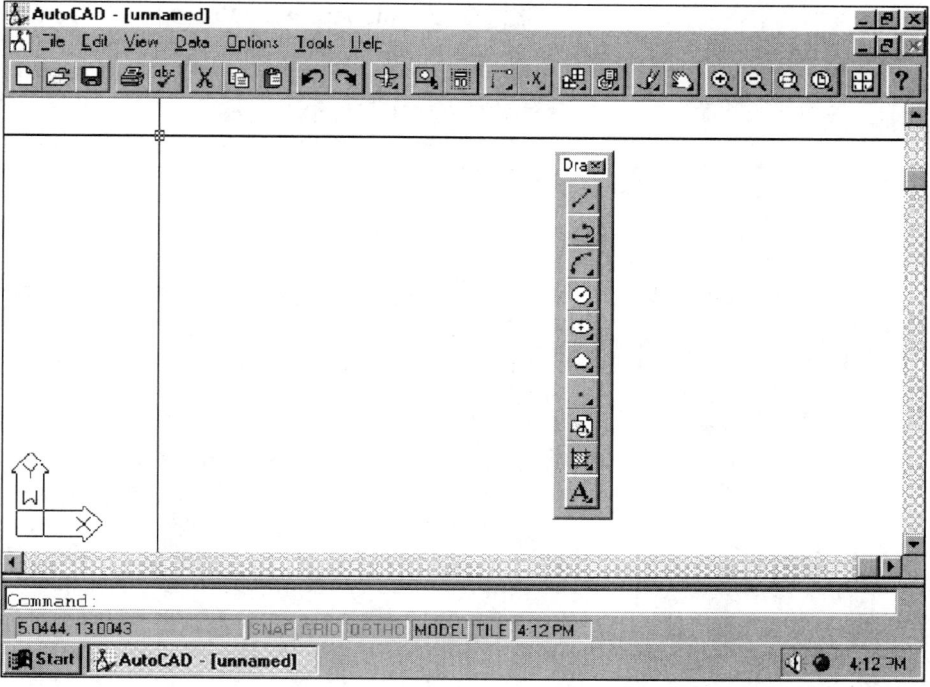

Figure 1-6

The Coordinate Display

The coordinate display at the bottom left of the status line keeps track of coordinates as you move the pointer. The coordinate display is controlled using the F6 key, or by double clicking on the coordinate display itself.

Move the cursor around slowly, and keep your eye on the pair of numbers at the bottom of the screen. They are probably moving very rapidly through four-place decimal numbers. When you stop moving, the numbers will be showing coordinates for the location of the pointer. These coordinates are standard ordered pairs in a coordinate system originating at (0,0) at the lower left corner. The first value is the x value, showing the horizontal position of the cross hairs, measuring left to right. The second value is y, or the vertical position of the cross hairs, measured from bottom to top. Points also have a z value, but it will always be 0 in two-dimensional drawing and can be ignored until you begin to draw in 3D (Chapter 12).

> Press F6 or double click with the arrow on the coordinate numbers to turn the coordinate display off.

The numbers will freeze and the display will turn gray.

> Move the cross hairs slowly.

Now when you move the cross hairs you will see that the coordinate display does not change. You will also see that it is grayed out, a standard Windows indication that this item is currently inactive or inaccessible.

> Press F6 or double click on the numbers again to turn the coordinate display on again.

The coordinate display actually has two different modes, but this will not be apparent until you enter a drawing command such as LINE (Task 3). For now, F6 or your mouse will simply turn the display on and off.

NOTE: The units AutoCAD uses for coordinates, for dimensions, and for measuring distances and angles can be changed at any time using the UNITS command (Chapter 2). For now, we will accept the AutoCAD default values, including the four-place decimals. In the next chapter we will be changing to two-place decimals. The F-keys are switches only; they cannot be used to change settings.

The Grid

> Press F7 or double click on the word "GRID" on the status bar to turn the grid on.

This will turn on the grid. When the grid is on, the word "GRID" will be black on the status bar.

The grid is simply a matrix of dots that helps you find your way around on the screen. It will not appear on your drawing when it is plotted, and it may be turned on and off at will. You may also change the spacing between dots, using the GRID command as we will be doing in Chapter 2.

The grid is presently set up to emulate the shape of an A-size (9 × 12) piece of paper. There are 10 grid points from bottom to top, numbered 0 to 9, and 13 points from left to right, numbered 0 to 12. The AutoCAD command that controls the outer size and shape of the grid is LIMITS, which will be discussed in Chapter 4. Until then we will continue to use the present format.

Also, you should be aware from the beginning that there is no need to scale AutoCAD drawings while you are working on them. That can be handled when you get ready to plot your drawing on paper. You will always draw at full scale, where one unit of length on the screen equals one unit of length in real space. This full-scale drawing space is called "model space". Notice the word "MODEL" on the status bar, indicating that you are in model space. The actual size of drawings printed out on paper will be handled through "paper space". When you are in paper space you will see the word "PAPER" on the status bar. For now, all your work will be done in model space, and you do not need to be concerned with paper space.

Snap

> Press F9, or double click on the word "SNAP" on the status bar.

The word should turn to black, indicating that snap mode is now on.

> Move the cursor slowly around the drawing area.

Notice how the cross hairs jump from point to point. If your grid is on, you will see that it is impossible to make the cross hairs touch a point that is not on the grid. Try it.

You will also see that the coordinate display shows only integer values and that the word SNAP is displayed in black on the status bar.

> Press F9 or double click on SNAP again.

Snap should now be off, and SNAP will be grayed out on the status bar again.

If you move the cursor in a circle now, you will see that the cross hairs move more smoothly, without jumping. You will also observe that the coordinate display moves rapidly through a series of four-place decimal values.

F9 turns snap on and off. With snap off you can, theoretically, touch every point on the screen. With snap on you can move only in predetermined increments. By default the snap is set to a value of 1.0000. In the next chapter you will learn how to change this setting using the SNAP command. For now we will leave it alone. A snap setting of 1 will be convenient for the drawings at the end of this chapter.

Using an appropriate snap increment is a tremendous timesaver. It allows for a degree of accuracy that is not possible otherwise. If all the dimensions in a drawing fall into one-inch increments, for example, there is no reason to deal with points that are not on a one-inch grid. You can find the points you want much more quickly and accurately if all those in between are temporarily eliminated. The snap setting will allow you to do that.

Ortho

F8 turns ortho mode on and off. You will not observe the ortho mode in action until you have entered the LINE command, however. We will try it out at the end of Task 3.

The User Coordinate System Icon

At the lower left of the screen you will see the User Coordinate System (UCS) icon (see *Figure 1-1*). These two arrows clearly indicate the directions of the x and y axes, which are currently aligned with the sides of your screen. In Chapter 12, when you begin to do 3D drawings, you will be defining your own coordinate systems that can be turned at any angle and originate at any point in space. At that time you will find that the icon is a very useful visual aid. However, it is hardly necessary in two-dimensional drawing and may be distracting. For this reason you may want to turn it off now and keep it turned off until you actually need it.

> Type "ucsicon".

Notice that the typed letters are displayed on the command line to the right of the colon.

> Press Enter.

AutoCAD will show the following prompt on the command line:

ON/OFF/All/Noorigin/ORigin <ON>:

As you explore AutoCAD commands, you will become familiar with many prompts like this one. It is simply a series of options separated by slashes (/). For now, we only need to know about "On" and "Off".

> Type "off" and press Enter.

The UCS icon will disappear from your screen. Any time you want to see it again, type "ucsicon" and then type "on". Alternatively, you can click on "Options" on the menu bar, then on "UCS" and then on "Icon". This will turn the icon on if it is off and off if it is on.

Task 3: Drawing a LINE

Procedure

(Remember, in this book procedure lists are provided at the beginning of some tasks as an overview and a reference only. *Do not try to complete the task using the procedure list alone.*)

1. Type "L" or select the Line tool from the Draw toolbar.
2. Pick a start point.
3. Pick an end point.
4. Pick another end point to continue in the LINE command, or press Enter to stop.

Discussion. You can communicate drawing instructions to AutoCAD by typing or by selecting items from a toolbar, a screen menu, a pull-down menu, or a tablet menu. Each method has its advantages and disadvantages depending on the situation. Often a combination of two or more methods is the most efficient way to carry out a complete command sequence. The instructions in this book are not always specific about which to use. All operators develop their own preferences. Consider the phrase "type or select" to include all five possibilities.

Each method is described briefly. You do not have to try them all out at this time. Read them over to get a feel for the possibilities, and then proceed to the LINE command. As a rule, we suggest learning the keyboard procedure first. It is the most basic, the most comprehensive, and changes the least from one release of AutoCAD to the next. But do not limit yourself by typing everything. As soon as you know the keyboard sequence, try out the other methods to see how they vary and how you can use them to save time. Ultimately, you will want to type as little as possible and use the differences between the menu systems to your advantage.

The Keyboard and the Command Line

The keyboard is the most primitive and fundamental method of interacting with AutoCAD. Toolbars, screen menus, pull-down menus, and tablet menus all function by automating basic command sequences as they would be typed on the keyboard. It is therefore useful to be familiar with the keyboard procedures even if the other methods are sometimes faster.

As you type commands and responses to prompts, the characters you are typing will appear on the command line after the colon. Remember that you must press Enter to complete your commands and responses. The command line can be

COMMAND ALIAS CHART	
LETTER + ENTER	= COMMAND
A ⏎	ARC
C ⏎	CIRCLE
E ⏎	ERASE
L ⏎	LINE
M ⏎	MOVE
P ⏎	PAN
R ⏎	REDRAW
Z ⏎	ZOOM

Figure 1-7

moved and reshaped, or you can switch to the text screen using F2 when you want to see more lines including previously typed entries.

It is very useful to know that some of the most often-used commands, such as LINE, ERASE, and CIRCLE, have "aliases." These one- or two-letter abbreviations are very handy. A few of the most commonly used aliases are shown in *Figure 1-7*.

Pull-Down Menus

All of the menu systems and the toolbars have the advantage that instead of typing a complete command, you can simply "point and shoot" to select an item. The pull-down menus contain commands primarily used in the management and arrangement of your drawing. You will use pull-down menus and submenus frequently, and it is good to become familiar with what is there and what is not there.

To use the pull-down menu, move the cross hairs up into the menu bar so that the selection arrow appears. Move the arrow to the menu heading you want. Select it with the pick button. A menu will appear. Run down the list of items to the one you want. Press the pick button again to select the item (see *Figure 1-8*). Items followed by a triangle have "cascading" submenus. Picking an item that is followed by an ellipsis (...) will call up a dialogue box.

Dialogue boxes (see Task 6) are familiar features in many Windows and Macintosh programs. They require a combination of pointing and typing that is fairly intuitive. We will discuss many dialogue boxes in detail as we go along.

Toolbars

Toolbars are comprised of buttons with icons that give one-click access to many of AutoCAD's commands. Seventeen of the most commonly used toolbars can be opened directly from the Tools pull-down menu in the same way that you opened the Standard toolbar. Thirty-three others are available through the Customize Toolbars dialogue box, which also can be found on the Tools pull-down menu.

Once opened, toolbars can "float" anywhere on the screen or can be "docked" along the edges of the drawing area. Toolbars can be a nuisance, since they cover portions of your drawing space. Do not use too many at once, and remember that you can use the scroll bars to move your drawing right, left, up, and down behind the toolbars.

The icons used on toolbars are also a mixed blessing. One picture may be worth a thousand words, but with all the pictures available, you may find that a few

Part I / Basic Two-Dimensional Entities

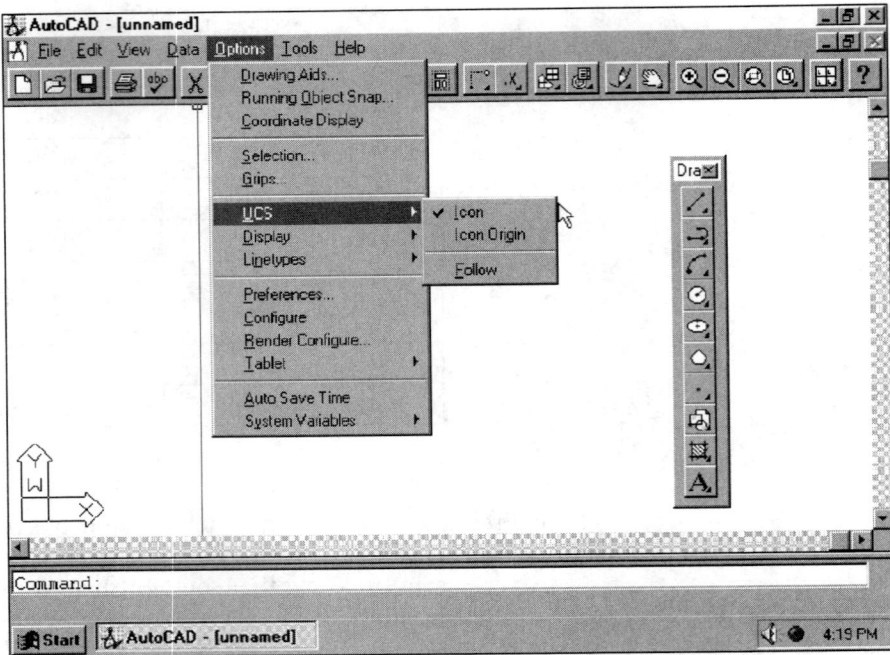

Figure 1-8

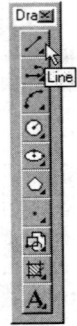

Figure 1-9

words can be very helpful as well. As in many other Windows applications, you can get a label for an icon simply by allowing the selection arrow to rest on the button for a moment without selecting it. These labels are called "Tooltips". Try this:

> Position the selection arrow on the top button of the Draw menu, as shown in *Figure 1-9*, but do not press the pick button.

You will see a yellow label that says "Line", as shown in the figure. This label identifies this button as the Line command button. Notice that the button also has a small black triangle at the bottom right. To float a docked toolbar, point within the gray border, press the pick button, and drag the toolbar across the screen. To dock a floating toolbar, drag it to any edge of the drawing area until it settles into a docked position. To close a toolbar, move it into a floating position and then click on the close button in the upper right corner. This indicates that a "flyout" is available, giving you access to other related commands or variations on the LINE command. If you press the pick button and hold it down, the flyout will appear. This flyout gives access to other variations of the LINE command.

NOTE: If you do not see the label, it is because "Tooltips" has been disabled in the Customize Toolbars dialogue box. Open the Tools menu and click on Customize Toolbars. In the Toolbars dialogue box, click in the box next to "Show Tooltips" and then Close the dialogue box.

The Screen Menu

There is an additional command selection option called the Screen Menu that appears at the right of the screen only when it is turned on in the Preferences dialogue box. We will not use it in this chapter.

Chap. 1

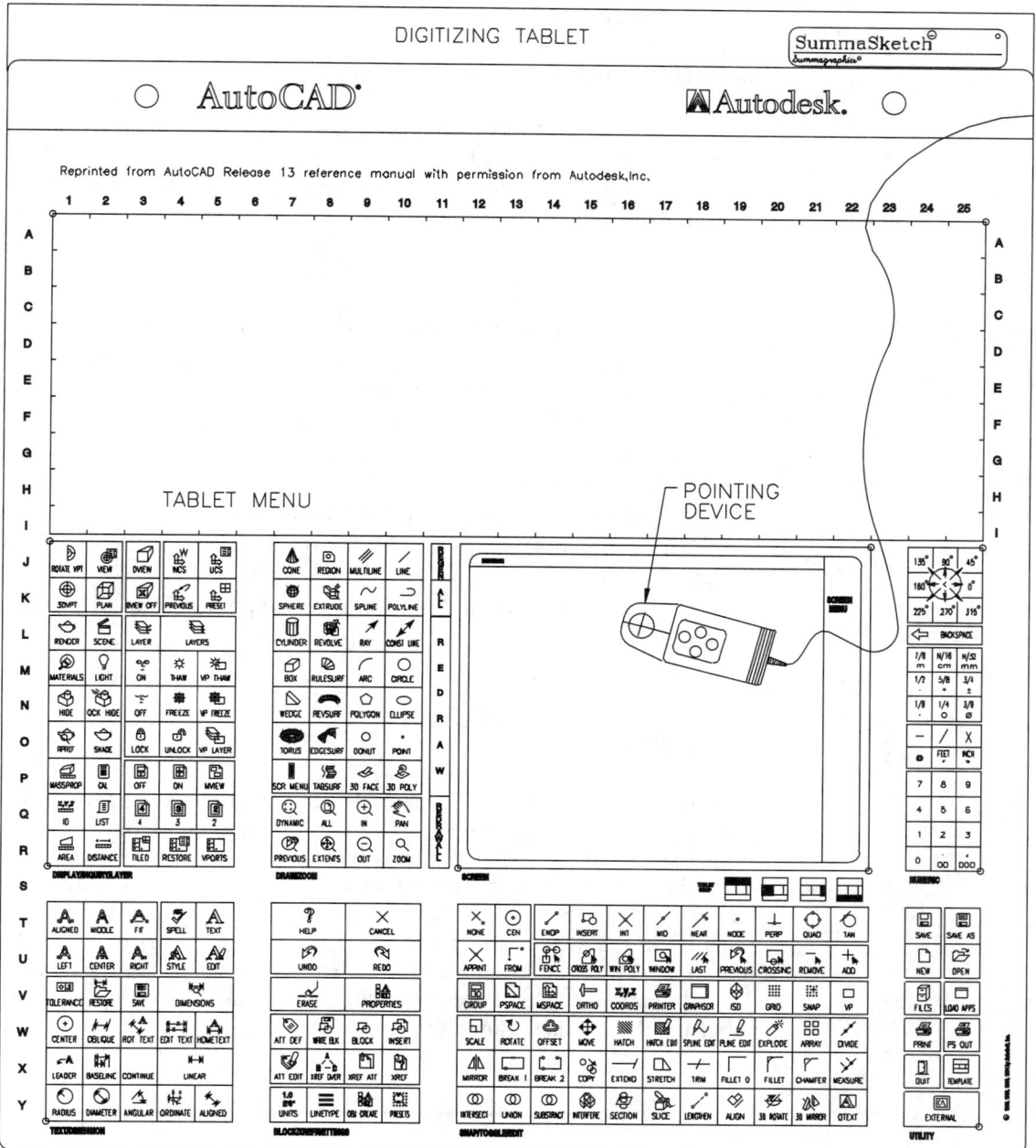

Figure 1-10

Tablet Menus

If you are using a digitizer with a tablet (as opposed to a mouse), you may have a tablet menu available. In some ways, locating a command on a tablet menu is the quickest method of all. With any good menu system there should be a large number of commands and subcommands available on the tablet, and you will not have to search through submenus or open toolbars and flyouts to find them. The major disadvantage of the tablet menu is that in order to use it you must take your eyes off the screen.

On a digitizing tablet, simply move the pointing device over the item you want and press the pick button (see *Figure 1-10*).

Now let's get started drawing.

The LINE command

> Type "L" or select the Line icon from the Draw toolbar (remember to press enter if you are typing).

Look at the command area. You should see this, regardless of how you enter the command:

From point:

This is AutoCAD's way of asking for a start point.

Also, notice that the pickbox disappears from the cross hairs when you have entered a drawing command.

Most of the time when you are drawing, you will want to point rather than type. In order to do this, you need to pay attention to the grid and the coordinate display.

> If snap is off, switch it on (F9 or double click on SNAP).
> Move the cursor until the display reads "1.0000,1.0000". Then press the pick button.

Now AutoCAD will ask for a second point. You should see this in the command area:

To point:

Rubber Band

Another thing to be aware of is the "rubber band" that extends from the start point to the cross hairs on the screen. If you move the cursor, you will see that this visual aid stretches, shrinks, or rotates like a tether, keeping you connected to the start point. You will also notice that when the rubber band and the cross hairs overlap (that is, when the rubber band is at 0, 90, 180, or 270 degrees), they both disappear in the area between the cross hairs and the start point, as illustrated in *Figure 1-11*. This may seem odd at first, but it is actually a great convenience. You will find many instances where you will need to know that the cross hairs and the rubber band are exactly lined up.

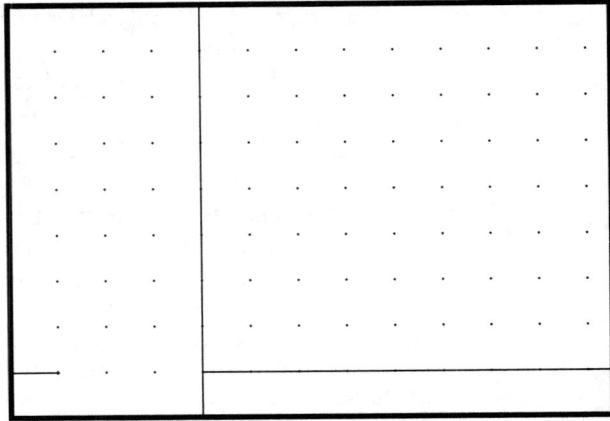

Figure 1-11

XY and Polar Coordinates

The other thing to watch is the coordinate display. If it is off (no change in coordinates when the cursor moves), press F6 to turn it on. Once it is on it will show either *xy* coordinates or polar coordinates. *xy* coordinates are the familiar ordered pairs discussed previously. They are lengths measured from the origin (0,0) of the coordinate system at the lower left corner of the grid. If your display shows two four-digit numbers, these are the *xy* coordinates.

If your display shows something such as "4.2426<45", it is set on polar coordinates.

> Press F6 and move your cursor.
Which type of coordinates is displayed?
> Press F6 and move your cursor again.
Observe the coordinate display.
You will see that there are three coordinate display modes: off (no change), *xy* (*x* and *y* values separated by a comma), and polar (length<angle).
> Press F6 once or twice until it shows polar coordinates.

Polar coordinates are in a length, angle format—4.0000<0 or 5.6569<45—and are given relative to the starting point of your line. The first number is the distance from the starting point of the line, and the second is an angle of rotation, with 0 degrees being straight out to the right and angles measured counterclockwise. In LINE, as well as most other draw commands, polar coordinates are very useful because they give you the length of the segment you are currently drawing.

> Press F6 to read *xy* coordinates.
> Pick the point (8.0000,8.0000).
Your screen should now resemble *Figure 1-12*. AutoCAD has drawn a line between (1,1) and (8,8) and is asking for another point.

To point:

This will allow you to stay in the LINE command to draw a whole series of connected lines if you wish. You can draw a single line from point to point, or a series of lines from point to point to point to point. In either case, you must tell AutoCAD when you are finished with a set of lines by pressing enter or the enter equivalent button on the cursor, or the space bar.

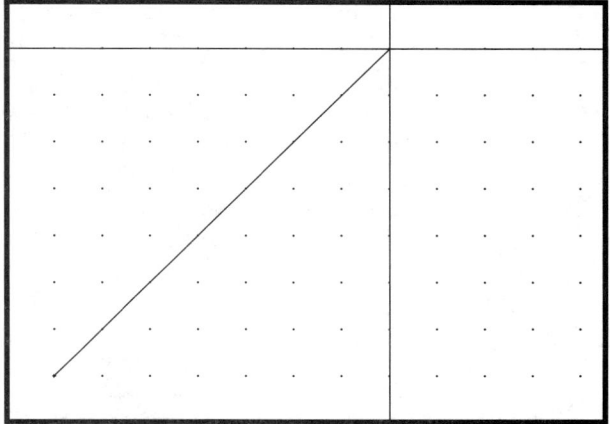

Figure 1-12

NOTE: When you are drawing a continuous series of lines, the polar coordinates on the display are given relative to the most recent point, not the original starting point.
> Press Enter or the space bar to end the LINE command.

You should be back to the "Command:" prompt again, and the pickbox will have reappeared at the intersection of the cross hairs.

Space Bar and Enter Key

In most cases AutoCAD allows you to use the space bar as a substitute for the enter or return key. This is a major convenience, since the space bar is easy to locate with one hand while the other hand is on the pointing device. For example, the LINE command can be entered without removing your right hand from your pointing device by typing the "L" on the keyboard and then hitting the space bar, both with the left hand. The major exception to the use of the space bar as an enter key is when you are entering text in the TEXT command (Chapter 7). Since a space may be part of a text string, the space bar must have its usual significance there.

NOTE: Hitting either the space bar or the Enter key at the command prompt will repeat the last command entered, another major convenience.

Relative Coordinates and "@"

AutoCAD also allows you to enter points using coordinates relative to the last point selected. To do this, use the "@" symbol. For example, after picking the point (1,1) in the last exercise you could have specified the point (8,8) by typing "@7,7", indicating the second point is over 7 and up 7 from the first point. Or, using polar coordinates relative to (1,1), you could type "@9.8995<45". All of these methods would give the same results.

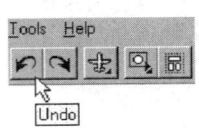

Figure 1-13

Undoing a Line Using U

> To undo the line you just drew, type "U" <Enter> or select the Undo tool from the Standard toolbar, as shown in *Figure 1-13*.
U undoes the last command, so if you have done anything else since drawing the line, you will need to type "U" <Enter> more than once. In this way you can step backwards through your drawing session, undoing your commands one by one.
> To bring the line back, type "REDO" <enter> or select the Redo tool, which is to the right of the Undo tool on the Standard toolbar.
NOTE: REDO only works immediately after U, and it only works once! That is, you can only REDO the last U and only if it was the last command executed.
NOTE: The Undo tool actually executes a command called U. AutoCAD also has a separate UNDO command, which can be entered at the command line. UNDO is more elaborate than U (see Appendix C). U is *not* an alias for UNDO. REDO can be used to reverse either U or UNDO.

Ortho

Before completing this section, we suggest that you try the ortho mode.

> Type "L" <enter> or select the Line tool from the Draw toolbar to enter the LINE command.

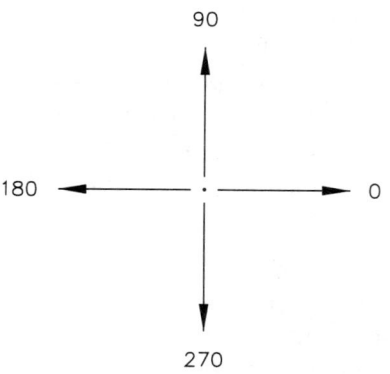

Figure 1-14

> Pick a starting point. Any point near the center of the screen will do.
> Press F8 or double click on the word "ORTHO" and move the cursor in slow circles.

Notice how the rubber band jumps between horizontal and vertical without sweeping through any of the angles between. Ortho forces the pointing device to pick up points only along the horizontal and vertical quadrant lines from a given starting point. With ortho on you can select points at 0, 90, 180, and 270 degrees of rotation from your starting point only (see *Figure 1-14*).

The advantages of ortho are similar to the advantages of snap mode, except that it limits angular rather than linear increments. It ensures that you will get precise and true right angles and perpendiculars easily when that is your intent. Ortho will become more important as drawings grow more complex. In this chapter it is hardly necessary, though it will be convenient in Drawings 1–1 and 1–3.

Escape

> While still in the LINE command, press the "Esc" (escape) key.

This will abort the LINE command and bring back the "Command:" prompt. Esc is used to cancel a command that has been entered.

Arrow Keys

There is one other way to control point selection. Using the arrow keys in lieu of the cursor can be useful when you are working with very small increments, when you want to move an exact number of snap points, or when you want to lock the cross hairs onto a point so that slight movements of the pointer will not affect point selection. An important limitation of the arrow keys is that you cannot use them to move diagonally.

> Press any of the arrow keys to initiate arrow key control of the cross hairs.
> Try moving the cross hairs up, down, left, and right with the appropriate arrow keys.

The arrow keys may be useful when you need a steadier motion than you can achieve with the cursor. One press will move the cross hairs one snap point if snap is on and one pixel (the smallest unit your monitor can display) if snap is off. Try it with snap on and off (press F9) to see what happens.

Holding down an arrow key will give you fast, continuous motion, much as it would on a word processor.

You can change the size of a single jump by using the page up and page down keys, but it is usually faster to use the pointing device in the usual manner to get the cursor near the point you want, then use the arrow keys close up.

When the cross hairs have reached the desired point, you can select that point by pressing Enter.

Object Selection Window

At some time during this chapter it is likely that you will accidentally or intentionally pick a point on the screen without entering a command. If you then drag the cursor away from the point you just picked, a box will appear and stretch as you move. At the same time, AutoCAD will be prompting you for the "Other corner:" of the box. But as soon as you pick it, the box will disappear. What is this? It's the object selection window, which allows you to select objects for editing. We will begin using it in Chapter 2. You can cancel the prompt for the other corner by pressing Esc.

Task 4: Review

Before going on to the drawings, quickly review the following items. If it all seems familiar, you should be ready for the next drawing task.

- F2 switches between text and graphics screens.
- F6 or double clicking on the coordinate display will turn coordinates on and off, and switch between polar and *xy* coordinates.
- F7 or double clicking on GRID turns the grid on and off.
- F8 or double clicking on ORTHO turns ortho on and off.
- F9 or double clicking on SNAP turns snap on and off.
- Commands may be entered by typing, or by selecting from a toolbar, a screen menu, a pull-down menu, or a tablet menu.
- Points may be selected by pointing or by typing coordinates.
- Once inside the LINE command, you can draw a single line or a whole series of connected lines.
- Press Enter or the space bar to end working in the LINE command.
- U will undo your most recent command.
- REDO will redo a U.
- Esc will cancel a command.
- The arrow keys may be used as an alternative way to control the cross hairs.

Task 5: Drawing and REDRAWing a Square

To practice what you have learned so far, reproduce, on your screen, the square shown in *Figure 1-15*. Then erase it using the U command as many times as necessary. The coordinates of the four corner points are (2,2), (7,2), (7,7), and (2,7).

CLOSEing a Set of Lines. AutoCAD provides a convenient Close option for drawing an enclosed figure using the LINE command. "Close" will connect the last in a continuous series of lines back to the starting point of the series. In drawing the square, for instance, you would simply type "C" <Enter> in lieu of drawing the last of the four lines. In order for this to work, the whole square must be drawn without leaving the LINE command.

REDRAW—Cleaning Up Your Act. You may have noticed that every time you select a point AutoCAD puts a "blip" on the screen in the form of a small cross.

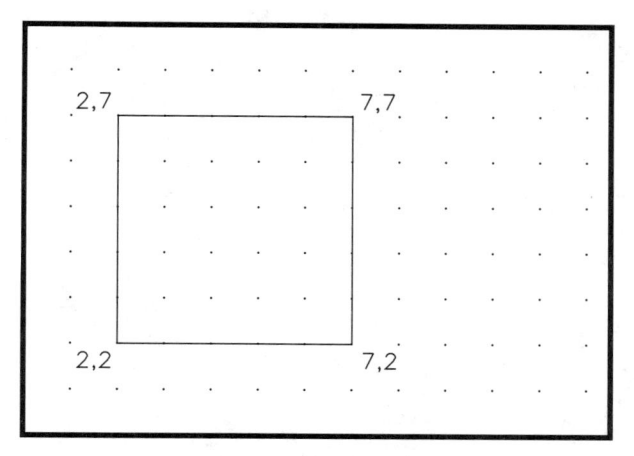

Figure 1-15

These are only temporary; they are not part of your drawing file database and will not appear on your drawing when it is plotted or printed. However, you will want to get rid of them from time to time to clean up the screen and avoid confusion.

> Type "r" <enter> or select the Redraw View tool from the Standard toolbar (as shown in *Figure 1-16*).

The display will be redrawn without the blips.

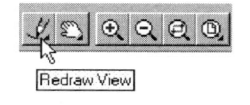

Figure 1-16

Task 6: Saving Your Drawings

Discussion. AutoCAD Release 13 for Windows has several commands that allow you to save drawings. Your choice of which to use will depend on whether you want to give the saved drawing a new name or keep it under the current drawing name. In all cases, a .dwg extension is added to file names to identify them as AutoCAD files. This is automatic when you name a file.

The SAVE Command

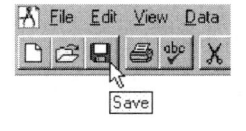

Figure 1-17

To save your drawing without leaving the editor, select "Save" from the File pull-down menu, or select the Save tool from the Standard toolbar, as shown in *Figure 1-17*.

If the current drawing is already named, Release 13 will save it without intervening dialogue. If the drawing is not named, the SAVEAS dialogue box will open automatically to allow you to name the drawing before it is saved. SAVEAS is described next.

The SAVEAS Command

To rename a drawing or name a previously unnamed drawing, type "Saveas", select "Saveas..." from the File pull-down menu, or, in an unnamed drawing, select the Save tool from the Standard Toolbar.

Any of these methods will call the Save Drawing As dialogue box (see *Figure 1-18*). The cursor will be blinking in the area labelled "Files:", waiting for you

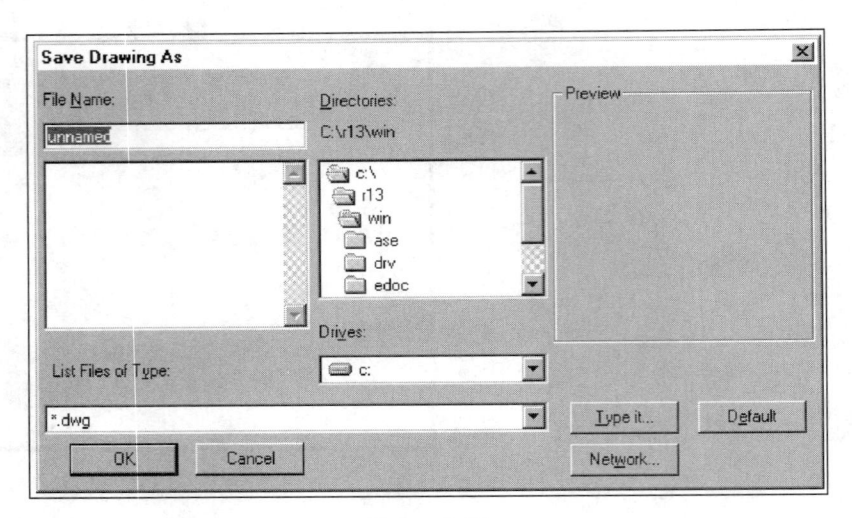

Figure 1-18

to enter a file name. Include a drive designation ("A:1-1") if you are saving your work on a floppy disk. AutoCAD will add the .dwg extension automatically. SAVEAS will also allow you to save different versions of the same drawing under different names while continuing to edit.

OPENing Saved Drawings

To open a previously saved drawing, type "open", select "Open" from the File pull-down menu, or select the Open tool from the Standard toolbar, as shown in *Figure 1-19*.

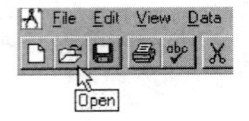

Figure 1-19

Once you have saved and closed a drawing, you will need to use the OPEN command to return to it. Entering the OPEN command by any method will bring up the Select File dialogue box shown in *Figure 1-20*. You can select a file directory in the box at the right and then a file from the box at the left. When you select a file, Release 13 will show a preview image of the selected drawing in the Preview image box at the right. This way you can make sure that you are opening the drawing you want.

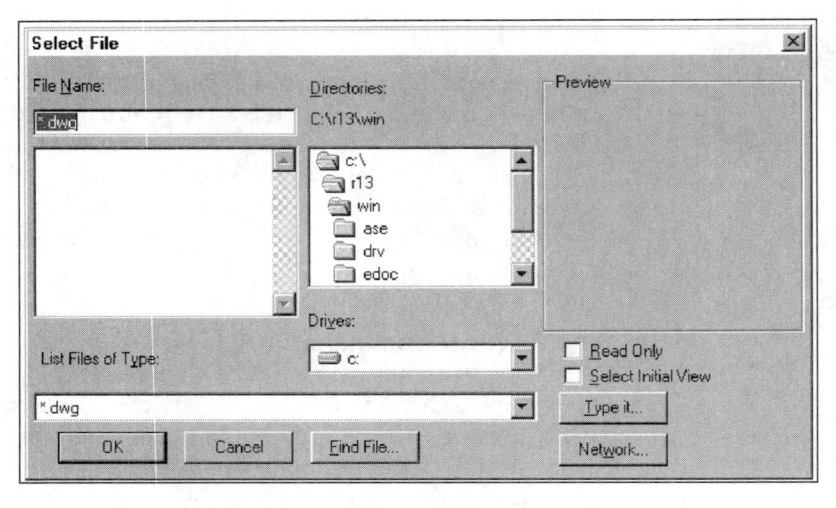

Figure 1-20

Exiting the Drawing Editor

To leave AutoCAD, open the File pull-down menu and select "Exit". If you have not saved your current drawing, AutoCAD will ask you if you wish to save your changes before exiting.

Tasks 7, 8, and 9: Three Simple Drawings

You are now ready to complete this chapter by creating Drawings 1–1, 1–2, and 1–3. If you wish to save your drawings, use SAVE or SAVEAS. Whenever you wish to start a new drawing, type "new" and enter a file name and the No Prototype option as we did at the beginning of the chapter. Remember to use a drive designation if you are saving your work on a floppy disk.

DRAWING 1-1: GRATE

Before beginning, look at the information below the drawing. Notice the F-key reminders and other information. The commands on the right are the new commands you will need to do this drawing. They are listed with aliases in parentheses.

The first two drawings in this chapter are given without dimensions. Instead, we have drawn them as you will see them on the screen, against the background of a one-unit grid. Remember that all of these drawings were done using a one-unit snap, and that all points will be found on one-unit increments.

DRAWING SUGGESTIONS

> If you are beginning a new drawing, select "New..." on the "File" menu, and then select "No Prototype" in the dialogue box.

> Remember to watch the coordinate display when searching for a point.

> Be sure that grid, snap, and the coordinate display are all turned on.

> Draw the outer rectangle first. It is 6 units wide and 7 units high, and its lower left-hand corner is at the point (3.0000,1.0000). The three smaller rectangles inside are 4 × 1.

If You Make a Mistake—U

The U command works nicely within the LINE command to undo the last line you drew, or the last two or three if you have drawn a series.

> Type "U" <enter>. The last line you drew will be gone or replaced by the rubber band awaiting a new end point. If you want to go back more than one line, type "U" <enter> again, as many times as you need.

> If you have already left the LINE command, U will still work, but instead of undoing the last line, it will undo the last continuous series of lines. In GRATE this could be the whole outside rectangle, for instance.

> Remember, if you have mistakenly undone something, you can get it back by typing "REDO" <enter>. You cannot perform other commands between U and REDO.

U is quick, easy to use, and efficient as long as you always spot your mistakes immediately after making them. Most of us, however, are more spontaneous in our blundering. We may make mistakes at any time and not notice them until the middle of next week. For us, AutoCAD provides more flexible editing tools, like ERASE, which is introduced in the next chapter.

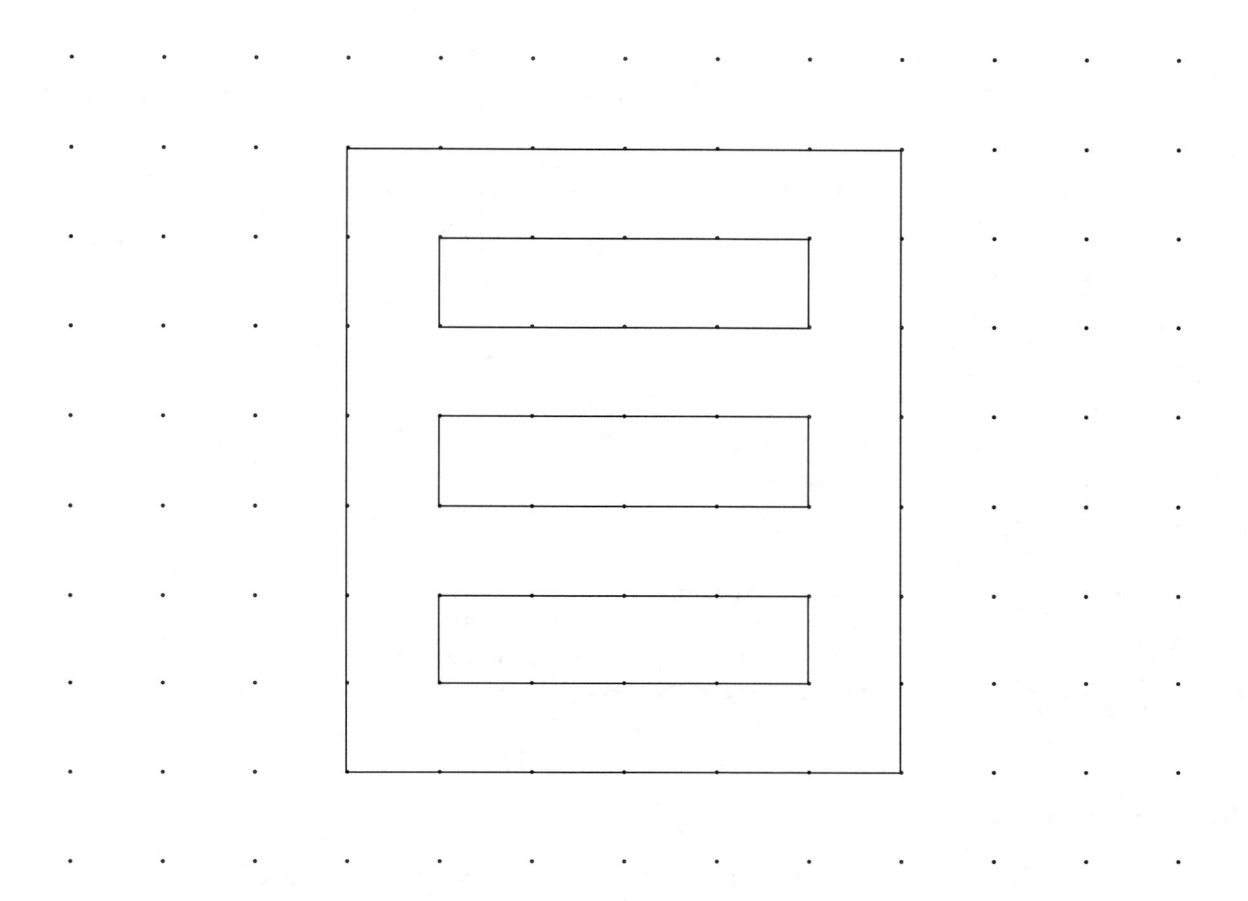

GRATE
Drawing 1-1

LAYER	0	LINE	(L)
UNITS	4-PLACE DECIMAL	U	
GRID	1.0000	REDO	
SNAP	1.0000	REDRAW	(R)

- F1 — HELP
- F2 — TEXT/GRAPHICS SCREEN
- F6 — ABSOLUTE/OFF/POLAR COORDS
- F7 — ON/OFF GRID
- F8 — ON/OFF ORTHO
- F9 — ON/OFF SNAP

DRAWING 1-2: DESIGN

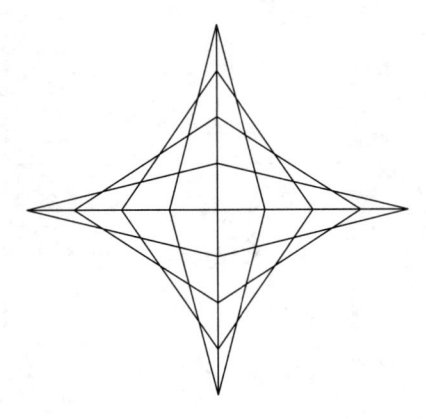

This design will give you further practice with the LINE command.

DRAWING SUGGESTIONS

> If you are beginning a new drawing, select "New..." on the "File" menu and then select "No Prototype" in the dialogue box.
> Draw the horizontal and vertical lines first. Each is eight units long.
> Notice how the rest of the lines work—outside point on horizontal to inside point on vertical, then working in, or vice-versa.

REPEATING A COMMAND

Remember, you can repeat a command by pressing Enter or the space bar at the Command: prompt. This will be useful in this drawing, since you have several sets of lines to draw.

Chap. 1

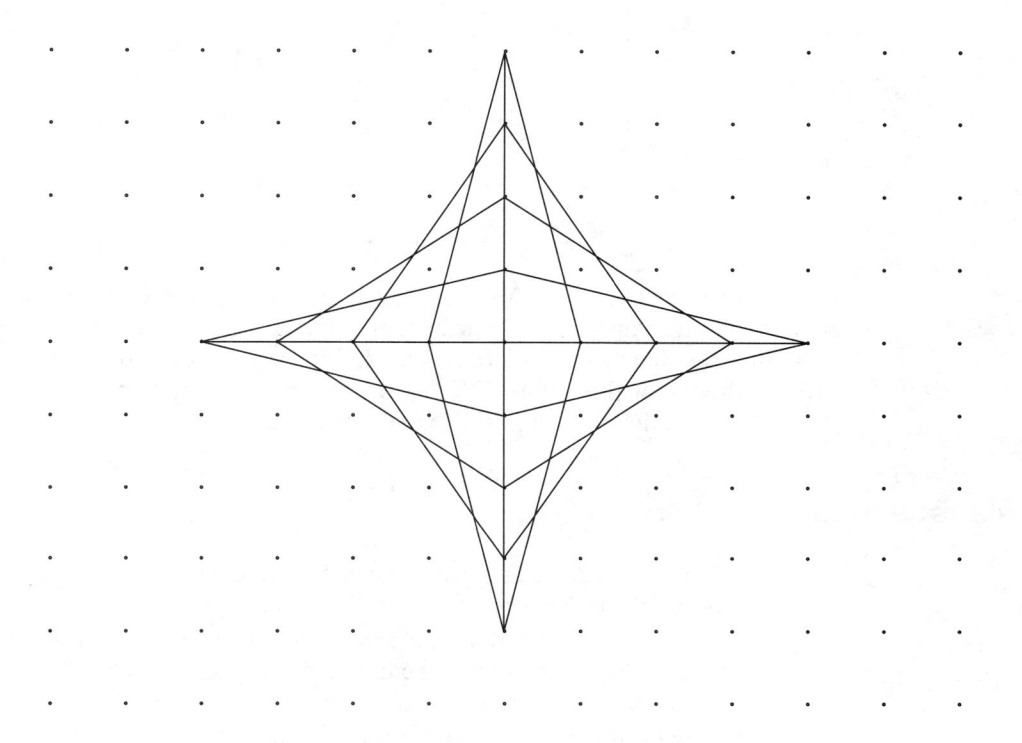

DESIGN # 1

Drawing 1-2

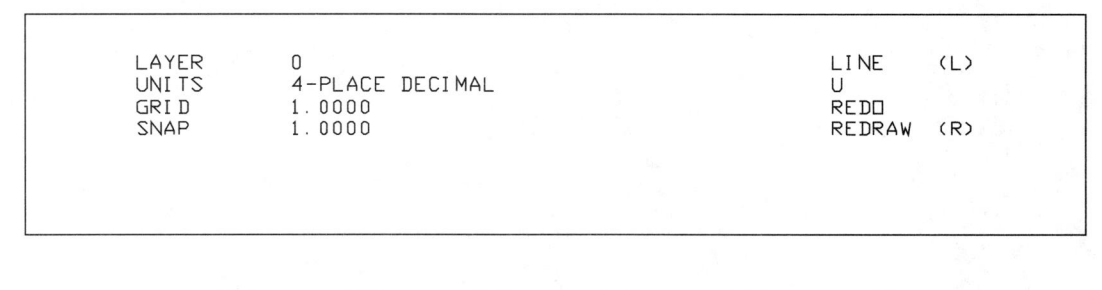

```
LAYER      0                          LINE    (L)
UNITS      4-PLACE DECIMAL            U
GRID       1.0000                     REDO
SNAP       1.0000                     REDRAW  (R)
```

| [F1] | [F2] | [F6] | [F7] | [F8] | [F9] |
| HELP | TEXT/GRAPHICS | ABSOLUTE/OFF/POLAR | ON/OFF | ON/OFF | ON/OFF |

DRAWING 1—3: SHIM

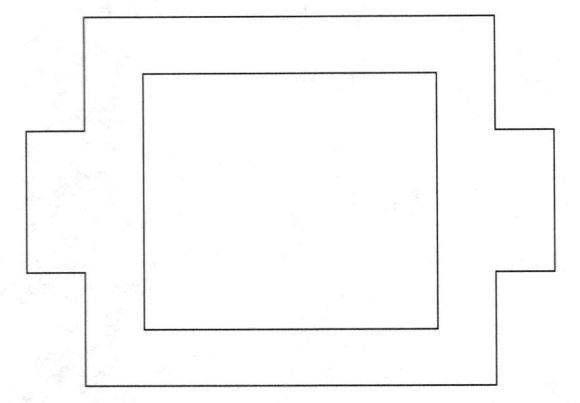

This drawing will give you further practice in using the LINE command. In addition, it will give you practice in translating dimensions into distances on the screen. Note that the dimensions are only included for your information; they are not part of the drawing at this point. Your drawing will look like the reference drawing that follows. Dimensioning is discussed in Chapter 8.

DRAWING SUGGESTIONS

> If you are beginning a new drawing, select "New..." on the "File" menu and then select "No Prototype" in the dialogue box.

> It is most important that you choose a starting point that will position the drawing so that it fits on your screen. If you begin with the bottom left-hand corner of the outside figure at the point (3,1), you should have no trouble.

> Read the dimensions carefully to see how the geometry of the drawing works. It is good practice to look over the dimensions before you begin drawing. Often the dimension for a particular line may be located on another side of the figure or may have to be extrapolated from other dimensions. It is not uncommon to misread, misinterpret, or miscalculate a dimension, so take your time.

Chap. 1

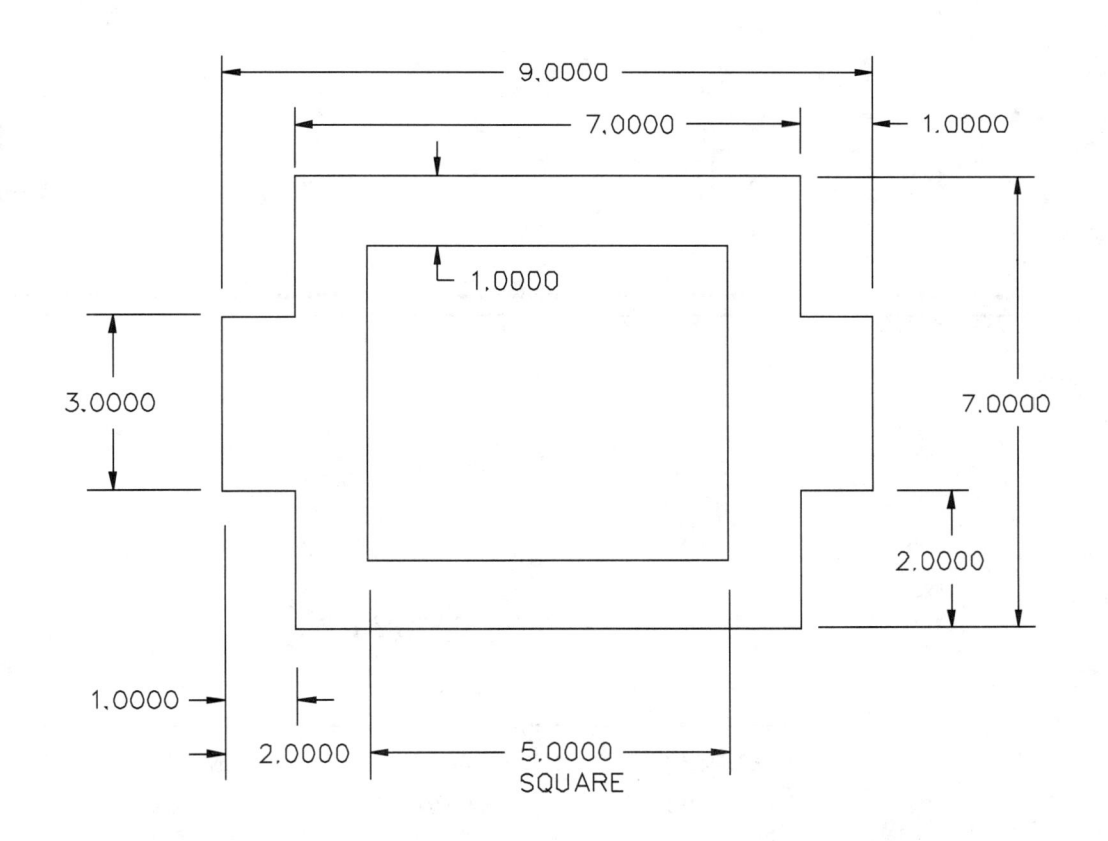

SHIM

Drawing 1-3

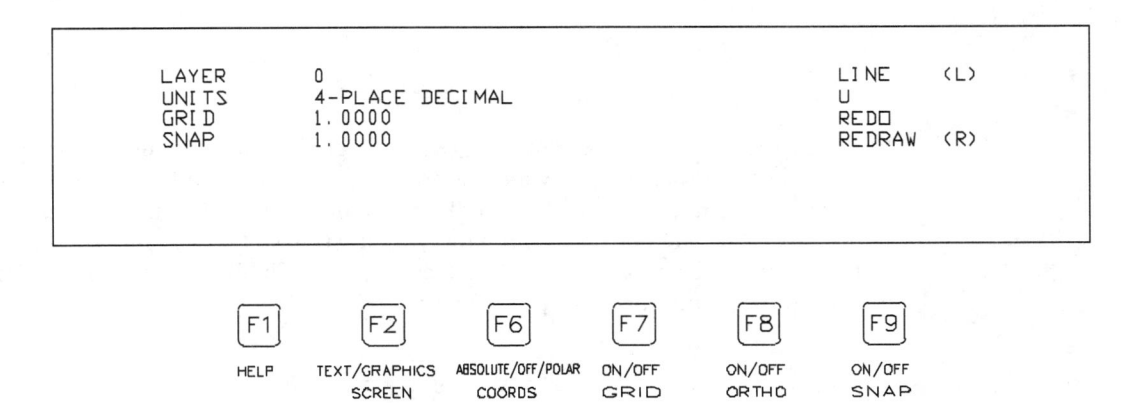

LAYER	0	LINE	(L)
UNITS	4-PLACE DECIMAL	U	
GRID	1.0000	REDO	
SNAP	1.0000	REDRAW	(R)

F1	F2	F6	F7	F8	F9
HELP	TEXT/GRAPHICS SCREEN	ABSOLUTE/OFF/POLAR COORDS	ON/OFF GRID	ON/OFF ORTHO	ON/OFF SNAP

CHAPTER 2

COMMANDS

OPTIONS	DRAW	MODIFY
DDRMODES	CIRCLE	ERASE
GRID		OOPS
SNAP		
	DATA	**OBJECT PROPERTIES**
	UNITS	DIST

OVERVIEW

In this chapter you will learn to change the spacing of the grid and the snap. You will also change the units in which coordinates are displayed. You will produce drawings containing straight lines and circles and learn to delete lines and circles selectively using the ERASE command. You will also learn to measure and mark distances on the screen using the DIST command. Finally, you begin to learn AutoCAD plotting and printing procedures.

TASKS

1. Change the snap spacing.
2. Change the grid spacing.
3. Change units.

4. Draw three concentric circles using the center point, radius method.
5. Draw three more concentric circles using the center point, diameter method.
6. ERASE the circles, using four selection methods.
7. Mark distances with DIST.
8. Print or plot a drawing.
9. Do Drawing 2–1 ("Aperture Wheel").
10. Do Drawing 2–2 ("Roller").
11. Do Drawing 2–3 ("Fan Bezel").
12. Do Drawing 2–4 ("Switch Plate").

Task 1: Changing the Snap

Procedure

1. Type "Snap" or select "Drawing Aids" from the Options pull down menu.
2. Enter a snap value.

Discussion. When you begin a new drawing using no prototype (prototypes are discussed in Chapter 4), the grid and snap are set with a spacing of 1. Moreover, they are linked so that changing one will change the other to the same value. In Task 2 we will set the grid independently. For now we will leave them linked.

In Chapter 1 all drawings were done without altering the grid and snap spacings from the prototype value of 1. Frequently you will want to change this, depending on your application. You may want a 10-foot snap for a building layout, or a 0.010 inch snap for a printed circuit diagram.

> To begin, type "new" or select "New" from the File pull down menu or the New tool from the Standard toolbar.

This will open the Create New Drawing dialogue box used in Chapter 1.
> Click on "No Prototype" to ensure that your drawing editor uses the default settings shown in this chapter.
> Using F7 and F9, be sure that grid and snap are both on.
> Type "snap" (we will no longer remind you to press Enter after typing a command or response to a prompt). Do not use the pull down or screen menu yet. We will get to those procedures momentarily.

The command area prompt will appear like this, with options separated by slashes (/):

Snap spacing or ON/OFF/Aspect/Rotate/Style <1.0000>:

You can ignore most of these options for now. The number <1.0000> shows the present setting. AutoCAD uses this format (<default>) in many command sequences to show you a present value or default setting. It usually comes at the end of a series of options. Pressing the Enter key or space bar at this point will give you the default setting.
> In answer to the prompt, type ".5" and watch what happens (of course you remembered to press Enter).

Because the grid is set to change with the snap, you will see the grid redrawn to a .5 increment.
> Move the cursor around to observe the effects of the new snap setting.
> Try other snap settings. Try 2, .25, and .125. Remember that you can repeat the last command, SNAP, by pressing Enter, the space bar, or the Enter key on your pointing device.

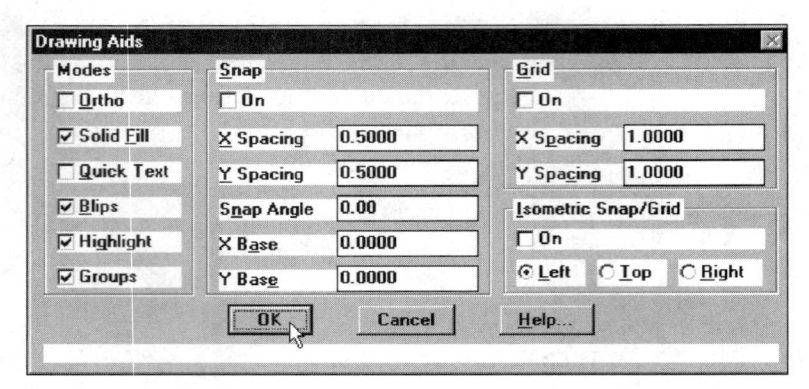

Figure 2-1

How small a snap will AutoCAD and your video display accept? Notice that when you get too small (smaller than .08 on our screen), the grid becomes too dense to display, but the snap can still be set smaller.

Using the Drawing Aids Dialogue Box

You can also change snap and grid settings using a dialogue box. The procedure is somewhat different, but the result is the same. Select "Options" from the pull down bar and then "Drawing Aids ..." from the menu. This method will call the Drawing Aids dialogue box shown in *Figure 2-1*. DDRMODES is the command that calls up this dialogue box, so you can actually open it from the keyboard as well. Most dialogue boxes are called by a command name beginning with DD, which stands for "Dynamic Dialogue".

Look at the Drawing Aids dialogue box. It contains some typical features, including check boxes, edit boxes, and radio buttons.

Check Boxes

You can turn ortho, snap, and grid on and off by moving the arrow inside the appropriate check box and pressing the pick button. A checked box is on, while an empty box is off. Notice that there are five other check boxes in the area on the left under "Modes". We will only have use for the snap and grid settings at this point, but for reference, "Solid fill" is discussed in Chapter 9 and "Quick text" in Chapter 7. If "Blips" is turned off, AutoCAD will not show blips on the screen as you draw. If "Highlight" is turned off, AutoCAD will not highlight selected entities. (We will get to highlighting at the end of this chapter when we discuss the ERASE command). If "Groups" is not selected then AutoCAD will not allow you to select grouped objects as a whole. (Groups are discussed briefly in this chapter and at length in Chapter 10.)

On the lower right you will see a box for isometric snap and grid control. We will have no use for these until Chapter 11. But notice the boxes in the lower line of the isometric snap/grid area labelled "Left", "Top", and "Right". These are examples of radio buttons, which are discussed in Task 3.

Also notice the "Help..." box at the bottom right. Again, any box with an ellipsis (...) calls another dialogue box that will overlay the current one. Picking this box would activate the HELP command. When you exited the HELP dialogue you would return to this Drawing Aids dialogue box.

Chap. 2

Edit Boxes

The snap and grid settings are shown in edit boxes. Edit boxes contain text or numerical information that can be edited the same as in a text editor. You can highlight the entire box to replace the text, or point anywhere inside to do partial editing.

To change the grid or snap setting, use the following procedure:

1. Move the arrow into the box in the table where the change is to be made ("X Spacing" under "Snap" or "Grid").
2. Double click to highlight the entire number.
3. Type a new value and press Enter. Notice that the Y spacing changes automatically when you change the X spacing (see note following).
4. Click on the OK box at the bottom to confirm changes, or "Cancel" to cancel changes.

NOTE: The dialogue box has places to set both X and Y spacing. It is unlikely that you will want to have a grid or snap matrix with different horizontal and vertical increments, but the capacity to do so is there. Also notice that you can change the snap angle. Setting the snap angle to 45, for example, would turn your snap and grid at a 45 degree angle.

Task 2: Changing the Grid

1. Type "grid" or open the Drawing Aids dialogue box.
2. Enter a value.

Discussion. Whether you are typing or using one of your menus, the process for changing the grid setting is the same as changing the snap. In fact, the two are similar enough to cause confusion. The grid is only a visual reference. It has no effect on selection of points. Snap is invisible, but it dramatically affects point selection. Grid and snap may or may not have the same setting.

> Using F7, be sure the grid is turned on.
> Type "grid" or use the Drawing Aids dialogue box, as discussed previously.
   If you are typing, the prompt will appear like this, with options separated by slashes (/):

   Grid spacing(X) or ON/OFF/Snap/Aspect <1.0000>:

> Type ".5".
> Try other grid settings. Try 2, .25, and .125. What happens when you try .0625?
> Now try setting snap to 1 and the grid spacing to .25. Notice how you cannot touch many of the dots. This is because the visible grid matrix is set to a smaller spacing than the invisible snap matrix.
   In practice this relationship is likely to be reversed. Since the grid is merely a visual aid, it will often be set "coarser" than the snap.
> Try setting the grid to .5 and the snap to .25.
   With this type of arrangement you can still pick exact points easily, but the grid is not so dense as to be distracting.

If you wish to keep snap and grid the same, set the grid to "0". The grid will then change to match the snap and will continue to change any time you reset the snap. To free the grid, just give it its own value again using the GRID command or the dialogue box.

Task 3: Changing Units

Procedure

1. Type "Units", or select "Units..." from the Data pull down menu.
2. Answer the prompts.
3. Press F2, if necessary to return to the drawing screen.

Discussion

> Type "Units" (do not use the pull down menu yet).

Presto! The text window appears and covers the graphics screen. We told you this would happen. The command area is too small to display the complete UNITS sequence, so it has been temporarily overlaid by the text screen. What function key will bring it back?

What you now see looks like this:

REPORT FORMATS: (EXAMPLES)
1. Scientific   1.55E+01
2. Decimal   15.50
3. Engineering   1'–3.50"
4. Architectural   1'–3 1/2"
5. Fractional   15 1/2

With the exception of Engineering and Architectural formats, these formats can be used with any basic unit of measurement. For example, decimal mode works for metric units as well as English units.

Enter choice, 1 to 5 <2>:

> Type "2" or simply press Enter, since the default system, and the one we will use, is decimal units.

Through most of this book we will stick to decimal units. Obviously, if you are designing a house you will want architectural units. If you are building a bridge you may want engineering-style units. You might want scientific units if you are doing research.

Whatever your application, once you know how to change units, you can do so easily and at any time. However, as a drawing practice you will want to choose appropriate units when you first begin work on a new drawing. Not only will coordinates be displayed in the units you select, but later, when you use AutoCAD's dimensioning features (see Chapter 8), your drawing will be dimensioned in these units.

AutoCAD should now be showing the following prompt:

Number of digits to right of decimal point, (0 to 8) <4>:

We will use two-place decimals because they are practical and more common than any other choice.

> Type "2" in answer to the prompt for the number of decimal places you wish to use.

AutoCAD now gives you the opportunity to change the units in which angles are measured. In this book we will use all of the default settings for angle measure, since they are by far the most common. If your application requires something different, the UNITS command is the place to make changes.

The default system is standard degrees without decimals, measured counter-clockwise, with 0 being straight out to the right (3 o'clock), 90 straight up (12 o'clock), 180 to the left (9 o'clock), and 270 straight down (6 o'clock).

> Press Enter four times, or until the "Command:" prompt reappears. Be careful not to press Enter again, or the UNITS command sequence will be repeated.

Looking at the coordinate display, you should now see values with only two digits to the right of the decimal. This setting will be standard in this book.

We suggest, as always, that you experiment with other choices in order to get a feel for the options that are available to you. You should also try the Units Control dialogue box described next.

The Units Control Dialogue Box

Activate the Units Control dialogue box by picking "Units..." from the Data pull down menu. You will see the command DDUNITS entered on the command line, and the dialogue box shown in *Figure 2-2* will appear. This box shows all of the settings that are also available through the UNITS command sequence. There are two dialogue box features here that we have not discussed previously.

Radio Buttons

First are the radio buttons in the columns labelled "Units" and "Angles". Radio buttons are used with lists of settings that are mutually exclusive. You should see that the Decimal button is shaded in the format column. All other buttons in this column are not shaded. You can switch settings by simply picking another button, but you can have only one button on at a time. Radio buttons are used here because you can use only one format at a time.

Pop Down Lists

The second new feature is the pop down lists at the bottom of the Units and Angles columns. You should try these to see how they function. You can change the precision (number of place values shown) by picking the arrow at the right of the box and then picking a setting, such as "0.000" for three-place decimals, from the list that appears.

Experiment as much as you like with the dialogue box. None of your changes will be reflected in the drawing editor until you click on the OK button or

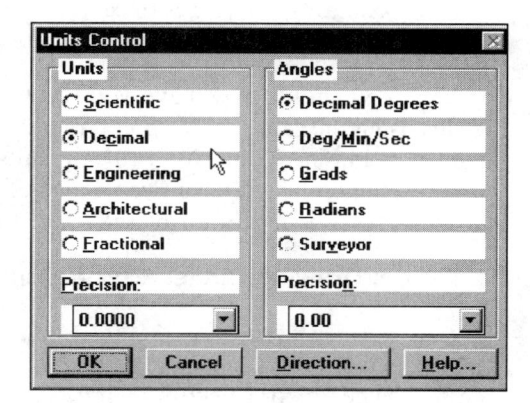

Figure 2-2

press Enter on the keyboard. When you are through, be sure to leave your units set for two-place decimals, your angle measure set for zero-place decimal degrees, and your angle zero direction set to East.

NOTE: All dialogue boxes can be moved on the screen. This is done by clicking in the gray title area at the top of the dialogue box, holding down the pick button, and dragging the box across the screen.

Task 4: Drawing Circles Giving Center Point and Radius

Procedure

1. Type "c" or select the Circle tool from the Draw toolbar.
2. Pick a center point.
3. Enter or drag a radius value.

Discussion. Circles can be drawn by giving AutoCAD three points on the circle's circumference, or two points that determine a diameter, two tangents and a radius, a center point and a radius, or a center point and a diameter. In this chapter we will use the latter two options.

We will begin by drawing a circle with radius 3 and center at the point (6,5). Then we will draw two smaller circles centered at the same point. Later we will erase them using the ERASE command.

> Using what you have just learned, set grid and snap to .5 and units to two-place decimal.

> Type "c" or select the Circle Center Radius tool from the Draw toolbar, illustrated in *Figure 2-3*. The prompt that follows will look like this:

3P/2P/TTR/<Center point>:

> Type coordinates or point to the center point of the circle you want to draw. In our case it will be the point (6,5). AutoCAD will assume that a radius or diameter will follow and will show the following prompt:

Diameter/<Radius>:

If we type or point to a value now, AutoCAD will take it as a radius, since that is the default.

> Type "3" or show by pointing that the circle has a radius of 3.

Notice how the rubber band works to drag out your circle as you move the cursor. Remember, if your coordinate display is not showing polar coordinates, press F6 once or twice until you see something like "3.00<0". When you are ready, press the pick button to show the radius end point.

You should now have your first circle complete. Next, draw two more circles using the same center point, radius method. They will be centered at (6,5) and have radii of 2.50 and 2.00. The results are illustrated in *Figure 2-4*.

Remember that you can repeat a command, in this case the CIRCLE command, by pressing Enter or the space bar.

Task 5: Drawing Circles Giving Center Point and Diameter

Procedure

1. Type "c" or select the Circle Center Diameter tool from the Circle flyout.
2. Pick a center point.

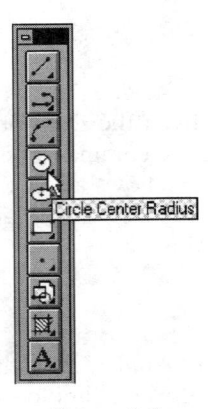

Figure 2-3

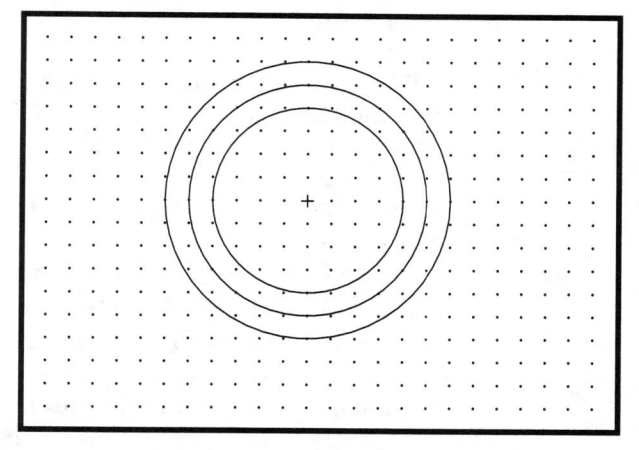

Figure 2-4

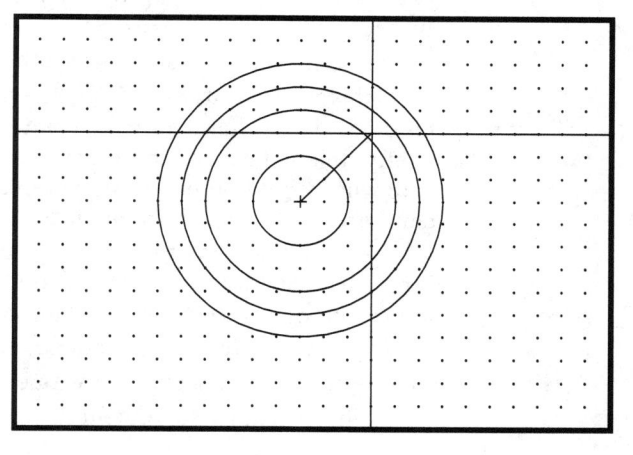

Figure 2-5

3. Respond to the prompt with a "d".
4. Type or drag a diameter length.

Discussion. We will draw three more circles centered on (6,5) having diameters of 2, 1.5, and 1. Drawing circles this way is almost the same as the radius method, except you will not use the default, and you will see that the rubber band works differently.

> Press Enter or the space bar to repeat the CIRCLE command. Type "c" or select the Circle tool from the Draw toolbar if you have done something else, such as a redraw, since drawing the first three circles. There is also a Circle Center Diameter tool on the Circle flyout which we will explore momentarily.
> Indicate the center point (6,5) by typing coordinates or pointing.
> Answer the prompt with a "d", for diameter.
   Notice that the cross hairs are now outside the circle you are dragging on the screen (see *Figure 2-5*). This is because AutoCAD is looking for a diameter, but the last point you gave was a center point. So the diameter is being measured from the center point out, twice the radius. Move the cursor around, in and out from the center point, to get a feel for this.
> Point to a diameter of 2.00, or type "2".
   You should now have four circles.

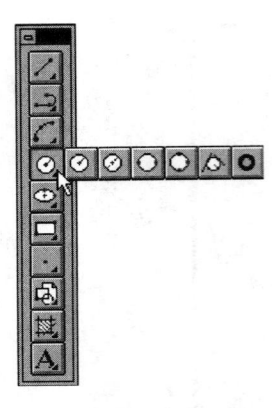

Figure 2-6

The Circle Flyout

We can use the Circle flyout menu bar to illustrate how flyouts work. As previously mentioned, the small black triangle in the corner of a tool button indicates that a flyout with other commands and options is available.

> Move the cursor arrow to the Circle tool, press the click button and hold it down.

The Circle flyout bar will appear as illustrated in *Figure 2-6*.

> Keep your finger on the button as you look at the flyout.

Notice that the first button is the same as the one on the main Draw toolbar. This the case in all flyouts.

> Continue holding down the button and move the arrow to the right slowly.

Notice how each button is "held down" as the arrow passes over it.

> Move to the second button and let the arrow rest there.

You will see a yellow tooltip indicating that this is the Circle Center Diameter tool.

> Release the cursor button while the Circle Center Diameter tool is down.

This will initiate the CIRCLE command with the diameter option. In this case "d" for diameter will be entered automatically at the second prompt. Briefly, this is because the menus and toolbars contain "macros" that automate what would otherwise be entered as keystrokes. If you watch the command area you will see frequent examples of this.

Notice also that the Circle Center Diameter tool replaces the Circle Center Radius tool on the Draw toolbar. It will stay there until you use the radius tool or another option again, or until you exit AutoCAD.

> Complete the command sequence to create a circle with a diameter of 1.5.
> Using the diameter tool, draw one more circle with a diameter of 1.0.

When you are done, your screen should look like *Figure 2-7*.

Sit back and admire your work, because we are about to erase it. In the meantime, studying *Figure 2-8* will give you a good introduction to the remaining options in the CIRCLE command. None of these is necessary to complete the drawings in this chapter. See the *AutoCAD Command Reference* for additional information.

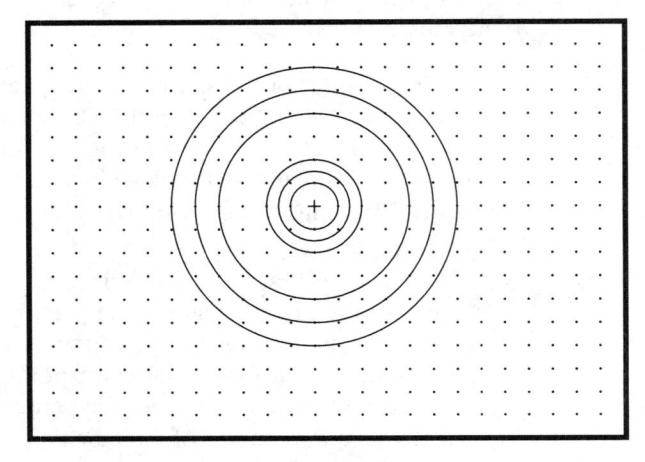

Figure 2-7

Chap. 2

TWO—POINT

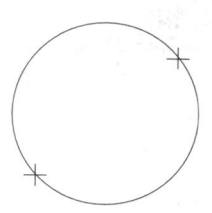

Pick two points.
Line between is used as diameter to construct circle.

THREE—POINT

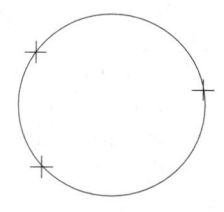

Pick three points
Arc through all three is completed to form circle.
Circle is visible on screen after second point selection.

TANGENT, TANGENT, RADIUS

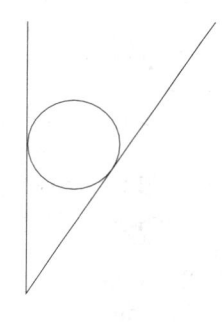

Select two objects on the screen ("Tangent Specs").
Type or show radius length.
AutoCAD constructs the circle that has the given radius and is tangent to both objects.

DONUT

Type or show inside diameter, type or show outside diameter, type or show the center of donut.
Donuts can be filled rings or solid filled circles.
Multiple copies can be created by picking new center points.
Select the Esc key to exit.

Figure 2-8

Task 6: Using the ERASE Command

Procedure

1. Type "e" or select the Erase tool from the Modify toolbar, as shown in *Figure 2-9*.
2. Select objects.
3. Press Enter.

38   Part I / Basic Two-Dimensional Entities

Figure 2-9

or

1. Select objects.
2. Type "e" or select the Erase tool.

Discussion. AutoCAD allows for many different methods of editing and even allows you to alter some of the basics of how edit commands work. Fundamentally, there are two different sequences for using most edit commands. These are called the Noun/Verb and the Verb/Noun methods.

In earlier versions of AutoCAD, most editing was carried out in a verb/noun sequence. That is, you would enter a command, such as ERASE (the verb), then select objects (the nouns), and finally press Enter to carry out the command. This method is still perfectly reasonable and effective, but AutoCAD now allows you to reverse the verb/noun sequence. You can use either method as long as "Noun/Verb" selection is enabled in your drawing.

In this task we will explore the traditional verb/noun sequence and then introduce the noun/verb or "pick first" method along with some of the many methods for selecting objects.

Verb/Noun Editing

> To begin this task you should have the six circles on your screen, as shown in *Figure 2-7*.

We will use verb/noun editing to erase the two outer circles. If you wish to be able to use the Erase tool, you will have to first open the Modify toolbar as follows:
1. Open the Tools pull down menu.
2. Open the Toolbars submenu.
3. Click on Modify.

> Type "e" or select the Erase tool from the Modify toolbar, as shown in *Figure 2-9*.

The cross hairs will disappear, but the pickbox will still be on the screen and will move when you move your cursor.

Also notice the command area. It should be showing this:

Select objects:

This is a very common prompt. You will find it in all edit commands and many other commands as well.

> Move your cursor so that the outer circle crosses the pickbox.

NOTE: In many situations you may find it convenient or necessary to turn snap off (F9) while selecting objects, since this gives you more freedom of motion.

> Press the pick button.

The circle will be highlighted (dotted). This is how AutoCAD indicates that an object has been selected for editing. It is not yet erased, however. You can go on and add more objects to the selection set and they, too, will become dotted.

> Use the box to pick the second circle. It too should now be dotted.

> Press Enter, the space bar, or the enter equivalent button on your pointing device to carry out the command.

This is typical of the verb/noun sequence in most edit commands. Once a command has been entered and a selection set defined, a press of the Enter key is required to complete the command. At this point the two outer circles should be erased.

Noun/Verb Editing

Now let's try the noun/verb sequence.

> Type "u" to undo the ERASE and bring back the circles.
> To ensure that noun/verb editing is enabled in your drawing, pick "Options" from the pull down menu and then "Selection...".

This will open the Object Selection Settings dialogue box.

> If the Noun/Verb Selection check box is not checked, click in the box to check it.
> Click on "OK" to exit the dialogue.

You are now ready to use pick first editing.

> Use the pickbox to select the outer circle.

The circle will be highlighted, and your screen should now resemble *Figure 2-10*. Those little blue boxes are called "grips". They are part of AutoCAD's autoediting system, which we will begin exploring in Chapter 3. For now you can ignore them.

> Pick the second circle in the same fashion.

The second circle will also become dotted and more grips will appear.

> Type "e" or select the Erase tool.

Your two outer circles will disappear as soon as you press Enter or pick the tool.

The two outer circles should now be gone. As you can see, there is not a lot of difference between the noun/verb and verb/noun sequences. One difference that is not immediately apparent is that there are a number of selection methods available in the older verb/noun system that cannot be activated when you pick objects first. We will get to other object select methods momentarily, but first try out the OOPS command.

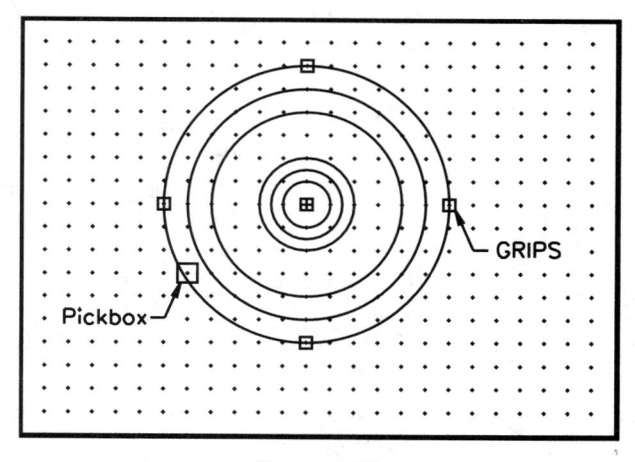

Figure 2-10

OOPS!

> Type or select "Oops" and watch the screen.

If you have made a mistake in your erasure, you can get your selection set back by typing (or selecting) "Oops". OOPS is to ERASE as REDO is to UNDO. You can use OOPS to undo an ERASE command, as long as you have not done another ERASE in the meantime. In other words, AutoCAD only saves your most recent ERASE selection set.

You can also use U to undo an ERASE, but notice the difference: U simply undoes the last command, whatever it might be; OOPS works specifically with ERASE to recall the last set of erased objects. If you have drawn other objects in the meantime, you can still use OOPS to recall a previously erased set. But if you tried to use U, you would have to backtrack, undoing any newly drawn objects along the way.

Other Object Selection Methods

You can select individual entities on the screen by pointing to them one by one, as we have done above, but in complex drawings this will often be inefficient. AutoCAD offers a variety of other methods, all of which have application in specific drawing circumstances. In this exercise we will select circles by the "windowing" and "crossing" methods, by indicating "last" or "L", meaning the last entity drawn, and by indicating "previous" or "P" for the previously defined set. There are also options to add or remove objects from the selection set and a crossing variation on the window option.

In addition, we suggest that you study *Figure 2-11* to learn about other methods. The number of selection options available may seem a bit overwhelming at first, but the time you take to learn them will be well spent. These same options will appear in numerous AutoCAD editing commands (MOVE, COPY, ARRAY, ROTATE, MIRROR) and should become part of your CAD vocabulary.

Selection by Window

In Releases 12 and 13, window and crossing selections can be initiated without entering a command. In other words, they are available for noun/verb selection. Also, whether you select objects first or enter a command first, you can force a window or crossing selection simply by picking points on the screen that are not on objects. AutoCAD will assume you want to select by windowing and will ask for a second point.

Let's try it. We will show AutoCAD that we want to erase all of the inner circles by throwing a temporary selection window around them. The window will be defined by two points moving left to right that serve as opposite corners of a rectangle. Only entities that lie completely within the window will be selected (see *Figure 2-12*).

> Pick point 1 at the lower left of the screen, as shown. Any point in the neighborhood of (3.5,1) will do.

AutoCAD will prompt for another corner:

Other corner:

> Pick point 2 at the upper right of the screen, as shown. Any point in the neighborhood of (9.5,8.5) will do. To see the effect of the window, be sure that it crosses the outside circle as in *Figure 2-12*.
> Type "e" or select the Erase tool.

The inner circles should now be erased.

> Type or select "Oops" to retrieve the circles once more. Since ERASE was the last command, typing "U" will work equally well.

OBJECT SELECTION METHOD	DESCRIPTION	ITEMS SELECTED
(W) WINDOW		THE ENTITIES WITHIN THE BOX
(C) CROSSING		THE ENTITIES CROSSED BY OR WITHIN THE BOX
(P) PREVIOUS		THE ENTITIES THAT WERE PREVIOUSLY PICKED
(L) LAST		THE ENTITY THAT WAS DRAWN LAST
(R) REMOVE		REMOVES ENTITIES FROM THE ITEMS SELECTED SO THEY WILL NOT BE PART OF THE SELECTED GROUP
(A) ADD		ADDS ENTITIES THAT WERE REMOVED AND ALLOWS FOR MORE SELECTION AFTER THE USE OF REMOVE
ALL		ALL ENTITIES CURRENTLY VISIBLE ON THE DRAWING
(F) FENCE		THE ENTITIES CROSSED BY THE FENCE
(WP) WPOLYGON		THE ENTITIES WITHIN THE THE POLYGON
(CP) CPOLYGON		THE ENTITIES CROSSED BY OR WITHIN THE PLOYGON

Figure 2-11

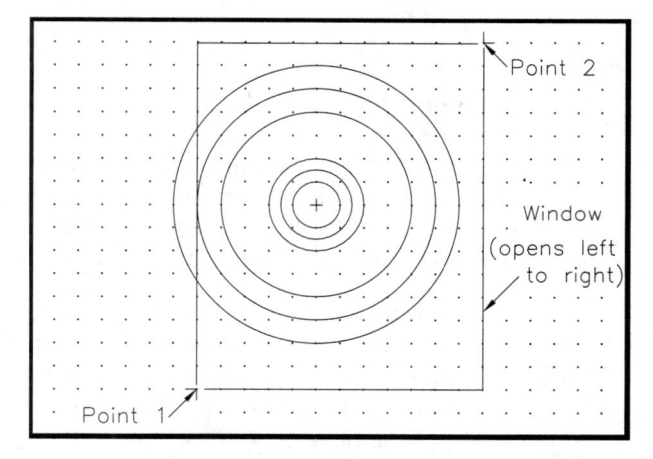

Figure 2-12

Selection by Crossing Window

Crossing is another alternative, useful in many cases where a standard window selection could not be performed. The selection procedure is the same, but a crossing box opens to the left instead of to the right and all objects that cross the box will be chosen, not just those that lie completely inside the box.

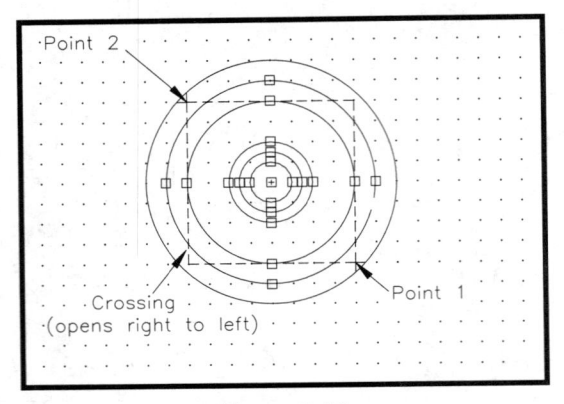

Figure 2-13

We will use a crossing box to select the inside circles.

> Pick point 1 close to (8.0,3.0) as in *Figure 2-13*.
AutoCAD prompts:

Other corner:

> Pick a point near (4.0,7.0). This point selection must be done carefully in order to demonstrate a crossing selection. Notice that the crossing box is shown with dotted lines, whereas the window box was shown with solid lines.
 Also, notice how the circles are now selected: those that cross *and* those that are completely contained within the box, but not those that lie outside.
 At this point we could enter the ERASE command to erase the circles, but instead we will demonstrate how to use the Esc key to cancel a selection set.
> Press the Esc key on your keyboard. This will cancel the selection set. The circles will no longer be highlighted, but you will see that the grips are still visible. To get rid of the grips you will need to cancel again.
> Press Esc again.
 The grips should now be gone as well.

Selecting the "Last" Entity

AutoCAD remembers the order in which new objects have been drawn during the course of a single drawing session. As long as you do not leave the drawing editor, you can select the last drawn entity using the "last" option. If you leave the drawing editor and return later, this information will no longer be available.

> Type "e" or select the Erase tool.
 Notice that there is no way to specify "last" before you enter a command. This option is only available as part of a command procedure. In other words, it only works in a verb/noun sequence.
> Type or select "L" or "last".
 The inner circle should be highlighted.
> Press Enter to carry out the command.
 The inner circle should be erased.

Selecting the "Previous" Selection Set

The P or Previous option works with the same procedure, but it selects the previous selection set rather than the last drawn entity. If the difference is not obvious to you now, don't worry: It will become clear as you work more with edit commands and selection sets.

Remove and Add

Together, the remove and add options form a switch in the object selection process. Under ordinary circumstances, whatever you select using any of the options above will be added to your selection set. By typing "r" at the "Select objects:" prompt you can switch over to a mode in which everything you pick is deselected or removed from the selection set. Then by typing "a" you can return to the usual mode of adding objects to the set.

Undoing a Selection

The ERASE command and other edit commands have an internal undo feature, similar to that found in the LINE command. By typing "u" at the "Select objects:" prompt you can undo your last selection without leaving the edit command you are in and without undoing previous selections. You can also type "u" several times to undo your most recent selections one by one. This allows you to back up one step at a time without having to cancel the command and start all over again.

ALL

"All" is a powerful option that should be used with care. By typing "all" at the "Select objects:" prompt you can select all objects currently visible in your drawing.

Fence

Type "f" or select "fence" at the "Select objects:" prompt and AutoCAD will prompt for a series of "fence points". These points will define a series of line segments called a fence. Any entity that the fence crosses or touches will be selected. This is a very useful option in tight, complex areas.

WPolygon and CPolygon

Type "wp" for "window polygon" or "cp" for "crossing polygon" at the "Select objects:" prompt. AutoCAD will ask for a series of polygon points. These will become the vertices of an irregular polygon of as many sides as you like. Objects will be selected as in window and crossing selections. That is, a window polygon will select only objects that lie completely within the window. A crossing polygon will select objects that cross or lie inside the polygon.

Group

Using the GROUP command, you can define a set of objects as a named group. Once defined, a group may be selected as a unit using the group option and the group name. Groups are discussed in Chapter 10.

Other Options

If you hit any key other than the ones AutoCAD recognizes at the "Select objects:" you will see the following prompt:

```
Expects a point or
Window/Last/Crossing/Box/All/Fence/WPolygon/Cpolygon/
Group/Add/Remove/Multiple/Previous/Undo/AUto/SIngle
Select objects:
```

Along with the options already discussed, you will see Box, Multiple, AUto, and SIngle. These options mostly are used in programming customized applications. See the *Release 13 AutoCAD Command Reference* under the SELECT command for additional information.

Task 7: Using the DIST command

Procedure

1. Type "Dist" or select the DIST tool from the Inquiry flyout on the Object Properties toolbar.
2. Pick first point.
3. Pick second point.
4. Read information in command area or use blips as guide points.

Discussion. The DIST command is one of AutoCAD's most useful inquiry commands. Inquiry commands give you information about your drawing. DIST works like a simple LINE command procedure, but gives you distances instead of actually drawing a line.

There are two principal uses of the DIST command. The most obvious is that it may be used to measure distances or the lengths of linear objects on the screen. The second use is less obvious, but may be more common. Like other commands that ask you to select points, DIST places blips on the screen. These can be very handy when used as guide points for drawing lines, circles, or other entities. This "guide" method is introduced later in the drawing suggestions for Drawing 2–4, "Switch Plate".

The following exercise will introduce you to the DIST command procedure.

> Type "Dist" or select the DIST tool from the Inquiry flyout on the Object Properties toolbar.

AutoCAD will prompt you to pick a point:

First point:

> Pick a point anywhere near the middle of the screen.

Notice that AutoCAD gives you a blip at the first point and a rubber band, just as if you were drawing a line. You are also prompted for a second point:

Second point:

> Pick any other point on the screen.

A blip is placed at the second point as well, but no line is drawn between the two points.
> Press F2 to open the text window.

You should see something like this below the command prompt:

Distance = 5.00 Angle in XY Plane = 53, Angle from XY Plane = 0
Delta X = 3.00, Delta Y = 4.00, Delta Z = 0.00

All of this information can be useful, depending on the situation. "Distance" gives the straight-line distance between the two selected points. "Angle in XY Plane" gives the angle that a line between the two points would make within the coordinate system in which 0 degrees represents a horizontal line out to the right.

Chap. 2

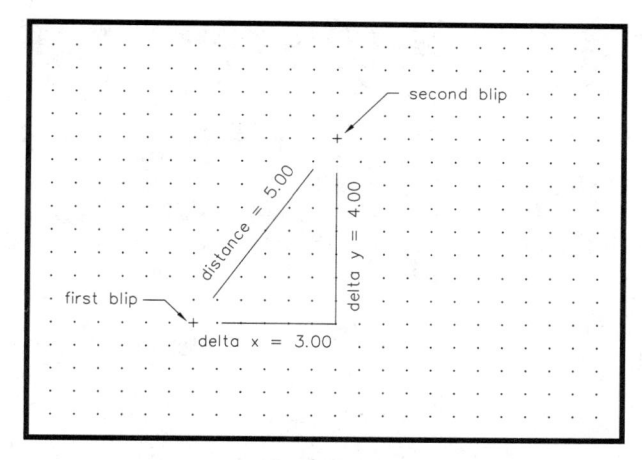

45

Figure 2-14

"Angle from XY Plane" is a 3D feature and will always be 0 in 2D drawings. "Delta X" is the horizontal displacement, which may be either positive or negative. Similarly, "Delta Y" is the vertical displacement. "Delta Z" is the displacement in the Z direction. It will always be 0 until we begin to explore AutoCAD's 3D drawing capabilities in Chapter 12.

Compare what is on your screen with *Figure 2-14*.

Task 8: Printing or Plotting a Drawing

Procedure

1. Type Ctrl-p, select the Print tool from the Standard toolbar, or select Print from the File pull down menu.
2. Click on "Window...".
3. Pick two points to define a window.
4. See that "Scaled to Fit" is checked.
5. Prepare printer or plotter.
6. Click on "OK".

Discussion. AutoCAD's printing and plotting capabilities are extensive and complex. In this book we will introduce you to them a little bit at a time. These presentations are intended to get your work out on paper efficiently.

For starters, we will show you how to do a very simple plot procedure. This procedure assumes that you do not have to change devices or configuration details. It should work adequately for the drawings in this chapter. One of the difficulties is that different types of plotters and printers work somewhat differently. We will try to present procedures that will work on whatever equipment you are using, assuming that it is appropriately configured to begin with.

We suggest that you now open the Plot Configuration dialogue box and work through this section without actually plotting anything. Then come back to it after you have completed one of the drawings in this chapter that you want to print out.

> Type "plot" or Ctrl-p, select the Print tool from the Standard toolbar, or select "Print..." from the File menu.

Any of these methods will call up the "Plot Configuration" dialogue box illustrated in *Figure 2-15*. You will become very familiar with it as you work

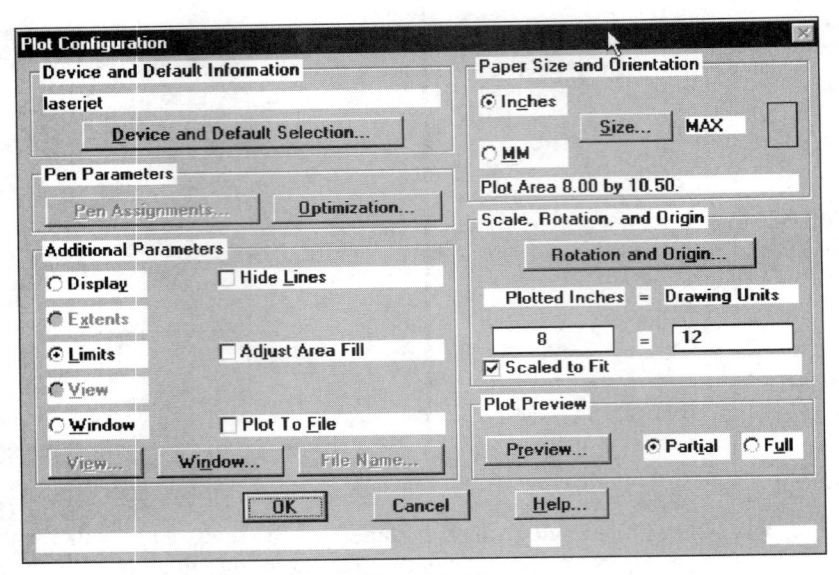

Figure 2-15

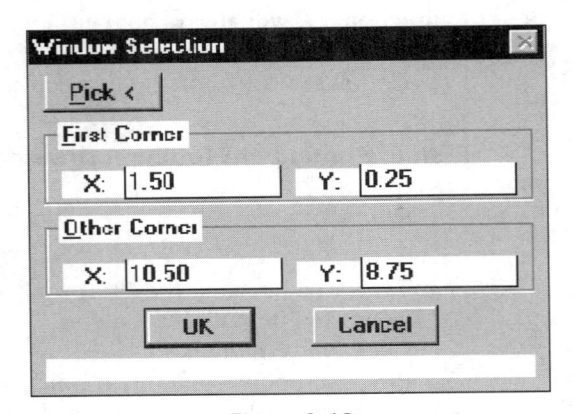

Figure 2-16

through this book. It is one of the most important working spaces in AutoCAD. It contains many options and will call many subdialogues, but for now we are going to look at only two settings.

Look at the box on the lower left labelled "Additional Parameters". The line of radio buttons on the left allows you to tell AutoCAD what part of your drawing you want to plot. For our purposes we will use "Window". For this exercise you will define a window around an object you have drawn. Windowing allows you to plot any portion of a drawing simply by defining the window. AutoCAD will base the size and placement of the printed drawing on the window you have defined on the screen. For now, any object will do.
> Click on "Window..." at the bottom middle of the Additional Parameters box.

This will call up the Window Selection dialogue box illustrated in *Figure 2-16*. It contains the *x* and *y* coordinates of the two corners of your window selection. To ensure that you get the window you want, you need to pick the two points, or type in the coordinates if you know them. We will pick points, using *Drawing 2-1* to illustrate.
> Click on "Pick <" at the top left of the dialogue box.

AutoCAD will temporarily close the Plot Configuration dialogue box so that you can pick points. You will be prompted:

First corner:

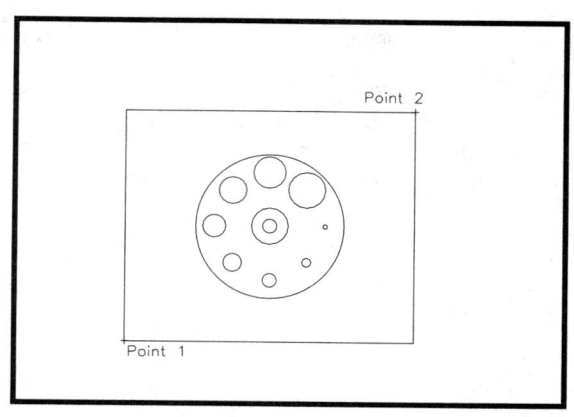

Figure 2-17

> Pick a point similar to point 1 in *Figure 2-17*. For this drawing, a point in the neighborhood of (1.5,.25) will do.

> Pick a point similar to point 2 in *Figure 2-17*. For this drawing, a point in the neighborhood of (10.5,8.75) will do.

As soon as you have picked the second point, AutoCAD will display the Window Selection box again, showing the coordinates you have chosen.

> Click on "OK".

This will bring you back to the Plot Configuration dialogue box. You are essentially done at this point. But before plotting, there is one thing to check. Look at the box at the middle right labeled "Scale, Rotation, and Origin". It should not be necessary to worry about any of these parameters at this point. If the "Scaled to Fit" box is checked, as it should be by default, then AutoCAD will plot your drawing at maximum size based on paper size and the window you have defined.

> If "Scaled to Fit" is not checked, click in the box to check it.

> If you are not actually going to print a drawing at this point, click on Cancel to close the Plot Configuration dialogue box.

At this point the exercise is complete. You should come back to it when you have a drawing ready to plot.

> If you are ready to proceed with a plot, look at your printer or plotter. Make sure that it is on, online, and that the paper is ready to go.

> Click on "OK".

This sends the drawing information out to be printed. You can sit back and watch the plotting device at work. If you need to cancel for any reason, click the Cancel button.

For now, that's all there is to it. If your plot does not look perfect, if it is not centered, for example, don't worry, you will learn all you need to know about plotting later on.

Tasks 9, 10, 11, and 12

You are now ready to complete Drawings 2–1 through 2–4. Remember to set grid, snap, and units before you begin each drawing. Use either ERASE or U if you make a mistake, depending on the situation. Use whichever form of the Circle command seems most appropriate or efficient to you. Be sure to try out DIST in Drawing 2–4.
Good luck!

DRAWING 2-1: APERTURE WHEEL

This drawing will give you practice drawing circles using the center point, radius method. Refer to the table below the drawing for radius sizes. With snap set at .25, some of the circles can be drawn by dragging and pointing. Other circles have radii that are not on a snap point. These circles can be drawn easily by typing in the radius.

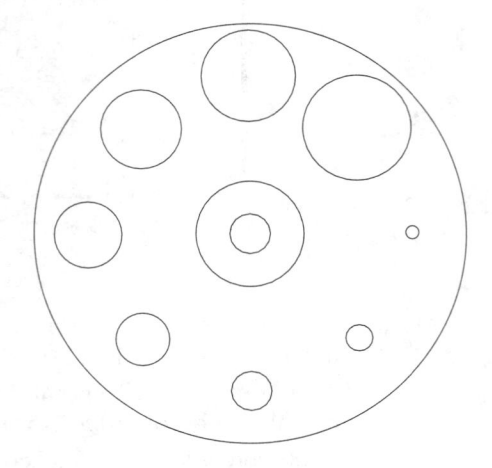

DRAWING SUGGESTIONS

GRID = .50
SNAP = .25

> A good sequence for doing this drawing would be to draw the outer circle first, followed by the two inner circles (h and c). These are all centered on the point (6.00, 4.50). Then you could begin at circle a and work around clockwise, being sure to center each circle correctly.

> Notice that there are two circles c and two circles h. This simply indicates that the two circles having the same letter are the same size.

> Remember, you may type any value you like and AutoCAD will give you a precise graphic image, but you cannot always show the exact point you want with a pointing device. Often it is more efficient to type a few values than to turn snap off or change its setting for a small number of objects.

Chap. 2

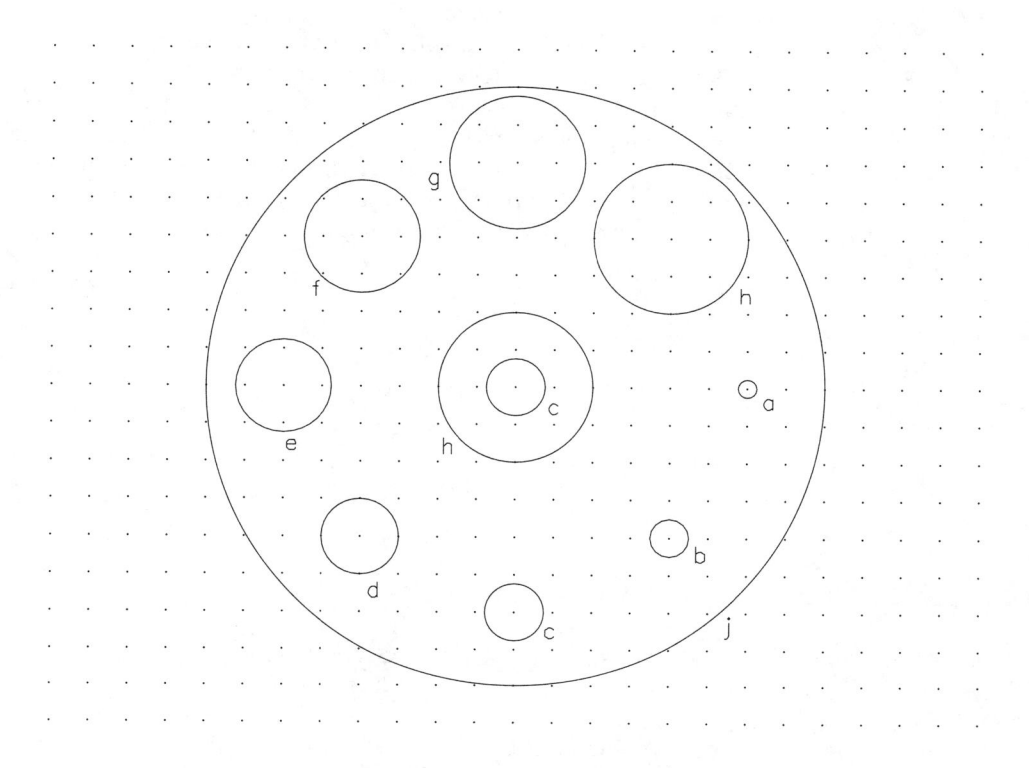

LETTER	a	b	c	d	e	f	g	h	j
RADIUS	.12	.25	.38	.50	.62	.75	.88	1.00	4.00

APERTURE WHEEL

Drawing 2-1

```
LAYER      0                        CIRCLE   (C)
UNITS      2-PLACE DECIMAL          ERASE    (E)
GRID       .50                      OOPS
SNAP       .25                      REDRAW   (R)
```

F1	F2	F6	F7	F8	F9
HELP	TEXT/GRAPHICS SCREEN	ABSOLUTE/OFF/POLAR COORDS	ON/OFF GRID	ON/OFF ORTHO	ON/OFF SNAP

DRAWING 2-2: ROLLER

This drawing will give you a chance to combine lines and circles and to use the center point, diameter method. It will also give you some experience with smaller objects, a denser grid, and a tighter snap spacing.

NOTE: Even though units are set to show only two decimal places, it is important to set the snap using three places (.125) so that the grid is on a multiple of the snap (.25 = 2 × .125). AutoCAD will show you rounded coordinate values, like .13, but will keep the graphics on target. Try setting snap to either .13 or .12 instead of .125, and you will see the problem for yourself.

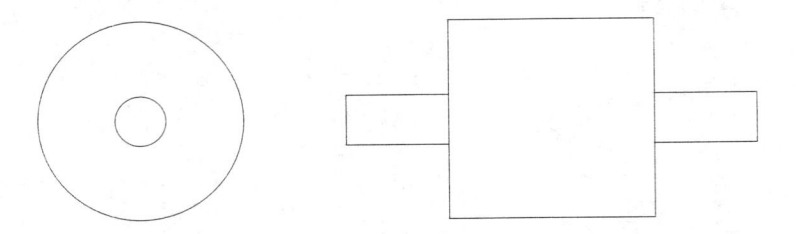

DRAWING SUGGESTIONS

GRID = .25
SNAP = .125

> The two views of the roller will appear fairly small on your screen, making the snap setting essential. Watch the coordinate display as you work and get used to the smaller range of motion.

> Choosing an efficient sequence will make this drawing much easier to do. Since the two views must line up properly, we suggest that you draw the front view first, with circles of diameter .25 and 1.00, and then use these circles to position the lines in the right side view.

> The circles in the front view should be centered in the neighborhood of (2.00, 6.00). This will put the upper left-hand corner of the 1 × 1 square at around (5.50, 6.50).

Chap. 2

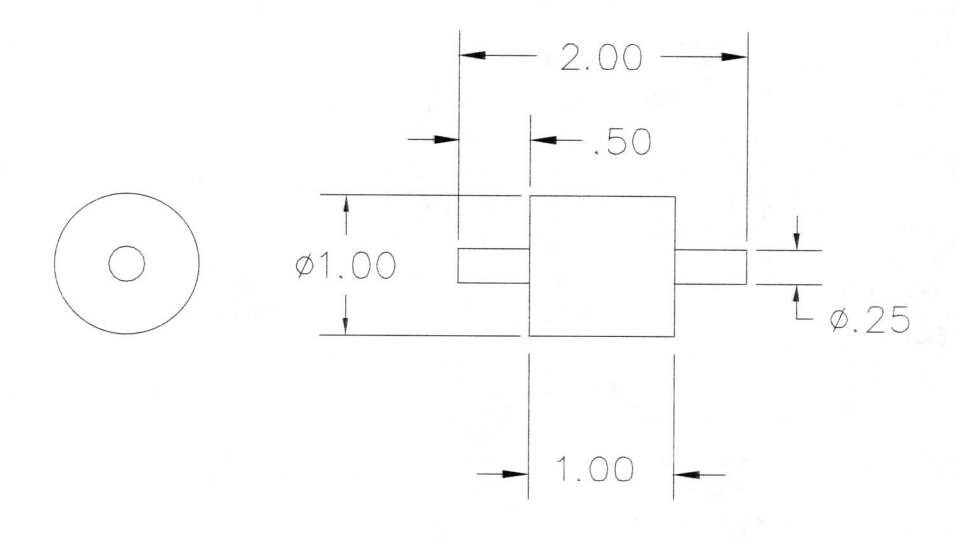

ROLLER
Drawing 2-2

LAYER	0	LINE	(L)
UNITS	2-PLACE DECIMAL	CIRCLE	(C)
GRID	.25	ERASE	(E)
SNAP	.125	OOPS	
		REDRAW	(R)

F1	F2	F6	F7	F8	F9
HELP	TEXT/GRAPHICS SCREEN	ABSOLUTE/OFF/POLAR COORDS	ON/OFF GRID	ON/OFF ORTHO	ON/OFF SNAP

DRAWING 2-3: FAN BEZEL

This drawing should be easy for you at this point. Set grid to .50 and snap to .25 as suggested, and everything will fall into place nicely.

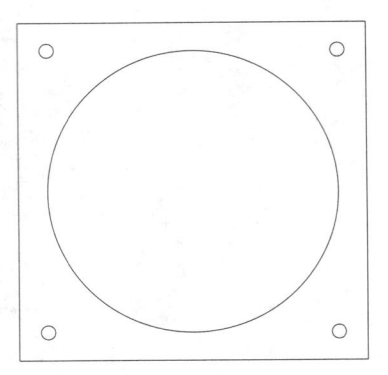

DRAWING SUGGESTIONS

GRID = .50
SNAP = .25

> Notice that the outer figure is a 6 × 6 square and that you are given diameters for the circles.

> You should start with the lower left-hand corner of the square somewhere near the point (3.00, 2.00) if you want to keep the drawing centered on your screen.

> Be careful to center the large inner circle at the center of the square.

Chap. 2

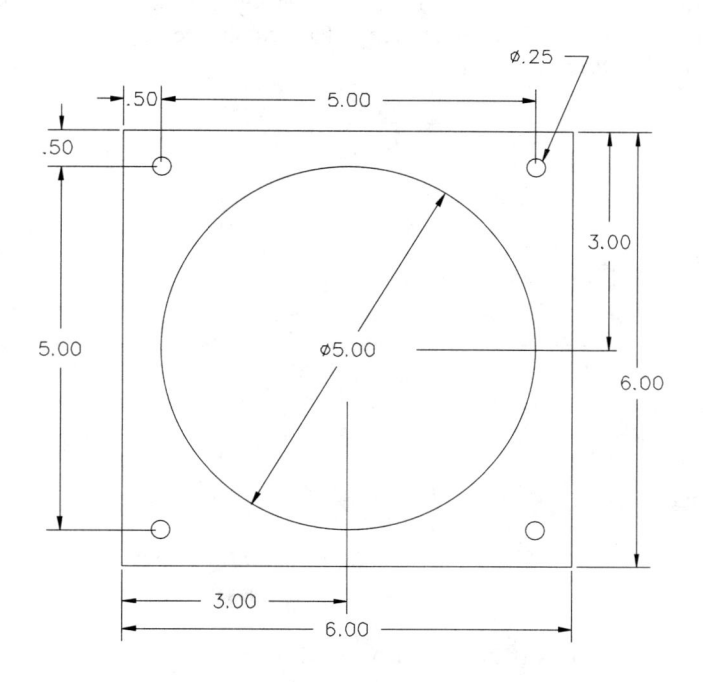

FAN BEZEL

Drawing 2-3

LAYER	0	LINE	(L)
UNITS	2-PLACE DECIMAL	CIRCLE	(C)
GRID	.50	ERASE	(E)
SNAP	.25	OOPS	
		REDRAW	(R)

[F1] HELP
[F2] TEXT/GRAPHICS SCREEN
[F6] ABSOLUTE/OFF/POLAR COORDS
[F7] ON/OFF GRID
[F8] ON/OFF ORTHO
[F9] ON/OFF SNAP

DRAWING 2-4: SWITCH PLATE

This drawing is similar to the last one, but the dimensions are more difficult, and a number of important points do not fall on the grid. It will give you practice using grid and snap points and the coordinate display. Refer to the table below the drawing for dimensions of the circles, squares, and rectangles inside the 7 × 10 outer rectangle. The placement of these smaller figures is shown by the dimensions on the drawing itself.

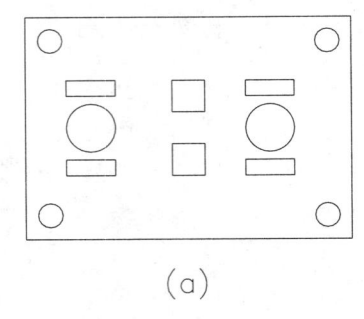

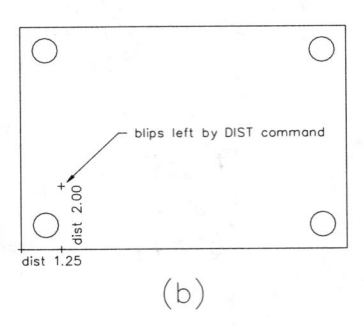

(a)   (b)

DRAWING SUGGESTIONS

GRID = .50
SNAP = .25

> Turn ortho on to do this drawing.
> A starting point in the neighborhood of (1, 1) will keep you well positioned on the screen.

GUIDE POINTS WITH DIST

The squares, rectangles, and circles in this drawing can be located easily using DIST to set up guide points. For example, set a first point at the lower left corner of the outer rectangle as in reference drawing b above. Then set the second point at 1.25 to the right along the bottom of the rectangle. Now repeat the DIST command and use this second point as the new first point. Set the new second point 2.00 up, and you will have a blip right where you want to begin the c rectangle. Look for other places to use this technique in this drawing.

THE RECTANG COMMAND

The RECTANG command is a quick and easy way to draw rectangles. Type or select the command and then pick two points at opposite corners of the rectangle you want to draw. It is just like creating a selection window, but the window remains as a single entity called a polyline. Polylines are discussed in Chapter 10. Type "Rectang" or select the Rectangle tool from the Draw toolbar.

Chap. 2

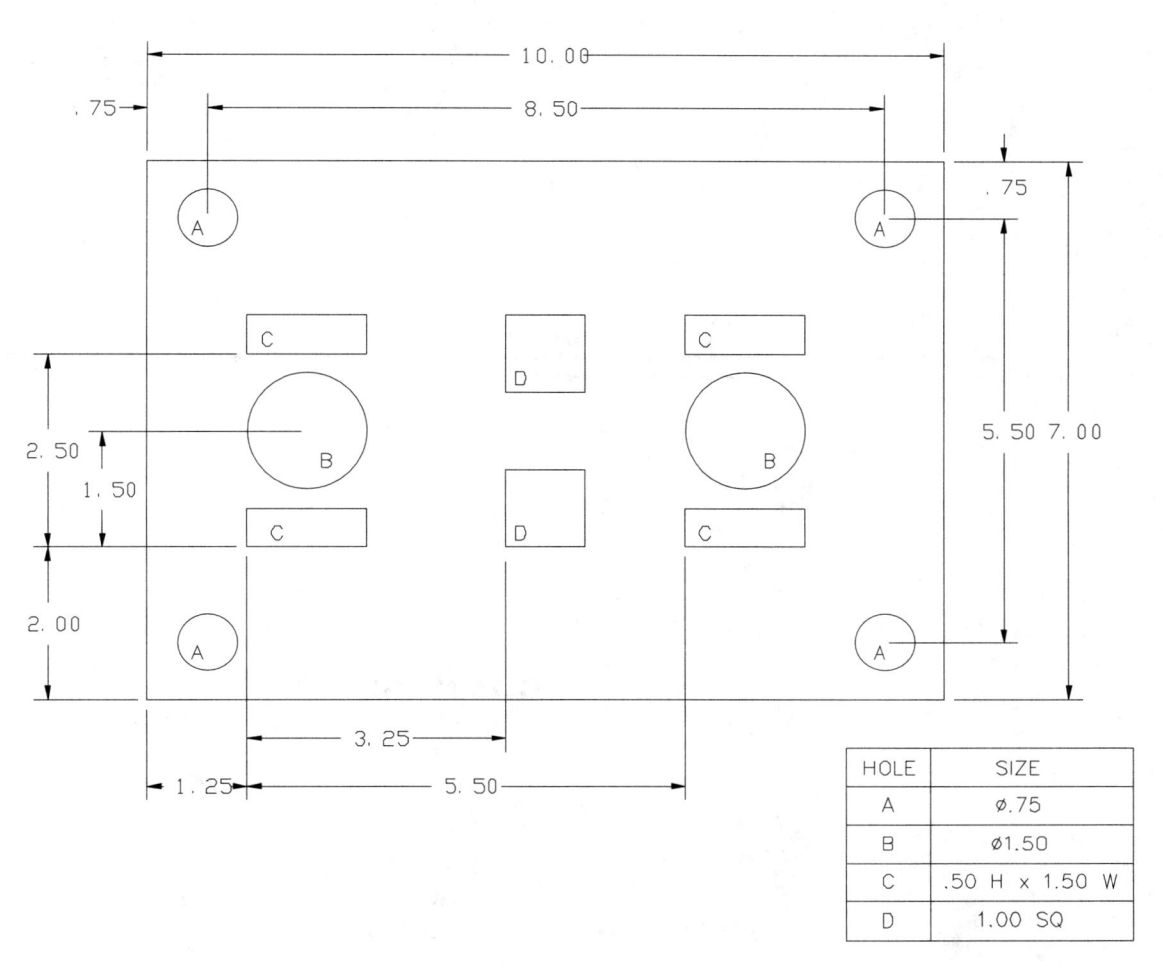

HOLE	SIZE
A	⌀.75
B	⌀1.50
C	.50 H x 1.50 W
D	1.00 SQ

SWITCH PLATE
Drawing 2-4

```
LAYER    0                          LINE     (L)
UNITS    2-PLACE DECIMAL            CIRCLE   (C)
GRID     .50                        ERASE    (E)
SNAP     .25                        OOPS
                                    REDRAW   (R)
```

F1	F2	F6	F7	F8	F9
HELP	TEXT/GRAPHICS SCREEN	ABSOLUTE/OFF/POLAR COORDS	ON/OFF GRID	ON/OFF ORTHO	ON/OFF SNAP

CHAPTER 3

COMMANDS

DATA	VIEW	MODIFY
DDLMODES	PAN	CHAMFER
LAYER	REGEN	FILLET
LTSCALE	VPORTS	
	ZOOM	

OVERVIEW

So far all the drawings you have done have been on a single white layer called "0". In this chapter you will create and use three new layers, each with its own associated color and linetype.

You will also learn to FILLET and CHAMFER the corners of previously drawn objects, to magnify portions of a drawing using the ZOOM command, and to move between adjacent portions of a drawing with the PAN command.

TASKS

1. Create three new layers.
2. Assign colors to layers.
3. Assign linetypes to layers.
4. Change the current layer.
5. FILLET the corners of a square.

6. CHAMFER the corners of a square.
7. ZOOM in and out using Window, Previous, and All.
8. PAN to display another area of a drawing.
9. Create multiple viewports (optional).
10. Use the Plot Preview feature.
11. Do Drawing 3–1 ("Mounting Plate").
12. Do Drawing 3–2 ("Stepped Shaft").
13. Do Drawing 3–3 ("Base Plate").
14. Do Drawing 3–4 ("Bushing").
15. Do Drawing 3–5 ("Half Block").

Task 1: Creating New Layers

Procedure

1. Select "Layers..." from the Data pull down menu.
2. Type a layer name in the edit box.
3. Click on "New".
4. Repeat for other new layers
4. Click on "OK" to leave the dialogue box.

Discussion. Layers allow you to treat specialized groups of entities in your drawing separately from other groups. For example, all of the dimensions in this book were drawn on a special dimension layer so that we could turn them on and off at will. We turned off the dimension layer in order to prepare the reference drawings for chapters 1 through 7, which are shown without dimensions. When a layer is turned off, all the objects on that layer become invisible, though they are still part of the drawing database and can be recalled at any time.

It is common to put dimensions on a separate layer, and there are many other uses of layers as well. Fundamentally, layers are used to separate colors and linetypes, and these in turn take on special significance depending on the drawing application. It is standard drafting practice, for example, to use small, evenly spaced dashes to represent objects or edges that would in reality be hidden from view. On a CAD system with a color monitor, these hidden lines can also be given their own color to make it easy for the designer to remember what layer he or she is working on.

In this book we will use a simple and practical layering system, most of which will be presented in this chapter. You should remember that there are many other systems in use, and many other possibilities. AutoCAD allows as many as 256 different colors and as many layers as you like.

You should also be aware that linetypes and colors are not restricted to being associated with layers. It is possible to mix linetypes and colors on a single layer. But while this may be useful for certain applications, we do not recommend it at this point.

> Begin a new drawing and use the No Prototype check box to ensure that you are using the same defaults as those used in this chapter.

The Layer Control Dialogue Box (DDLMODES)

In this instance we will introduce the dialogue box procedures first because they are more efficient than the command line methods. The main advantage of using the dialogue box is that a table of layers will be displayed in front of you as you make changes, and you will be able to make several changes at once.

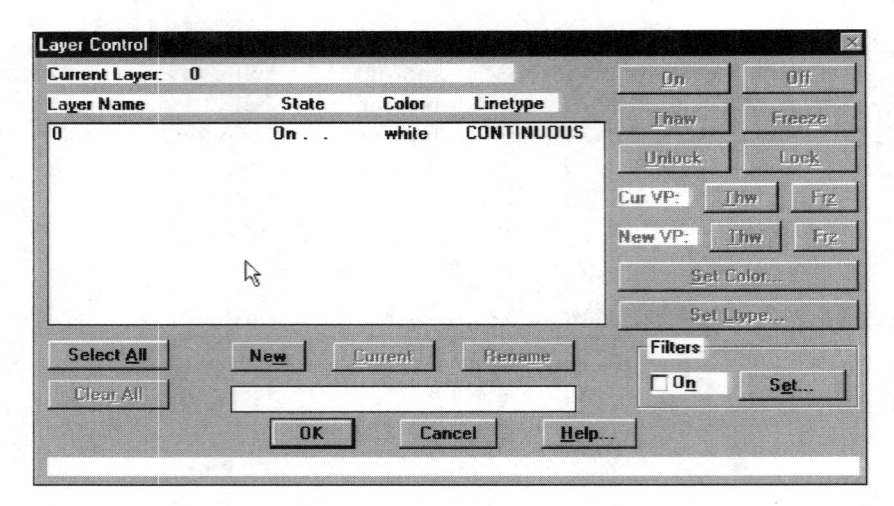

Figure 3-1

> Select "Layers..." from the Data pull down menu.

This will call the Layer Control dialogue box illustrated in *Figure 3-1*. At the top left you will see that the current layer is 0. Below that you will see a box that lists layers defined in the current drawing. In our case "0" is the only defined layer. It is on, uses the color white, and the continuous linetype.

Now we will create three new layers. You should see a blinking line in the edit box at the bottom. This shows that AutoCAD is ready to accept typed input into this box.

> Type "1". There is no need to press Enter when using an edit box.
> Click on "New", just above the edit box.

The newly defined layer, layer 1, will be entered immediately in the layer name box. You will see that it is currently defined with characteristics identical to layer 0. We will alter these momentarily. But first, define two more layers.

Layer names may be up to 31 characters long, although only 18 characters will be displayed in the layer name list. We have chosen single-digit numbers as layer names because they are easy to type and because we can match them to AutoCAD's color numbering sequence.

You can also create several new layers at once by typing names in the edit box separated by commas. Try it.

> Type "2,3" in the edit box and click on "New" to create layers 2 and 3.

At this point your layer name list should look like this:

Layer name	State	Color	Linetype
0	On..	white	CONTINUOUS
1	On..	white	CONTINUOUS
2	On..	white	CONTINUOUS
3	On..	white	CONTINUOUS

NOTE: If you do not see the layer in the layer list it will not be created. In order to create a new layer you must click on "New". A common error is to type names in the edit box and then click on "OK". This will accomplish nothing. Also, if you cancel the dialogue box, all changes will be cancelled, including the creation of new layers.

Task 2: Assigning Colors to Layers

Procedure

1. Select "Layers…" from the Data pull down menu if you are not already in the Layer Control dialogue box.
2. Select a layer name.
3. Click on "Set Color…".
4. Type a color name or number, or select a color.
5. Click on "OK".

Discussion. We now have four layers, but they are all pretty much the same. Obviously we have more changes to make before our new layers will have useful identities.

Layer 0 has some special features, which will be discussed in Chapter 10. Because of these it is common practice to leave it defined the way it is. We will begin our changes on layer 1.

> (If for any reason you have left the Layer Control dialogue box, reenter it by selecting "Layers…" from the Data pull down menu.)

Before you can change the qualities of a layer, you must have it selected in the layer name box. Until you do, all of the boxes on the right, including color and linetype, will be grayed out (inaccessible).

> Move the cursor arrow anywhere on the layer 1 line and click to select layer 1.
  You will know the layer is selected when the line changes color.
> Click on "Set Color…".

This will call the Select Color dialogue box illustrated in *Figure 3-2*. There are nine standard colors at the top, followed by gray shades and a palette of colors.

AutoCAD can display up to 256 different color shades. The 9 standard colors shown at the top of the box are numbered 1 through 9 and are the same for all color monitors. Color numbers 10–249 are shown in the full color palette and numbers 250–255 are the gray shades shown in between.

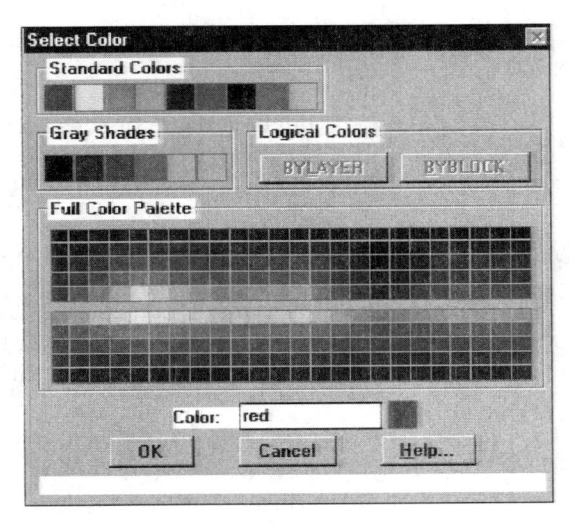

Figure 3-2

> Select the red box or type "1" or "red" in the edit box.

All of these methods will have the same result.

> Click on "OK".

> Type "1" or "red" or select the red box on the left. If you type, pressing Enter will complete the process and close the box. If you select, you will need to click on "OK" to complete the process.

You will now see that layer 1 is defined with the color red in the layer name list box.

Next we will assign the color yellow to layer 2. In order to do this we need to select layer 2 in the box and de-select layer 1.

> Click on layer 2.

The layer 2 line should now be highlighted. Notice that layer 1 is still highlighted. This would allow you to set the layer qualities of more than one layer at once if the layers' qualities were to be the same.

> Click on the layer 1 line to de-select layer 1.

This line should no longer be highlighted.

> Click on "Set Color..." and assign the color yellow (color #2) to layer 2.

> Select layer 3, and de-select layer 2.

> Click on "Set Color..." again and assign the color green (color #3) to layer 3.

Look at the layer list. It should look like this:

Layer name	State	Color	Linetype
0	On. .	white	CONTINUOUS
1	On. .	red	CONTINUOUS
2	On. .	yellow	CONTINUOUS
3	On. .	green	CONTINUOUS

Task 3: Assigning Linetypes

Procedure

1. Select "Layers..." from the Data pull down menu if not already in the Layer Control dialogue box.
2. Select a layer.
3. Select "Set Ltype".
4. Type a linetype name or select a linetype from the dialogue box.
5. Click on "OK".
6. Click on "OK" again to exit the Layer Control dialogue box.

Discussion. AutoCAD has a standard library of linetypes that can be assigned easily to layers. There are 40 standard types in addition to continuous lines. If you do not assign a linetype, AutoCAD will assume you want continuous lines. In addition to continuous lines we will be using hidden and center lines. We will put hidden lines in yellow on layer 2 and center lines in green on layer 3.

> (If for any reason you have left the Layer Control dialogue box, reenter it by clicking the Data pull down menu and selecting "Layers...").

> Select layer 2 in the layer name box. Make sure other layers are not highlighted.

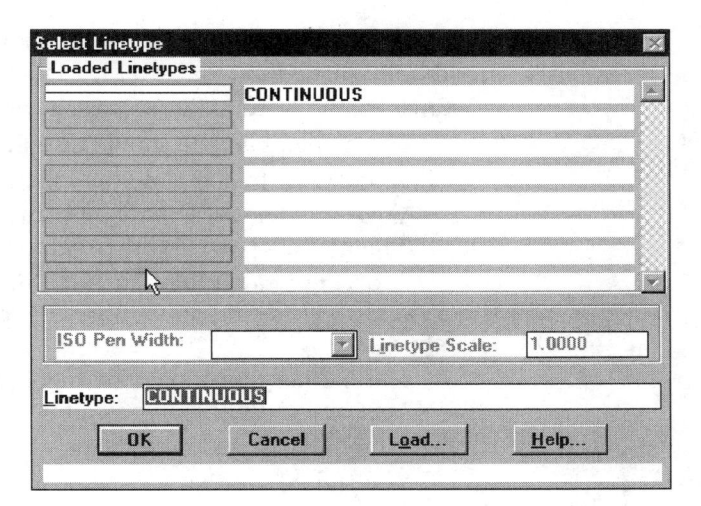

Figure 3-3

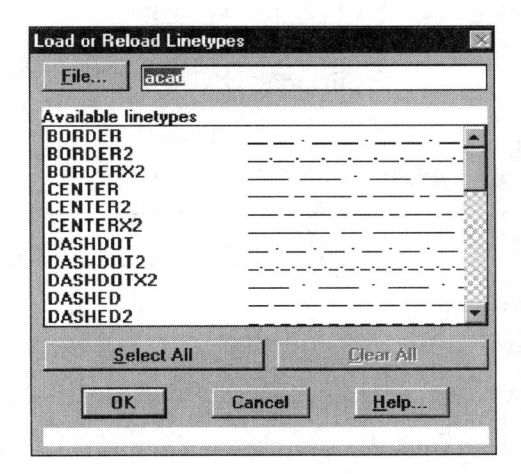

Figure 3-4

> Click on "Set Ltype...".

This will call up the Select Linetype dialogue box illustrated in *Figure 3-3*. The box containing a list of loaded linetypes currently only shows the continuous linetype. We can fix this by selecting the "Load..." button at the bottom of the dialogue box.

> Click on "Load...".

This will call a second dialogue box, the Load or Reload Linetypes box illustrated in *Figure 3-4*. Here you can pick from the list of linetypes available from the standard "acad" file or from other files containing linetypes, if there are any on your system. You also have the option of loading all linetypes from any given file at once. The linetypes are then defined in your drawing and you can assign a new linetype to a layer at any time. This makes things easier. It does, however, use up more memory.

For our purposes we will load only the hidden and center linetypes we are going to be using.

> Click on the word "Center" or anywhere on the center line.

The complete line for this linetype should now be highlighted.

> Move the cursor arrow to the down arrow on the scroll box at the right and scroll down until you see the "Hidden" linetype on the list.
> Click on the word "Hidden" or anywhere on the hidden line.

The hidden linetype should also be highlighted now.

> Click on "OK" to complete the loading process.

You should now see the center and hidden linetypes added to the list of loaded linetypes. Now that these are loaded, we can assign them to layers.

> Click on the hidden line illustrated in the box. You will notice that you can't select by clicking on the word "Hidden" this time. You have to select the line itself.

The hidden line should be highlighted in white and the word "HIDDEN" entered in the Linetype edit box.

> Click on "OK" to close the box.

You should see that layer 2 now has the hidden linetype.

Next assign the center linetype to layer 3.

> De-select layer 2 and select layer 3.
> Click on "Set Ltype...".
> Select the center linetype.
> Click on "OK".

Examine your layer list again. It should look like the one following. If not, use the other dialogue boxes to fix it.

Layer name	State	Color	Linetype
0	On..	white	CONTINUOUS
1	On..	red	CONTINUOUS
2	On..	yellow	HIDDEN
3	On..	green	CENTER

Task 4: Changing the Current Layer

Procedure

1. Open the Layer Control dialogue box from the Data pull down menu.
2. Select one layer.
3. Click on "Current".
4. Click on "OK".

Discussion. In order to draw new entities on a layer, you must make it the currently active layer. Previously drawn objects on other layers also will be visible and will be plotted if that layer is turned on, but new objects will go on the current layer.

> (If for any reason you have left the Layer Control dialogue box, reenter it by opening the Data pull down menu and selecting "Layers...".)
> Select layer 1.

All other layers must be de-selected or the "Current" box will be inaccessible.

> Click on "Current".

The current layer indicator at the top left of the dialogue box will show layer 1.

> When layer 1 and the current box are both highlighted, click on "OK".

At this point we suggest that you try drawing some lines to see that you are, in fact, on layer 1 and drawing in red, continuous lines.

When you are satisfied with the red lines you have drawn, go into the Layer Control dialogue box again (click twice on "Data") and set the current layer to 2. Now draw more lines and see that they are "hidden" yellow lines.

Set layer 3 as the current layer and draw some green center lines.

Finally, set layer 1 as the current layer again before moving on.

Other Options in the Layer Control Box

In the upper right-hand corner of the Layer Control dialogue box you will see three pairs of layer mode settings. These settings probably will not be useful to you until later on, but we introduce them briefly here for your information.

"On" and "Off" affect only the visibility of objects on a layer. Objects on layers that are off are not visible or plotted, but are still in the drawing and are considered when the drawing is "regenerated". Regeneration is the process by which AutoCAD translates the very precise numerical data that make up a drawing file database into the less precise values of screen graphics. Regeneration can be a slow process in large, complex drawings. As a result it may be useful not to regenerate all the time. This is where "Freeze" comes in. Frozen layers are not only invisible but are ignored in regeneration. "Thaw", of course, reverses this setting. Thawed layers will always be regenerated.

"Lock" and "Unlock" do not affect visibility, but do affect availability of objects for editing. Objects on locked layers are visible but cannot be edited. "Unlock" reverses this setting.

In addition to "Set Color..." and "Set Ltype..." there are two other boxes with ellipses. As you recall, boxes like these will always call other dialogue boxes. One is the standard Help button. For the other, look in the lower right-hand corner of the box in the "Filters" section and you will see "Set...". By selecting this you call a dialogue box that allows you to limit the layers listed in the Layer Name box. This is a useful feature in large drawings where it is not unusual to have 30 or more layers. Using filters you could, for example, list only the green-colored layers, or only layers with red, continuous lines. The On box allows you to turn filtering on and off once filtering criteria are defined.

The Layer Command

As an alternative to the use of the dialogue box, there is a LAYER command that allows you to control layer characteristics and settings from the command line. You can enter LAYER by typing "la". AutoCAD will issue a prompt that looks like this:

?/Make/Set/New/ON/OFF/Color/Ltype/Freeze/Thaw/LOck/Unlock:

Here is a brief look at how the options work. "?" will bring up a list of defined layers similar to the list in the dialogue box. You can limit the list by using the MS-DOS wild card characters ? and *. The * represents any string of characters in a layer name, while the ? represents any individual character.

"Make" is used to create a single new layer, which automatically becomes the current layer. "Set" is the option used to set a new current layer when the layer is already defined. "New" is used to define new layers.

All the other options are the same as in the dialogue box. If you use the LAYER command you will not have to load individual linetypes. However, you will have to know the linetype you want and type its name correctly.

The Purge Command

You will notice that there is no option for deleting layers in either the LAYER command or the Layer Control dialogue box. Deleting layers is handled through the PURGE command. To use PURGE, type "purge" at the command prompt, or select it from the Data menu. In either case you will see a list of the types of named objects that can be purged from a drawing database. The list includes layers and linetypes, among other things. Only unused objects may be purged. In other words, you cannot purge a layer that has been drawn on, or a linetype definition that is used in the drawing.

Task 5: The Screen Menu

Procedure

1. From the Options pull down menu, select "Preferences...".
2. In the Preferences dialogue box, check the Screen Menu box.

Discussion. AutoCAD has one more method of entering commands and options besides the commands, toolbars, and pull down menus you now know how to use. The screen menu is a complete menu hierarchy that appears on the right side of the display area when it is turned on. It contains all of the AutoCAD command set and options. One of the advantages of having the screen menu on is that command options will appear there regardless of how you enter a command. You may find that it is efficient to enter a command from the keyboard or a toolbar and then pick an option from the screen menu.

We will show you how to turn the screen menu on and off and how it coordinates with other methods. After that, we will leave it to you to decide when to use it.

> Open the Options pull down menu.
> Select "Preferences...".

This will open the Preferences dialogue box illustrated in *Figure 3-5*. On the left in the area labelled "AutoCAD Graphics Window", you will see a box labelled "Screen Menu". It will probably be empty.

> Click on the Screen Menu box.
> When the Screen Menu box shows an ✓, click on the OK button.

The screen menu will be added to the right of your screen as shown in *Figure 3-6*.

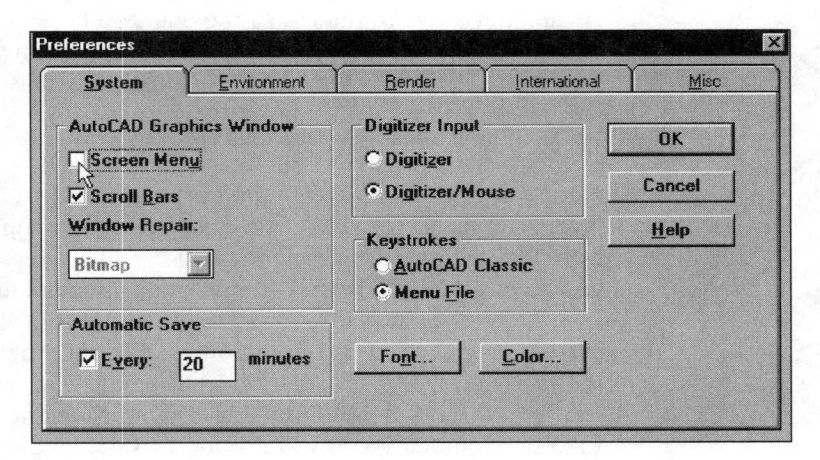

Figure 3-5

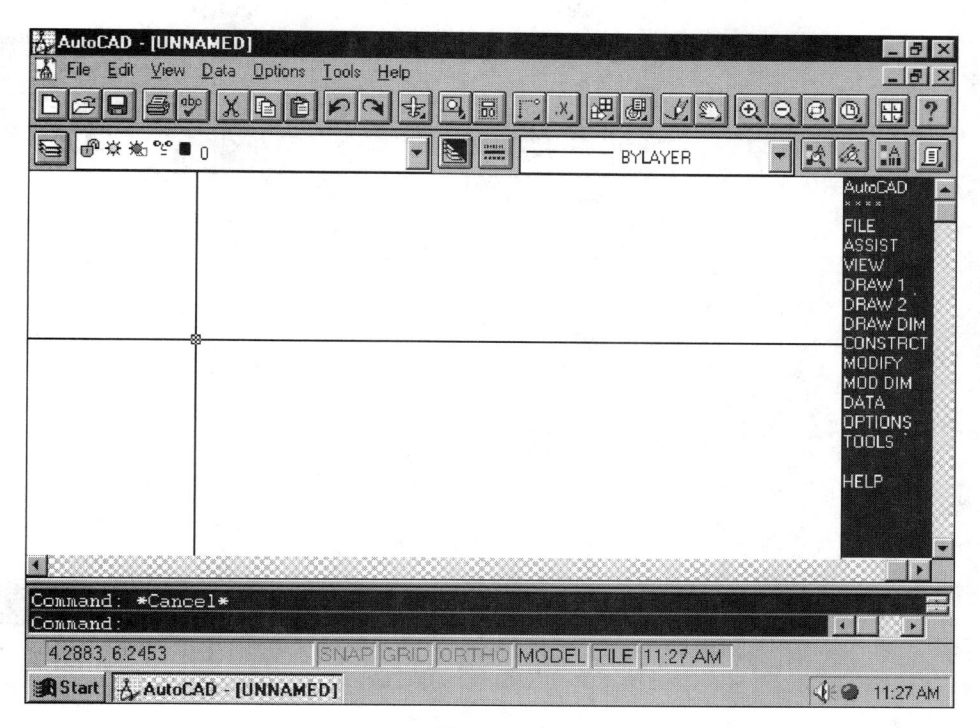

Figure 3-6

> Move the cursor into the screen menu area and run up and down the menu.

As you do this you will see the different menu labels highlighted. To pick a menu, press the pick button when the menu label is highlighted. For example, try opening the FILE menu.

> Move the cursor so that "FILE" is highlighted.
> Press the pick button.

This will bring you to the first submenu, shown in *Figure 3-7*. The options here will work in familiar ways. Selecting "Saveas:", for example, will call up the Saveas dialogue box.

> Click on "AutoCAD" at the top of the screen menu.

This will return you to the main menu. You will see more about how the screen menu works as you work through the FILLET command.

Task 6: Editing Corners Using FILLET

Procedure

1. Type or select the Fillet tool from the Modify toolbar, Feature flyout.
2. Type "r" or select "radius".
3. Enter a radius value.
4. Press Enter to repeat the FILLET command.
5. Select two lines that meet at a corner.

Discussion. Now that you have a variety of linetypes to use, you can begin to do some more realistic mechanical drawings. All you will need is the ability to create filleted (rounded) and chamfered (cut) corners. The two work similarly, and AutoCAD makes them easy. Fillets may also be created between circles and arcs, but the most common usage is the type of situation demonstrated here.

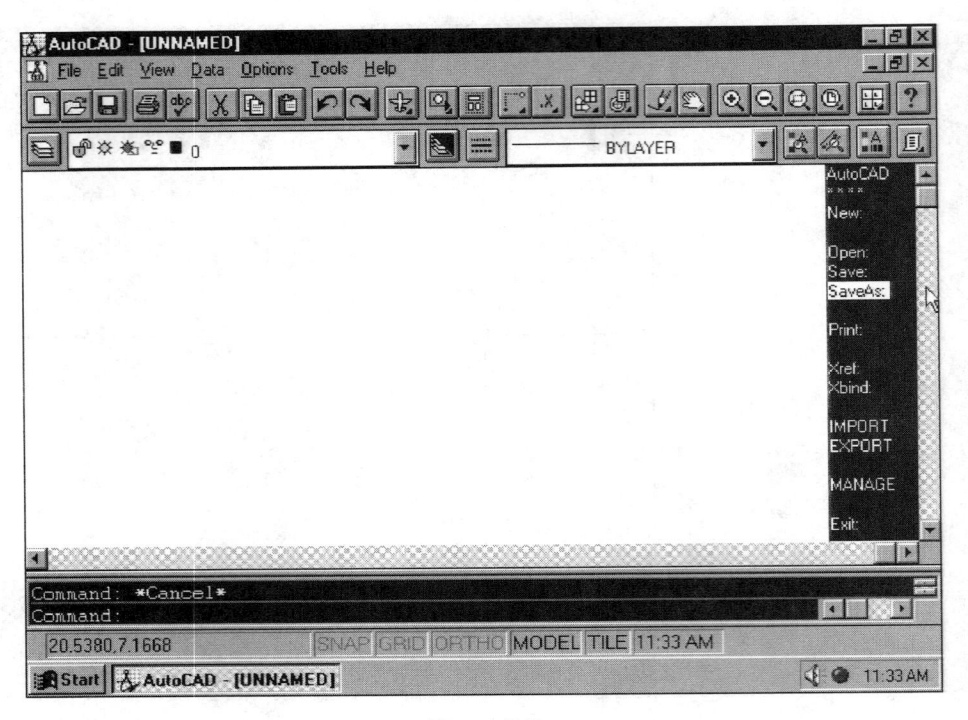

Figure 3-7

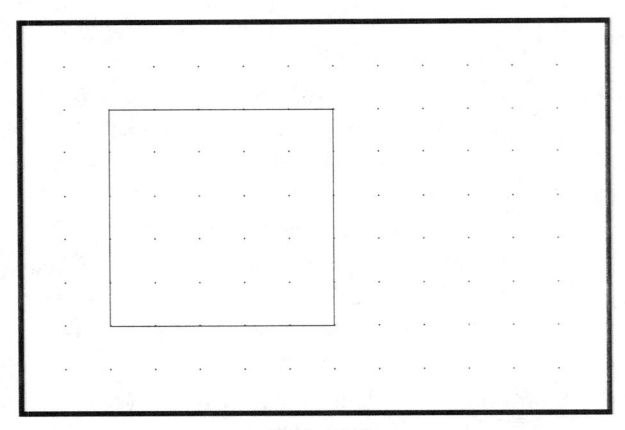

Figure 3-8

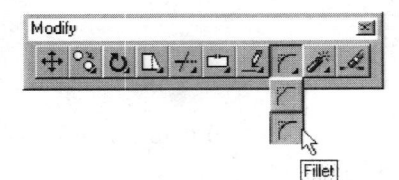

Figure 3-9

> Erase any lines left on the screen from previous exercises.

> If you have not already done so, set layer 1 as the current layer.

> Draw a 5 × 5 square on your screen, as in *Figure 3-8*. We will use this figure to practice fillets and chamfers. Exact coordinates and lengths are not significant.

> Type "Fillet" or open the Modify toolbar and select the Fillet tool from the Feature flyout, as shown in *Figure 3-9*.

A prompt with options will appear in the command area, and you will also see these options listed on the screen menu. Whenever you enter a command, options will be listed on the screen menu and can be selected if the screen menu is visible. The prompt is as follows:

(TRIM mode) Current fillet radius = 0.0000
Polyline/Radius/Trim<Select first object>:

Polylines are discussed in Chapter 8. Trim mode is discussed at the end of this exercise.

The first thing you must do is determine the degree of rounding you want. Since fillets are really arcs, they can be defined by a radius.

> Type "r" or select "Radius" from the screen menu.

AutoCAD prompts:

Enter fillet radius <0.0000>:

The default is 0 because no fillet radius has been defined for this drawing yet. You can use a 0 fillet radius to connect two lines at a corner or, more commonly, you can define a fillet radius by typing a value or showing two points that define the radius length.

> Type ".5" or show two points .5 units apart.

You have set .5 as the standard fillet radius for this drawing. You can change it at any time, but it will not affect previously drawn fillets.

> Press Enter or the space bar to repeat FILLET.

The prompt is the same as before:

(TRIM mode) Current fillet radius = 0.5000
Polyline/Radius/Trim<Select first object>:

You will notice that you have the pickbox on the screen now. Use it to select two lines that meet at any corner of your square.

Behold! A fillet! You did not even have to press Enter. AutoCAD knows that you are done after selecting two lines.

> Press Enter or the space bar to repeat FILLET. Then fillet another corner.

We suggest that you proceed to fillet all four corners of the square. When you are done your screen should resemble *Figure 3-10*.

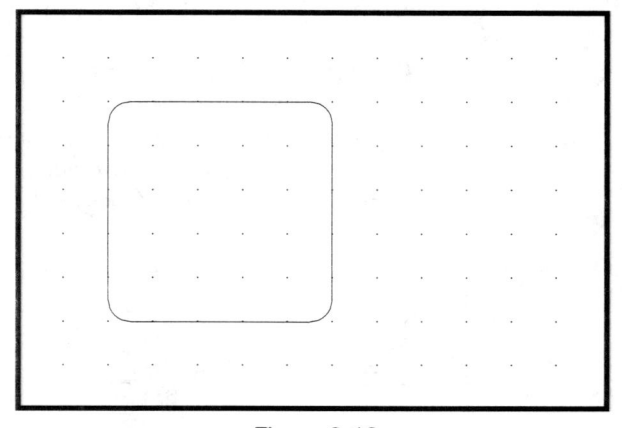

Figure 3-10

Part I / Basic Two-Dimensional Entities

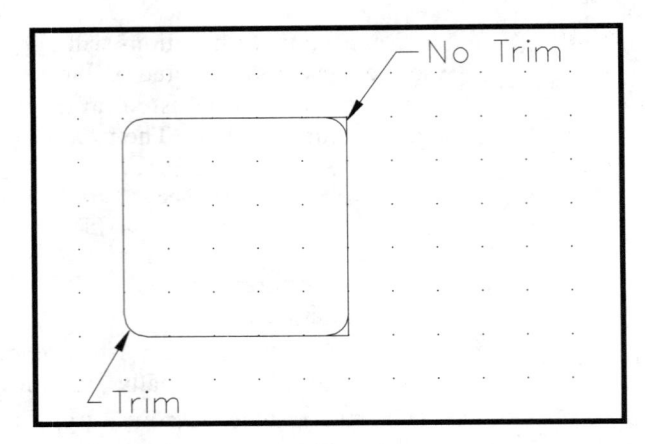

Figure 3-11

Trim Mode

Trim mode is new in Release 13. It allows you to determine whether or not you want AutoCAD to remove square corners as it creates fillets and chamfers. Examples of fillets created with Trim mode on and off are shown in *Figure 3-11*. In most cases, you will want to leave trim mode on. To turn it off, enter FILLET and select "No Trim" from the screen menu, or type "t" for "Trim" and then "n" for "No Trim".

Task 7: Editing Corners with CHAMFER

Procedure

1. Type "Chamfer" or select the Chamfer tool from the Modify toolbar, Feature flyout.
2. Type "d" or select "Distance".
3. Enter a chamfer distance.
4. Press Enter to repeat the CHAMFER command.
5. Select two lines that meet at a corner.

Discussion. The CHAMFER command sequence is almost identical to the FILLET command, with the exception that chamfers may be uneven. That is, you may cut back farther on one side of a corner than on the other. To do this you must give AutoCAD two distances instead of one.

> Prepare for this exercise by undoing all your fillets using the U command as many times as necessary.

> Type "Chamfer" or select the Chamfer tool from the Feature flyout on the Modify toolbar, as shown in *Figure 3-12*. (You can also select Chamfer from the screen menu under "Construct".)

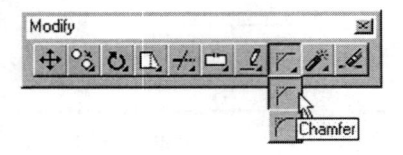

Figure 3-12

AutoCAD prompts:

> (TRIM mode) Current chamfer Dist1 = 0.0000, Dist2 = 0.0000
> Polyline/Distance/Angle/Trim/Method/<Select first line>:

> Type "d" or select "Distance".
  The next prompt will be:

> Enter first chamfer distance <0.0000>:

The present default is 0 because we have yet to define a chamfer distance for this drawing.
> Type ".25".

AutoCAD asks for another distance with a prompt like this:

> Enter second chamfer distance <0.25>:

The first distance has become the default and most of the time it will be used. If you want an asymmetric chamfer, enter a different value for the second distance.
> Press enter to accept the default, making the chamfer distances symmetrical.
  If you have selected "Distance" from the screen menu, CHAMFER will repeat automatically at this point.
> If necessary, press Enter to repeat the CHAMFER command.
> Answer the prompt by pointing to a line this time.
> Point to a second line, perpendicular to the first.
  You should now have a neat chamfer on your square.

The MULTIPLE Command Modifier

If you are creating many fillets or chamfers at once you might want to use the MULTIPLE command modifier to force automatic repetition of the command. At the "Command:" prompt, type the command modifier "multiple" before the command itself, with a space between, like this: "multiple chamfer". Then you can proceed to chamfer one corner after another without having to reenter the command. MULTIPLE can be used with other drawing and editing commands as well. When you are ready to move on to another command, press Esc "Cancel" to return to the command prompt. We suggest that you continue this exercise by chamfering the other three corners of your square, using multiple chamfer if you wish. When you are done, your screen should resemble *Figure 3-13*.

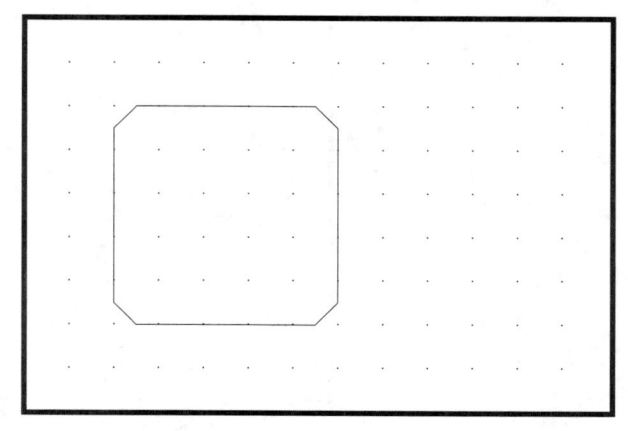

Figure 3-13

Task 8: ZOOMing Window, Previous, and All

Procedure

1. Type "z" or select a Zoom tool from the Standard toolbar.
2. Enter a ZOOM method or magnification value.
3. Enter values or points if necessary, depending on choice of method.

Discussion. The capacity to zoom in and out of a drawing is one of the more impressive benefits of working on a CAD system. When drawings get complex it often becomes necessary to work in detail on small portions of the drawing space. Especially with a small monitor, the only way to do this is by making the detailed area larger on the screen. This is easily done with the ZOOM command. You should have a square with chamfered corners on your screen from the previous exercise. If not, a simple square will do just as well, and you should draw one now.

> Type "z" or select the Zoom Window tool from the Standard toolbar, as illustrated in *Figure 3-14*.

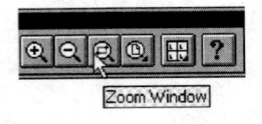

Figure 3-14

The prompt that follows, in the command area and on the screen menu, includes the following options:

All/Center/Dynamic/Extents/Left/Previous/Vmax/Window/<Scale(X/XP)>:

If you have used the Zoom Window tool, the Window option will be entered automatically.

We are interested, for now, in All, Previous, and Window, which we will explore in reverse order. See the *AutoCAD Command Reference* for further information.

As in ERASE and other edit commands, you can force a window selection by typing "w" or selecting "Window". However, this is unnecessary. The windowing action is automatically initiated if you pick a point on the screen after entering ZOOM.

> Pick a point just below and to the left of the lower left-hand corner of your square (point 1 in *Figure 3-15*).

AutoCAD asks for another point:

Other corner:

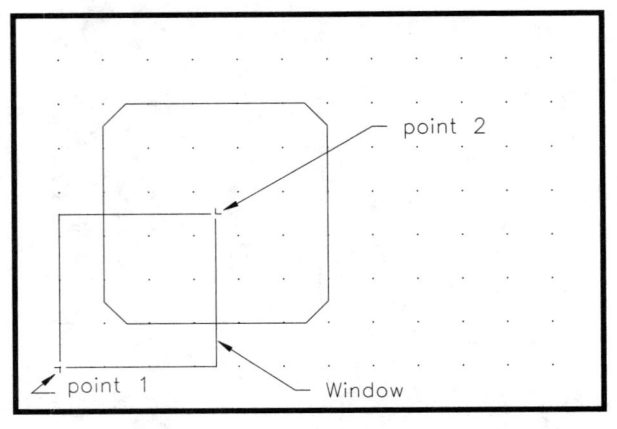

Figure 3-15

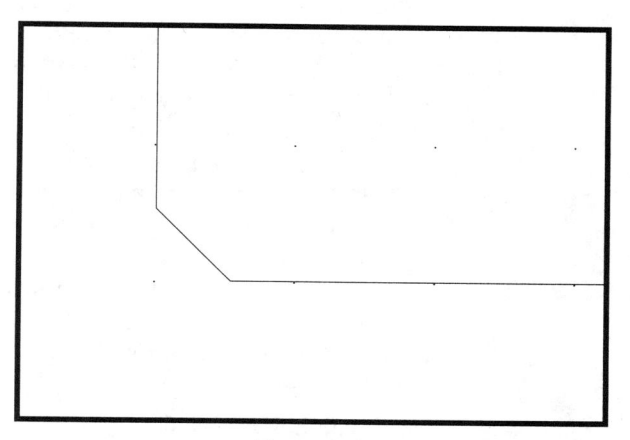

Figure 3-16

You are being asked to define a window, just as in the ERASE command. This window will be the basis for what AutoCAD displays next. Since you are not going to make a window that exactly conforms to the screen size and shape, AutoCAD will interpret the window this way: Everything in the window will be shown, plus whatever additional area is needed to fill the screen. The center of the window will become the center of the new display.

> Pick a second point near the center of your square (point 2 in the figure).

The lower left corner of the square should now appear enlarged on your screen, as shown in *Figure 3-16*.

> Using the same method, try zooming up further on the chamfered corner of the square. If snap is on you may need to turn it off (F9).

Remember that you can repeat the ZOOM command by pressing Enter or the space bar.

At this point, most people cannot resist seeing how much magnification they can get by zooming repeatedly on the same corner or angle of a chamfer. Go ahead. After a couple of zooms the angle will not appear to change. An angle is the same angle no matter how close you get to it. But what happens to the spacing of the grid and snap as you move in?

When you are through experimenting with window zooming, try zooming out to the previous display.

> Press Enter to repeat the ZOOM command. Do not use any of the ZOOM tools.
> Type "p" or select "Previous".

You should now see your previous display.

AutoCAD keeps track of your most recent displays. The exact number of displays it stores depends on the version you are using. Releases 13 remembers ten previous displays.

> ZOOM "Previous" as many times as you can until you get a message that says:

No previous display saved.

Zoom All

ZOOM All zooms out to display the whole drawing. It is useful when you have been working in a number of small areas of a drawing and are ready to view the whole scene. You do not want to have to wade through previous displays to find your way back. ZOOM All will take you there in one jump.

In order to see it work, you should be zoomed in on a portion of your display before executing ZOOM All.

> Press Enter or type "z" to repeat the ZOOM command, or select the Zoom All tool to the right of the Zoom Window tool, illustrated previously in *Figure 3-14*.

The Zoom All tool automatically enters the "All" option. If you have entered the ZOOM command by typing or using the screen menu, you will have the following additional step.

> If necessary, type "a" or select "All" from the screen menu.

There you have it.

NOTE: The Zoom All tool has a flyout that includes tools for all of the ZOOM command options.

Other ZOOM Tools

The other ZOOM tools, Zoom In and Zoom Out, are easy to use, but provide less flexible movement. Zoom In always zooms in by magnifying the image by a factor of 2. Zoom Out reverses this by using a constant factor of 0.5. Try these if you like. At any time you can return to the whole drawing by using the Zoom All tool.

Task 9: Moving the Display Area with PAN

Procedure

1. Type "p" or select the Pan tool from the Standard toolbar.
2. Pick a displacement base point.
3. Pick a second point to show displacement.

Discussion. As soon as you start to use ZOOM you are likely to need PAN as well. While ZOOM allows you to magnify portions of your drawing, PAN allows you to shift the area you are viewing in any direction.

In Windows you have the option of panning with the scrollbars at the edges of the drawing area, but the PAN command allows more precision and flexibility.

> Type "p" or select the Pan tool from the Standard toolbar (as illustrated in *Figure 3-17*).

AutoCAD will prompt you to show a displacement:

Displacement:

Imagine that your complete drawing is hidden somewhere behind your monitor, and that the display area is now functioning like a microscope with the lens focused on one portion. If the ZOOM command increases the magnification of the lens, then PAN moves the drawing like a slide under the lens, in any direction you want.

To move the drawing you will indicate a displacement by picking two points on the screen. The line between them will serve as a vector, showing the distance and direction you want to PAN. Notice that the objects on your screen will move in the direction you indicate; if your vector moves to the right, so will the objects.

Figure 3-17

Chap. 3

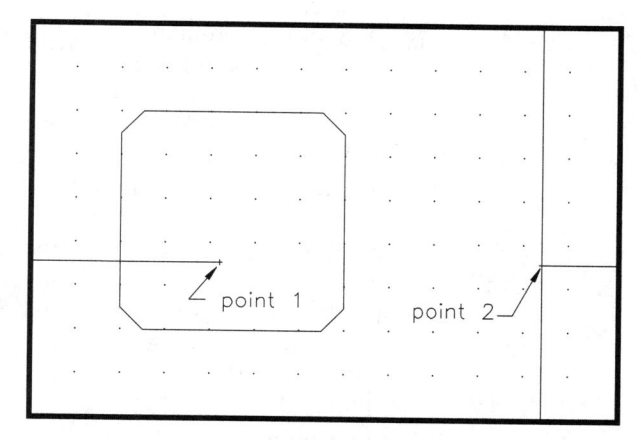

Figure 3-18

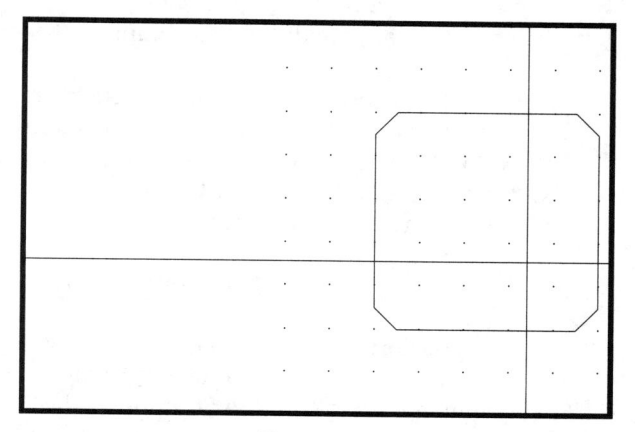

Figure 3-19

> Pick point 1 to begin your displacement vector, as shown in *Figure 3-18*. You will be prompted for another point:

Second point:

> Pick point 2 to the right of your first point.

As soon as you have shown AutoCAD the second point, objects on the screen will shift to the right, as in *Figure 3-19*.
> Press Enter or the space bar to repeat the PAN command.
> Indicate a displacement to the left, moving objects back near their previous positions.

Experiment with the PAN command, moving objects up, down, left, right, and diagonally. You should also compare the effect of using the scrollbars with the PAN command. What function key would make it impossible to PAN diagonally? Hint: The name of the function begins and ends with an "o" and the F-key that turns it on and off begins with an "F" and ends with an "8".

Transparent Commands

If you have used the toolbar or the screen menu to enter the ZOOM and PAN commands, you may have noticed that they place an apostrophe and an underline before the name of the command. If you select the Pan tool, for example, you will see the following in the command area:

Command: '_pan

The apostrophe is a command modifier that makes the command transparent. This means that you can enter it in the middle of another command sequence, and when you are done you will still be in that sequence. For example, you can pan while drawing a line. This is a major convenience if you already have selected the first point and then realize that the second point will be off the screen. A sample procedure using transparent PAN would be as follows:

1. Type "l" or select "Line".
2. Pick a first point.
3. Type "'p" (notice the apostrophe) or select the Pan tool.
4. Show a displacement vector.
5. Pick a second point to complete the line.

The major limitation in the use of transparency is that a command cannot be used transparently if its use would require a regeneration of the drawing. This would happen, for example, if you tried to pan beyond the limits of a drawing (see the section on LIMITS in Chapter 4). Then AutoCAD would give you this message in the command area:

** Requires a regen, cannot be transparent **

and your previous command sequence would be resumed without change.

The underline character (_) you see after the apostrophe and before many commands that AutoCAD sends to the command line is added to commands in menu systems to ensure that AutoCAD interprets the commands in English. Foreign language versions of AutoCAD have their own command names, but can still use menus developed in English, as long as the underline is there as a flag.

Task 10: Creating Multiple Viewports in 2D (Optional)

Procedure

1. Type "vports" or select "Tiled Viewports" and then "Layout ..." from the View pull down menu.
2. Type or select the number of viewports (2, 3, or 4).
3. Specify horizontal and vertical arrangement of windows.

Discussion. Although it may not be critical at this point, you have the ability to create multiple viewports, or windows, on your screen. You can position viewports anywhere on the screen, vary their size, and plot any configuration of viewports. These features are most useful in 3D drawings and will be discussed in depth in Chapters 13 and 15.

Multiple viewports also may be used in 2D to allow you to view different parts of a drawing or a complete drawing and a zoomed portion simultaneously. With multiple viewports you have the advantage of switching views less frequently, but this must be weighed against the disadvantage of working in smaller viewing windows.

There are two types of viewports: tiled and non-tiled. Tiled viewports cover the whole screen and do not overlap. They must be plotted one at a time. Nontiled viewports can be placed in any configuration on the screen and can be plotted as they appear on the screen. They can only be created in paper space.

In this exercise we will create a simple tiled two-viewport configuration with a full view in one window and a zoomed view in the other.

> To begin this exercise, you should have a full view of the chamfered square, as shown previously in *Figure 3-13*.

> Type "vports". (Avoid the pull down menu for now.)

AutoCAD will prompt:

Save/Restore/Delete/Join/SIngle/?/2/<3>/4:

You will see the same options on the screen menu, if it is available. "Save", "Restore", and "Delete" allow you to keep viewport configurations in memory once they have been created. "Join" will reduce the number of viewports by joining two adjacent windows. "SIngle" returns you to a single window. "?" will give you a list of viewport configurations you have previously saved. The numbers 2, 3, and 4 specify numbers of windows. We will use two windows in this exercise.

> Type or select "2" from the screen menu.

AutoCAD still needs to know which way to split the screen:

Horizontal/<Vertical>:

> Type "v" or select "Vertical" (you can also simply press Enter since vertical is the default).

Your screen will be redrawn as shown in *Figure 3-20*.

> Now move your cursor back and forth between the two windows.

You will see the cross hairs whenever you are in the right viewport and an arrow when you are in the left viewport. You will also notice that the right viewport is surrounded by a black border. This indicates that the right viewport is currently active. You can perform drawing or editing in the current viewport only. However, any changes you make will be immediately reflected in all viewports.

> Move the cursor to the left viewport and press the pick button.

The cross hairs will appear on the left. The left viewport is now active and its border will be black. If you move back to the right you will see the arrow. Often you can switch viewports while you are in the middle of a command sequence. With some commands, such as ZOOM and PAN, this will not work.

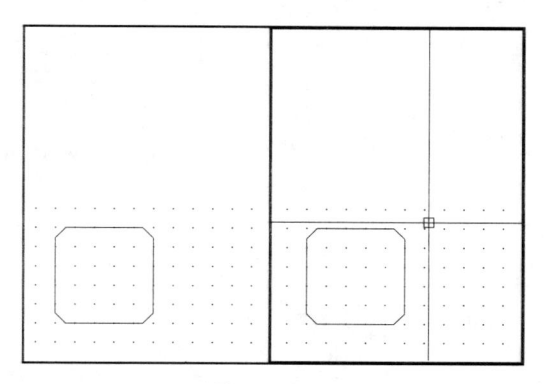

Figure 3-20

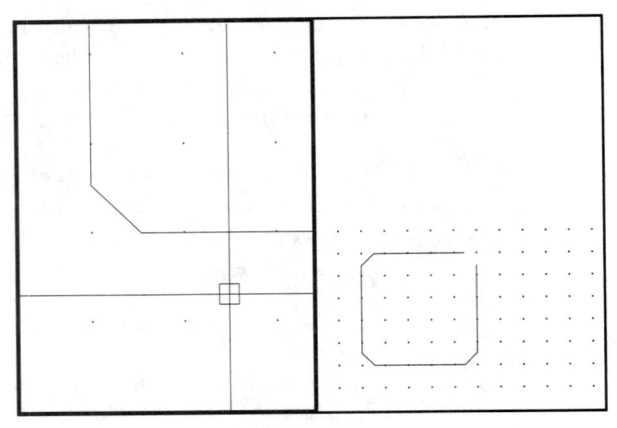

Figure 3-21

> With the left viewport active, enter the ZOOM command and zoom in on a window around the lower left corner of the square.
Your screen should now resemble *Figure 3-21*.

To complete this exercise, you may want to do some simple drawing and editing in each viewport and observe how your changes appear in both viewports.

None of the two-dimensional drawings in this book will require multiple viewports, but you may try them at any time if you wish. If you want more information, see the *AutoCAD User's Guide*.

The Tiled Viewport Layout Dialogue Box

Before going on, return to a single viewport by using the Single option in the "Tiled Viewport Layout" dialogue box.

> Select "Tiled Viewports...", and then "Layout" from the View pull down menu, or "VIEW" and then "DDvport:" on the screen menu.

This will call up a Tiled Viewport Layout dialogue box, illustrated in *Figure 3-22*. This box shows 12 standard viewport configurations on the right. These configurations are named in order on the left of the box.

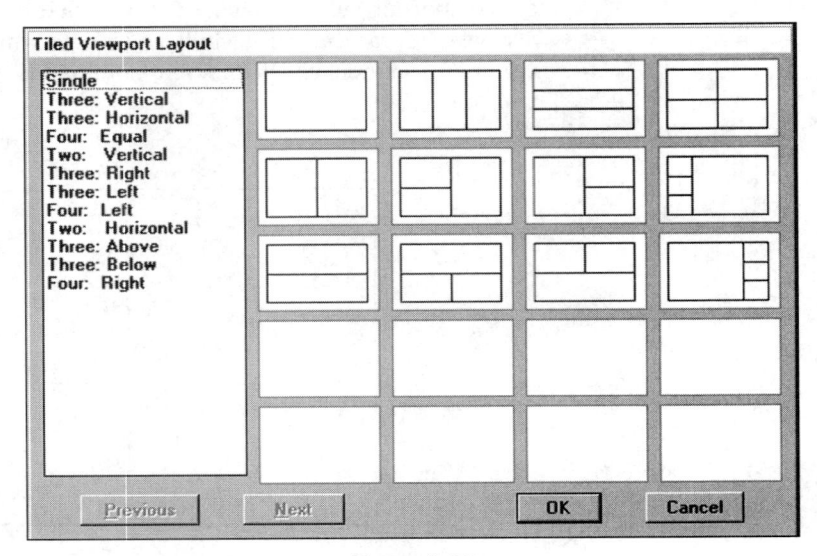

Figure 3-22

Chap. 3

> Select "Single" by picking the top left layout box or the top line of the list.
> Click on "OK".

Notice that the new display is derived from whichever viewport was active before you executed the Single option. You may need to do a ZOOM All to return to the original display.

Task 11: Using Plot Preview

Procedure

1. Type "Plot" or select the Print tool from the Standard toolbar.
2. Change parameters as needed.
3. Select Partial or Full preview.
4. Select "Preview...".

Discussion. The plot preview feature of the Plot Configuration dialogue box is an essential tool in carrying out efficient plotting and printing. Plot configuration is complex and the odds are good that you will waste time and paper by printing drawings directly without first previewing them on the screen. In this task we are still significantly limited in our use of plot configuration parameters, but learning to use the plot preview will make all of your future work with plotting and printing more effective.

> To begin this task you should have a drawing on your screen ready to preview. Any drawing will do, but we will illustrate using Drawing 3–4.

> Type "plot" or select the Print tool from the Standard toolbar as illustrated in *Figure 3-23*.

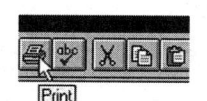

Figure 3-23

This will open the Plot Configuration dialogue box. Plot Preview is at the lower right of the dialogue box. There are two types of preview, "Partial" and "Full". A partial preview will show you an outline of the effective plotting area in relation to the paper size, but will not show an image of the plotted drawing. NOTE: We will address paper sizes in the next chapter. For now, we will assume that your plot configuration is correctly matched to the paper in your printer or plotter. If you do not get good results with this task, the problem may very well lie here.

Partial previews are quick and should be accessed frequently as you set plot parameters that affect how paper will be used and oriented to print your drawing. Full previews take longer and may be saved for when you think you have got everything right.

We will look at a partial preview first.

> If the "Partial" radio button is not selected in your dialogue box, select it now.
> Click on "Preview...".

You will see a preview image similar to the one shown in *Figure 3-24*. The exact image will depend on your plotting device, so it may be different from the one shown here. The elements of the preview will be the same, however. The red rectangle represents your drawing paper. It may be oriented in landscape (horizontally) or portrait (vertically). Typically, printers are in portrait, and plotters in landscape.

Part I / Basic Two-Dimensional Entities

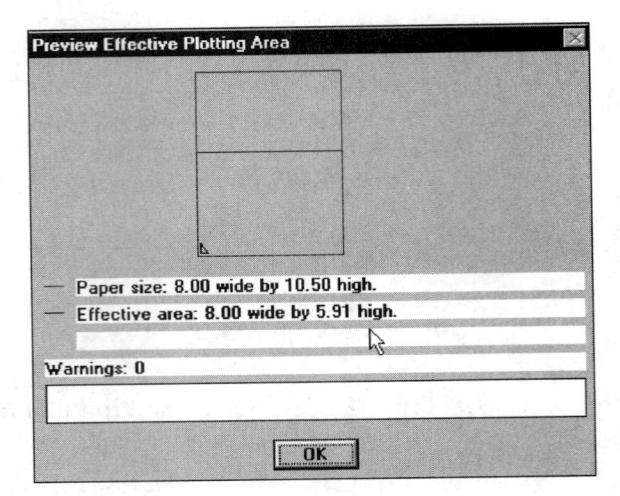

Figure 3-24

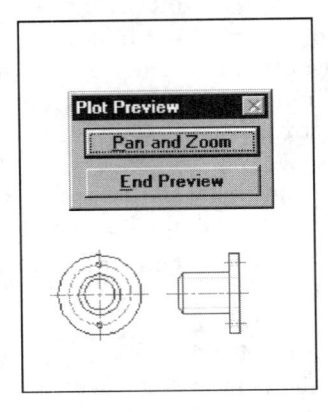

Figure 3-25

The blue rectangle inside the red one illustrates the effective plotting area. It is quite possible that the blue and red rectangles will overlap. The blue represents the size and shape of the area that AutoCAD can actually use given the shape of the drawing in relation to the size and orientation of the paper. The effective area is dependent on many things, as you will see. We will leave it as is for now and return later when you begin to alter the plot configuration.

In one corner of the red rectangle you will see a small triangle. This is the rotation icon. It shows the corner of the plotting area where the plotter will begin plotting (the origin).

> Click on "OK" to exit the preview box.
> Click on the "Full" radio button to switch to a full preview.
> Click on "Preview...".

The dialogue box will disappear temporarily and you will see a preview similar to the one in *Figure 3-25*. We have used Drawing 3–4 to illustrate. You will see whatever drawing you are previewing, with orientation and placement depending on your plotting device.

The small Plot Preview box in the middle can be moved aside like any dialogue box. Just move the cursor to the gray title area, press the pick button, and hold it down as you move the box.

The "Pan and Zoom" feature allows you to look closely at small areas in the drawing, to check text or dimensions, for example. Panning and zooming in the preview has no effect on the plot parameters.

> Click on "Pan and Zoom".

Selecting "Pan and Zoom" will cause the box to disappear and be replaced by a rectangle with an **x** in the middle. This feature functions like the pan and zoom box in the "dynamic" option of the ZOOM command (Chapter 11). The box shows the portion of the drawing that will be shown when the pan/zoom is executed. With the **x** showing, you are in "pan" mode. You can move the box to any portion of the drawing you want to examine. Pressing Enter while in pan mode will cause AutoCAD to show you an image of the portion of your drawing that is within the pan box.

> Press the pick button once. (Do not press Enter or the enter button on your cursor yet.)

When you press the pick button once, the **x** will be replaced by an arrow at the right side of the box. Then you will be able to shrink or stretch the box by moving the cursor left or right. This is the "zoom" mode, which allows you to focus on larger or smaller segments of the drawing. Notice that you cannot move the box to the left. You can only cause it to expand or contract to the right. To move to the left you need to press the pick button again to get back into pan mode. To get the precise area you want you may need to switch back and forth between pan and zoom several times. When you have moved and stretched the box so that it windows the area you want to see, press the second button on your cursor, or press Enter. This will execute the magnification and you will see an enlarged image. We suggest that you try it on whatever drawing you are looking at.

> Pan and zoom to window an area of your drawing that contains objects.

> Press Enter, the space bar, or the enter button on your pointing device.

You will see an enlarged image of that portion of your drawing.

> Click on "Zoom Previous" to return to the full drawing preview.

> Click on "End Preview" to exit the full preview.

This will bring you back to the Plot Configuration dialogue.

This ends our initial preview of your drawing. In ordinary practice, if everything looked right in the preview you would move on to plot or print your drawing now by clicking on "OK". In the chapters that follow, we will explore the rest of the plot configuration dialogue box and will use plot preview extensively as we change plot parameters. For now, get used to using plot preview. If things are not coming out quite the way you want, you will be able to fix them soon.

Tasks 12, 13, 14, 15, and 16

With layers, colors, linetypes, fillets, chamfers, zooming, and panning you are ready to do the drawings for Chapter 3.

Remember to set grid, snap, and units and to define layers before you begin each drawing. Use the ZOOM and PAN commands whenever you think they would help you to draw more efficiently. When you are ready to plot a drawing, take full advantage of the plot preview feature in the Plot Configuration dialogue box.

DRAWING 3-1: MOUNTING PLATE

This drawing will give you experience using center lines and chamfers. Since there are no hidden lines, you will have no need for layer 2, but we will continue to use the same numbering system for consistency. Draw the continuous lines in red on layer 1 and the center lines in green on layer 3.

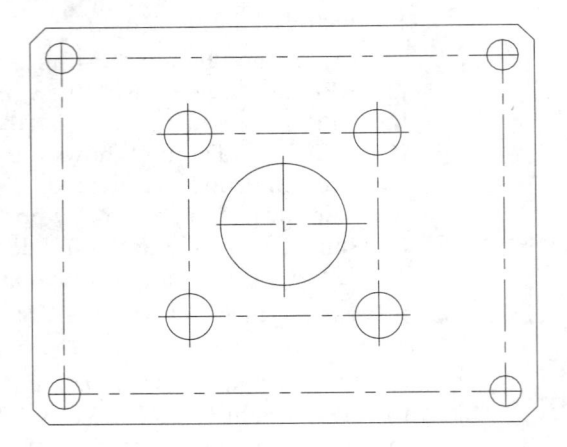

DRAWING SUGGESTIONS

GRID = .5
SNAP = .25
LTSCALE = .5

LTSCALE

The size of the individual dashes and spaces that make up center lines, hidden lines, and other linetypes is determined by a global setting called "LTSCALE". By default it is set to a factor of 1.00. In smaller drawings this setting will be too large and will cause some of the shorter lines to appear continuous regardless of what layer they are on.

To remedy this, change LTSCALE as follows:

1. Type "ltscale" or select "Linetypes" and then "Global Linetype Scale" from the Options pull down menu.
2. Enter a value.

For the drawings in this chapter use a setting of .50. See *Figure 3-26* for some examples of the effect of changing LTSCALE.

> Draw the chamfered rectangle and the nine circles on layer 1 first. Then set current layer to 3 and draw the center lines.

NOTE: In manual drafting it would be more common to draw the center lines first and use them to position the circles. Either order is fine, but be aware that what is standard practice in pencil and paper drafting may not be efficient or necessary on a CAD system.

——— — ——— LTSCALE = 1.00

—— — —— — LTSCALE = .50

— — — — — — — LTSCALE = .25

Figure 3-26

Chap. 3

.25 x .25 CHAMFER
4 PLACES

4.00
2.50
3.00

Ø.75
4 HOLES

3.00

Ø2.00

3.25

1.75

5.50 6.50

.50

.50

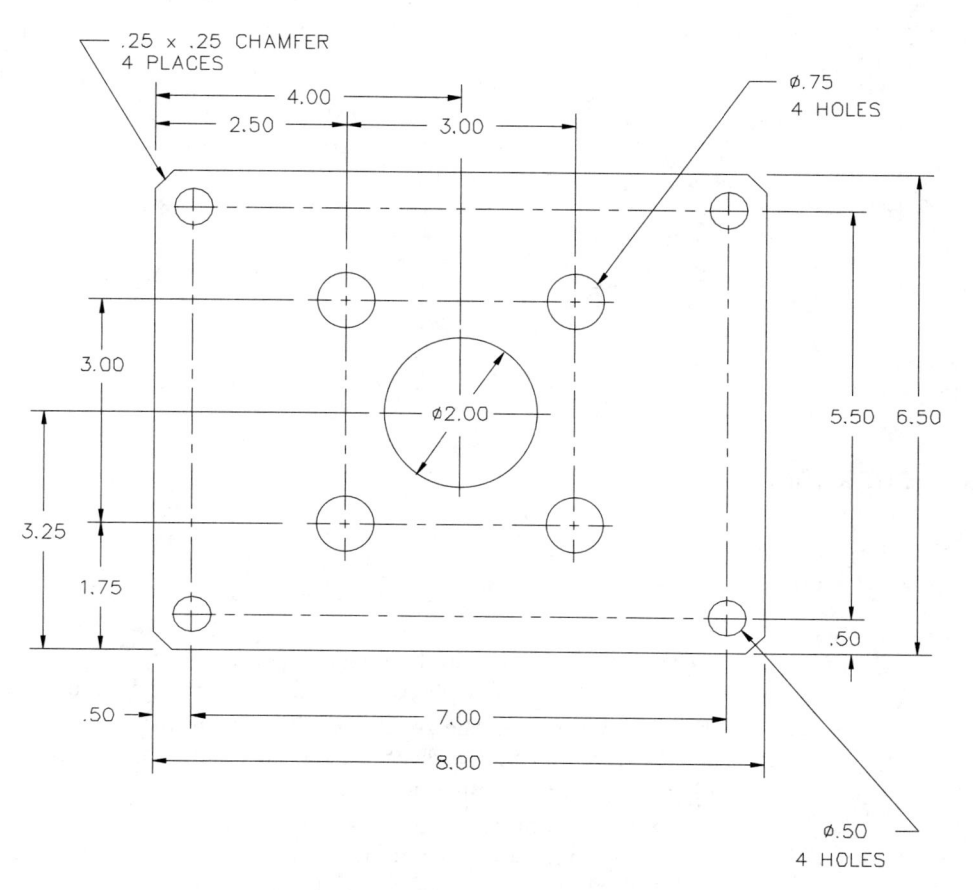

7.00

8.00

Ø.50
4 HOLES

MOUNTING PLATE
Drawing 3-1

LAYERS	NAME	COLOR	LINETYPE		
	0	WHITE	———— CONTINUOUS	LINE	(L)
	1	RED	———— CONTINUOUS	CIRCLE	(C)
	3	GREEN	– – – – CENTER	CHAMFER	
				ZOOM	(Z)

F1 — HELP
F2 — TEXT/GRAPHICS SCREEN
F6 — ABSOLUTE/OFF/POLAR COORDS
F7 — ON/OFF GRID
F8 — ON/OFF ORTHO
F9 — ON/OFF SNAP

DRAWING 3-2: STEPPED SHAFT

This two-view drawing uses continuous lines, center lines, chamfers, and fillets. You may want to zoom in to enlarge the drawing space you are actually working in, and pan right and left to work on the two views.

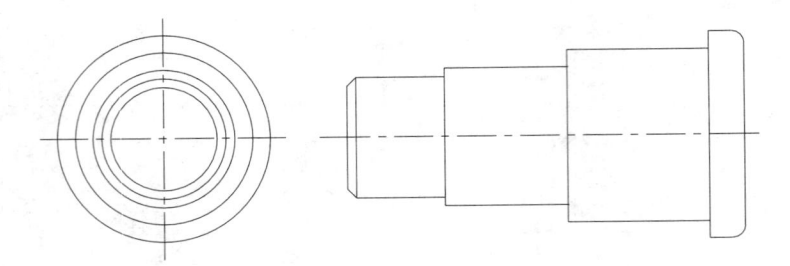

DRAWING SUGGESTIONS

GRID = .25
SNAP = .125
LTSCALE = .5

> Center the front view in the neighborhood of (2,5). Then the right side view will have a starting point at about (5,4.12), before the chamfer cuts this corner off.

> Draw the circles in the front view first, using the vertical dimensions from the side view for diameters. Save the inner circle until after you have drawn and chamfered the right side view.

> Draw a series of rectangles for the side view, lining them up with the circles of the front view. Then chamfer two corners of the leftmost rectangle and fillet two corners of the rightmost rectangle.

> Use the chamfer on the side view to line up the radius of the inner circle.

> Remember to set current layer to 3 before drawing the center line through the side view.

Chap. 3

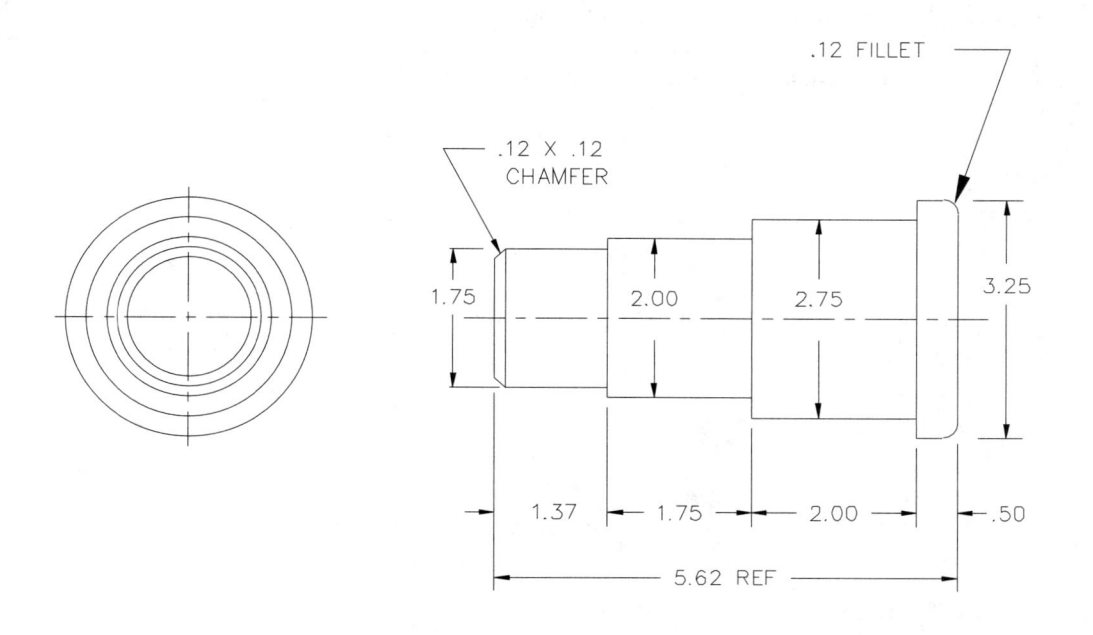

.12 FILLET

.12 X .12 CHAMFER

1.75   2.00   2.75   3.25

1.37   1.75   2.00   .50

5.62 REF

STEPPED SHAFT
Drawing 3-2

LAYERS	NAME	COLOR	LINETYPE	
	0	WHITE	CONTINUOUS	
	1	RED	CONTINUOUS	
	3	GREEN	CENTER	

LINE (L)
CIRCLE (C)
CHAMFER
FILLET
ZOOM (Z)

F1	F2	F6	F7	F8	F9
HELP	TEXT/GRAPHICS SCREEN	ABSOLUTE/OFF/POLAR COORDS	ON/OFF GRID	ON/OFF ORTHO	ON/OFF SNAP

83

DRAWING 3-3: BASE PLATE

This drawing uses continuous lines, hidden lines, center lines, and fillets. The side view should be quite easy once the front view is drawn. Remember to change layers when you want to change linetypes.

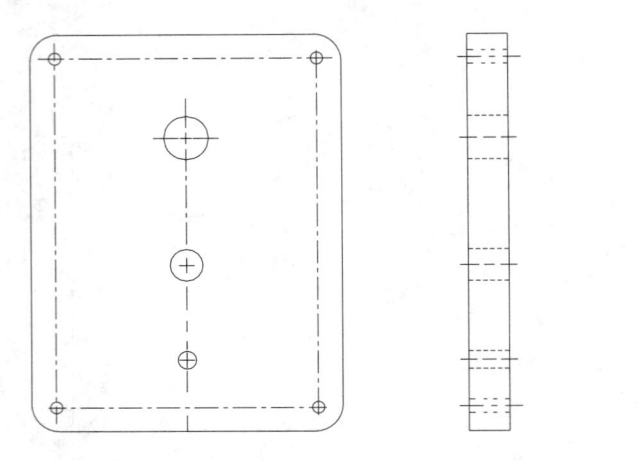

DRAWING SUGGESTIONS

GRID = .25
SNAP = .125
LTSCALE = .5

> Study the dimensions carefully and remember that every grid increment is .25, while snap points not on the grid are exactly halfway between grid points. The four circles at the corners are .38 (actually .375 rounded off) over and in from the corner points. This is three snap spaces (.375 = 3 × .125).

> Position the three circles along the center line of the rectangle carefully. Notice that dimensions are given from the center of the screw holes at top and bottom.

> Use the circle perimeters to line up the hidden lines on the side view, and the centers to line up the center lines.

Chap. 3

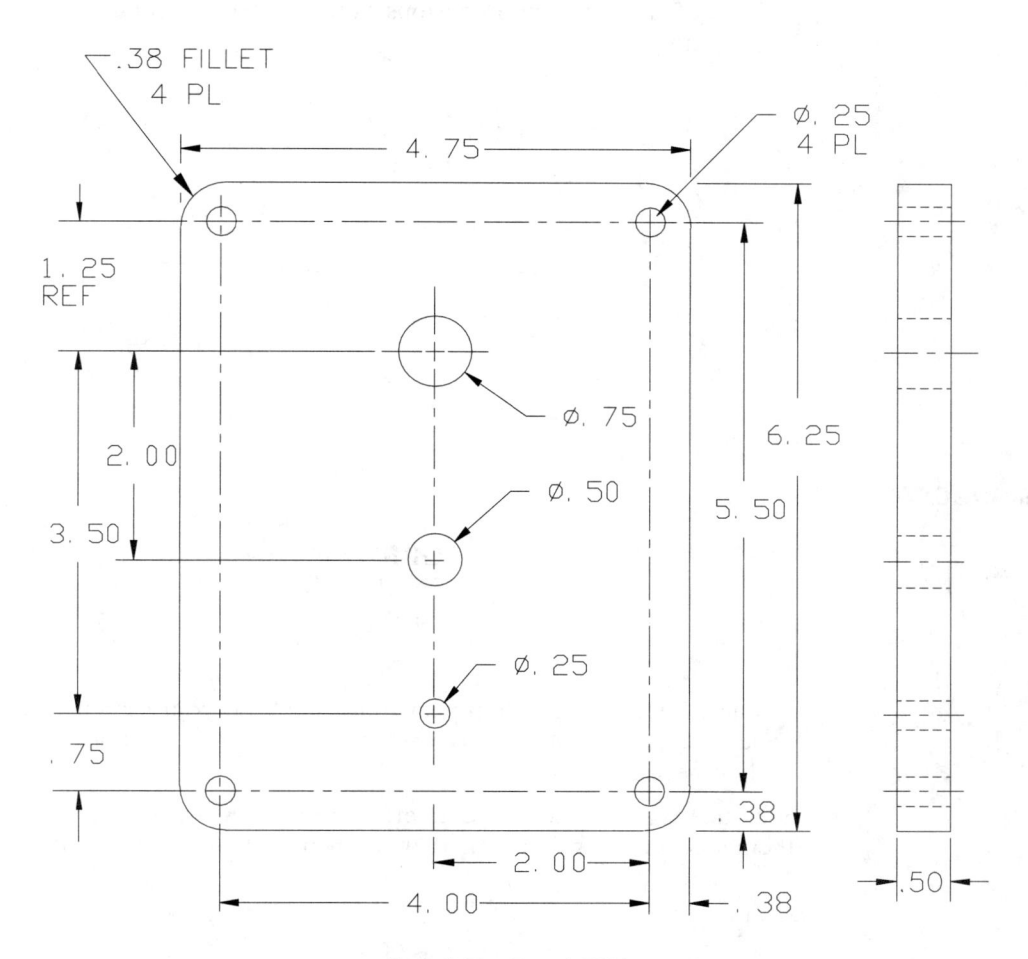

BASE PLATE
Drawing 3-3

- .38 FILLET 4 PL
- Ø.25 4 PL
- 4.75
- 1.25 REF
- Ø.75
- 2.00
- Ø.50
- 3.50
- 6.25
- 5.50
- Ø.25
- .75
- .38
- 2.00
- .38
- 4.00
- .50

LAYERS	NAME	COLOR	LINETYPE
	0	WHITE	———— CONTINUOUS
	1	RED	———— CONTINUOUS
	2	YELLOW	-------- HIDDEN
	3	GREEN	— — — CENTER

LINE (L)
CIRCLE (C)
FILLET
ZOOM (Z)

- [F1] HELP
- [F2] TEXT/GRAPHICS SCREEN
- [F6] ABSOLUTE/OFF/POLAR COORDS
- [F7] ON/OFF GRID
- [F8] ON/OFF ORTHO
- [F9] ON/OFF SNAP

DRAWING 3-4: BUSHING

This drawing will give you practice with chamfers, layers, and zooming. Notice that because of the smaller dimensions here, we have recommended a smaller LTSCALE setting.

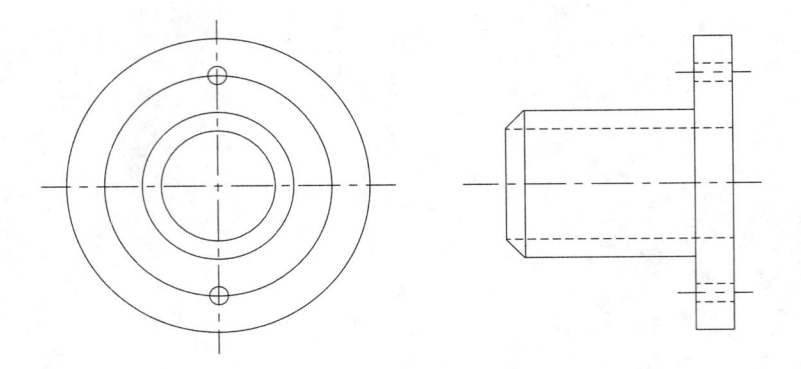

DRAWING SUGGESTIONS

GRID = .25
SNAP = .125
LTSCALE = .25

> Since this drawing will appear quite small on your screen, it would be a good idea to ZOOM in on the actual drawing space you are using, and use PAN if necessary.

> Notice that the two .25-diameter screw holes are 1.50 apart. This puts them squarely on grid points that you will have no trouble finding.

REGEN

When you zoom you may find that your circles turn into many-sided polygons. AutoCAD does this to save time. These time savings are not noticeable now, but when you get into larger drawings they become very significant. If you want to see a proper circle, type "Regen". This command will cause your drawing to be regenerated more precisely from the data you have given.

You may also notice that REGENs happen automatically when certain operations are performed, such as changing the LTSCALE setting after objects are already on the screen.

Chap. 3
87

.25 DIA THRU
2 HOLES EQ SP
ON 1.50 B.C

.75 DIA THRU

.25

1.00

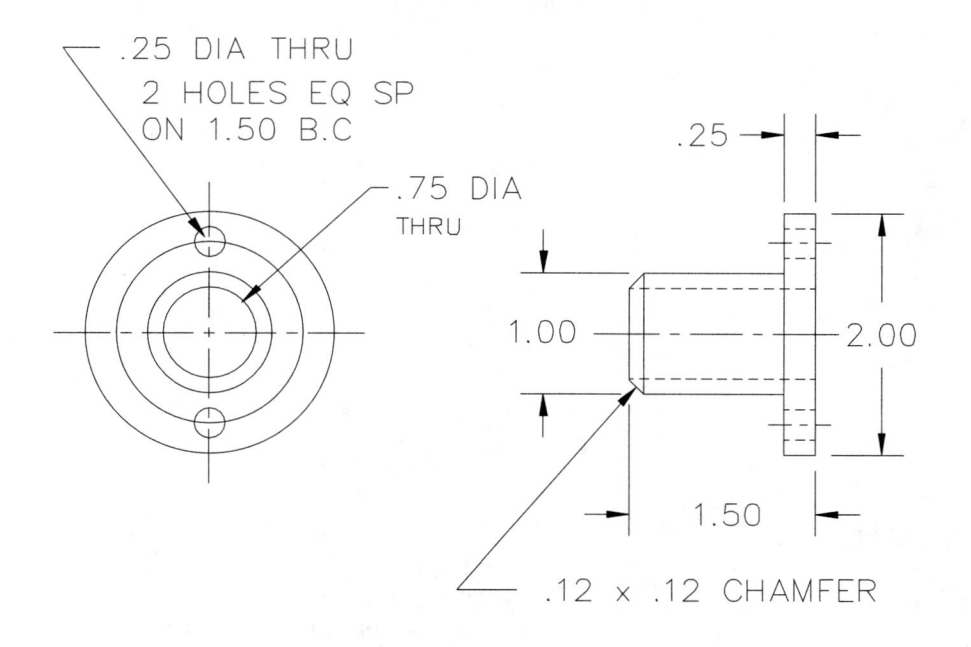

2.00

1.50

.12 x .12 CHAMFER

BUSHING
Drawing 3-4

LAYERS	NAME	COLOR	LINETYPE	
	0	WHITE	————	CONTINUOUS
	1	RED	————	CONTINUOUS
	2	YELLOW	- - - - - -	HIDDEN
	3	GREEN	— - —	CENTER

LINE (L)
CIRCLE (C)
CHAMFER
ZOOM (Z)

F1 HELP
F2 TEXT/GRAPHICS SCREEN
F6 ABSOLUTE/OFF/POLAR COORDS
F7 ON/OFF GRID
F8 ON/OFF ORTHO
F9 ON/OFF SNAP

DRAWING 3-5: HALF BLOCK

This cinder block is the first project using architectural units in this book. Set units, grid, and snap as indicated, and everything will fall into place nicely.

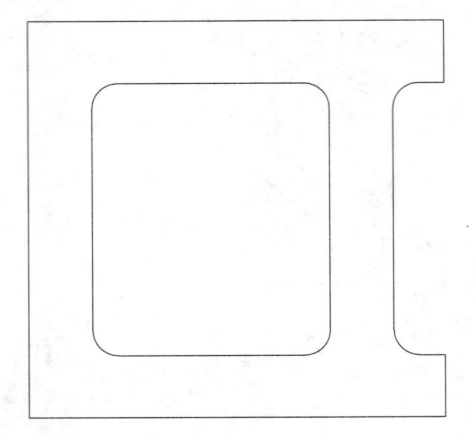

DRAWING SUGGESTIONS

UNITS = Architectural
smallest fraction = 4 (1/4")
GRID = 1/4"
SNAP = 1/4"

> Start with the lower left corner of the block at the point (0'-1",0'-1") to keep the drawing well placed on the display.

> After drawing the outside of the block with the 5 1/2" indentation on the right, use the DIST command to locate the inner rectangle 1 1/4" in from each side.

> Set the FILLET radius to 1/2" or .5. Notice that you can use decimal versions of fractions. The advantage is that they are easier to type.

> You can use MULTIPLE FILLET to fillet the six corners.

Chap. 3

.5 RAD. FILLET
6 PLACES

8"

1 1/4"

5 1/2"

1 1/4"

1"

8"

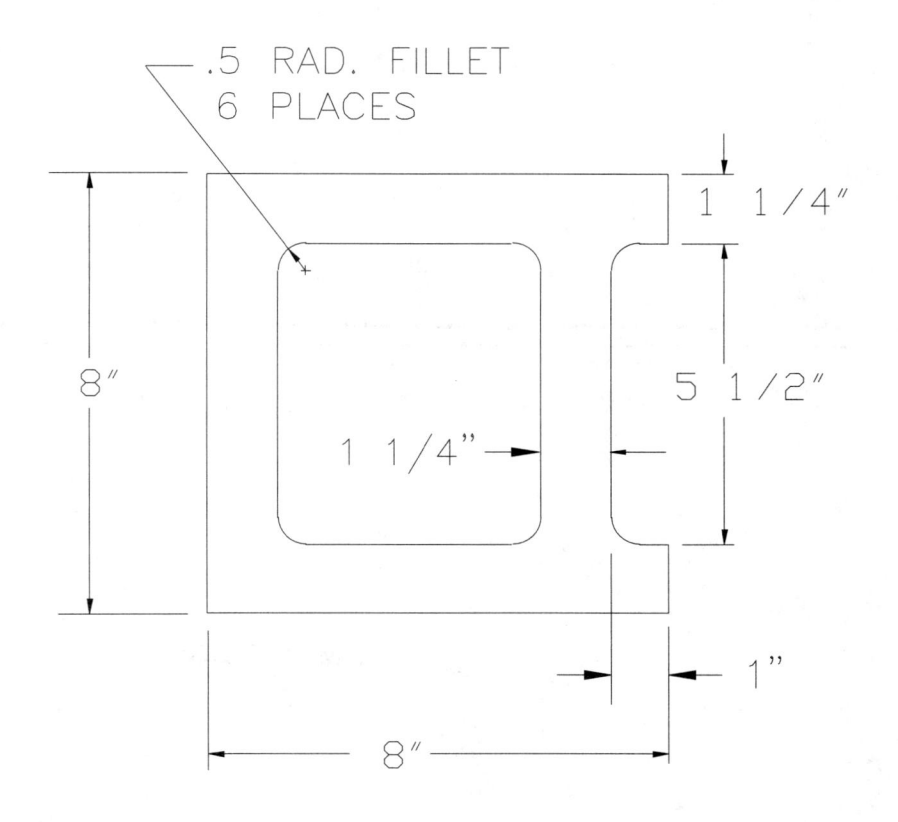

HALF BLOCK

Drawing 3-5

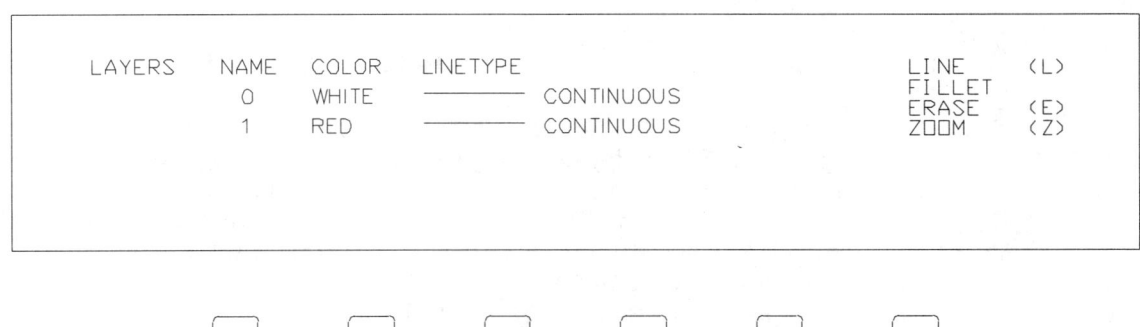

LAYERS	NAME	COLOR	LINETYPE			
	0	WHITE	———————— CONTINUOUS		LINE	(L)
	1	RED	———————— CONTINUOUS		FILLET	
					ERASE	(E)
					ZOOM	(Z)

F1 — HELP
F2 — TEXT/GRAPHICS SCREEN
F6 — ABSOLUTE/OFF/POLAR COORDS
F7 — ON/OFF GRID
F8 — ON/OFF ORTHO
F9 — ON/OFF SNAP

CHAPTER 4

COMMANDS

MODIFY	**DATA**
ARRAY (rectangular)	LIMITS
COPY	
MOVE	

Special Topic: Prototype drawings

OVERVIEW

In this chapter you will learn some real timesavers. If you have grown tired of defining the same three layers, along with units, grid, snap, and ltscale, for each new drawing, read on. You are about to learn how to use prototype drawings. With prototypes, you can begin each new drawing with whatever setup you want. In addition, you will learn to reshape the grid using the LIMITS command, and to COPY, MOVE, and ARRAY objects on the screen so that you do not have to draw the same thing twice. We will begin with LIMITS, since we will want to change the limits as part of defining your first prototype.

TASKS

1. Change the shape of the grid using the LIMITS command.
2. Create a prototype drawing.

Chap. 4

3. Select your drawing as the prototype.
4. MOVE an object in a drawing.
5. COPY an object in a drawing.
6. Create a rectangular ARRAY.
7. Change Plot Configuration parameters.
8. Do Drawing 4–1 ("Pattern").
9. Do Drawing 4–2 ("Grill").
10. Do Drawing 4–3 ("Weave").
11. Do Drawing 4–4 ("Test Bracket").
12. Do Drawing 4–5 ("Floor Framing").

Task 1: Setting LIMITS

Procedure

1. Type "Limits" or select "Drawing Limits" from the Data pull down menu.
2. Enter lower left-hand coordinates.
3. Enter upper right-hand coordinates.
4. ZOOM All.

Discussion. You have changed the density of the screen grid many times, but always within the same 12 × 9 space, which basically represents an A-size sheet of paper. Now you will learn how to change the shape, by setting new limits to emulate other sheet sizes or any other space you want to represent. But first, a word about model space and paper space.

Model Space and Paper Space

"Model space" is an AutoCAD concept that refers to the imaginary space in which we create and edit objects. In model space, objects are always drawn full scale (1 screen unit = 1 unit of length in the real world). The alternative to model space is "paper space", in which screen units represent units of length on a piece of drawing paper. Paper space is most useful in plotting multiple views of 3D drawings. In Part I of this book all of your work will be done in model space.

In this exercise we will reshape our model space to emulate different drawing sheet sizes. This will not be necessary in actual practice. With AutoCAD you can scale your drawing to fit any drawing sheet size when it comes time to plot. Model space limits should be determined by the size and shapes of objects in your drawing, not by the paper you are going to use when you plot. However, you set limits in model space and in paper space in exactly the same way, so what you learn here will translate very easily when you begin using paper space.

> Begin a new drawing using "No Prototype".

After we are finished exploring the LIMITS command, we will create the new settings we want and save this drawing as your B-size prototype.

> Use F7 to turn the grid on.

> Type "Limits" or select "Drawing Limits" from the Data pull down menu.

AutoCAD will prompt you as follows:

Reset Model Space limits
ON/OFF/<lower left corner> <0.0000,0.0000>:

Part I / Basic Two-Dimensional Entities

The ON and OFF options determine what happens when you attempt to draw outside the limits of the grid. With LIMITS off, nothing will happen. With LIMITS on, AutoCAD will not accept any attempt to begin an entity outside of limits, notifying you with the message "Attempt to draw outside of limits". You can extend objects beyond the limits as long as they were started within them. By default, LIMITS is off, and we will leave it that way.

> Press Enter.

This will enter the default values for the lower left corner (0,0). AutoCAD will give you a second prompt:

Upper right corner <12.0000,9.0000>:

Notice the default coordinates. These determine the size and shape of the grid you have been working with. We will set the limits to emulate a B-size sheet of paper.

> Type "18,12".

The grid will be regenerated to cover the screen, but you will not see any change in size. Under the new limits the complete grid has become larger than the present display, and you are now only seeing part of it. Whenever you set limits larger or smaller than the current display, you will have to do a ZOOM All to see the display defined according to the new limits.

> Type "z" or select the Zoom All tool from the Standard toolbar.
> If necessary (i.e., if you are typing), type "a" or select "All".

You should have an 18 x 12 grid on your screen. Place the cursor on the upper right-hand grid point to check its coordinates. This is the grid you will use for a B-size prototype.

We suggest that you continue to experiment with setting limits, and that you try some of the possibilities listed in *Figure 4-1*, which is a table of sheet sizes.

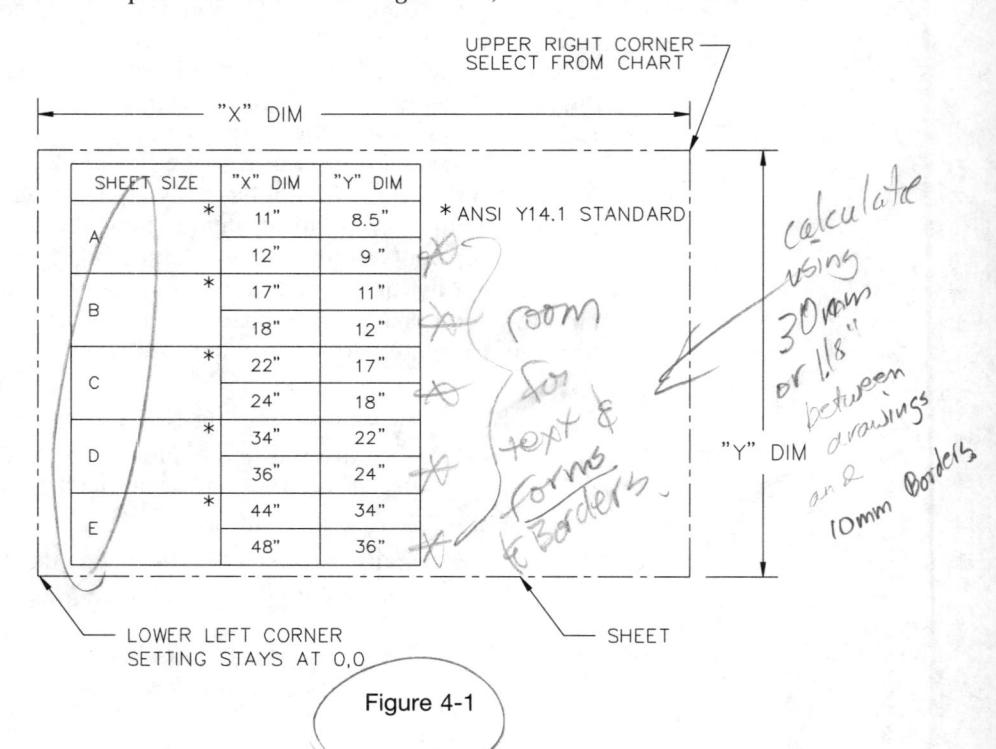

SHEET SIZE	"X" DIM	"Y" DIM
A	* 11"	8.5"
	12"	9"
B	* 17"	11"
	18"	12"
C	* 22"	17"
	24"	18"
D	* 34"	22"
	36"	24"
E	* 44"	34"
	48"	36"

*ANSI Y14.1 STANDARD

Figure 4-1

Notice that there are two sets of standards commonly in use. Sometimes the standard you use will be determined by your plotter. This is particularly true for the larger sheet sizes. Some plotters that plot on C-size paper, for example, will take a 24 × 18 inch sheet but not a 22 × 17.

> When you are done experimenting, return LIMITS to (0,0) and (18,12), using the LIMITS command, and then ZOOM All.

You are now in the drawing that we will use for your prototype, so it is not necessary to begin a new one for the next section.

Task 2: Creating a Prototype

Procedure

1. Define layers and change settings (grid, snap, units, limits, ltscale, etc.) as desired.
2. Save the drawing, giving it an appropriate name for a prototype.

Discussion. To make your own prototype, so that new drawings will begin with the settings you want, all you have to do is create a drawing that has those settings and then tell AutoCAD that this is the drawing you want to use to define your initial drawing setup. The first part should be easy for you now, since you have been doing your own drawing setup for each new drawing in this book.

> Make changes to the present drawing as follows:

GRID	1.00 ON (F7)	COORD	ON (F6)
SNAP	.25 ON (F9)	LTSCALE	.5
UNITS	2-place decimal	LIMITS	(0,0) (18,12)

> Load all linetypes in the standard ACAD linetype file.
> Create the following layers and associated colors and linetypes.

Remember that you can make changes to your prototype at any time. The layers called "text", "hatch", and "dim" will not be used until Chapters 7 and 8, in which we introduce text, hatch patterns, and dimensions to your drawings. Creating them now will save time and avoid confusion later on.

Layer 0 is already defined.

Layer name	State	Color	Linetype
0	On	7 (white)	CONTINUOUS
1	On	1 (red)	CONTINUOUS
2	On	2 (yellow)	HIDDEN
3	On	3 (green)	CENTER
TEXT	On	4 (cyan)	CONTINUOUS
HATCH	On	5 (blue)	CONTINUOUS
DIM	On	6 (magenta)	CONTINUOUS

> When all changes are made, save your drawing as "B".

NOTE: Do not leave anything drawn on your screen or it will come up as part of the prototype each time you open a new drawing. For some applications this may be useful. For now we want a blank prototype.

If you have followed instructions up to this point, B.dwg should be on file. Now we will use it as the prototype for a new drawing.

Task 3: Selecting a Prototype Drawing

Procedure

1. Type "new", select "New..." from the File pull down menu, or select the New tool from the Standard toolbar.
2. Enter your prototype drawing name in the Prototype drawing edit box.
3. Press Enter or click on "OK".

Discussion. The procedure for designating a prototype drawing makes use of a dialogue box and is quite simple.

> Type "new", select "New..." from the File pull down menu, or select the New tool at the far left of the Standard toolbar.

This will call up the familiar Create New Drawing dialogue box shown in *Figure 4-2*. The edit box on the top right holds the name of the current prototype drawing. In effect, the drawing named in this box will appear when a new drawing is created, unless you specifically tell AutoCAD to do otherwise. If there is no name in the box, then AutoCAD will use its own ACAD.dwg.

The simplest way to change the prototype is to type the name of a new prototype drawing in this box.

> To change the prototype drawing, double click inside the Prototype drawing name box.

If there is already a name in the box, it will become highlighted.

If the box is grayed out, you will notice that the box next to "No Prototype" is checked. Clicking in this box will remove the ✓ and make the Prototype name box accessible.

If you prefer to select from a list, you can pick the "Prototype..." box, which will call up a Standard file list box. You can select any file in the list to become the prototype for your new drawing.

> Type "b" or select B.dwg from the file list to make B.dwg the current prototype.

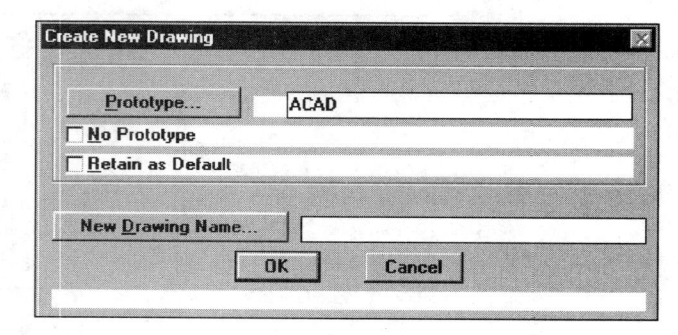

Figure 4-2

If your prototype is to be found in a directory other than the one in which ACAD.exe, the AutoCAD program, is found, you will need to include a drive designation. For example "A:B" means B.dwg is on a floppy disk in drive A.

> Click on "OK".

Your B drawing is now designated as the prototype for the new drawing you are about to open. If you also want to retain B as the default prototype, so that it comes up every time you open any new drawing, you will need to click in the Retain as Default check box. If you are using this book in a course, ask your instructor about setting up a default prototype. Since other people probably use your workstation, your instructor will want to manage your use of a prototype carefully.

> Click inside the New Drawing Name edit box, and then type "4-1" or "A:4-1".
> Click on "OK" to exit the edit box and begin the new drawing.

You will find that the new drawing includes all the changes made to B.dwg.

NOTE: There are other ways to control your initial drawing setup. Suppose you have created three or four different prototypes that you want to use at different times for different projects. You might, for example, have C-, D-, and E-size prototypes as well as a B-size. With B as the default prototype it is still easy to begin a drawing using some other drawing file for the initial setup.

To open a new drawing called GIZMO.dwg and use the setup from C.dwg, for example, you would use the following procedure:

1. Type "New" or select "New..." from the File menu or the New tool from the Standard toolbar.
2. In the edit box next to "New Drawing Name" type "GIZMO=C" or "GIZMO=A:C".

The format for this response, then, is:

<new drawing name>=<alternate prototype>

This is the equivalent of typing "Gizmo" in the Prototype box in place of your default prototype, but without clicking on "Retain as Default".

Finally, if you wanted to return to the AutoCAD prototype settings that you have been using up until now, you could simply drop the second name, like this:

<new drawing name>=

This is the equivalent of clicking on "No Prototype".

Task 4: Using the MOVE command

Procedure

1. Type "m" or select the Move tool from the Modify toolbar.
2. Define a selection set. (If noun/verb selection is enabled, you can reverse steps 1 and 2.)
3. Choose the base point of a displacement vector.
4. Choose a second point.

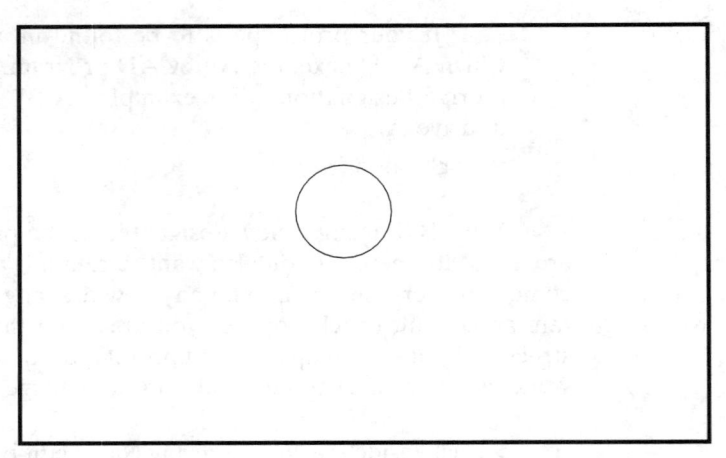

Figure 4-3

Figure 4-4

Discussion. The ability to copy and move objects on the screen is one of the great advantages of working on a CAD system. It can be said that CAD is to drafting as word processing is to typing. Nowhere is this analogy more appropriate than in the "cut and paste" capacities that the COPY and MOVE commands give you.

> Draw a circle with a radius of 1 somewhere near the center of the screen (9,6), as shown in *Figure 4-3*.

As discussed in Chapter 2, Release 13 allows you to pick objects before or after entering an edit command. In this exercise we will use MOVE both ways, beginning with the noun/verb or "pickfirst" method. We will pick the circle you have just drawn, but be aware that the selection set could include as many entities as you like, and that a group of entities can be selected with a window or crossing box.

> Type "m" or select the Move tool from the Modify toolbar, as shown in *Figure 4-4*.

You will be prompted to select objects to move.

> Point to the circle.

As in the ERASE command, your circle will become dotted.

In the command area, AutoCAD will tell you how many objects have been selected and prompt you to select more. You may need to open the text screen (F2) to see this. When you are through selecting objects you will need to press Enter to move on.

> Press Enter.

AutoCAD prompts:

Base point or displacement:

Most often you will show the movement by defining a vector that gives the distance and direction you want the object to be moved.

NOTE: In order to define movement with a vector, all AutoCAD needs is a distance and a direction. Therefore, the base point does not have to be on or near the object you are moving. Any point will do, as long as you can use it to show how you want your objects moved. This may seem strange at first, but it will soon become quite natural. Of course, you may choose a point on the object if you wish. With a circle, the center point may be convenient.

> Point to any location not too near the right edge of the screen.

AutoCAD will give you a rubber band from the point you have indicated and will ask for a second point:

Second point of displacement:

As soon as you begin to move the cursor, you will see that AutoCAD also gives you a circle to drag so you can immediately see the effect of the movement you are indicating. Let's say you want to move the circle 3.00 to the right. Watch the coordinate display and stretch the rubber band out until the display reads "3.00<0" (press F6 to get polar coordinates), as in *Figure 4-5*.

> Pick a point 3.00 to the right of your base point.

The rubber band and your original circle disappear, leaving you a circle in the new location.

Now, if ortho is on, turn it off (F8) and try a diagonal move. This time we will use the previous option to select the circle.

> Type "m" or select the Move tool, or press Enter to repeat the command.

AutoCAD follows with the "Select objects:" prompt.

> Reselect the circle by typing "p" for previous.
> Press Enter to end the object selection process.
> Select a base point.
> Move the circle diagonally in any direction you like.

Figure 4-6 is an example of how this might look.

Try moving the circle back to the center of the screen. It may help to choose the center point of the circle as a base point this time, and choose a point at or near the center of the grid for your second point.

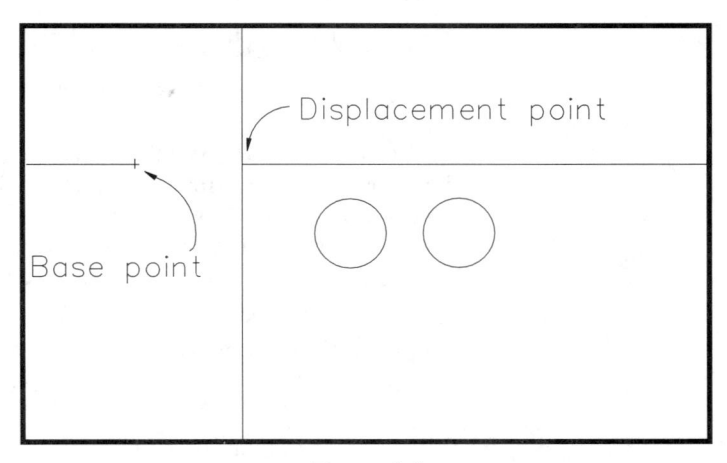

Figure 4-5

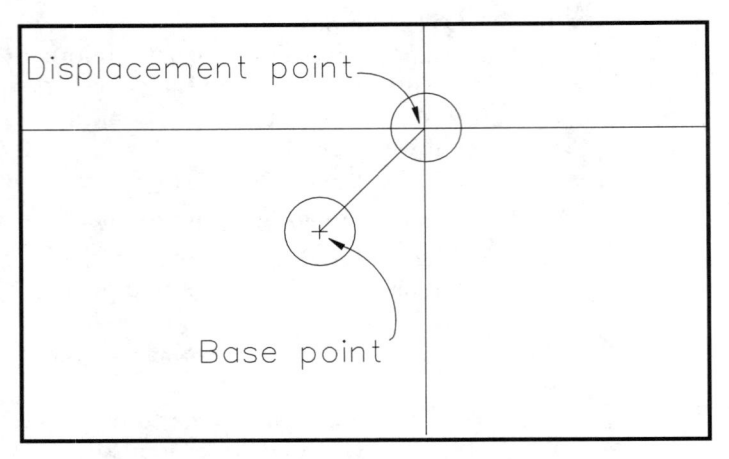

[Figure: rectangle divided by crosshairs with "Displacement point" circle in upper right area and "Base point" circle near center, with arrow between them]

Figure 4-6

Moving with Grips

You can use grips to perform numerous editing procedures without ever entering a command. This is probably the simplest of all editing methods, called "autoediting". It does have some limitations, however. In particular, you can only select by pointing, windowing, or crossing.

> Point to the circle.

It will become highlighted and grips will appear.

Notice that grips for a circle are placed at quadrants and at the center. In more involved editing procedures the choice of which grip or grips to use for editing is significant. In this exercise you will do fine with any of the grips.

> Move the pickbox slowly over one of the grips. If you do this carefully you will notice that the pickbox "locks onto" the grip as it moves over it. You will see this more clearly if snap is off (F9).

> When the pickbox is locked on a grip, press the pick button.

The selected grip will become filled and change colors (from blue to red).

In the command area you will see this:

```
** STRETCH **
<Stretch to point>/Base point/Copy/Undo/eXit:
```

Stretching is the first of a series of five autoediting modes that you can activate by selecting grips on objects. The word "stretch" has many meanings in AutoCAD and they are not always what you expect. We will explore the stretch autoediting mode and the STRETCH command in Chapter 6. For now, we will bypass stretch and use the MOVE mode.

> Press Enter, the enter button on your cursor, or the space bar to bring up the MOVE autoedit mode.

You should see the following in the command area:

```
** MOVE **
<Move to point>/Base point/Copy/Undo/eXit:
```

Chap. 4

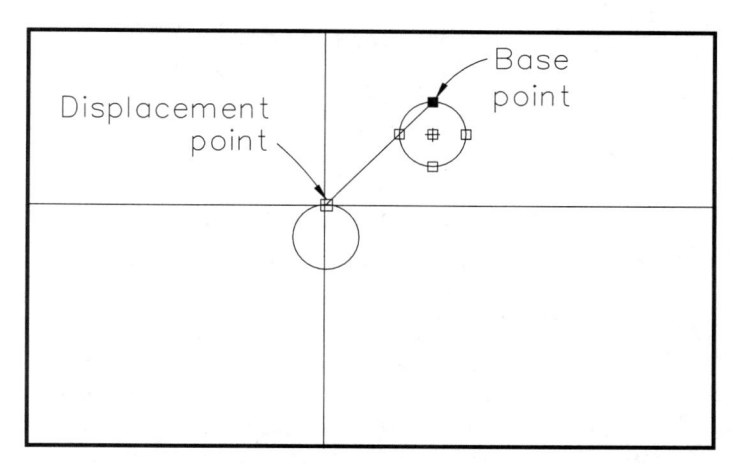

Figure 4-7

Move the cursor now and you will see a rubber band from the selected grip to the same position on a dragged circle, as illustrated in *Figure 4-7*.

> Pick a point anywhere on the screen.

The circle will move where you have pointed.

Moving by Typing a Displacement

There is one more way to use the MOVE command. Instead of showing Auto-CAD a distance and direction, you can type a horizontal and vertical displacement. For example, to move the circle 3 units to the right and 2 units up, you would follow this procedure. There is no autoediting equivalent for this procedure.

1. Press Esc twice to remove grips.
2. Pick the circle.
3. Type "m" or select the Move tool.
4. Type "3,2" in response to the prompt for base point or displacement.
5. Press Enter in response to the prompt for a second point.

Task 5: Using the COPY command

Procedure

1. Type "Copy" or select the Copy tool from the Modify toolbar (*not from the Standard toolbar*).
2. Define a selection set (steps 1 and 2 can be reversed if noun/verb selection is enabled).
3. Choose a base point.
4. Choose a second point.

Discussion. The COPY command works so much like the MOVE command that you should find it quite easy to learn at this point, and we will not give you specific instructions. The main difference is that the original object will not disappear when the second point of the displacement vector is given. Also, there is the additional option of making multiple copies of the same object, which we will explore in a moment.

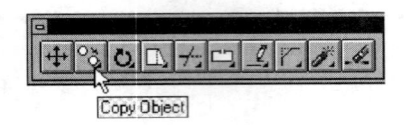

Figure 4-8

But first, we suggest that you try making several copies of the circle in various positions on the screen. Try using both noun/verb and verb/noun sequences.

> To initiate COPY, type "copy" or select the Copy tool from the Modify toolbar, as shown in *Figure 4-8*.

Notice that "c" is not an alias for COPY. Also, notice that there is a Copy tool on the Standard toolbar that initiates the COPYCLIP command. This tool has a very different function. It is used to copy objects to the Windows Clipboard and then into other applications. It has no effect on objects within your drawing, other than to save them on the clipboard.

When you are satisfied that you know how to use the basic COPY command, move on to the Multiple copy option.

The Multiple Copy Option

This option allows you to show a whole series of vectors starting at the same base point, with AutoCAD placing copies of your selection set accordingly.

> Type "Copy" or select the Copy tool from the Modify toolbar.
> Point to one of the circles on your screen.
> Press Enter to end the selection process.
> Type "m" or select "Multiple" from the screen menu, if available.
> Show AutoCAD a base point.
> Show AutoCAD a second point.

You will see a new copy of the circle, and notice also that the prompt for a "Second point of displacement" has returned in the command area. AutoCAD is waiting for another vector, using the same base point as before.

> Show AutoCAD another second point.
> Show AutoCAD another second point.

Repeat as many times as you wish. If you get into this you may begin to feel like a magician pulling ring after ring out of thin air and scattering them across the screen. The results will appear something like *Figure 4-9*.

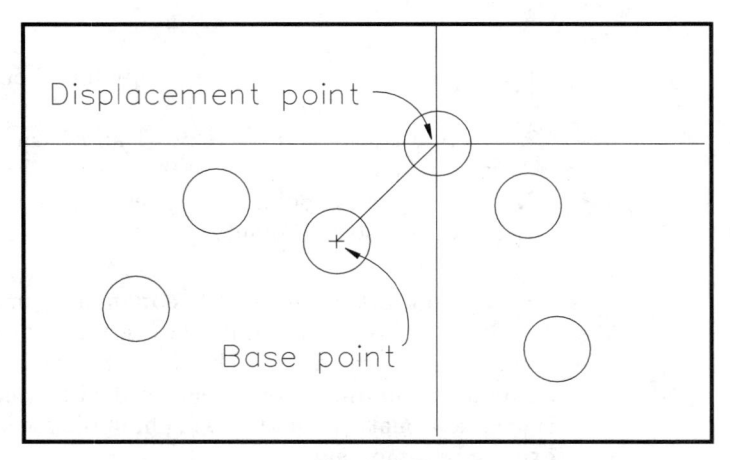

Figure 4-9

Chap. 4

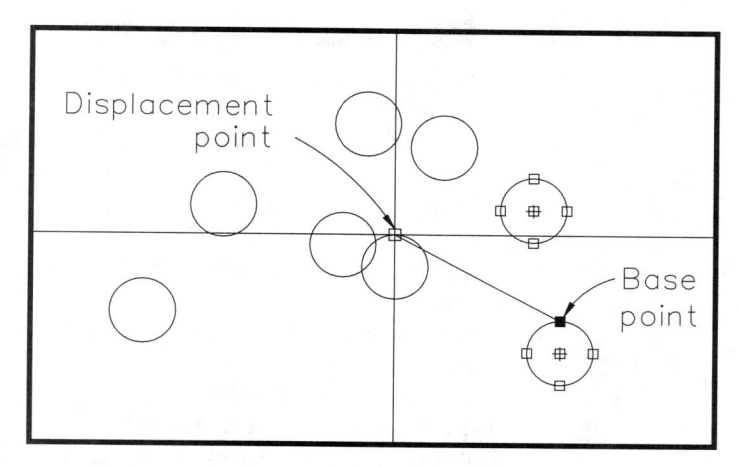

Figure 4-10

Copying with Grips

The grip editing system includes a variety of special techniques for creating multiple copies in all five modes. For now we will stick with the copy option in the MOVE mode, which provides a shortcut for the same kind of process you just went through with the COPY command.

Since you should have several circles on your screen now, we will take the opportunity to demonstrate how you can use grips on more than one object at a time. This can be a real timesaver if your drawing contains two or more objects that maintain the same relationship with each other at different locations in your drawing.

> Pick any two circles.

The circles you pick should become highlighted and grips should appear on both, as illustrated in *Figure 4-10*.

> Pick any grip on either of the two highlighted circles.

The grip should change colors.

> Press Enter, the enter button on your cursor, or the space bar.

This should bring you into MOVE mode. Notice the prompt:

```
** MOVE **
<Move to point>/Base point/Copy/Undo/eXit:
```

> Type "c" to initiate copying.

The prompt will change to:

```
** MOVE (multiple) **
<Move to point>/Base point/Copy/Undo/eXit:
```

You will find that all copying in the grip editing system is multiple copying. Once in this mode AutoCAD will continue to create copies wherever you press the pick button until you exit by typing "x" or pressing Enter.

> Move the cursor and observe the two dragged circles.

> Pick a point to create copies of the two highlighted circles.

> Pick another point to create two more copies.

> When you are through, press Enter to exit the grip editing system.
> Press Esc twice to remove grips.

Task 6: Using the ARRAY Command—Rectangular Arrays

Procedure

1. Type "Array" or select the Array tool from the Copy flyout on the Modify toolbar.
2. Define a selection set. (Steps 1 and 2 can be reversed if noun/verb editing is enabled.)
3. Press Enter to end selection.
4. Type "r" or select "rectangular".
5. Enter the number of rows in the array.
6. Enter the number of columns.
7. Enter the distance between rows.
8. Enter the distance between columns.

Discussion. The ARRAY command gives you a powerful alternative to simple copying. An array is a repetition in matrix form of the same figure. This command takes an object or group of objects and copies it a specific number of times in mathematically defined, evenly spaced, locations.

There are two types of arrays. Rectangular arrays are linear and defined by rows and columns. Polar arrays are angular and based on the repetition of objects around the circumference of an arc or circle. The dots on the grid are an example of a rectangular array; the lines on any circular dial are an example of a polar array.

Both types are common. We will explore rectangular arrays in this chapter and polar arrays in the next.

In preparation for this exercise, erase all the circles from your screen. This is a good opportunity to try the ERASE All option.

> Type "e" or select the Erase tool from the Modify toolbar.
> Type "all".
> Press Enter.
> Now draw a single circle, radius .5, centered at the point (2,2).
> Type "Array" or select the Rectangular Array tool from the Copy flyout on the Modify toolbar, as shown in *Figure 4-11*.

You will see the "Select objects" prompt.

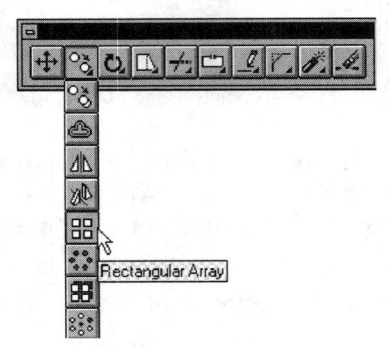

Figure 4-11

> Point to the circle.
> Press Enter to end the selection process.

AutoCAD will ask which type of array you want:

Rectangular or Polar array (R/P) <R>:

> Type "r" or select "Rectang" from the screen menu. Or, you can press Enter if R is the default.

AutoCAD will prompt you for the number of rows in the array.

Number of rows (---) <1>:

The (---) is to remind you of what a row looks like, i.e., it is horizontal.

The default is 1. So if you press Enter you will get a single row of circles. The number of circles in the row will depend, then, on the number of columns you specify. We will ask for three rows instead of just one.
> Type "3".

AutoCAD now asks for the number of columns in the array:

Number of columns (|||) <1>:

Using the same format (|||), AutoCAD reminds you that columns are vertical. The default is 1 again. What would an array with three rows and only one column look like?

We will construct a five-column array.
> Type "5".

Now AutoCAD needs to know how far apart to place all these circles. There will be 15 of them in this example—three rows with five circles in each row. AutoCAD prompts:

Unit cell or distance between rows (---):

"Unit cell" means that you can respond by showing two corners of a window. The horizontal side of this window would give the space between columns; the vertical side would give the space between rows. You could do this exercise by showing a 1 × 1 window. We will use the more basic method of typing values for these distances. The distance between rows will be a vertical measure.
> Type "1".

AutoCAD now asks for the horizontal distance between columns:

Distance between columns (| | |):

> Type "1" again.

You should have a 3 × 5 array of circles, as shown in *Figure 4-12*.

Notice that AutoCAD builds arrays up and to the right. This is consistent with the coordinate system, which puts positive values to the right on the horizontal *x* axis, and upwards on the vertical *y* axis. Negative values can be used to create arrays in other directions.

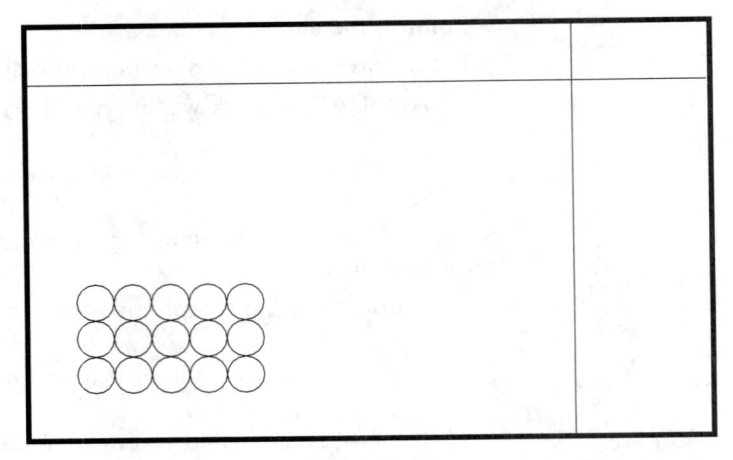

Figure 4-12

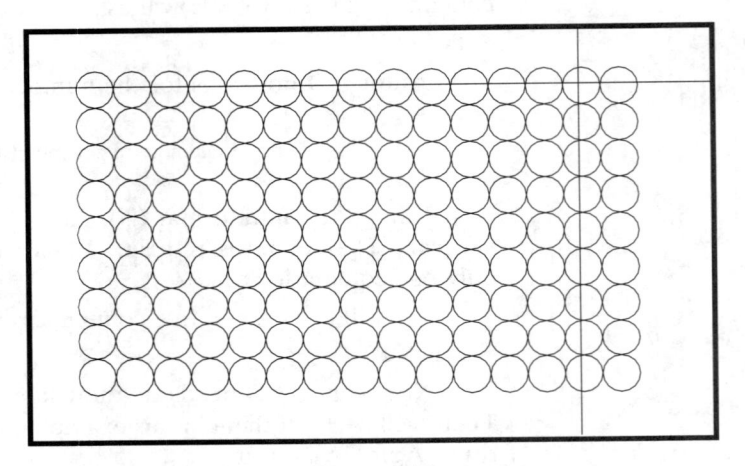

Figure 4-13

We will use the array now on your screen as the selection set to create another array. We will specify an array that has three rows and three columns, with 3.00 between rows and 5.00 between columns. This will keep our circles touching without overlapping.

> Press Enter to repeat the ARRAY command.

> Using a window, select the whole array of 15 circles.

> Press Enter to end the selection process.

> Type "r" or select "Rectang" or press Enter.

> Type "3" for the number of rows.

> Type "3" for the number of columns.

> Type "3" for the distance between rows.

> Type "5" for the distance between columns.

You should have a screen full of circles, as in *Figure 4-13*.

When you are ready to move on, use the U command to undo the last two arrays.

> Type "u" to undo the second array.

> Type "u" again to undo the first array.

Now you should be back to your original circle centered at (2,2). Notice that the U command works nicely to undo an incorrectly drawn array quickly. This is important to know, because it is easy to make mistakes creating arrays. Be aware, however, that for other purposes the objects in an array are treated as separate entities, just as if you had drawn them one by one.

Try using some negative distances to create an array down and to the left.

> First, use the MOVE command or grips to move your circle to the middle of the screen.

> Type "Array" or select the Array tool.

> Select the circle by pointing or typing "L" for last.

> Press Enter to end the selection process.

> Type "r", select "Rectang", or press Enter.

> Type "3" for the number of rows.

> Type "3" for the number of columns.

> Type "−2" for the distance between rows.

> Type "−2" for the distance between columns.

Your array should be built down and to the left. The −2 distance between rows causes the array to be built going down. The −2 distance between columns causes the array to be built across to the left.

Task 7: Changing Plot Configuration Parameters

Discussion. In the previous chapter you began using the plot preview feature of the Plot Configuration Dialogue box. In this chapter we encourage you to continue to learn about plot configuration by exploring several more areas of the dialogue box. We have used no specific drawing for illustration. Now that you know how to use plot preview, you can observe the effects of changing plot parameters with any drawing you like and decide at any point whether you actually want to print out the results. We will continue to remind you to look at a plot preview after making any change in configuration. This is the best way to learn about plotting.

We will start with device selection and move on to pen parameters and additional parameters. In the next chapter we will complete the introduction to the dialogue box with paper size, orientation, scaling, rotation, and origin.

> To begin this exploration, you should have a drawing or drawn objects on your screen so that you can observe the effects of various configuration changes you will be making.

> Type "plot", select "Print..." from the "File" pull down menu, or select the Print tool from the Standard toolbar.

This will open up the Plot Configuration dialogue box.

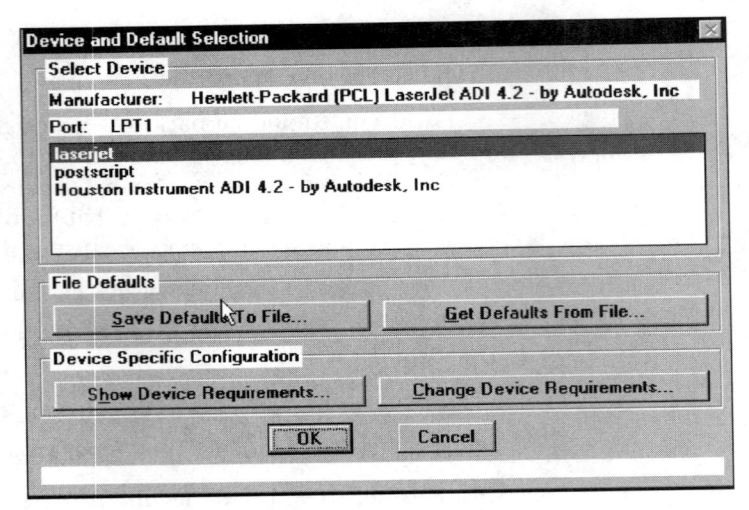

Figure 4-14

Device and Default Information

The device box should contain the name of the printer or plotter you are planning to use. If not, you can get a list of available options through the subdialogue illustrated in *Figure 4-14*.

> Click on "Device and Default Selection..." or type "d".

You should see a subdialogue box similar to the one shown in the figure. The list of devices will be your own, of course. If there is a need to change plotters or printers you can do so by selecting from the list. If the device you want is not on the list, you will need to make sure the device driver is properly installed and then use the CONFIG command to add it to the list. See the *AutoCAD Installation Guide for DOS* for additional information.

Along with the list of available plotting devices, this dialogue box allows you to save plotting specifications to ASCII files and get them back later. AutoCAD automatically saves your most recent plot parameters in a file called ACAD.cfg. However, for more permanent storage, you can create a separate file. Such files are saved with a "pcp" extension ("Plot Configuration Parameters"). There are many parameters to deal with in plotting, including as many as 256 pen colors. So saving a set of parameters to a file may be far more efficient than specifying them manually each time you plot. You may have one set of parameters for one device, and another set for a different device. Or you may have different setups for different types of drawings.

In addition, some plotting devices have special configuration requirements not needed or not available on other devices. If this is the case with your device, the boxes under "Device Specific Configuration" will be accessible. The specific parameters and options will be determined by the device driver for your plotter. See the *AutoCAD Installation Guide for Windows* for more information.

> Click on "OK" or "Cancel" to exit the Device and Default Selection dialogue.

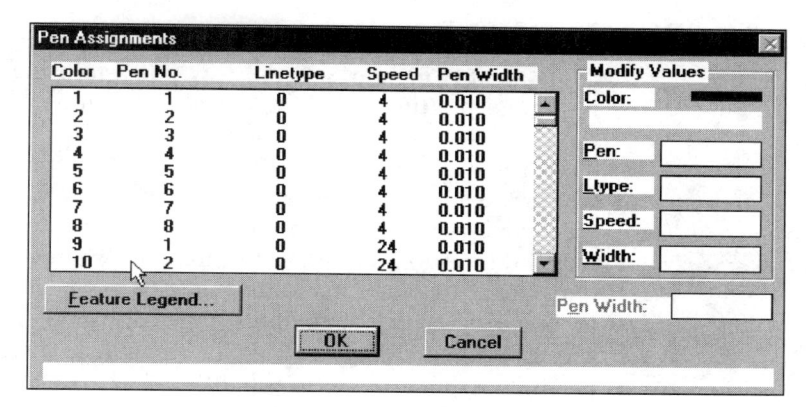

Figure 4-15

This will bring you back to the Plot Configuration dialogue box. Assuming the device named in the Device and Default Information box is the correct one, you are ready to move on. However, if you have made any changes, we recommend that you do a plot preview. Changing devices may bring about changes in paper size and orientation, for example, and you will see these changes reflected graphically in the partial and full previews.

Pen Parameters

If you are using a plotter with multiple pens, you can assign colors, linetypes, widths, and speeds to each pen individually. If you are using a printer, you will find that the Pen Assignments box is grayed out. If you do have access, we suggest you look at the subdialogue now, even though you may not want to make changes.

> Click on "Pen Assignments..." or type "p".

This will call the dialogue box shown in *Figure 4-15*. If you select any pen, you will see its color, number, linetype, speed, and width displayed in the Modify Values box at the right. Changes can be made in these edit boxes in the usual manner.

The specifications made here are designed to relate pen numbers on your plotter to pen colors. If pen numbers are correctly related to pen colors, then layers will automatically be plotted in their assigned colors. The linetypes assigned to layers in AutoCAD are also plotted automatically and do not need to be assigned to pens at this point.

NOTE: If your plotter supports multiple linetypes, you will reach a subdialogue showing numbered linetypes by clicking on "Feature Legend...". These are not to be confused with the linetypes created within your AutoCAD drawing associated with layers. They should be used in special applications to vary the look of "continuous" AutoCAD lines only. Otherwise you will get a confused mixture of linetypes when your plotter tries to break up lines that AutoCAD has already drawn broken.

> Click on "OK" or "Cancel" to exit the "Pen Assignments" subdialogue.

Additional Parameters

This is a crucial area of the dialogue box that allows you to specify the portion of your drawing to be plotted. You have some familiarity with this from Chapter 2, where you plotted using a window selection. Changes here will have a very significant impact on the effective plotting area. Be sure to use plot preview any time you make changes in these parameters.

Also available in this area are hidden line removal (for 3D drawings), fill area adjustment, which affects the way pen width is interpreted when drawing wide lines, and plotting to a file instead of to an actual plotter. These are discussed briefly at the end of this section.

The radio buttons on the left show the options for plotting area. "Display" will create a plot using whatever is actually on the screen. If you used the ZOOM command to enlarge a portion of the drawing before entering PLOT and then selected this option, AutoCAD would plot whatever you have zoomed in on. "Extents" refers to the actual drawing area in which you have drawn objects. It may be larger or smaller than limits of the drawing. Drawing limits, as you know, are specified by you using the LIMITS command. If you are using our standard B-size prototype, they will go from (0,0) to (18,12). "View" will be accessible only after you have defined views in the drawing using the VIEW command (Chapter 11). "Window" will not be accessible until you define a window (if you have defined a window in a previous drawing, it may be saved in ACAD.cfg, the plot configuration file).

> As an exercise, we suggest that you try switching among Display, Extents, Limits, and Window selections and use plot preview to see the results. Use both partial and full previews to ensure that you can clearly see what is happening. This can be very instructive.

Whenever you make a change, also observe the changes in the boxes showing Plotted Inches = Drawing Units. Assuming that "Scaled to Fit" is checked, you will see significant changes in these scale ratios as AutoCAD adjusts scales according to how much area it is being asked to plot.

A few brief words about the other "Additional Parameters" options before moving on. "Hide Lines" is relevant only to 3D drawings. Lines that would be obstructed from the current point of view on a 3D surface or solid model can be removed from the display using the HIDE command. When it comes to plotting, however, they will not be removed unless the "Hide Lines" box is checked. Hidden line removal is discussed in Chapter 13.

"Adjust Area Fill" is only relevant in drawings that must be precise to specifications less than a pen's width. In these cases, you can tell your plotter to compensate for pen width when it draws thick lines, such as wide polylines, solids, and traces (Chapter 9).

"Plot to File" saves the plot information so that it can be used later or sent to another site for plotting. This may be a more efficient way to plot if, for example, a number of files can be plotted at one time using a "plot spooler." Plot spoolers are software programs that plot a series of plot files one after another. Plots saved to a file are given the same name as the drawing but with a .plt extension.

We will explore the last two areas of Plot Configuration, "Paper Size and Orientation" and "Scale, Rotation, and Origin" in the next chapter. In the meantime, you should continue to experiment with plotting and plot previewing as you complete the drawings that follow.

Tasks 8, 9, 10, 11, and 12

All the drawings in this chapter will use your new prototype. Whether you have defined a prototype in the Create New Drawing dialogue box or use the equal sign to load your prototype, the settings and layers should be as you have defined them.

Do not expect, however, that you will never need to change them. Layers will stay the same throughout this book, but limits will change from time to time, and grid and snap will change frequently.

The main thing you should be focused on in doing these drawings is to become increasingly familiar with the COPY and ARRAY commands. When you finish each drawing, go into Plot Configuration and try a plot preview even if you do not intend to print on paper.

DRAWING 4-1: PATTERN

This drawing will give you practice using the COPY command. There are numerous ways in which the drawing can be done. The key is to try to take advantage of the repetition in the pattern by copying in an efficient manner. The following figures suggest one way it can be done.

DRAWING SUGGESTIONS

$$GRID = .5$$
$$SNAP = .25$$

> Begin with a 6 × 6 square. Then draw the first set of lines as in *Reference 4-1a*.
> Copy the first set down .5 to produce *Reference 4-1b*.
> Draw the first set of v-shaped lines. Then use a multiple copy to produce *Reference 4-1c*.
> Finally, make a single copy of all the lines you have so far, using a window or crossing box for selection. (Be careful not to select the outside lines.) Watch the displacement carefully and you will produce *Reference 4-1d*, the completed drawing.

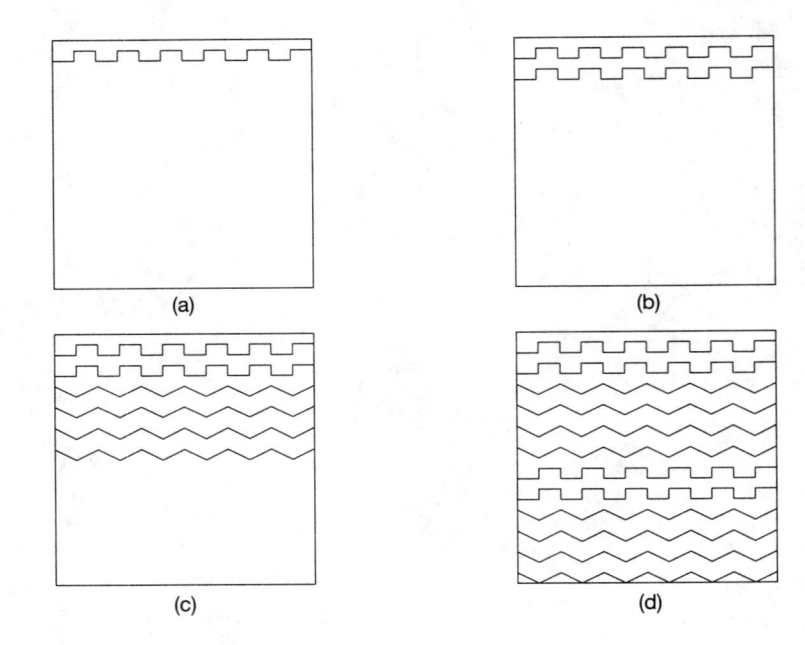

(a)

(b)

(c)

(d)

Chap. 4

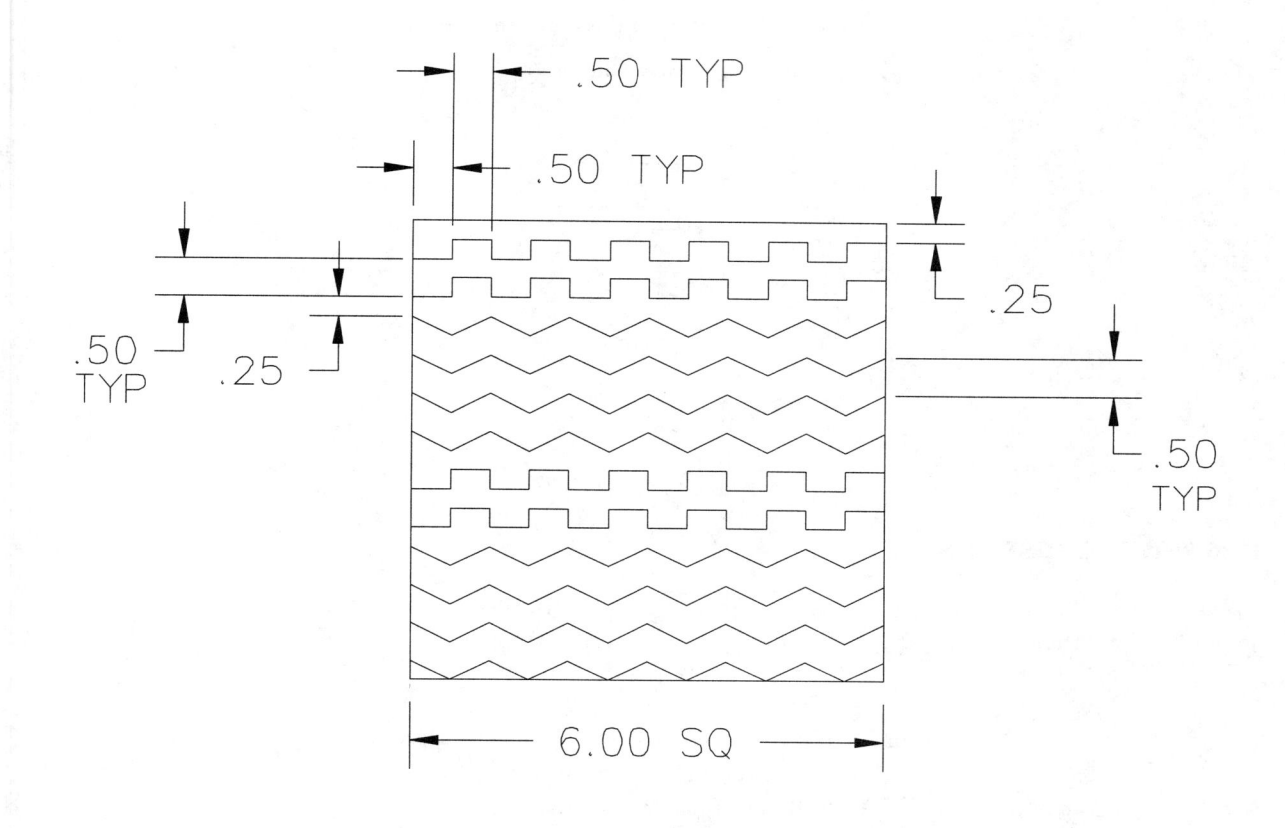

.50 TYP
.50 TYP
.50 TYP
.25
.25
.50 TYP

6.00 SQ

PATTERN

Drawing 4-1

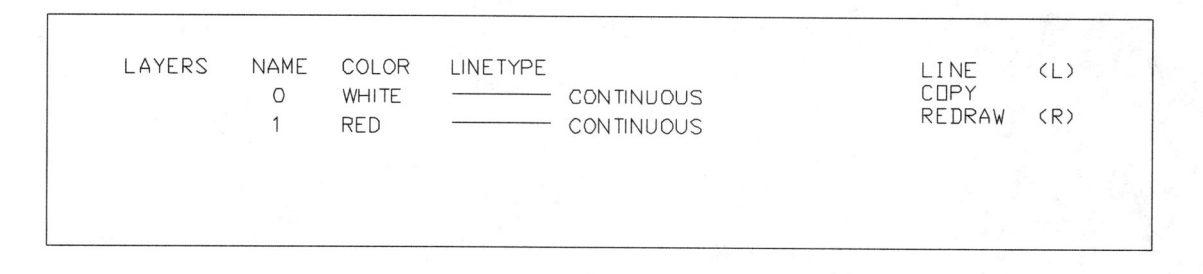

LAYERS	NAME	COLOR	LINETYPE		
	0	WHITE	———— CONTINUOUS	LINE	(L)
	1	RED	———— CONTINUOUS	COPY	
				REDRAW	(R)

[F1] HELP
[F2] TEXT/GRAPHICS SCREEN
[F6] ABSOLUTE/OFF/POLAR COORDS
[F7] ON/OFF GRID
[F8] ON/OFF ORTHO
[F9] ON/OFF SNAP

DRAWING 4–2: GRILL

This drawing should go very quickly if you use the ARRAY command.

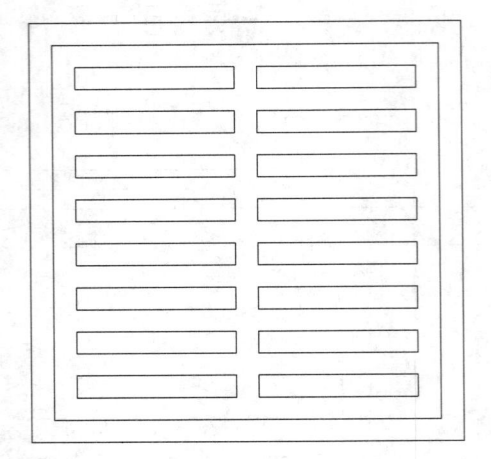

DRAWING SUGGESTIONS

GRID = .5
SNAP = .25

> Begin with a 4.75 × 4.75 square.
> Move in .25 all around to create the inside square.
> Draw the rectangle in the lower left-hand corner first, then use the ARRAY command to create the rest.
> Also remember that you can undo a misplaced array using the U command.

Chap. 4

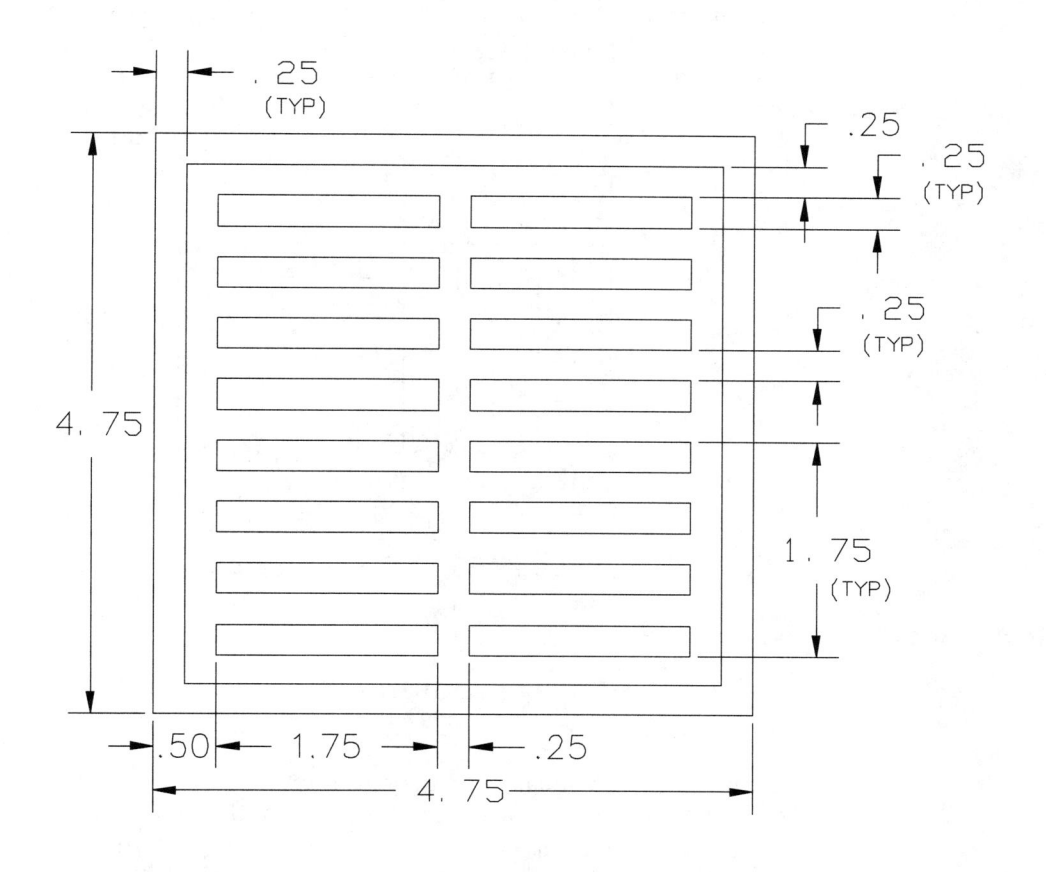

.25
(TYP)

.25

.25
(TYP)

4.75

.25
(TYP)

1.75
(TYP)

.50 1.75 .25
4.75

GRILL
Drawing 4-2

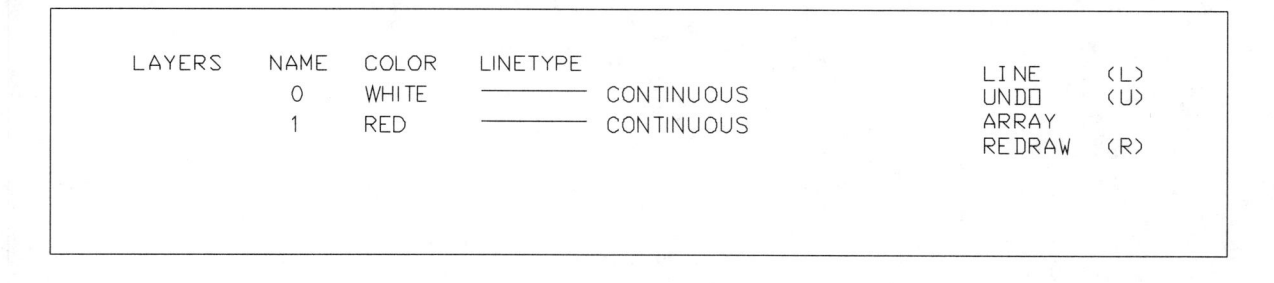

LAYERS	NAME	COLOR	LINETYPE		
	0	WHITE	————	CONTINUOUS	
	1	RED	————	CONTINUOUS	

LINE   (L)
UNDO   (U)
ARRAY
REDRAW   (R)

F1	F2	F6	F7	F8	F9
HELP	TEXT/GRAPHICS SCREEN	ABSOLUTE/OFF/POLAR COORDS	ON/OFF GRID	ON/OFF ORTHO	ON/OFF SNAP

DRAWING 4-3: WEAVE

As you do this drawing, watch AutoCAD work for you and think about how long it would take to do by hand! The finished drawing will look like *Reference 4-3*. For clarity, the drawing on the next page shows only one cell of the array and its dimensions.

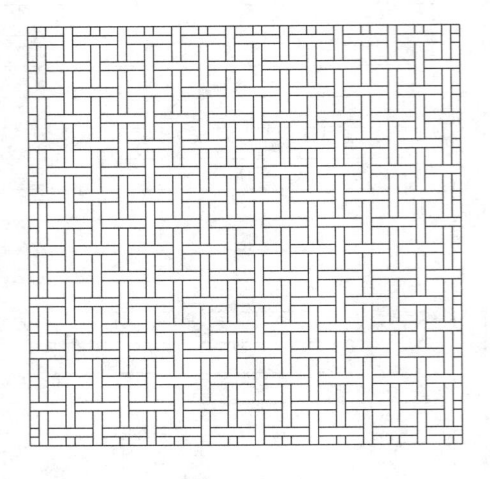

DRAWING SUGGESTIONS

GRID = .5
SNAP = .25

> Draw the 6 × 6 square, then zoom in on the lower left using a window. This will be the area shown in the lower left of the dimensioned drawing.

> Observe the dimensions and draw the line patterns for the lower left corner of the weave. You could use the COPY command in several places if you like, but the time gained will be minimal. Don't worry if you have to fuss with this a little to get it correct; once you've got it right the rest will be easy.

> Use ARRAY to repeat the lower left-hand cell in an 8 × 8 matrix.

> If you get it wrong, use U and try again.

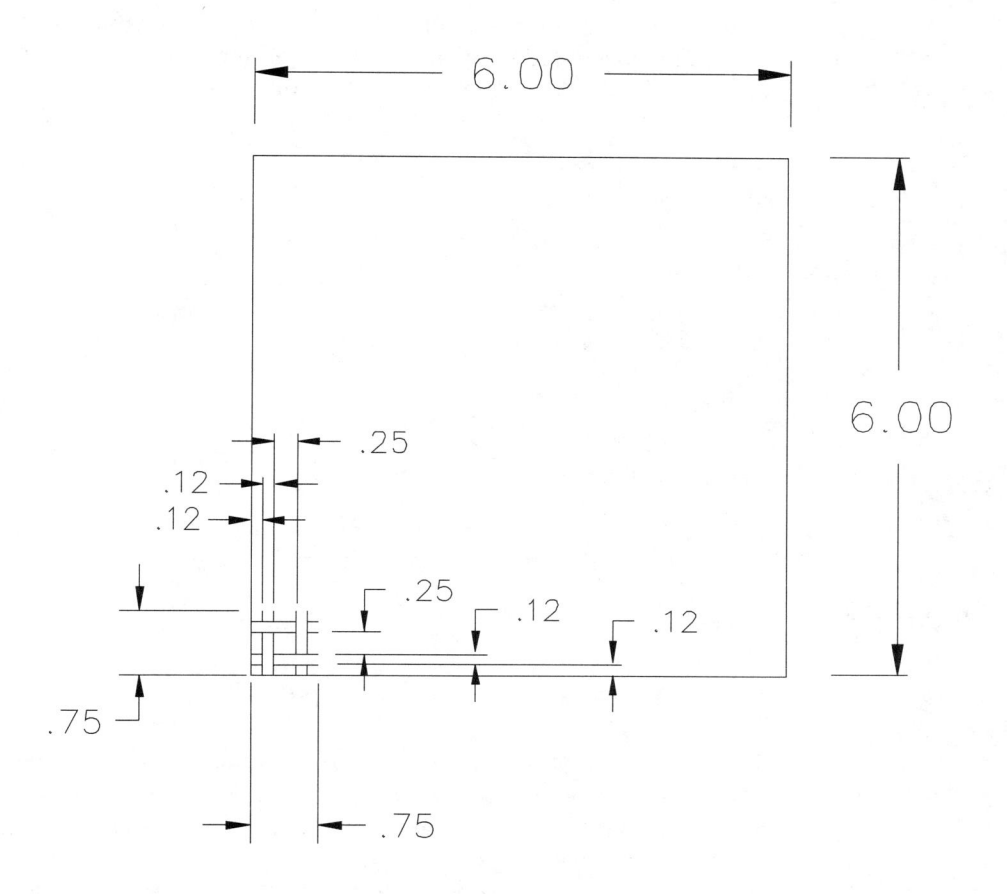

WEAVE

Drawing 4-3

LAYERS	NAME	COLOR	LINETYPE
	0	WHITE	———— CONTINUOUS
	1	RED	———— CONTINUOUS

- LINE (L)
- COPY
- ARRAY
- UNDO (U)
- REDRAW (R)
- ZOOM (Z)

F1	F2	F6	F7	F8	F9
HELP	TEXT/GRAPHICS SCREEN	ABSOLUTE/OFF/POLAR COORDS	ON/OFF GRID	ON/OFF ORTHO	ON/OFF SNAP

DRAWING 4-4: TEST BRACKET

This is a great drawing for practicing much of what you have learned up to this point. Notice the suggested snap, grid, ltscale, and limit settings, and use the AR-RAY command to draw the 25 circles on the front view.

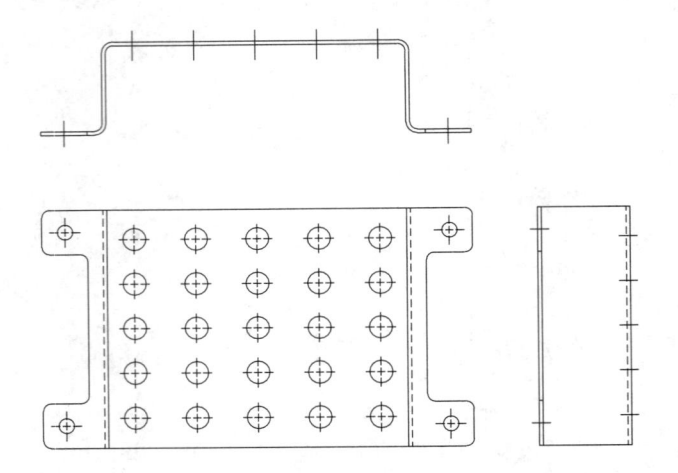

DRAWING SUGGESTIONS

GRID = .5   LTSCALE = .50
SNAP = .25   LIMITS = (0,0) (24,18)

> Be careful to draw all lines on the correct layers, according to their linetypes.
> Draw center lines through circles before copying or arraying them, otherwise you will have to go back and draw them on each individual circle or repeat the array process.
> A multiple copy will work nicely for the four .50 diameter holes. A rectangular array is definitely desirable for the twenty-five .75 diameter holes.

CREATING CENTER MARKS WITH THE DIMCEN SYSTEM VARIABLE

There is a simple way to create the center marks and center lines shown on all the circles in this drawing. It involves changing the value of a dimension variable called "dimcen" (dimension center). Dimensioning and dimension variables are discussed in Chapter 8, but if you would like to jump ahead, the following procedure will work nicely in this drawing.

> Type "dimcen".
    The default setting for dimcen is .09, which will cause AutoCAD to draw a simple cross as a center mark. Changing it to −.09 will tell AutoCAD to draw a cross that reaches across the circle.
> Type "−.09".
> After drawing your first circle, and before arraying it, type "dim". This will put you in the dimension command.
> Type "cen", indicating that you want to draw a center mark. This is a very simple dimension feature.
> Point to the circle.

Chap. 4 117

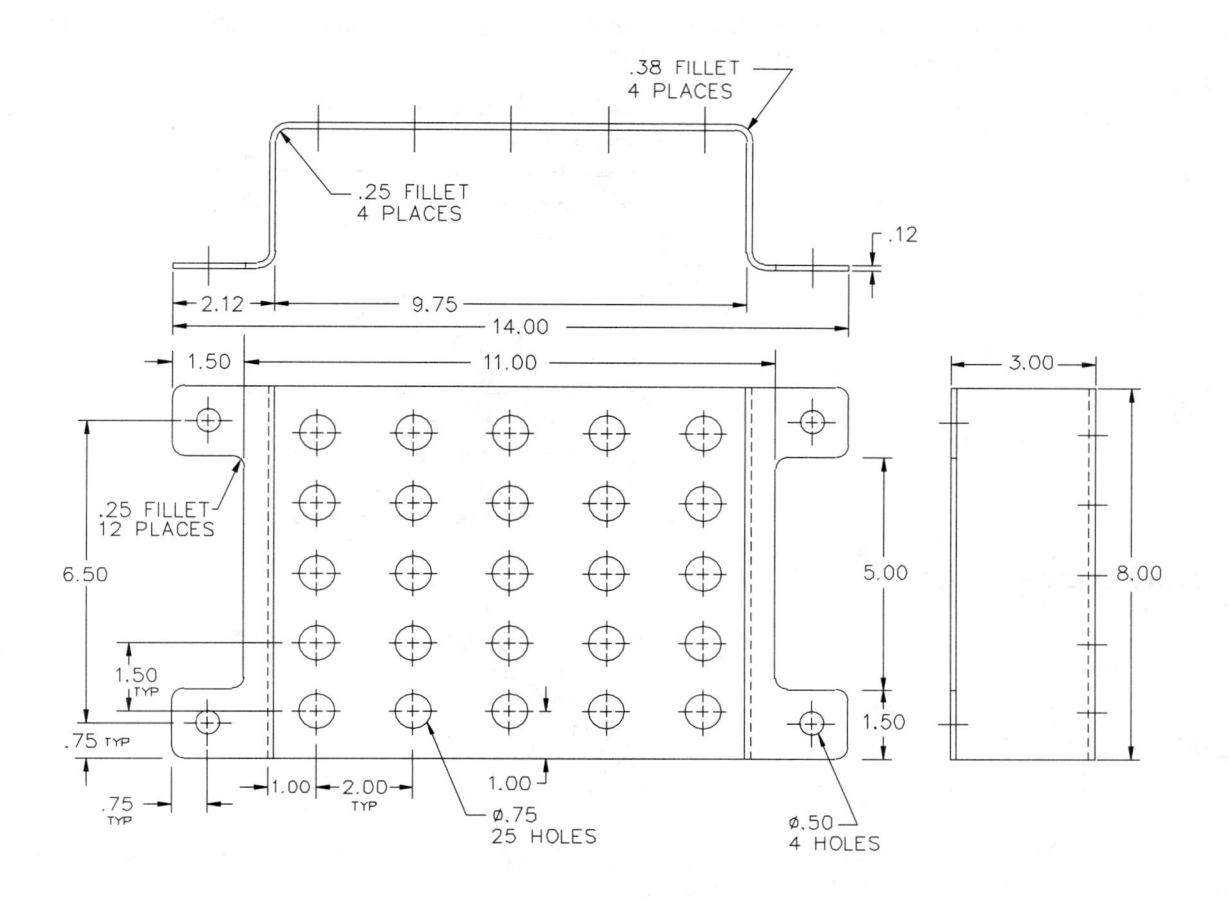

TEST BRACKET
Drawing 4-4

LAYERS	NAME	COLOR	LINETYPE		
	0	WHITE	———— CONTINUOUS	LINE	(L)
	1	RED	———— CONTINUOUS	CIRCLE	(C)
	2	YELLOW	------ HIDDEN	FILLET	
	3	GREEN	— — CENTER	ARRAY	
				ZOOM	(Z)

- F1 — HELP
- F2 — TEXT/GRAPHICS SCREEN
- F6 — ABSOLUTE/OFF/POLAR COORDS
- F7 — ON/OFF GRID
- F8 — ON/OFF ORTHO
- F9 — ON/OFF SNAP

DRAWING 4-5: FLOOR FRAMING

This architectural drawing will require changes in many features of your drawing setup. Pay close attention to the suggested settings.

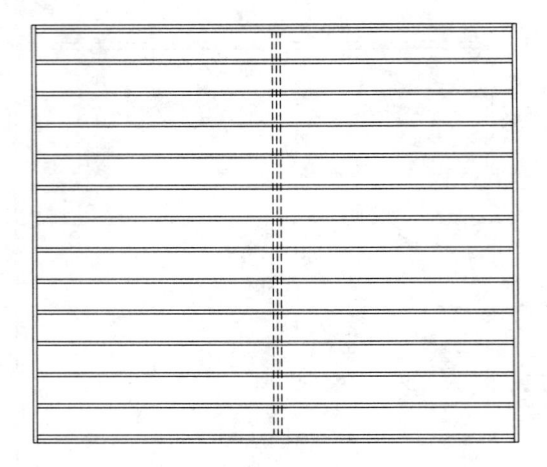

DRAWING SUGGESTIONS

UNITS = Architectural,
        smallest fraction = 1″
LIMITS = 36′, 24′
GRID = 1′
SNAP = 2″
LTSCALE = 12

> Be sure to use foot (′) and inch (″) symbols when setting limits, grid, and snap (but not ltscale).

> Begin by drawing the 20′ × 17′-10″ rectangle, with the lower left corner somewhere in the neighborhood of (4′,4′).

> Complete the left and right 2 × 10 joists by copying the vertical 17′-10″ lines 2″ in from each side. You may find it helpful to use the arrow keys when working with such small increments.

> Draw a 19′-8″ horizontal line 2″ up from the bottom and copy it 2″ higher to complete the double joists.

> Array the inner 2 × 10 in a 14-row by 1-column array, with 16″ between rows.

> Set to layer 2 and draw the three 17′-4″ hidden lines down the center.

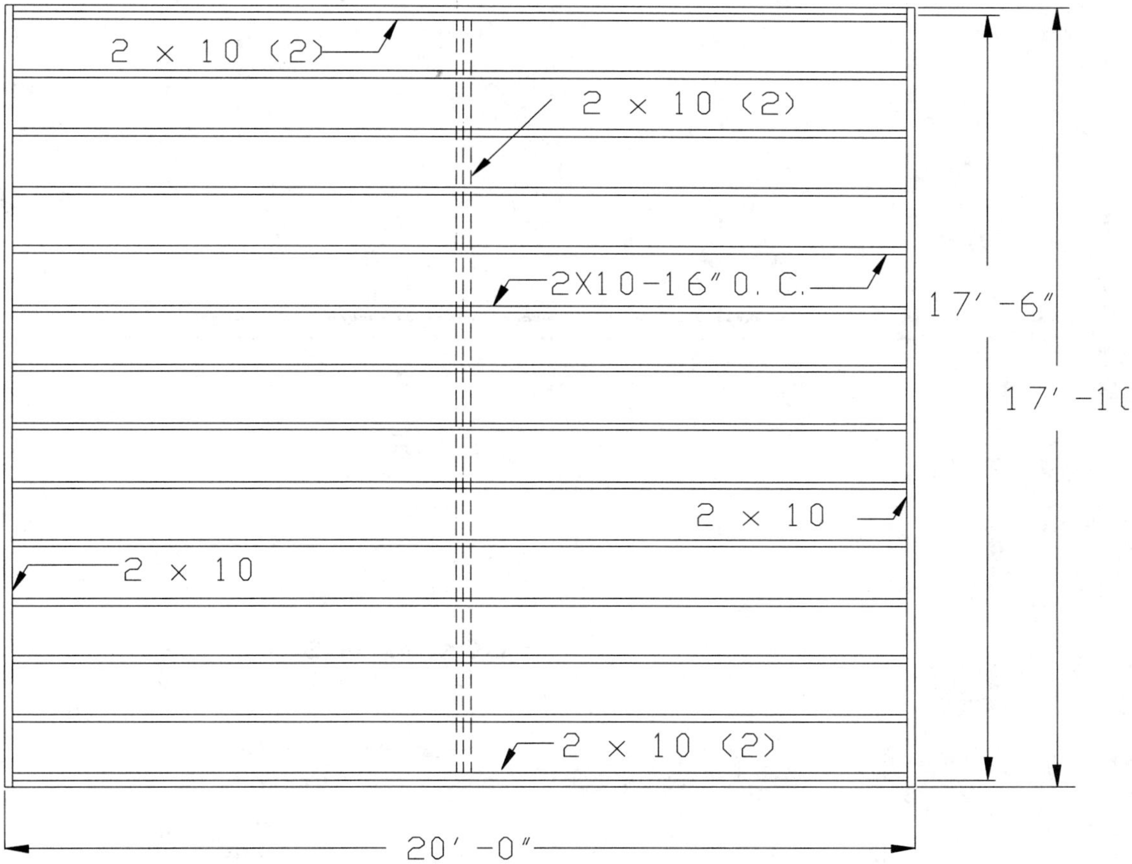
2 × 10 (2)
2 × 10 (2)
2X10-16" O. C.
2 × 10
2 × 10
2 × 10 (2)
17' -6"
17' -1(
20' -0"

FLOOR FRAMING

Drawing 4-5

LAYERS	NAME	COLOR	LINETYPE	
	0	WHITE	————	CONTINUOUS
	1	RED	————	CONTINUOUS
	2	YELLOW	- - - - -	HIDDEN

LINE (L)
COPY
ARRAY
REDRAW (R)
ZOOM (Z)

F1	F2	F6	F7	F8	F9
HELP	TEXT/GRAPHICS SCREEN	ABSOLUTE/OFF/POLAR COORDS	ON/OFF GRID	ON/OFF ORTHO	ON/OFF SNAP

CHAPTER 5

COMMANDS

DRAW	MODIFY
ARC	ARRAY (polar)
	MIRROR
	ROTATE

OVERVIEW

So far, every drawing you have done has been composed of lines and circles. In this chapter you will learn a third major entity, the ARC. In addition, you will expand your ability to manipulate objects on the screen. You will learn to ROTATE objects and create their MIRROR images. But first, we will pick up where we left off in Chapter 4 by showing you how to create polar arrays.

TASKS

1. Create three polar arrays.
2. Draw arcs in eight different ways.
3. Rotate a previously drawn object.
4. Create mirror images of previously drawn objects.
5. Change Paper Size, Orientation, Plot Scale, Rotation, and Origin.
6. Do Drawing 5–1 ("Flanged Bushing").
7. Do Drawing 5–2 ("Guide").

Chap. 5

8. Do Drawing 5–3 ("Dials").
9. Do Drawing 5–4 ("Alignment Wheel").
10. Do Drawing 5–5 ("Hearth").

Task 1: Creating Polar Arrays

Procedure

1. Type "Array" or select the Array tool from the Copy flyout on the Modify toolbar.
2. Define a selection set. (Steps 1 and 2 can be reversed if noun/verb selection is enabled.)
3. Type "p" or select "polar".
4. Pick a center point.
5. Enter the number of items to be in the array (or press Enter).
6. Enter the angle to fill (or 0).
7. Enter the angle between items.
8. Tell whether or not to rotate items.

Discussion. The procedure for creating polar arrays is lengthy and requires some explanation. The first two steps are the same as in rectangular arrays. Step 3 is also the same, except that you respond with "polar" or "p" instead of "rectangular" or "r". From here on the steps will be new. First you will pick a center point, and then you will have several options for defining the array.

There are three qualities that define a polar array, but two are sufficient. A polar array is defined by two of the following: 1) a certain number of items, 2) an angle that these items span, and 3) an angle between each item and the next. However you define your polar array, you will have to tell AutoCAD whether or not to rotate the newly created objects as they are copied.

> Begin a new drawing using the B = size prototype.
> In preparation for this exercise, draw a vertical 1.00 line at the bottom center of the screen, near (9.00,2.00), as shown in *Figure 5-1*. We will use a 360 degree polar array to create *Figure 5-2*.
> Type "Array" or select the Array tool from the Copy flyout on the Modify toolbar, as illustrated in *Figure 5-3*.
> Select the line.

Figure 5-1

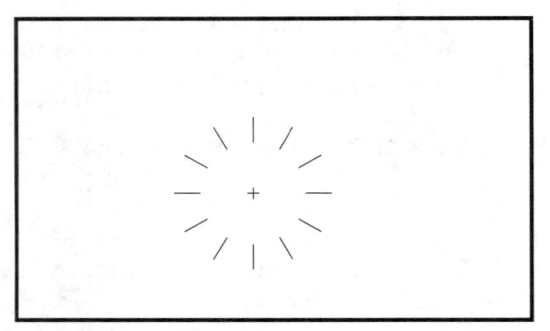

Figure 5-2

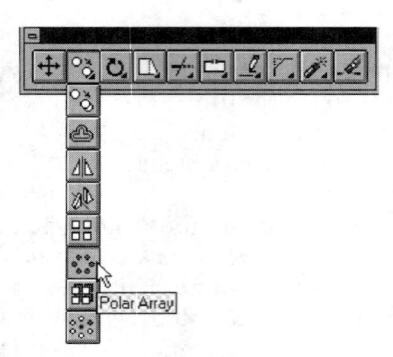

Figure 5-3

> Type "p" or select "polar".

So far, so good. Nothing new up to this point. Now you have a prompt that looks like this:

Center point of array:

Rectangular arrays are not determined by a center, so we did not encounter this prompt before. Polar arrays, however, are built by copying objects around the circumferences of circles or arcs, so we need a center to define one of these.

> Pick a point directly above the line and somewhat below the center of the screen. Something in the neighborhood of (9.00,4.50) will do. The next prompt is:

Number of items:

Remember that we have a choice of two out of three among number of items, angle to fill, and angle between items. This time we will give AutoCAD the first two.

> Type "12".

Now that AutoCAD knows that we want 12 items, all it needs is either the angle to fill with these, or the angle between the items. It will ask first for the angle to fill:

Angle to fill (+=ccw,-=cw) <360>:

The symbols in parentheses tell us that if we give a positive angle the array will be constructed counterclockwise; if we give a negative angle, it will be constructed clockwise. Get used to this; it will come up frequently.

The default is 360 degrees, meaning an array that fills a complete circle.

If we did not give AutoCAD an angle (that is, if we responded with a "0"), we would be prompted for the angle between. This time around we will give 360 as the angle to fill.

> Press Enter to accept the default, a complete circle.

AutoCAD now has everything it needs, except that it doesn't know whether we want our lines to retain their vertical orientation or to be rotated along with the angular displacement as they are copied. AutoCAD asks:

Rotate objects as they are copied? <Y>:

Notice the default, which we will accept.
> Press Enter or type "y".

Your screen should resemble *Figure 5-2*. Now let's try some of the other options. We will define an array that has 20 items placed 15 degrees apart and not rotated.

> Type "U" to undo the first array.
> Type "Array" or select the Array tool.
> Select the line again.
> Press Enter to end object selection.
> Type "p" or select "polar".
> Pick the same center point as before.
> Type "20" for the number of items.
> Type "0" for the angle to fill.

As mentioned, this response tells AutoCAD to issue a prompt for the angle between items:

Angle between items (+=ccw,-=cw):

The symbols in parentheses are familiar from the "angle to fill" prompt. Notice that there is no default angle here.
> Type "15" for the angle between items.

All that remains is to tell AutoCAD not to rotate the lines as they are copied.
> Type "n".

Your screen should now resemble *Figure 5-4*.

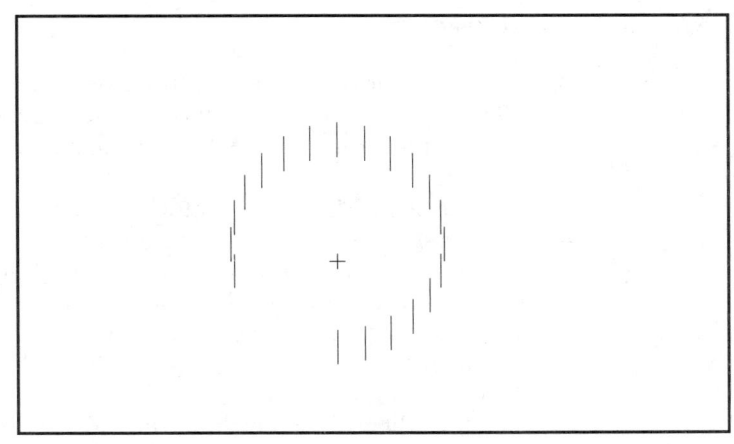

Figure 5-4

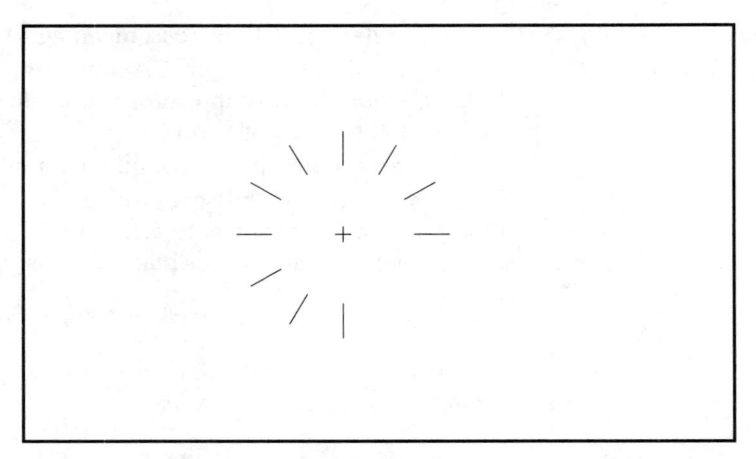

Figure 5-5

Try one more and then you will be on your own with polar arrays. For this one, define an array that fills 270 degrees moving clockwise and has 30 degrees between each angle, as in *Figure 5-5*.

> Undo the last array.
> Repeat the first four steps, up to the "number of items" prompt.
> Press Enter to skip the "Number of items" prompt.
This tells AutoCAD to issue the other two prompts instead.
> Type "−270" for the angle to fill.
    What will the negative angle do?
> Type "30" for the angle between.
> Press Enter to rotate items as they are copied.
    Your screen should resemble *Figure 5-5*.

This ends our discussion of polar arrays. With the options AutoCAD gives you there are many possibilities that you may want to try out. As always, we encourage experimentation. When you are satisfied, erase everything on the screen and do a REDRAW in preparation for learning the ARC command.

Task 2: Drawing Arcs

Procedure

1. Type "a" or select the Arc tool from the Draw toolbar.
2. Type or show where to start the arc, where to end it, and what circle it is a portion of, using any of the 11 available methods.

Discussion. Learning AutoCAD's Arc command is an exercise in geometry. In this section we will give you a firm foundation for understanding and drawing arcs so that you will not be confused by all the options that are available. The information we give you will be more than enough to do the drawings in this chapter and most drawings you will encounter elsewhere. Refer to the *AutoCAD Command Reference* and the chart at the end of this section (*Figure 5-8*) if you need additional information.

AutoCAD gives you eight distinct ways to draw arcs, eleven if you count variations in order. With so many choices, some generalizations will be helpful.

First, notice that every option requires you to specify three pieces of information: where to begin the arc, where to end it, and what circle it is theoretically a part of. To get a handle on the range of options, look at the following standard screen menu abbreviations and their meanings.

	Screen Menu	Information needed
1	3-point:	Three points on arc
2	St,C,End:	Start,Center,End
3	St,C,Ang:	Start,Center,Angle
4	St,C,Len:	Start,Center,Length of chord
5	St,E,Ang:	Start,End,Angle
6	St,E,Dir:	Start,End,Starting direction
7	St,E,Rad:	Start,End,Radius
8	Ce,S,End:	Center,Start,End
9	Ce,S,Ang:	Center,Start,Angle
10	Ce,S,Len:	Center,Start,Length of chord
11	ArcCont:	Start given as end point of previous line or arc; Circle tangent to previous line or arc; End required
12	LinCont:	Begins a straight line at the end point of the last line or arc

Notice that options 8, 9, and 10 are simply reordered versions of 2, 3, and 4. This is how we end up with 11 options instead of 8. Also notice that "LinCont" does not draw an arc at all, and so is not counted.

More important, "start" is always included. In every option, a starting point must be specified, though it does not have to be the first point given.

The options arise from the different ways you can specify the end and the circle from which the arc is cut. The end may be shown as an actual point (all End or E options) or inferred from a specified angle or length of chord (all Ang and Len options).

The circle that the arc is part of may be specified directly by its center point (all Ce and C options) or inferred from other information, such as a radius length (Rad options), an angle between two given points (Ang options), or a tangent direction (St,E,Dir, and ArcCont).

With this framework in mind, we will begin by drawing an arc using the simplest method, which is also the default, the three-point option. The geometric key to this method is that any three points not on the same line determine a circle or an arc of a circle. AutoCAD uses this in the CIRCLE command (the 3P option) as well as in the ARC command.

> Type "a" or select the Arc tool from the Draw toolbar, as shown in *Figure 5-6*.

AutoCAD's response will be this prompt:

Center/<Start point>:

Accepting the default by specifying a point will leave open all those options in which the start point is specified first.

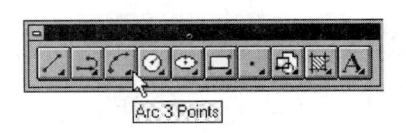

Figure 5-6

If you instead type a "c", AutoCAD will prompt for a center point and follow with those options that begin with a center.
> Select a starting point near the center of the screen.
AutoCAD prompts:

Center/End/<Second point>:

We will continue to follow the default three-point sequence by specifying a second point. You may want to refer to the chart (*Figure 5-8*) as you draw this arc.
> Select any point one or two units away from the previous point. Exact coordinates are not important.

Once AutoCAD has two points, it gives you an arc to drag. By moving the cursor slowly in a circle and in and out you can see the range of what the third point will produce.

AutoCAD also knows now that you have to provide an end point to complete the arc, so the prompt has only one option:

End point:

Any point you select will do, as long as it produces an arc that fits on the screen.
> Pick an end point.

As you can see, three-point arcs are easy to draw. It is much like drawing a line, except that you have to specify three points instead of two. In practice, however, you do not always have three points to use this way. This necessitates the broad range of options in the ARC command. The dimensions you are given and the objects already drawn will determine what options are useful to you.

Next, we will create an arc using the start, center, end method, the second option illustrated in *Figure 5-8*.

> Type "U" to undo the three-point arc.
> Type "a" or select the Arc Start Center End tool from the Arc flyout as shown in *Figure 5-7*.
> Select a point near the center of the screen as a start point.

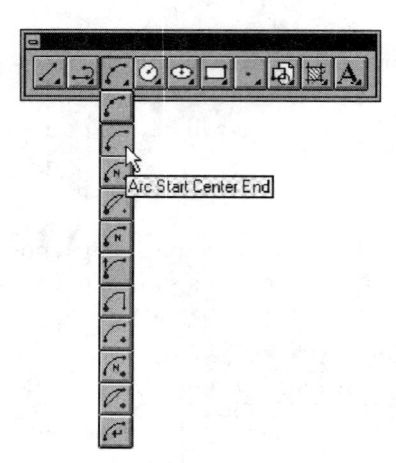

Figure 5-7

The prompt that follows is the same as for the three-point option, but we will not use the default this time:

Center/End/<Second point>:

We will choose the Center option.

NOTE: If you choose options from the screen menu, you will find some steps automated. If you select "St,C,End" for example, the "c" will be entered automatically.

> Type "c".

This tells AutoCAD that we want to specify a center point next, so we see this prompt:

Center:

> Select any point roughly one to three units away from the start point.

The circle from which the arc is to be cut is now clearly determined. All that is left is to specify how much of the circle to take, which can be done in one of three ways, as the prompt indicates:

Angle/Length of chord/<End point>:

We will simply specify an end point by typing coordinates or pointing. But first, move the cursor slowly in a circle and in and out to see how the method works. As before, there is an arc to drag, and now there is a radial direction rubber band as well. If you pick a point anywhere along this rubber band, AutoCAD will assume you want the point where it crosses the circumference of the circle.

NOTE: Here, as in the polar arrays in this chapter, AutoCAD is building arcs *counterclockwise*, consistent with its coordinate system.

> Select an end point to complete the arc.

We will draw one more arc, using the start, center, angle method, before going on. This method has some peculiarities in the use of the rubber band that are typical of the ARC command and can be confusing. An example of how the start, center, angle method may look is shown in *Figure 5-8*.

> Type "U" to undo the last arc.
> Type "a" or select the Arc tool.

AutoCAD will ask for a center or start point:

Center/<Start point>:

> Pick a start point near the center of the screen.

AutoCAD prompts:

Center/End/<Second point>:

> Type "c".

AutoCAD prompts for a center point:

Center:

> Pick a center point one to three units below the start point.

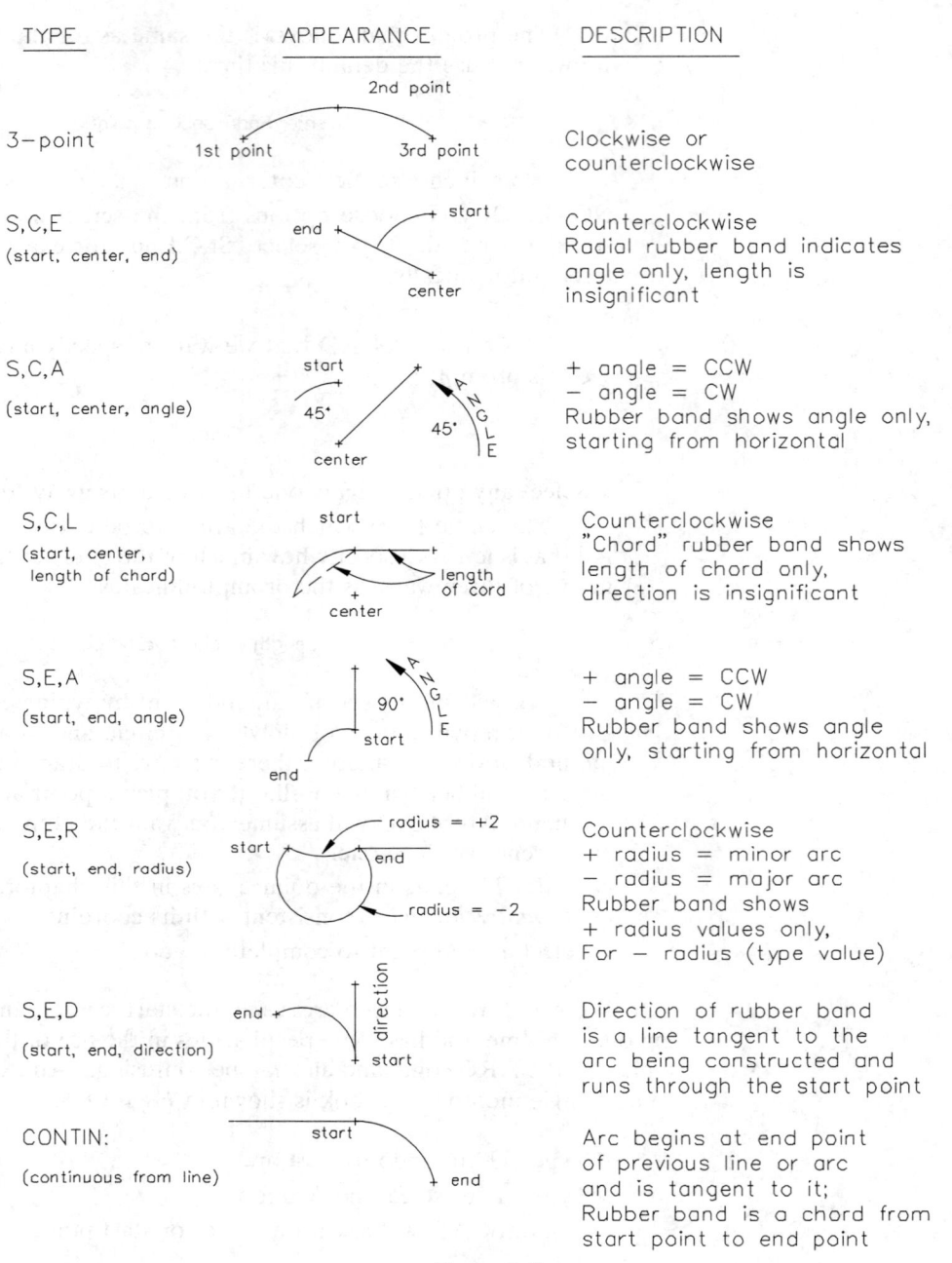

TYPE	APPEARANCE	DESCRIPTION
3-point	1st point, 2nd point, 3rd point	Clockwise or counterclockwise
S,C,E (start, center, end)	end, start, center	Counterclockwise Radial rubber band indicates angle only, length is insignificant
S,C,A (start, center, angle)	start, 45°, center, 45°, ANGLE	+ angle = CCW − angle = CW Rubber band shows angle only, starting from horizontal
S,C,L (start, center, length of chord)	start, length of cord, center	Counterclockwise "Chord" rubber band shows length of chord only, direction is insignificant
S,E,A (start, end, angle)	90°, start, end, ANGLE	+ angle = CCW − angle = CW Rubber band shows angle only, starting from horizontal
S,E,R (start, end, radius)	start, end, radius = +2, radius = −2	Counterclockwise + radius = minor arc − radius = major arc Rubber band shows + radius values only, For − radius (type value)
S,E,D (start, end, direction)	end, start, direction	Direction of rubber band is a line tangent to the arc being constructed and runs through the start point
CONTIN: (continuous from line)	start, end	Arc begins at end point of previous line or arc and is tangent to it; Rubber band is a chord from start point to end point

Figure 5-8

AutoCAD will prompt as before:

Angle/Length of chord/<End point>:

> Type "a" to indicate that you will specify an angle.

You can type an angle specification or show an angle on the screen. Notice that the rubber band now shows an angle only; its length is insignificant. The indicated angle is being measured from the horizontal, but the actual arc begins at the start point and continues counterclockwise, as illustrated in *Figure 5-8*.

> Type "45" or show an angle of 45 degrees. (Remember, you can use F6 to change to polar coordinates that will show the angle.)

Now that you have tried three of the basic methods for constructing an arc, we strongly suggest that you study the chart and then try out the other options. The notes in the right-hand column will serve as a guide to what to look for.

The differences in the use of the rubber band from one option to the next can be confusing. You should understand, for instance, that in some cases the linear rubber band is only significant as a distance indicator; its angle is of no importance and is ignored by AutoCAD. In other cases it is just the reverse; the length of the rubber band is irrelevant, while its angle of rotation is important.

NOTE: One additional trick you should try out as you experiment with arcs is as follows: If you press Enter or the space bar at the "Center/<Start point>" prompt, AutoCAD will use the end point of the last line or arc you drew as the new starting point and construct an arc tangent to it. This is the same as the Continue option on the pull down menu and the ArcCont option on the screen menu.

This completes the present discussion of the Arc command. Constructing arcs, as you may have realized, can be tricky. Another option that is available and often useful is to draw a complete circle and then use the TRIM or BREAK commands to cut out the arc you want. BREAK and TRIM are introduced in the next chapter.

Task 3: Using the ROTATE command

Procedure

1. Type "Rotate" or select the Rotate tool from the Modify toolbar.
2. Define the selection set. (Steps 1 and 2 can be reversed if noun/verb selection is enabled.)
3. Pick a base point.
4. Indicate an angle of rotation.

Discussion. ROTATE is a fairly straightforward command, and it has some uses that might not be apparent immediately. For example, it frequently is easier to draw an object in a horizontal or vertical position and then ROTATE it rather than drawing it in a diagonal position.

In addition to the ROTATE command there is also a rotate mode in the grip edit system, which we will introduce at the end of the exercise.

> In preparation for this exercise, clear your screen and draw a horizontally oriented arc near the center of your screen, as in *Figure 5-9*. Exact coordinates and locations are not important.

We will begin by rotating the arc to the position shown in *Figure 5-10*.
> Select the arc.
> Type "Rotate" or select the Rotate tool from the Modify toolbar, as shown in *Figure 5-11*.

You will be prompted for a base point.

Base point:

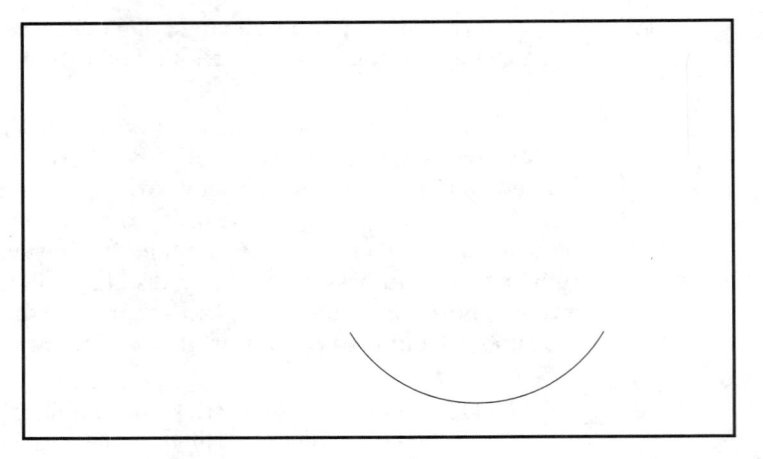

Figure 5-9

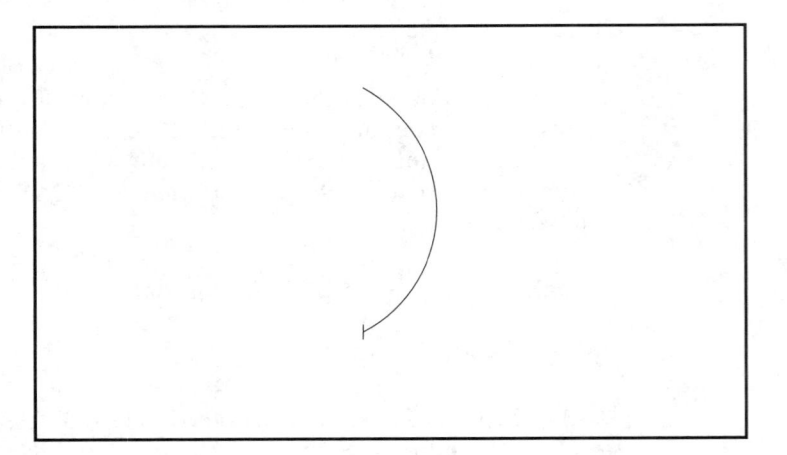

Figure 5-10

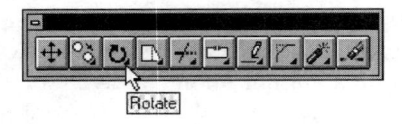

Figure 5-11

This will be the point around which the object is rotated. The results of the rotation, therefore, are dramatically affected by your choice of base point. We will choose a point at the left tip of the arc.
> Point to the left tip of the arc.

The prompt that follows looks like this:

<Rotation angle>/Reference:

The default method is to indicate a rotation angle directly. The object will be rotated through the angle specified and the original object deleted.

Move the cursor in a circle and you will see that you have a copy of the object to drag into place visually. If ortho or snap are on, turn them off to see the complete range of rotation.

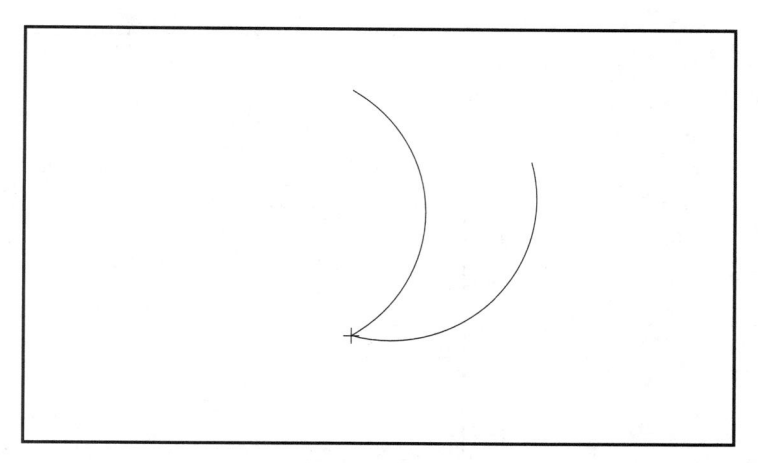

Figure 5-12

> Type "90" or point to a rotation of 90 degrees (use F6 if your coordinate display is not showing polar coordinates).

The results should resemble *Figure 5-10*.

Notice that when specifying the rotation angle directly like this, the original orientation of the selected object is taken to be 0 degrees. The rotation is figured counterclockwise from there. However, there may be times when you want to refer to the coordinate system in specifying rotation. This is the purpose of the "reference" option. To use it, all you need to do is specify the present orientation of the object relative to the coordinate system, and then tell AutoCAD the orientation you want it to have after rotation. Look at *Figure 5-12*. To rotate the arc as shown, you either can indicate a rotation of −45 degrees or tell AutoCAD that it is presently oriented to 90 degrees and you want it rotated to 45 degrees. Try this method for practice.

> Press Enter to repeat the ROTATE command.
> Select the arc.
> Press Enter to end selection.
> Choose a base point at the lower tip of the arc.
> Type "r" or select "Referenc".

AutoCAD will prompt for a reference angle:

Reference angle <0>:

> Type "90".

AutoCAD prompts for an angle of rotation:

Rotation angle:

> Type "45".

Your arc should now resemble the solid arc in *Figure 5-12*.

Rotating with Grips

Rotating with grips is simple and there is a very useful option for copying, but your choice of object selection methods is limited, as always, to pointing and windowing. Try this:

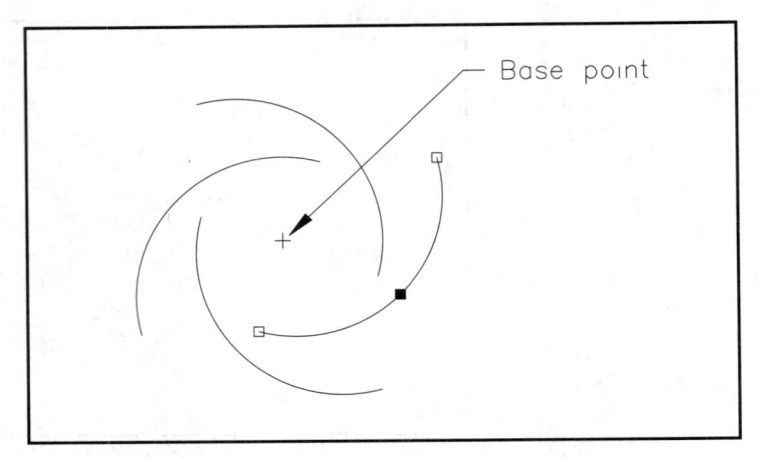

Figure 5-13

> Pick the arc.
  The arc will become highlighted and grips will appear.
> Pick the center grip.
  Notice that as soon as you pick a grip, a Grip Edit Mode menu appears in the screen menu area, if available. You can pick "Rotate" from the menu or press Enter twice to bypass Stretch and Move.
> Select "Rotate" from the screen menu, or press Enter twice.
  Move your cursor in a circle and you will see the arc rotating around the grip at the center of the arc.
> Now, type "b" to select "Base pt" from the screen menu.
  This will allow you to pick a base point other than the selected grip.
> Pick a base point above and to the left of the grip, as shown in *Figure 5-13*.
  Move your cursor in circles again. You will see the arc rotating around the new base point.
> Type "c" or select "Copy" from the menu.
  Notice the Command area prompt, which indicates you are now in a rotate and multiple copy mode.
> Pick a point showing a rotation angle of 90 degrees, as illustrated by the top arc in *Figure 5-13*.
> Pick a second point showing a rotation angle of 180 degrees, as illustrated by the arc at the left in the figure.
> Pick point 3 at 270 degrees to complete the design shown in *Figure 5-13*.
> Press Enter to exit the grip mode.

This capacity to create rotated copies is very useful, as you will find when you do the drawings at the end of the chapter.

Task 4: Creating Mirror Images of Objects on the Screen

Procedure

1. Type "Mirror" or select the Mirror tool from the Copy flyout on the Modify toolbar.
2. Define a selection set. (Steps 1 and 2 can be reversed if noun/verb selection is enabled.)

Chap. 5   133

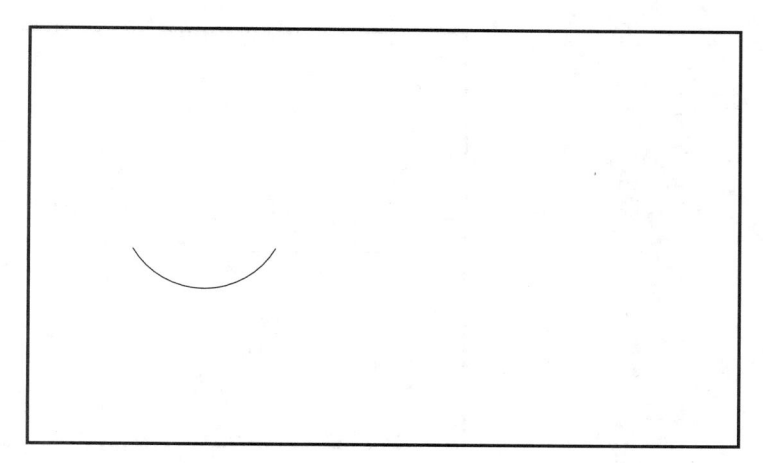

Figure 5-14

3. Point to two ends of a mirror line.
4. Indicate whether or not to delete original object.

Discussion. There are two main differences between the command procedures for Mirror and Rotate. First, in order to mirror an object you will have to define a mirror line, and second you will have an opportunity to indicate whether you want to retain the original object or delete it. In the Rotate sequence the original is always deleted.

There is also a mirror mode in the grip edit system, which we will explore at the end of the task.

> To begin this exercise, undo the rotate copy process of the former exercise so that you are left with a single arc. Rotate it and move it to the left so that you have a bowl-shaped arc placed left of the center of your screen, as in *Figure 5-14*.

Except where noted, you should have snap and ortho on to do this exercise.
> Select the arc.
> Type "Mirror" or select the Mirror tool from the Copy flyout on the Modify toolbar, as shown in *Figure 5-15*.

Now AutoCAD will ask you for the first point of a mirror line.

First point of mirror line:

A mirror line is just what you would expect; the line serves as the "mirror" and all points on your original object will be reflected across the line at an equal distance and opposite orientation.

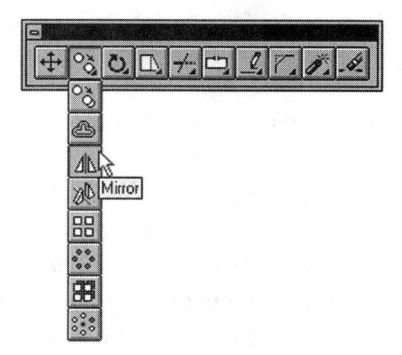

Figure 5-15

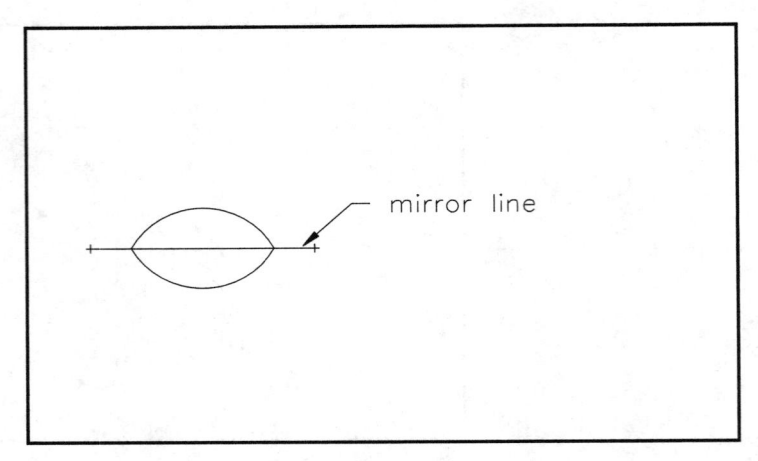

Figure 5-16

We will show a mirror line even with the top of the arc, so that the end points of the mirror images will be touching.

> Select a point even with the left end point of the arc, as in *Figure 5-16*.

You are prompted to show the other end point of the mirror line:

Second point:

The length of the mirror line is not important. All that matters is its orientation. Move the cursor slowly in a circle, and you will see an inverted copy of the arc moving with you to show the different mirror images that are possible, given the first point you have specified. Turn ortho off to see the whole range of possibilities, then turn it on again to complete the exercise.

We will select a point at 0 degrees from the first point, so that the mirror image will be directly above the original arc, and touching at the end points as in *Figure 5-16*.

> Select a point directly to the right (0 degrees) of the first point.

The dragged object will disappear until you answer the next prompt, which asks if you want to delete the original object or not.

Delete old objects? <N>:

This time around we will not delete the original.

> Press Enter to retain the old object. Your screen will look like *Figure 5-16*, without the mirror line in the middle.

Now let's repeat the process, deleting the original this time, and using a different mirror line, to produce *Figure 5-18*.

> Press Enter to repeat the MIRROR command.
> Select the original (lower) arc.
> Press Enter to end selection.

We will create a mirror image above the last one by choosing a mirror line slightly above the two arcs as in *Figure 5-17*.

> Select a first point of the mirror line slightly above and to the left of the figure.
> Select a second point directly to the right of the first point.

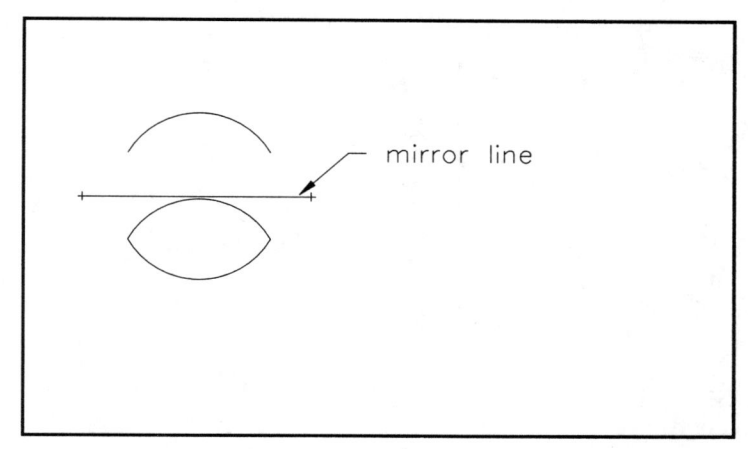

Figure 5-17

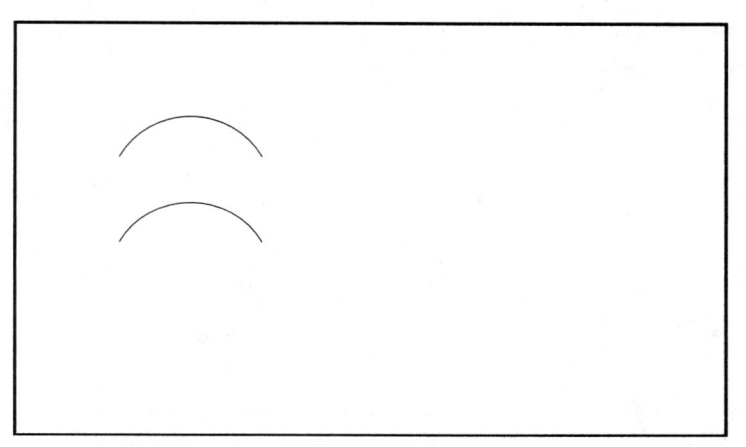

Figure 5-18

> Type "y" indicating that you want the old object, the lower arc, deleted. Your screen should now resemble *Figure 5-18*.

Mirroring with Grips

Mirror is the fifth grip mode, after stretch, move, rotate, and scale. It works exactly like the rotate mode, except that the rubber band will show you a mirror line instead of a rotation angle. The option to retain or delete the original is obtained through the copy option, just as in the Rotate mode. Try it.

> Select the two arcs on your screen by pointing or windowing.

The arcs will be highlighted and grips will be showing.

> Pick any of the grips.
> Pass to the Mirror mode by pressing Enter four times, or by selecting "MIrror" from the screen menu.

Move the cursor and observe the dragged mirror images of the arcs. Notice that the rubber band operates as a mirror line, just as in the Mirror command.

> Type "b" or select "Base pt".

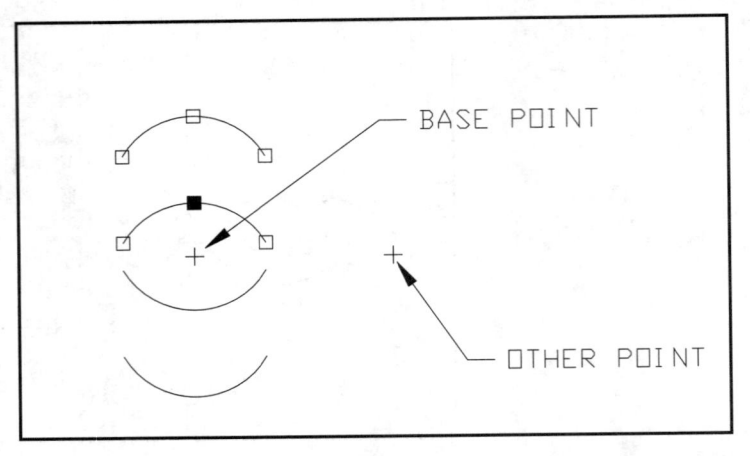

Figure 5-19

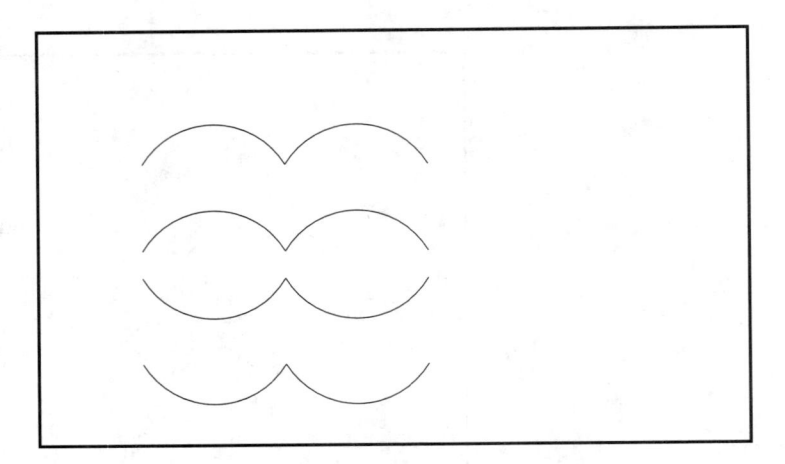

Figure 5-20

This frees you from the selected grip and allows you to create a mirror line from any point on the screen. Notice the "Base point:" prompt in the command area.

> Type "c" or select "Copy".

As in the Rotate mode, this is how you retain the original in a grip edit mirroring sequence.

> Pick a base point slightly below the arcs.
> Pick a second point to the right of the first.

Your screen should resemble *Figure 5-19*.

We suggest that you complete this exercise by using the Mirror grip edit mode with the copy option to create *Figure 5-20*.

Task 5: Changing Paper Size, Orientation, Plot Scale, Rotation, and Origin

Discussion. This discussion will complete our exploration of the basic features of the Plot Configuration dialogue box. The parameters involved will dramatically impact the results of your hard copy output. In particular, putting all of these variables together with each other and previously discussed parameters takes a lot of skill and knowhow. You can gain this expertise through experience with actual plotting and plot previewing. As you become more comfortable with what is going on, it is especially valuable to plot using more than one device and different paper sizes.

Paper Size and Orientation

This box gives critical information and choices about the size and orientation of your drawing sheet. To begin with, you can choose to see information presented in inches or millimeters by selecting one of the two radio buttons. Inches is the default.

> Type "plot" or select the Print tool from the standard tool bar to open the Plot Configuration dialogue box.
> Click on "MM".

You will see that both the plot area and the scale values are changed to reflect metric units.

> Click on "Inches".

On the right you will see a rectangle showing the orientation of the paper in the plotting device. It will be either landscape (horizontal) or portrait (vertical). This orientation is part of the device driver and cannot be changed directly. If you want to plot horizontally when your device is configured vertically, or vice-versa, you must rotate the plot using the Rotation and Origin subdialogue described in the next section.

The plot area is shown below the radio buttons and is also determined by the plotting device. The default size will be the maximum size available on your printer or plotter. If you are using a printer, for example, you may have the equivalent of an A-size sheet. In this case the plot area will be close to 8.00 × 11.00.

> Click on "Size...".

This will open the Paper Size subdialogue box shown in *Figure 5-21*. The standard sizes listed in the box on the left are device specific and will depend on your plotter. If you are using a printer, for example, you may see only the A size on the list. The "USER" boxes on the right allow you to

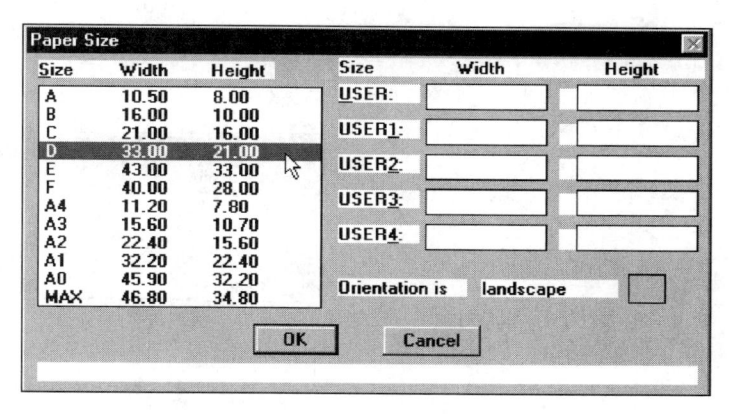

Figure 5-21

define plotting areas of your own. This means, for example, that you can plot in a 5.00 × 5.00 area on an 8.00 × 11.00 or larger sheet of paper.

Paper size can be changed by picking any of the sizes on the list at the left.
> Change the paper size, if you wish, and then click on "OK" to exit the subdialogue.

If you have changed sizes, the new size will be named next to the Size box, and the new plot area will be listed below. The change also may be reflected in the scale box ("Plotted Inches = Drawing Units").

Once again, if you have changed paper sizes we suggest that you do a plot preview. Paper size is one of the important factors in determining effective plotting area.

Scale, Rotation, and Origin

Plots can be scaled to fit the available plot area, or given an explicit scale of paper units to drawing units. "Scaled to Fit" is the default, as shown by the ✓ in the check box. With this setting, the area chosen for plotting in the Additional Parameters box (Display, Extents, Limits, etc.) will be plotted as large as possible within the plot area specified in the Paper Size and Orientation box. Fitting the chosen area to the available plot area will dictate the scale shown in the edit boxes. Plotted inches or millimeters are shown in relation to drawing units. If either the area to be plotted or the paper size is changed, the change will be reflected in the scale boxes.

If "Scaled to Fit" is not checked, the scale will default to 1 = 1. In this case drawing units will be considered equivalent to paper size units. 1-to-1 scale is definitely preferred when plotting from Paper Space (Chapter 6). Other scales can be specified explicitly by typing in the edit boxes. When you change the drawing scale, the area to be plotted may be affected. If the area is too large for the paper size given the scale, then only a portion of the chosen area will be plotted. If the area becomes smaller than the available paper, some blank space will be left. Changing scales should be followed by a partial preview.

The area of the paper that is actually used for plotting may also be affected by the rotation and origin of the plot. If your device is configured with paper oriented vertically (portrait style), and you want to plot horizontally (landscape), then you will need to rotate 90 degrees. This is done with the radio buttons in the Plot Rotation and Origin subdialogue box.

> Click in the Rotation and Origin box.

This will call the dialogue box shown in *Figure 5-22*. You can rotate to 0, 90, 180, or 270 degrees as shown. Rotating a plot by 90 degrees will have

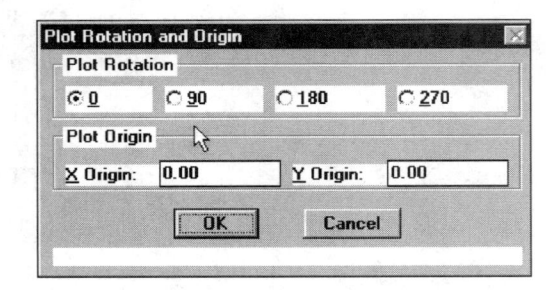

Figure 5-22

a very significant impact on the relationship between paper size and effective drawing area.

This box will also allow you to change the origin of the plot. Plots usually originate in the lower left-hand corner of the page, but you can alter this. For example, let's say you wanted to plot a 5 × 5 area in the upper right of an 8 × 11 sheet, landscape orientation. You could do this by creating a 5 × 5 "User" paper size and then moving the origin from (0,0) to (6,3).

> Change the plot rotation if you wish, and then Click on "OK" to exit the dialogue box.

At this point, you have been through all the major parameters of plot configuration. It is important that you gain experience in using the configuration parameters available. When you have a drawing ready, open the dialogue box and make whatever adjustments you think are necessary. You should access at least one partial and one full preview along the way. When everything looks right, check your plotting device and paper and then click on "OK" to start it rolling.

Tasks 6, 7, 8, 9, and 10

You have learned some complex sequences in this chapter, especially in the Arc and polar Array commands, so take your time doing the next five drawings, and be sure that you understand the commands involved. Your knowledge of AutoCAD and CAD operation is increasing rapidly at this point, and it will be important that you practice what you have learned carefully.

DRAWING 5-1: FLANGED BUSHING

This drawing makes use of a polar array to draw eight screw holes in a circle. It also will review the use of layers and linetypes.

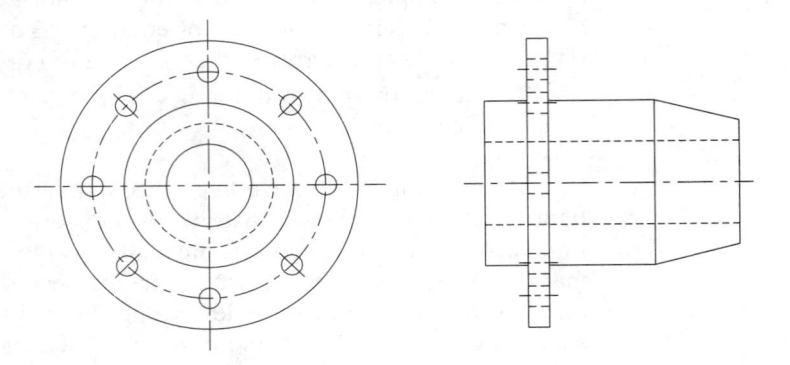

DRAWING SUGGESTIONS

GRID = .25   LTSCALE = .50
SNAP = .25   LIMITS = (0,0) (18,12)

> Draw the concentric circles first, using dimensions from both views. Remember to change layers as needed.

> Once you have drawn the 2.75-diameter bolt circle, use it to locate one of the bolt holes. Any of the circles at a quadrant point (0, 90, 180, or 270 degrees) will do.

> Draw a center line across the bolt hole, and then array the hole and the center line 360 degrees. Be sure to rotate the objects as they are copied, otherwise you will get strange results from your center lines.

Chap. 5

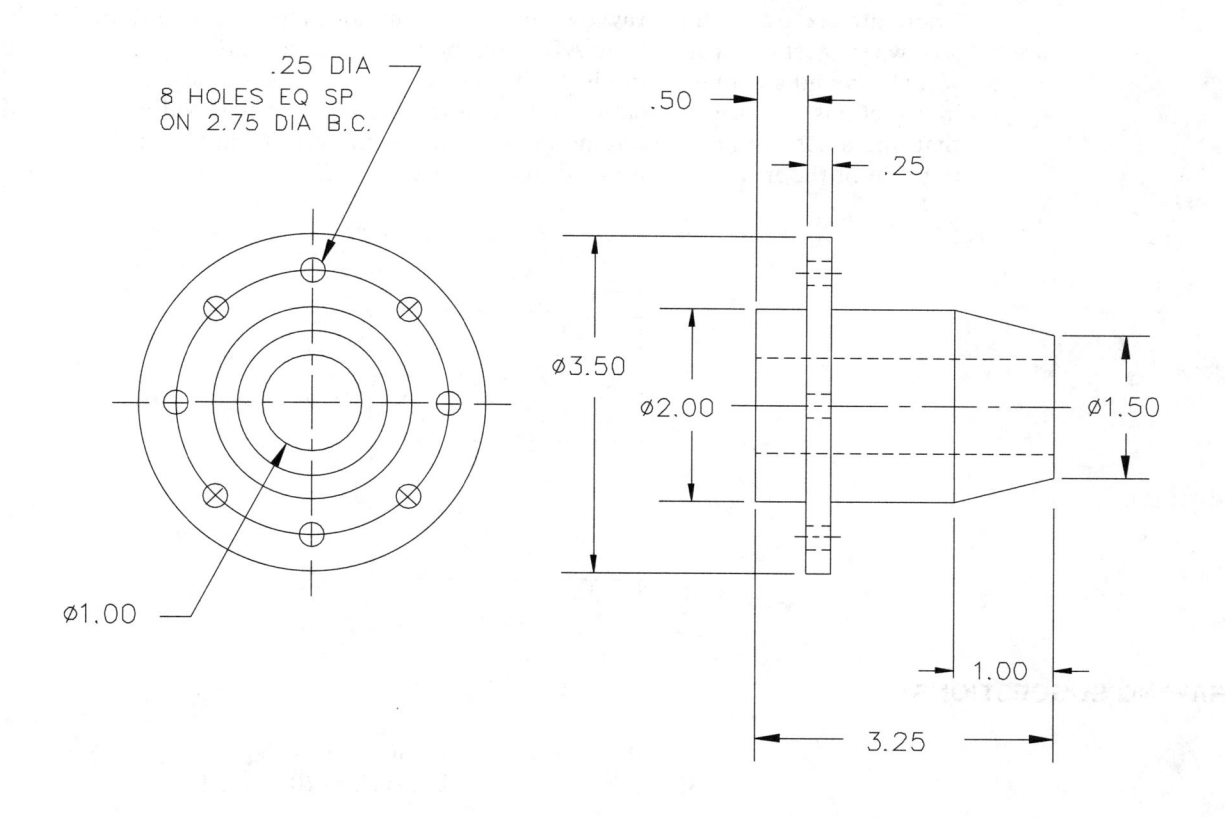

.25 DIA
8 HOLES EQ SP
ON 2.75 DIA B.C.

Ø1.00

.50
.25

Ø3.50
Ø2.00
Ø1.50

1.00
3.25

FLANGED BUSHING

Drawing 5-1

LAYERS	NAME	COLOR	LINETYPE	
	0	WHITE	————	CONTINUOUS
	1	RED	————	CONTINUOUS
	2	YELLOW	- - - - -	HIDDEN
	3	GREEN	— - —	CENTER

LINE (L)
CIRCLE (C)
ARRAY
MIRROR
ZOOM (Z)

[F1] HELP
[F2] TEXT/GRAPHICS SCREEN
[F6] ABSOLUTE/OFF/POLAR COORDS
[F7] ON/OFF GRID
[F8] ON/OFF ORTHO
[F9] ON/OFF SNAP

DRAWING 5-2: GUIDE

There are six arcs in this drawing, and while some of them could be drawn as fillets, we suggest that you use the ARC command for practice. By drawing arcs you will also avoid a common problem with fillets. Since fillets are designed to round intersections at corners, creating a fillet in the middle of a line will erase part of that line unless you turn Trim mode off. This would affect the center line on the left side of the front view of this drawing, for example.

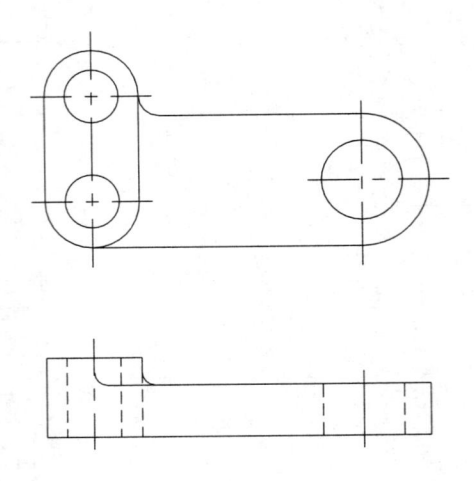

DRAWING SUGGESTIONS

GRID = .25   LTSCALE = .50
SNAP = .125   LIMITS = (0,0) (12,9)

> The three large arcs in the top view all can be drawn easily using Start, Center, End.

> The smaller .375 arc in the top view could be drawn by filleting the top arc with the horizontal line to its right. However, we suggest you try an arc giving start, center, end or start, center, angle. Note that you can easily locate the center by moving .375 to the right of the end point of the upper arc.

> The same method will work to draw the .25 arc in the front view. Begin by dropping a line down .25 from the horizontal line. Start your arc at the end of this line, and move .25 to the right to locate its center. Then the end will simply be .25 down from the center (or you could specify an angle of 90 degrees).

> Similarly, the arc at the center line can be drawn from a start point .25 up from the horizontal. It will have a radius of .25 and make an angle of 90 degrees.

Chap. 5

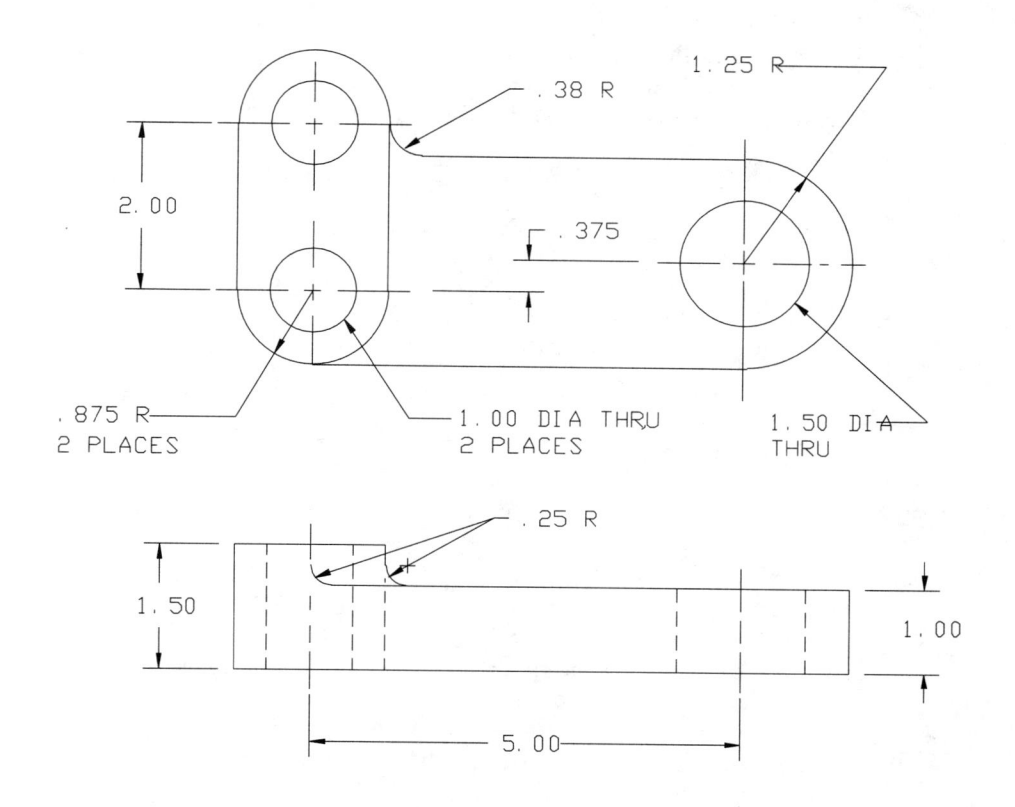

GUIDE
Drawing 5-2

LAYERS	NAME	COLOR	LINETYPE
	0	WHITE	CONTINUOUS
	1	RED	CONTINUOUS
	2	YELLOW	HIDDEN
	3	GREEN	CENTER

LINE (L)
CIRCLE (C)
ARC (A)
COPY
ZOOM (Z)

F1 HELP
F2 TEXT/GRAPHICS SCREEN
F6 ABSOLUTE/OFF/POLAR COORDS
F7 ON/OFF GRID
F8 ON/OFF ORTHO
F9 ON/OFF SNAP

DRAWING 5-3: DIALS

This is a relatively simple drawing that will give you some good practice with polar arrays and the ROTATE and COPY commands.

Notice that the needle drawn at the top of the next page is only for reference; the actual drawing includes only the plate and the three dials with their needles.

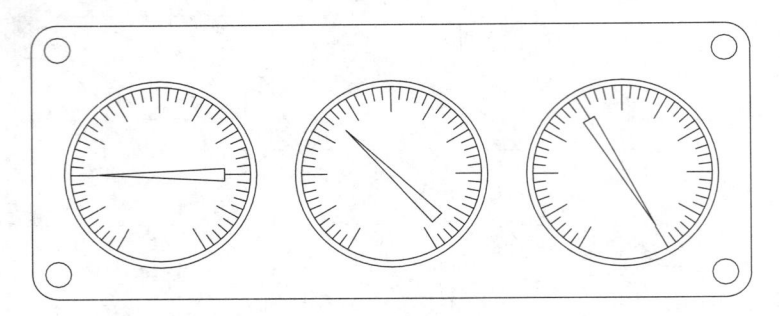

DRAWING SUGGESTIONS

GRID = .25 LTSCALE = .50
SNAP = .125 LIMITS = (0,0) (12,9)

> After drawing the outer rectangle and screw holes, draw the leftmost dial, including the needle. Draw a .50 vertical line at the top and array it to the left (counterclockwise—a positive angle) and to the right (negative) to create the 11 larger lines on the dial. Use the same operation to create the 40 small (.25) markings.

> Complete the first dial and then use a multiple copy to produce two more dials at the center and right of your screen. Be sure to use a window to select the entire dial.

> Finally, use the ROTATE command to rotate the needles as indicated on the new dials. Use a window to select the needle, and rotate it around the center of the dial.

Chap. 5

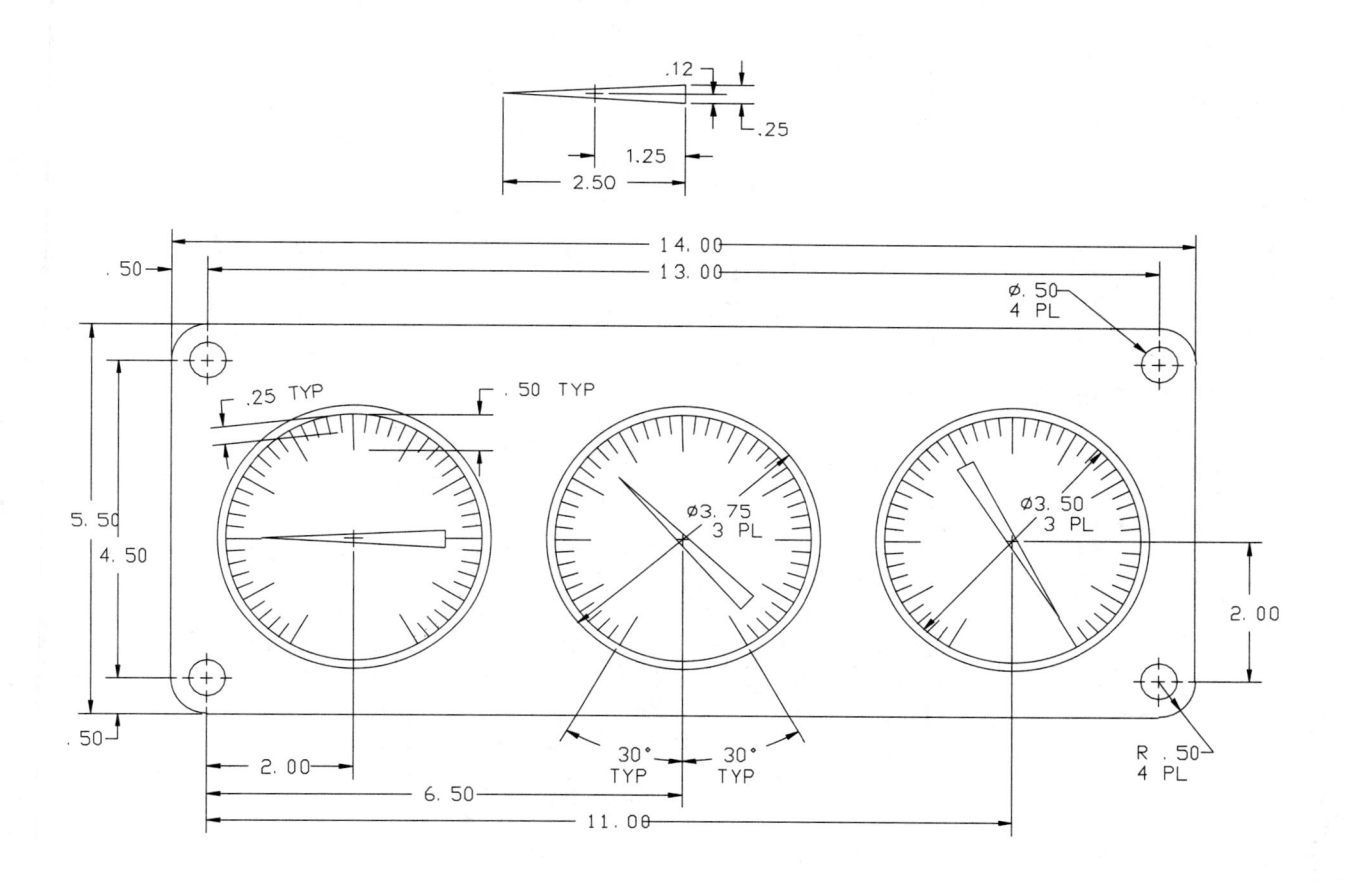

DIALS
Drawing 5-3

LAYERS	NAME	COLOR	LINETYPE		
	0	WHITE	———— CONTINUOUS		
	1	RED	———— CONTINUOUS		
	3	GREEN	— — — CENTER		

LINE (L)
CIRCLE (C)
ARRAY
COPY
FILLET
ROTATE
ZOOM (Z)

F1 HELP
F2 TEXT/GRAPHICS SCREEN
F6 ABSOLUTE/OFF/POLAR COORDS
F7 ON/OFF GRID
F8 ON/OFF ORTHO
F9 ON/OFF SNAP

DRAWING 5-4: ALIGNMENT WHEEL

This drawing shows a typical use of the MIRROR command. Carefully mirroring sides of the symmetrical front view will save you from duplicating some of your drawing efforts. Notice that you will need a small snap setting to draw the vertical lines at the chamfer.

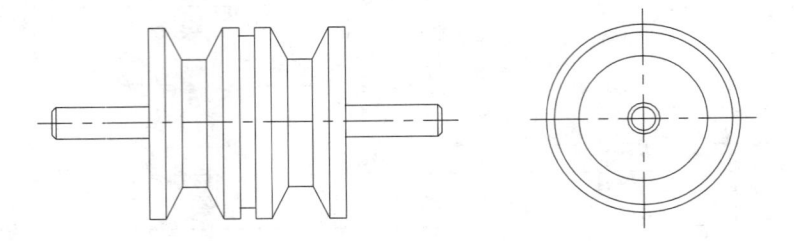

DRAWING SUGGESTIONS

GRID = .25 LTSCALE = .50
SNAP = .125 LIMITS = (0,0) (12,9)

> There are numerous ways to use Mirror in drawing the front view. As the reference shows, there is top–bottom symmetry as well as left–right symmetry. The exercise for you is to choose an efficient mirroring sequence.

> Whatever sequence you use, consider the importance of creating the chamfer and the vertical line at the chamfer before this part of the object is mirrored.

> Once the front view is drawn, the right side view will be easy. Remember to change layers for center and hidden lines and to line up the small inner circle with the chamfer.

Chap. 5

(ORTHO ON)

MIRROR LINES

REFERENCE

.25
2.88
.37
.25
27° REF
.06 X 45° CHAMFER BOTH ENDS
Ø2.00
Ø2.75
Ø3.00
Ø.50
.25
1.38
3.00
1.50
6.00

ALIGNMENT WHEEL
Drawing 5-4

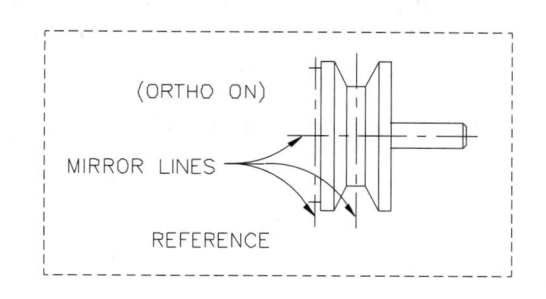

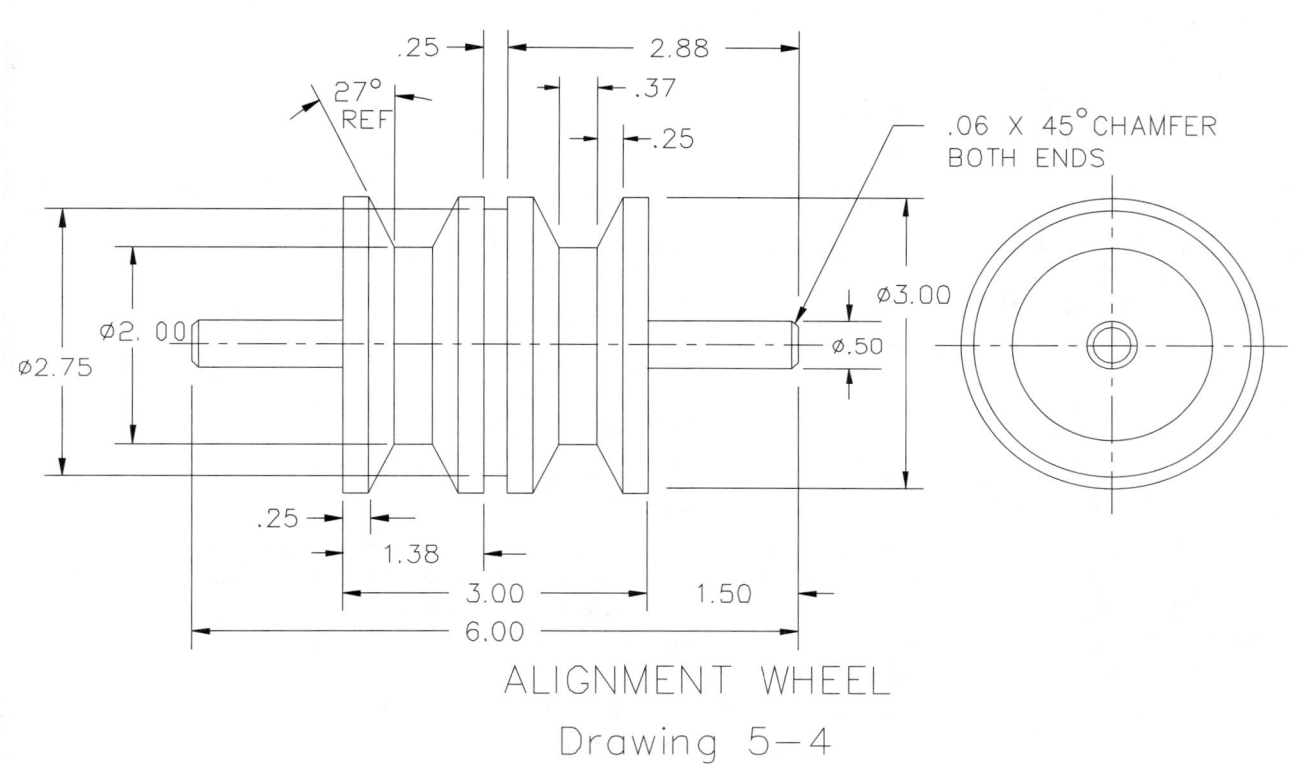

LAYERS	NAME	COLOR	LINETYPE			
	0	WHITE	————	CONTINUOUS	LINE	(L)
	1	RED	————	CONTINUOUS	CIRCLE	(C)
	2	YELLOW	— — —	HIDDEN	CHAMFER	
	3	GREEN	— — —	CENTER	MIRROR	
					ZOOM	(Z)

F1	F2	F6	F7	F8	F9
HELP	TEXT/GRAPHICS SCREEN	ABSOLUTE/OFF/POLAR COORDS	ON/OFF GRID	ON/OFF ORTHO	ON/OFF SNAP

DRAWING 5-5: HEARTH

Once you have completed this architectural drawing as it is shown, you might want to experiment with filling in a pattern of firebrick in the center of the hearth. The drawing itself is not complicated, but little errors will become very noticeable when you try to make the row of 4 × 8 bricks across the bottom fit with the arc of bricks across the top, so work carefully.

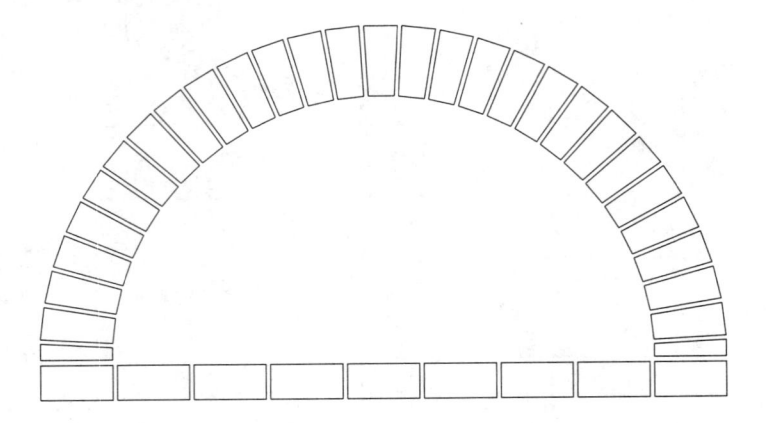

DRAWING SUGGESTIONS

UNITS = Architectural
   smallest fraction = 8 (1/8")
LIMITS = (0,0) (12',9')
GRID = 1'
SNAP = 1/8"

> Zoom in to draw the wedge-shaped brick indicated by the arrow on the right of the dimensioned drawing. Draw half of the brick only and mirror it across the center line as shown. (Notice that the center line is for reference only.) It is very important that you use Mirror so that you can erase half of the brick later.
> Array the brick in a 29 item, 180 degree polar array.
> Erase the bottom halves of the end bricks at each end.
> Draw a new horizontal bottom line on each of the two end bricks.
> Draw a 4 × 8 brick directly below the half brick at the left end.
> Array the 4 × 8 brick in a 1 row, 9 column array, with 8.5" between columns.

Chap. 5

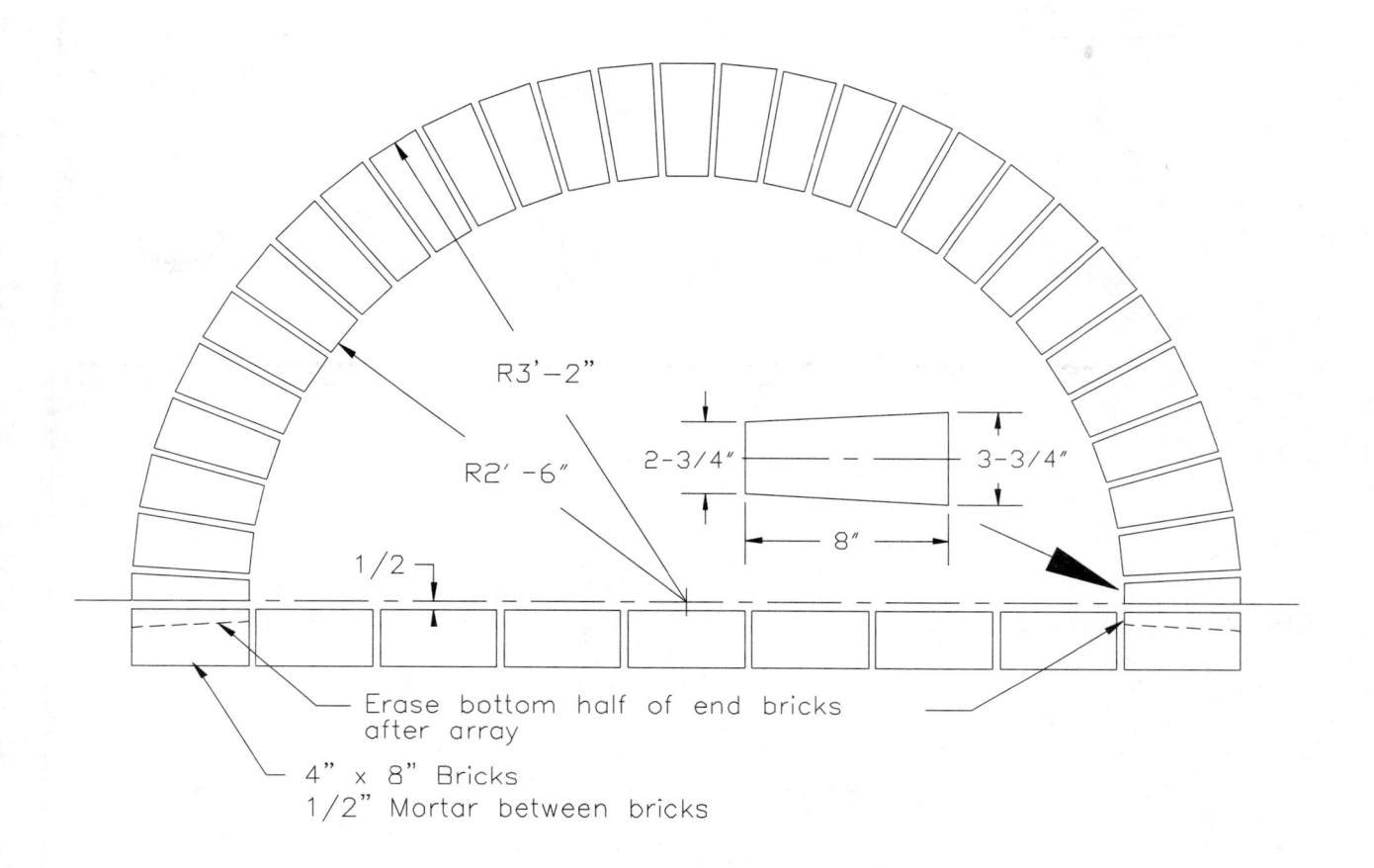

R3'-2"
R2'-6"
2-3/4"
3-3/4"
8"
1/2"

— Erase bottom half of end bricks after array

— 4" x 8" Bricks
1/2" Mortar between bricks

HEARTH
Drawing 5-5

Drawing Compliments of Thomas Casey

LAYERS	NAME	COLOR	LINETYPE		
	0	WHITE	———————— CONTINUOUS	LINE	(L)
	1	RED	———————— CONTINUOUS	ERASE	(E)
				MIRROR	
				ARRAY	
				MOVE	(M)
	3	GREEN	— — — CENTER	ZOOM	(Z)

F1	F2	F6	F7	F8	F9
HELP	TEXT/GRAPHICS SCREEN	ABSOLUTE/OFF/POLAR COORDS	ON/OFF GRID	ON/OFF ORTHO	ON/OFF SNAP

CHAPTER 6

COMMANDS

MODIFY

BREAK
TRIM
EXTEND
STRETCH

Special Topic: Object Snap (OSNAP)

OVERVIEW

This chapter will continue to expand your repertoire of editing commands. You will learn to BREAK entities on the screen into pieces so that they may be manipulated or erased separately. You will also learn to shorten entities using the TRIM command, or to lengthen them with the EXTEND command.

But most important, you will begin to use a very powerful tool called Object Snap that will take you to a new level of accuracy and efficiency as a CAD operator.

TASKS

1. Use object snap to select specifiable points on an entity using single-point overrides.
2. Select points with OSNAP using running modes.

Chap. 6   151

3. Use BREAK to break a previously drawn entity into two separate entities.
4. Use TRIM to shorten entities.
5. Use EXTEND to lengthen entities.
6. Use STRETCH to move selected objects while retaining their connections to other objects.
7. Plot from Multiple Viewports in paper space.
8. Do Drawing 6–1 ("Bike Tire").
9. Do Drawing 6–2 ("Archimedes Spiral").
10. Do Drawing 6–3 ("Spiral Designs").
11. Do Drawing 6–4 ("Grooved Hub").
12. Do Drawing 6–5 ("Cap Iron").
13. Do Drawing 6–6 ("Deck Framing").

Task 1: Selecting Points with Object Snap (Single-Point Override)

Procedure

1. Enter a drawing command, such as LINE, CIRCLE, or ARC.
2. Type or select the name of an object snap mode.
3. Point to a previously drawn object.

Discussion. Some of the drawings in the last two chapters have pushed the limits of what you can accomplish accurately on a CAD system with incremental snap alone. Object snap is a related tool that works in a very different manner. Instead of snapping to points defined by the coordinate system, it snaps to geometrically specifiable points on objects that you already have drawn.

Let's say you want to begin a new line at the end point of one that is already on the screen. If you are lucky, it may be on a snap point, but it is just as likely not to be. Turning snap off and using the arrow keys may appear to work, but chances are that when you zoom in you will find that you have actually missed the point. Using object snap is the only precise way, and it is as precise as you could want. Let's try it.

> To prepare for this exercise, draw a 6 × 6 box with a circle inside, as in *Figure 6-1*. Exact sizes and locations are not important; however, the circle should be centered within the square.

> Now enter the LINE command (type "l" or select the Line tool).

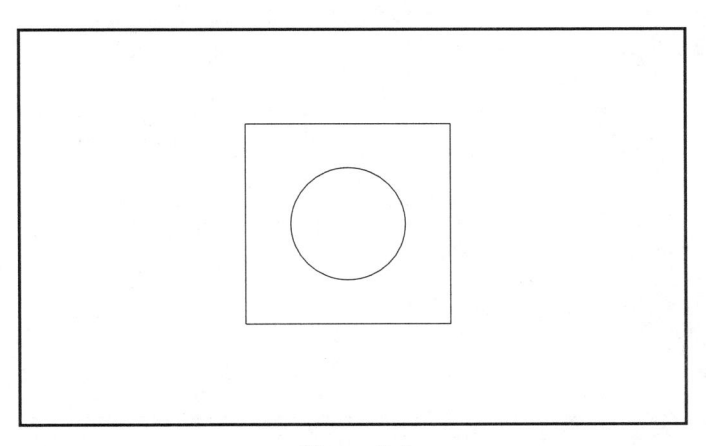

Figure 6-1

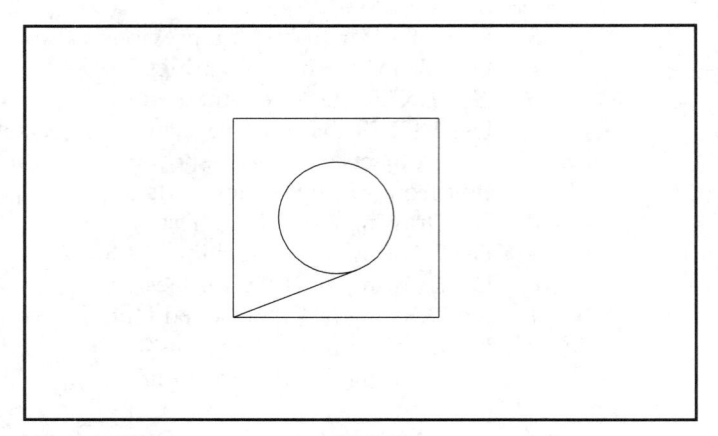

Figure 6-2

We are going to draw a line from the lower left corner of the square to a point on a line tangent to the circle, as shown in *Figure 6-2*. This task would be extremely difficult without object snap. The corner is easy to locate, since you probably have drawn it on snap, but the tangent may not be.

We will use an "end point" object snap to locate the corner and a "tangent" object snap to locate the tangent point.

> At the "From point:" prompt, instead of specifying a point, type "end" or select the Snap to Endpoint tool from the Object Snap flyout on the Standard toolbar, as illustrated in *Figure 6-3*.

You may also have a cursor menu which can be accessed by holding down the Shift key and pressing the Enter (right) button on a two button mouse. This is a very convenient feature. You should get used to using it if you have it.

Entering "Endpoint" by any of these methods tells AutoCAD that you are going to select the start point of the line by using an end point object snap rather than by direct pointing or entering coordinates.

Now that AutoCAD knows that we want to begin at the end point of a previously drawn entity, it needs to know which one.

The pickbox at the intersection of the cross hairs is now a target box. Its size can be set separately from the size of the pickbox using the APERTURE command, as discussed later. To be selected, a point or an entity containing the point must be within the aperture, as in *Figure 6-4*.

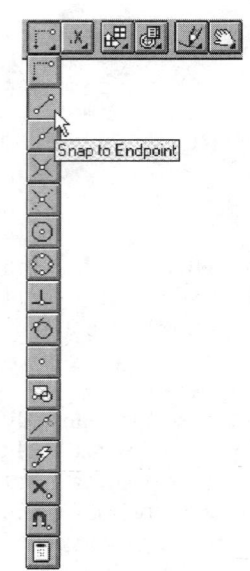

Figure 6-3

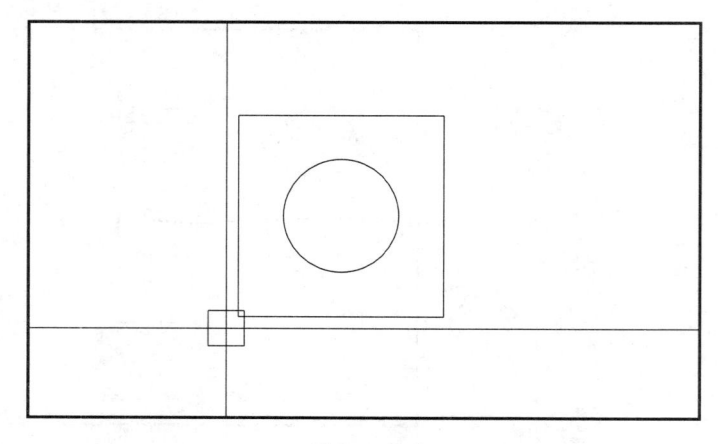

Figure 6-4

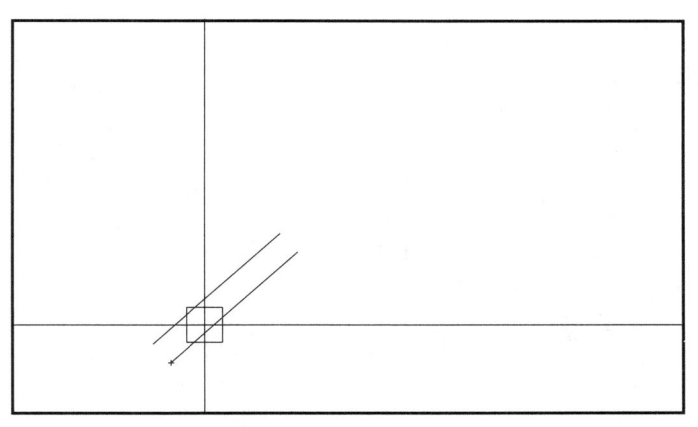

Figure 6-5

> Position the cursor so that the lower left corner of the square is within the target box, then press the pick button.

  Now we will draw the tangent.

> At the "To point:" prompt, type "tan" or select "Tangent".

> Move the cursor to the right and position the cross hairs so that the circle crosses the target box. Press the pick button. AutoCAD will locate the tangent point and draw the line.

> Press Enter to exit the LINE command. Your screen should now resemble *Figure 6-2*.

NOTE: In more complex drawings it is quite possible that there will be more than one point that fits the definition of the osnap mode you have selected (for example, two or more distinct end points or objects with end points within the box, as in *Figure 6-5*). In this case AutoCAD will first search for all possible candidates and will then select the one nearest the intersection of the cross hairs. An exception to this can be made using the "quick" mode described in the chart at the end of this discussion (see *Figure 6-9*).

We will repeat the process now, but start from the midpoint of the bottom side of the square instead of its end point.

> Repeat the LINE command.

> At the prompt for a point, type "mid" or select "Midpoint".

> Position the aperture anywhere adjacent to the bottom side of the square and press the pick button.

> At the prompt for a second point, type "tan" or select "Tangent".

> Position the aperture along the lower right side of the circle and press the pick button.

> Press Enter or the space bar to exit the LINE command.

  At this point your screen should resemble *Figure 6-6*.

That's all there is to it. Remember the steps: 1) enter a command; 2) when AutoCAD asks for a point, type or select an object snap mode instead; 3) select an object to which the mode can be applied and AutoCAD will find the point.

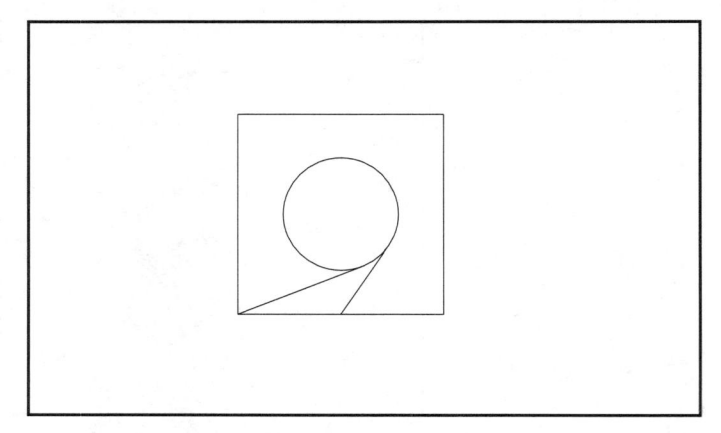

Figure 6-6

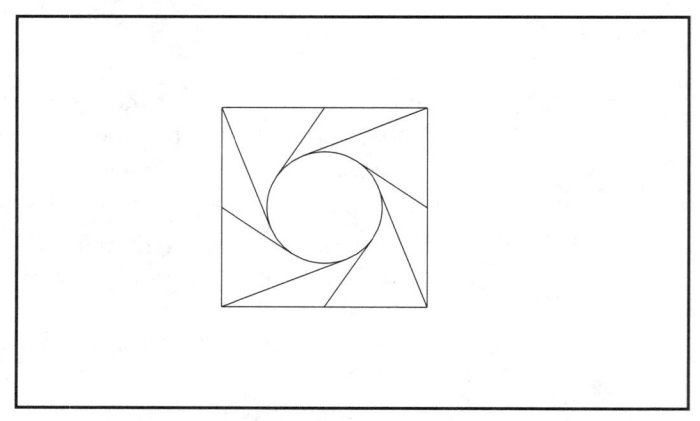

Figure 6-7

Task 2: Selecting Points with OSNAP (Running Mode)

Procedure

1. Type or select "OSNAP" or pick "Running Object Snap..." under "Options" on the pull down menu.
2. Type or select one or more OSNAP modes.
3. Enter drawing commands.

Discussion. So far we have been using object snap one point at a time. Since object snap is not constantly in use for most applications, this single-point method is probably most common. But if you find that you are going to be using one or a number of object snap types repeatedly and will not need to select many points without them, there is a way to keep object snap modes on so that they affect all point selection. These are called "running object snap modes". We will use this method to complete the drawing shown in *Figure 6-7*. Notice how the lines are drawn from midpoints and corners to tangents to the circle. This is easily done with object snap.

In order to turn on a running osnap mode you can enter the OSNAP command at the command line or through the screen menu, or use the DDOSNAP dialogue box from the pull down or screen menu. We recommend the dialogue box because it is quick, easy, and also gives you the chance to change the aperture size.

Chap. 6   155

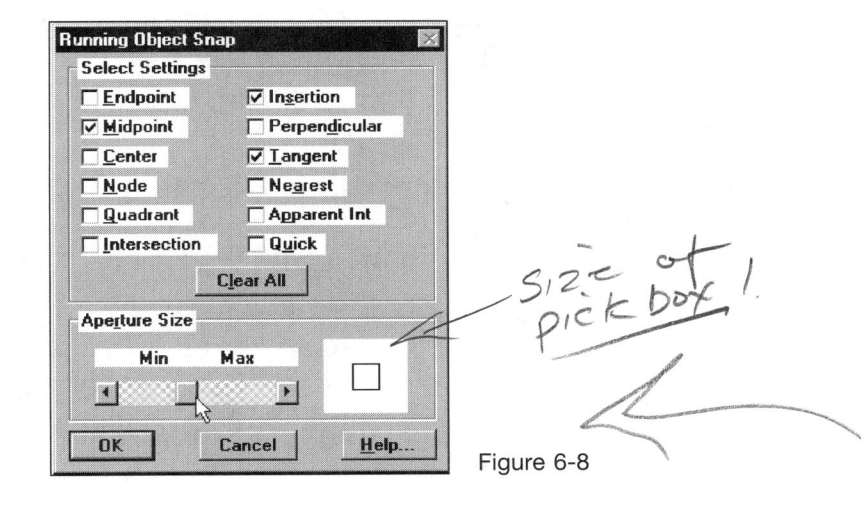

Figure 6-8

> Select "Options" and then "Running Object Snap..." from the pull down menu.

You will see the dialogue box illustrated in *Figure 6-8*. This box can also be called by the DDOSNAP command. At the top is a list of object snap modes with check boxes. At the bottom is a box with a scroll bar where you can change the object snap aperture size.

You will find a description of all of the object snap modes on the chart (*Figure 6-9*) at the end of this task, but for now we will be using three: midpoint, tangent, and intersect. Midpoint and tangent you already know. Intersect snaps to the point where two entities meet or cross. We will use intersect instead of end point to select the remaining three corners of the square.

> Click on the check boxes next to "Midpoint", "Tangent", and "Intersection".

Before you leave the dialogue box, try changing the aperture size.

Changing the Size of the Aperture

The aperture can be changed visually using the scroll bar in the usual manner, or by entering the APERTURE command and typing a number. If you type the command, you will be asked to specify the aperture size in pixels (from 1 to 50, one pixel being the smallest unit your monitor can display).
NOTE: The aperture size is a "system variable." This means that its setting will remain in effect when you enter other drawings.

> Click on the box in the middle of the scroll bar and drag it to the right, or click on the right arrow.

Watch the aperture in the black box on the right growing larger.

> Set the aperture by moving the scroll bar box to the left of center, as shown in *Figure 6-8*. The aperture itself should be somewhat larger than the pickbox you are used to seeing.

Remember, the aperture is distinct from the pickbox. Changing the aperture has no effect on the size of the object selection pickbox. The size of this box is controlled by another system variable called PICKBOX.

The best size for your aperture depends on your drawing. If you are doing a lot of point selection in tight spaces, and especially if you are using multiple osnap modes, you may want a smaller aperture to avoid confusion. If you have plenty of room to work in, you may want a larger aperture to make the selection process looser and faster.

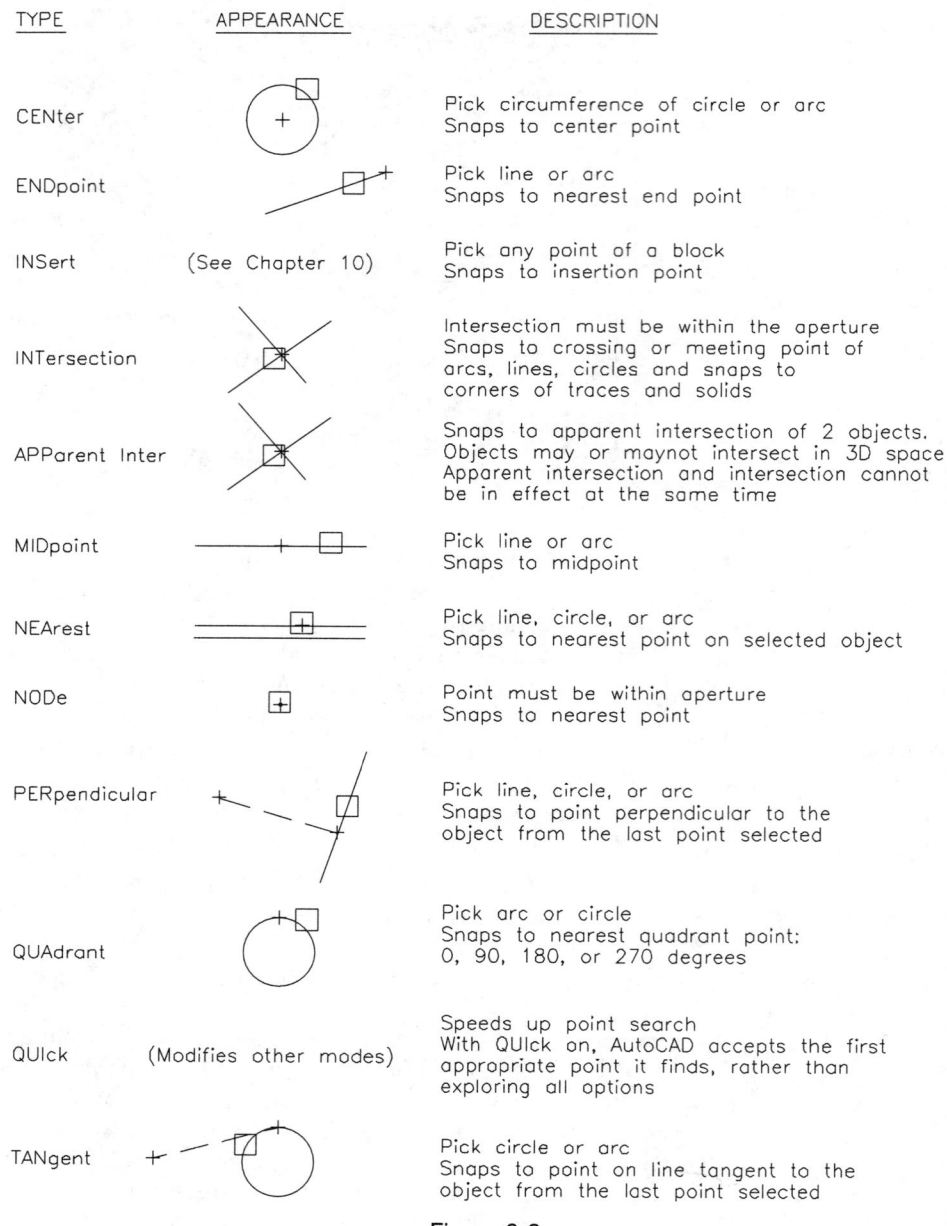

TYPE	APPEARANCE	DESCRIPTION
CENter		Pick circumference of circle or arc Snaps to center point
ENDpoint		Pick line or arc Snaps to nearest end point
INSert	(See Chapter 10)	Pick any point of a block Snaps to insertion point
INTersection		Intersection must be within the aperture Snaps to crossing or meeting point of arcs, lines, circles and snaps to corners of traces and solids
APParent Inter		Snaps to apparent intersection of 2 objects. Objects may or maynot intersect in 3D space. Apparent intersection and intersection cannot be in effect at the same time
MIDpoint		Pick line or arc Snaps to midpoint
NEArest		Pick line, circle, or arc Snaps to nearest point on selected object
NODe		Point must be within aperture Snaps to nearest point
PERpendicular		Pick line, circle, or arc Snaps to point perpendicular to the object from the last point selected
QUAdrant		Pick arc or circle Snaps to nearest quadrant point: 0, 90, 180, or 270 degrees
QUIck	(Modifies other modes)	Speeds up point search With QUIck on, AutoCAD accepts the first appropriate point it finds, rather than exploring all options
TANgent		Pick circle or arc Snaps to point on line tangent to the object from the last point selected

Figure 6-9

> Click on "OK" to exit the dialogue box.

AutoCAD returns you to the "Command:" prompt and you are ready to draw with the running osnap modes in effect. We will draw tangent lines from the corners of the square and from the midpoints of its sides to produce *Figure 6-7*.

Now back to our drawing.

> Enter the LINE command.

Notice the size of the aperture on the cross hairs. The change in size tells you that you are looking at the object snap aperture instead of the pickbox and that there are osnap modes in effect. When you select points now, AutoCAD will look for the point nearest the center of the aperture that fulfills the geometric requirements of one of the three running osnap modes you have chosen. If there is more than one point, it will select the one nearest the intersection of the cross hairs.

> Position the aperture so that the lower right corner is within the box and press the pick button.

AutoCAD will select the intersection of the bottom and the right sides and give you the rubber band and the prompt for a second point.

Notice that the aperture is still on the cross hairs.

> Move the cross hairs up and along the right side of the circle and press the pick button.

Be sure that the intersection of the previous tangent and the circle is not within the aperture.

AutoCAD will construct a new tangent from the lower right corner to the circle.

> Press Enter to complete the command sequence.
> Press Enter again to repeat LINE so you can begin with a new start point.

We will continue to move counterclockwise around the circle. This should begin to be easy now.

> Position the aperture along the right side of the square and press the pick button. Be sure the corner is not within the aperture.

AutoCAD snaps to the midpoint of the side.

> Move up along the upper right side of the circle and press the pick button.
> Press Enter to exit LINE.
> Press Enter again to repeat LINE and continue around the circle drawing tangents like this: upper right corner to top of circle, top side midpoint to top left of circle, upper left corner to left side, left side midpoint to lower left side.

Remember that running osnap modes should give you both speed and accuracy, so push yourself a little to see how quickly you can complete the figure.

Your screen should now resemble *Figure 6-7*.

Before going on we need to turn off the running osnap modes.

> Click twice on "Options" on the pull down menu bar.

Notice that AutoCAD remembers your pull down menu selections. You can re-open a dialogue box by clicking twice on the heading at the top of the menu.

> Click in all the check boxes that are showing ✓'s.
> Click on "OK" to exit the dialogue box.

AutoCAD will return you to the command prompt, and when you begin drawing again, you will see that the aperture is gone.

NOTE: You can also turn off all running osnap modes by typing "osnap" and then pressing Enter when asked for osnap modes.

Now we will move on to four very useful and important new editing commands: BREAK, TRIM, EXTEND, and STRETCH. Before leaving Object Snap, be sure to study the chart, *Figure 6-9*.

Task 3: BREAKing Previously Drawn Objects

Procedure

1. Type "Break" or select the Break tool from the Modify toolbar.
2. Select an object to be broken.

158 Part I / Basic Two-Dimensional Entities

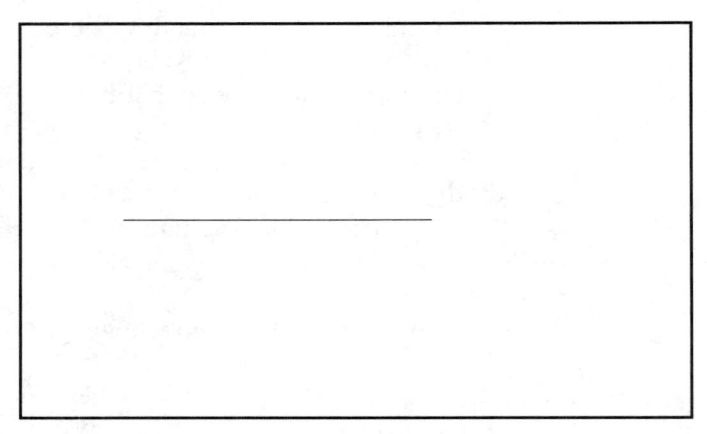

Figure 6-10

3. Show the first point of the break.
4. Show the second point of the break.

Discussion. The BREAK command allows you to break an object on the screen into two entities, or to cut a segment out of the middle or off the end. The command sequence is similar for all options. The action taken will depend on the points you select for breaking. BREAK works on lines, circles, arcs, traces, and polylines (traces and polylines are discussed in Chapter 9).

> In preparation for this section, clear your screen of any objects left over from Task 2 and draw a 5.0 horizontal line across the middle of your screen, as in *Figure 6-10*. Exact lengths and coordinates are not important. Also, be sure to turn off any running osnap modes that may be on from the last exercise.

AutoCAD allows for four different ways to break an object, depending on whether the point you use to select the object is also to be considered a break point. You can break an object at one point or at two points, and you have the choice of using your object selection point as a break point or not.

We begin by breaking the line you have just drawn into two independent lines using a single break point, which is also the point used to select the line. This procedure is labeled "Sel Pt" (select point) on the screen menu.

> Type "Break" or select the Break tool from the Modify toolbar.

Be aware that the noun/verb or pick first sequence does not work with BREAK.

AutoCAD will prompt you to select an object to break:

Select object:

You may select an object in any of the usual ways, but notice that you can only break one object at a time. If you try to select more—with a window, for example—AutoCAD will give you only one. Because of this you will best indicate the object you want to break by pointing to it.

NOTE: Object snap modes work well in edit commands such as BREAK. If you wish to break a line at its midpoint, for example, you can use the midpoint object snap mode to select the line and the break point.

> Select the line by picking any point near its middle. (The exact point is not critical; if it were, we could use a midpoint object snap.)

The line has now been selected for breaking, and since there can be only one object, you do not have to press Enter to end the selection process as you often do in other editing commands. AutoCAD will prompt as follows:

Enter second point (or F for first point):

When you are selecting an object by pointing, AutoCAD will assume that the point you use for selection is also the first point of the break. It will be most efficient, therefore, if you do select the object with a break point. Then you can proceed by selecting the second point immediately. If not, type "f" and you will be prompted for the first break point, as the parentheses tell you.

Having selected the object and the first break point, we now want to select a point that will break the object in two without erasing anything. To do this, simply pick the same point again.

> Point to the same point that you just used to select the line, or type "@".

The "@" symbol is shorthand for the last point entered.

The break is complete. In order to demonstrate that the line is really two lines now, we will select the right half of it for our next break.

> Press Enter or the space bar to repeat the BREAK command.
> Point to the line on the right side of the last break.

The right side of the line should become dotted, as in *Figure 6-11*. Clearly the original line is now being treated as two separate entities.

We will shorten the end of this dotted section of the line. Assume that the point you just used to select the object is the point where you want it to end; now all you need to do is to select a second point anywhere beyond the right end of the line.

> Select a second point beyond the right end of the line.

Your line should now be shortened, as in *Figure 6-12*.

Next we will cut a piece out of the middle of the left side.

> Press Enter or the space bar to repeat BREAK.
> Select the left side of the original line with a point toward the left end.

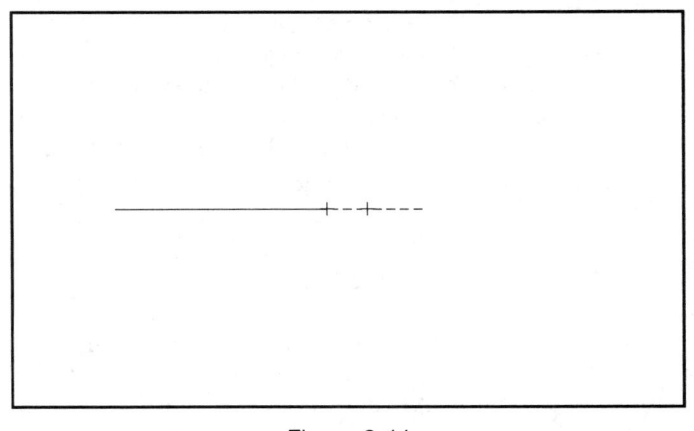

Figure 6-11

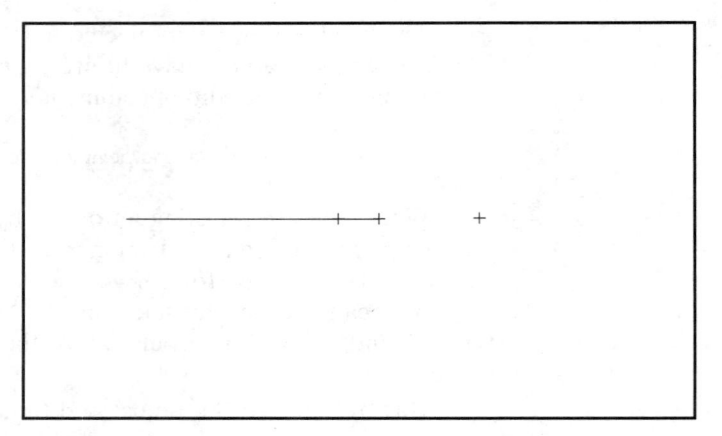

Figure 6-12

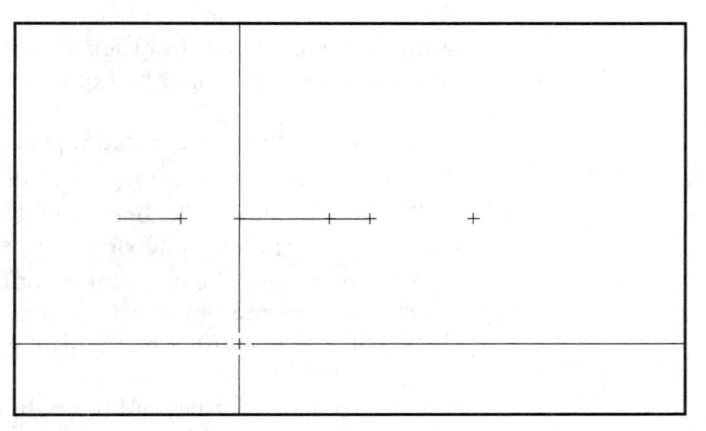

Figure 6-13

We want to cut a piece out of the middle of the left side, so the next point needs to be to the right of the first point, but still toward the middle of the left-hand line.

NOTE: It is actually not necessary that the second point be on the line at all. It could be above or below it, as in *Figure 6-13*. AutoCAD will break the line along a perpendicular between the point we choose and the line we are breaking. The same system would apply if we were breaking a polyline or a trace. An arc or a circle would be broken along a line between the selected point and the center of the arc or circle.

> Select a second point on or off the line, somewhat to the right of the first point.

Your line should now have a piece cut out, as in *Figure 6-13*. Notice that there are now three lines on the screen, one to the left and two to the right of the last break.

BREAK is a very useful command, but there are times when it is cumbersome to shorten objects one at a time. The TRIM command has some limitations that BREAK does not have, but it is much more efficient in situations where you want to shorten objects at intersections.

Chap. 6 161

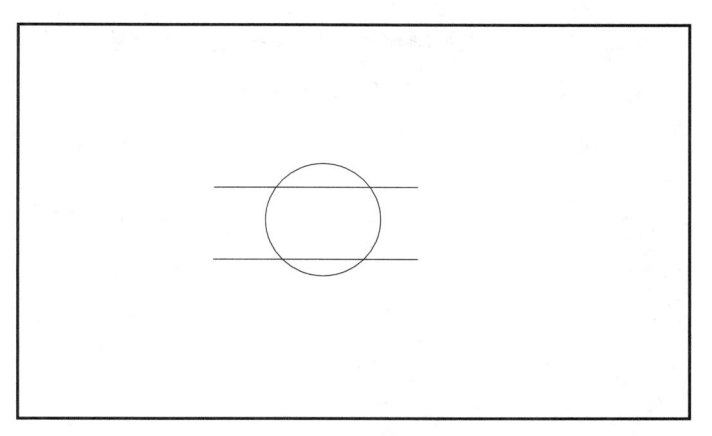

Figure 6-14

Task 4: Using the TRIM Command

Procedure

1. Type "Trim" or select the Trim tool from the Trim flyout on the Modify toolbar.
2. Select a cutting edge or edges.
3. Press Enter to end the cutting edge selection process.
4. Select object to trim.
5. Select other objects to trim.
6. Press Enter to return to "Command" prompt.

Discussion. The TRIM command works wonders in many situations where you want to shorten objects at their intersections with other objects. It will work with lines, circles, arcs, and polylines (see Chapter 9). The only limitation is that you must have at least two objects and they must cross or meet. If you are not trimming to an intersection, use BREAK.

> In preparation for exploring TRIM, clear your screen and then draw two horizontal lines crossing a circle, as in *Figure 6-14*. Exact locations and sizes are not important.

First we will use the TRIM command to go from *Figure 6-14* to *Figure 6-15*.

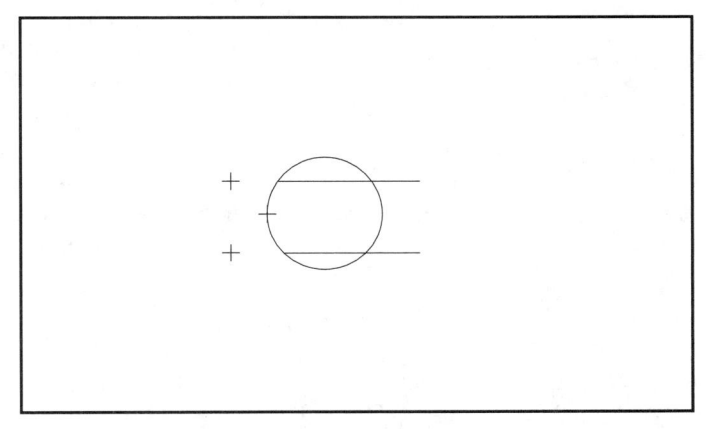

Figure 6-15

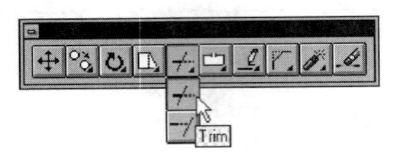

Figure 6-16

> Type "Trim" or select the Trim tool from the Trim flyout on the Modify toolbar, as illustrated in *Figure 6-16*.

The first thing AutoCAD will want you to specify is at least one cutting edge. A cutting edge is an entity you want to use to trim another entity. That is, you want the trimmed entity to end at its intersection with the cutting edge. You may have to press F2 to see the complete prompt, which looks like this:

Select cutting edge(s): (Projmode = UCS, Edgemode = No extend)
Select objects:

The first line reminds you that you are selecting edges first—the objects you want to trim will be selected later. The option of selecting more than one edge is a useful one, which we will get to shortly. The notations in parentheses are relevant to 3D drawing and need not concern you at this point. For your information, Projmode and Edgemode are system variables that determine the way AutoCAD will interpret boundaries and intersections in 3D space.

For now we will select the circle as an edge and use it to trim the upper line.

> Point to the circle.

The circle becomes dotted and will remain so until you leave the TRIM command. AutoCAD will prompt for more objects until you indicate that you are through selecting edges.

> Press Enter or the space bar to end the selection of cutting edges.

You will be prompted for an object to trim:

<Select object to trim>/Project/Edge/Undo:

We will trim off the segment of the upper line that lies outside the circle on the left. The important thing is to point to the part of the object you want to *remove*, as shown by the blips in *Figure 6-15*.

> Point to the upper line to the left of where it crosses the circle.

The line is trimmed immediately, but the circle is still dotted, and AutoCAD continues to prompt for more objects to trim. Note how this differs from the BREAK command, in which you could only break one object at a time.

Also notice that you have an undo option, so that if the trim does not turn out the way you wanted, you can back up without having to leave the command and start over.

> Point to the lower line to the left of where it crosses the circle.

Now you have trimmed both lines.

> Press Enter or the space bar to end the TRIM operation.

Your screen should resemble *Figure 6-15*.

This has been a very simple trimming process, but more complex trimming is just as easy. The key is that you can select as many edges as you like and that an entity may be selected as both an edge and an object to trim, as we will demonstrate.

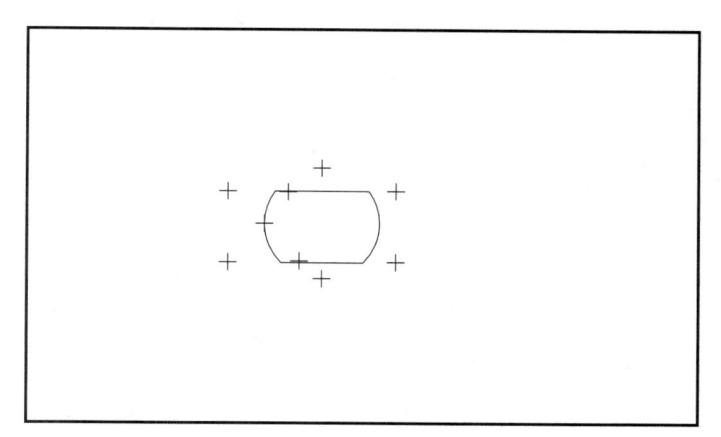

Figure 6-17

> Repeat the TRIM command.
> Select both lines and the circle as cutting edges.
This can be done with a window or with a crossing box.
> Press Enter to end the selection of edges.
> Point to each of the remaining two line segments that lie outside the circle on the right, and to the top and bottom arcs of the circle to produce the band-aid shaped object in *Figure 6-17*.
> Press Enter to exit the TRIM command.

Task 5: Using the EXTEND Command

Procedure

1. Type "Extend" or select the Extend tool from the Trim flyout on the Modify toolbar.
2. Select a boundary, or boundaries.
3. Press Enter to end the boundary selection process.
4. Select object to extend.
5. Select other objects to extend.
6. Press Enter to return to the command prompt.

Discussion. If you compare the procedures of the EXTEND command and the TRIM command you will notice a remarkable similarity. Just substitute the word "boundary" for "cutting edge" and the word "extend" for "trim" and you've got it. These two commands are so quick to use that it is sometimes efficient to draw a temporary cutting edge or boundary on your screen and erase it after trimming or extending.

> Leave *Figure 6-17*, the band-aid, on your screen and draw a vertical line to the right of it, as in *Figure 6-18*. We will use this line as a boundary to which to extend the two horizontal lines, as in *Figure 6-19*.
> Type "Extend" or select the Extend tool from the Trim flyout on the Modify toolbar, as shown in *Figure 6-20*.

You will be prompted for objects to serve as boundaries:

Select boundary edge(s): (Projmode = UCS, Edgemode = No extend)
Select objects:

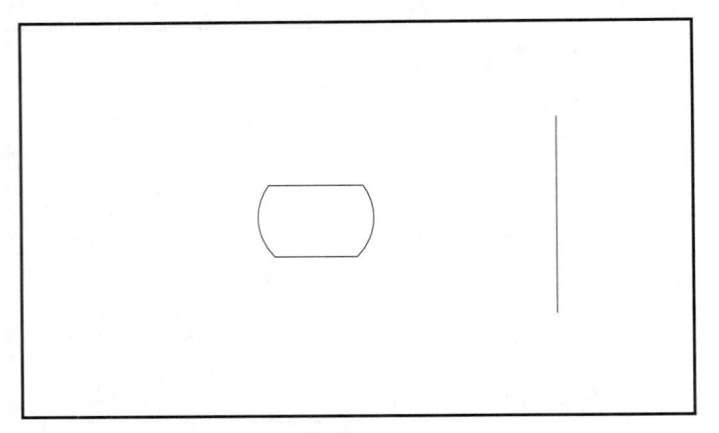

Figure 6-18

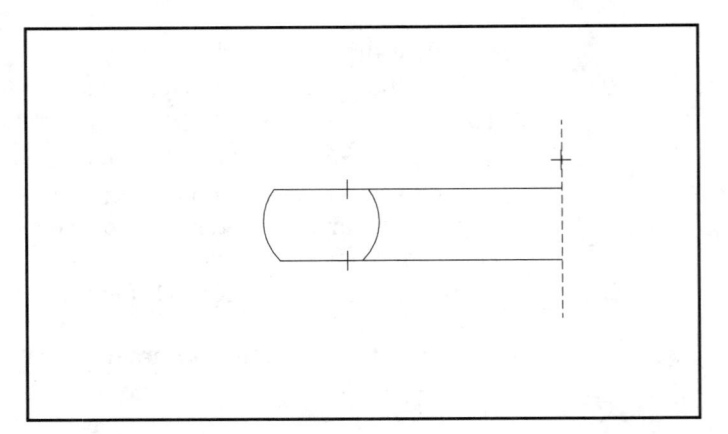

Figure 6-19

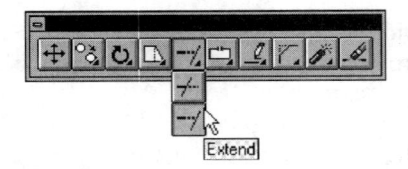

Figure 6-20

Look familiar? As with the TRIM command, any of the usual selection methods will work. For our purposes, simply point to the vertical line.
> Point to the vertical line on the right.

You will be prompted for more boundary objects until you press Enter.
> Press Enter or the space bar to end the selection of boundaries.

AutoCAD now asks for objects to extend:

<Select objects to extend>/Project/Edge/Undo:

> Point to the right half of one of the two horizontal lines.

Notice that you have to point to the line on the side closer to the selected boundary. Otherwise AutoCAD will look to the left instead of the right and give you the following message:

Object does not intersect an Edge

Note also that you only can select objects to extend by pointing. Windowing, crossing, or last selections will not work.

> Point to the right half of the other horizontal line. Both lines should be extended to the vertical line.

Your screen should resemble *Figure 6-19*.

> Press Enter to exit the EXTEND command.

Task 6: Using the STRETCH Command

Procedure

1. Type "Stretch" or select the Stretch tool from the Resize flyout on the Modify toolbar.
2. Select objects to stretch, using at least one window or crossing selection.
3. Press Enter to end selection.
4. Show first point of stretch displacement.
5. Show second point of stretch displacement.

Discussion. The STRETCH command is a phenomenal timesaver in special circumstances in which you want to move objects without disrupting their connections to other objects. Often STRETCH can take the place of a whole series of moves, trims, breaks, and extends. It is commonly used in such applications as moving doors or windows within walls without having to redraw the walls.

The term "stretch" must be understood to have a special meaning in AutoCAD. When a typical stretch is performed, some objects are lengthened, while others are shortened, and others are simply moved.

There is also a stretch mode in the grip edit system, as we have seen previously. We will take a look at it at the end of the exercise.

First, we will do a simple stretch on the objects you have already drawn on your screen. This will give you a good basic understanding of the STRETCH command. Further experimentation on your own is also recommended.

> Type "Stretch" or select the Stretch tool from the Stretch flyout on the Modify toolbar, illustrated in *Figure 6-21*.

AutoCAD will prompt for objects to stretch in the following manner:

    Select objects to stretch by crossing-window or polygon...
    Select objects:

The first line of this prompt reminds you of a unique quality of the STRETCH command procedure. You must include at least one crossing-window or crossing-polygon selection in your selection set. Beyond that you can include other selection types as well. This ensures that you will include all the objects in an intersection in the stretch procedure. If this is not your intent, you probably should be using a different modifying command.

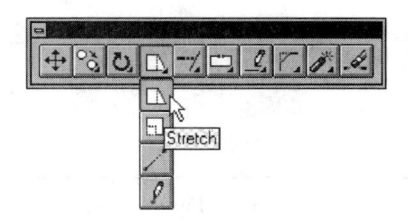

Figure 6-21

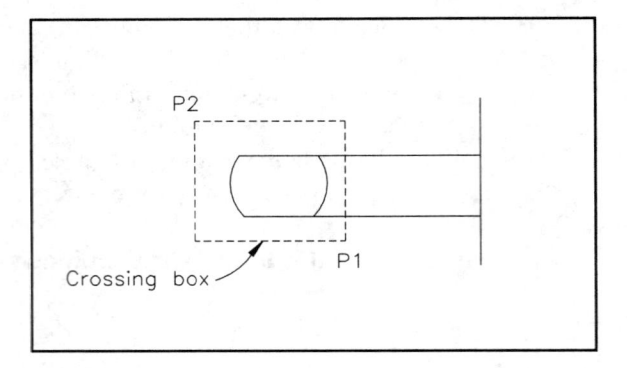

Figure 6-22

> Point to the first corner of a crossing box, as shown by point 1 (P1) in *Figure 6-22*.

AutoCAD will prompt for a second corner:

Other corner:

> Point to a second corner, as shown by point 2 (P2) in the figure.

AutoCAD will continue to prompt for objects, so we need to show that we are through selecting.
> Press Enter or the space bar to end the selection process.

Now you will need to show the degree and direction of stretch you want. In effect, you will be showing AutoCAD how far to move the objects that are completely within the box. Objects that cross the box will be extended or shrunk so that they remain connected to the objects that move.

The prompt sequence for this action is the same as the sequence for a move:

Base point or displacement:

> Pick any point near the middle of the screen, leaving room to indicate a horizontal displacement to the right, as illustrated in *Figure 6-23*.

AutoCAD prompts:

Second point of displacement:

> Pick a second point to the right of the first, as shown in *Figure 6-23*. Having ortho on will ensure a horizontal move (F8).

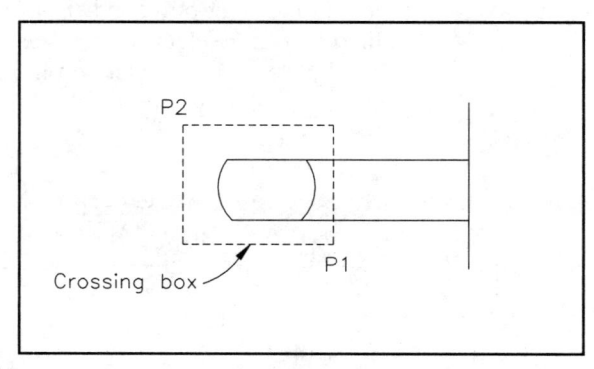

Figure 6-23

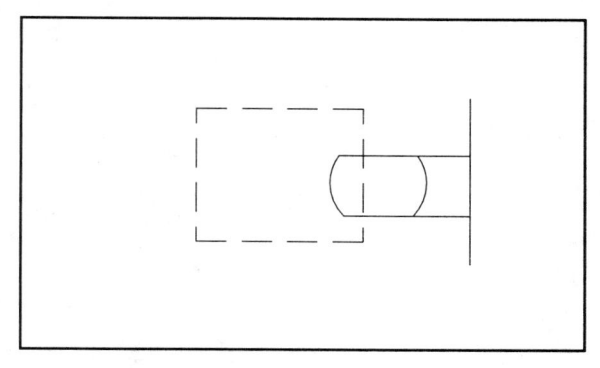

Figure 6-24

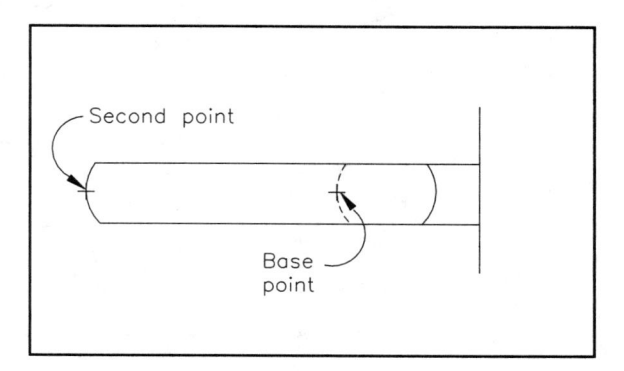

Figure 6-25

The arcs will be moved to the right and the horizontal lines will be shrunk as shown. Notice that nothing here is literally being stretched. The arcs are being moved and the lines are being compressed. This is one of the ways STRETCH can be used.

Try performing another stretch like the one illustrated in *Figures 6-24* and *6-25*. Here the lines are being lengthened, while one arc moves and the other stays put, so that the original band-aid is indeed stretched.

Stretching with Grips

Stretching with grips is a simple operation and is best reserved for simple stretches. Stretches like the ones you have just performed with the STRETCH command are possible in grip editing, but they require very careful selection of multiple grips. The results are not always what you expect and it takes more time to complete the process. The type of stretch that works best with grips is illustrated in the following exercise.

> Pick the lower horizontal line.
The line will be highlighted and grips will appear.
> Pick the vertical line.
Now both lines should appear with grips, as in *Figure 6-26*. We will use one grip on the horizontal line and one on the vertical line to create *Figure 6-27*.
> Pick the grip at the right end of the horizontal line.

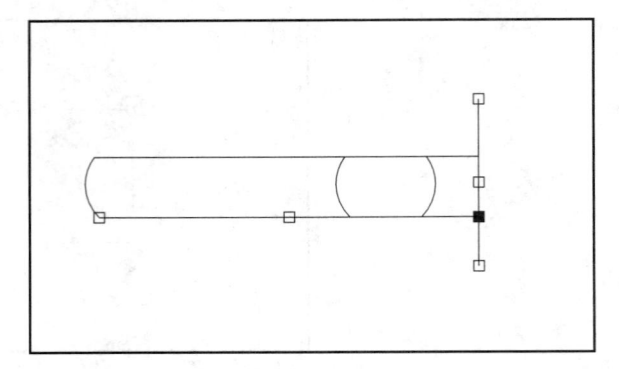

Figure 6-26

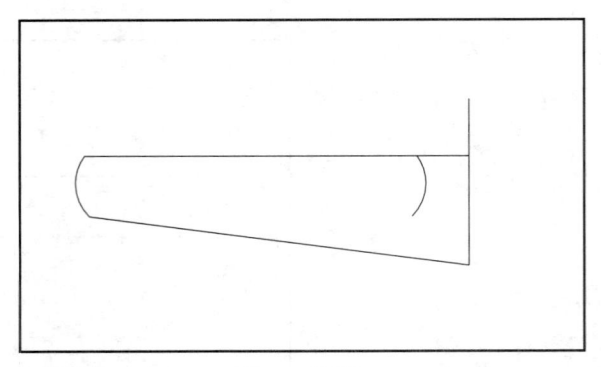

Figure 6-27

As soon as you press the pick button, the autoedit system puts you into STRETCH mode and the grip will change color.

In the command area you will see the following:

```
** STRETCH **
<Stretch to point>/Base point/Copy/Undo/eXit:
```

We will stretch the line to end at the lower end point of the vertical line.
> Move the cross hairs slowly downward and observe the screen.

If ortho is off, you will see two rubber bands. One represents the line you are stretching, and the other connects the cross hairs to the grip you are manipulating.
> Pick the grip at the bottom of the vertical line.

Your screen should resemble *Figure 6-27*. Notice how the grip on the vertical line works like an object snap point.

Try one more grip stretch to create *Figure 6-28*. You will move the end point of the upper line just as you did the lower.

In the next task you will take a giant leap in plotting technique as you begin to use paper space and multiple viewports.

Task 7: Plotting from Multiple Viewports in Paper Space

Procedure

1. Set "Tilemode" to 0, by typing or using a pull down menu or toolbar selection.
2. Use MVIEW to create paper space layout.

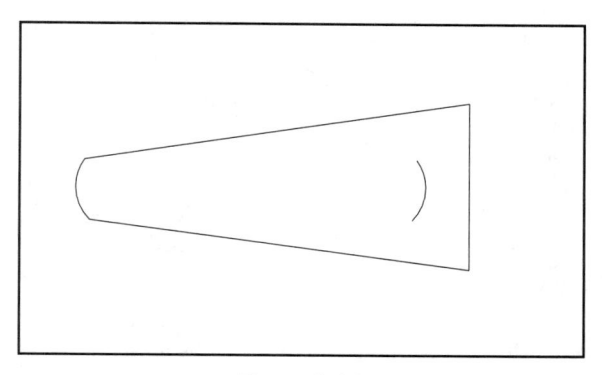

Figure 6-28

3. Switch to model space to position or edit objects in the drawing.
4. Switch to paper space to plot.
5. Type or select "Plot".
6. Preview plot, change parameters, and execute plotting as usual.

Discussion. In this plotting exercise you will begin to use paper space and multiple floating viewports for the first time. We have used Drawing 6-4 to illustrate. We recommend that you read through this section now and then return to it after you complete Drawing 6-4.

You have a completed drawing on your screen and you are now considering how to present it on paper. In the days of the drafting board, all drawings were committed to paper from the start. This meant that people doing drafting were inevitably conscious of scale, paper size, and rotation from start to finish. When draftspeople first began using CAD systems, they still tended to think in terms of the final hard copy their plotter would produce even as they were creating lines on the screen. But to take full advantage of the powers of a CAD system, it is usually more efficient to conceive of screen images as representing objects at full scale, rather than as potential drawings on a piece of paper. After all, the units on a screen grid can just as easily represent miles as inches. This little world of the screen in which we can think and draw in full scale is called "model space" in AutoCAD lingo.

Using model space to its fullest potential, we can allow ourselves to ignore scale and other drawing paper issues entirely, if we wish, until it is time to plot. At that time, we may want to make use of AutoCAD's "paper space." Paper space overlays model space and allows us to create a paper-scale world on top of the full-scale world we have been drawing in.

This is the concept of paper space. In actual practice you may find paper space unnecessary for common two-dimensional plotting. As we have seen in previous plotting exercises, the PLOT command has a very efficient previewing system and scaling features of its own that will allow you to move easily between 2D model space and the sheet of drawing paper waiting in your plotter.

Where paper space really begins to pay off is when you want to create multiple views of a single object and plot them all simultaneously. Model space tiled viewports can only be plotted one at a time. With paper space viewports you can create multiple views of the same object, position them wherever you like, and print the whole configuration as one drawing.

In this task we will create a plot of Drawing 6-4, the "Grooved Hub." The plotted drawing will include the original two views plus two close-up views. This will be done in paper space using three viewports. You should be able to generalize from the techniques demonstrated here to create a variety of multiple view

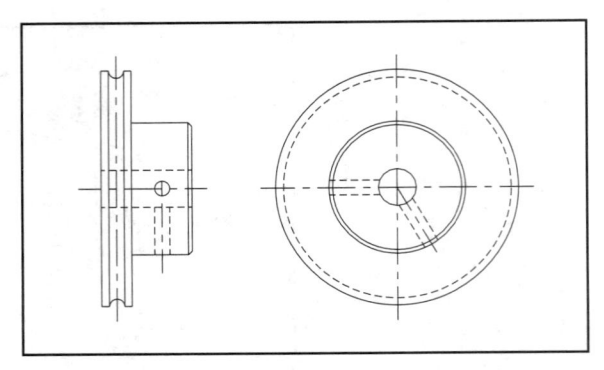

Figure 6-29

drawings with whatever drawing you may be working on. Later on, when you get into 3D drawing you will be able to draw an object and view it from different angles, placing different views in different viewports and placing these where you want them in your completed drawing.

> To begin this exercise you should have on your screen a drawing you want to plot showing some close-up views. We have used Drawing 6-4, shown in *Figure 6-29*, for illustration.
> Before leaving model space, turn off the grid (F7). You will see why shortly.

In order to enter paper space you must change the value of the "Tilemode" variable from 1 ("On") to 0 ("Off"). When Tilemode is on you can only create the type of nonoverlapping viewports we showed in Chapter 3. These viewports cannot be moved or plotted simultaneously.

You can change Tilemode at the command line, the Standard toolbar, or from the pull down menu.
> Type "Tilemode" or select "Paper Space" from the View pull down, or the Paper Space tool from the Tilemode flyout on the Standard toolbar, as shown in *Figure 6-30*.
> Type "0".

Your screen will go blank and AutoCAD will regenerate your drawing. If "Ucsicon" is "On", you will see the paper space icon in the left-hand corner of your screen. This icon appears in place of the UCS icon whenever you switch to paper space. For this reason it is a good idea to have the icon turned on when you are going back and forth between the two types of spaces.
> If necessary, turn the UCS icon on by typing "ucsicon" and then "on".

You are now looking at a blank sheet of paper in paper space. You can imagine that your drawing is behind the paper space screen. We will need to create viewports before we can see it again. Viewports are like windows from paper space into model space. Until a window is created, you cannot see what is beyond the paper.

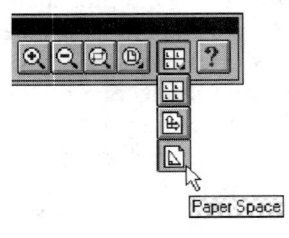

Figure 6-30

But first, we need to think about the paper our drawing will be on. This, after all, is the whole point of paper space. Before opening viewports, we will set up limits and a grid in paper space to emulate the drawing sheet we are going to plot on. For purposes of illustration, let's say that we are going to plot on a D-size sheet of paper. If your plotter will take a D-size sheet you will be able to find the actual plotting area available by looking in the PLOT dialogue paper size list box.

> Type "Plot", or select the Print tool from the Standard toolbar, or "Print..." from the File pull down menu.

> Type "s" or select "Size...".

You will see the dialogue box illustrated previously in *Figure 5-21*. Ours shows us that the Houston Instruments plotter we are using plots in an area 33.00 by 21.00 on a D-size sheet. If yours is different, or if you have no D-size option, use another sheet size and plotting area from your list. We will also include some instructions for A-size paper as we go along since most people have access to a printer. You should expect to make adjustments, however, if your drawing size does not match ours.

> Cancel the Paper Size subdialogue.

> Cancel the Plot Configuration dialogue.

This should bring you back to your blank paper space screen.

> Type "Limits" or select "Drawing Limits..." from the Data pull down menu.

> Set paper space limits to (0,0) and (33,21), or whatever is appropriate for your plotter. If you are working with A-size, it will be approximately (12,9) for most printers.

> Turn the grid on (F7).

The grid is now on in paper space and off in model space.

> Zoom all.

> Reset your grid and snap to a 1.00 increment.

Your screen is now truly representative of a D-size drawing sheet. The plot will be made 1-to-1, with one paper space screen unit equaling one inch on the drawing sheet. There is little reason to do it any other way, since the whole point of paper space is to emulate the paper on the screen.

Now it is time to create viewports.

> Type "Mview" or select "Floating Model Space" from the View pull down menu or the Floating Model Space tool from the Tilemode flyout on the Standard toolbar.

The Floating Model Space selections simply initiate the MVIEW command and return you to model space at the same time.

AutoCAD prompts:

ON/OFF/Hideplot/Fit/2/3/4/Restore/<First Point>:

We will deal only with the default option in this exercise. With this option you create a viewport just as you would a selection window.

> Pick a point at the lower left of your screen as shown in *Figure 6-31*. Our actual point is (1.00,1.00). All of the coordinate values in this exercise will need to be adjusted if you are using other than a D-size sheet of paper. Exact correspondence is not critical. As long as your viewports resemble our illustrations, you will be fine.

> Pick a second point up 13 and over 9 from point 1. The coordinate display will show (10.00,14.00).

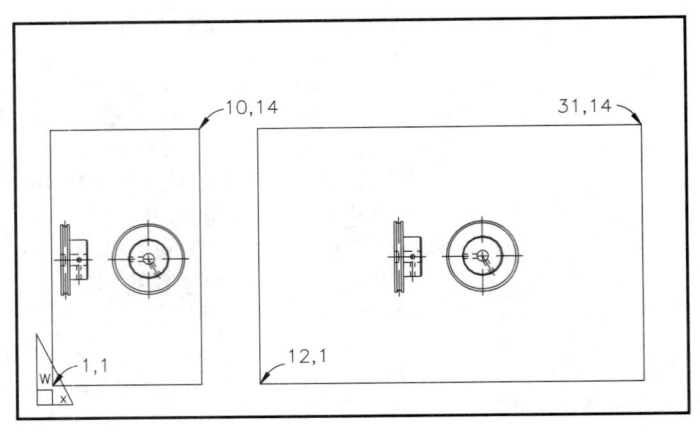

Figure 6-31

Your screen will be redrawn with the drawing shown at small scale in the viewport you have just created. We will create a second viewport next.

If you had not turned off the model space grid at this point you would see model space and paper space grids overlapping. Having both grids on is useless and confusing.

Now we will create a second viewport to the right of the first.

> Repeat MVIEW.
> Pick point (13.00,1.00), as shown in the figure.
> Pick point (31.00,13.00), as shown.

You have now created a second viewport. Notice that the images in the two viewports are the same. Before we go on to create a third viewport, we will create different zoom-magnifications inside the two viewports. To do this we need to switch back to model space.

> Type "ms" or select "Floating Model Space" from the pull down menu or the Standard toolbar.

You will see that the paper space icon disappears and UCS icons are shown in the corners of the viewports. You will also see that the viewport on the right is outlined in black, indicating that it is currently active. If you have not used multiple viewports before, take a moment to explore the way the cursor works. You can have only one viewport active at a time. When the cursor is within that viewport, you will see the cross hairs. Otherwise you will see an arrow. To switch viewports, move the arrow into the desired viewport and press the pick button.

> Make the right viewport active.

We are going to zoom in so that the two-view drawing fills the right viewport. We could do this by windowing, but we can maintain more precise scale relationships if we use the ZOOM "Center" and "XP" options. We will see the importance of paper space and model space scale relationships in later chapters.

> Type "z" or select the Zoom center tool from the Zoom flyout on the Standard toolbar.
> If you are typing, type "c" or select "Center" from the screen menu.

AutoCAD prompts for a center point.

> Pick a point roughly halfway between the two views in the viewport.

AutoCAD will prompt for a magnification value. Accepting the default would simply center the image in the viewport. We will take an extra step by

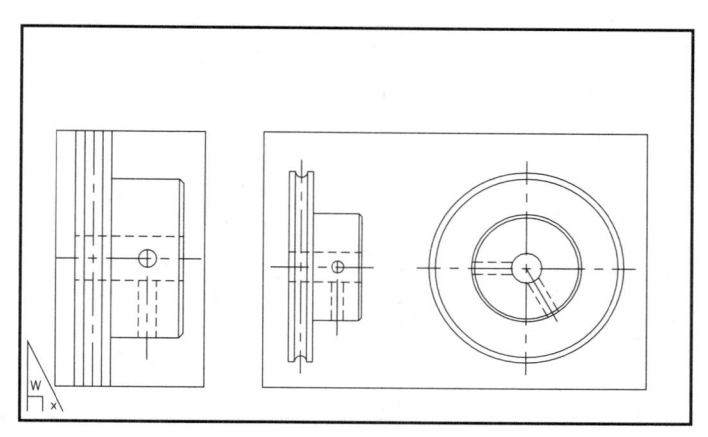

Figure 6-32

using the "XP" option here. "XP" means "times paper." It allows you to zoom relative to paper space units. If you zoom 1xp, then a model space unit will take on the size of a current paper space unit, which in turn equals one inch of drawing paper. We will zoom 2xp (.5xp if you are using A-size paper). This will mean that one unit in the viewport will equal 2 paper space units, or 2 inches on paper (in A size, 1 unit will equal .5 inches on paper).
> Type "2xp" (or .5xp for A-size paper).

Your right viewport will be redrawn to resemble the one in *Figure 6-32*. You may need to pan slightly to the left or right to position the image in the viewport. Notice that you cannot use the scrollbars to pan inside a viewport.

Next, we will enlarge the image on the left so that we get a close-up of the left side view.
> Make the left viewport active.
> Type "z" or select the Zoom center tool.
> Type "c" or select "Center".
> Pick a center point in the middle of the left side view.
> Type "4xp" (1xp for A-size paper).

This will create an enlarged image in which one model space unit equals 4 inches in the drawing sheet (1=1 A size).
> Pan left or right to position the enlargement in the viewport, as shown in *Figure 6-32*.

Now that you have the technique, we will create one more enlargement, focusing on the center of the hub.
> Type "Mview" or select "Floating Viewports" from the View pull down menu and then "1 Viewport".
> Pick point (23.00,15.00).
> Pick point (31.00, 21.00).

Notice that the new viewport is created from the most recent viewport image.
> Use PAN in model space to bring the hub center into the new viewport.
> Zoom on the center of the hub at 6 times paper (1.5xp for an A sheet) in the new viewport.
> Type or select "Regenall" to regenerate the display and create truer circles.

Your screen should resemble *Figure 6-33*.

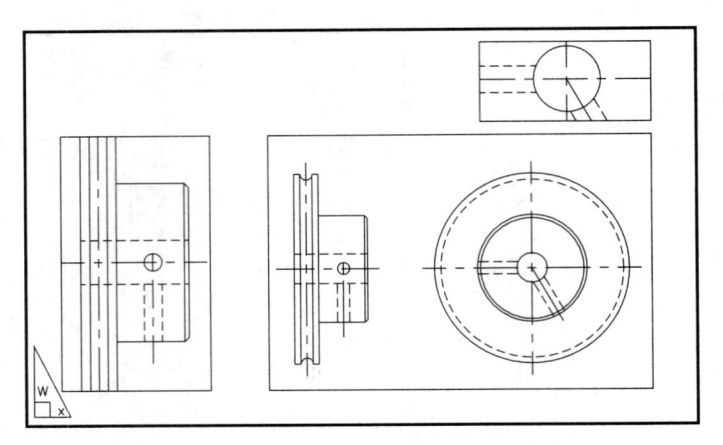

Figure 6-33

Great! Now we are ready to plot. Plotting a multiple viewport drawing is no different from plotting from a single view, but you have to make sure you plot from paper space. Otherwise AutoCAD will plot only the currently active viewport.

> Type "ps" or select the Paper space icon from the Tilemode flyout on the Standard toolbar.
> Type "Plot" or select the Print tool from the Standard toolbar, or "Print..." from the File pull down menu.
> Click on "Limits" in the Additional Parameters box.
> Click on "Size" in the Paper Size and Orientation box.

We looked into this box for information before, but we cancelled the command. Now it is time to choose the paper size we have been preparing for.

> Select the D-size option, or whatever you have chosen for this exercise.
> Click on "OK" in the Size subdialogue box.
> If the Scaled to Fit box is selected, click on it so the ✓ is removed.

When Scaled to Fit is deselected, the scale boxes should show 1 = 1. If not, you should edit them to show 1 = 1.

> Do a partial preview of the plot.

The effective area should match the paper size, because we are set to plot limits, and our limits match the effective drawing area of this paper size for this plotter.

> Do a full preview of the plot.

Your screen should resemble *Figure 6-34*. (We have moved the Plot Preview box to the upper left corner of the screen.)

Excellent. You are now ready to plot.

> Click on "End Preview".
> Prepare your plotter. (Make sure you use the right size paper.)
> Click on "OK".
> Press Enter and watch it go.

NOTE: Be sure to SAVE this drawing in its multiple viewport form before leaving, because we will return to it in Chapter 8 to explore scaling dimensions between model space and paper space.

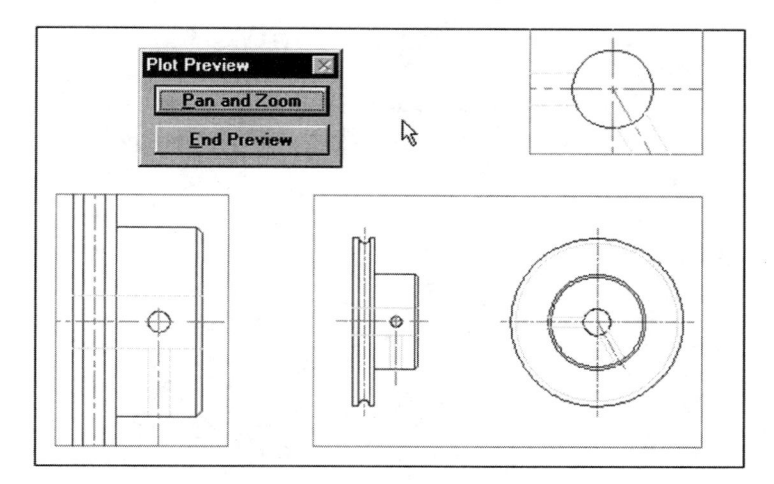

Figure 6-34

Tasks 8, 9, 10, 11, 12, and 13

The drawings that follow will bring you to the end of Part I of this book. With Object snap and the new editing commands and plot procedures you have learned in this chapter, you have reached a significant plateau. Most of the fundamental drawing, editing, and printing tools are now in your repertoire of CAD skills. The six drawings that follow will give you the opportunity to practice what you have learned. Notice that BREAK and TRIM often are used deliberately as part of a planned drawing sequence, whereas EXTEND and STRETCH tend to appear more frequently as "quick fixes" when something needs to be moved or changed.

DRAWING 6-1: BIKE TIRE

This drawing can be done very quickly with the tools you now have. It makes use of one object snap, three trims, and a polar array. Be sure to set the limits large, as suggested.

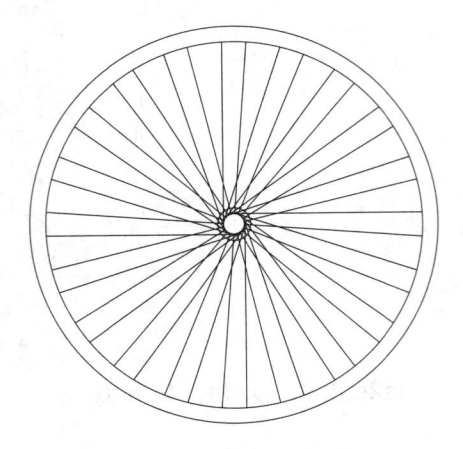

DRAWING SUGGESTIONS

GRID = 1.00   LIMITS = (0,0) (48,36)
SNAP = .25

> Begin by drawing the 1.25, 2.50, 24.00, and 26.00 diameter circles centered on the same point near the middle of your display.

> Draw line (a) using a QUADrant object snap to find the first point on the inside circle. The second point can be anywhere outside the 24 circle at 0 degrees from the first point. The exact length of the line is insignificant since we will be trimming it back to the circle.

> Draw line (b) from the center of the circles to a second point anywhere outside the 24 circle at an angle of 14 degrees. Remember to use the coordinate display to construct this angle. This line also will be trimmed.

> Trim lines (a) and (b) using the 24 circle as a cutting edge.

> Trim the other end of line (b) using the 1.25 circle as a cutting edge.

> Construct a polar array, selecting lines (a) and (b). There are 20 items in the array, and they are rotated as they are copied.

Chap. 6   **177**

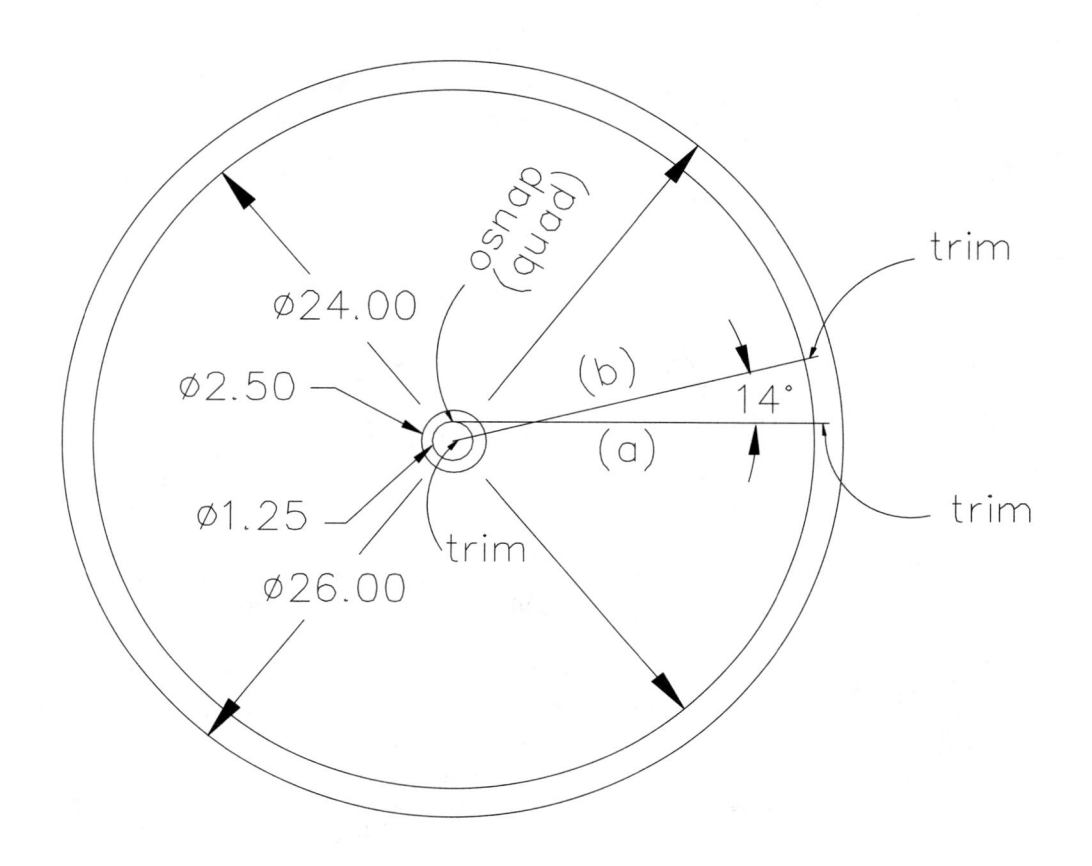

Ø24.00
Ø2.50
Ø1.25
Ø26.00
(osnap quad)
(a)
(b)
14°
trim
trim
trim

BIKE TIRE

Drawing 6-1

LAYERS	NAME	COLOR	LINETYPE			
	0	WHITE	———— CONTINUOUS		LINE	(L)
	1	RED	———— CONTINUOUS		CIRCLE	(C)
					ARRAY	
					TRIM	
					ZOOM	(Z)

[F1] HELP
[F2] TEXT/GRAPHICS SCREEN
[F6] ABSOLUTE/OFF/POLAR COORDS
[F7] ON/OFF GRID
[F8] ON/OFF ORTHO
[F9] ON/OFF SNAP

DRAWING 6-2: ARCHIMEDES SPIRAL

This drawing and the next go together as an exercise you should find interesting and enjoyable. These are not technical drawings, but they will give you valuable experience with important CAD commands. You will be creating a spiral using a radial grid of circles and lines as a guide. Once the spiral is done, you will use it to create the designs in the next drawing, 6–3, "Spiral Designs."

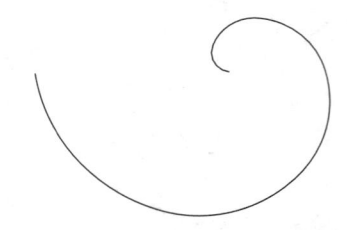

DRAWING SUGGESTIONS

GRID = .5   LIMITS = (0,0) (18,12)
SNAP = .25   LTSCALE = .5

> The alternating continuous and hidden lines work as a drawing aid. If you use different colors and layers they will be even more helpful.

> Begin by drawing all the continuous circles on layer 0, centered near the middle of your display. Use the continuous circle radii as listed.

> Draw the continuous horizontal line across the middle of your six circles and then array it in a three-item polar array.

> Set to layer 2 for the hidden lines. The procedure for the hidden lines and circles will be the same as for the continuous lines, except the radii are different and you will array a vertical line instead of a horizontal one.

> Set to layer 1 for the spiral itself.

> Turn on a running object snap to intersection mode and construct a series of three-point arcs. Start points and end points will be on continuous line intersections; second points always will fall on hidden line intersections.

> When the spiral is complete, turn off layers 0 and 2. There should be nothing left on your screen but the spiral itself. Save it or go on to Drawing 6–3.

GROUPing objects

Here is a good opportunity to use Release 13's GROUP command. GROUP is discussed more fully in Chapter 10, but you will find it useful here. GROUP defines a collection of objects as a single entity so that they may be selected and modified as a unit. The spiral you have just drawn will be used in the next drawing and it will be easier to manipulate if you GROUP it. For more information, see Chapter 10.

1. Type "Group" or select the Object Group tool from the Standard toolbar.
2. Type "Spiral" for a group name.
3. Click on "New <".
4. Select the six arcs with a window.
5. Press Enter to end selection.
5. Click on "OK".

The spiral can now be selected, moved, rotated, and copied as a single entity.

Chap. 6

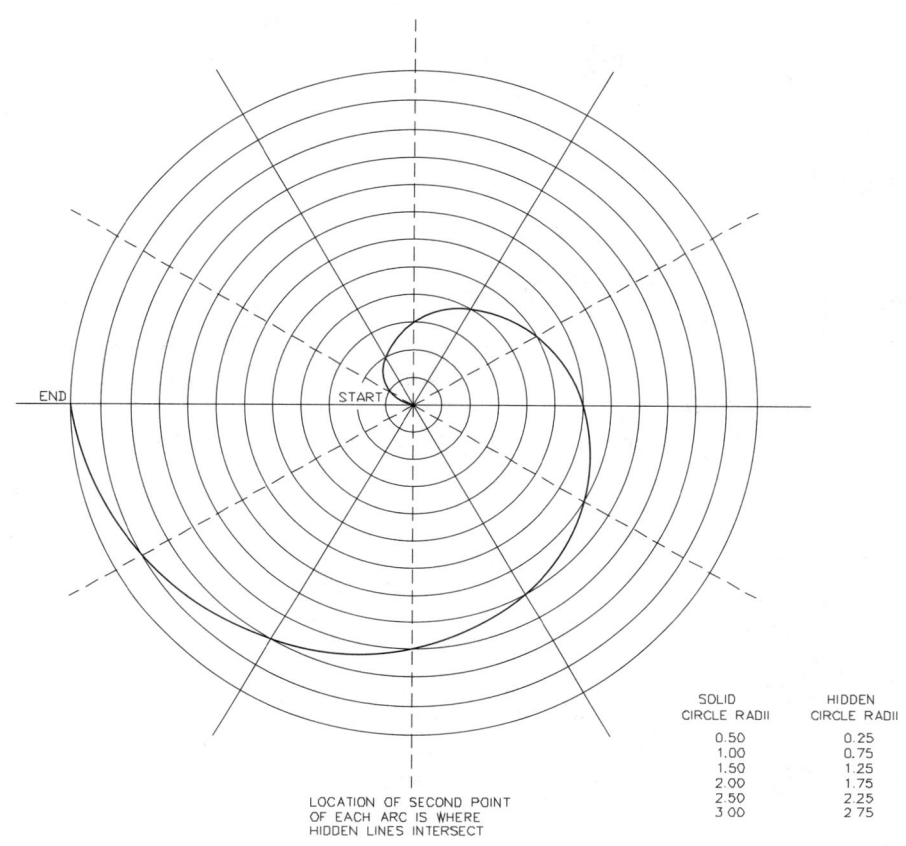

179

LOCATION OF SECOND POINT
OF EACH ARC IS WHERE
HIDDEN LINES INTERSECT

SOLID CIRCLE RADII	HIDDEN CIRCLE RADII
0.50	0.25
1.00	0.75
1.50	1.25
2.00	1.75
2.50	2.25
3.00	2.75

NOTE: THIS DRAWING IS USED
ON DRAWING 6-3
SAVE THIS DRAWING!

ARCHIMEDES SPIRAL

Drawing 6-2

LAYERS	NAME	COLOR	LINETYPE			
	0	WHITE	———— CONTINUOUS		LINE	(L)
	1	RED	———— CONTINUOUS		CIRCLE	(C)
	2	YELLOW	— — — HIDDEN		ARC	(A)
					ARRAY	
					PAN	(P)
					ZOOM	(Z)

[F1]	[F2]	[F6]	[F7]	[F8]	[F9]
HELP	TEXT/GRAPHICS SCREEN	ABSOLUTE/OFF/POLAR COORDS	ON/OFF GRID	ON/OFF ORTHO	ON/OFF SNAP

DRAWING 6-3: SPIRAL DESIGNS

These designs are different from other drawings in this book. There are no dimensions and you will use only edit commands now that the spiral is drawn. Below the designs is a list of the edit commands you will need. Don't be too concerned with precision. Some of your designs may come out slightly different from ours. When this happens, try to analyze the differences.

DRAWING SUGGESTIONS

$$\text{LIMITS} = (0,0)\ (34,24)$$

These large limits will be necessary if you wish to draw all of these designs on the screen at once.

In some of the designs and in Drawing 6-4 you will need to rotate a copy of the spiral and keep the original in place. You can accomplish this using the grip edit rotate procedure with the copy option, or by making a copy of the objects before you enter the ROTATE command. Both procedures are listed following.

HOW TO ROTATE AN OBJECT AND RETAIN THE ORIGINAL

Using Grip Edit

1. Select the spiral.
2. Pick the grip around which you want to rotate, or any of the grips if you are not going to use the grip as a base point for rotation.
3. Type "b" or select "Base point", if necessary. In this exercise the base point you choose for rotation will depend on the design you are trying to create.
4. Type "c" or select "Copy".
5. Show the rotation angle.
6. Press Enter to exit the grip edit system.

Using the ROTATE Command

1. Use COPY to make a copy of the objects you want to rotate directly on top of their originals. In other words, give the same point for the base point and the second point of displacement. When the copy is done, your screen will not look any different, but there will actually be two spirals there, one on top of the other.
2. Enter ROTATE and give "p" or "previous" in response to the "Select objects:" prompt. This will select all the original objects from the last COPY sequence, without selecting the newly drawn copies.
3. Rotate as usual, choosing a base point dependent on the design you are creating.
4. After the ROTATE sequence is complete, you will need to do a REDRAW before the objects copied in the original position will be visible.

Chap. 6

SPIRAL DESIGNS

(Make from Drawing 6-2)

Drawing 6-3

LAYERS	NAME	COLOR	LINETYPE			
	0	WHITE	——————— CONTINUOUS		LINE	(L)
	1	RED	——————— CONTINUOUS		COPY	
					MOVE	(M)
					ROTATE	
					ARRAY	
					MIRROR	
					PAN	(P)
					ZOOM	(Z)

F1 HELP
F2 TEXT/GRAPHICS SCREEN
F6 ABSOLUTE/OFF/POLAR COORDS
F7 ON/OFF GRID
F8 ON/OFF ORTHO
F9 ON/OFF SNAP

DRAWING 6-4: GROOVED HUB

This drawing includes a typical application of the rotation technique just discussed. The hidden lines in the front view must be rotated 120 degrees and a copy retained in the original position. There are also good opportunities to use MIRROR, object snap, and TRIM.

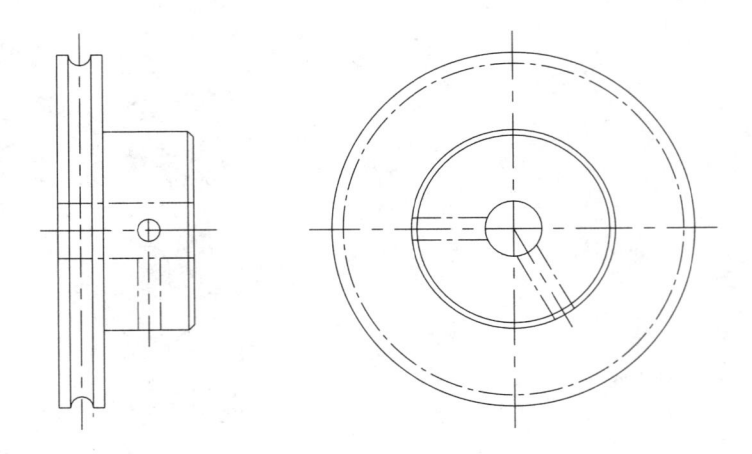

DRAWING SUGGESTIONS

GRID = .5 LIMITS = (0,0) (18,12)
SNAP = .0625 LTSCALE = 1

> Draw the circles in the front view and use these to line up the horizontal lines in the left side view.

> There are several different planes of symmetry in the left side view, which suggests the use of mirroring. We leave it up to you to choose an efficient sequence.

> A quick method for drawing the horizontal hidden lines in the left side view is to use a quadrant osnap to begin a line at the top and bottom of the .62 diameter circle in the front view. Draw this line across to the back of the left side view, and use TRIM to erase the excess on both sides.

> The same method can be used to draw the two horizontal hidden lines in the front view. Snap to the top and bottom quadrants of the .25 diameter circle in the left side view as a guide and draw lines through the front view. Then trim to the 2.25 diameter circle and the .62 diameter circle.

> Once these hidden lines are drawn, rotate them, retaining a copy in the original position.

Plotting in Paper Space with Multiple Viewports

As you near the completion of Part I, it is time to explore paper space and the use of multiple viewports to plot different views in a drawing. This drawing is used in Task 7 to illustrate multiple viewport plotting techniques. Once you have completed the drawing as shown, return to the chapter and create the drawing layout in paper space with two close-up views. Save the multiple view layout as well because it will be used again in Chapter 8.

Chap. 6

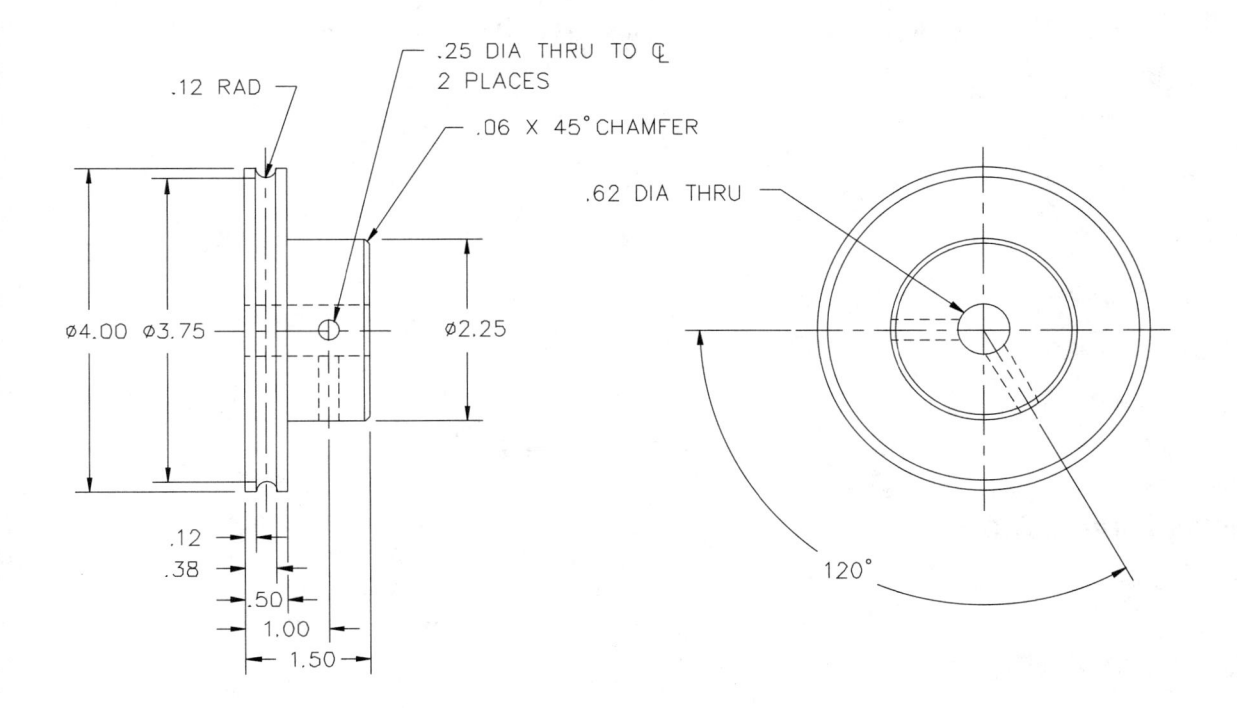

183

.12 RAD

.25 DIA THRU TO ℄
2 PLACES

.06 X 45° CHAMFER

.62 DIA THRU

Ø4.00 Ø3.75

Ø2.25

.12
.38
.50
1.00
1.50

120°

GROOVED HUB
Drawing 6-4

LAYERS	NAME	COLOR	LINETYPE	
	0	WHITE	————	CONTINUOUS
	1	RED	————	CONTINUOUS
	2	YELLOW	- - - - -	HIDDEN
	3	GREEN	— - —	CENTER

LINE   (L)
CIRCLE   (C)
ARC   (A)
CHAMFER
COPY
BREAK
TRIM
MIRROR
ROTATE
ZOOM   (Z)

F1 - HELP
F2 - TEXT/GRAPHICS SCREEN
F6 - ABSOLUTE/OFF/POLAR COORDS
F7 - ON/OFF GRID
F8 - ON/OFF ORTHO
F9 - ON/OFF SNAP

DRAWING 6-5: CAP IRON

This drawing is of a type of blade used in a wood plane. When wood is planed, the cap iron causes it to curl up out of the plane so that it does not jam. There are several good applications for the TRIM command here.

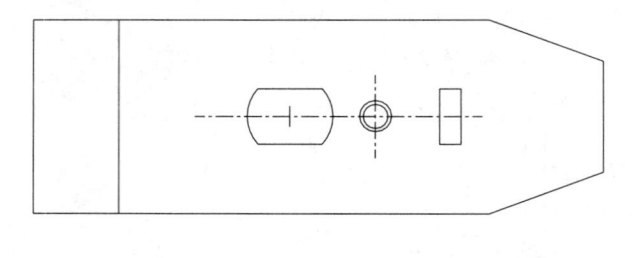

DRAWING SUGGESTIONS

GRID = 1.00   LIMITS = (0,0) (18,12)
SNAP = .25   LTSCALE = .25

> The circle with a hidden line outside a continuous line indicates a tapped hole. The dimension is given to the hidden line; the continuous inner line is drawn with a slightly smaller radius that is not specified.

> You may find it helpful to use the DIST command to position the smaller figures within the top view.

> The figure near the center of the top view that has two arcs with .38 radii can be drawn exactly the same way as the "band-aid," *Figure 6-18* in Task 4 of this chapter. Draw a circle and two horizontal lines and then trim it all down.

> The .54 and .58 arcs in the front view can be drawn using Start, End, Radius.

> The small vertical hidden lines in the front view can be done using a system introduced in the previous drawing. Draw lines down from the figures in the top view and then trim them. For the tapped hole and the arced opening in the middle, you will have to use object snaps to right and left quadrant points to locate the start of these lines.

Chap. 6

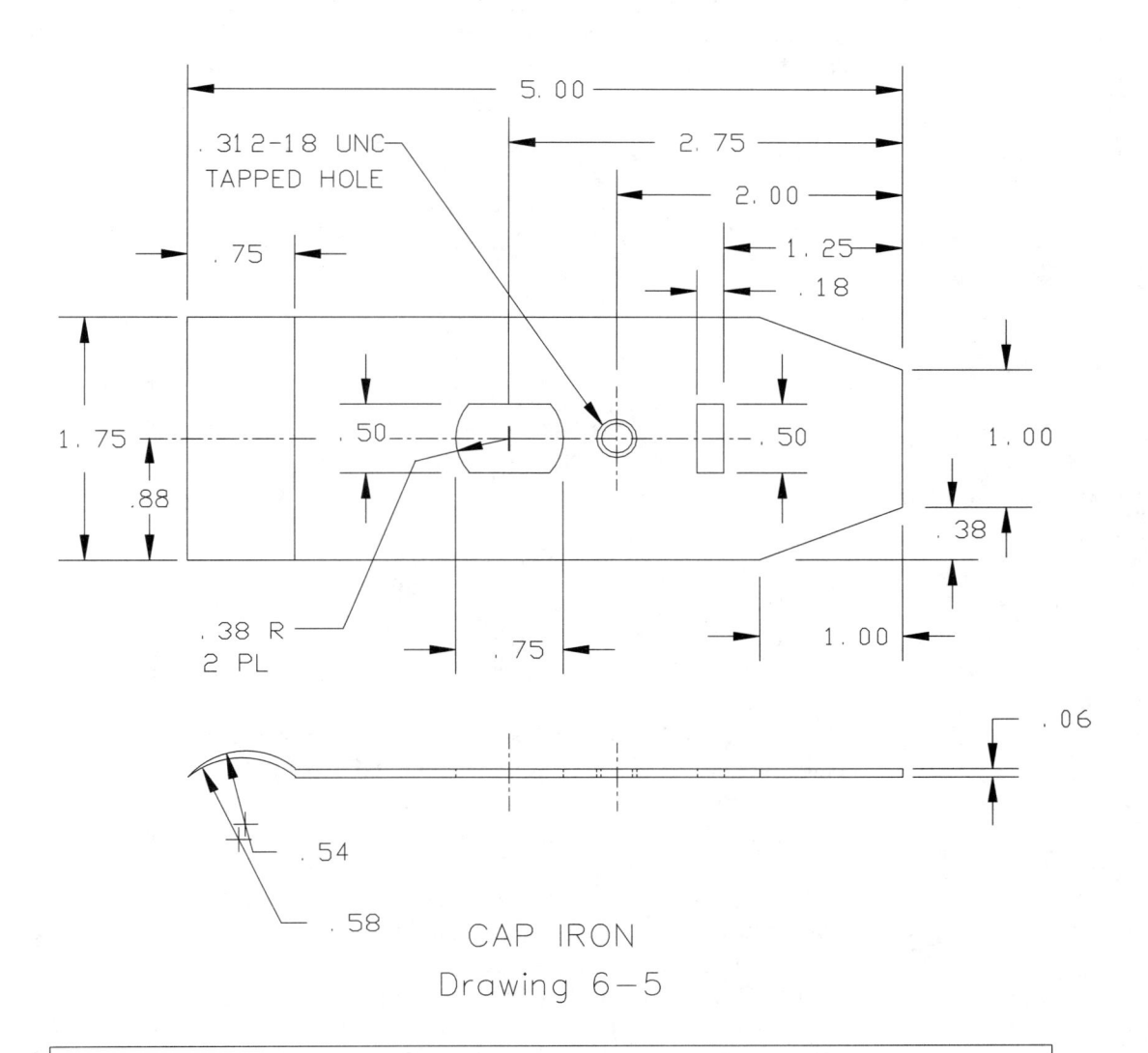

CAP IRON
Drawing 6-5

LAYERS	NAME	COLOR	LINETYPE		
	0	WHITE	——— CONTINUOUS	LINE	(L)
	1	RED	——— CONTINUOUS	CIRCLE	(C)
	2	YELLOW	------- HIDDEN	ARC	(A)
	3	GREEN	—·—·— CENTER	BREAK	
				TRIM	
				CHAMFER	
				ZOOM	(Z)

F1	F2	F6	F7	F8	F9
HELP	TEXT/GRAPHICS SCREEN	ABSOLUTE/OFF/POLAR COORDS	ON/OFF GRID	ON/OFF ORTHO	ON/OFF SNAP

DRAWING 6-6: DECK FRAMING

This architectural drawing may take some time, although there is nothing in it you have not done before. Notice that the settings are quite different from our standard prototype, so be sure to change them before beginning.

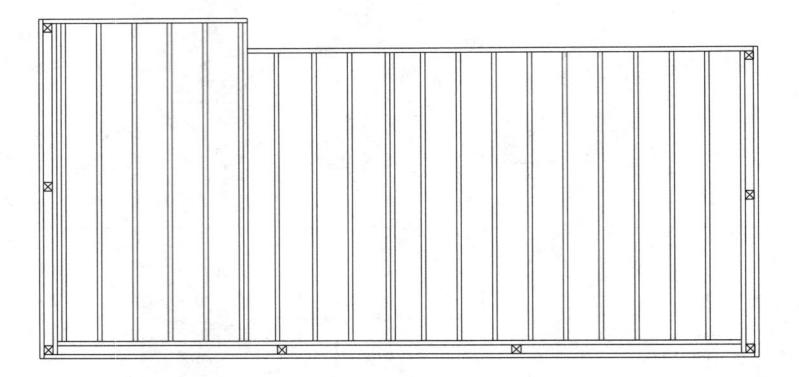

DRAWING SUGGESTIONS

UNITS = Architectural
    smallest fraction = 1
LIMITS = (0,0) (48,36)
GRID = 1'
SNAP = 2"

> Whatever order you choose for doing this drawing, we suggest that you make ample use of COPY, ARRAY, and TRIM.

> Keep ortho on, except to draw the lines across the middle of the squares.

> With snap set at 2" it is easy to use the arrow keys to copy lines 2" apart, as you will be doing frequently to draw the 2" × 8" studs.

> You may need to turn snap off when you are selecting lines to copy, but be sure to turn it on again to specify displacements.

> Notice that you can use ARRAY effectively, but that there are three separate arrays. They are all 16" on center, but the double boards in several places make it inadvisable to do a single array of studs all the way across the deck. What you can do, however, is to draw, copy, and array all the vertical studs first and then go back and trim them to their various lengths using the horizontal boards as cutting edges.

Chap. 6

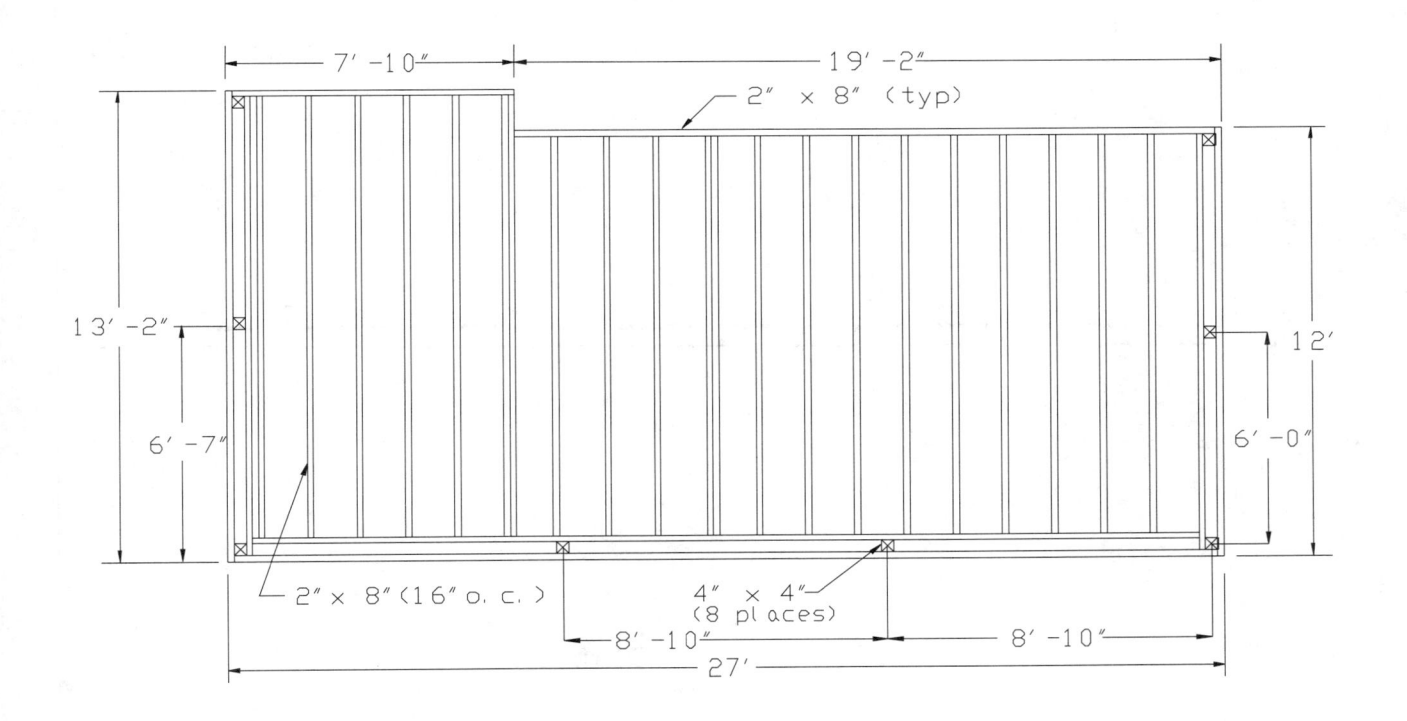

DECK FRAMING
Drawing 6-6

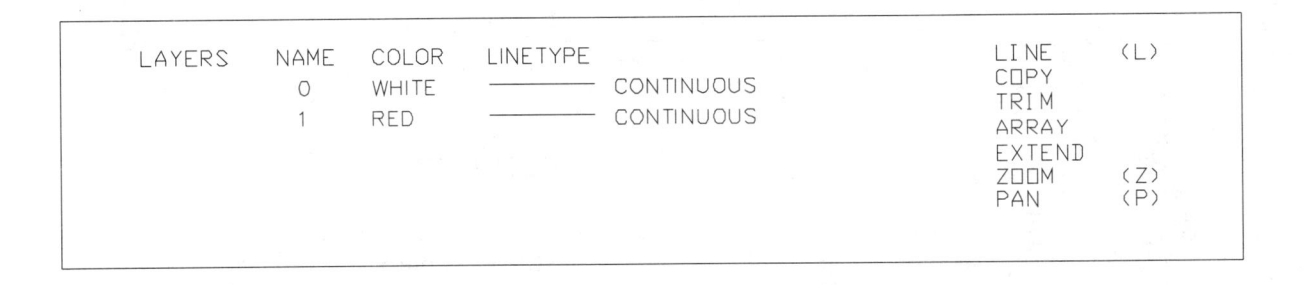

LAYERS	NAME	COLOR	LINETYPE		
	0	WHITE	———— CONTINUOUS	LINE	(L)
	1	RED	———— CONTINUOUS	COPY	
				TRIM	
				ARRAY	
				EXTEND	
				ZOOM	(Z)
				PAN	(P)

F1	F2	F6	F7	F8	F9
HELP	TEXT/GRAPHICS SCREEN	ABSOLUTE/OFF/POLAR COORDS	ON/OFF GRID	ON/OFF ORTHO	ON/OFF SNAP

PART II
Text, Dimensions, and Other Complex Entities

CHAPTER 7

COMMANDS

DRAW	**MODIFY**	**DATA**	**OBJECT PROPERTIES**
DTEXT	CHANGE	STYLE	DDEMODES
MTEXT	CHPROP		
TEXT	DDCHPROP		**TOOLS**
	DDEDIT		SPELL
	DDMODIFY		
	SCALE		

OVERVIEW

This chapter begins Part II of the book. Part I focused on basic 2D entities such as lines, circles, and arcs. In the next five chapters you will be learning to draw a number of AutoCAD entities that are constructed as *groups* of lines, circles, and arcs. Text, dimensions, polylines, and blocks are all entities made up of basic 2D entities, but you will not have to treat them line by line, arc by arc. Also in Part II, you will continue to learn AutoCAD editing features.

Now it's time to add text to your drawings. In this chapter you will learn to find your way around Release 13's three text commands, TEXT, DTEXT, and MTEXT. In addition, you will learn many new editing commands that are often used with text but that are equally important for editing other objects.

TASKS

1. Enter left-justified text using the DTEXT command.
2. Enter text using six different justification options.
3. Enter text on an angle and text using character codes.
4. Enter paragraph text using MTEXT.
5. Use DDEDIT to edit previously drawn text.
6. Use DDMODIFY to change text properties.
7. Check spelling of text in a drawing.
8. Change fonts and styles.
9. Use CHANGE to edit previously drawn text.
10. Use CHANGE points to edit other entities.
11. Use SCALE to change the size of objects on the screen.
12. Do Drawing 7-1 ("Title Block").
13. Do Drawing 7-2 ("Gauges").
14. Do Drawing 7-3 ("Stamping").
15. Do Drawing 7-4 ("Control Panel").

Task 1: Entering Left-Justified Text Using DTEXT

Procedure

1. Type "Dtext" or select the Dtext tool from the Text flyout on the Draw toolbar.
2. Pick a start point.
3. Answer prompts regarding height and rotation.
4. Type text.
5. Press Enter to exit the command.

Discussion. Release 13 provides three different commands for entering text in a drawing. TEXT, the oldest of the three, allows you to enter single lines of text at the command prompt. DTEXT uses all of the same options as TEXT but shows you the text on the screen as you enter it, as well as allowing you to enter multiple lines of text and to backspace through them to make corrections. MTEXT is a new command that allows you to type paragraphs of text in a dialogue box and then positions them in a windowed area in your drawing. All of these commands have numerous options for placing text and a variety of fonts to use and styles that can be created from them. In the first three tasks we will focus on the basic placement features of the three commands, sticking with the standard style and font. In Task 4 we will do a spell check. In Task 5 we will explore other styles and fonts.

We will begin with standard text and the DTEXT command. Most of what you learn will apply to the TEXT command as well, but DTEXT has more features and is easier to use.

> To prepare for this exercise, draw a 4.00 horizontal line beginning at (1,1). Then create a 6 row by 1 column array with 2.00 between rows, as shown in *Figure 7-1*. These lines are for orientation in this exercise only; they are not essential for drawing text.

> Type "Dtext" or select the Dtext tool from the Text flyout on the Draw toolbar, as shown in *Figure 7-2*.

You will see a prompt with three options in the command area:

Justify/Style/<Start point>:

"Style" will be explored in Task 5. In this task we will be looking at different options for placing text in a drawing. These are all considered text justification methods and will be listed if you choose the "Justify" option at the

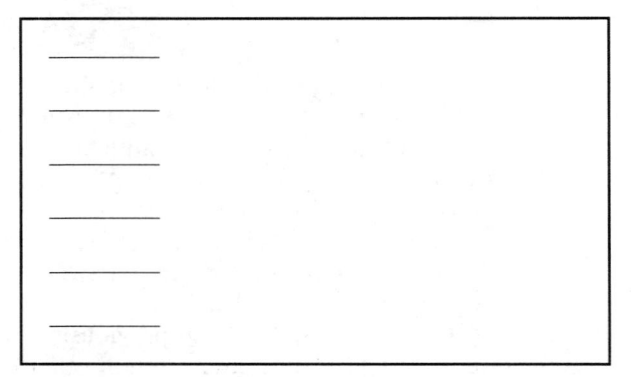

Figure 7-1

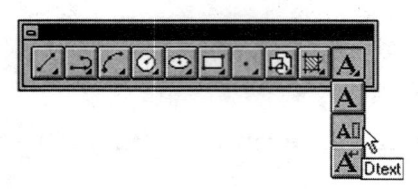

Figure 7-2

command prompt. However, the justification options are shown automatically in the screen menu area regardless of how you enter the DTEXT command. We will explore these momentarily.

First we will use the default method by picking a start point. This will give us left-justified text. This is what you would expect. The text we enter will be inserted left to right from the point we pick.
> Pick a start point at the left end of the upper line.

Look at the prompt that follows and be sure that you do not attempt to enter text yet:

Height <0.20>:

This gives you the opportunity to set the text height. The number you type specifies the height of uppercase letters in the units you have specified for the current drawing. For now we will accept the default height.
> Press Enter to accept the default height (0.20).

The prompt that follows allows you to place text in a rotated position.

Rotation angle <0>:

The default of 0 degrees orients text in the usual horizontal manner. Other angles can be specified by typing a degree number relative to the polar coordinate system, or by showing a point. If you show a point, it will be taken as the second point of a baseline along which the text string will be placed. For now we will stick to horizontal text.
> Press Enter to accept the default angle (0).

Now, at last, it is time to enter the text itself. AutoCAD prompts:

Text:

Notice also that a small box has appeared at the start point. Move your cross hairs away from this point and you will see that the box stays. This shows where the first letter you type will be placed. It is a feature of DTEXT

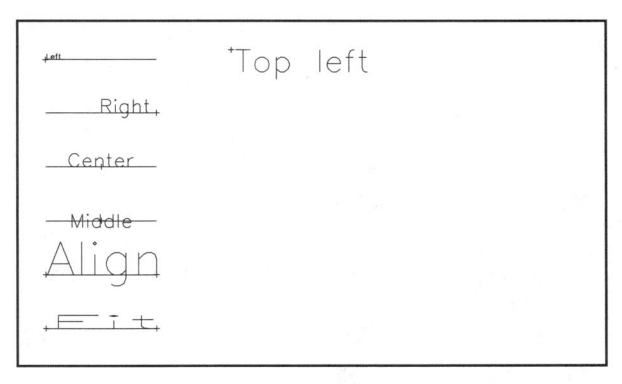

Figure 7-3

that you would not find in the TEXT command. For our text we will type the word "Left" since this is an example of left-justified text. Watch the screen as you type and you will see dynamic text at work.
> Type "Left" and press Enter. (Remember, you cannot use the space bar in place of the enter key when entering text.)

Notice that the text box jumps down below the line when you hit Enter. Also notice that you are given a second "Text:" prompt in the command area.
> Type "Justified" and press Enter.

The text box jumps down again and another "Text:" prompt appears. This is how DTEXT allows for easy entry of multiple lines of text directly on the screen in a drawing. To exit the command, you need to press Enter at the prompt.
> Press Enter to exit DTEXT.

This completes the process and returns you to the command prompt.

Figure 7-3 shows the left-justified text you have just drawn, along with the other options as we will demonstrate them in the rest of this exercise.

Before proceeding with other text justification options, we will demonstrate two additional features of DTEXT.

> Press Enter to repeat the DTEXT command.

If you press Enter again at this point instead of showing a new start point or selecting a justification option, you will go right back to the "Text:" prompt as if you had never left the command. Try it.
> Press Enter.

You will see the "Text:" prompt in the command area and the text box will reappear on the screen just below the word "Justification".
> Type "Text" and press Enter.

At this point you will still be in the DTEXT command with the "Text:" prompt showing. You could press Enter to exit the command or continue typing lines. Instead try this:
> Move the cross hairs to any part of the screen and press the pick button.

The text box will move to whatever point you have selected. This means that you can type text in several areas of the screen without ever leaving DTEXT, as long as the text is the same height, angle, and style. You do not even have to press Enter before you move the text box. Try it again.
> Move the cross hairs once again and press the pick button.

The dynamic text box will move wherever you want.

> Type "here" in the new spot.

> Move the text box again and type "and there".

Now, before leaving DTEXT, use the backspace feature to erase the last two lines.

> Backspace through "and there" and "here".

This demonstrates how you can backspace dynamically through text created in DTEXT even if the text is in different areas. However, this only works before you exit the command.

> Press Enter again to exit the command.

Once you have left DTEXT there are other ways to edit text, which we will explore in Tasks 5 and 6.

Task 2: Using Other Text Justification Options

Procedure

1. Type "Dtext" or select the DText tool from the Text flyout on the Draw toolbar.
2. Type or select an option.
3. Pick a location.
4. Answer prompts regarding height and rotation.
5. Type text.
6. Press Enter to exit the command.

Discussion. We will now proceed to try out some of the other text placement options, beginning with right-justified text, as shown on the second line of *Figure 7-3*. We will also specify a change in height.

Right-Justified Text

Right-justified text is constructed from an end point backing up, right to left.

> Repeat the DTEXT command. You will see the same prompt as before.

> Type "r" or select "Right" from the screen menu.

Now AutoCAD prompts you for an end point instead of a start point:

End point:

We will choose the right end of the second line.

> Point to the right end of the second line.

This time we will change the height to .50. Notice that AutoCAD gives you a rubber band from the end point. It can be used to specify height and rotation angle by pointing, if you like.

> Type ".5" and press Enter or show a height of .50 by pointing.

> Press Enter to retain 0 degrees of rotation. You are now prompted to enter text.

> Type "Right" and press Enter.

Here you should notice an important fact about the DTEXT command. Initially, DTEXT ignores your justification choice, entering the letters you type from left to right as usual. The justification will be carried out only when you exit the command.

At this point you should have the word "Right" showing to the right of the second line. Watch what happens when you press Enter a second time to exit the command.
> Press Enter.

The text will jump to the left, onto the line. Your screen should now include the second line of text in right-justified position as shown in *Figure 7-3*.

Centered Text

Centered text is justified from the bottom center of the text.

> Repeat the DTEXT command.
> Type "c" or select "Center".
AutoCAD prompts:

Center point:

> Point to the midpoint of the third line.
> Press Enter to retain the current height, which is now set to .50.
> Press Enter to retain 0 degrees of rotation.
> Type "Center" and press Enter.

Notice again how the letters are displayed on the screen in the usual left to right manner.

> Press Enter again to complete the command.

The word "Center" should now be centered as shown in *Figure 7-3*.

Middle Text

Middle text is justified from the middle of the text both horizontally and vertically, rather than from the bottom center.

> Repeat DTEXT.
> Type "m" or select "Middle".
AutoCAD prompts:

Middle point:

> Point to the midpoint of the fourth line.
> Press Enter to retain the current height of .50.
> Press Enter to retain 0 degrees of rotation.
> Type "Middle" and press Enter.
> Press Enter again to complete the command.

Notice the difference between center and middle. Center refers to the midpoint of the baseline below the text. Middle refers to the middle of the text itself, so that the line now runs through the text.

Aligned Text

Aligned text is placed between two specified points. The height of the text is calculated proportional to the distance between the two points and the text is drawn along the line between the two points.

> Repeat DTEXT.
> Type "a" or select "Align".
   AutoCAD prompts:

First text line point:

> Point to the left end of the fifth line.   AutoCAD prompts for another point:

Second text line point:

> Point to the right end of the fifth line.
   Notice that there is no prompt for height. AutoCAD will calculate a height based on the space between the points you chose. There is also no prompt for an angle, because the angle between your two points (in this case 0) will be used. You could position text at an angle using this option.
> Type "Align" and press enter.
> Press Enter again to complete the command.
   Notice that the text jumps in size and placement to fill the line.

Text Drawn to Fit Between Two Points

The Fit option is similar to the Aligned option, except that the specified text height is retained.

> Repeat DTEXT.
> Type "f" or select "fit".
   You will be prompted for two points as in the "align" option.
> Point to the left end of the sixth line.
> Point to the right end of the sixth line.
> Press Enter to retain the current height.
   As in the align option, there will be no prompt for an angle of rotation.
> Type "Fit" and press Enter.
> Press Enter again to complete the command.

This time the text will be stretched horizontally to fill the line without a change in height. This is the difference between fit and align. In the align option, text height is determined by the width you show. With fit, the specified height is retained and the text is stretched or compressed to fill the given space.

Other Justification Options

Before proceeding to the next task, take a moment to look at the list of justification options. They are on the screen menu, if it is available, starting with "Top Left". These same options will be listed on the command line if you enter TEXT or DTEXT and type "j". The command line prompt looks like this:

Align/Fit/Center/Middle/Right/TL/TC/TR/ML/MC/MR/BL/BC/BR:

The letter options are spelled out in the chart shown in *Figure 7-4*. We already have explored the first five plus the default option. For the others, study the figure. As shown on the chart, T is for top, M is for middle, and B is for bottom. L, C, and R stand for left, center, and right. All of these options work the same

Chap. 7   **195**

TEXT JUSTIFICATION	
<START POINT> TYPE ABBREVIATION	TEXT POSITION + INDICATES START POINT or PICK POINT
A	ALIGN
F	FIT
C	CENTER
M	MIDDLE
R	RIGHT
TL	TOP LEFT
TC	TOP CENTER
TR	TOP RIGHT
ML	MIDDLE LEFT
MC	MIDDLE CENTER
MR	MIDDLE RIGHT
BL	BOTTOM LEFT
BC	BOTTOM CENTER
BR	BOTTOM RIGHT

Figure 7-4

way. Notice that it is not necessary to type "j" and see the list before entering the option. Just enter TEXT or DTEXT and then the one or two letters of the option. Let's try one.

> Repeat DTEXT and then type "tl" or select "Top Left" from the screen menu.

AutoCAD will ask for a "Top/left point". As shown in the chart, *Figure 7-4*, top left refers to the highest potential text point at the left of the word.

> Pick a top left point as shown in *Figure 7-3* above the words "top left".

> Press Enter twice to accept the height and rotation angle settings and arrive at the "Text:" prompt.

> Type "top left" and press Enter.

> Press Enter again to complete the command.

As before, the text will jump into top left justified position when you exit the command. Your screen should now resemble *Figure 7-3*.

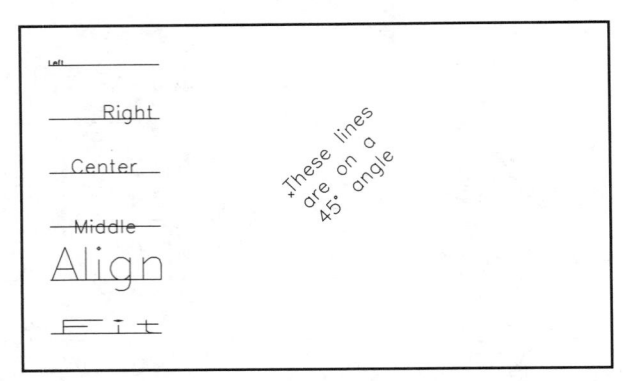

Figure 7-5

Task 3: Entering Text on an Angle and Text Using Character Codes

Procedure

1. Enter TEXT or DTEXT.
2. Specify start point and text height.
3. Specify rotation angle.
4. Type text, including character codes as needed.
5. Press Enter to exit command.

Discussion. We have already seen how you can use DTEXT to enter multiple lines of text. In this task we will explore this further by entering several lines on an angle, adding special character symbols along the way. We will create three lines of left-justified text, one below the other, all rotated 45 degrees, as shown in *Figure 7-5*.

> Repeat the DTEXT command.
  You will see the familiar prompt:

  Justify/Style/<Start point>:

> Pick a starting point near (12.00,8.00), as shown by the blip next to the word "These" in *Figure 7-5*.
> Type ".3" to specify a smaller text size.
> Type "45" or show an angle of 45 degrees.
  Notice that the text box is shown at the specified angle.
> Type "These lines" and press Enter.
  The text will be drawn on the screen at a 45 degree angle and you will be returned to the "Text:" prompt. Notice that the text box on the screen is still at the specified angle.
> Type "are on a" and press Enter.
  You should be at the "Text:" prompt.

The Degree Symbol and Other Special Characters

The next line contains a degree symbol. Since you do not have this character on your keyboard, AutoCAD provides a special method for drawing it. Type the text

Chap. 7   **197**

CONTROL CODES AND SPECIAL CHARACTERS	
Type at TEXT PROMPT	TEXT on Drawing
%%O OVERSCORE	$\overline{\text{OVERSCORE}}$
%%U UNDERSCORE	$\underline{\text{UNDERSCORE}}$
180%%D	180°
2.00 %%P.01	2.00 ±.01
%%C4.00	⌀4.00

Figure 7-6

with the %% signs just as shown following and then study *Figure 7-6*, which lists other special characters that can be drawn in the same way.

> Type "45%%d angle" and press Enter.

DTEXT will initially type the character code directly to the screen, just as you have typed it. When you exit the command, the character code will be translated and redrawn. Watch.

> Press Enter again to complete the command sequence.

Your screen should now resemble *Figure 7-5*.

Task 4: Entering Paragraph Text Using MTEXT

Procedure

1. Type "Mtext" or select the Text tool from the Text flyout on the Draw toolbar.
2. Specify options.
3. Pick an insertion point.
4. Pick a second corner.
5. Type text.
6. Save and Exit the text editor.

Discussion. Release 13 includes a new text command that allows you to create paragraphs of text in a dialogue box and position them within a defined window in your drawing. Like TEXT and DTEXT, MTEXT has nine options for text justification and its own set of character codes.

We begin by creating a simple left-justified paragraph.

> Type "Mtext" or select the Text tool from the Text flyout on the Draw toolbar, as illustrated in *Figure 7-7*. (The label on the tool says "Text", but this is the MTEXT command.)

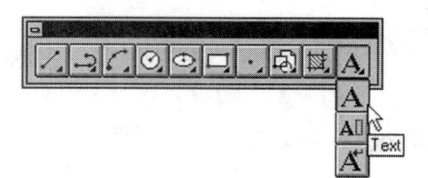

Figure 7-7

You will see the following prompt in the command area:

Attach/Rotation/Style/Height/Direction/<Insertion point>:

We will discuss options momentarily, after you see how the command works.

Fundamentally, MTEXT lets you define the width of a paragraph of text that you will create in a text editor. The word paragraph is used loosely here to designate any text with multiple lines that wrap around within a specified area. When the text is entered using MTEXT, AutoCAD formats it to conform to the specified width and justification method and draws the text on your screen. The width can be defined in several ways. The default method for specifying a width is to draw a window on the screen. This can be misleading. MTEXT does not attempt to place text inside the window, but only within its width. The first point of the window becomes the insertion point of the text. How AutoCAD uses this insertion point depends on the "Attachment" option, which is the MTEXT version of justification. The second window point defines the width. We will begin by using this default method and the default "Top Left" attachment option.

> Pick an insertion point near the middle of your drawing area, in the neighborhood of (9.00,6.00).

AutoCAD will begin a window at the selected point and give you a new prompt. It is the same as the previous prompt except that two options have been added and the default has been change from "Insertion point" to "Other corner".

We will continue with the default options by picking a second corner. The only important thing about the window you define is its width, as you will see. For purposes of demonstration we suggest a window 3.00 wide and no more than 1.00 high. The window can be drawn to the left or right, up or down, and it can be any height. The results will be the same as long as the width is 3.00.

> Pick a second point to define a window 3.00 wide and about 1.00 high.

As soon as you pick the second point, AutoCAD will open the Edit MText dialogue box, as illustrated in *Figure 7-8*. The most important feature

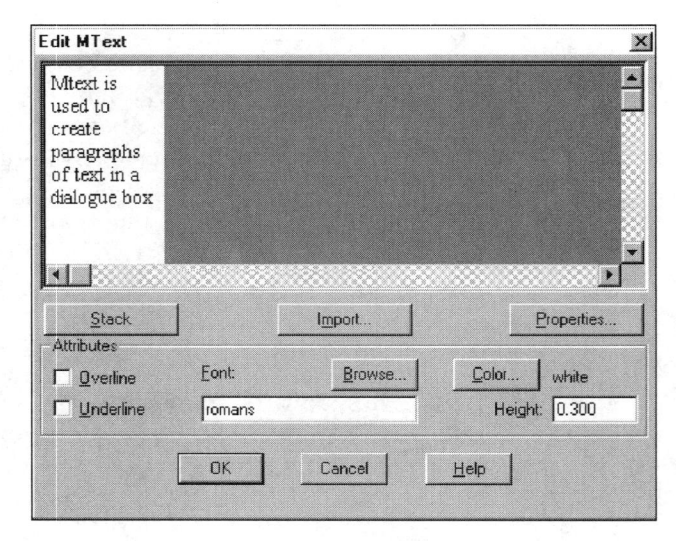

Figure 7-8

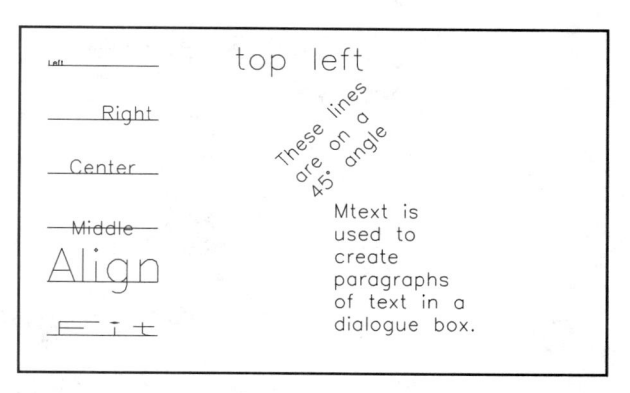

Figure 7-9

of this dialogue box is the editing area at the top of the screen. The right side is black, and the white area on the left represents the width of the paragraph text area you have just defined in your drawing. When you enter text in this area it will wrap around as it will in your drawing.

> Type "Mtext is used to create paragraphs of text in a dialogue box."
> Click on "OK" to leave the dialogue box.

You will be returned to the drawing editor and the new text will be added as shown in *Figure 7-9*. Notice that the text you typed has been wrapped around to fit within the 3.00 width window. However, the .30 height of the text has been retained and the 1.00 height of the text window you defined has been ignored. Also notice that the text is drawn left to right from the insertion point, regardless of how you drew the window. You will see more about how this works as we proceed to modify this text and explore other options in the next task.

Task 5: Editing Text with DDEDIT

Procedure

1. Type "ddedit" or select the Edit Text tool from the Special Edit flyout on the Modify toolbar.
2. Select text to edit.
3. Edit text in the edit box.
4. Click on "OK".

Discussion. There are several ways to modify text that already exists in your drawing. You can change wording and spelling as well as properties such as layer, style, and justification. Commands that you will use to alter text include CHANGE, CHPROP, DDCHPROP, DDEDIT, and DDMODIFY. CHANGE, DDMODIFY, and DDEDIT can be used to change words as well as text properties, CHPROP AND DDCHPROP can change only properties.

For text editing you will most often use DDEDIT and DDMODIFY. In both cases there will be minor variations in how the commands work depending on whether the text you are editing was created using DTEXT or MTEXT. We will begin with some simple DDEDIT text editing. In Task 5, we will use the property modification powers of DDMODIFY to show different attachment options of MTEXT paragraphs.

> Type "ddedit" or select the Edit Text tool from the Special Edit flyout on the Modify toolbar, as shown in *Figure 7-10*.

Figure 7-10

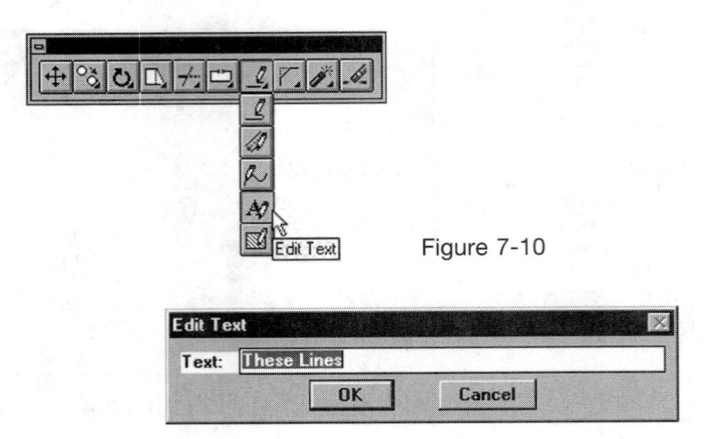

Figure 7-11

Regardless of how you enter the command, AutoCAD will prompt you to select an object for editing:

<Select an annotation object>/Undo:

Annotation objects will include all objects that have text, including text, dimensions, and attributes. Dimensions are the subject of Chapter 8. Attributes are discussed in Chapter 10.

We will select one line of the angled text.

> Select the words "These lines" by clicking on any of the letters.

As soon as you select the text, it will appear in a small edit box, as illustrated in *Figure 7-11*. This is the DDEDIT dialogue box for text created with DTEXT and TEXT. If you had selected text created with MTEXT you would be in the Mtext Edit box with the paragraph text showing. We will demonstrate momentarily. Now we will add the word "three" to the middle of this line.

> Move the dialogue box arrow to the center of the text in the edit box, between "These" and "lines", and press the pick button.

The text should no longer be highlighted and a flashing cursor should be present indicating where text will be added if you begin typing.

> Type the word "three" and add a space so that the line reads "These three lines".

> Click on "OK".

The dialogue box will disappear and your text will be redrawn with the word "three" added as shown in *Figure 7-12*.

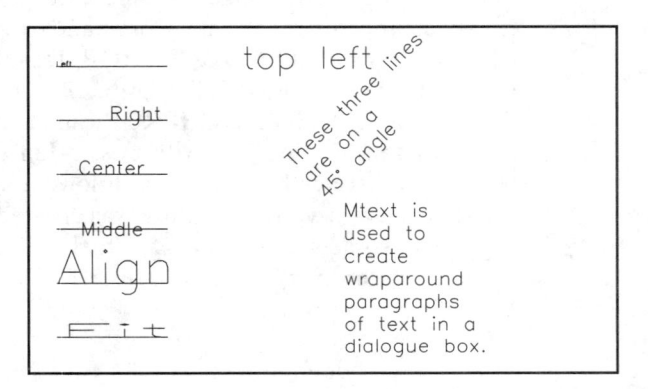

Figure 7-12

Now let's try it with the text you created in MTEXT. The first difference you will notice is that since MTEXT creates text as paragraphs, you cannot select a single line of text. When you click, the whole paragraph will be selected.

DDEDIT repeats automatically. So you should have the following prompt in the command area before proceeding:

<Select an annotation object>/Undo:

If not, repeat DDEDIT.

> Select the text beginning with "Mtext is".

This will call up the Edit Mtext dialogue box with the chosen paragraph showing in the white space.

> Move the screen cursor to the second line, after "create", and press the pick button.

You should now have a flashing cursor on the line after "create".

> Add "wraparound", so that the paragraph will read "Mtext is used to create wraparound paragraphs of text in a dialogue box."

> Click on "OK".

You will return to the drawing editor, with the new text added and reformatted as shown in *Figure 7-12*. That's it for DDEDIT. Next we will explore DDMODIFY along with more MTEXT placement options.

Task 6: Modifying Text with DDMODIFY

Procedure

1. Type "ddmodify" or select the Properties tool from the Object Properties toolbar or "Properties" from the Edit pull down menu.
2. Select text to modify (steps 1 and 2 can be reversed if noun/verb editing is enabled).
3. Use the dialogue box to change properties.
4. Click on "OK".

Discussion. DDMODIFY is one of several commands that can be used to change properties of objects in a drawing. It is used with many other kinds of objects besides text. In this exercise you will learn how to use DDMODIFY and at the same time explore the MTEXT attachment options. Attachment is one of the properties you will be able to modify, and this is an efficient way to explore the options without having to input a lot of new text. We will end this exercise with a summary of MTEXT placement options.

> Draw a 3.00 line just above the MTEXT paragraph, as shown in *Figure 7-13*.

This line is only for reference. It should begin at the same snap point that was used as the insertion point for the text. The left end of the line will show the insertion point and the length will show the width of the paragraph. We have used the point (9.00,6.00) and the 3.00 width.

> Type "ddmodify" or select the Properties tool from the Object Properties toolbar, shown in *Figure 7-14*, or "Properties..." from the Edit pull down menu.

The pull down menu selection will actually execute a program called propchk. Both the DDMODIFY command and the program will first check what type of object you have selected and then open the appropriate dialogue box. The only difference is that propchk will allow you to select more than

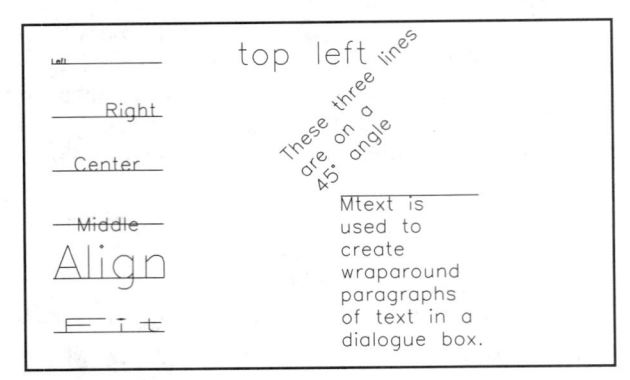

Figure 7-13

Figure 7-14

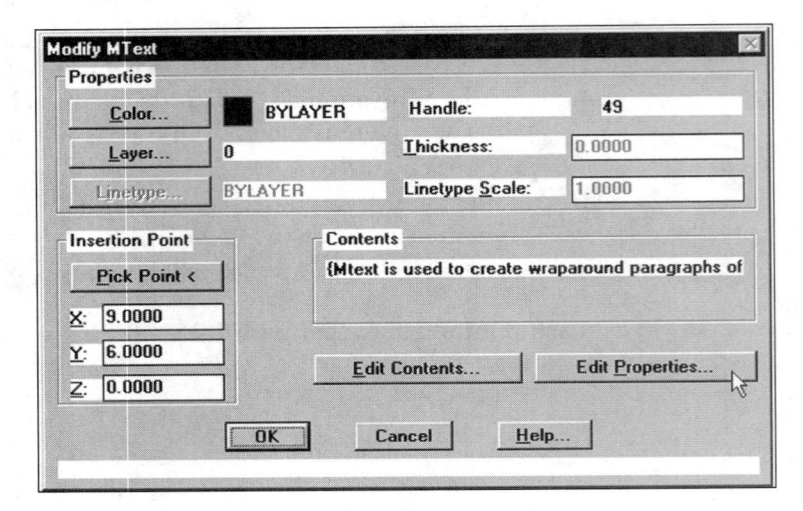

Figure 7-15

one object and then decide what you can do depending on what you have chosen. DDMODIFY will only allow one selection.

> Select the paragraph beginning with "Mtext is".

If you typed the DDMODIFY command, you will go directly to a dialogue box. If you selected "Properties..." from the pull down, you will have to press Enter to end object selection.

> If necessary, press Enter to end object selection.

You should now be seeing the Modify Mtext dialogue box illustrated in *Figure 7-15*. Take a look at it. The options in the top box, including color, layer, linetype, handle, thickness, and linetype scale are standard changeable properties for all objects. All DDMODIFY dialogue boxes will include these. These are also the common properties that can be changed using CHANGE, CHPROP or the DDCHPROP dialogue box.

The area below the Properties box is unique to text drawn with MTEXT. The content of the text is shown in the middle for reference only. If you wish to edit the contents, click on "Edit Contents...". This will call up the Edit Mtext box, and will work much like DDEDIT.

> Click on "Edit Properties...".

This will call the MText Properties dialogue box illustrated in *Figure 7-16*. Here you can modify style, height, direction (horizontal or vertical), attachment, paragraph width, and rotation. We will demonstrate two differ-

Chap. 7   203

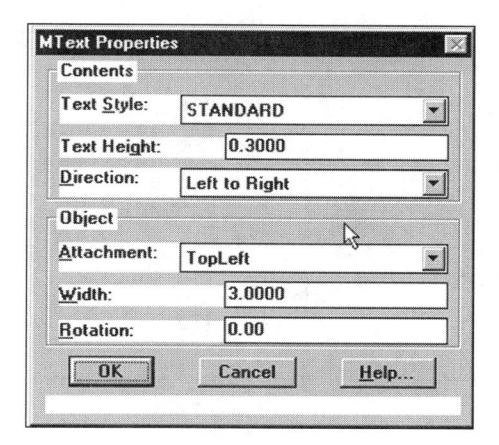

Figure 7-16

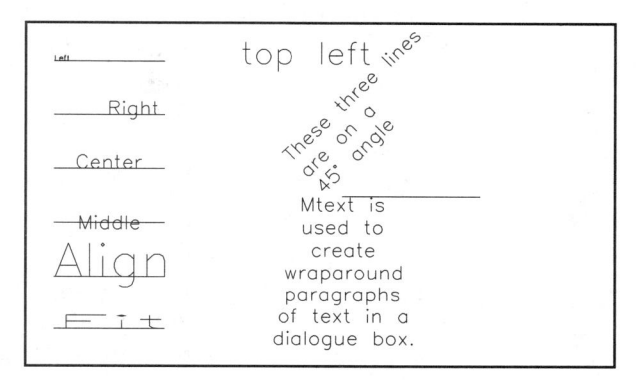

Figure 7-17

ent attachment options; other options are illustrated in *Figure 7-19* at the end of this exercise.

> Click on the arrow at the right end of the "Attachment:" box.

This will open up a list box with a list of the nine attachment options. The list should look familiar to you, since it includes the same choices as the text justification options introduced previously. The only difference is that attachment places and justifies an entire paragraph at once rather than one line at a time.

Notice that the default attachment is Top Left. We will change it to Top Center, the second option on the list.

> Click on "TopCenter".

The list box will close and "TopCenter" should now be shown in the Attachment edit box.

> Click on "OK" to exit MText Properties.
> Click on "OK" again to exit Modify MText.

Your text will be redrawn as shown in *Figure 7-17*. The paragraph will now be in centered format, with the original insertion point used as a top center point. Try it once more. This time we will use a vertical text direction.

> Repeat DDMODIFY.
> Select the paragraph again.
> If necessary, press Enter to end object selection.

This should bring you back to the Modify MText dialogue box.

> Click on "Edit Properties...".

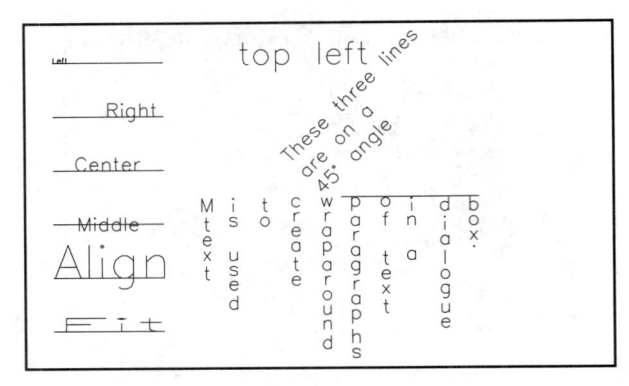

Figure 7-18

This will open the MText Properties dialogue box again.
> Click on the arrow to the right of the Direction edit box.

On the command line in the MTEXT command text directions are labeled horizontal and vertical. Here they are Left to Right and Top to Bottom.
> Change the direction to "Top to Bottom".
> Click on "OK" to exit "MText Properties".
> Click on "OK" to exit "Modify MText".

Your text will be redrawn as shown in *Figure 7-18*. The insertion point is still top center, but the words in the paragraph are now printed vertically. In vertical text, the width specification is used vertically instead of horizontally. In this case the paragraph covers about 5.00 units horizontally, but Au-

Figure 7-19

toCAD has attempted to limit the vertical boundary to 3.00. However, MTEXT will not split words, so that "wraparound" and "paragraphs" extend down about 4.50 units. This suggests the following summary of how Mtext handles boundaries.

1. Mtext only works with one dimension, the "width".
2. Width is horizontal in horizontal text and vertical in vertical text.
3. Mtext will not split words, but will wrap around between words. It will not begin a new word outside the boundary.
4. The boundary is measured from the insertion point in a manner dependent on the attachment option and the text direction.

You may wish to continue with other attachment options, or study *Figure 7-19,* which illustrates the options.

Task 7: Using the SPELL Command

Procedure

1. Type "Spell" or select the Spelling tool from the Standard toolbar.
2. Select objects.
3. Press Enter to end selection.
4. Use the dialogue box to ignore, change, or add words the spell checker does not recognize.

Discussion. Release 13 is the first AutoCAD version to have an internal spell checker to check spelling of text in a drawing. It is simple to use and will be very familiar to anyone who has used spell checkers in word processing programs. We will use the SPELL command to check the spelling of all the text we have drawn so far.

Figure 7-20

> Type "spell" or select the Spelling tool from the Standard toolbar, as illustrated in *Figure 7-20.*

You will see a "Select objects:" prompt on the command line. At this point you could point to individual objects. Any object may be selected, although no checking will be done if you select a line, for example.

For our purposes we will use an "All" selection to check all the spelling in the drawing.

> Type "all".

AutoCAD will continue to prompt for object selection until you press Enter.

> Press Enter to end object selection.

This will bring you to the Check Spelling dialogue box shown in *Figure 7-21.* If you have followed the exercise so far and not misspelled any words along the way, you will see "Mtext" in the Current word box and "Text" as a suggested correction. We will ignore this change, but before you leave SPELL, look at what is available: You can ignore a word the checker does not recognize, or change it. You can change a single instance of a word, or change all instances in the currently selected text. You can add a word to a customized dictionary but you cannot add words to the main dictionary. For this reason, Add is probably grayed out in your dialogue box. Selecting "Change Dictionaries..." will call up another dialogue box where you can create a customized dictionary and add words to it.

> Click on "Ignore".

If your drawing does not contain other spelling irregularities, you should now see an AutoCAD Alert message that says:

Spelling check complete.

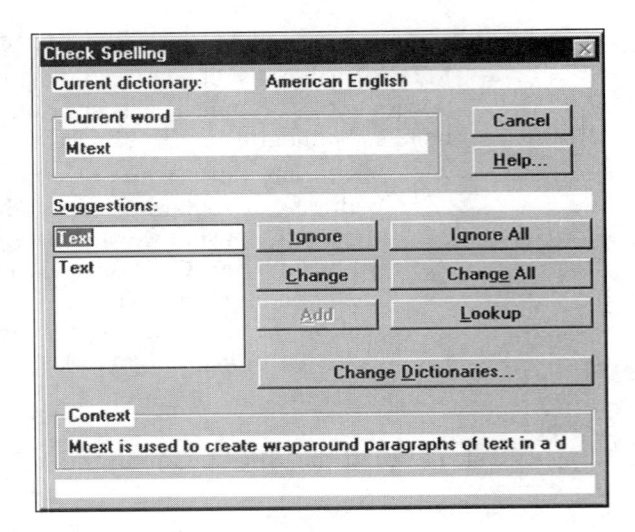

Figure 7-21

> Click on "OK" to end the spell check.

If you have made any corrections in spelling they will be incorporated into your drawing at this point.

Task 8: Changing Fonts and Styles

Procedure

1. Type "Style" or select "Text Style" from the Data pull down menu.
2. Type a new style name.
3. Type a font file name.
4. Answer prompts for height, width, angle, and orientation.

Discussion. By default, the current text style in any AutoCAD drawing is one called "STANDARD". It is a specific form of a font called "txt" that comes with the software. All the text you have entered so far has been drawn with the standard style of the "txt" font.

Changing fonts is a simple matter. However, there is room for confusion in the use of the words "style" and "font." You can avoid this confusion if you remember that fonts are the basic patterns of character and symbol shapes that can be used with the TEXT, DTEXT, and MTEXT commands, while styles are variations in the size, orientation, and spacing of the characters in those fonts. It is possible to create your own fonts, but for most of us this is an esoteric activity. In contrast, creating your own styles is easy and practical.

We will begin by creating a variation of the STANDARD style you have been using.

> Type "Style" or select "Text Style" from the Data pull down menu.

You will be prompted as follows:

Text style name (or ?) <STANDARD>:

By now you should be familiar with the elements of this prompt. We will use the "?" first to see a list of available styles.

> Type "?" or select "List?" from the screen menu.

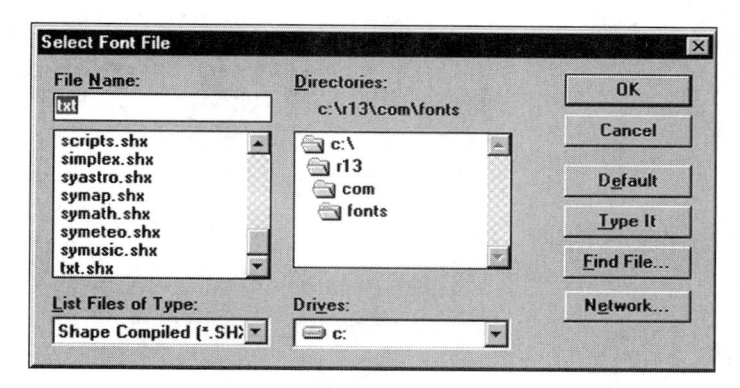

Figure 7-22

AutoCAD will offer you the opportunity to limit the list of styles by using wild card characters.

Text style(s) to list <*>:

> Press Enter to list all available styles.

AutoCAD will switch over to the text screen and give you the following information:

Text styles:

Style name: STANDARD   Font files: txt
Height: 0.00   Width factor: 1.00   Obliquing angle: 0   Generation: Normal

Current text style: STANDARD

If anyone has used text commands in your prototype drawing, it is possible that there will be other styles listed. However, STANDARD is the only one that is certain to be there, because it is created automatically. We will create our own variation of the STANDARD style and call it "VERTICAL". It will use the same "txt" character font, but will be drawn down the display instead of across.

> Press Enter to repeat the STYLE command.

You will see this prompt again:

Text style name (or ?) <STANDARD>:

> Type "vertical".

AutoCAD will respond by displaying the Select Font File dialogue box shown in *Figure 7-22*.

> Press Enter to retain the current txt font.

AutoCAD closes the font dialogue box and prompts:

Height <0.00>:

It is important to understand what 0 height means in the STYLE command. It does not mean that your characters will be drawn 0.00 units high. It means that there will be no fixed height, so you will be able to specify a height whenever you use this style. Notice that STANDARD currently has no fixed height. That is why you are prompted for a height whenever you

use it. In general, it is best to leave height variable unless you know that you will be drawing a large amount of text with one height. For practice, try giving our new "VERTICAL" style a fixed height.
> Type ".5".
AutoCAD prompts:

> Width factor <1.00>:

This prompt allows you to stretch or shrink characters in the font based on a factor of one. Let's double the width to see how it looks.
> Type "2".
AutoCAD prompts:

> Obliquing angle:

This allows you to put any font on a slant, right or left, creating an italic effect. We will leave this one alone for the moment.
> Press Enter to retain 0 degrees of slant.
AutoCAD follows with a series of three prompts regarding the orientation of characters. The first one is:

> Backwards? <N>:

Obviously this is for special effects. You can try this one in a moment.
> Press Enter to retain "frontwards" text.
The second orientation prompt is even more peculiar:

> Upside down? <N>:

> Press Enter if you want your text to be drawn right side up.
Finally, the one we've been waiting for:

> Vertical? <N>:

This is what allows us to create a vertical style text.
> Type "y".
Before returning the "Command:" prompt AutoCAD will tell you that your new style is now current:

> VERTICAL is now the current text style.

To see your new style in action you will need to enter some text.
> Type or select "DTEXT".
> Pick a start point, as shown by the blip near the letter "V" in *Figure 7-23*.
Notice that you are not prompted for a height because the current style has height fixed at .50.
> Press Enter to retain 270 degrees of rotation.
> Type "Vertical".
> Press Enter to end the line.
Before going on, notice that the DTEXT text placement box has moved up to begin a new column of text next to the word vertical.
> Press Enter to exit DTEXT.
Your screen should resemble *Figure 7-23*.

Chap. 7   **209**

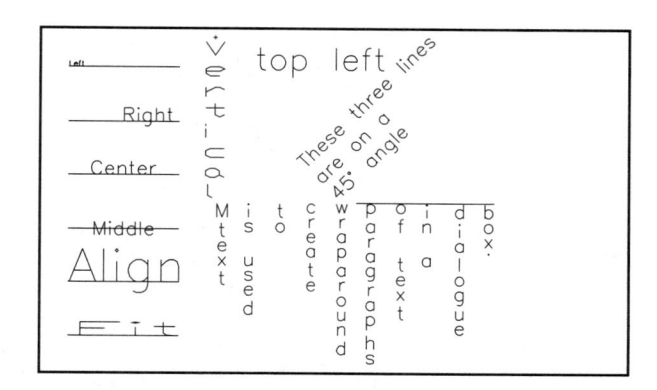

Figure 7-23

There are now two text styles in the current drawing. Both use the txt font. Next we will create a third style using a different font and some of the other style options.

> Type "Style" or select "Text Style" from the Data pull down menu.

The prompt now shows "Vertical" as the current style.

Text style name (or ?) <VERTICAL>:

> Type "third" and press Enter.

This gives our third text style the name "Third".

AutoCAD will tell you that Third is a new style and will open a Select Font File dialogue box so that you can begin to define it. The dialogue box is illustrated in *Figure 7-22*. This box has a directory list on the left and a font file list with a scroll bar on the right. At the top you will see a Pattern edit box showing the file name extensions that are included in AutoCAD's font library. Shx files are AutoCAD's own fonts, pfa and pfb files are postscript files that will print only on postscript printers, ttf files are TrueType font files. You will see many of each type listed in the files list box. Samples of each font are shown in Appendix C of the Release 13 *AutoCAD User's Guide*.

> Click on the scroll up arrow on the right side of the "Files": box.

You will see many font files scrolling by.

> Scroll to "romand.shx" and stop.

Romand stands for "Roman Duplex", an AutoCAD font.

> Click on "romand.shx" so that it becomes highlighted.

"romand.shx" will also be entered into the "File": edit box at the top.

> Click on "OK".

The dialogue box will disappear, leaving you in the middle of the STYLE command sequence with a prompt for a text height:

Height <0.00>:

> Type "0" or press Enter to specify variable height.

The rest of the command sequence will be familiar from the STYLE command. We will retain all the defaults except for the obliquing angle.

> Type "1" to specify the standard width factor.

> Type "45" and press Enter.

This will cause your text to be slanted 45 degrees to the right. For a left slant, you would type a negative number.

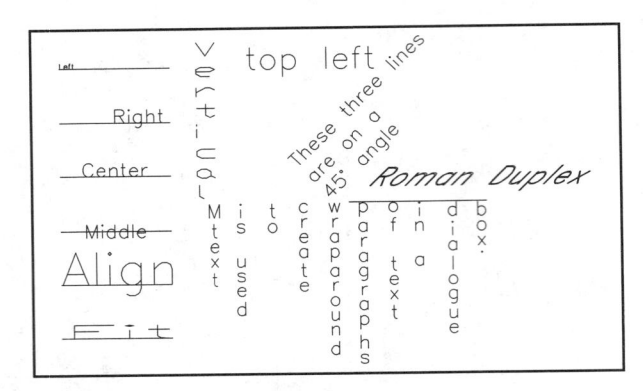

210 Part II Text, Dimensions, and Other Complex Entities

Figure 7-24

> Press Enter to retain frontward text.
> Press Enter to retain rightside up text.
> Press Enter to retain horizontal text.

AutoCAD will tell you, though you may need to press F2 to see it:

THIRD is now the current text style.

Now enter some text to see how this slanted Roman Duplex style looks.
> Type or select "DTEXT" and answer the prompts to draw the words "Roman Duplex" with a .50 height, as shown in *Figure 7-24*. We started this text at the point (6.00, 7.00)

Switching the Current Style

All new text is created in the current style. The style of previously drawn text can be changed, as we will show later. In this exercise we will talk only about switching the current style.

Once you have a number of styles defined in a drawing, you can switch from one to another with the Style option of the TEXT and DTEXT commands. This option is only for switching previously defined styles; it will not allow you to define new ones. In addition, you can switch styles using the Select Text Style dialogue box. This is a subdialogue of the DDEMODES command. It can be reached by typing "DDemodes", selecting the DDEMODES tool from the Object Properties toolbar, or selecting "Object Creation..." from the Data pull down menu. We will use the menu.

> Select "Object Creation..." under "Data" on the pull down menu.

This brings up the Object Creation Modes dialogue box shown in *Figure 7-25*.
> Click on "Text Style...".

This will open the Select Text Style box shown in *Figure 7-26*. Third will be highlighted as the current text style, and will be listed along with standard and vertical. A sample of the selected text style will be shown in the black box to the right. The sample text will be ABC, but you can change this by typing in the Sample Text edit box.
> Click on "Vertical".

When Vertical is highlighted you will see the sample box change to vertical text. This is a convenient way to view and switch among text styles. But remember, it can only show you styles that you have already created.

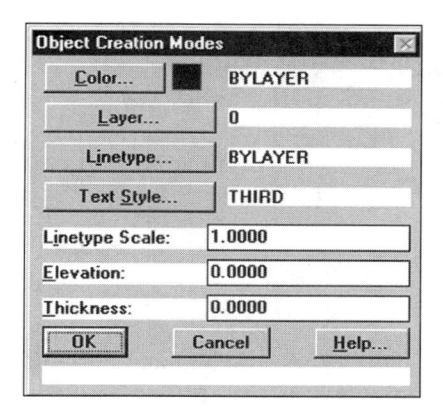

Figure 7-25

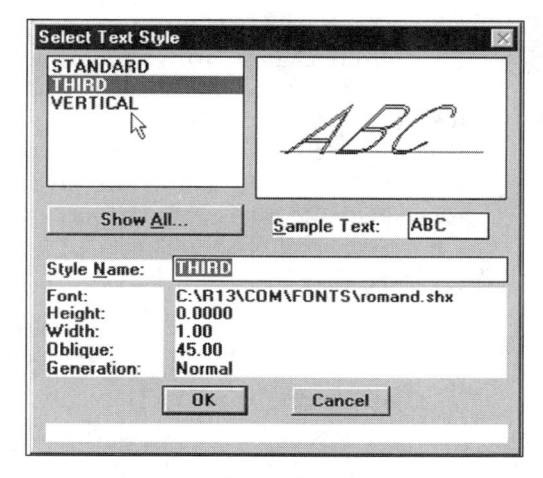

Figure 7-26

Before leaving, we suggest that you return to the Standard text style.
> Click on "Standard" so that it becomes highlighted.
> Click on "OK" to exit Select Text Style.
> Click on "OK" to exit Object Creation Modes.

NOTE: If you change the definition of a text style, all text previously drawn in that style will be regenerated with the new style specifications.

Task 9: Changing Previously Drawn Text with CHANGE

Procedure

1. Type "Change" or select the Change tool from the Resize flyout on the Modify toolbar.
2. Select objects (text). (Steps 1 and 2 can be reversed if noun/verb selection is enabled.)
3. Pick a new location or press Enter for no change.
4. Type or select a new text style or press Enter for no change.
5. Type or show a new height or press Enter for no change.
6. Type or show a new rotation angle or press Enter for no change.
7. Type new text or press Enter for no change.

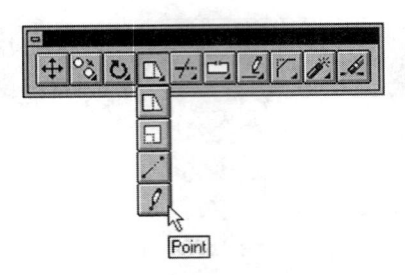

212   Part II Text, Dimensions, and Other Complex Entities

Figure 7-27

Discussion. The CHANGE command is another useful tool that allows you to change a number of different entities, text being one of them. CHANGE works from the command line and will allow most of the same changes that you find in DDMODIFY. However, *CHANGE will not work with MTEXT paragraphs.* The main advantage of CHANGE is that you can select more than one object and work through the changes without leaving the command. The qualities of previously drawn text that can be changed are location, style, height, rotation angle, and the text itself. You can change all the properties at once if need be, but more often you will be changing only one or two. Properties you do not wish to change are retained by pressing Enter. In this exercise we will use the CHANGE command to change the style of some previously drawn text. In task 7, we will use CHANGE to alter some lines.

> Type "Change" or select the Change point tool from the Resize flyout on the Modify toolbar, as shown in *Figure 7-27*.

You will be prompted to select objects.

> Point to the words "top left" at the top of your drawing.
> Press Enter to end selection.

AutoCAD will issue the first of a series of prompts that ask you to specify what you would like to change:

Properties/<Change point>:

"Properties" refers to a standard list of options, including color, layer, and linetype, which can also be changed using CHPROP, DDMODIFY, or DDCHPROP. CHPROP works exactly the same as CHANGE, except that it skips this prompt and moves directly to property change options. DDCHPROP provides the same options but in a dialogue box format.

"Change point" has different meanings with different types of entities. In the case of text, it allows you to relocate the text (this can also be done with the MOVE command or by moving a grip point).

> Press Enter to skip property changes.

AutoCAD prompts:

Enter text insertion point:

This option allows you to move text in a drawing.

> Press Enter to leave the text where it is.

The next prompt will allow you to change styles:

Text style: Standard
New style or RETURN for no change:

Let's change to our Third text style.

> Type "third".

You are now prompted for a change in height:

New height <0.50>:

> Press Enter to retain the ".50" height.

The next prompt is for a change in rotation angle:

New rotation angle <0>:

We will retain this angle.

> Press Enter to retain horizontal orientation.

Finally, AutoCAD prompts for a change in the characters themselves:

New Text <top left>:

This gives you yet another way to change wording and spelling. It is especially useful in a procedure where you create an array of one text item and then change the text of some or all of the items in the array. This is often more efficient than creating a large number of related text items independently. We will show you this technique in Drawing 7-2, "Gauges."

> Press Enter to retain the current text.

This will terminate the command and your screen will be redrawn with the words "top left" in the Third text style.

NOTE: Grips can be used to edit text in the usual grip edit modes of moving, copying, rotating, mirroring, and scaling. The stretch mode works the same as moving. Grips on text are located at the left-justified start point and at the original point actually used to position the text. Grips cannot be used to reword, respell, or change text properties.

Task 10: Using Change Points with Other Entities

Procedure

1. Type "Change" or select the Change point tool from the Resize flyout on the Modify toolbar.
2. Define a selection set. (Steps 1 and 2 can be reversed if noun/verb selection is enabled.)
3. Show a change point.

Discussion. You can use a change point to alter the size of lines and circles. With lines, CHANGE will perform a function similar to the EXTEND command, but without the necessity of defining an extension boundary. With circles, CHANGE will cause them to be redrawn so that they pass through the change point.

> Repeat the CHANGE command.

You will be prompted to:

Select objects:

> Select the first two lines, under the words "Left" and "Right".
> Press Enter to end sel   ection.

AutoCAD prompts:

Properties/<Change point>:

We will use a change point first to alter the selected lines, as shown in *Figure 7-28.*

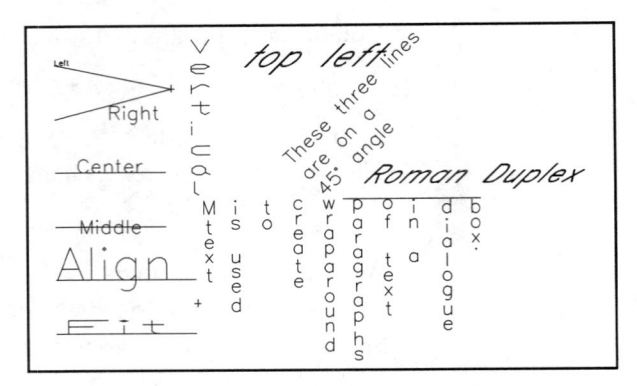

214   Part II Text, Dimensions, and Other Complex Entities

Figure 7-28

> If ortho is on, turn it off (F8).
> Pick a point between the two lines and to the right, in the neighborhood of (6.50,10.00).

The lines will be redrawn so that the change point becomes the new end point of both lines.

To maintain horizontal or vertical orientation of lines while using the change point option of the CHANGE command, turn ortho on. Try it.
> Turn ortho on.
> Repeat the CHANGE command.
> Select the fifth, and sixth lines where the words "Align", and "Fit" are drawn.
> Press Enter to end selection.
> Pick a change point to the right of the lines, as shown by the blip in *Figure 7-28*.

Be careful not to pick this point too low or too high. This could cause AutoCAD to redraw one or more of the lines vertically. Both lines will be extended horizontally, as in *Figure 7-28*.

NOTE: If you use the change point option to edit a circle, the circle will be redrawn so that it passes through the change point. See *Figure 7-29*.

Task 11: SCALEing Previously Drawn Entities

Procedure

1. Type "Scale" or select the Scale tool from the Resize flyout on the Modify toolbar.
2. Select objects. (Steps 1 and 2 can be reversed if noun/verb selection is enabled.)

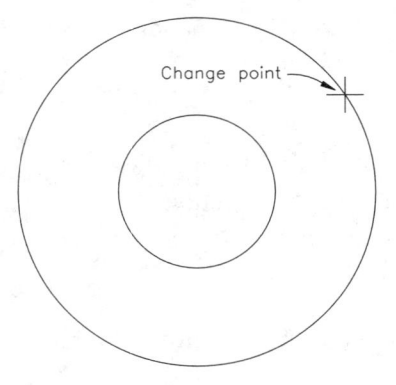

Figure 7-29

Chap. 7 215

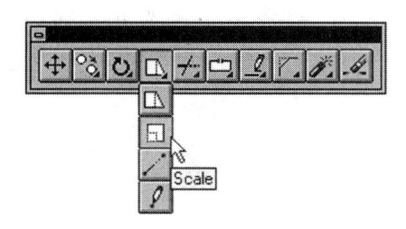

Figure 7-30

3. Pick a base point.
4. Enter a scale factor.

Discussion. Any object or group of objects can be scaled up or down using the SCALE command or the grip edit scale mode. In this exercise we will practice scaling some of the text and lines that you have drawn on your screen. Remember, however, that there is no special relationship between SCALE and text and that other types of entities can be scaled just as easily.

> Type "Scale" or select the Scale tool from the resize flyout on the Modify toolbar, as shown in *Figure 7-30*.

AutoCAD will prompt you to select objects.

> Use a crossing box (right to left) to select the set of six lines and text drawn in Task 1.
> Press Enter to end selection.

You will be prompted to pick a base point:

Base point:

Imagine for a moment that you are looking at a square and you want to shrink it using a scale-down procedure. All the sides will, of course, be shrunk the same amount, but how do you want this to happen? Should the lower left corner stay in place and the whole square shrink toward it? Or should everything shrink toward the center? Or toward some other point on or off the square (see *Figure 7-31*)? This is what you will tell AutoCAD when you pick a base point. In most applications you will choose a point somewhere on the object.

> Pick a base point at the left end of the bottom line of the selected set (the blip in *Figure 7-32*).

AutoCAD now needs to know how much to shrink or enlarge the objects you have selected:

<Scale factor>/Reference:

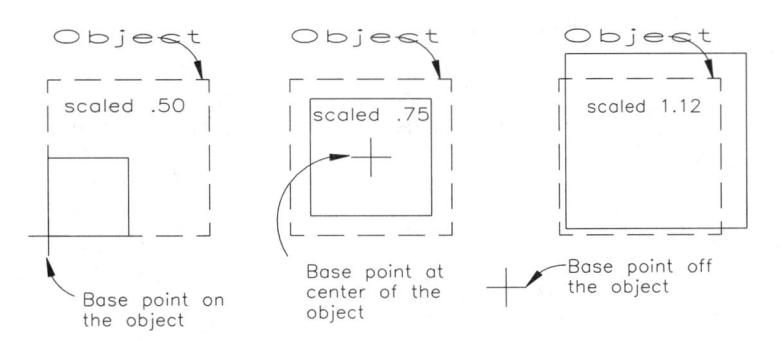

Figure 7-31

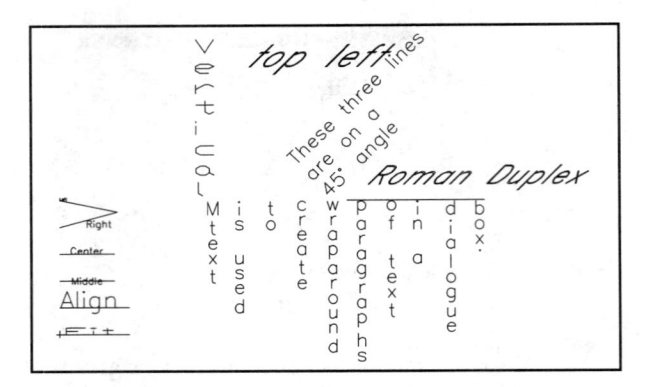

Figure 7-32

We will get to the reference method in a moment. When you enter a scale factor, all lengths, heights, and diameters in your set will be multiplied by that factor and redrawn accordingly. Scale factors are based on a unit of 1. If you enter .5, objects will be reduced to half their original size. If you enter 2, objects will become twice as large.

> Type ".5" and press Enter.

Your screen should now resemble *Figure 7-32*.

SCALEing by Reference

This option can save you from doing the arithmetic to figure out scale factors. It is useful when you have a given length and you know how large you want that length to become after the scaling is done. For example, we know that two of the lines we just scaled are now 2.00 long (the middle two that we did not alter with CHANGE). Let's say that we want to scale them again to become 2.33 long (a scale factor of 1.165, but who wants to stop and figure that out?). This could be done using the following procedure:

1. Enter the SCALE command.
2. Select the "previous" set.
3. Pick a base point.
4. Type "r" or select "reference".
5. Type "2" for the reference length.
6. Type "2.33" for the new length.

NOTE: You can also perform reference scaling by pointing. In the procedure above, you could point to the ends of the 2.00 line for the reference length and then show a 2.33 line for the new length.

Scaling with Grips

Scaling with grips is very similar to scaling with the SCALE command. To illustrate this, try using grips to return the text you just scaled back to its original size.

> Use a window or crossing box to select the six lines and the text drawn in Task 1 again.

There will be a large number of grips on the screen, three on each line and two on most of the text entities. Some of these will overlap or duplicate each other.

> Pick the grip at the lower left corner of the word "Fit," the same point used as a base point in the last scaling procedure.

> Select "SCale" from the screen menu, or press Enter three times to bypass stretch, move, and rotate.
> Move the cursor slowly and observe the dragged image.

AutoCAD will use the selected grip point as the base point for scaling unless you specify that you want to pick a different base point.

Notice that you also have a reference option as in the SCALE command. Unlike the SCALE command you also have an option to make copies of your objects at different scales.

As in SCALE, the default method is to specify a scale factor by pointing or typing.
> Type "2" or show a length of 2.00.

Your text will return to its original size and your screen will resemble *Figure 7-28* again.
> Press Esc twice to clear grips.

Tasks 12, 13, 14, and 15

The drawings that follow contain typical applications of the text and modification commands you have just explored. Pay particular attention to the suggestions on the use of DTEXT and MTEXT in the first drawing, and CHANGE in the second, third, and fourth drawings. These will save you time and help you to become a more efficient CAD operator.

DRAWING 7-1: TITLE BLOCK

This title block will give you practice in using a variety of text styles and sizes. You may want to save it and use it as a title block for future drawings. In Chapter 10 we will show you how to insert one drawing into another, so you will be able to incorporate this title block into any drawing.

QTY REQ'D	DESCRIPTION		PART NO.	ITEM NO.
	BILL OF MATERIALS			
UNLESS OTHERWISE SPECIFIED DIMENSIONS ARE IN INCHES	DRAWN BY: B. A. Cad Designer	DATE	YOUR CAD CO.	
REMOVE ALL BURRS & BREAK SHARP EDGES	APPROVED BY:			
TOLERANCES FRACTIONS ± 1/64 DECIMALS ANGLES ± 0°-15' XX ± .01 XXX ± .005	ISSUED:		DRAWING TITLE:	
MATERIAL:	FINISH:	SIZE C	CODE IDENT NO. 38178	DRAWING NO.	REV.
		SCALE:	DATE:	SHEET	OF

DRAWING SUGGESTIONS

GRID = 1
SNAP = .0625

> Make ample use of DIST and TRIM as you draw the line patterns of the title block. Take your time and make sure that at least the major divisions are in place before you start entering text into the boxes.

> Set to the "text" layer before entering text.

> Use DTEXT with all the STANDARD, .09, left-justified text. This will allow you to do all of these in one command sequence, moving the cursor from one box to the next and entering the text as you go.

> Remember that once you have defined a style, you can make it current using the TEXT or DTEXT commands. This will save you from having to restyle more than necessary.

> Use "%%D" for the degree symbol and "%%P" for the plus or minus symbol.

Chap. 7   **219**

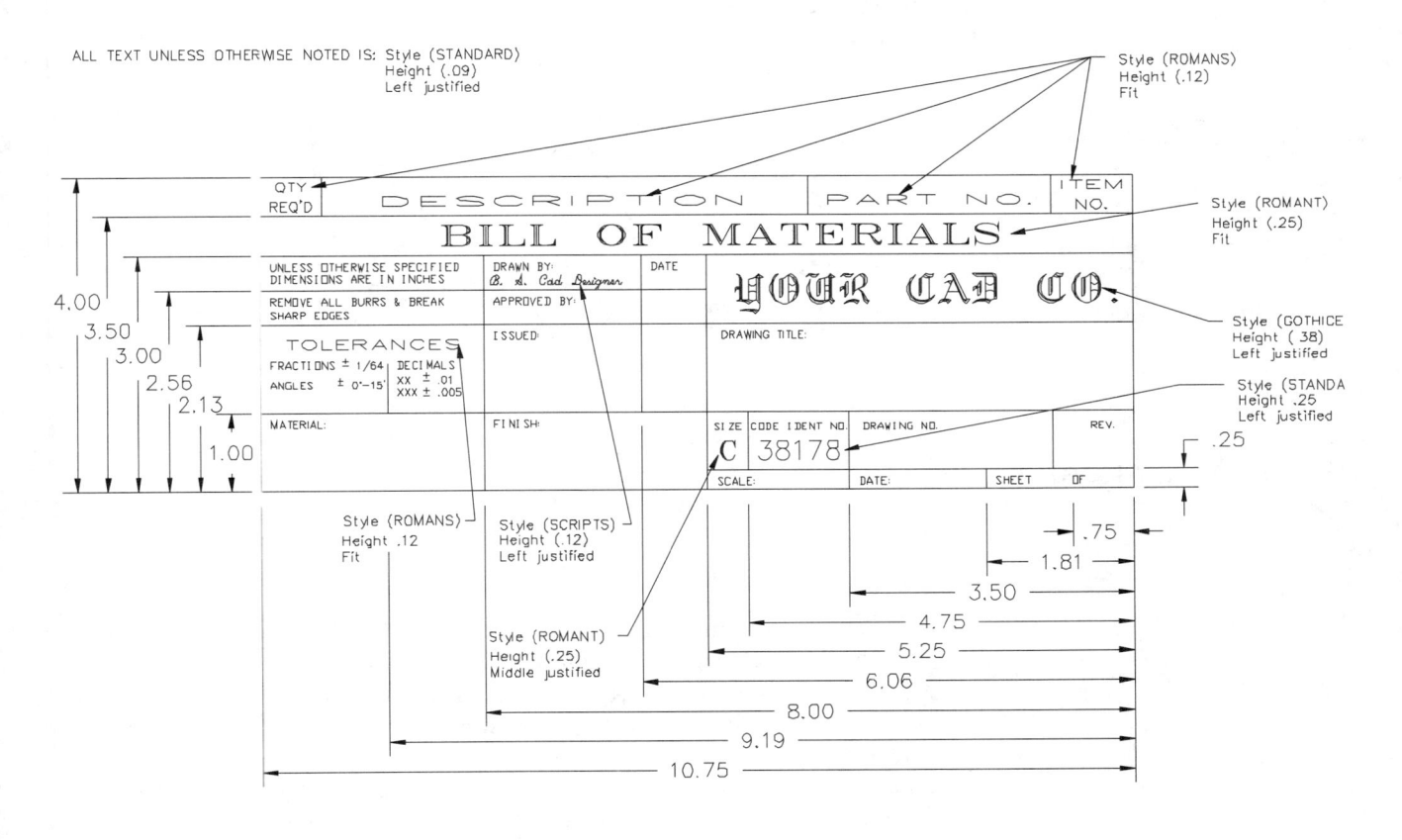

ALL TEXT UNLESS OTHERWISE NOTED IS: Style (STANDARD)
                                    Height (.09)
                                    Left justified

Style (ROMANS)
Height (.12)
Fit

QTY REQ'D	DESCRIPTION	PART NO.	ITEM NO.

BILL OF MATERIALS

Style (ROMANT)
Height (.25)
Fit

UNLESS OTHERWISE SPECIFIED
DIMENSIONS ARE IN INCHES

REMOVE ALL BURRS & BREAK SHARP EDGES

DRAWN BY: B. A. Cad Designer

APPROVED BY:

DATE

ISSUED:

𝔜𝔒𝔘𝔕 𝔒𝔄𝔇 𝔒𝔒.

Style (GOTHICE)
Height (.38)
Left justified

TOLERANCES
FRACTIONS ± 1/64   DECIMALS
ANGLES   ± 0°-15'   XX ± .01
                     XXX ± .005

DRAWING TITLE:

Style (STANDA
Height .25
Left justified

MATERIAL: FINISH: SIZE CODE IDENT NO. DRAWING NO.   REV.
                            C   38178
                            SCALE: DATE: SHEET   OF

.25

Style (ROMANS)
Height .12
Fit

Style (SCRIPTS)
Height (.12)
Left justified

Style (ROMANT)
Height (.25)
Middle justified

Dimensions: 4.00, 3.50, 3.00, 2.56, 2.13, 1.00
.75, 1.81, 3.50, 4.75, 5.25, 6.06, 8.00, 9.19, 10.75

TITLE BLOCK
Drawing 7-1

LAYERS	NAME	COLOR	LINETYPE		
	0	WHITE	———— CONTINUOUS		
	1	RED	———— CONTINUOUS		
	TEXT	CYAN	———— CONTINUOUS		

LINE   (L)
TEXT
DDEDIT
CHANGE
PAN   (P)
ZOOM   (Z)

F1	F2	F6	F7	F8	F9
HELP	TEXT/GRAPHICS SCREEN	ABSOLUTE/OFF/POLAR COORDS	ON/OFF GRID	ON/OFF ORTHO	ON/OFF SNAP

DRAWING 7-2: GAUGES

This drawing will teach you some typical uses of the SCALE and CHANGE commands. Some of the techniques used will not be obvious, so read the suggestions carefully.

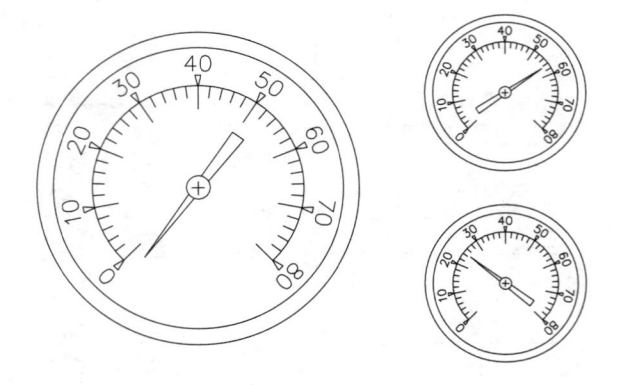

DRAWING SUGGESTIONS

GRID = .5
SNAP = .125

> Draw three concentric circles at diameters of 5.0, 4.5, and 3.0. The bottom of the 3.0 circle can be trimmed later.

> Zoom in to draw the arrow-shaped tick at the top of the 3.0 circle. Then draw the .50 vertical line directly below it and the number "0" (middle-justified text) above it.

> These three objects can be arrayed to the left and right around the perimeter of the 3.0 circle using angles of +135 and −135 as shown.

> Use the CHANGE command to change the arrayed zeros into 10, 20, 30, etc.

> Draw the .25 vertical tick directly on top of the .50 mark at top center and array it left and right. There will be 20 marks each way.

> Draw the needle horizontally across the middle of the dial.

> Make two copies of the dial; use SCALE to scale them down as shown. Then move them into their correct positions.

> Rotate all three needles as shown.

Chap. 7

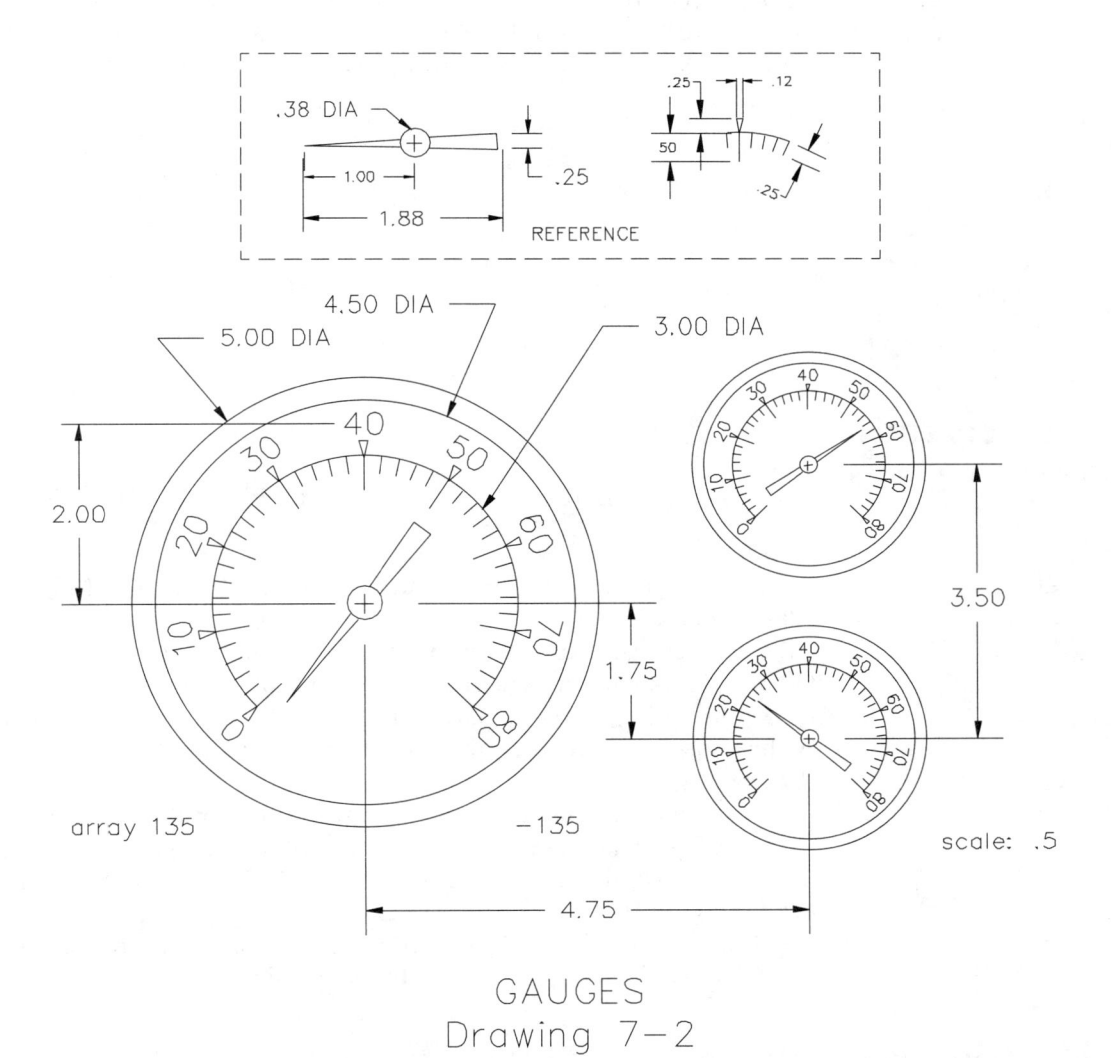

.38 DIA
1.00
1.88
.25
.25 .12
.50
.25
REFERENCE

5.00 DIA
4.50 DIA
3.00 DIA
2.00
array 135
−135
1.75
4.75
3.50
scale: .5

GAUGES
Drawing 7−2

LAYERS	NAME	COLOR	LINETYPE	
	0	WHITE	————	CONTINUOUS
	1	RED	————	CONTINUOUS
	3	GREEN	– – – –	CENTER
	TEXT	CYAN	————	CONTINUOUS

LINE   (L)
CIRCLE   (C)
TEXT
SCALE
ROTATE
COPY
ARRAY
CHANGE
DDEDIT

F1	F2	F6	F7	F8	F9
HELP	TEXT/GRAPHICS SCREEN	ABSOLUTE/OFF/POLAR COORDS	ON/OFF GRID	ON/OFF ORTHO	ON/OFF SNAP

DRAWING 7-3: STAMPING

This drawing is trickier than it appears. There are many ways that it can be done. The way we have chosen not only works well but makes use of a number of the commands and techniques you have learned in the last two chapters. Notice that a change in limits is needed to take advantage of some of the suggestions.

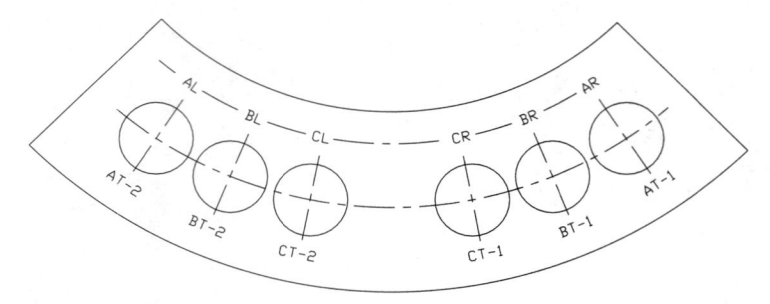

DRAWING SUGGESTIONS

GRID = .50   LIMITS = (0,0) (24,18)
SNAP = .25

> Draw two circles, radius 10.25 and 6.50, centered at about (13,15). These will be trimmed later.
> Draw a vertical line down from the center point to the outer circle. We will copy and rotate this line to form the ends of the stamping.
> Use the rotate, copy mode of the grip edit system to create copies of the line rotated 45 degrees and −45 degrees (coordinate display will show 315 degrees).
> Trim the lines and the circles to form the outline of the stamping.
> Draw a 1.50 diameter circle in the center of the stamping, 8.50 down from (13,15). Draw middle-justified text, "AR", 7.25 down, and "AT-1" down 9.75 from (13,15).
> Follow the procedure below to create offset copies of the circle and text, then CHANGE all text to agree with the drawing.

GRIP COPY MODES WITH OFFSET SNAP LOCATIONS

Here is a good opportunity to try out another grip edit feature. If you hold down the shift key while picking multiple copy points, AutoCAD will be constrained to place copies only at points offset from each other the same distance as your first two points. For example, try this:

1. Select the circle and the text.
2. Select any grip to initiate grip editing.
3. Type "RO" or select "Rotate".
4. Type "b" or select "Base pt".
5. Pick the center of the stamping (13,15) as the base point.
6. Type "c" or select "Copy".
7. Hold down Shift and move the cursor to rotate a copy 11 degrees from the original.
8. Keep holding down the shift key as you move the cursor to create other copies. All copies will be offset 11 degrees.

Chap. 7

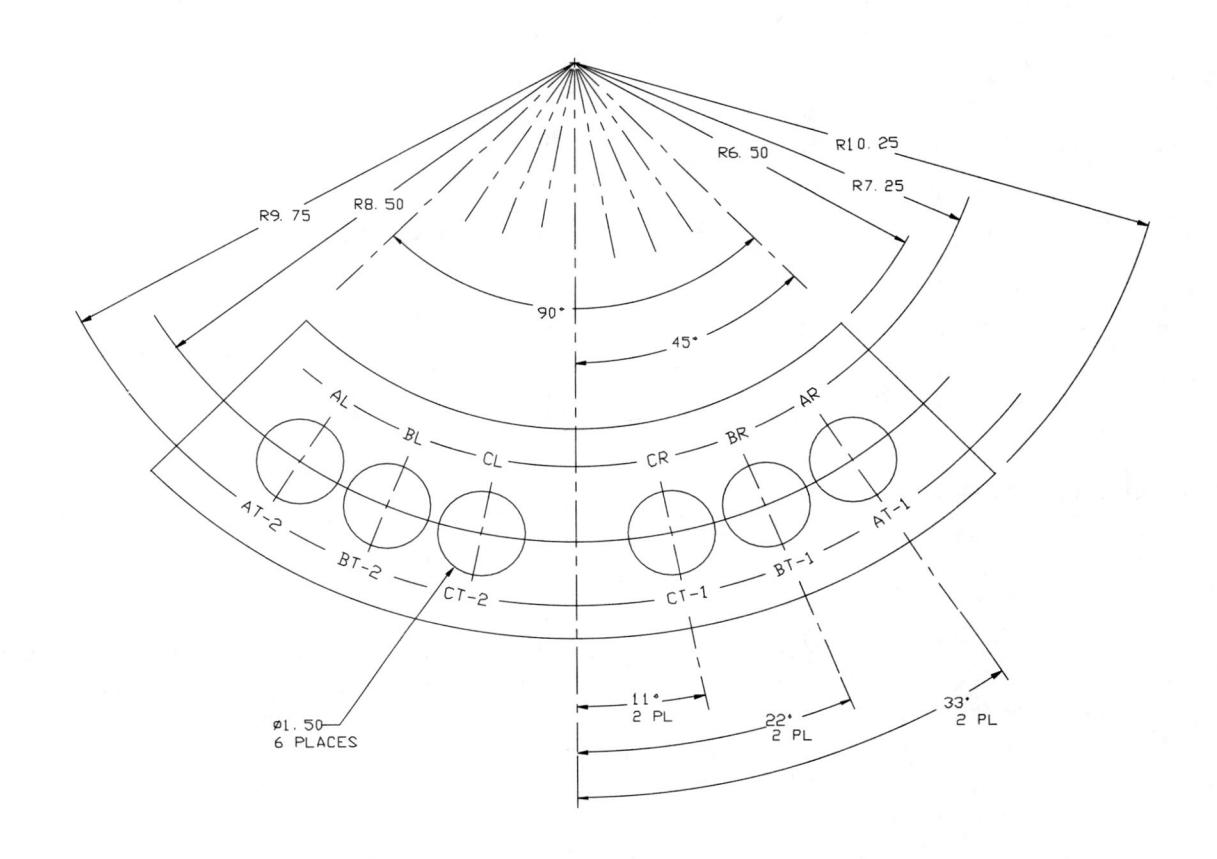

STAMPING
Drawing 7-3

LAYERS	NAME	COLOR	LINETYPE	
	0	WHITE	——————	CONTINUOUS
	1	RED	——————	CONTINUOUS
	3	GREEN	— — — —	CENTER
	TEXT	CYAN	——————	CONTINUOUS

LINE (L)
CIRCLE (C)
TEXT
COPY
TRIM
ROTATE
BREAK
CHANGE
DDEDIT

F1	F2	F6	F7	F8	F9
HELP	TEXT/GRAPHICS SCREEN	ABSOLUTE/OFF/POLAR COORDS	ON/OFF GRID	ON/OFF ORTHO	ON/OFF SNAP

DRAWING 7-4: CONTROL PANEL

Done correctly, this drawing will give you a good feel for the power of the commands you now have available to you. Be sure to take advantage of combinations of ARRAY and CHANGE as described. Also, read the suggestion on moving the origin before you begin.

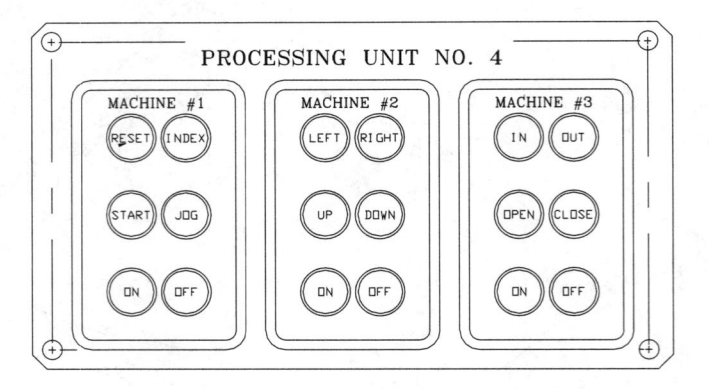

DRAWING SUGGESTIONS

GRID = .50
SNAP = .0625

> After drawing the outer rectangles, draw the double outline of the left button box, and fillet the corners. Notice the different fillet radii.
> Draw the "on" button with its text at the bottom left of the box. Then array it 2 × 3 for the other buttons in the box.
> CHANGE the lower right button text to "off" and draw the MACHINE # text at the top of the box.
> ARRAY the box 1 × 3 to create the other boxes.
> CHANGE text for buttons and machine numbers as shown.
> Complete the drawing.

MOVING THE ORIGIN WITH THE UCS COMMAND

The dimensions of this drawing are shown in ordinate form, measured from a single point of origin in the lower left-hand corner. In effect, this establishes a new coordinate origin. If we move our origin to match this point, then we will be able to read dimension values directly from the coordinate display. This may be done by setting the lower left-hand limits to $(-1,-1)$. But it also may be done using the UCS command to establish a User Coordinate System with the origin at a point you specify. User Coordinate Systems are discussed in depth in Chapter 12. For now, here is a simple procedure:

> Type "ucs".
> Type "o" for the "Origin" option.
> Point to the new origin.

That's all there is to it. Move your cursor to the new origin and watch the coordinate display. It should show "0.00,0.00", and all values will be measured from there.

Chap. 7 225

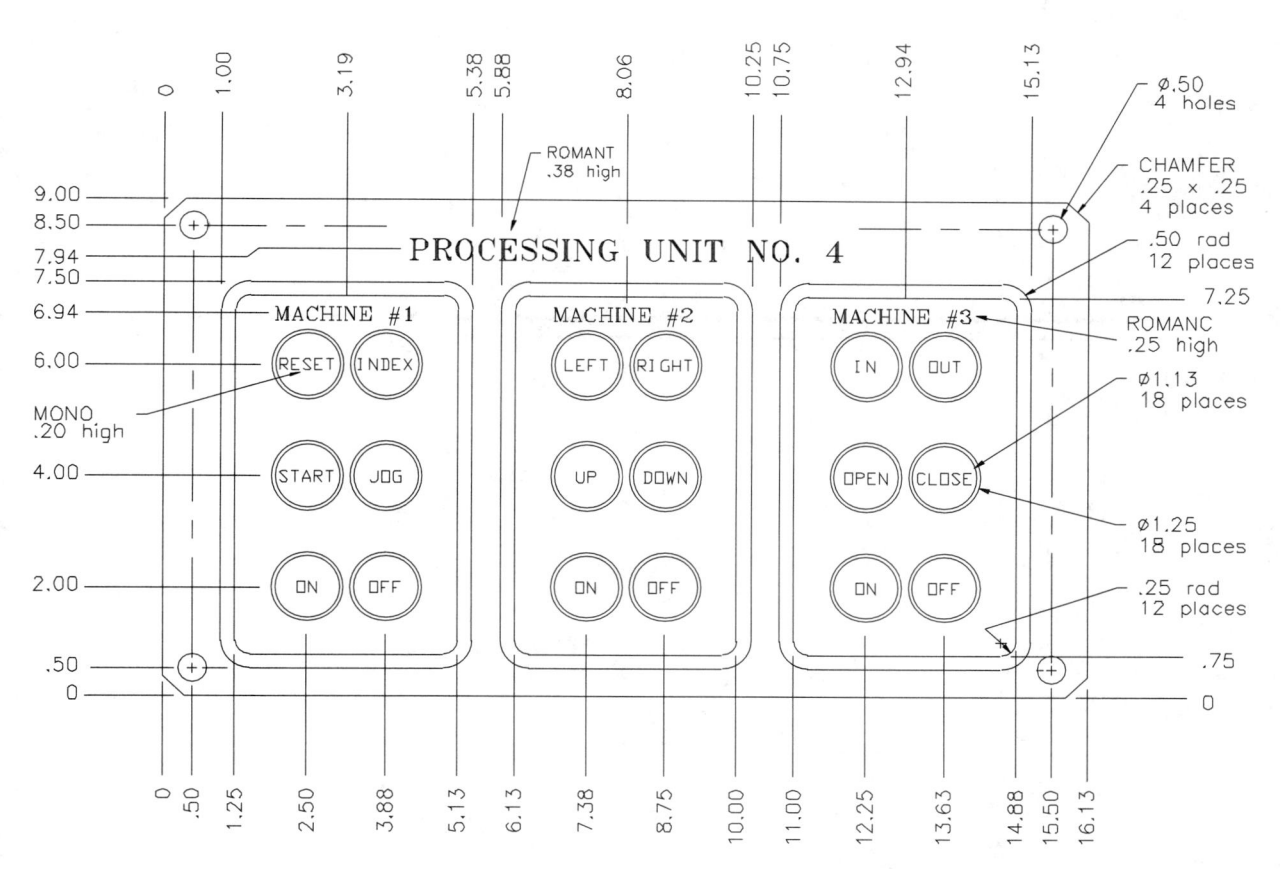

CONTROL PANEL
Drawing 7-4

Dimensions (top, left to right): 0, 1.00, 3.19, 5.38, 5.88, 8.06, 10.25, 10.75, 12.94, 15.13

Dimensions (left, top to bottom): 9.00, 8.50, 7.94, 7.50, 6.94, 6.00, 4.00, 2.00, .50, 0

Dimensions (bottom, left to right): 0, .50, 1.25, 2.50, 3.88, 5.13, 6.13, 7.38, 8.75, 10.00, 11.00, 12.25, 13.63, 14.88, 15.50, 16.13

Dimensions (right): 7.25, .75, 0

Labels:
- PROCESSING UNIT NO. 4 — ROMANT .38 high
- MACHINE #1: RESET, INDEX, START, JOG, ON, OFF
- MACHINE #2: LEFT, RIGHT, UP, DOWN, ON, OFF
- MACHINE #3: IN, OUT, OPEN, CLOSE, ON, OFF — ROMANC .25 high
- MONO .20 high
- Ø.50 4 holes
- CHAMFER .25 x .25 4 places
- .50 rad 12 places
- Ø1.13 18 places
- Ø1.25 18 places
- .25 rad 12 places

LAYERS	NAME	COLOR	LINETYPE	
	0	WHITE	————	CONTINUOUS
	1	RED	————	CONTINUOUS
	3	GREEN	— — —	CENTER
	TEXT	CYAN	————	CONTINUOUS

LINE   (L)
CIRCLE   (C)
TEXT
COPY
ARRAY
FILLET
CHAMFER
DDEDIT

F1	F2	F6	F7	F8	F9
HELP	TEXT/GRAPHICS SCREEN	ABSOLUTE/OFF/POLAR COORDS	ON/OFF GRID	ON/OFF ORTHO	ON/OFF SNAP

CHAPTER 8

COMMANDS

DRAW	DATA	MODIFY
BHATCH	DDIM	DIMEDIT
BPOLY		DIMTEDIT

DIMENSIONING

DIMALIGNED
DIMANGULAR
DIMBASELINE
DIMCONTINUE
DIMLINEAR
DIMOVERRIDE
DIMSTYLE
LEADER

OVERVIEW

The ability to dimension your drawings and add crosshatch patterns will greatly enhance the professional appearance and utility of your work. AutoCAD's dimensioning feature is a complex system of commands, subcommands, and variables that automatically measure objects and draw dimension text and extension lines. With AutoCAD's dimensioning tools and variables, you can create dimensions in a wide variety of formats, and these formats can be saved as styles. The time saved through not having to draw each dimension line by line is very significant.

TASKS

1. Define and save a dimension style.
2. Draw linear dimensions (horizontal, vertical, and aligned).
3. Draw baseline and continued linear dimensions.
4. Draw angular dimensions.
5. Draw center marks and diameter and radius dimensions.
6. Draw leaders to dimension objects.
7. Draw ordinate dimensions.
8. Change dimension variable settings.
9. Change dimension text with DIMEDIT.
10. Add cross-hatching to previously drawn objects.
11. Scale dimensions between model space and paper space.
12. Do Drawing 8–1 ("Tool Block").
13. Do Drawing 8–2 ("Flanged Wheel").
14. Do Drawing 8–3 ("Shower Head").
15. Do Drawing 8–4 ("Nose Adaptor").
16. Do Drawing 8–5 ("Plot Plan").
17. Do Drawing 8–6 ("Panel").

Task 1: Creating and Saving a Dimension Style

Procedure

1. Type "ddim" or select "Dimension Style..." from the Data pull down menu.
2. Give your dimension style a name.
3. From the Family box, select which type of dimension you want to style first.
4. Set Geometry, Format, and Annotation styles.
5. Save settings.
6. Select other dimension types from the Family box and set these.
7. Save settings and exit.

Discussion. Dimensioning in AutoCAD is highly automated and very easy compared to manual dimensioning. In order to achieve a high degree of automation while still allowing for the broad range of flexibility required to cover all dimension styles, the AutoCAD dimensioning system is necessarily quite complex. In the exercises that follow we will guide you through the system, show you some of what is available, and give you a good foundation for understanding how to get what you want out of AutoCAD dimensioning. We will create a basic dimension style and use it to draw standard dimensions and tolerances. We will leave it to you to explore the many variations that are possible.

In Release 13 it is best to begin by defining a dimension style. A dimension style is a set of dimension variable settings that control the text and geometry of all types of AutoCAD dimensions. In previous releases, the default styles for most dimensions would parallel the drawing units set through the Units Control dialogue box or the UNITS command. Release 13 dimensions, however, are quite independent of drawing units and must be set separately. We recommend that you create the new dimension style in your prototype drawing and save it. Then you will not have to make these changes again when you start new drawings.

> To begin this exercise, type "open" or select the Open tool from the Standard toolbar.

This calls the Select File dialogue box.

> In the File Name box, type "b" or select whatever drawing you are using as a prototype.

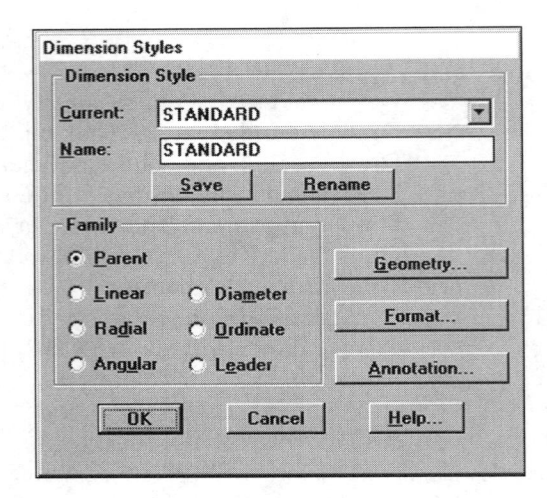

Figure 8-1

When "B" is highlighted you should see the preview image in the black box at the right. This will be blank if your prototype drawing has no objects drawn in it.

> Click on "OK".

This will open your prototype drawing. Now we will make some changes in dimension style settings so that all dimensions showing distances will be presented with two decimal places and angular dimensions will have no decimals.

> Type "ddim" or select "Dimension Style..." from the Data pull down menu.

This will call the Dimension Styles dialogue box shown in *Figure 8-1*. You will see that the current dimension style is called "Standard". Among other things, the AutoCAD Standard dimension style uses four-place decimals in all dimensions, including angular dimensions.

On the left below the Dimension Style name box you will see the Family box with a set of radio buttons for the different types of dimensions. A family is a complete group of dimension settings for the different types of dimensions. The types of dimensions are shown with radio buttons: Linear, Radial, Angular, etc. You can set these individually or use the Parent radio button to set them all at once to a single format. In this exercise we will first use the Parent button to set all types of dimensions to two-place decimals. Then we will set angular dimensions individually to show no decimal places.

But first, let's give the new dimension style a name. We will use "B" to go along with our B prototype.

> Double click in the Name: edit box to highlight the word "Standard".
> Type "B".
> Click on "Save".

This will create the new dimension style and make it current, so that subsequent dimensions will be drawn using the B style.

> Check to make sure that the Parent radio button is selected. It should be by default.

Before moving on, look at the three call boxes at the right. We will make changes only in the Annotation... subdialogue, but you may wish to look at the others while you are here. If you do, simply open the dialogue boxes and cancel them when you are through looking. Geometry... calls a subdialogue that allows you to adjust aspects of the lines, arrowheads, extension lines, and center marks that make up a dimension. Format... allows for

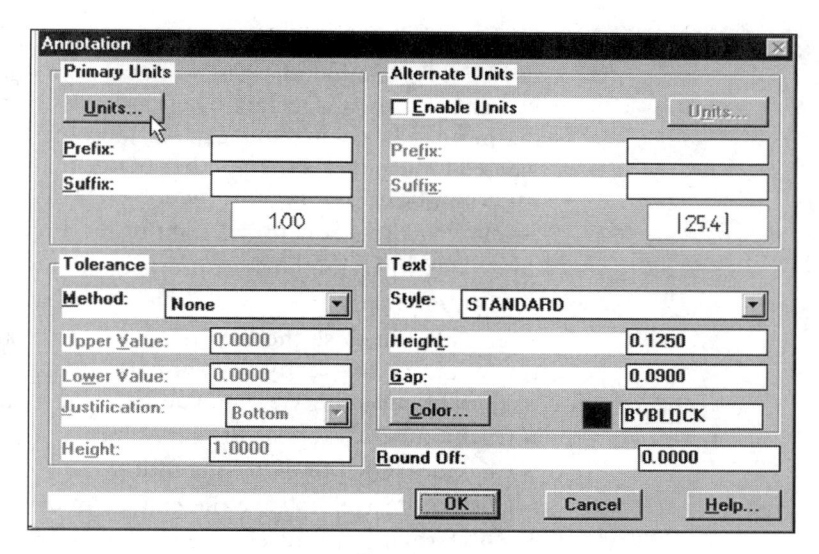

Figure 8-2

changes in the placement of dimension text relative to dimension geometry. Annotation... allows changes in the text and measurements provided for AutoCAD dimensions.

> Click on "Annotation...".

This will call the Annotation dialogue box shown in *Figure 8-2*. There are areas here for adjusting Primary Units, which is what we are interested in, Tolerance, Alternate Units, and Text style. We will explore tolerances later. Alternate units are dimension units that may be automatically presented in parentheses along with primary units. Text styles you know about from the last chapter. Standard will be the default text style for dimensions, but if you have another text style defined in your drawing, you could select it here. Then all dimensions drawn with this dimension style would have the selected text style.

> Click on "Units..." in the Primary Units box on the upper left of the dialogue box.

This will bring up the Primary Units dialogue box shown in *Figure 8-3*. There are adjustments available for units, dimension precision, angular units,

Figure 8-3

and tolerances. The lists under Units and Angles are the same lists used by the UNITS command. The Units should show "Decimal" and the Angles box should show "Decimal Degrees". If for any reason these are not showing in your box you should make these changes now. For our purposes all we need to change is the number of decimal places showing in the Dimension Precision box. By default it will be 0.0000. We will change it to 0.00.
> Click on the arrow to the right of the Precision box.

This will open a list of precision settings ranging from 0 to 0.00000000.
> Click on 0.00.

This will close the list box and show 0.00 as the selected precision. At this point we are ready to complete this part of the procedure by returning to the Dimension Style dialogue box and saving our changes.
> Click on "OK" to exit Primary Units.
> Click on "OK" to exit Annotation.
> Click on "Save" to save the change in dimension precision.

This will save the change in dimension style B. At this point dimension style B has all the AutoCAD default settings except that all dimensions, linear and angular, will be shown as two-place decimals. Next we will set the angular precision separately to 0 places.
> Click on the Angular radio button.
> Click on Annotation ....
> Click on Units....
> Change Dimension Precision to 0 decimal places.

Note that you are only changing angular dimension precision; all other dimensions in the family will keep the parent setting of 0.00.

Be sure to make the change in the same Precision box that you used before. It is the one on the left, under Dimension, not the one on the right under Tolerance. The two boxes are identical and since the Tolerance box is directly under the Angle box it may seem natural to make the change here. But the Tolerance box only changes the precision of tolerances, which we are not using right now. The Dimension box is used to adjust the precision of all types of dimensions.
> Click on "OK" to exit Primary Units.
> Click on "OK" to exit Annotation.
> Click on "Save" to save the changes to B.
> Click on "OK" to exit the Dimension Styles dialogue box.
> Finally, go to the File menu, save prototype drawing B with the new dimension style B, and use New to open a new drawing.

If the new drawing is opened with the B prototype, the B dimension style will be current for the next task.

Task 2: Drawing Linear Dimensions

Procedure

1. Type "Dimlin" or select the Linear Dimension tool from the Dimensioning toolbar.
2. Select an object or show two extension line origins.
3. Show the dimension line location.

Discussion. AutoCAD Release 13 has many commands and features that aid in the drawing of dimensions. Prior to Release 13 all AutoCAD dimension-

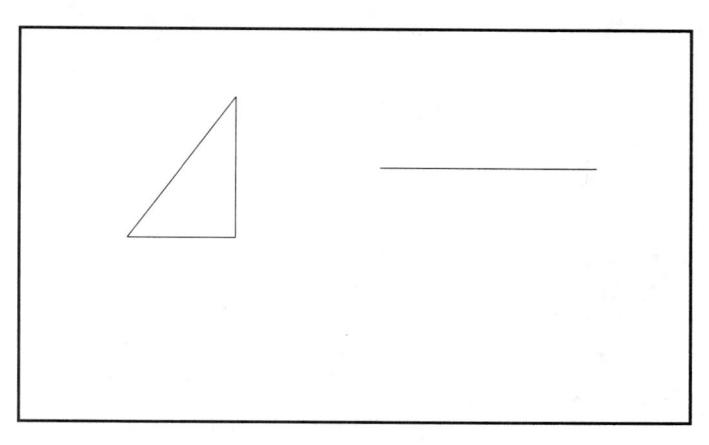

Figure 8-4

ing was handled through the DIM command, which was really a subsystem of commands for different types of dimensions. In Release 13 the DIM subcommands have become commands that can be accessed directly from the command prompt.

In this exercise you will create some basic linear dimensions in the now-current B style.

> To prepare for this exercise, draw a triangle (ours is 3.00, 4.00, 5.00) and a line (6.00) above the middle of the display, as shown in *Figure 8-4*. Exact sizes and locations are not critical.

We will begin by adding dimensions to the triangle.

The new Release 13 dimensioning commands are streamlined and efficient. Their full names, however, are all rather long. They all begin with "dim" and are followed by what used to be the DIM command options. For example: DIMLINEAR, DIMALIGNED, and DIMANGULAR. They do have somewhat shorter aliases, which we will show you as we go along. We encourage you to use the Dimensioning toolbar to avoid typing these names.

We begin by placing a linear dimension below the base of the triangle.

> To open the Dimensioning toolbar, select "Toolbars" and then "Dimensioning" from the Tools pull down menu.

This will open the Dimensioning toolbar shown in *Figure 8-5*.

> Type "dimlin" or select the Linear Dimension tool from the Dimensioning toolbar, as shown in the figure.

All of these methods will bring you into the DIMLINEAR command, with the following prompt in the command area:

First extension line origin or RETURN to select:

There are two ways to proceed at this point. One is to show where the extension lines should begin, and the other is to select the base of the triangle itself and let AutoCAD position the extension lines. In most simple applications the latter method is faster.

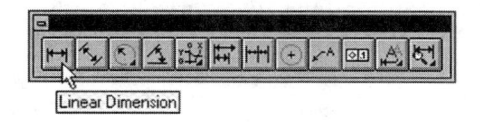

Figure 8-5

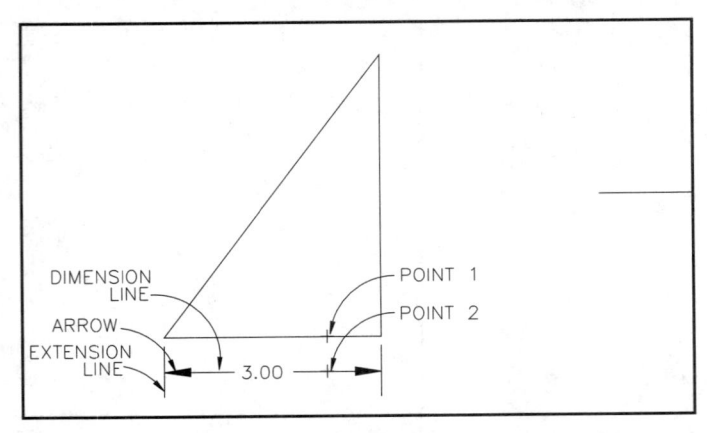

Figure 8-6

> Press Enter (RETURN) to indicate that you will select an object.

AutoCAD will replace the cross hairs with a pickbox and prompt for your selection:

Select object to dimension:

> Select the horizontal line at the bottom of the triangle, as shown by point 1 in *Figure 8-6*.

AutoCAD immediately creates a dimension, including extension lines, dimension line, and text, that you can drag out away from the selected line. AutoCAD will place the dimension line and text where you indicate, but will keep the text centered between the extension lines. The prompt is as follows:

Dimension line location
(Text/Angle/Horizontal/Vertical/Rotated):

In the default sequence, you will simply show the location of the dimension. If you wish to alter the text you can do so using the "Text" option, or you can change it later with a command called DIMEDIT. "Angle", "Horizontal", and "Vertical" allow you to specify the orientation of the text. Horizontal text is the default for linear text. "Rotated" allows you to rotate the complete dimension, so that the extension lines move out at an angle from the object being dimensioned (text remains horizontal).

NOTE: If the dimension variable "dimsho" is set to 0 (off), you will not be given an image of the dimension to drag into place. The default setting is 1 (on), so this should not be a problem. If, however, it has been changed in your drawing, type "dimsho" and then "1" to turn it on again.

> Pick a location about .50 below the triangle, as shown by point 2 in *Figure 8-6*.

Bravo! You have completed your first dimension.

Notice that our figure and others in this chapter are shown zoomed in on the relevant object for the sake of clarity. You may zoom or not as you like.

At this point, take a good look at the dimension you have just drawn to see what it consists of. As in *Figure 8-6*, you should see the following components: two extension lines, two "arrows," a dimension line on each side of the text, and the text itself.

Notice also that AutoCAD has automatically placed the extension line origins a short distance away from the triangle base (you may need to zoom

Chap. 8

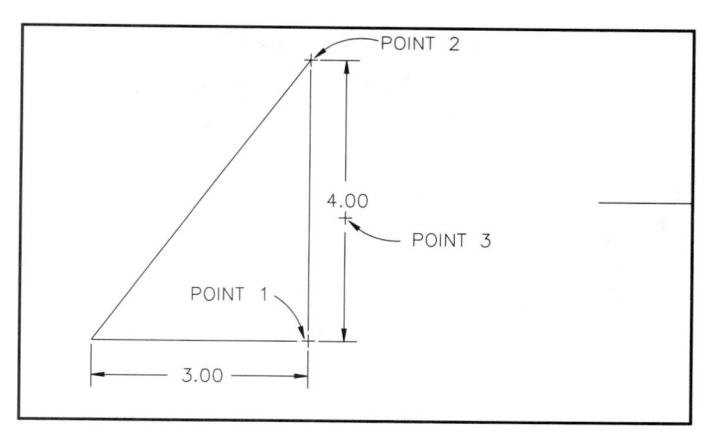

233

Figure 8-7

in to see this). This distance is controlled by a dimension variable called "dimexo", which can be changed in the Dimension Style dialogue box under Geometry. It is one of many variables that control the look of AutoCAD dimensions. Another example of a dimension variable is "dimasz", which controls the size of the arrows at the end of the extension lines. Variables are discussed in Task 7.

Next, we will place a vertical dimension on the right side of the triangle. You will see that DIMLINEAR handles both horizontal and vertical dimensions.

> Repeat the DIMLINEAR command.

You will be prompted for extension line origins as before:

First extension line origin or RETURN to select:

This time we will show the extension line origins manually.
> Pick the right-angle corner at the lower right of the triangle, point 1 in *Figure 8-7*. AutoCAD will prompt for a second point:

Second extension line origin:

Even though you are manually specifying extension line origins, it is not necessary to show the exact point where you want the line to start. AutoCAD will automatically set the dimension lines slightly away from the line as before, according to the setting of the dimexo dimension variable.
> Pick the top intersection of the triangle, point 2 in the figure.

From here on, the procedure will be the same as before. You should have a dimension to drag into place, and the following prompt:

Dimension line location
(Text/Angle/Horizontal/Vertical/Rotated):

> Pick a point .50 to the right of the triangle, point 3 in the figure.

Your screen should now include the vertical dimension, as shown in *Figure 8-7*.

Now let's place a dimension on the diagonal side of the triangle. For this we will need the DIMALIGNED command.

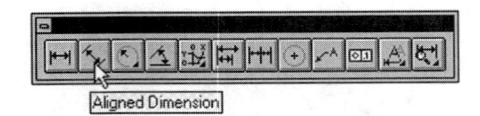

234   Part II Text, Dimensions, and Other Complex Entities

Figure 8-8

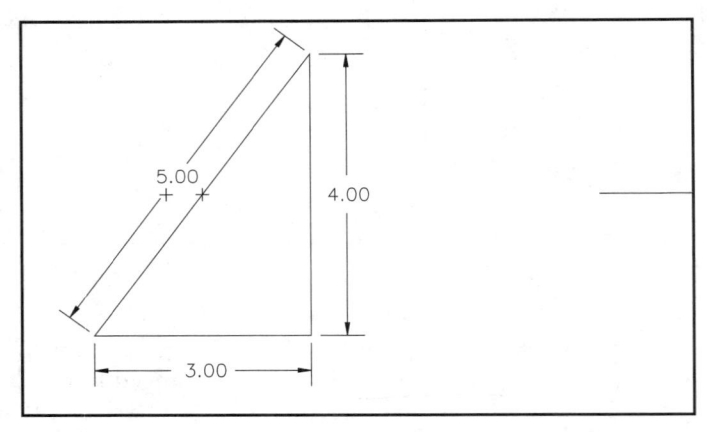

Figure 8-9

> Type "dimali" or select the Aligned Dimension tool from the Dimensioning toolbar as shown in *Figure 8-8*.

> Press Enter (RETURN), indicating that you will select an object.

AutoCAD will give you the pickbox and prompt you to select an object to dimension.

> Select the hypotenuse of the triangle.

> Pick a point approximately .50 above and to the left of the line.

Your screen should resemble *Figure 8-9*. Notice that AutoCAD retains horizontal text in aligned and vertical dimensions as the default.

Task 3: Drawing Multiple Linear Dimensions—Baseline and Continue

Procedure

1. Draw an initial linear dimension.
2. Type "dimbase" or "dimcont" or select the Baseline or Continue Dimension tool from the Dimensioning toolbar.
3. Pick a second extension line origin.
4. Pick another second extension line origin...
5. Press Enter to exit the command.

Discussion. DIMBASELINE and DIMCONTINUE allow you to draw multiple linear dimensions more efficiently. In baseline format you will have a series of dimensions all measured from the same initial origin. In continued dimensions there will be a string of dimensions in which the second extension line for one dimension becomes the first extension for the next.

> To prepare for this exercise, be sure that you have a 6.00 horizontal line as shown in *Figure 8-4* at the beginning of Task 2. Although the figures in this exercise will show only the line, leave the triangle in your drawing, because we will come back to it in the next task.

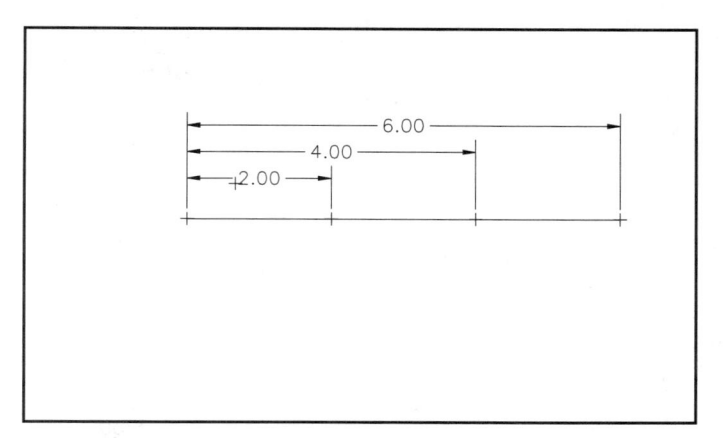

Figure 8-10

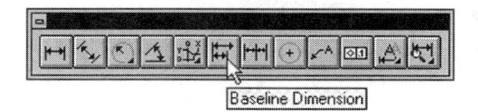

Figure 8-11

In this exercise we will be placing a set of baseline dimensions on top of the line and a continued series on the bottom. In order to use either Baseline or Continue, you must have one linear dimension already drawn on the line you wish to dimension. So we will begin with this.

> Select the Linear Dimension tool from the Dimensioning toolbar.
> Pick the left end point of the line for the origin of the first extension line.
> Pick a second extension origin 2.00 to the right of the first, as shown in *Figure 8-10*.
> Pick a point .50 above the line for dimension text.

You should now have the initial 2.00 dimension shown in *Figure 8-10*. We will use DIMBASELINE to add the other dimensions above it.

> Type "dimbase" or select the Baseline Dimension tool from the Dimensioning toolbar, as shown in *Figure 8-11*.

AutoCAD uses the first extension line origin you picked again and prompts for a second:

Second extension line origin or RETURN to select:

> Pick a point 4.00 to the right of the first extension line (in other words, 4.00 from the left end of the 6.00 line).

The second baseline dimension shown in *Figure 8-10* should be added to your drawing. We will add one more. AutoCAD leaves you in the DIMBASELINE command so that you can add as many baseline dimensions as you want.

> Pick the right end point of the line.

Your screen should resemble *Figure 8-10*. See how quickly AutoCAD draws dimensions? As long as you have your dimension style defined the way you want it, this can make dimensioning go very quickly.

AutoCAD will still be prompting for another second extension line origin. We will need to press Enter twice to exit DIMBASELINE.

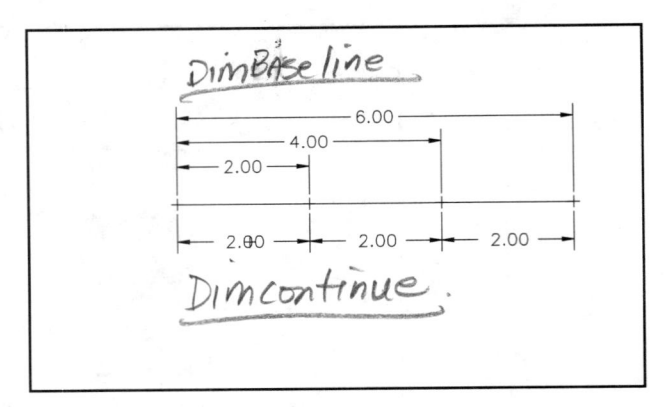

236   Part II Text, Dimensions, and Other Complex Entities

Figure 8-12

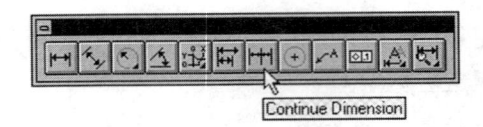

Figure 8-13

> Press Enter to end extension line selection.
    The first time you press Enter, AutoCAD will show you a new prompt:

Select base dimension:

This prompt would allow you to begin a new series of baseline dimensions from a dimension other than the last one you drew. Bypassing this prompt will take you back to command prompt.
> Press Enter to exit DIMBASELINE.

Continued Dimensions

Now we will place three continued dimensions along the bottom of the line, as shown in *Figure 8-12*. The process is very similar to the baseline process so you should need little help at this point.

> Begin by using DIMLINEAR to place an initial horizontal dimension .50 below the line, showing a length of 2.00 from the left end, as shown in *Figure 8-12*.
> Type "dimcont" or select the Continue Dimension from the Dimensioning toolbar, as shown in *Figure 8-13*.
> Pick a second extension line origin 2.00 to the right of the last extension line.
    Be sure to pick this point on the 6.00 line, otherwise the extension line will be left hanging.
> Pick another second extension line at the right end of the line.
> Press Enter to end the continued series.
> Press Enter to exit DIMCONTINUE.
    Done!

Task 4: Drawing Angular Dimensions

Procedure

1. Type "Dimang" or select the Angular Dimension tool from the Dimensioning toolbar.

Chap. 8 237

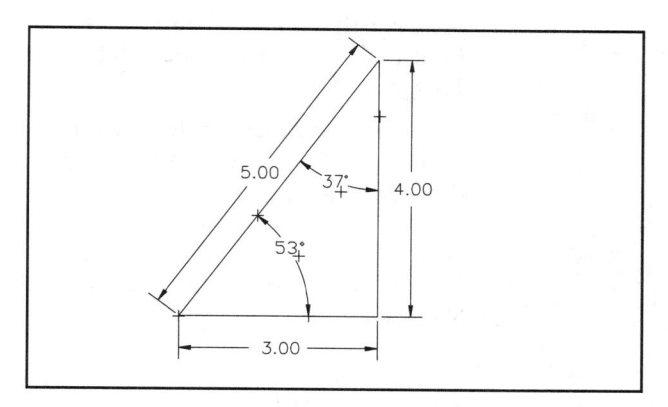

Figure 8-14

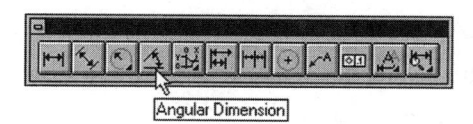

Figure 8-15

2. Select two lines that form an angle.
3. Pick a dimension location.

Discussion. Angular dimensioning works much like linear dimensioning, except that you will be prompted to select objects that form an angle. AutoCAD will compute an angle based on the geometry that you select (two lines, an arc, part of a circle, or a vertex and two points) and construct extension lines, a dimension arc, and text specifying the angle.

For this exercise we will return to the triangle and add angular dimensions to two of the angles as shown in *Figure 8-14*.

> Type "dimang" or select the Angular Dimension tool from the Dimensioning toolbar, as shown in *Figure 8-15*.

The first prompt will be:

Select arc, circle, line, or RETURN:

The prompt shows that you can use angular dimensions to specify angles formed by arcs and portions of circles as well as angles formed by lines. If you press Enter (RETURN), you can specify an angle manually by picking its vertex and a point on each side of the angle. We will begin by picking lines, the most common use of angular dimensions.

> Select the base of the triangle.

You will be prompted for another line:

Second line:

> Select the hypotenuse.

As in linear dimensioning, AutoCAD now shows you the dimension lines and lets you drag them into place (assuming dimsho is on). The prompt asks for a dimension arc location and also allows you the option of changing the text or the text angle.

Dimension arc line location (Text/Angle):

> Move the cursor around to see how the dimension may be placed and then pick a point between the two selected lines, as shown by the blip in *Figure 8-14*.

The lower left angle of your triangle should now be dimensioned, as in *Figure 8-14*. Notice that the degree symbol is added by default in angular dimension text.

We will dimension the upper angle by showing its vertex, using the RETURN option.

> Repeat DIMANGULAR.
> Press Enter (RETURN).

AutoCAD prompts for an angle vertex.

> Point to the vertex of the angle at the top of the triangle.

AutoCAD prompts:

First angle endpoint:

> Pick a point along the hypotenuse.

In order to be precise this should be a snap point. The most dependable one will be the lower left corner of the triangle.

AutoCAD prompts:

Second angle end point:

> Pick any point along the vertical side of the triangle.

There should be many snap points on the vertical line, so you should have no problem.

> Move the cursor slowly up and down within the triangle.

Notice how AutoCAD places the arrows outside the angle when you approach the vertex and things get crowded. Also notice that if you move outside the angle, AutoCAD switches to the outer angle.

> Pick a location for the dimension arc as shown in *Figure 8-14*.

Angular Dimensions on Arcs and Circles

You can also place angular dimensions on arcs and circles. In both cases AutoCAD will construct extension lines and a dimension arc. When you dimension an arc with an angular dimension, the center of the arc becomes the vertex of the dimension angle, and the end points of the arc become the start points of the extension lines. In a circle the same format is used, but the dimension line origins are determined by the point used to select the circle and a second point, which AutoCAD prompts you to select. These options are illustrated in *Figure 8-16*.

Chap. 8   **239**

ANGULAR DIM ON CIRCLE   ANGULAR DIM ON ARC

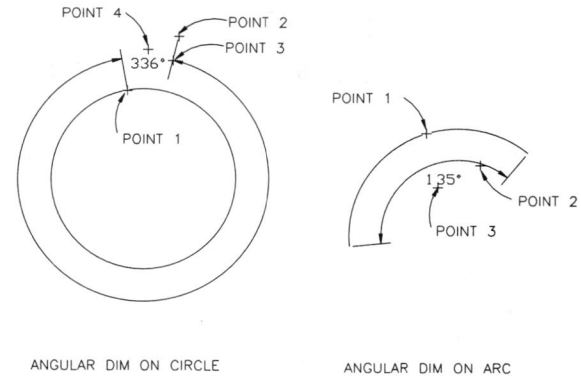

Figure 8-16

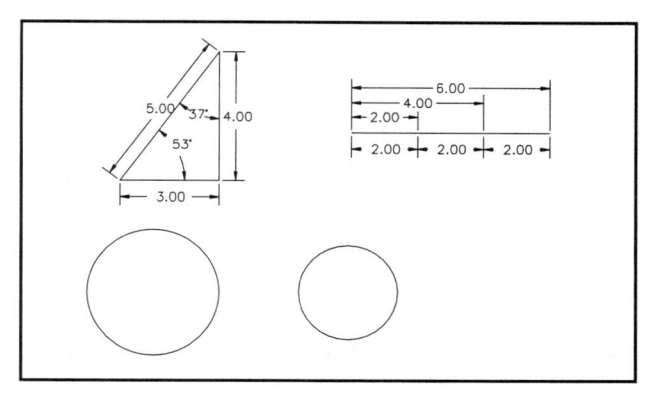

Figure 8-17

Task 5: Dimensioning Arcs and Circles

Procedure

1. Type "dimdia" or "dimrad" or select the Radius or Diameter Dimension tool from the Radial dimension flyout on the Dimensioning toolbar.
2. Pick the arc or circle at the point where you want the dimension line or leader to start.
3. Type text or press Enter.
4. Pick a leader line end point location.

Discussion. The basic process for dimensioning circles and arcs is as simple as those we have already covered. It can get tricky, however, when AutoCAD does not place the dimension where you want it. Text placement can be controlled by adjusting dimension variables. In this exercise we will create a center mark and some diameter and radius dimensions.

> To prepare for this exercise, draw two circles at the bottom of your screen, as shown in *Figure 8-17*. The circles we have used have radii of 2.00 and 1.50.

Although the remaining figures in this section will show the circles only, keep the triangle and the line in your drawing, because they will be used again in Task 7.

> Type "dimcenter" or select the Center Mark tool from the Dimensioning toolbar, as shown in *Figure 8-18*.

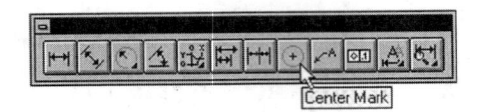

240 Part II Text, Dimensions, and Other Complex Entities

Figure 8-18

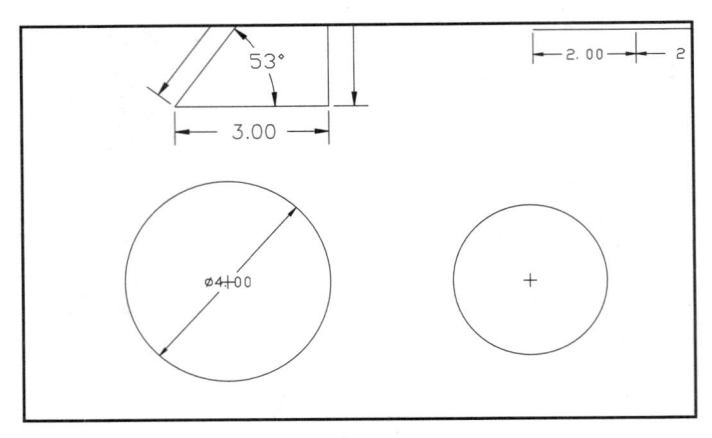

Figure 8-19

You cannot use "dimcen" as the command name because that is the name of the dimension variable that controls the style of the center mark.

Center marks resemble blips, but they are actual lines and will appear on a plotted drawing. They are the simplest of all dimension features to create and are created automatically as part of some radius and diameter dimensions.

AutoCAD prompts:

Select arc or circle:

> Select the smaller circle.

A center mark will be drawn in the 1.50 circle, as shown in *Figure 8-19*. You may want to REDRAW your display to see the difference between blips and center marks. Blips are in white and if you are drawing on layer 1, your center mark will be red.

NOTE: A different type of center mark can be produced by changing the dimension variable "dimcen" from .09 to −.09. The result is shown in the dimension variables chart, *Figure 8-22*, later in this chapter. You may recall that this technique was introduced previously in Drawing 4–4.

Now we will add the diameter dimension shown on the larger circle in *Figure 8-19*.

> Type "dimdia" or select the Diameter Dimension tool from the Radial dimension flyout on the Dimensioning toolbar, as shown in *Figure 8-20*.

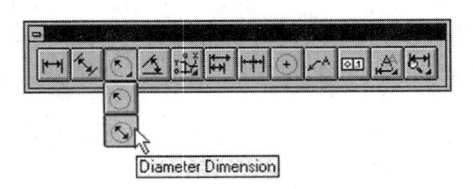

Figure 8-20

Chap. 8   **241**

AutoCAD will prompt:

Select arc or circle:

> Select the larger circle.

AutoCAD will show a diameter dimension with the dimension text at the center of the circle and ask for Dimension line location. The Text and Angle options allow you to change the dimension text or put it at an angle. If you move your cursor around you will see that you can position the dimension line anywhere around the circle.

> Pick a dimension position so that your screen resembles *Figure 8-19*.

Notice that the diameter symbol prefix is added automatically by default.

The placement of diameter dimensions is an important consideration. Diameter dimensions are often shown as this one is, at the center of the circle. This can be problematic if other dimensions, text, or objects are in the way. Release 13 offers substantial flexibility through the grip editing system and the DIMTEDIT command.

Using Grips to Move Dimension Text

Suppose you want to move the dimension text "4.00" away from the center of the circle, but keep it within the extension lines. This is easily done using grips.

> Pick the diameter dimension just drawn.

Dimensions are block entities and can be selected by picking any part of the block. Blocks are collections of objects treated as one entity. They are covered in Chapter 10.

You will know when you have picked the dimension by looking for the three blue grips boxes. You will find that the grip stretch mode works just like the move mode when you are working with a block.

> Pick the box at the center near the dimension text.

After picking the grip box you will find that you can move both the dimension line and the text around inside the circle. Actually you can move outside the circle as well. If you do this, AutoCAD will place the text outside and draw a leader to it from the dimension line.

> Pick a point above and to the right of the center to produce the text placement shown in *Figure 8-21*. Ortho must be off to do this.

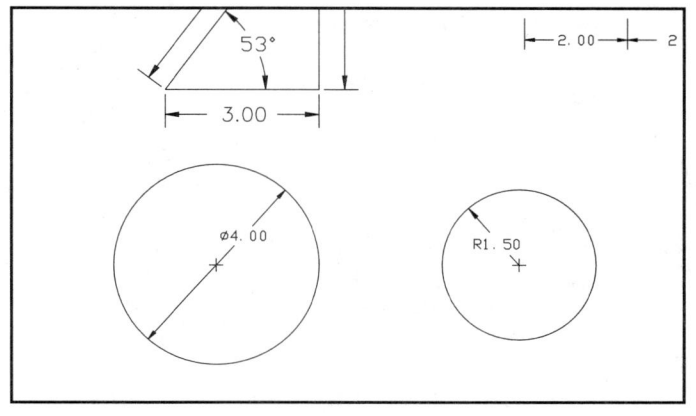

Figure 8-21

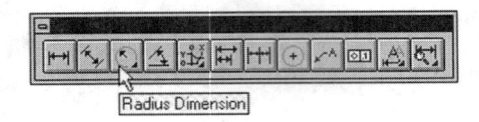

Figure 8-22

The DIMTEDIT command can be used to accomplish the same purpose, following this procedure:

1. Type "Dimted".
2. Select a dimension.
3. Enter a new text location.

DIMTEDIT also allows you to rotate the text angle.

Radius Dimensions

The procedures for radius dimensioning are exactly the same as those for diameter dimensions. We will quickly draw a radius dimension on the smaller circle.

> Type "Dimrad" or select the Radius Dimension tool from the Radial Dimension flyout on the Dimensioning toolbar, as shown in *Figure 8-22*.
> Select the 1.50 (smaller) circle.
> Move the cursor outside and around the circle.

Wherever you move, the dimension will remain within the circle. If you had drawn a smaller circle so that the dimension text would not easily fit inside, AutoCAD would place it outside using a leader.

> Pick a point to complete the dimension as shown in *Figure 8-21*.

The "R" for radius is added automatically.

Task 6: Dimensioning with Leaders

Procedure

1. Type "lead" or select the Leader tool from the Dimensioning toolbar.
3. Select a start point.
4. Select an end point.
5. Select another end point...
6. Type dimension text.

Discussion. Leaders are useful for attaching annotation to all kinds of objects. They may be used to dimension objects in crowded areas of a drawing and to attach paragraph text to an object. Unlike other dimension formats in which you select an object or show a length, a leader is simply a line or series of lines with an arrow at the end to connect an object with its annotation. The LEADER command does not recognize and measure a selected object, so you will need to know the dimension text you want to use *before* you begin.

In this exercise we will create two leaders with associated text. One will be as simple as we can make it and the other will be more complex.

> Type "lead" or select the Leader tool from the Dimensioning toolbar, as shown in *Figure 8-23*.

Chap. 8   243

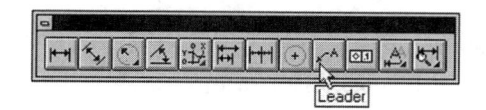

Figure 8-23

AutoCAD will prompt you for a point as in the LINE command:

From point:

Usually you will want the leader arrow to start on the object, not offset as an extension line would be. This suggests that an object snap may be in order.
> Type "nea", or select the Snap to Nearest tool from the Object Snap flyout on the Standard toolbar.

This specifies that you want to snap to the nearest point on the circle. You will see that the pickbox has been added to the cross hairs.
> Position the cross hairs so that the upper right side of the 1.50 radius circle crosses the aperture and press the pick button.

The leader will be snapped to the circle and a rubber band shown extending to the cross hairs. AutoCAD will prompt for a second point just as in the LINE command:

To point:

> Pick a second point for the leader up and to the right of the first point, as shown on the smaller circle in *Figure 8-24*.

After the first point has been entered, the prompt will change:

To point (Format/Annotation/Undo)<Annotation>:

The default option "Annotation" will allow you to begin creating the text you want. We will save the other options for the next leader.
> Press Enter to indicate that you are ready to create the annotation.
AutoCAD prompts:

Annotation (or RETURN for options):

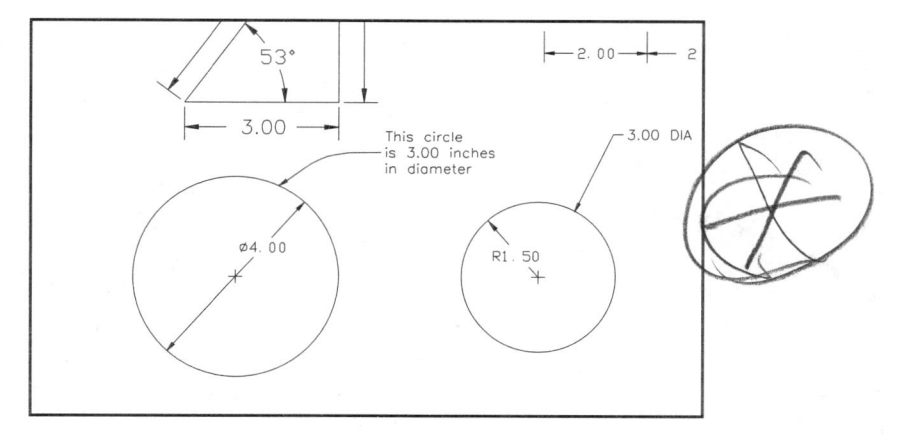

Figure 8-24

244   Part II Text, Dimensions, and Other Complex Entities

We will not use the other options in this exercise, but will discuss them shortly.
> Type "3.00 DIA" and press Enter.

After you have entered this text, AutoCAD will prompt you for more:

MText:

This shows that if you continue entering text, it will be added beneath the first line in MTEXT paragraph form. We will try this with our next leader. You should be aware that all text created in the LEADER command is created as Mtext and can therefore be edited using all the tools available for Mtext, including the DDMODIFY command, width boundaries, attachment options, and the Edit Mtext dialogue box for editing contents.
> Press Enter to complete the command.

The annotated leader illustrated on the smaller circle in *Figure 8-24* should be added to your drawing. If you look closely, you will notice that a short horizontal line segment is added automatically to "connect" the text to the leader.

Next we will create a more complex curved leader attached to three lines of Mtext.

> Repeat the "Leader" command.
> Type "Nea" or select the Nearest object snap tool again.
> Pick a leader start point on the upper right side of the larger, 2.00 radius circle.
> Pick a second point for the leader at about 45 degrees up and to the right of the first point.

After the second point has been entered, the prompt will change to:

To point (Format/Annotation/Undo)<Annotation>:

This time we will use the "Format" option to draw a curved leader. Leaders made up of a number of straight line segments or curves are often useful for maneuvering around other objects in a crowded drawing.
> Type "f" or select "Format" from the screen menu, if available.

AutoCAD issues this prompt:

Spline/STraight/Arrow/None/<Exit>:

"Spline" is the option we want. "STraight" (you must type "st" to distinguish this option from spline) would switch us back to straight segments. "Arrow" would draw an arrow at the start point of the leader, but this is done by default. "None" would suppress the arrow.
> Type "s" to create a spline curve.
> Move the cursor slowly around the second point.

You will see that the line now bends and curves to the new point you are about to select.
> Pick the third point slightly above and to the right of the second to create a curved leader similar to the one in *Figure 8-24*.
> Press Enter to end the leader at this point.

AutoCAD will now prompt for an annotation:

Annotation (or RETURN for options):

The options available if you were to press Return here are as follows: "Tolerance" calls up a tolerance symbol dialogue box so that you can add tolerancing symbols to your annotation; "Copy" lets you copy previously created text and attach it to the end of your leader; "Block" lets you attach a block to your leader (blocks are discussed in Chapter 10); "None" exits the command without adding any annotation; "Mtext" is the default. Pressing Enter here would call up the Edit Mtext dialogue box for Mtext paragraph creation.

For our purposes we can simply begin entering text. This will also put us into Edit Mtext

> Type "This circle" and press Enter.

You are now in the Edit Mtext dialogue.

The multiple lines we create will be automatically justified and attached in the middle to the leader as illustrated.

> Type "is 3.00 inches" and press Enter.

> Type "in diameter".

> Click on "OK" to complete the command.

Your screen should now resemble *Figure 8-24*.

Task 7: Drawing Ordinate Dimensions

Procedure

1. Define a coordinate system with origin at the corner of the object to be dimensioned.
2. Type "Dimord" or select the Ordinate Dimension tool from the Dimensioning toolbar.
3. Select a location to be dimensioned.
4. Pick a leader end point.
5. Press Enter or change dimension text.

Discussion. Ordinate, or datum line, dimensions are another way to specify linear dimensions. They are used to show multiple horizontal and vertical distances from a single point or the corner of an object. Since these fall readily into a coordinate system, it is efficient to show these dimensions as the x and y displacements from a single point of origin. AutoCAD will ordinarily specify points based on the point (0,0) on your screen, therefore it will be necessary to move the origin so that DIMORDINATE will show the appropriate dimension text. Drawing 7-4 in the last chapter was dimensioned in this way.

> To prepare for this exercise, erase the baseline and continued dimensions created in Task 3. This is a good opportunity to apply the "remove" option in the ERASE command, as follows:

1. Enter the ERASE command.
2. Select all of the baseline and continued dimensions with a window or crossing box. This also will select the line.
3. Type "r" or select "Remove".
4. Select the line only.
5. Press Enter to carry out the command.

The dimensions will be erased, but not the line, since it has been removed from the selection set.

> Now draw a 3.00 vertical line at the left end of the 6.00 horizontal line, as shown in *Figure 8-25*.

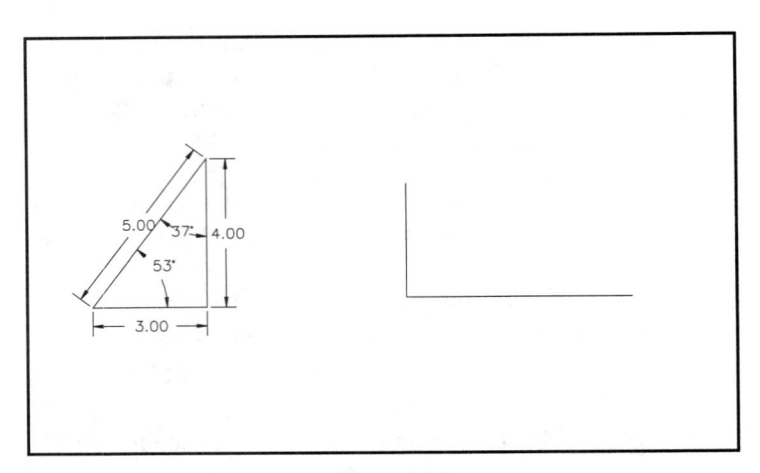

Figure 8-25

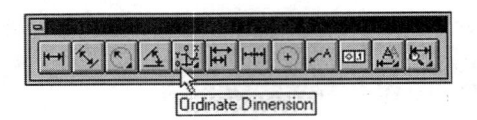

Figure 8-26

We will use ordinate dimensions to specify a series of horizontal and vertical distances from the intersection of the two lines. First, we need to define a temporary User Coordinate System with its origin at the intersection. User coordinate systems are crucial in 3D drawing and are explored in depth in Chapter 12.

> Type "Ucs" or select "Set UCS" from the View pull down menu.
> Type "o" or select "Origin".

Specifying a new coordinate system by moving the point of origin is the simplest of many options in the UCS command. AutoCAD prompts:

Origin point <0,0,0>:

> Pick the intersection of the two lines.

If you move your cursor to the intersection and watch the coordinate display, you will see that this point is now read as (0.00,0.00).

> Type "dimord" or select the Ordinate Dimension from the Dimensioning toolbar, as shown in *Figure 8-26*.

AutoCAD prompts:

Select Feature:

In actuality, all you will do is show AutoCAD a point and then an end point for a leader. Depending on where the end point is located relative to the first point, AutoCAD will show dimension text for either an *x* or a *y* displacement from the origin of the current coordinate system.

> Pick a point along the 6.00 line, 1.00 to the right of the intersection, as shown in *Figure 8-27*.

AutoCAD prompts:

Leader endpoint (Xdatum/Ydatum/Text):

Chap. 8 247

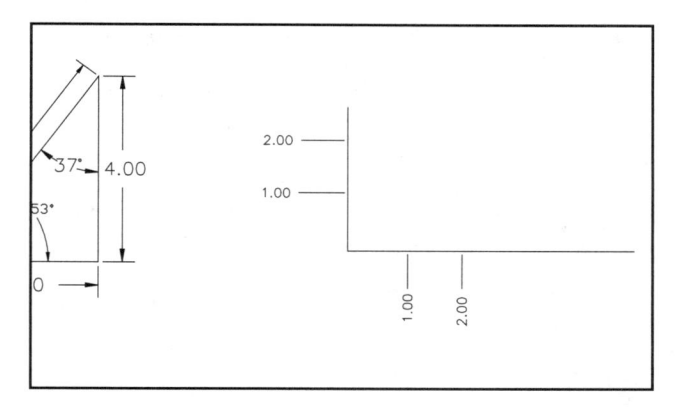

Figure 8-27

You can manually indicate whether you want the *x* or *y* coordinate by typing "x" or "y". However, if you choose the end point correctly, AutoCAD will pick the right coordinate automatically. You can also provide your own text, but that would defeat the purpose of setting up a coordinate system that will give you the distances from the intersection of the two lines.

> Pick an endpoint .5 below the line, as shown in *Figure 8-27*.

Your screen should now include the 1.00 ordinate dimension shown in the figure.

> To complete this exercise, repeat the ordinate option three times and add the other ordinate dimensions shown.

When you are done, you should return to the world coordinate system. This is the default coordinate system and the one we have been using all along.

> Type "Ucs" or select "Set UCS" and then "World" from the View pull down menu.

> If you are typing, type "w" or press Enter to return to the world coordinate system.

This will return the origin to its original position at the lower left of your screen.

Task 8: Changing and Overriding Dimension Variables

Procedure

1. Type a variable name.
2. Type a new value.
3. Enter the DIMSTYLE command.
4. Type "a" or select "apply".
5. Select dimensions to apply new variable value to.

or

1. Type "dimover" or select "Overrid:" from the screen menu under "MOD DIM".
2. Type a dimension variable name.
3. Type a new value.
4. Select dimensions you want to alter.

Discussion. As you know from Task 1, you can save and restore dimension styles using the Dimension Style dialogue box. When a new style is created it becomes current and all subsequent dimensions will be drawn using the new style.

Sometimes, however, you may not want to create a whole new style in order to draw one or two dimensions that are slightly different from the others in your drawing. Or, you may want to create a new style and apply it to some previously drawn dimensions. The first case is handled using a dimension override, the DIMOVERRIDE command. The second is done by changing dimension variables and then using the "apply" option in the DIMSTYLE command. We will demonstrate both, beginning with an override, and then look at a complete listing of all the dimension variables and their current settings.

> Type "dimover" or select "Overrid:" from the screen menu under "MOD DIM".

AutoCAD prompts:

Dimension variable to override (or Clear to remove overrides)

We can create some very easily visible changes by altering the scale of a dimension using the dimscale variable.
> Type "dimscale".

AutoCAD gives you the current value and prompts for a change:

Current value <1.00> New value:

> Type "2".

AutoCAD continues to prompt for variables to override, so that we can change more than one at a time.
> Press Enter.

Now that we have provided a new temporary dimension scale, we need to select dimensions that we want to show this scale. We can use all of our usual selection methods here including windowing and the all option. In this case we will change one dimension only.
> Select the 3.00 linear dimension at the base of the triangle.
> Press Enter to end object selection.

You will see that the 3.00 dimension text is redrawn twice as large, as shown in *Figure 8-28*. This alteration in dimension style is a one-time-only override. The change in dimscale has not been retained in memory, and any new dimensions drawn would have dimscale of 1.00. To make a more permanent change in style we could go to the dialogue box as before. Changes made in this way, however, will be applied to all dimensions previously drawn

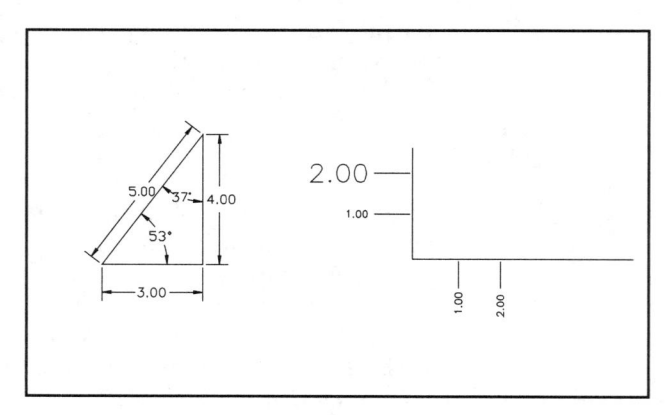

Figure 8-28

in the current dimension style. By changing a dimension variable at the command line, we can also gain the option of applying the change to selected dimensions only.

In order to change a variable at the command line, just type its name, and then enter the new value.

> Type "dimscale".

AutoCAD prompts:

New value for DIMSCALE <1.00>:

> Type "2".

This brings you back to the command prompt. The variable has been changed in the current dimension style, as you would see by opening the Dimension Style dialogue box, or by creating a new dimension. In order to apply the change to previously drawn dimensions you need the DIMSTYLE command.

> Type "dimstyle" or select "DimStyl:" under "MOD DIM" on the screen menu.

The DIMSTYLE command is not the same as the DDIM command, which calls the Dimension Style dialogue box. It will list variables that have been changed and then prompt with options for other types of changes. You may have to press F2 to see this:

dimension style overrides:
DIMSCALE 2.00
Dimension Style Edit (Save/Restore/STatus/Variables/Apply/?) <Restore>:

Do not be confused by the use of the word override here. There is a difference between one-time overrides like the one we did using the DIMOVERRIDE command, and running overrides like this one which are retained in the current style until the style is restored to its original configuration.

We will use the "apply" option to apply the change in dimscale to one of our previously drawn dimensions.

> Type "a" or select "Apply".

AutoCAD needs to know which dimensions we want to apply the change to:

Select objects:

> Select the 2.00 top ordinate dimension.
> Press Enter to end object selection.

The 2.00 dimension text will be enlarged as shown in *Figure 8-28*.

While we are on the DIMSTYLE command, use it to look at a list of all the dimension variables and their current settings. Setting dimension variables is easy, but the sheer number (58 in Release 13) can be overwhelming. The chart included in this chapter (*Figure 8-29*) will show you some of the most commonly used variables. By studying it carefully you will gain a better sense of the possibilities. For more information, see the *AutoCAD User's Guide*.

> Repeat DIMSTYLE.
> Type "st" or select "Status".

You will see 58 variables listed with their current settings and a phrase describing the effect of each setting. You will have to press Enter (RETURN) twice to get to the end of the list. As you may notice, these variables

COMMONLY USED DIMENSION VARIABLES

VARIABLE	DEFAULT VALUE	APPEARANCE	DESCRIPTION	NEW VALUE	APPEARANCE
dimaso	on	All parts of dim are one entity	Associative dimensioning	off	All parts of dim are separate entities
dimscale	1.00	├─2.00─┤	Changes size of text & arrows, not value	2.00	├─2.00─┤
dimasz	.18	▶	Sets arrow size	.38	▶
dimcen	.09	+	Center mark size and appearance	−.09	⊕
dimdli	.38		Spacing between continued dimension lines	.50	
dimexe	.18		Extension above dimension line	.25	
dimexo	0.06		Extension line origin offset	.12	
dimtp	0.00	1.50	Sets plus tolerance	.01	$1.50^{+0.01}_{-0.00}$
dimtm	0.00	1.50	Sets minus tolerance	.02	$1.50^{+0.00}_{-0.02}$
dimtol	off	1.50	Generate dimension tolerances (dimtp & dimtm must be set) (dimtol & dimlim cannot both be on)	on	$1.50^{+0.01}_{-0.02}$
dimlim	off	1.50	Generate dimension limits (dimtp & dimtm must be set) (dimtol & dimlim cannot both be on)	on	1.51 1.48
dimtad	off	├─1.50─┤	Places text above the dimension line	on	├─1.50─┤
dimtxt	.18	1.50	Sets height of text	.38	1.50
dimtsz	.18	├─1.50─┤	Sets tick marks & tick height	.25	├─1.50─┤
dimtih	on	1.50	Sets angle of text When off rotates text to the angle of the dimension	off	1.50
dimtix	off	Ø0.71 +	Forces the text to inside of circles and arcs. Linear and angular dimensions are placed inside if there is sufficient room	on	Ø0.71

Figure 8-29

affect the same characteristics shown in the Dimension Style dialogue box. In fact when you make changes there you are actually changing variable settings. As you glance over this list, it also would be a good time to look at *Figure 8-29* to get a sense of what a few dimension variables can do in the way of changing the look of dimensions.

Finally, before moving on, use the "restore" option to remove the change in dimscale.

> Type "r", select "Restore" or press Enter, since Restore is the default option. AutoCAD prompts:

?/Enter dimension style name or RETURN to select dimension:

> Type "b" or the name of your current dimension style.
This will restore the original values of the B dimension style.

Task 9: Changing Dimension Text with Dimedit

Procedure

1. Type or select "Dimedit".
2. Type "n" or select "New".
3. Enter the new text.
4. Select the dimension you want to change.

Discussion. There is one more dimension command you should know about before we move on to hatching. DIMEDIT allows you to change the text of previously drawn dimensions. You can add text or change the wording or numbers in the text, alter the rotation or obliquing angle of the text, or return text to its "home" position after it has been moved.

> Type or select "Dimedit" (under "MOD DIM" on the screen menu).
AutoCAD prompts with options:

Dimension Edit (Home/New/Rotate/Oblique) <Home>:

> Type "n" or select "New".
This indicates that you want to enter new text. Accordingly, AutoCAD opens the Edit Mtext box and waits for you to enter text. You will see two arrows in the edit box (<>). Whatever you type will be added to the existing dimension text. If you type to the left of the arrows, you will add text to the left, if you type to the right, text will be added to the right.
We will change the 5.00 aligned dimension to read 5.00 mm.
> Click on the right side of <> so that the flashing cursor moves to the right.
> Type "mm".
The text will appear in the edit box.
> Click on "OK" or press Enter to return to the drawing.
AutoCAD prompts for objects to receive the new text:

Select Objects:

> Select the 5.00 aligned dimension on the hypotenuse of the triangle.
> Press Enter to end object selection.
The text will be redrawn, as shown in *Figure 8-30*. This command is very convenient when all you want to do is add text to a dimension.

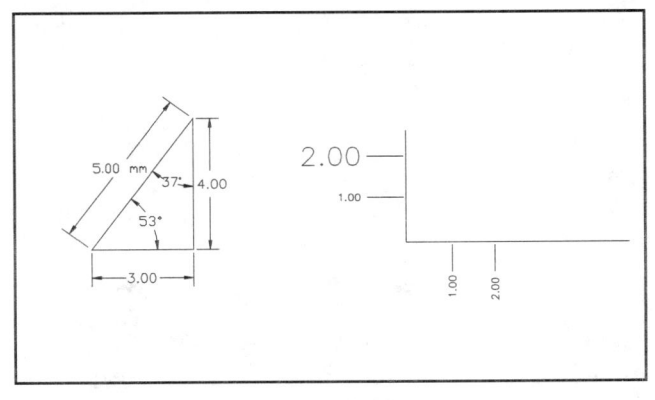

Figure 8-30

Task 10: Using the BHATCH Command

Procedure

1. Type "bhatch" or select the Hatch tool from the Draw toolbar.
2. Select a pattern.
3. Define style parameters.
4. Define boundaries of object to be hatched.

Discussion. Automated hatching is another immense timesaver. Release 13 includes two commands for use in cross hatching. Of the two, BHATCH and HATCH, BHATCH is more powerful and easier to use. BHATCH differs from HATCH in that it automatically defines the nearest boundary surrounding a point you have specified. The HATCH command requires you to manually specify each segment of the boundary. In other words, with BHATCH you can point to the area you want to hatch and AutoCAD will go looking for its boundaries, while with HATCH you select the boundaries and AutoCAD hatches what's inside.

> To prepare for this exercise, clear your screen of all previously drawn objects and then draw three rectangles, one inside the other, with the word "TEXT" at the center, as shown in *Figure 8-31*.

> Type "bhatch" or select the Hatch tool from the Draw toolbar, as shown in *Figure 8-32*.

Hatch on the toolbar actually enters the BHATCH command. Whether typed or selected, BHATCH always calls the Boundary Hatch dialogue box shown in *Figure 8-33*. At the top of the box you will see the Pattern Type box. Before we can hatch anything we need to specify a pattern. Later we will show AutoCAD what we wish to hatch using the Pick Points method.

The Pattern type currently shown in the image box is a predefined pattern. There are about 68 of these patterns. But we will first use a simple user-defined pattern of straight lines on a 45 degree angle.

> Click on the arrow to the right of "Predefined".

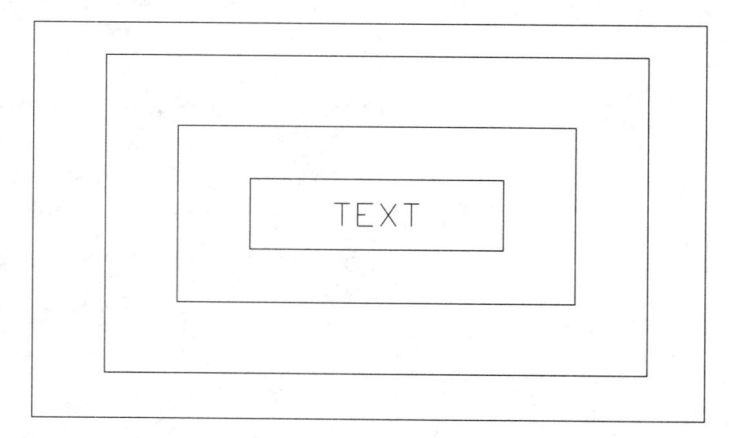

Figure 8-31

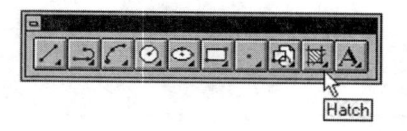

Figure 8-32

Chap. 8 253

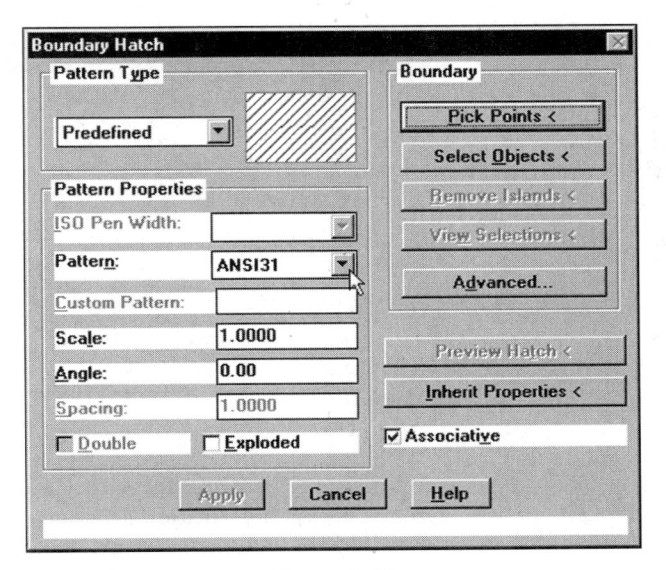

Figure 8-33

    This opens a list including Predefined, User-defined and Custom patterns.
> Click on "User-defined".

    When you select a user-defined pattern there will be nothing shown in the image box.

    When you create a user-defined pattern you will need to specify an angle and a spacing.
> Double click in the Angle edit box, and then type "45".
> Double click in the Spacing edit box, and then type ".5".

    The remaining boxes in this area are Double and Exploded. Double hatching creates double hatch lines running perpendicular to each other according to the specified angle. Hatch patterns are created as a single entity within the specified boundary. If they are created with Exploded checked, each line of the pattern will be a separate entity.

    Next we need to show AutoCAD where to place the hatching. To the right in the dialogue box is the Boundary area. The first two options are "Pick Points" and "Select Objects". Using the "Pick Points" option, you can have AutoCAD locate a boundary when you point to the area inside it. The "Select Objects" option can be used to create boundaries in the way that the HATCH command works, by selecting entities that lie along the boundaries.
> Click on "Pick Points <".

    The dialogue box will disappear temporarily and you will be prompted as follows:

                        Select internal point:

> Pick a point inside the largest, outer rectangle, but outside the smaller rectangles.

    AutoCAD displays these messages, though you may have to press F2 to see them:

                        Selecting everything visible...
                        Analyzing the selected data...
                        Analyzing internal islands...

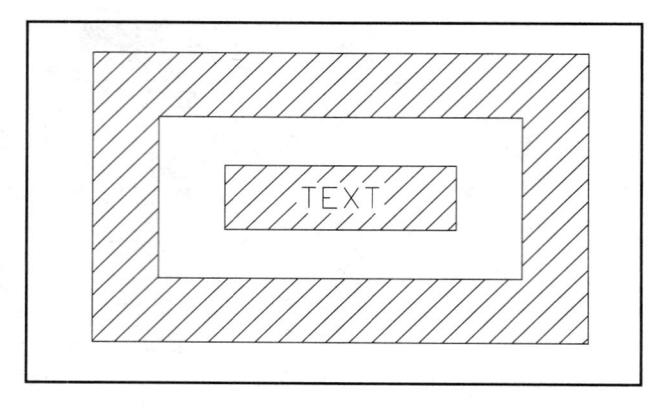

Figure 8-34

In a large drawing this process can be time consuming, as the program searches all visible entities to locate the appropriate boundary. When the process is complete, all of the rectangles and the text will be highlighted. It will happen very quickly in this case.

AutoCAD continues to prompt for internal points so that you can define multiple boundaries. Let's return to the dialogue box and see what we've done so far.

> Press Enter to end internal point selection.

The dialogue box will reappear. You may not have noticed, but several of the options that were "grayed out" before are now accessible. We will make use of the "Preview Hatch" option. This allows us to preview what has been specified without leaving the command, so that we can continue to adjust the hatching until we are satisfied.

> Click on "Preview Hatch <".

Your screen should resemble *Figure 8-34*, except that you will have to move the Boundary Hatch - Continue box away from the center of the display as we have done. This demonstrates the "normal" style of hatching in which multiple boundaries are hatched or left clear in alternating fashion, beginning with the outermost boundary and working inward. You can see the effect of the other styles by looking at the Advanced Options dialogue box. Notice that BHATCH has recognized the text as well as the other interior boundaries.

> Click on Continue to return to the Boundary Hatch dialogue box.

You could complete the hatching operation at this point by clicking on Apply, but let's take a look at a few more details while we are here.

> Click on "Advanced...".

This calls the Advanced Options dialogue box shown in *Figure 8-35*. In the middle you will see the hatching style area. There are three basic options that determine how BHATCH will treat interior boundaries. "Normal" is the current style.

> Click on the arrow to the right of "Normal".

You will see the other two styles listed. "Normal" hatches alternate areas moving inward, "Outer" hatches only the outer area, and "Ignore" hatches through all interior boundaries. There is an image box that shows an example of the current style, as shown in *Figure 8-35*.

> Click on "Outer" and watch the image box.

It now shows the "Outer" style in which only the area between the outermost boundary and the first inner boundary is hatched.

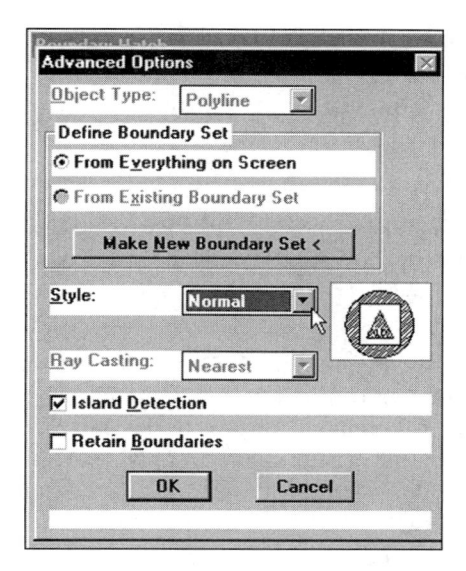

Figure 8-35

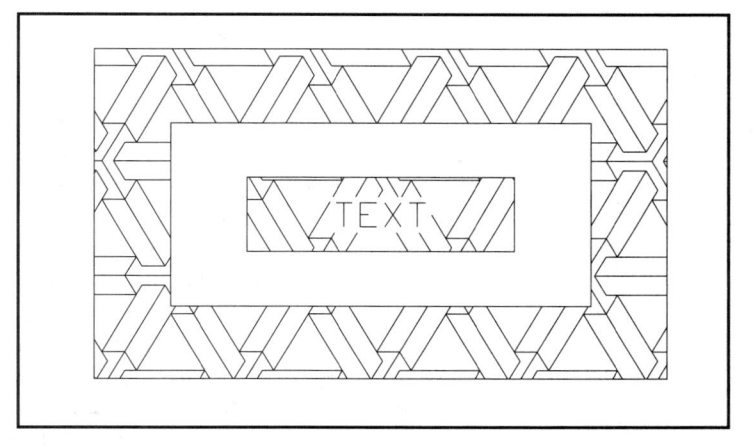

Figure 8-36

> Click on the arrow again and then on "Ignore" and watch the image box.

In the "Ignore" style, all interior boundaries are ignored and the entire area including the text is hatched.

You can see the same effects in your own drawing, if you like, by clicking on "OK" and then "Preview Hatch" after changing from the "Normal" style to either of the other styles. Of course, the three styles are indistinguishable if you do not have boundaries within boundaries to hatch.

> When you are done experimenting, you should select "Normal" style hatching again and return to the Boundary Hatch dialogue box.

Now let's take a look at some of the fancier stored hatch patterns that AutoCAD provides.

> Click on the arrow to the right of "User-Defined" and select "Predefined".
> Now click on the arrow to the right of "Pattern" in the Pattern box.

This opens a long list of AutoCAD's predefined hatch patterns. To produce the hatched image in *Figure 8-36*, we chose the Escher pattern.

> Move down the list until you come to "Escher".
> Select "Escher".

As soon as the pattern is selected you will see it illustrated in the pattern type image box.

To produce the figure we also used a larger scale in this hatching.

> Double click in the "Scale:" edit box and type "1.5".
> Double click in the "Angle:" edit box and type "0".
> Click on "Preview Hatch <".

Your screen should resemble *Figure 8-36*, but remember this is still just the preview. When you are through adjusting hatching, you have the choice of canceling the BHATCH command, so that no hatching is added to your drawing, or completing the process by clicking on "Apply". Apply will confirm the most recent choices of boundaries, patterns, and scales, making them part of your drawing.

> Click on Continue.
> Click on "Apply" to exit BHATCH and confirm the hatching.

Other Advanced Options and the BPOLY Command

There are a number of worthwhile options and techniques that we have not explored in this exercise. Some of these options are available from the Advanced Options subdialogue box. For your information we offer the following notes:

1. When AutoCAD locates a boundary, it temporarily creates a polyline entity that completely outlines the boundaried area. A polyline (Chapter 9) is a single entity, which may be comprised of many straight and curved line segments. By default, the temporary polyline borders used by BHATCH are deleted after hatching is drawn. They may be retained for other uses, however, by checking the Retain Boundaries box in the Advanced Options dialogue box.
2. Using the BPOLY command, the same procedures that are used to create polyline hatch boundaries can be used to create polyline outlines independent of any hatching operation. BPOLY calls a dialogue box similar to the Advanced Options dialogue, but with no intervening steps through the BHATCH dialogues.
3. In very complex drawings it may be efficient to limit the number of entities AutoCAD needs to consider when looking for boundaries. This can be done using the Make New Boundary Set option. The boundary set does not need to be precise. By including all the entities in one portion of a drawing, for example, you could still substantially reduce the magnitude of AutoCAD's task. To specify a boundary set, click on "Make New Boundary Set" in the Advanced Options dialogue box.
4. "Ray casting" is an alternative method AutoCAD can use to search out boundaries. The default method is called "island detection". If you deselect Island Detection you will see that the first option for ray casting is called "nearest". In this method AutoCAD begins by looking at the nearest entity that could be part of a border. Other options force the program to look in a specified direction relative to the coordinate system. You will see these options listed as +X, −X, +Y, and −Y on a pop up list under "Ray Casting:" in "Advanced Options". For most purposes island detection is all you will

need. The other methods can speed up the boundary-making process in tight, complex situations. See the *AutoCAD User's Guide* for further information.

Task 11: Scaling Dimensions Between Paper Space and Model Space

Procedure

1. Use ZOOM XP to set scale in viewports.
2. Set Dimtxt to a desirable text size.
3. Set Dimscale to 0.
4. Create dimensions in model space.

Discussion. There are numerous scaling problems that arise when you are working with viewports and paper space. The ZOOM XP feature introduced in Chapter 6 allows you to create precise scale relationships between model space images and paper space units. Numerous other issues arise when you begin to use text and dimensions in paper space multiple-viewport drawings. We will begin by illustrating some of the problems.

> To begin this task, you should have the multiple-view layout of Drawing 6-4 on your screen. If this drawing is unavailable, any similar multiple-viewport drawing will do, though it may be more difficult to follow the steps given here if you are looking at a different drawing.

NOTE: This exercise assumes that the variable Dimscale is initially set to 1, and that Dimtxt is set to 0.18. These are default settings. If they have been changed in your drawing, you will not get the exact results shown here. Also, we assume that your current text style has a height setting of 0, meaning that it is variable. This is a default setting as well.

Draw Text in Paper Space

There are certain basic principles that are useful in adding text and dimensions to a multiple-view drawing in paper space. The first is that most text be created in paper space. To see why, try entering some text in paper space and model space as follows.

> First, check to see that tilemode is off (0) and that you are in paper space (look for the paper space icon). If necessary, type "Tilemode" and then "0" to set tilemode. Type "ps" to enter paper space.

> Type "Dtext" or select the Dtext tool from the Text flyout on the Draw toolbar.

> Pick a start point outside any of the viewports. Our text begins about 3 units over the center of the left viewport, as shown in *Figure 8-37*.

> Type "1" for a text height of one unit. This assumes that you are using the D-size paper space limits from Chapter 6. If not, you will have to adjust for your own settings.

> Press Enter for 0 rotation.

> Type "Drawing 6-4".

> Press Enter twice.

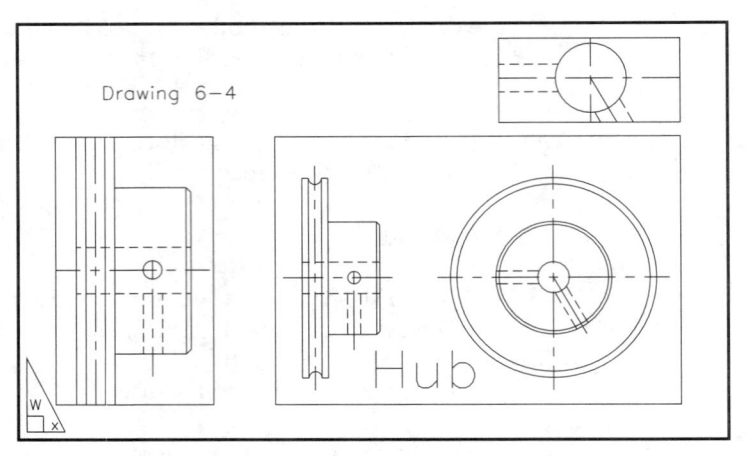

Figure 8-37

Your screen should have text added as shown in *Figure 8-37*.
> Type "ms" to switch to model space.
> Make the largest viewport active.
> Type "Dtext".
> Pick a start point below the two views, as shown.
> Press Enter to retain a height of 1.00 units.
> Press Enter for 0 rotation.
> Type "Hub".

Your screen should resemble *Figure 8-37*.

What has happened here? Why is the "Hub" drawn twice as big as "Drawing 6-4" (or some other size, depending on your limit and zoom factor settings)? Do you remember the zoom xp scale factor we used in this viewport? This viewport is enlarged by two times paper space. So any text you draw inside it will be enlarged by a factor of two as well. If you want, try drawing text in either of the other two viewports. You will find that text in the left viewport is magnified four times the paper space size and text in the uppermost viewport is magnified six times.

You could compensate for these enlargements by dividing text height by factors of 2, 4, and 6, but that would be cumbersome. Furthermore, if you decided to change the zoom factor at a later date, you would have to recreate any text drawn within the altered viewport. Otherwise, your text sizes in the overall drawing would be inconsistent.

For this reason, it is recommended that text be drawn in paper space.

Dimension Model Space Objects in Model Space

When it comes to dimensions, however, the rule is just the opposite. Dimensions should be kept in model space with the objects they refer to. The main reason is that dimensions in AutoCAD are associative. They will change when the objects they document are changed. This is true if they are in the same space. It will not be true if a model space object is dimensioned in paper space.

The rule is simple, but it requires some manipulation of variables to maintain consistency in dimension text size. As we proceed, we will also encounter some layering problems.

Chap. 8   259

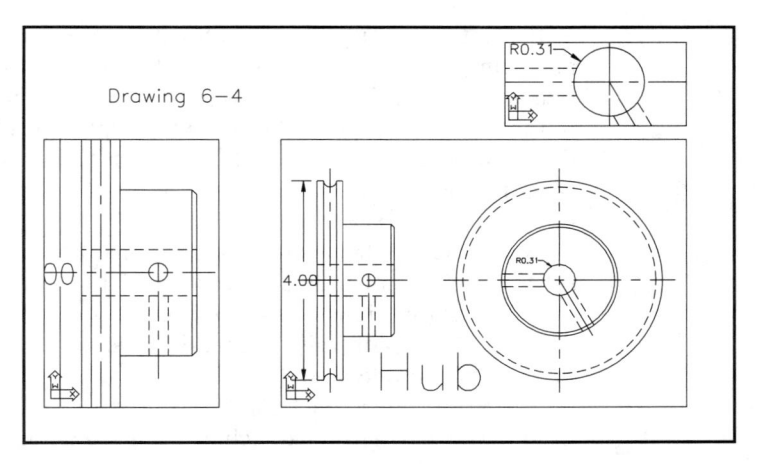

Figure 8-38

> Check to be sure that you are in model space before beginning. If not, type "ms".
> Make the "dim" layer current.
> Make the large, central viewport active.
> Type "Dimlin" or select the Linear Dimension tool from the Dimensioning toolbar.
> Pick the top of the left side view for the first extension line origin.
> Pick the bottom of the same side for the second extension line origin.
> Pick a dimension line location about .25 to the left of the object. This may seem a little close, but it will help to illustrate an important point.
> Press Enter to accept the dimension text (4.00).
   Your screen should resemble *Figure 8-38*.

Two things to notice: The dimension looks fine in the active viewport, but it is duplicated in the enlargement on the left at twice the size and may be cut off. This illustrates our two main problems. We want all our dimensions to appear the same size, and we do not want dimensions intended for one viewport to appear in others. The first problem is a scaling issue, while the second involves layering. We will pursue scaling in this task and leave layer control for the next exercise.
   To get more of a flavor of what's going on, try one more dimension.

> Make the upper viewport active.
> Type "Dimrad" or select the Radius Dimension tool from the Dimensioning toolbar.
> Select the circle in the upper viewport.
> Pick a dimension line location that allows you to see the dimension text clearly.
> Look at the size of the dimension.
      Obviously it is way too big.
> Undo (U) the radial dimension.

In fact, the dimension shown in the upper viewport was three times as big as the dimension in the central viewport and twice as big as the duplicate dimension in the left viewport. As you may have guessed, the dimensions in each viewport are being magnified just as the text was previously. The default dimension text size, set to .18 by the dimtxt variable, is being doubled (2 times paper size) to .36 in the central viewport. So the text "4.00" has a height of .36 paper space units in that viewport. But in the left viewport it has a height of .72 units (4 times paper space). The radial dimension in the upper viewport had a height of 1.08 units, or 6 times the dimtxt setting.

AutoCAD has a simple fix for this problem. When the variable dimscale is set to 0 instead of the default value of 1 or some other explicit scaling factor, dimension text in viewports is adjusted according to the model space to paper space zoom factor. With this setting, dimensions in all viewports can be maintained at the same desirable size.

For our purposes, let's say we are satisfied with the .36 size we see in the central viewport. In order to achieve this size in all viewports simultaneously, we will need to set dimscale to 0 and dimtxt to .36.

> Type "dimtxt".

AutoCAD shows you the current value and asks for a new value.

> Type ".36".

> Type "dimscale".

> Type "0".

Now let's try drawing the radial dimension in the upper viewport again.

> Type "Dimrad" or select the Radius Dimension tool from the Dimensioning toolbar.
> Select the circle in the upper viewport.
> Position the dimension as shown in *Figure 8-38*.

Wonderful, except that now we have a tiny duplicate of the radial dimension showing in the central viewport. This is another example of the layering problem, which we will explore next.

Manipulating Layer Visibility in Multiple Viewports

The duplicate dimensions in your drawing are just one example of the need to control layer visibility separately in different viewports. This can be done using the **VPLAYER** command.

> You should be in model space to begin. If you're not, type "ms".

Our goal will be to make dimensions intended for the central viewport invisible in other viewports and vice-versa. In order to accomplish this, we need at least two dimension layers. If you wanted independent dimensions in all three viewports, you would need three layers.

> Make the upper viewport active.

> Open the Viewport Layer Control dialogue box from the Data pull down menu.

> Type "Dim-u" (for dimensions in the upper viewport) in the edit box.

> Click on "New".

> Select the new "DIM-U" layer from the layer list.

> Use the Set Color subdialogue to give it color number 4, cyan.

This should be the same color as your regular DIM layer.

> Click on "OK" to return to the main dialogue.

> Click on "OK" to exit the dialogue box.

Now that we have two dimension layers we can freeze dimensions in the viewports where they are not wanted. But first we must move some of the previously drawn dimensions to the newly created layer.

> Type or select "Chprop".

> Select the radial dimension.

> Press Enter to end object selection.

> Type "La" or select "LAyer".

> Type "Dim-u" for the new layer.

> Press Enter to exit the CHPROP command.

Now the 4.00 vertical dimension and the 0.31 radial dimension are on different layers, although they appear the same. We need to freeze DIM in the top and left viewports, and freeze DIM-U in the central viewport.

> Type "Vplayer" or select Viewport Layer Controls from the Data pull down menu.

If you are typing, AutoCAD will prompt as follows:

?/Freeze/Thaw/Reset/Newfrz/Vpvisdflt:

If you use the menu you will see the same options listed. "?" or the "List" option will give you a list of layers currently frozen in a selected viewport. "Freeze" and "Thaw" will allow you to freeze and thaw layers in selected viewports. "Reset" sets layers in selected viewports to default visibility settings. These defaults are established using the "Default Visibility" option. The "New Freeze" option provides an efficient sequence for controlling layers in multiple viewports. With "New Freeze" you create a new layer which is frozen in all viewports. Then you can thaw the new layer in selected viewports where visibility is desired.

For our purposes we only need the freeze option.

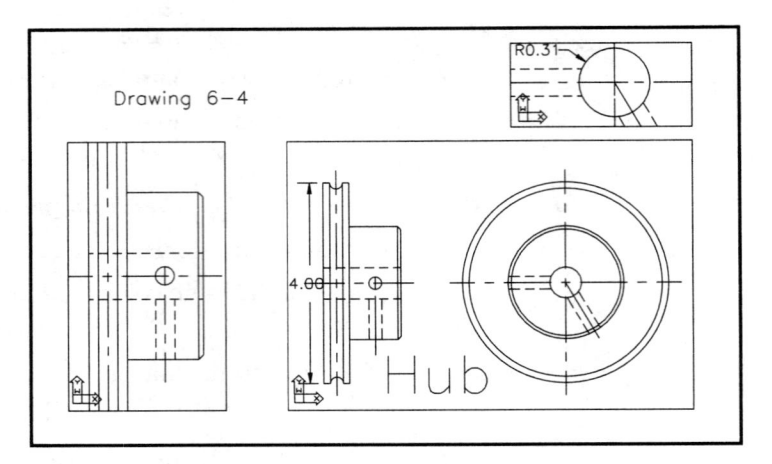

Figure 8-39

> Type "f" or select "Freeze".

> Type "Dim".

> Type "s" or select "Select".

AutoCAD temporarily switches to paper space so that you can select viewport entities.

> Pick any point on the border of the left viewport.

> Pick any point on the border of the top viewport.

> Press Enter to end object selection.

We also need to freeze DIM-U in the central viewport.

> Type "f" or select "Freeze".

> Type "dim-u".

> Type "s" or select "Select".

> Select any point on the border of the central viewport.

> Press Enter to end object selection.

> Press Enter to exit the VPLAYER command.

Your screen will be regenerated to resemble *Figure 8-39*.

Turning Viewport Borders Off

We have used the borders of our viewports as part of our plotted drawing in this drawing layout. Frequently, you will want to turn them off. In a typical three-view drawing, for example, you do not draw borders around the three views.

In multiple-viewport paper space drawings the visibility of viewport borders is easily controlled by putting the viewports on a separate layer and then turning the layer off before plotting. You can make a "border" layer, for example, and make it current while you create viewports. Or you can use CHPROP to place viewports on the border layer later.

Tasks 12, 13, 14, 15, 16, and 17

Dimensioning and Hatching are two of AutoCAD's most powerful features. They will do vast amounts of work for you and perform very well if used correctly. In general, you will complete other drawing procedures first and save hatching and dimensioning until the end. Dimensions and hatch patterns should also be allotted separate layers of their own so that they can be turned on and off at will.

Both dimensioning and hatching can be time consuming and require careful attention. But remember, in most applications your drawings will be of little use until the dimensions and appropriate hatching are clearly and correctly placed.

DRAWING 8-1: TOOL BLOCK

In this drawing the dimensions should work well without editing. The hatch is a simple user-defined pattern used to indicate that the front and right views are sectioned views.

DRAWING SUGGESTIONS

GRID = 1.0
SNAP = .125
HATCH line spacing = .125

> As a general rule, complete the drawing first, including all cross-hatching, then add dimensions and text at the end.

> Place all hatching on the hatch layer. When hatching is complete, set to the dim layer and turn the hatch layer off so that hatch lines will not interfere when you select lines for dimensioning.

> Zooming in on the area being hatched is advisable to see that the whole boundary is defined clearly.

> The section lines in this drawing can be easily drawn as leaders in the DIM command. Set the "dimasz" variable to .38 first. Check to see that ortho is on, then begin the leader at the tip of the arrow, and make a right angle as shown. After picking the other end point of the leader, press Enter to bring up the "Annotation (or RETURN for options)" prompt. Then press Enter (RETURN) to call up options. Type "n" for None so that you will have no text.

> You will need to set the dimtix variable to "on" in order to place the 3.25 diameter dimension at the center of the circle in the top view, and "off" to create the leader style diameter dimension in the front section.

> Remember multiple lines of text can be drawn with the LEADER command and will be centered on the Leader.

Chap. 8

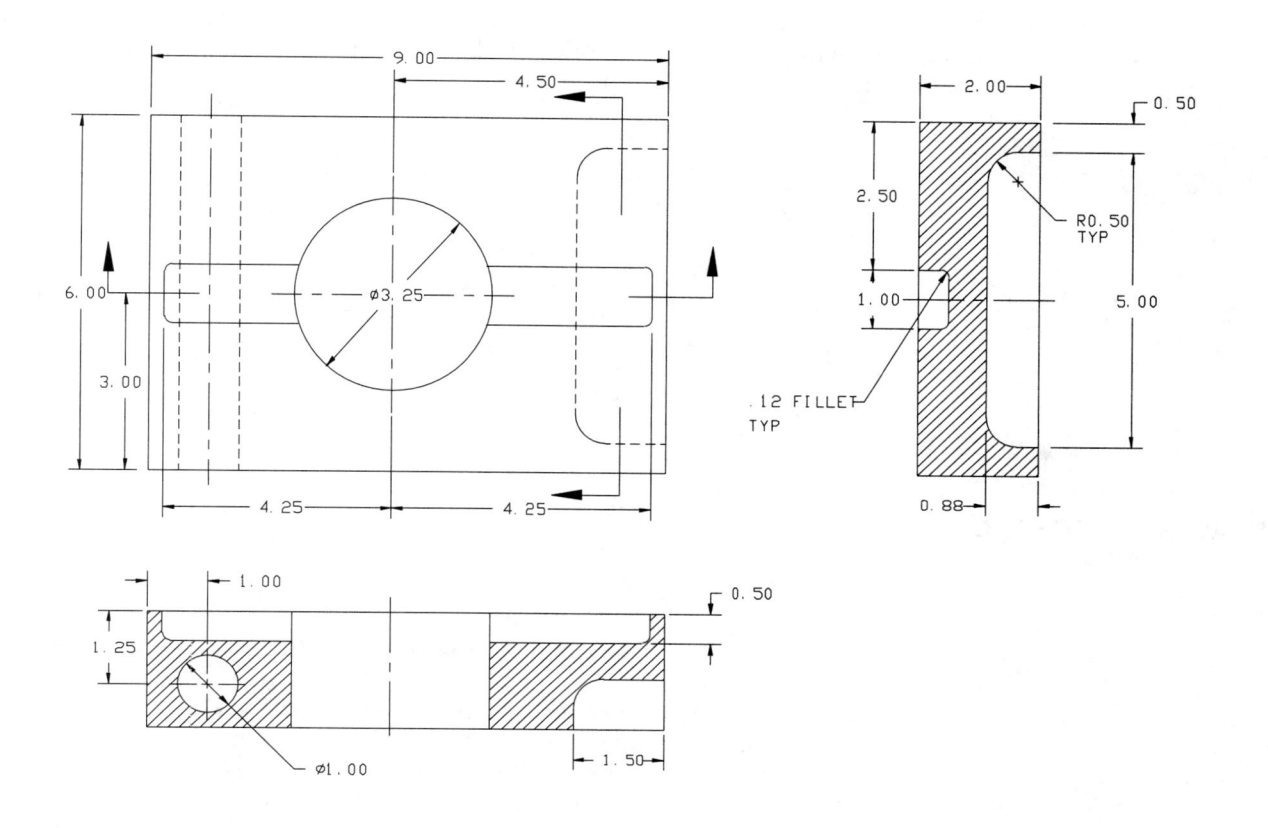

TOOL BLOCK
Drawing 8-1

LAYERS	NAME	COLOR	LINETYPE
	0	WHITE	CONTINUOUS
	1	RED	CONTINUOUS
	2	YELLOW	HIDDEN
	3	GREEN	CENTER
	TEXT	CYAN	CONTINUOUS
	HATCH	BLUE	CONTINUOUS
	DIM	MAGENTA	CONTINUOUS

LINE (L)
CIRCLE (C)
HATCH
BREAK
FILLET
ZOOM (Z)

F1 HELP
F2 TEXT/GRAPHICS SCREEN
F6 ABSOLUTE/OFF/POLAR COORDS
F7 ON/OFF GRID
F8 ON/OFF ORTHO
F9 ON/OFF SNAP

DRAWING 8-2: FLANGED WHEEL

Most of the objects in this drawing are straightforward. The keyway is easily done using the TRIM command. Use DIMTEDIT or grips to move the diameter dimension as shown in the reference following.

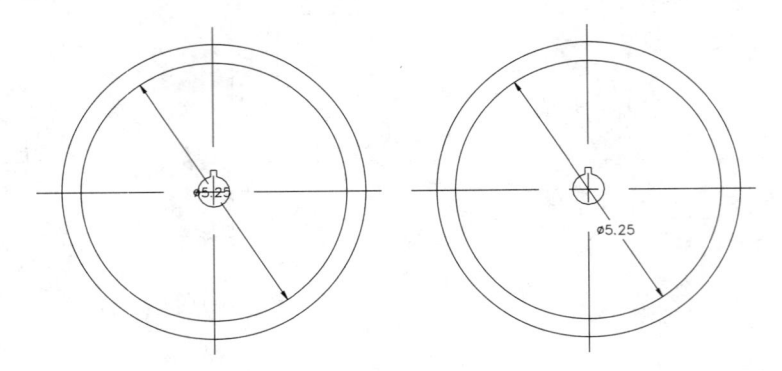

DRAWING SUGGESTIONS

GRID = .25
SNAP = .0625
HATCH line spacing = .50

> You will need a .0625 snap to draw the keyway. Draw a .125 × .125 square at the top of the .63 diameter circle. Drop the vertical lines down into the circle so they may be used to TRIM the circle. TRIM the circle and the vertical lines, using a window to select both as cutting edges.

> Remember to set to layer "hatch" before hatching, layer "text" before adding text, and layer "dim" before dimensioning.

Chap. 8

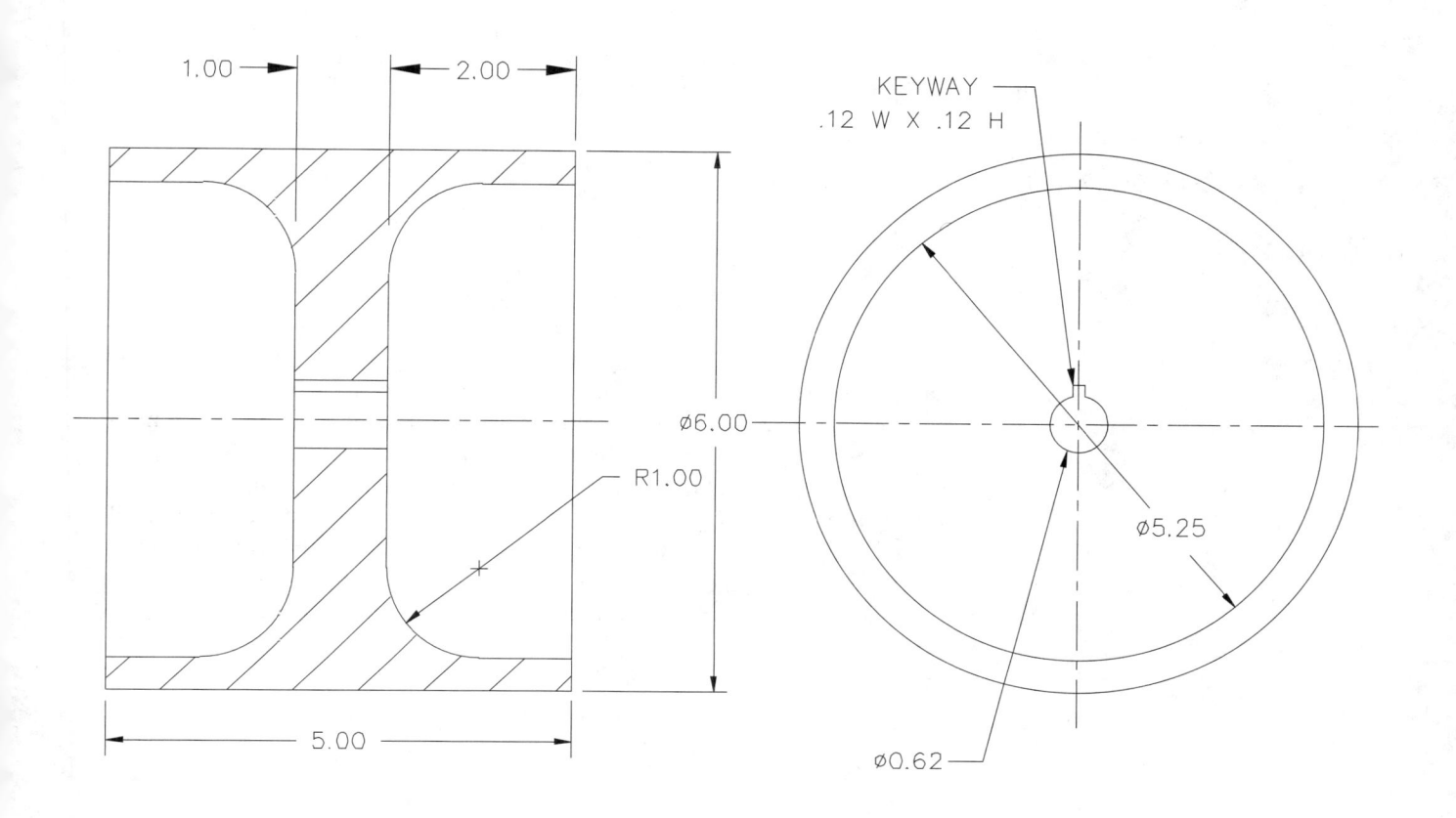

FLANGED WHEEL

Drawing 8-2

LAYERS	NAME	COLOR	LINETYPE	
	0	WHITE	————————	CONTINUOUS
	1	RED	————————	CONTINUOUS
	3	GREEN	— — — —	CENTER
	TEXT	CYAN	————————	CONTINUOUS
	HATCH	BLUE	————————	CONTINUOUS
	DIM	MAGENTA	————————	CONTINUOUS

LINE   (L)
CIRCLE (C)
MOVE   (M)
BREAK
HATCH
FILLET
DIM
ZOOM   (Z)

KEYWAY .12 W X .12 H

F1	F2	F6	F7	F8	F9
HELP	TEXT/GRAPHICS SCREEN	ABSOLUTE/OFF/POLAR COORDS	ON/OFF GRID	ON/OFF ORTHO	ON/OFF SNAP

DRAWING 8-3: SHOWER HEAD

This drawing makes use of the procedures for hatching and dimensioning you learned in the last two drawings. In addition, it uses an angular dimension, baseline dimensions, leaders, and "%%c" for the diameter symbol.

DRAWING SUGGESTIONS

GRID = .50
SNAP = .125
HATCH line spacing = .25

> You can save some time on this drawing by using MIRROR to create half of the right side view. Notice, however, that you cannot hatch before mirroring, because the mirror command will reverse the angle of the hatch lines.

> To achieve the angular dimension at the bottom of the right side view, you will need to draw the vertical line coming down on the right. Select this line and the angular line at the right end of the shower head, and the angular extension will be drawn automatically. Add the text "2 PL" using the DTEXT command.

> Notice that the diameter symbols in the vertical dimensions at each end of the right side view are not automatic. Use %%c to add the diameter symbol to the text.

Chap. 8   269

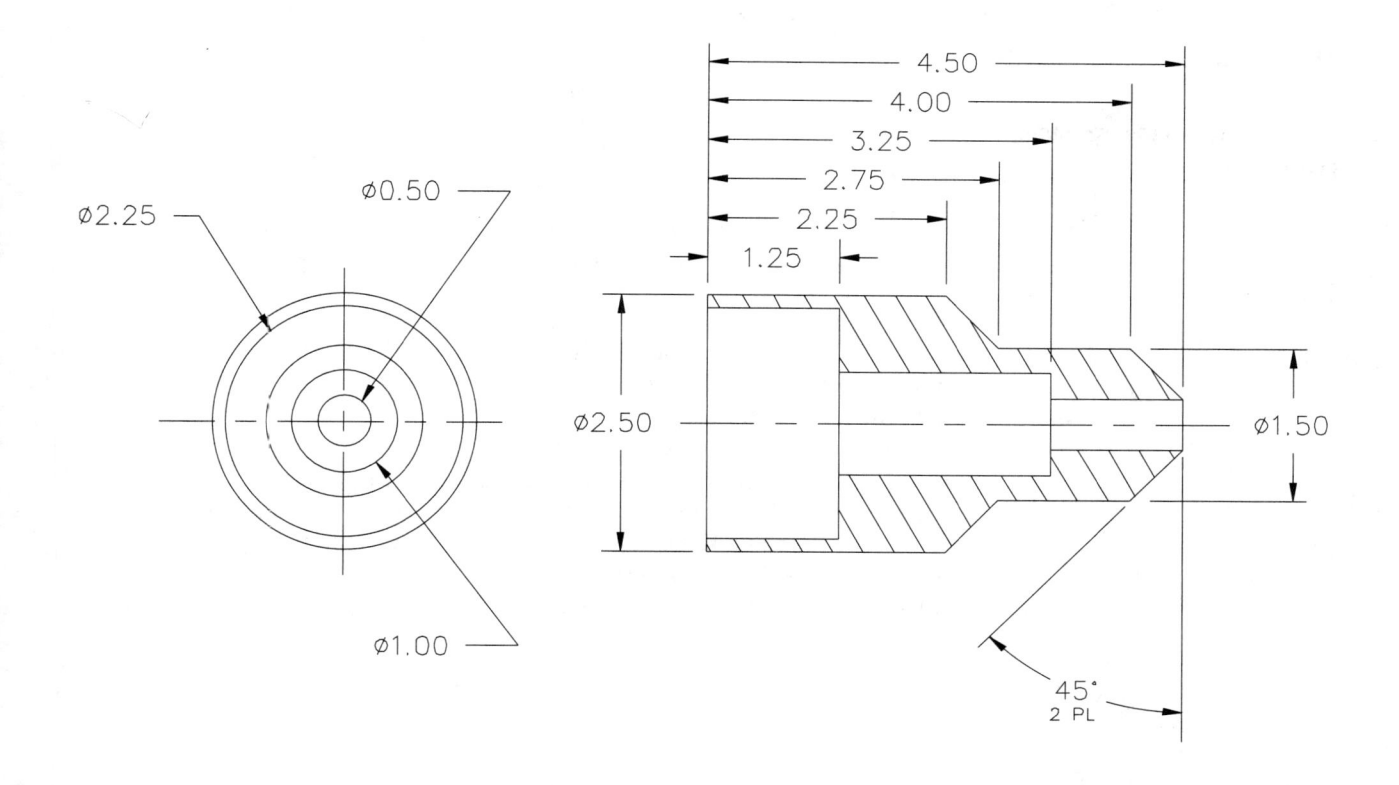

SHOWER HEAD

Drawing 8-3

LAYERS	NAME	COLOR	LINETYPE	
	0	WHITE	————	CONTINUOUS
	1	RED	————	CONTINUOUS
	2	YELLOW	————	HIDDEN
	3	GREEN	—·—·—	CENTER
	TEXT	CYAN	————	CONTINUOUS
	HATCH	BLUE	————	CONTINUOUS
	DIM	MAGENTA	————	CONTINUOUS

LINE   (L)
CIRCLE (C)
MIRROR
HATCH
DIM
ZOOM   (Z)

F1	F2	F6	F7	F8	F9
HELP	TEXT/GRAPHICS SCREEN	ABSOLUTE/OFF/POLAR COORDS	ON/OFF GRID	ON/OFF ORTHO	ON/OFF SNAP

DRAWING 8-4: NOSE ADAPTOR

Make ample use of ZOOM to work on the details of this drawing. Notice that the limits are set larger than usual, and the snap is rather fine by comparison.

DRAWING SUGGESTIONS

LIMITS = (0,0) (36,24)
GRID = .50 SNAP = .125
HATCH line spacing = .25

> You will need a .125 snap to draw the thread representation shown in the reference. Understand that this is nothing more than a standard representation for screw threads; it does not show actual dimensions. Zoom in close to draw it and you should have no trouble.

> This drawing includes two examples of "simplified drafting" practice. The thread representation is one, and the other is the way in which the counter bores are drawn in the front view. A precise rendering of these holes would show an ellipse, since the slant of the object dictates that they break through on an angle. However, to show these ellipses in the front view would make the drawing more confusing and less useful. Simplified representation is preferable in such cases.

(thread representation)

30°
TYP

0.12

Reference

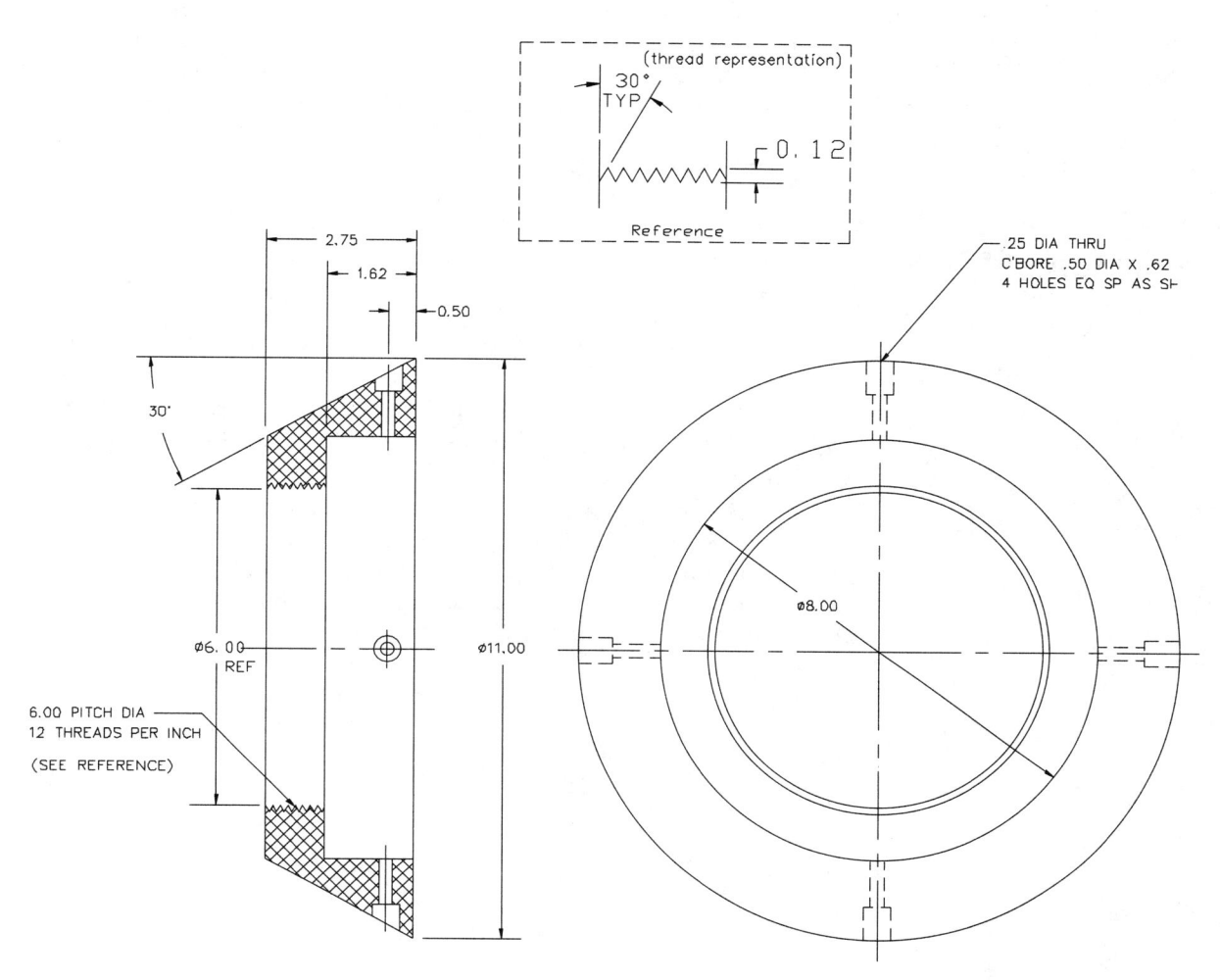

2.75
1.62
0.50

30°

.25 DIA THRU
C'BORE .50 DIA X .62
4 HOLES EQ SP AS SH

Ø6.00 REF
Ø11.00
Ø8.00

6.00 PITCH DIA
12 THREADS PER INCH
(SEE REFERENCE)

NOSE ADAPTOR
Drawing 8-4

LAYERS	NAME	COLOR	LINETYPE	
	0	WHITE	———— CONTINUOUS	LINE (L)
	1	RED	———— CONTINUOUS	CIRCLE (C)
	2	YELLOW	---- HIDDEN	HATCH
	3	GREEN	— — CENTER	BREAK
	TEXT	CYAN	———— CONTINUOUS	TRIM
	HATCH	BLUE	———— CONTINUOUS	COPY
	DIM	MAGENTA	———— CONTINUOUS	ARRAY

MIRROR
DIM
SCALE

F1 HELP
F2 TEXT/GRAPHICS SCREEN
F6 ABSOLUTE/OFF/POLAR COORDS
F7 ON/OFF GRID
F8 ON/OFF ORTHO
F9 ON/OFF SNAP

DRAWING 8-5: PLOT PLAN

This architectural drawing makes use of three hatch patterns and several dimension variable changes. Be sure to make these settings as shown. Notice that we have simplified the format of the drawing page for this drawing. This is because the drawings are becoming more involved and because you should need less information to complete them at this point. We will continue to show drawings this way for the remainder of the book.

DRAWING SUGGESTIONS

GRID = 10'   LIMITS = 180',120'
SNAP = 1'   LTSCALE = 2'

> The "trees" shown here are symbols for oaks, willows, and evergreens.
> Use the DIST command to find start points for the inner rectangular objects (the garage, the dwelling, etc.).
> BHATCH will open a space around text inside a defined boundary; however, sometimes you will want more white space than BHATCH leaves. The simple solution is to draw a box around the text area as an inner boundary. If the BHATCH style is set to "Normal" it will stop hatching at the inner boundary. Later you can erase the box, leaving an island of white space around the text.

Chap. 8   **273**

EXAMPLE OF TREES
draw a pattern in
a circle as shown
and array.

REFERENCE

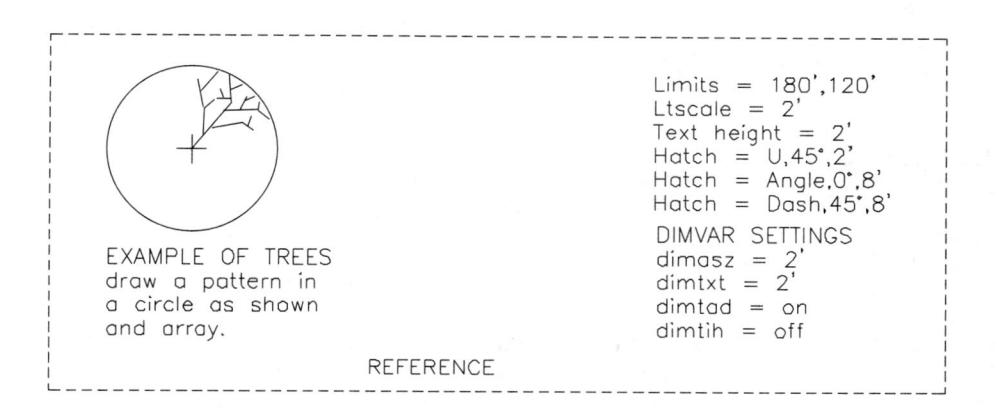

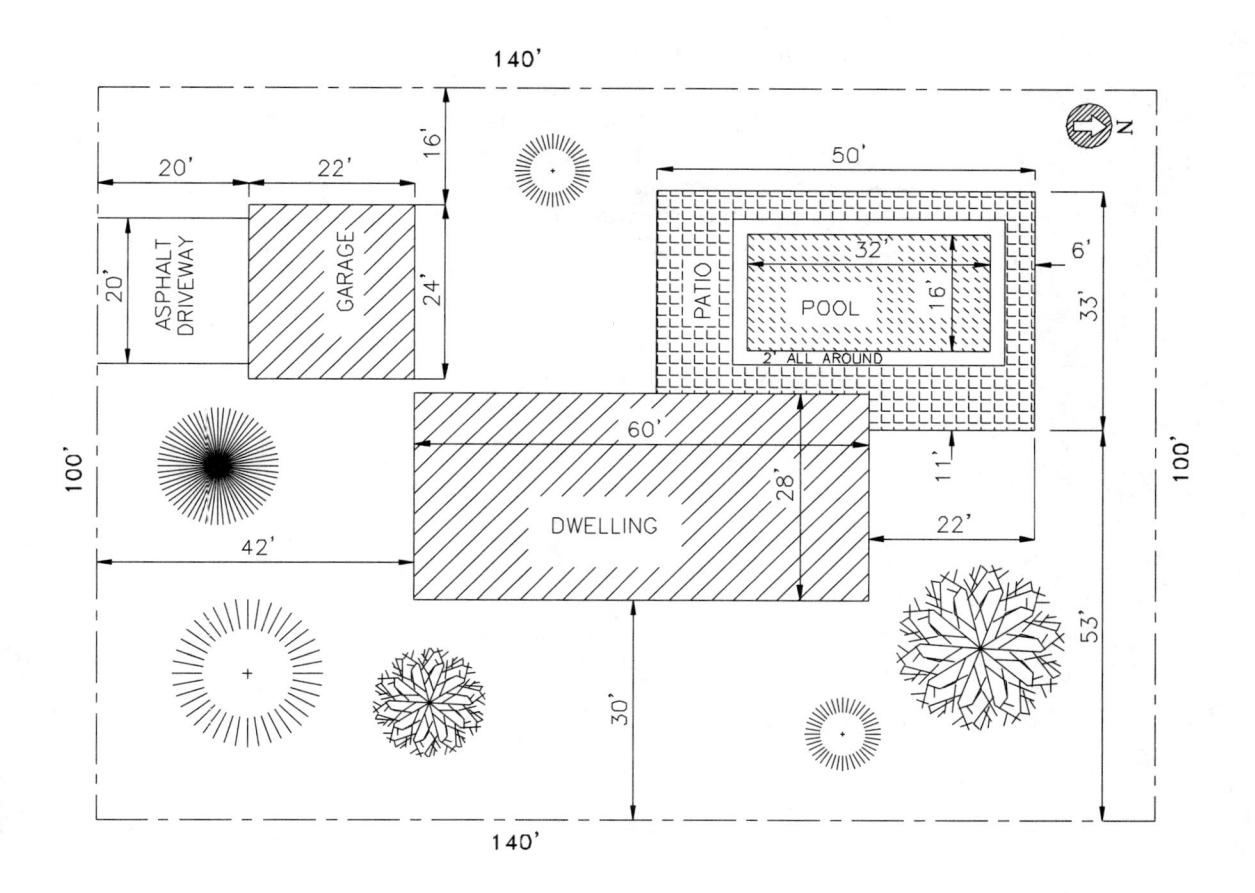

Limits = 180',120'
Ltscale = 2'
Text height = 2'
Hatch = U,45°,2'
Hatch = Angle,0°,8'
Hatch = Dash,45°,8'
DIMVAR SETTINGS
dimasz = 2'
dimtxt = 2'
dimtad = on
dimtih = off

PLOT PLAN
Drawing 8-5

DRAWING 8-6: PANEL

This drawing is primarily an exercise in using ordinate dimensions. Both the drawing of the objects and the adding of dimensions will be facilitated dramatically by this powerful feature.

DRAWING SUGGESTIONS

GRID = .50
SNAP = .125
UNITS = 3-place decimal

> After setting grid, snap, and units, create a new user coordinate system with the origin moved in and up about 1 unit each way. This technique was introduced in Task 6. For reference, here is the procedure:

1. Type or select "UCS".
2. Type "o" for "Origin".
3. Pick a new origin point.

> From here on all of the objects in the drawing can be easily placed using the *x* and *y* displacements exactly as they are shown in the drawing.

> When objects have been placed, switch to the dim layer and begin dimensioning using the ordinate dimension feature. You should be able to move along quickly, but be careful to keep dimensions on each side of the panel lined up. That is, the leader end points should end along the same vertical or horizontal line.

Chap. 8

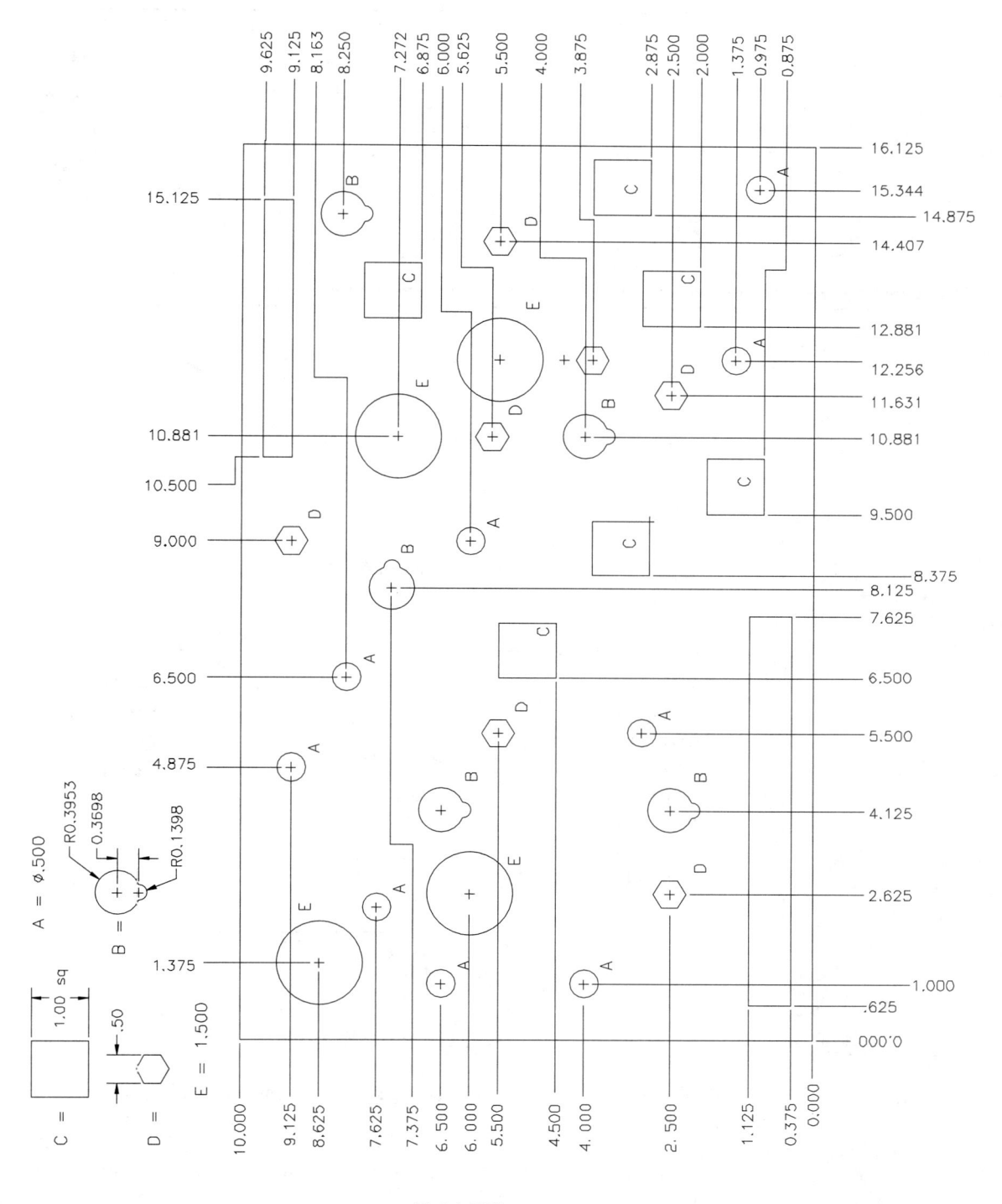

PANEL
DRAWING 8-6

CHAPTER 9

COMMANDS

DRAW	**DATA**	**MODIFY**
DONUT	MLSTYLE	MLEDIT
MLINE		OFFSET
PLINE	**TOOLS**	PEDIT
POINT	VSLIDE	
POLYGON	MSLIDE	
SKETCH		
SOLID	**OPTIONS**	
	FILL	

OVERVIEW

This chapter should be fun. As you can see by the preceding list, you will be learning a large number of new commands. You will see new things happening on your screen with each command. The commands in this chapter are used to create special entities, some of which cannot be drawn any other way. All of them, are complex objects made up of lines, circles, and arcs (like the text, dimensions, and hatch patterns discussed in the previous chapter), but they are stored and treated as singular entities. Some of them, such as polygons and donuts, are familiar geometric figures, while others, like polylines, are peculiar to CAD.

TASKS

1. Draw POLYGONs.
2. Draw DONUTs.
3. Use the FILL command.
4. Draw straight polyline segments.
5. Draw polyline arc segments.
6. Edit polylines with PEDIT.
7. Use the OFFSET command to create parallel objects.
8. Draw SOLIDs.
9. Make and view slides.
10. Draw and edit Multilines.
11. Draw POINTs in various styles (optional).
12. Draw freehand lines using SKETCH (optional).
13. Do Drawing 9–1 ("Backgammon Board").
14. Do Drawing 9–2 ("Dart Board").
15. Do Drawing 9–3 ("Printed Circuit Board").
16. Do Drawing 9–4 ("Carbide Tip Saw Blade").
17. Do Drawing 9–5 ("Gazebo").

Task 1: Drawing POLYGONs

Procedure

1. Type "Polygon" or select the Polygon tool from the Polygon flyout on the Draw toolbar.
2. Type number of sides.
3. Pick center point.
4. Indicate "Inscribed" or "Circumscribed".
5. Show radius of circle.

Discussion. Among the most interesting and flexible of the entities you can create in AutoCAD is the polyline. In this chapter we will begin with two regularly shaped polyline entities, polygons and donuts. These entities have their own special commands, separate from the general PLINE command (Tasks 4 and 5), but are created as polylines and can be edited just as any other polyline would be.

Polygons with any number of sides can be drawn using the POLYGON command. (Rectangles can be drawn by showing two corners using the RECTANG command, which draws polyline rectangles.) In the default sequence, AutoCAD will construct a polygon based on the number of sides, the center point, and a radius. Optionally, the "edge" method allows you to specify the number of sides and the length and position of one side (see *Figure 9-1*).

Inscribed   Circumscribed   Edge

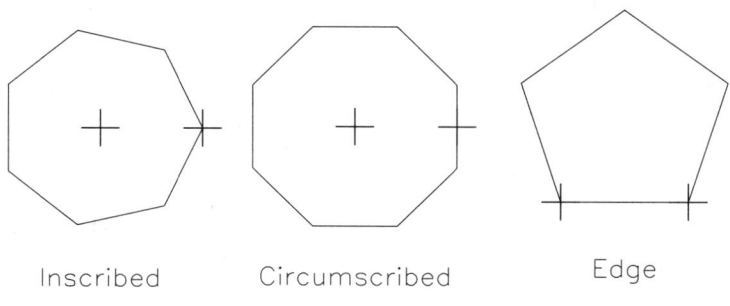

Figure 9-1

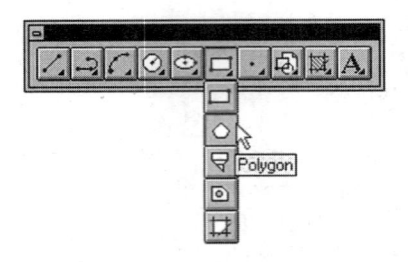

Figure 9-2

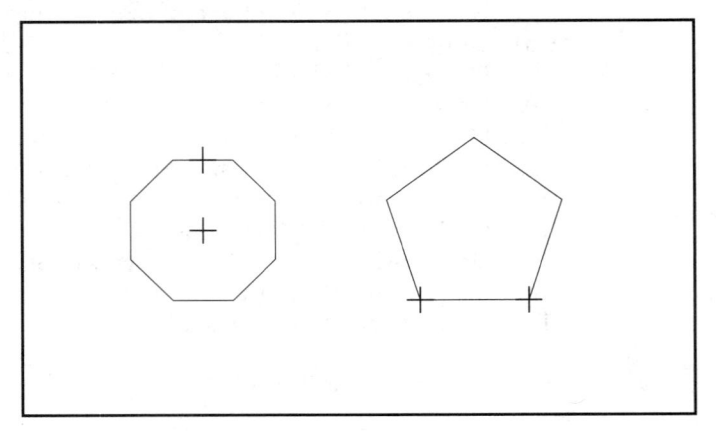

Figure 9-3

> Type "polygon" or select the Polygon tool from the Polygon flyout on the Draw toolbar as shown in *Figure 9-2*.

AutoCAD's first prompt will be for the number of sides:

Number of sides <4>:

> Type "8".

Now you are prompted to show either a center point or the first point of one edge:

Edge/<Center of polygon>:

> Pick a center point as shown by the blip on the left in *Figure 9-3*.

From here the size of the polygon can be specified in one of two ways, as shown in *Figure 9-1*. The radius of a circle will be given and the polygon drawn either inside or outside the imaginary circle. Notice that in the case of the "inscribed" polygon, the radius is measured from the center to a vertex, while in the "circumscribed" polygon it is measured from the center to the midpoint of a side. You can tell AutoCAD which you want by typing "i" or "c" or selecting from the screen.

Inscribed in circle/Circumscribed about circle (I/C) <I>:

The default is currently "inscribed". We will use the "circumscribed" method instead.

> Type "c" or select "circumscribed" ("C-scribe" on the screen menu).

Now you will be prompted to show a radius of this imaginary circle (that is, a line from the center to a midpoint of a side).

Radius of circle:

Chap. 9   **279**

> Show a radius similar to the one in *Figure 9-3*.
 We leave it to you to try out the "inscribed" option.
We will draw one more polygon, using the "edge" method.
> Press Enter to repeat the POLYGON command.
> Type "5" for the number of sides.
> Type "e" or select "Edge".
 AutoCAD will issue a different series of prompts:

First endpoint of edge:

> Pick a point as shown on the right in *Figure 9-3*.
 AutoCAD prompts:

Second endpoint of edge:

> Pick a second point as shown.
Your screen should resemble *Figure 9-3*.

Task 2: Drawing "DONUTs"

Procedure

1. Type "donut" or select the Donut tool from the Circle flyout on the Draw toolbar.
2. Type or show an inside diameter.
3. Type or show an outside diameter.
4. Pick a center point.
5. Pick another center point.
6. Press Enter to exit the command.

Discussion. The DONUT command is logical and easy to use. You show inside and outside diameters and then draw as many donut-shaped objects of the specified size as you like.

> Clear your display of polygons before continuing.
> Type "donut" or select the Donut tool from the Circle flyout on the Draw toolbar, as shown in *Figure 9-4*.
 AutoCAD prompts:

Inside diameter <0.50>:

We will change the inside diameter to 1.00.

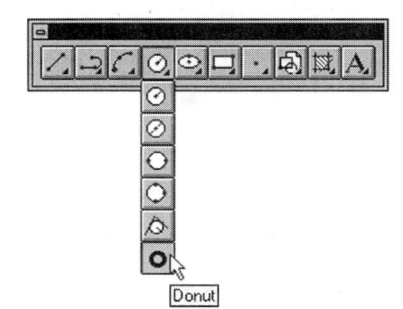

Figure 9-4

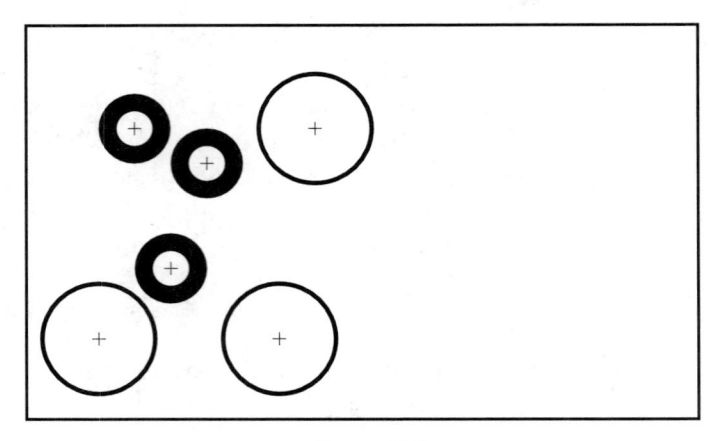

Figure 9-5

> Type "1".

AutoCAD prompts:

Outside diameter <1.00>:

We will change the outside diameter to 2.00.
> Type "2".

AutoCAD gives you a donut to drag into place and prompts:

Center of doughnut:

> Pick any point.

A donut will be drawn around the point you chose, as shown by the "fat" donuts in *Figure 9-5*. (If your donut is not filled, see Task 3.)
AutoCAD stays in the DONUT command, allowing you to continue drawing donuts.
> Pick a second center point.
> Pick a third center point.

You should now have three "fat" donuts on your screen as shown.
> Press Enter to exit the DONUT command.

Now reenter the donut command, change the inside diameter to 3.00 and the outer diameter to 3.25, and draw three or four "thin" donuts as shown in *Figure 9-5*. When you are done, leave the donuts on the screen so that you can see how they are affected by the FILL command.

Task 3: Using the FILL command

Procedure

1. Type "Fill".
2. Type "on" or "off".
3. Type or select "regen".

Discussion. Donuts, polylines (Tasks 4 and 5), and 2D solids (Task 8) are all affected by FILL. With FILL on, these entities are displayed and plotted as solid filled objects. With FILL off, only the outer boundaries are displayed (donuts are shown with radial lines between the inner and outer circles). Since filled objects are slower to regenerate than outlined ones, you may want to set FILL off as you are working on a drawing and turn it on when you are ready to print or plot.

> For this exercise you should have at least one donut on your screen from Task 2.
> Type "fill" or open the Drawing Aids (DDRMODES) dialogue box (on the Options pull down menu).

If you are typing, AutoCAD prompts:

ON/OFF <ON>:

If you are at the dialogue box, Solid Fill will be the second check box under "Modes" on the left.
> Type "off" or click in the Solid Fill check box, and then click on "OK" to exit the box.

You will not see any immediate change in your display when you do this. In order to see the effect, you will have to regenerate your drawing.
> Type or select "regen".

Your screen will be regenerated with FILL off and will resemble *Figure 9-6*. Many of the special entities that we will be discussing in the remainder of this chapter can be filled, so we encourage you to continue to experiment with FILL as you go along.

Task 4: Drawing Straight Polyline Segments

Procedure

1. Type "pl" or select the Polyline tool from the Polyline flyout on the Draw toolbar.
2. Pick a start point.
3. Type or select width, halfwidth, or other options.
4. Pick other points.

Discussion. In AutoCAD there are several ways in which collections of entities can be treated as one unit. In the last two chapters you saw how text, dimensions, and hatch patterns are all created as complex entities that can be selected and treated as single objects. In the next chapter you will see how to create

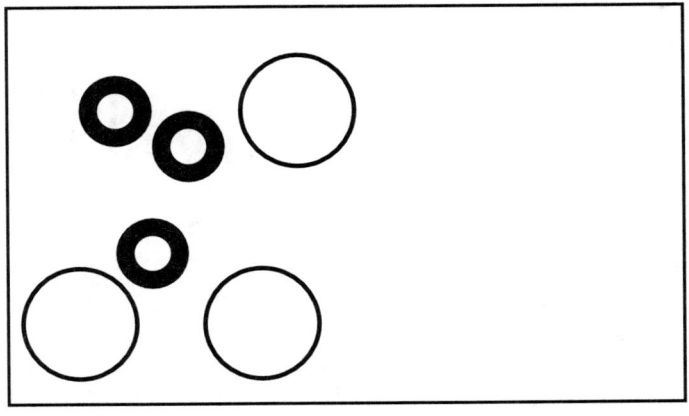

Figure 9-6

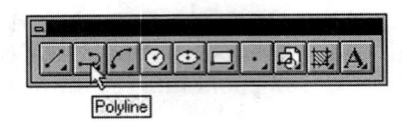

Figure 9-7

blocks from separate entities. Here you will see another kind of conglomerate entity, the polyline. You have already drawn several polylines without going through the PLINE command. Donuts and polygons both are drawn as polylines and therefore can be edited using the same edit commands that work on other polylines. You can, for instance, fillet all the corners of a polygon at once. Using the PLINE command itself, you can draw anything from a simple line to a series of lines and arcs with varying widths. Most important, polylines can be edited using many of the ordinary edit commands as well as a whole set of specialized editing procedures found in the PEDIT command.

We will begin by creating a simple polyline rectangle. The process will be much like drawing a rectangular outline with the LINE command, but the result will be a single object, rather than four distinct line segments.

> Clear your display of donuts before continuing.
> Type "pl" or select the Polyline tool from the Polyline flyout on the Draw toolbar, as shown in *Figure 9-7*.

AutoCAD begins with a prompt for a starting point:

From point:

> Pick a start point, such as P1 in *Figure 9-8*.

From here the PLINE prompt sequence becomes more complicated:

Current line width is 0.00
Arc/Close/Halfwidth/Length/Undo/Width/<Endpoint of line>:

The prompt begins by giving you the current line width, left from any previous use of the PLINE command.

Then the prompt offers options in the usual format. "Arc" will lead you into another set of options that deal with drawing polyline arcs. We will save polyline arcs for Task 5. "Close" works as in the LINE command to connect the last end point in a sequence to the original starting point. We will get to the other options momentarily.

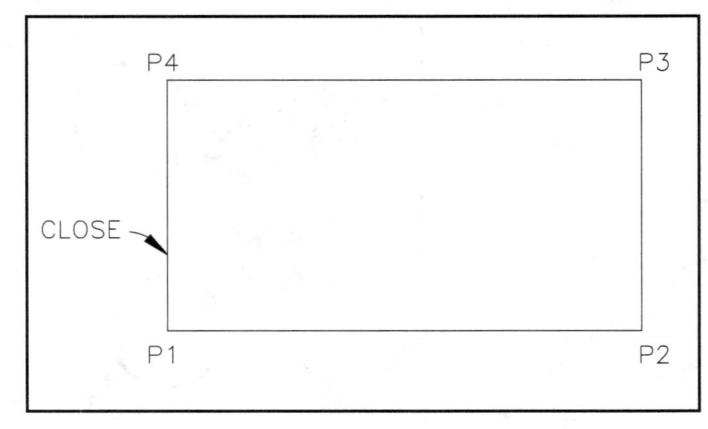

Figure 9-8

Chap. 9
283

This time around we will draw a series of 0 width segments, just as we would in the LINE command.

> Pick an end point, such as P2 in the figure.

AutoCAD will draw the segment and repeat the prompt.

> Pick another end point, say, P3 in the figure.
> Pick another end point, P4 in the figure.
> Type "c" or select "Close" to complete the rectangle, as shown in the figure.
> Now, select the rectangle by pointing to any of its sides.

You will see that the entire rectangle is selected, rather than just the side you pointed to. This means, for example, that you can FILLET or CHAMFER all four corners of the rectangle at once. Try it if you like, using the following procedure:

1. Type "Fillet" or select the Fillet tool from the Modify toolbar.
2. Type "r" or select "Radius".
3. Specify a radius.
4. Repeat the FILLET command.
5. Type "p" or select "Polyline" to indicate that you want to fillet an entire polyline.
6. Select the rectangle.

Note: If a corner is left without a fillet, it is probably because you did not use the close option when you completed the rectangle.

Now let's create a rectangle with wider lines.

> Type "pl" or select the Pline tool from the Draw toolbar.
> Pick a starting point as shown by P1 in *Figure 9-9*.

AutoCAD prompts:

Arc/Close/Halfwidth/Length/Undo/Width/<Endpoint of line>:

This time we need to make use of the "Width" option.

> Type "w" or select "width" from the screen menu, if available.

AutoCAD will respond with:

Starting width <0.00>:

You will be prompted for two widths, a starting width and an ending width. This makes it possible to draw tapered lines. For this exercise, our lines will have the same starting and ending width.

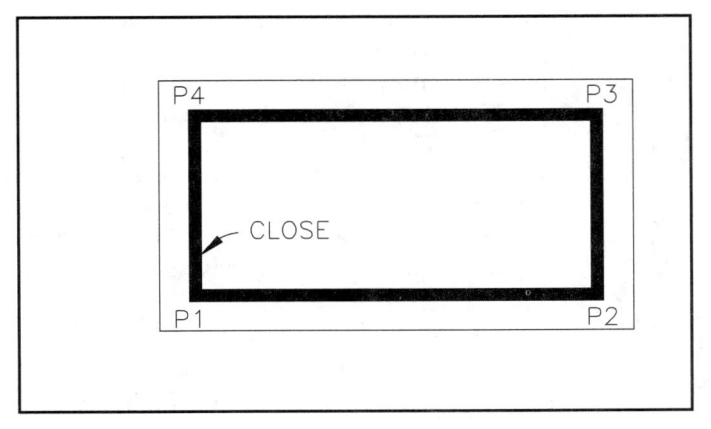

Figure 9-9

NOTE: The "halfwidth" option differs from "width" only in that the width of the line to be drawn is measured from the center out. With either option you can specify by showing rather than typing a value.

> Type ".25".

AutoCAD prompts:

Ending width <0.25>

Notice that the starting width has become the default for the ending width. To draw a polyline of uniform width, we accept this default.

> Press Enter to keep starting width and ending width the same.

AutoCAD now returns to the previous prompt:

Arc/Close/Halfwidth/Length/Undo/Width/<Endpoint of line>:

> Pick an end point as shown by P2 in *Figure 9-9*.

> Continue picking points to draw a second rectangle as shown in the figure. Be sure to use the close option to draw the last side, otherwise the last two sides will overlap rather than join.

The only options we have not discussed in this exercise are "Length" and "Undo". "Length" allows you to type or show a value, and then draws a segment of that length starting from the end point of the previous segment and continuing in the same direction (if the last segment was an arc, the length will be drawn tangent to the arc). "Undo" undoes the last segment, just as in LINE.

In the next task we will draw some pline arc segments.

Task 5: Drawing Polyline Arc Segments

Procedure

1. Enter the Pline command.
2. Pick a start point.
3. Specify a width.
4. Type "a" or select "arc".
5. Type or select options or pick an end point.

Discussion. A word of caution: Because of the flexibility and power of the PLINE command, it is tempting to think of polylines as always having weird shapes, tapered lines, and strange sequences of lines and arcs. Most books perpetuate this by consistently giving peculiar examples to show the range of what is possible with polylines. This is useful but misleading. Remember, polylines are practical entities even for relatively simple applications such as the rectangles drawn in Task 4.

Having said that, we will proceed to add our own bit of strangeness to the lore of the polyline. We will draw a polyline with three arc segments and one tapered straight line segment, as shown in *Figure 9-10*. We call this thing a "goose-necked funnel." You may have seen something like it at your local garage.

> Type "pl" or select the Pline tool from the Draw toolbar.

> Pick a new start point as shown by P1 in *Figure 9-10*.

> Type "w" or select "width" to set new widths.

> Type "0" for the starting width.

Chap. 9 285

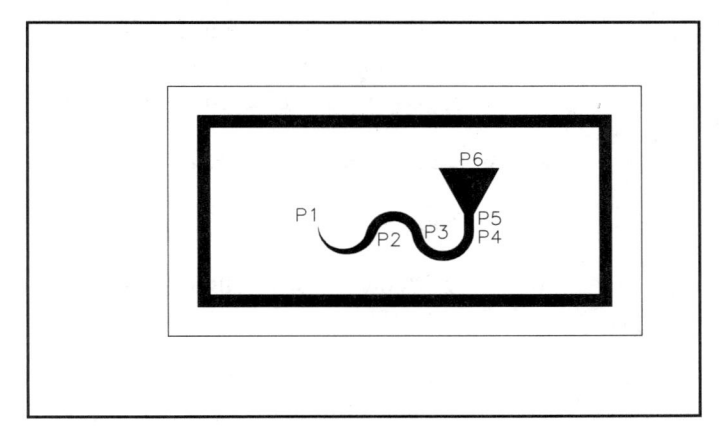

Figure 9-10

> Type ".5" for the ending width.
> Type "a" or select "Arc". This will bring up the arc prompt, which looks like this (press F2 to see it, if necessary):

Angle/CEnter/CLose/Direction/Halfwidth/Line/Radius/Second pt/Undo/Width

Let's look at this prompt for a moment. To begin with there are four options that are familiar from the previous prompt. "CLose", "Halfwidth", "Undo", and "Width" all function exactly as they would in drawing straight polyline segments. The "Line" option returns you to the previous prompt so that you can continue drawing straight line segments after drawing arc segments.

The other options, "Angle", "CEnter", "Direction", "Radius", "Second pt", and "Endpoint of arc", allow you to specify arcs in ways similar to the ARC command. One difference is that AutoCAD assumes that the arc you want will be tangent to the last polyline segment entered. This is often not the case. The "center" and "direction" options let you override this assumption where necessary, or you can begin with a short line segment to establish direction before entering the arc prompt.

> Pick an end point to the right, as shown by P2 in the figure, to complete the first arc segment.

NOTE: If you did not follow the order shown in the figures and drew your previous rectangle clockwise, or if you have drawn other polylines in the meantime, you will find that the arc does not curve downward as shown in *Figure 9-10*. You can fix this by using the Direction option. Type "d" and then point straight down. Now you can pick an end point to the right as shown.

AutoCAD prompts again (press F2, if necessary):

Angle/CEnter/CLose/Direction/Halfwidth/Line/Radius/Second pt/Undo/Width/
<Endpoint of arc>:

For the remaining two arc segments, retain a uniform width of .50.
> Enter points P3 and P4 to draw the remaining two arc segments as shown.

Now we will draw two straight line segments to complete the polyline.
> Type "L" or select "line" (this takes you back to the original prompt).
> Pick P5 straight up about 1.00 as shown.
> Type "w" or select "width".
> Press Enter to retain .50 as the starting width.

> Type "3" for the ending width.
> Pick an end point up about 2.00 as shown.
Your screen should resemble *Figure 9-10*.

Task 6: Editing Polylines with PEDIT

Procedure

1. Type "Pedit" or select the Pedit tool from the Special Edit flyout on the Modify toolbar.
2. Select a polyline.
3. Type or select a PEDIT option.
4. Follow the prompts.

Discussion. The PEDIT command provides a whole subsystem of special editing capabilities that work only on polylines. We will not attempt to have you use all of them; some you may never need. Most important is that you be aware of the possibilities so that when you find yourself in a situation calling for a PEDIT procedure you will know what to look for. After executing the following task, study *Figure 9-14*, the PEDIT chart. For further information see the *AutoCAD User's Guide*.

We will perform two edits on the polylines already drawn.

> Type "Pedit" or select the Pedit tool from the Special Edit flyout on the Modify toolbar, as shown in *Figure 9-11*.

You will be prompted to select a polyline:

Select polyline:

> Select the outer 0-width polyline rectangle drawn in Task 4.

Notice that PEDIT works on only one object at a time and that selected polylines *do not* become dotted. You are prompted as follows:

Open/Join/Width/Edit vertex/Fit/Spline/Decurve/Ltype gen/Undo/eXit/ <X>:

"Open" will be replaced by "Close" if your polyline has not been closed. "Undo" and "eXit" are self-explanatory. Other options are illustrated in *Figure 9-14*. "Edit vertex" brings up the subset of options shown on the right side of the chart. When you do vertex editing, AutoCAD will mark one vertex at a time with an **x**. You can move the **x** to other vertices by pressing Enter, typing "n", or selecting "Next".

Now we will edit the selected polyline by changing its width.
> Type "w" or select "width".

This option allows you to set a new uniform width for an entire polyline. All tapering and variation is removed when this edit is performed.

AutoCAD prompts:

Enter new width for all segments:

> Type ".25".

Your screen will be redrawn to resemble *Figure 9-12*.

You should be at the "Close/Join/Width/Edit vertex..." prompt before continuing. The last polyline is still selected so that you can continue shaping it with other PEDIT options.

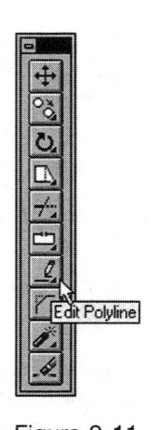

Figure 9-11

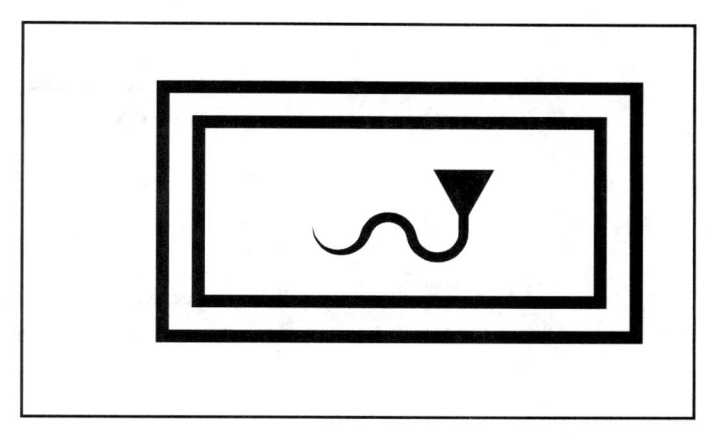

Figure 9-12

> Press Enter to exit PEDIT.
> Press Enter to repeat PEDIT.

This exiting and reentering is necessary in order to select another polyline to edit.

> Select the "gooseneck funnel" polyline.

This time we'll try out the "Decurve" option. Decurve straightens all curves within the selected polyline.

> Type "d" or select "Decurve".

Your screen will resemble *Figure 9-13*.

To complete this exercise, we suggest that you try out some of the other editing options. In particular, you will get interesting results from "Fit" and "Spline". Be sure to study the PEDIT chart *Figure 9-14* before going on to the next task.

Task 7: Creating Parallel Objects with OFFSET

Procedure

1. Type "Offset" or select the Offset tool from the Special Edit flyout on the Modify toolbar.
2. Type or show an offset distance.
3. Select object to offset.
4. Show which side to offset.

Discussion. Offset creates parallel copies of lines, circles, arcs, or polylines. You will find a number of typical applications in the drawings at the end of this chapter. In this brief exercise we will perform an offset operation to add a third border, as shown in *Figure 9-15*.

> Type "Offset" or select the Offset tool from the Special Edit flyout on the Modify toolbar.

AutoCAD prompts:

Offset distance or Through <Through>:

There are two methods. You can type or show a distance or you can show a point that you want the new copy to run through. We will use the

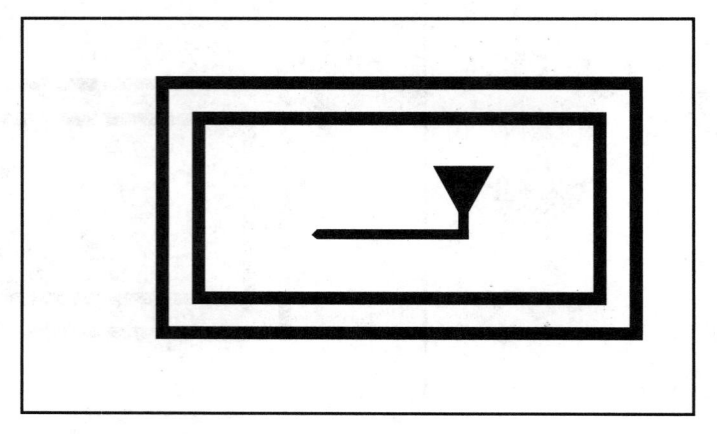

Figure 9-13

Figure 9-14

Chap. 9   **289**

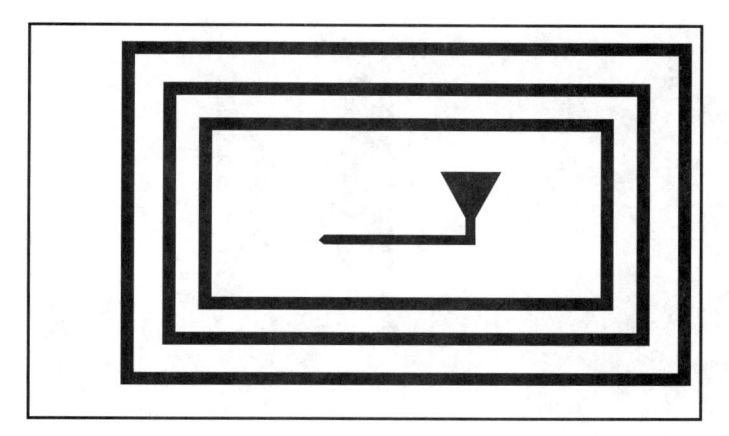

Figure 9-15

distance method. Then if you like you can undo the command and try it again using the "through point" system.
> Type ".75".
   AutoCAD prompts for an object:

Select object to offset:

> Point to the outer rectangle.
   AutoCAD now needs to know whether to create the offset image to the inside or outside of the rectangle:

Side to offset:

> Pick a point anywhere outside the rectangle.
   Your screen should now resemble *Figure 9-15*. AutoCAD continues to prompt for objects to offset, so you will need to press Enter when you are done.
> Press Enter to exit the OFFSET command.

To create the same border using the through point method, follow this procedure:

1. Enter the OFFSET command.
2. Type "t" or select "through".
3. Select the rectangle.
4. Pick a "through point" 0.75 out from any of the sides of the rectangle.

Task 8: Drawing "SOLIDs"

Procedure

1. Type "Solid" or select the 2D Solid tool from the Polygon flyout on the Draw toolbar.
2. Pick a first point.
3. Pick a second point.
4. Pick a third point.

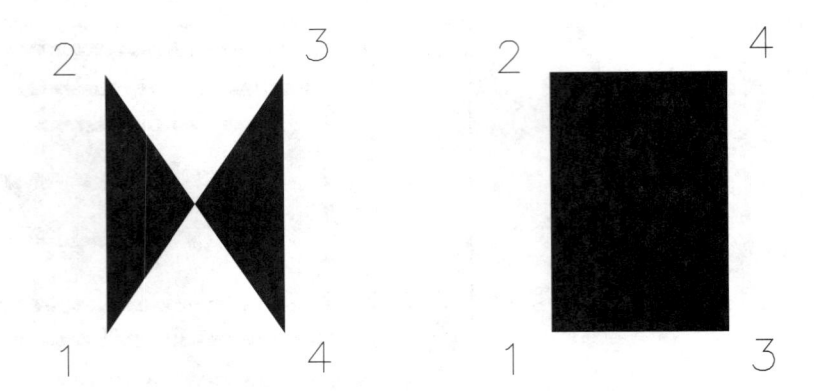

Figure 9-16

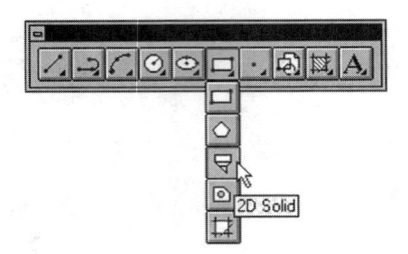

Figure 9-17

5. Pick a fourth point or press Enter to draw a triangular section.
6. Pick another third point or press Enter to exit the command.

Discussion. SOLID allows you to draw rectangular and triangular solid-filled shapes in two dimensions by specifying points that become corners or vertices. There is a trick to using SOLID for rectangular sections involving the order in which you enter points. If you enter them in the wrong order you will get the bow tie effect shown in *Figure 9-16*. It is natural to enter points in a rectangle by moving around the perimeter. However, AutoCAD solids are drawn with edges between point 1 and point 3, and between point 2 and point 4, so you need to be careful about the order in which you pick points.

> To begin this task, clear the screen of polylines left over from Task 7.
> FILL and ORTHO should be on for this exercise. We will begin with a rectangular solid.
> Type "Solid" or select the 2D Solid tool from the Polygon flyout on the Draw toolbar, as shown in *Figure 9-17*.

AutoCAD will prompt for a series of points, beginning with:

First point:

> Pick a point similar to P1 in *Figure 9-18*.
AutoCAD prompts:

Second point:

> Pick a point similar to P2.

Chap. 9   **291**

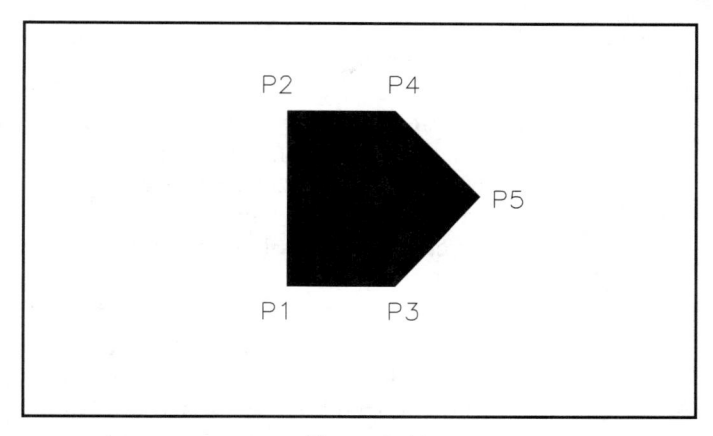

Figure 9-18

These first two points will become the end points of one side of a rectangular solid. AutoCAD prompts:

Third point:

> Pick a point similar to P3.

Remember that a side will be drawn between point 1 and point 3. AutoCAD prompts:

Fourth point:

> Pick a point similar to P4 in *Figure 9-18*.

When the fourth point is entered, AutoCAD will draw a solid rectangle and continue to prompt for points.

Third point:

If you continue entering points, the previous points 3 and 4 will become points 1 and 2 of the new section. You can draw a triangular section by picking a third point and then pressing Enter in response to the prompt for a fourth point. This also means that you will need to press Enter twice when you want to exit SOLID. We will draw a triangular solid before exiting.
> Turn ortho off and pick a point similar to P5 in *Figure 9-18*.
> Press Enter in response to the "Fourth point:" prompt.

Your screen should resemble *Figure 9-18*.
> Press Enter again to exit the command.

Task 9: Making and Viewing Slides

Procedure

1. Type "Mslide" or "Vslide" or select "Slide" from the Tools menu and then "Save" or "View".
2. Type or select the name of a .sld file.

Discussion. Slides are simply "snapshots" of AutoCAD drawings that are saved in a reduced format so they can be loaded very quickly. They cannot be plotted or edited, but often are used in developing business presentations that can be shown on a computer screen.

Slides are very easily created using MSLIDE. Once created they can be displayed using the VSLIDE command. Since slides resemble drawings, it is important that you understand the primary difference: Slides cannot be edited, added to, or changed in any way. To change a slide you must overwrite the slide file with a new one of the same name.

To create a slide of your present display, follow this procedure:

> Type "Mslide" or select "Slide" from the Tools menu and then "Save".

MSLIDE stands for "make slide." It creates a slide from your current screen display. When the command is entered, you will see a Create Slide File dialogue box. This is a standard file list box, listing files that have a .sld extension. When the box opens, the cursor will be blinking in the File: edit box so that you can type in a name for the slide you want to create.

> Type a name for the file, like "9-1" or "solid."
> Press Enter or Click on "OK".

It's that simple. Your display will be saved as a file with a .sld extension. To see that it is really there, you must first alter your screen in some way and then load the file using VSLIDE.

> Erase the solid from your screen.
> Type "Vslide" or select "Slide" from the Tools menu and then "View".

You will see another standard file list dialogue box. This one will be titled "Select Slide File".

> Type or select the name of the file you just created with MSLIDE.
> Press Enter or click on "OK".

Your slide will appear.

> Try to select the solid or any other objects that appear in your slide.

You will find that you cannot. It is possible to draw new objects while a slide is showing on your screen. These are not part of the slide, but are part of your current drawing. If you REDRAW the screen, the newly drawn objects will remain and the slide will disappear.

> To clear the slide from your screen, type "r" or select "Redraw".

Most slide applications use a series of slides, exactly as you would in a photographic slide show. This process can be automated and timed using a special kind of file called a script file. There are a number of commands used in the making of a script file, including SCRIPT, DELAY, RESUME, and RSCRIPT, in addition to MSLIDE and VSLIDE. See the *AutoCAD User's Guide* for further information if your goals include the use of slide presentations.

Task 10: Drawing and Editing Multilines

Procedure

1. Type "mline" or select the Multiline tool from the Polyline flyout on the Draw toolbar.
2. Pick a from point.
3. Pick a to point.
4. Pick another to point, or press Enter to exit the command.

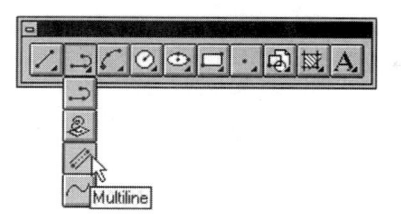

Figure 9-19

Discussion. Multilines are a new Release 13 entity. They are groups of parallel lines with various forms of intersections and end caps. Each individual line is called an element and you can have up to 16 elements in a single multiline style. Drawing multilines is about as simple as drawing lines. The complexity comes in defining multiline styles and in editing intersections. In this task we will draw standard multilines, create a new style, and edit the intersection of two multilines.

> To begin this exercise, clear the screen of solids or other objects left from previous exercises.

First, we will draw some standard multilines.

> Type "mline" or select the Multiline tool from the Polyline flyout on the Draw toolbar, as shown in *Figure 9-19*.

AutoCAD will issue the following prompt:

Justification/Scale/Style/<From point>:

If you stick with the default option you will see that the MLINE sequence is exactly like drawing a line. "Justification" refers to the way elements are positioned in relation to the points you pick on the screen. The default justification is "Top". This means that the top element of the multiline will be positioned at the cross hairs when you pick points. Try it and we will discuss the other options later.

> Pick a "from point" similar to P1 in *Figure 9-20*.

AutoCAD gives you a standard, two-element multiline to drag and prompts for another point:

To Point:

Move the cursor and notice how the cross hairs continue to connect with the top element. The other two options for justification are "Zero" and

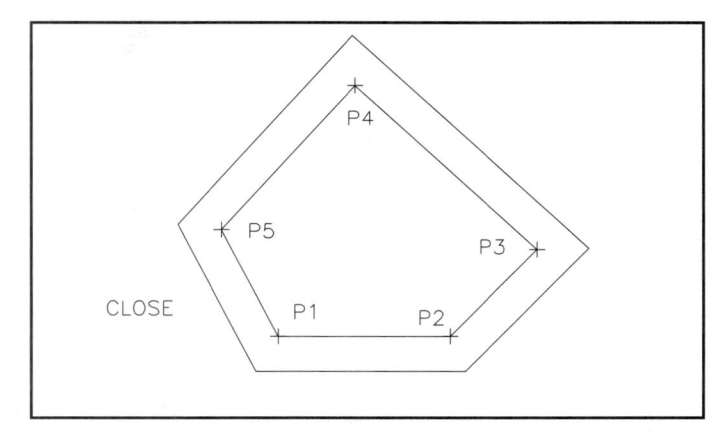

Figure 9-20

"Bottom". Zero lines up in the middle of the elements, at the zero point or origin. You will understand this better after we create a new style. Bottom lines up on the bottom element.

> Pick a "to point" similar to P2 in the figure.

Exact lengths and angles are not important.

Move the cursor around and notice how AutoCAD adjusts the corner to maintain parallel line elements.

AutoCAD has added an undo option now that you have one multiline segment complete.

Undo/<To point>:

> Pick P3 as in the figure.

Once you have two complete multiline segments, AutoCAD adds a close option:

Close/Undo/<To point>:

> Pick P4 as in the figure.
> Pick P5 as in the figure.
> Type "c" or select "Close" to complete the figure.

Creating Multiline Styles

The real power of multilines comes when you learn to create your own multiline style. This is done through the Multiline Styles dialogue box, called by the ML-STYLE command.

> Type "mlstyle" or select "Multiline Style..." from the Data pull down menu.

This will call the dialogue box shown in *Figure 9-21*. Standard is the name of the current multiline style, which, as we have seen, includes two continuous line elements. A word of caution here; the Multiline Styles dialogue box is not as user friendly as some. It will not respond well if you do not do things in the prescribed order. In particular, you must first establish element

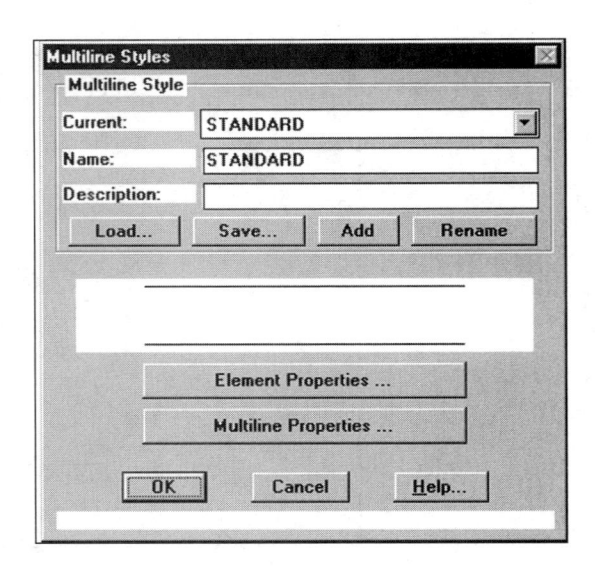

Figure 9-21

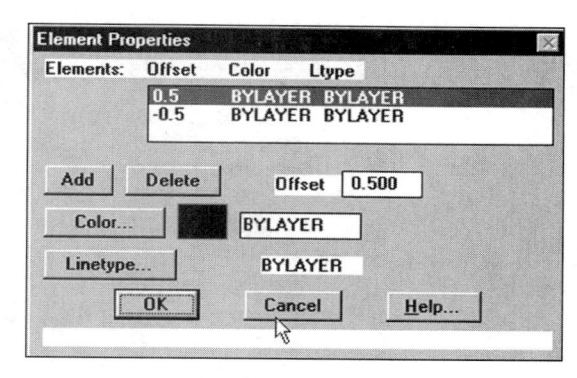

Figure 9-22

and multiline properties, then give the style a name, save it, and add it to the list of available styles. Any variation in this order will cause problems.

We will begin by adding a third element.

> Select "Element Properties...".

This calls the Element Properties dialogue box shown in *Figure 9-22*. First look at the elements box. It shows that there are now only two elements, one is offset 0.5 above the origin point of the multiline (0.0) and the other is offset −0.5, or 0.5 below the origin. This is consistent with our previous discussion of multiline justification options. You will recall that standard multilines have a zero point between the two lines, but since the default justification is top, the cross hairs line up on the top element. With zero justification they would line up at 0.0. With Bottom justification they would line up on the −0.5 element.

> Click on "Add".

This is how we begin to add a new element. As soon as you click "Add", a third element is added to the box. Notice that it is offset 0.0. In other words, it is right on the zero line between the two offset lines. For this style we will leave it there. If we needed to offset it we would type a new offset number in the offset box.

Next, notice that all three elements are listed as having BYLAYER color and linetype. This means that the color and linetype will be determined by whatever layer the multiline is drawn on. For the sake of learning, we will change the linetype of our newly added middle element. This element should be highlighted in blue. If it is not, click on it to highlight it before proceeding.

> Click on "Linetype...".

This calls the "Select Linetype" dialogue box shown in *Figure 9-23*. This box contains all the loaded linetypes in your drawing. From past exercises, you should at least have the hidden and center linetypes loaded, so we will use one of these. (If for any reason your prototype drawing does not have the HIDDEN linetype or if you want to use a linetype that is not loaded, you could select "Load..." from this dialogue box and load them now.)

> Run down the list until you see "HIDDEN".
> Select "HIDDEN".
> Click on "OK".

Notice that the element at 0.0 now has the HIDDEN linetype style.

> Click on "OK" again.

When you return to the Multiline Styles dialogue box you should see that the middle element has been added to the image box, but is shown as a

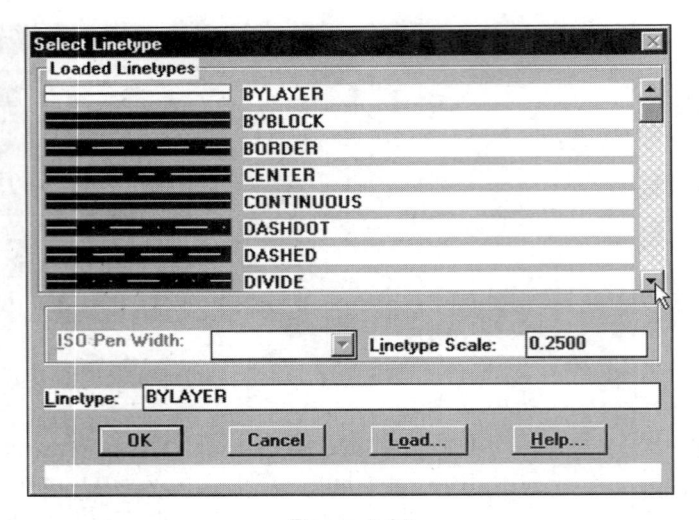

Figure 9-23

Figure 9-24

continuous line. The image box shows elements by position but does not show color or linetype.

Now let's look at the Multiline Properties dialogue box.

> Click on "Multiline Properties...".

This calls up the dialogue box shown in *Figure 9-24*. This box controls the way joints and ends of multilines are treated. The variety of options is shown in *Figure 9-25*. For our purposes it will not be necessary to add joints or end caps at this point.

> Click on "OK" or "Cancel" to exit the Multiline Properties box.

At this point we are ready to give the new style a name, save it, make it current and then exit the dialogue.

> Double click in the "Name" box to highlight "Standard".

> Type in a new name, such as "3", for the 3 elements in this style.

> Click on "Save" to save the new style.

This will call a Save Multiline Style dialogue box.

> Click on "OK" to save the new style in the "ACAD" file.

> Click on "Add" to add the new style to the list of available multiline styles.

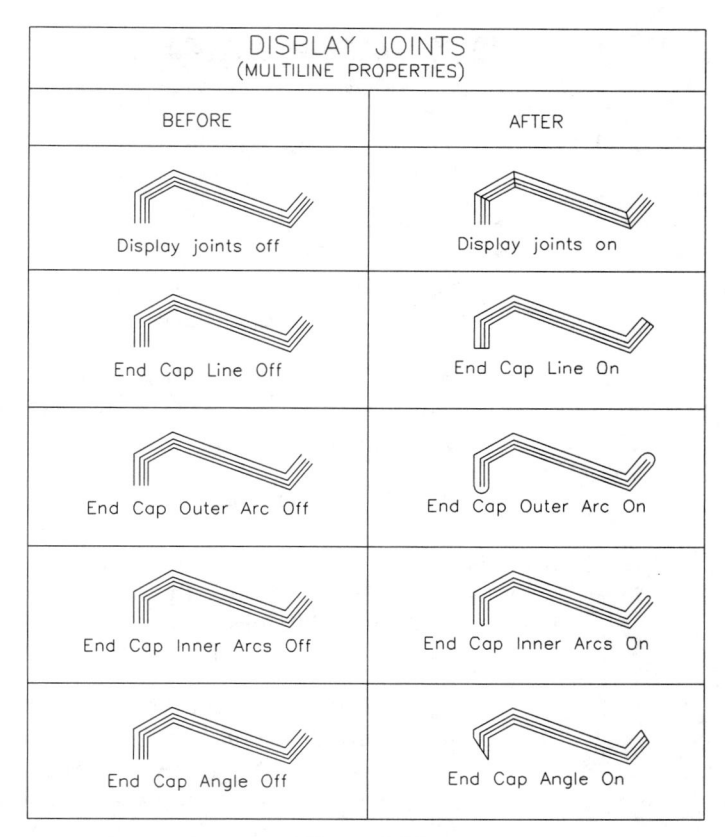

Figure 9-25

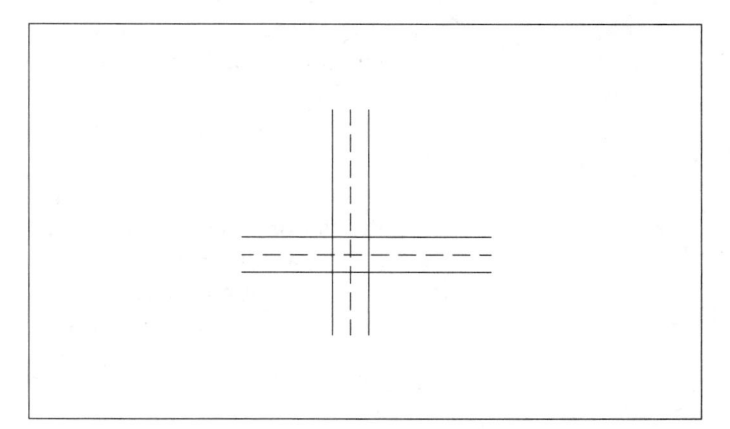

Figure 9-26

When you do this, your new style will be added and made current. The new name should appear in the current box. If you click on the arrow to the right of the box you will see that "Standard" is on the list as an alternative.

Once your style has been defined, named, saved, and added as the current style, you are ready to leave the box and draw some new multilines.

> Click on "OK" to exit the dialogue box.

> Type "mline" or select the Multiline tool from the Polyline flyout on the Draw toolbar.

> Pick two points to draw the horizontal multiline shown in *Figure 9-26*.

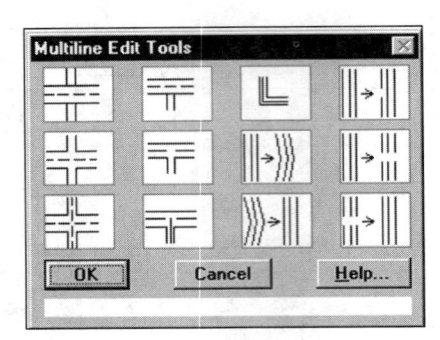

Figure 9-27

> Press Enter to exit the MLINE command.
> Repeat MLINE and pick two more points to draw the vertical multiline shown in the figure.

Editing Multiline Intersections

Multilines can be modified using many of the same edit commands that are used with other entities. In addition there is a special MLEDIT command for editing the intersection of two multilines. The possibilities will be easy to see since the dialogue box illustrates the options using a figure similar to the one you have just drawn.

> Type "mledit" or select the Multiline Edit tool from the Special Edit flyout on the Modify toolbar.

This calls the Multiline Edit Tools dialogue box shown in *Figure 9-27*. When you select any of the twelve images in the box, the name of that type of edit will be shown at the lower left corner of the box. Since the figure on your screen is similar to the one used in these image boxes, what you see is pretty much what you will get when you perform any of these edits.
> Click on the top left image box.

As you see, this choice is called a Closed Cross.
> Click on "OK".

Now you must select the two multilines to edit.
> Pick the vertical multiline.

The order in which you pick is clearly significant with this and many other of the multiline edits. In this case the second multiline selected does not change and will appear to "cross over" the first.
> Pick the horizontal multiline.

Your screen should resemble *Figure 9-28*.

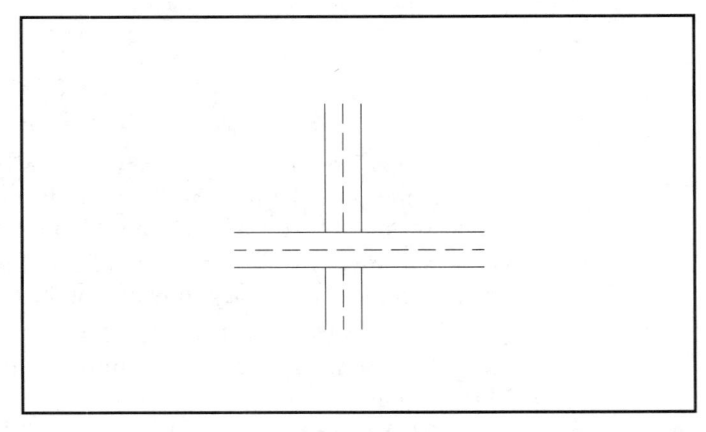

Figure 9-28

Chap. 9   299

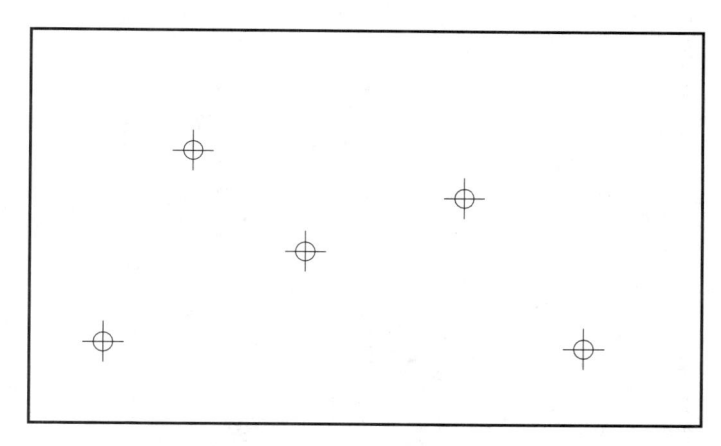

Figure 9-29

As you can now imagine, the possibilities available with up to 16 elements, 256 colors, 58 standard linetypes, plus the different endcap forms, and the various types of intersection edits are substantial. We would encourage you to experiment before going on.

Task 11: Drawing "POINTs" (Optional)

Procedure

1. Type "Point" or select the Point tool from the Draw toolbar.
2. Pick a point.

Discussion. On the surface this is the simplest DRAW command in AutoCAD. However, if you look at *Figure 9-29*, you will see figures that were drawn with the POINT command that do not look like ordinary points. This capability adds a bit of power and complexity to this otherwise simple command.

> Erase objects from previous exercises.
> Turn off the grid (F7).
> Type "Point" or select the Point tool from the Draw toolbar.
> Pick a point anywhere on the screen.

AutoCAD will place a blip at the point and return you to the "Command:" prompt.

In order to see what has really happened, you will need to perform a REDRAW to clear away the blip.

> Type "r" or select the Redraw View tool from the Standard toolbar.

Look closely and you will see the point you have drawn. Besides those odd instances in which you may need to draw tiny dots like this, points can also serve as object snap "nodes." See the OSNAP chart, *Figure 6-8* in Chapter 6.

But what about those circles and crosses in *Figure 9-29*? AutoCAD has 18 other simple forms that can be drawn as points. Before we change the point form, we need to see our options.

> Type "ddptype" or select "Display" and then "Point Style..." from the Options pull down menu.

AutoCAD displays a Point Style dialogue box with an icon menu, as shown in *Figure 9-30*. It shows you graphic images of your choices. You can

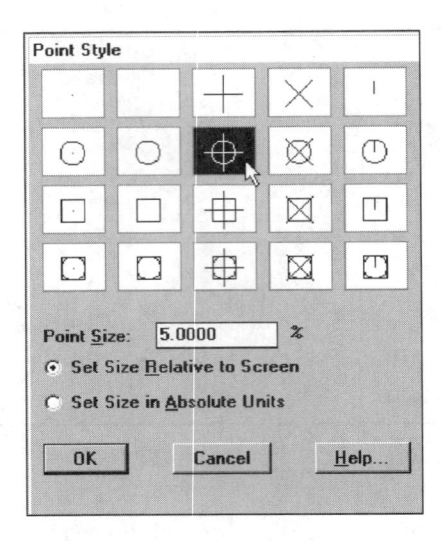

Figure 9-30

pick any of the point styles shown by pointing. You can also change the size of points using the Point Size edit box.

> Pick the style in the middle of the second row.

> Click on "OK" to exit the dialogue box.

> Type "Point" or select the Point tool from the Draw toolbar.

> Pick a point anywhere on your screen.

AutoCAD will draw a point in the chosen style, as shown in the figure.

If you have selected the POINT command from the toolbar, AutoCAD will continue to draw points wherever you pick them until you exit the command. If you have entered it from the command line, you will have to repeat it to draw more points.

> Repeat POINT, if necessary, and pick another point.

Draw a few more points, or return to the dialogue box to try another style if you wish. If you have entered POINT from a menu you will have to cancel it to exit.

> If necessary, cancel the POINT command.

Task 12: Using the SKETCH command (Optional)

Procedure

1. Type "Sketch" or select the Sketch tool from the Miscellaneous toolbar.
2. Type an increment.
3. Pick a start point (pen down).
4. Move cursor to sketch lines.
5. Pick an end point (pen up).
6. Record, exit, quit, or erase.

Discussion. The SKETCH command allows you to draw freehand lines. We include it here as an optional task so that you will know that it is available. It is not used in any of the drawings that follow.

Chap. 9

The key to SKETCH is becoming familiar with its pen up, pen down action. Also, get used to the idea that SKETCHed lines are not part of your drawing until you "record" them or exit the SKETCH command.

> Type "Sketch" or select the Sketch tool from the Miscellaneous toolbar.

AutoCAD prompts:

SKETCH record increment <0.10>:

This will allow you to decide how fine or coarse you want your lines to be. Remember also that AutoCAD will continue to observe your snap. If you want a small record increment, turn snap off.

> Press Enter to accept .10 as the record increment, or change it if you like.

You will see the following prompt:

Sketch. Pen eXit Quit Record Erase Connect.

We will discuss these options in a moment. They will make more sense after you have done some sketching.

> In order to begin sketching, choose any point on your screen and press the pick button once.

This puts your imaginary sketching pen down.

> Move the cursor and watch the lines that appear on the screen.

> Press the pick button again.

This picks your imaginary pen up again, resulting in an end point. If you move the cursor again, no new lines will be drawn.

> Press the pick button once again and move the cursor. The pen is down and you can continue sketching from a new start point.

Now look at the other options:

Sketch. Pen eXit Quit Record Erase Connect.

"P" picks the imaginary pen up and down, but the pick button is more convenient. "X" records the lines you have drawn and exits the command. "Q" exits without recording. "R" records without exiting. "E" allows you to erase some of the lines you have sketched in the last sequence. The action of this erase option is interesting and you should try it out. "C" connects you to the point where you last picked up your pen. "." draws a straight line from the point where you left off to the current position of the cross hairs.

NOTE: Since SKETCHed objects are made up of large numbers of very small lines, they take up a great deal of memory.

Tasks 13, 14, 15, 16, and 17

You now know how to draw nearly all of AutoCAD's two-dimensional entities. In the next chapter we will explore ways to create and manipulate groups and blocks made up of multiple entities, all of which will be drawn and edited using the commands you already know. The drawings you are about to do are intended to be fun and interesting as well as to give you experience with the new entities you have learned in this chapter.

DRAWING 9-1: BACKGAMMON BOARD

This drawing should go very quickly. It is a good warm-up and will give you practice with MLINE, PLINE, and SOLID. Remember that the dimensions are always part of your drawing now, unless otherwise indicated.

DRAWING SUGGESTIONS

GRID = 1.00
SNAP = .125

> First create the multiline line style for the frame with three elements 0.25, 0.00, and −.50 and joints on as shown. Then draw the 15.50 × 17.50 multiline frame.

> Draw a 0-width 15.50 × 13.50 polyline rectangle and then OFFSET it .125 to the inside. The inner polyline is actually .25 wide; but it is drawn on center, so the offset must be half the width.

> Enter the PEDIT command and change the width of the inner polyline to .25. This will give you your wide filled border.

> Draw the four triangles at the left of the board and then array them across. The filled triangles are drawn with the SOLID command; the others are just outlines drawn with LINE or PLINE. (Notice that you cannot draw some solids filled and others not filled.)

> The dimensions in this drawing are quite straightforward and should give you no trouble. Remember to set to layer "dim" before dimensioning.

Chap. 9

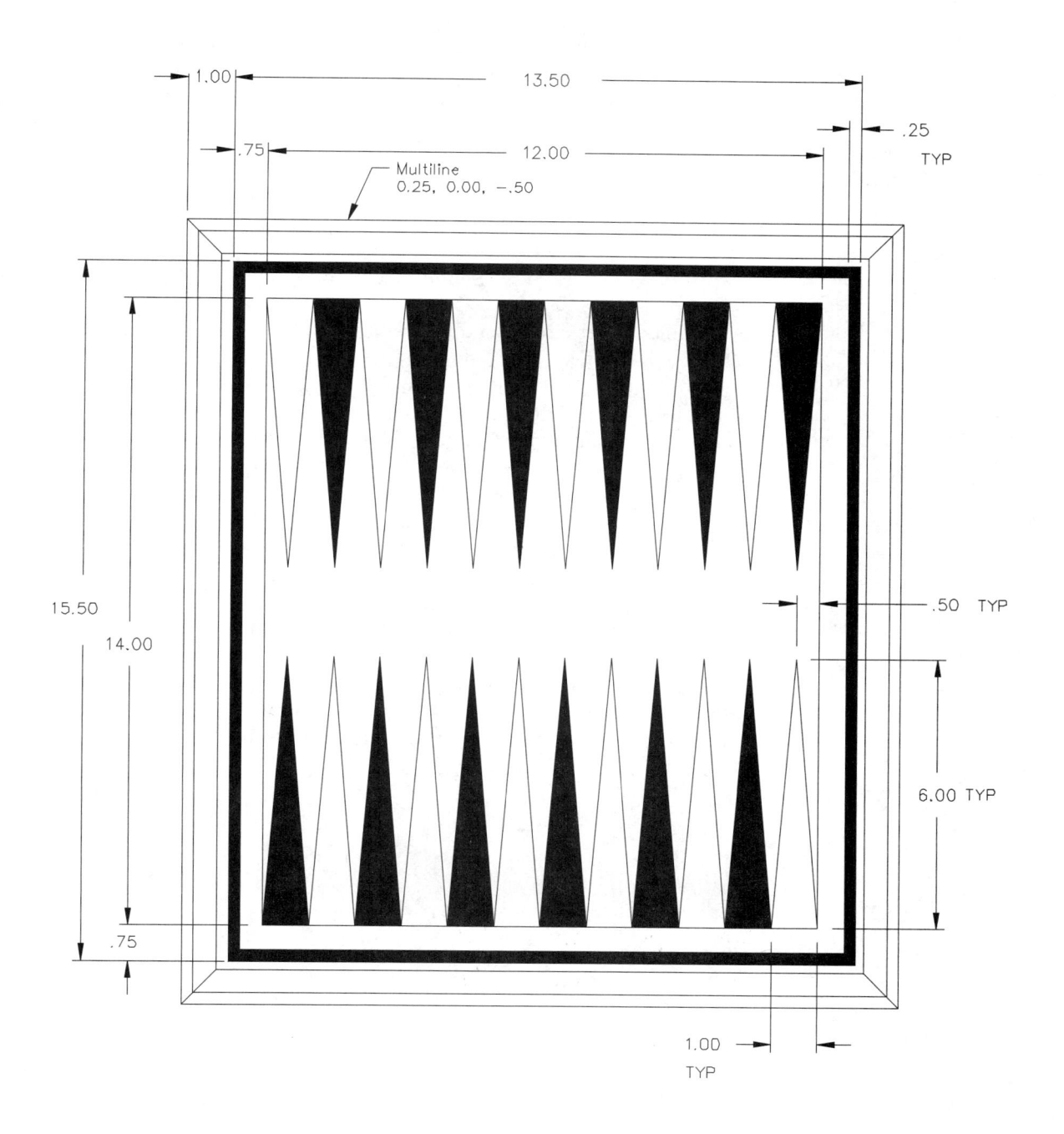

BACKGAMMON BOARD
Drawing 9-1

DRAWING 9-2: DART BOARD

Although this drawing may seem to resemble the previous one, it is quite a bit more complex and is drawn in an entirely different way. Using SOLID to create the filled areas here would be impractical because of the arc-shaped edges. We suggest you use DONUTs and TRIM them along the radial lines.

DRAWING SUGGESTIONS

LIMITS = (0.0) (24,18)
GRID = 1.00
SNAP = .125

> The filled inner circle is a donut with 0 inner and .62 outer diameters.

> The second circle is a simple 1.50 diameter circle. From here, draw a series of donuts. The outside diameter of one will become the inside diameter of the next. The 13.00 and 17.00 diameter outer circles must be drawn as circles rather than donuts so they will not be filled.

> Draw a radius line from the center to one of the quadrants of the outer circle and array it around the circle.

> You may find it easier and quicker to turn fill off before trimming the donuts. Also, use layers to keep the donuts separated visually by color.

> To TRIM the donuts, select the radial lines as cutting edges. This is easily done using a very small crossing box around the center point of the board. Otherwise you will have to pick each line individually in the area between the 13.00 and 17.00 circle.

> Draw the number 5 at the top of the board using a "middle" text position and a rotation of 2 degrees. Array it around the circle and then use the DDEDIT command to change the copied fives to the other numbers shown.

Chap. 9

CIRCLE DIAMETERS

⌀.62
⌀1.50
⌀7.50
⌀8.25
⌀13.00
⌀17.00

DART BOARD

Drawing 9-2

DRAWING 9-3: PRINTED CIRCUIT BOARD

This drawing uses donuts, solids, and polylines. Also notice the ordinate dimensions.

DRAWING SUGGESTIONS

UNITS = 4-place decimal
LIMITS = (0,0) (18,12)
GRID = 0.5000
SNAP = 0.1250

> Because this drawing uses ordinate dimensions, moving the 0 point of the grid using the UCS command will make the placement of figures very easy.

> The 26 rectangular tabs at the bottom can be drawn as polylines or solids. We drew solids and used DIST to lay out corners before entering the SOLID command.

> After placing the donuts according to the dimensions, draw the connections to them using polyline arcs and line segments. These will be simple polylines of uniform .03125 halfwidth. The triangular tabs will be added later.

> Remember, AutoCAD begins all polyline arcs tangent to the last segment drawn. Often this is not what you want. One way to correct this is to begin with a line segment that establishes the direction for the arc. The line segment can be extremely short and still accomplish your purpose. Thus many of these polylines will consist of a line segment, followed by an arc, followed by another line segment.

> There are two sizes of the triangular tabs, one on top of the rectangular tabs and one at each donut. Draw one of each size in place and then use multiple COPY, MOVE, and ROTATE commands to create all the others.

Chap. 9

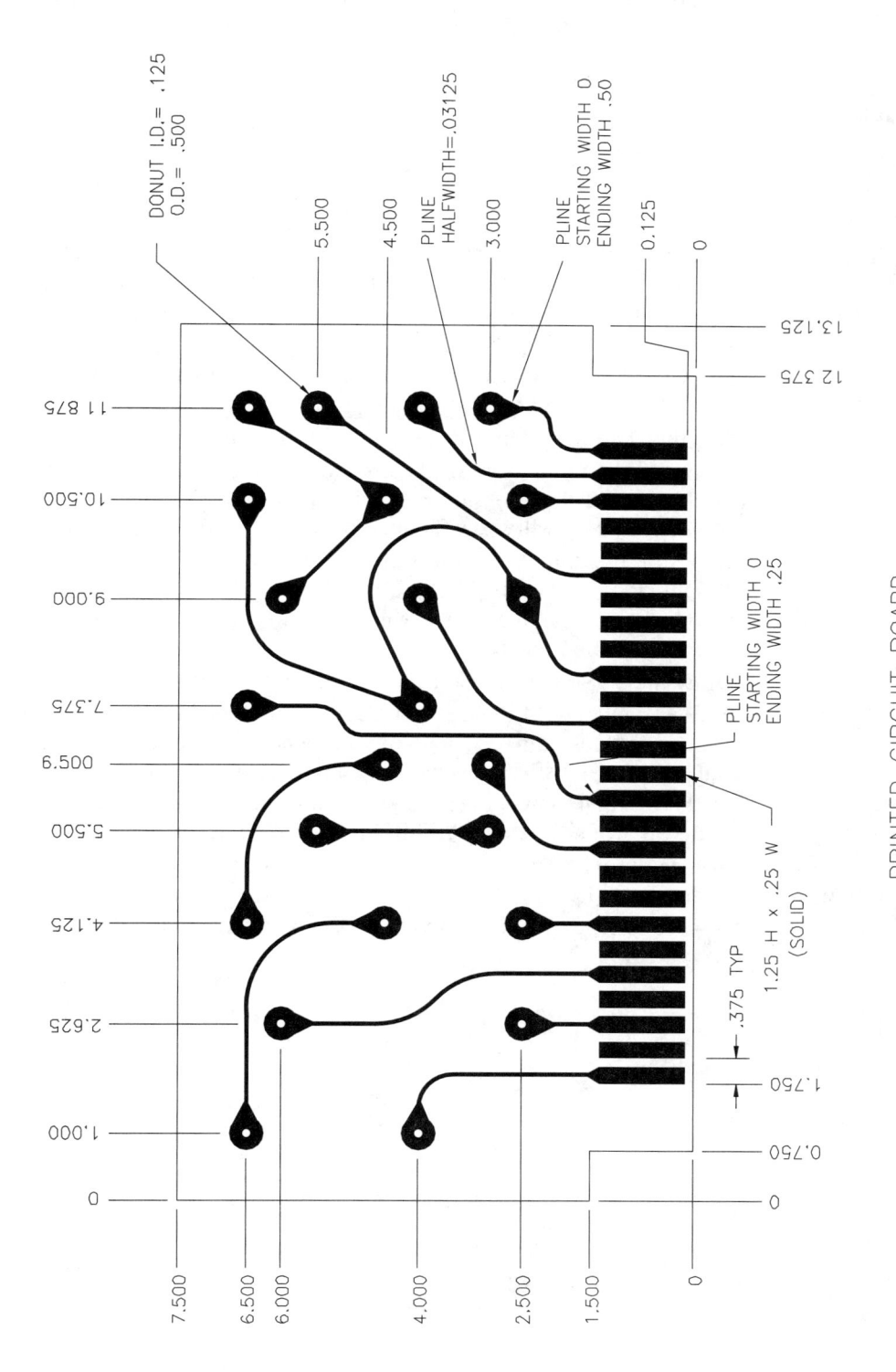

PRINTED CIRCUIT BOARD
DRAWING 9-3

DRAWING 9-4: CARBIDE TIP SAW BLADE

This is a nice drawing that will give you some good experience with the OFFSET command. How would you draw the sides of the carbide tip if you could not use OFFSET?

DRAWING SUGGESTIONS

GRID = 1.00
SNAP = .125

> After drawing the 7.25 diameter circle, draw a vertical line 1.50 over from the center line. This line will become the left side of the detailed "cut."

> Use DIST with an object snap to the intersection of the circle and the vertical line to locate the .58 vertical distance.

> Draw the horizontal center line through the .58 point and the vertical center line .16 to the right.

> Use the center lines in drawing the .16 radius arc.

> From the right end point of the arc, draw a line extending out of the circle at 80 degrees. The dimension is given as 10 degrees from the vertical, but the coordinate display will show 80 degrees from the horizontal instead.

> OFFSET this line .06 to the right and left to create the lines for the left and right sides of the carbide tip.

> Draw a horizontal line .12 up from the center line. TRIM it with the sides of the carbide tip and create .06 radius fillets right and left.

> Draw the 3.68 radius circle to locate the outside of the tip.

> BREAK and TRIM the three 80 degree lines, leaving three extension lines for use in dimensioning. Then copy the whole area out to the right for the detail. When you start working on the detail, SCALE it up 2.00.

> In the original view, erase the extension lines and then array the cut and carbide tip around the circle. TRIM the circle out of the new cuts and tips.

> You can use a "Rotated" dimension at 10 degrees to create the .12 and .06 dimensions in the detail.

> Be sure to type in your own values as you dimension the detail, since it has been scaled.

Chap. 9

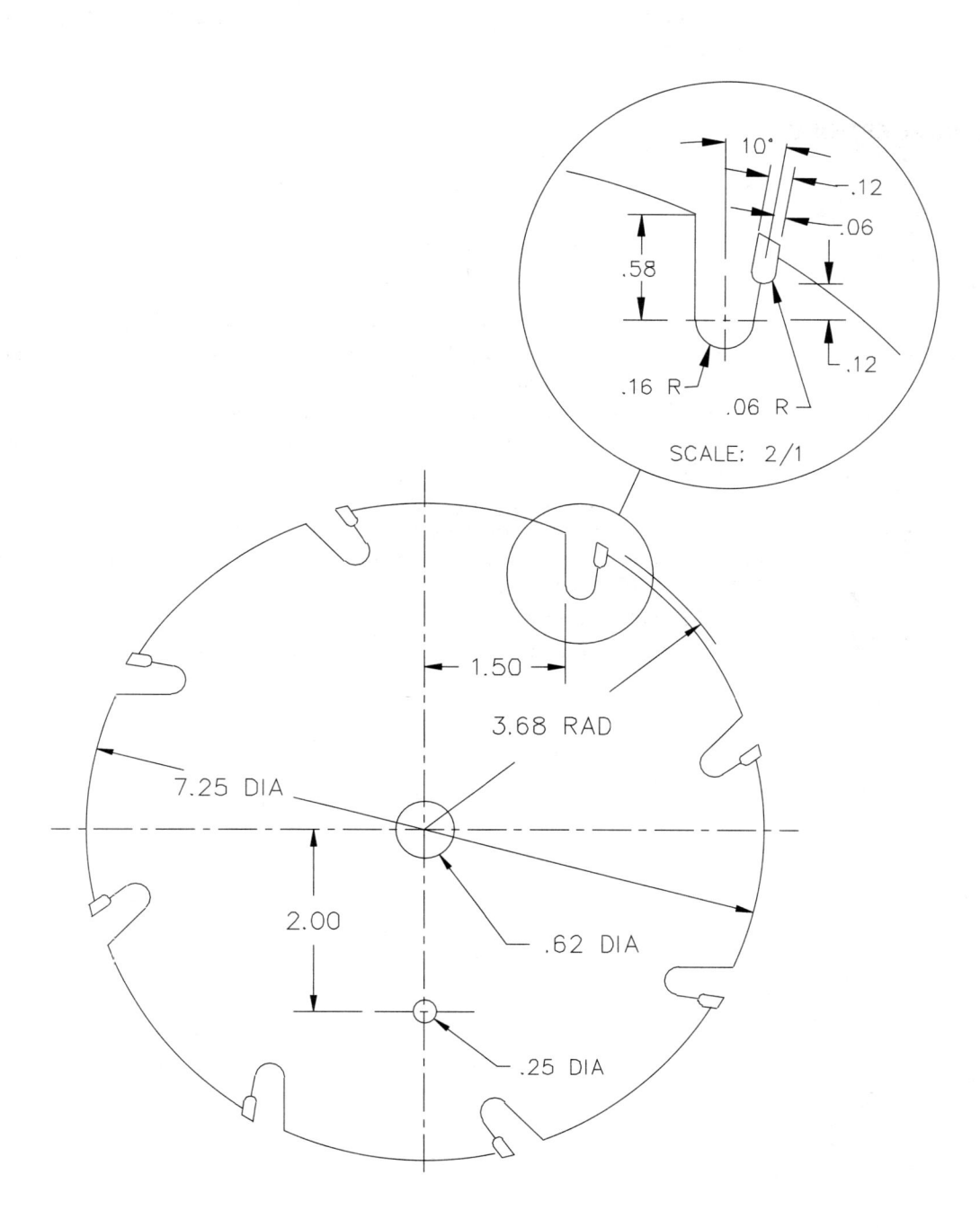

CARBIDE TIP SAW BLADE
Drawing 9-4

DRAWING 9-5: GAZEBO

This architectural drawing makes extensive use of both the POLYGON command and the OFFSET command.

DRAWING SUGGESTIONS

UNITS = Architectural
GRID = 1'
SNAP = 2"
LIMITS = (0',0') (48',36')

> All radii except the 6" polygon are given from the center point to the midpoint of a side. In other words, the 6" polygon will be "inscribed," while all the others will be "circumscribed."

> Notice that all polygon radii dimensions are given to the outside of the 2" × 4". OFFSET to the inside to create the parallel polygon for the inside of the board.

> Create radial studs by drawing a line from the midpoint of one side of a polygon to the midpoint of the side of another, or the midpoint of one to the vertex of another as shown, then offset 1" each side and erase the original. Array around the center point.

> TRIM lines and polygons at vertices.

> You can make effective use of MIRROR in the elevation.

Chap. 9

Polygon radii 6"

Polygon radii 2'-0"

Polygon radii 6'-0"

Polygon radii 6'-4"

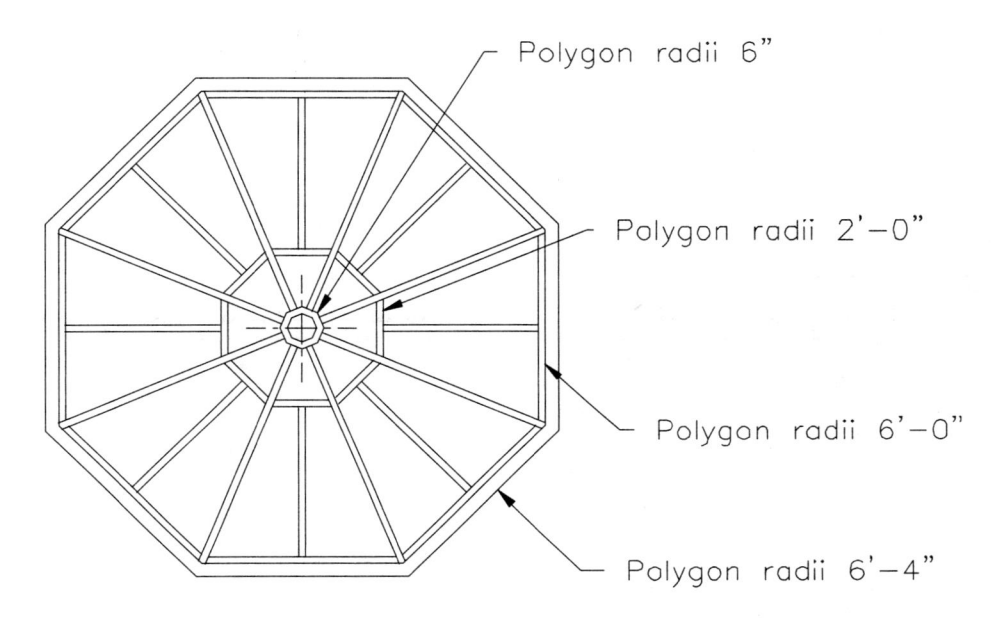

ROOF FRAMING

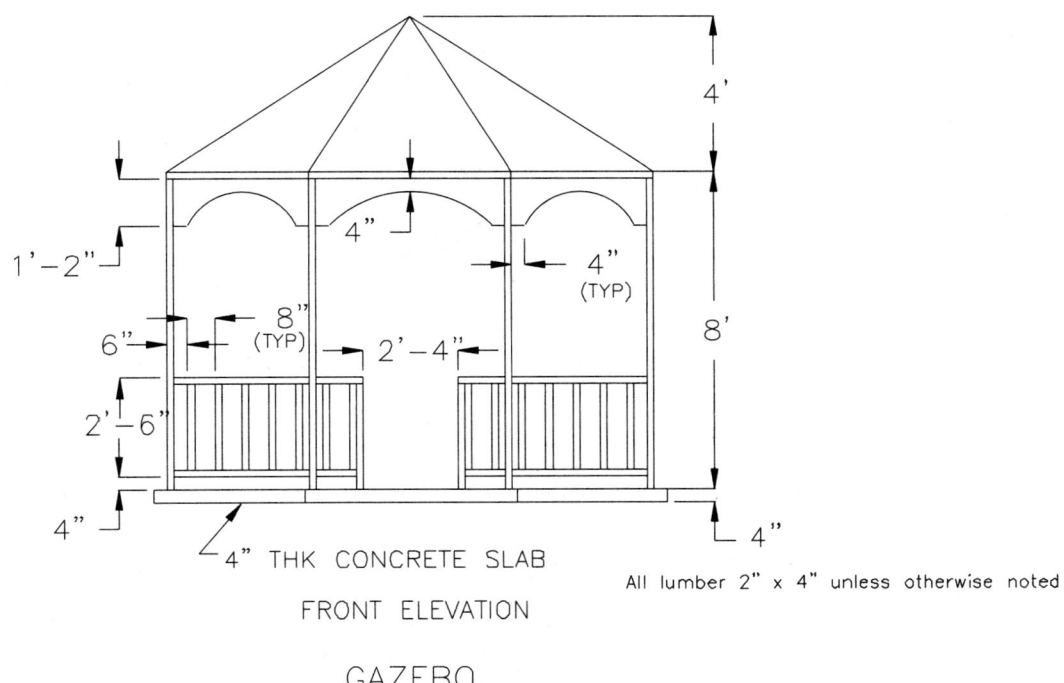

4'

1'-2"

4"

4" (TYP)

8" (TYP)

6"

2'-4"

8'

2'-6"

4"

4"

4" THK CONCRETE SLAB

All lumber 2" x 4" unless otherwise noted

FRONT ELEVATION

GAZEBO
Drawing 9-5

CHAPTER 10

COMMANDS

DRAW	**ATTRIBUTE**	**EXTERNAL REFERENCE**
BLOCK	ATTDEF	XBIND
INSERT	ATTDISP	XREF
WBLOCK	ATTEDIT	
	ATTEXT	**STANDARD**
	DDATTDEF	GROUP
	DDATTE	COPYCLIP

OVERVIEW

You have seen several ways in which AutoCAD can treat a complex object as a single entity. In this chapter you will learn to create "groups" and "blocks." A group is simply a set of objects that can be selected, named, and manipulated collectively. A block is a set of objects more permanently defined as a single entity. Blocks can be inserted repeatedly in many drawings and also can be given attributes. An attribute is an item of information about a block, such as a part number or price, that is stored along with the block definition. All the information stored in attributes can be extracted from a drawing and used to produce itemized reports. This is a powerful feature of CAD that has no direct counterpart in manual drafting.

Blocks may be stored within individual drawings or saved as complete drawings in themselves. In the latter case they can then be inserted into other drawings as blocks or linked to other drawings as "external references," using the XREF command. These features allow you to create symbol libraries made up of commonly used objects.

TASKS

1. Create groups using GROUP.
2. Create blocks using BLOCK.
3. INSERT and assemble blocks.
4. Copy objects to other applications using the Windows clipboard.
5. Create attributes using ATTDEF.
6. Edit attributes using DDATTE and ATTEDIT.
7. EXPLODE blocks.
8. Do Drawing 10-1 ("CAD Room").
9. Do Drawing 10-2 ("Base Assembly").
10. Do Drawing 10-3 ("Double Bearing Assembly").
11. Do Drawing 10-4 ("Scooter Assembly").

Task 1: Creating GROUPs

Procedure

1. Type "Group" or select the Object Group tool from the Standard toolbar.
2. Type a name.
3. Click on "New".
4. Select objects to be included in the group definition.
5. Press Enter to end object selection.
6. Click on "OK" to exit the dialogue.

Discussion. The simplest way to create a complex entity from previously drawn entities is to group them into a unit with the GROUP command, which is new in Release 13. Groups are given names and can be selected for all editing processes if they are defined as selectable.

In this exercise we will form groups from objects that also will be used later to define blocks. In this way you will get a feel for the different functions of these two methods of creating collections of objects. You will be creating simple symbols for a computer, monitor, digitizer, and keyboard as seen from above, looking down. Once created, these may also be used in Drawing 10-1 at the end of the chapter.

> Begin by making the following changes in the drawing setup:
  1. Set to layer 0 (the reason for doing this is discussed in the NOTE following this list).
  2. Change to architectural units, with smallest fraction = 1.
  3. Set GRID = 1'.
  4. Set SNAP = 1".
  5. Set LIMITS = (0',0') (48',36').

NOTE: Blocks created on layer 0 will be inserted on the current layer. Blocks created on any other layer will stay on the layer on which they are created. Inserting blocks is discussed in Task 3.

> Zoom into an area approximately 12' × 9'.

> Draw the four objects in *Figure 10-1*.

Draw the geometry only; the text and dimensions in the figure are for your reference only and should not be on your screen.

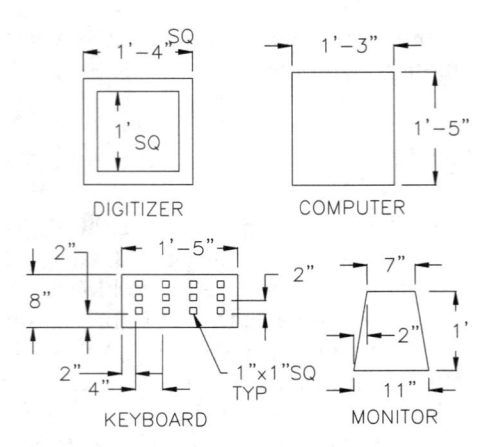

Figure 10-1

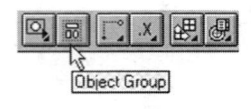

Figure 10-2

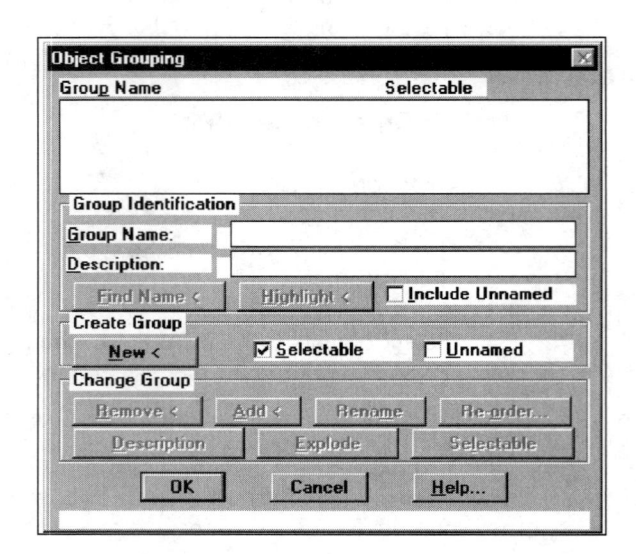

Figure 10-3

We will define the "keyboard" as a group.

> Type "Group" or select the Object Group tool from the Standard toolbar, as shown in *Figure 10-2*.

Either method will call the Object Grouping dialogue box shown in *Figure 10-3*. At the top of the box is the Group Name list box. It will be empty now since there are no groups defined in this drawing. Below that is the Group Identification area with edit boxes for entering a group name (up to 31 characters) and a group description (up to 64 characters). The flashing cursor bar should be in the group name box so that you can enter a name. Our first group will be the set of rectangles you have drawn as a symbol for a keyboard.

> Type "keyboard" in the Group Name edit box.

Now look at the Create Group area. The three boxes here are "New <", "Selectable", and "Unnamed". In order to create a group, you must indicate that it is a new group. But first, you need to be sure that the group will be defined as selectable, if that is your intention, as it most often will be. Unnamed groups are usually groups that have been created by copying named groups. In these cases AutoCAD assigns names beginning with *A and followed by a number.

> Be sure that "Selectable" is checked.
> Click on "New <" in the Create Group area.

At this point the dialogue box will disappear to give you access to objects in your drawing. You will see a "Select Objects:" prompt at the command line.

> Select the keyboard outer rectangles and small rectangles using a window.
> Press Enter to end object selection.

This will bring back the dialogue box. "KEYBOARD" should now be in the list box, with a "Yes" to the right indicating that it is a selectable group.

> Click on "OK" to exit the dialogue box.

The keyboard is now defined in the drawing as a selectable group. To see that this is so, try selecting it.

> Position the pick box anywhere on the "Keyboard" and press the pick button.

You will see from the highlights and blue grip boxes that the complete group is selected. That is all you need to do with groups at this point. Groups are useful for copying and manipulating groups of objects that tend to stay together. The following notes will help you to go further with groups if you wish.

1. If you click on "Find Name" and then select any object that is part of group, AutoCAD will show you the name (or names) of the group (or groups) that the object belongs to.
2. Unnamed groups are only included in the Group Name list if Include Unnamed is checked.
3. In editing commands you can select a group by pointing or by typing "group" at the Select Objects prompt, and then typing the name of the group.
4. If the PICKSTYLE variable is set to 0 (default value is 1), you will only be able to select groups by typing their names, not by pointing. This variable is changed if you pick "Group Selection" from the "Assist" pull down menu.

Concerning the Change Group area of the dialogue box...

1. Remove and Add allow you to remove or add individual objects of a previously defined group.
2. The objects in a group have a defined order, which can be changed using the Group Order dialogue box. Select "Re-order..." in the Object Grouping dialogue box.
3. You can change the description of a previously defined group by highlighting the name on the group list, typing or editing the description, and then clicking on Description.
4. You can delete a group definition by highlighting its name on the group list and then clicking on Explode.
5. To switch the selectability status of a defined group between yes and no, use the Selectable box at the bottom right of the dialogue box.

Task 2: Creating BLOCKs

Procedure

1. Type "Block" or select the Block tool from the Block flyout on the Draw toolbar.
2. Type a name.
3. Pick an insertion point.
4. Select objects to be included in the block definition.

Discussion. Blocks are more permanent than groups. Blocks can be stored as part of an individual drawing or as separate drawings, and can be inserted into any drawing. In general, the most useful blocks are those that will be used repeatedly in many drawings and therefore can become part of a library of predrawn objects used by you and others in your work group. In mechanical drawing, for instance, you may want a set of screws drawn to standard sizes that you can call out any time you wish. Or, if you are doing architectural drawing, you might find a library of doors and windows useful.

In this chapter we are creating a set of simple symbols for some of the tools we know you will be using no matter what kind of CAD you are doing—namely, computers, monitors, keyboards, digitizers, plotters, and printers. We define them as blocks and then assemble them into a workstation. Later we will insert workstations into an architectural drawing called "CAD ROOM."

> Type "Block" or select the Block tool from the Block flyout on the Draw toolbar.

The first thing AutoCAD wants is a name for the block:

Block name (or ?):

A "?" will get you a list of blocks defined within the current drawing. Right now there are none.

> Type "computer".

AutoCAD prompts:

Insertion base point:

Insertion points and insertion base points are critical in the whole matter of using blocks. The insertion base point is the point on the block which will be at the intersection of the cross hairs when you insert the block. Therefore, when defining a block, try to anticipate the point on the block you would most likely use to position the block on the screen.

> Use a midpoint osnap to pick the middle of the bottom line of the computer as the insertion point, as shown in *Figure 10-4*.

Finally, AutoCAD needs to know what to include in the block.

Select objects:

> Use a window to select the whole computer box.

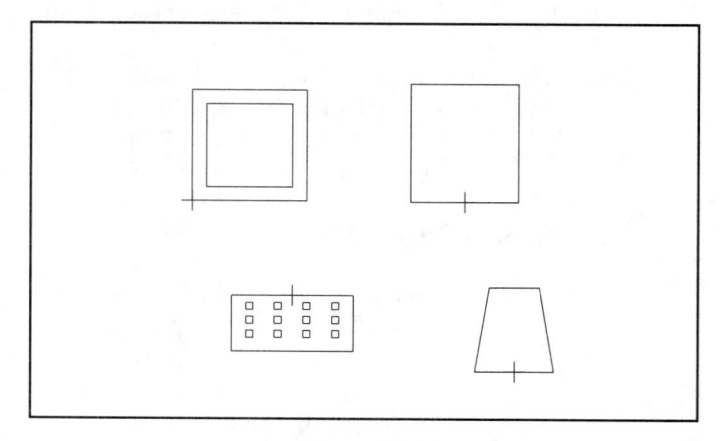

Figure 10-4

When a block is defined, the first thing that happens is that it is erased from the display. The block definition is now part of the drawing database, and you can insert the block anywhere in the drawing, but the original is gone. This facilitates the practice of creating a number of blocks, one after the other, and then assembling them at the end. If the originals did not disappear you would have the added step of erasing them or panning to another part of the display to find room for the next block.

NOTE: If for any reason you want the original back right away, the OOPS command will bring it back, just as it does in the ERASE command. Do not use U, because this would undo the block definition.

You have created a "computer" block definition. Now repeat the process to make a "keyboard" block.

> Type "Block" or select the Block tool from the Draw toolbar.
> Type "keyboard".
> Pick the midpoint of the top line of the keyboard as the insertion base point.
> Select the keyboard.

Since you have already defined the keyboard as a selectable group, one pick should select the whole thing. In the command area AutoCAD will show how many individual objects are in the selection set, and also that there is one group in the set. The group definition of the keyboard will now become part of the block definition.

> Press Enter to end object selection.

Repeat the blocking process two more times to create "monitor" and "digitizer" blocks, with insertion base points as shown in *Figure 10-4*. When you are done, your screen should be blank. Look at this description of the WBLOCK command before proceeding to Task 3.

WBLOCK

The WBLOCK command is very similar to BLOCK, except that it writes a block out to a separate file so that it may be inserted in other drawings. You can WBLOCK a previously defined block or create a new block definition as you write the block out. You can also WBLOCK an entire drawing. This can be quite useful, since a WBLOCKed drawing takes up less memory than a SAVEd one. We will be using WBLOCK as well as BLOCK extensively in the drawings at the end of this chapter.

Task 3: INSERTing Previously Defined Blocks

Procedure

1. Type "ddinsert" or select the Insert Block tool from the Block flyout on the Draw toolbar.
2. Type a block name.
3. Pick an insertion point.
4. Answer prompts for horizontal and vertical scale and rotation angle.

Discussion. The INSERT and DDINSERT commands are used to bring blocks into a drawing. The four block definitions you created in Task 1 are now part of the drawing database and can be inserted in this drawing anywhere you like.

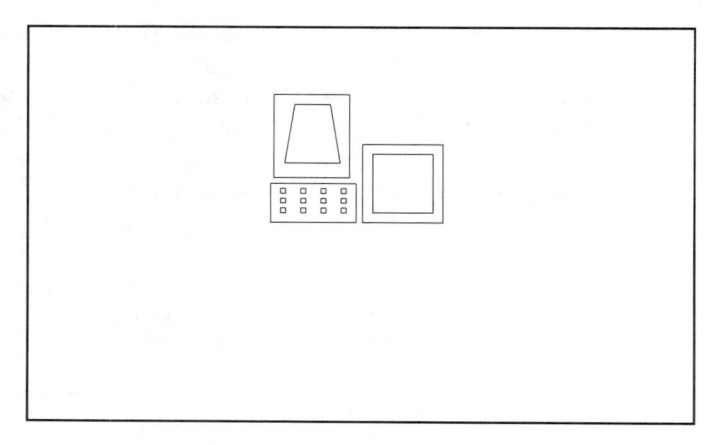

Figure 10-5

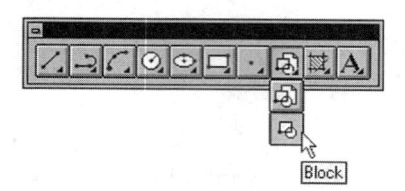

Figure 10-6

INSERT or DDINSERT, the dialogue box version, also can be used to insert complete drawings into other drawings. Among other things, these procedures are very useful in creating assembly drawings. You will find that assembling blocks can be done efficiently using appropriate OSNAP modes to place objects in precise relation to one another. Assembly drawing will be the focus of the drawing tasks at the end of this chapter.

In this task we will insert the computer, monitor, keyboard, and digitizer back into the drawing to create the "workstation" assembly shown in *Figure 10-5*. We will also discuss other options for drawing file management, including the use of complete drawings as blocks or as "external references."

> If you are still on layer 0, switch to layer 1.
> Type "ddinsert" or select the Insert Block tool from the Block flyout on the Draw toolbar, as shown in *Figure 10-6*.

This will bring up the Insert dialogue box shown in *Figure 10-7*. Now is a good time to see that your block definitions are still in your database, even though they are no longer on the screen.

> Click on "Block..." in the dialogue box.

You should see a Defined Blocks dialogue box with a list like this:
COMPUTER
DIGITIZER
KEYBOARD
MONITOR

> Select "COMPUTER" from the list, then click on "OK" to return to the Insert dialogue, and then again to begin the insertion.

From here on you will follow prompts from the command line. AutoCAD now needs to know where to insert the computer and you will see this prompt:

Insertion point:

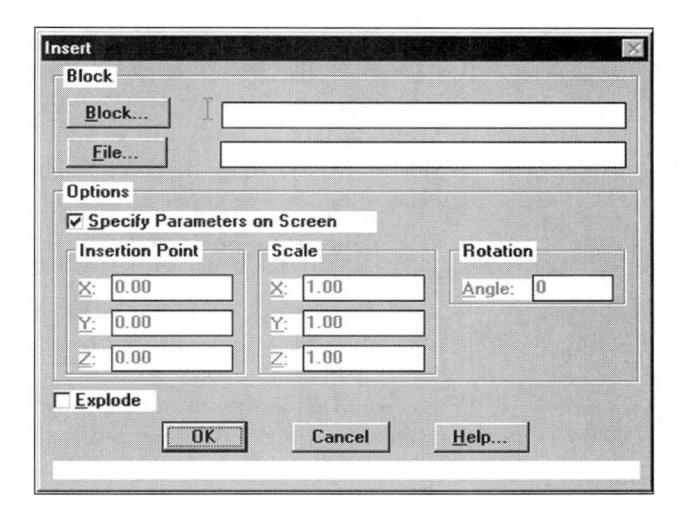

Figure 10-7

Notice that AutoCAD gives you a block to drag into place and that it is positioned with the block's insertion base point at the intersection of the cross hairs.

> Pick a point near the middle of the screen, as shown in *Figure 10-5*.

What comes next is a set of prompts that allow you to scale and rotate the block as you insert it. This vastly increases the flexibility and power of the blocking system, although in many instances, including this one, you will accept all the defaults.

The first prompt asks for a scale factor:

X scale factor <1> / Corner / XYZ:

Unlike the SCALE command, which automatically scales both horizontally and vertically, blocks can be stretched or shrunk in either direction independently as you insert them. You can type an X scale factor or specify both an X and a Y factor at once by showing two corners of a window using the Corner option. The third option, XYZ, is reserved for 3D applications. Pressing Enter will retain the block's present length.

> Press Enter to retain an X scale factor of 1.

AutoCAD follows with a prompt for vertical scale:

Y scale factor (default=X):

> Press Enter to retain a Y factor of 1.

You now have the opportunity to rotate the object:

Rotation angle <0>:

> Press Enter to retain 0 degrees of rotation.

Notice that the block is inserted on layer 1 even though it was created on layer 0. Remember that this only works with blocks drawn on layer 0. Blocks drawn on other layers stay on the layer they were drawn on when they are inserted.

Now let's add a monitor.

> Repeat the DDINSERT command.

Notice that the last block inserted becomes the default block name in the Block name box. This facilitates procedures in which you insert the same block in several different places in a drawing.

> Select "Block..." in the Insert dialogue box.

> Select "MONITOR" in the Defined Blocks dialogue box.

> Click on "OK" in both dialogue boxes.

> Pick an insertion point two or three inches above the insertion point of the computer, as shown.

> Press Enter three additional times to retain X and Y scale factors of 1, and a rotation of 0.

You should have the monitor sitting on top of the computer, and be back at the "command" prompt. We will insert the keyboard, as shown in *Figure 10-5*.

> Repeat DDINSERT.

> Click on "Block...".

> Click on "KEYBOARD".

> Exit both dialogue boxes.

> Pick an insertion point one or two inches below the computer, as shown.

> Press Enter three additional times to retain X and Y scale factors of 1, and a rotation of 0.

You should now have the keyboard in place.

> Repeat DDINSERT once more and place the digitizer block to the right of the other blocks as shown.

Congratulations, you have completed your first assembly. Now that you are familiar with BLOCK, WBLOCK, and DDINSERT, you have the primary tools needed to create and utilize a symbol library. Tasks 5 and 6 introduce you to attributes. We will create attributes to hold information about CAD workstations and include them in the definition of a new "ws" block. Then we will insert several workstations into our drawing and edit some of the attribute information. But before going on, let's look at "external references" and the Windows clipboard, two other ways to bring information from one drawing into another.

External References

An external reference is a drawing that is "attached" to another drawing through the use of the XREF command. External references are similar to blocks and can be used for many of the same purposes. They are particularly important in network environments.

In the previous exercise we inserted blocks that were defined within our current drawing. We can use exactly the same procedure with the DDINSERT command to insert a complete drawing file into our current drawing. The inserted drawing would then become a block within the current drawing, although its original drawing file would still exist separately. The XREF command is an alternative to inserting complete drawings. The principal difference between inserted drawings and externally referenced drawings is that inserted drawings are actually merged with the current drawing database, whereas externally referenced drawings are only linked. You cannot edit an external reference from within the current drawing. However, if the XREFed drawing is changed, the changes will be reflected in the current drawing the next time it is loaded, or when the Reload option of the XREF command is executed. This allows several people at separate workstations to work on different aspects of a single master drawing, which is updated automatically as changes are made in the various referenced drawings.

Since XREF only loads enough information to "point to" the externally referenced drawing, it does not increase the size of the current drawing file as significantly as INSERT does. The options of the XREF command are as follows:

?	Produces a list of external references attached to the current drawing.
Bind	Merges an external reference completely into the current drawing. The end result is the same as INSERTing a drawing, but binding does not have to occur until the final version of the drawing is complete. There is also an XBIND command that allows you to exclude certain types of information when you bind an external reference. The dimensions, for example, can be left out if they are drawn on a separate layer.
Detach	Removes the link between the current drawing and specified external references. Detached objects are no longer seen in your drawing.
Path	Tells AutoCAD where to locate an external reference. This option is used to update a link when file structure is changed, or the externally referenced drawing is moved. Otherwise, the link cannot be maintained.
Reload	Reloads an external reference without leaving the current drawing. This is most useful in networked environments in which one person may be working on a drawing that is referenced in another person's drawing. Using this option, the most recent changes can be brought into the current drawing.
Overlay	Overlays the xref drawing without altering your current drawing so that you can see how your drawing relates to others in your network.
Attach	Creates a link between the current drawing and another drawing.

Management of Named Objects

What happens when an externally referenced or inserted drawing has layers, linetypes, text styles, dimension styles, blocks, or views with names that conflict with those in the current drawing? Good question. In the case of INSERTed drawings, name definitions in the current drawing override those in the inserted block. In the case of XREFed drawings, named objects are given special designations that eliminate the confusion. For example, if drawing A is attached to drawing B and both have a layer called FLOOR, a new layer is created in B called A|FLOOR.

Task 4: Using the Windows Clipboard

Procedure

1. Select the Cut or Copy tool from the Standard toolbar.
2. Move to another Windows application.
3. Type Ctrl-V or select "Paste" in that application.

Discussion. The Windows clipboard makes it very easy to copy objects from an AutoCAD drawing into other Windows applications. You will use the Copy and Cut tools from the Standard toolbar, which activate the COPYCLIP AND

COPYCUT commands. Cut will remove the selected objects from your AutoCAD drawing, while Copy will leave them. When you send objects to the Clipboard, using COPYCLIP or CUTCLIP, the objects will be defined as a block and given a random name. This is not the best procedure for creating blocks within AutoCAD, however, since you have no control over the name.

In this task we will go through the steps to copy part of an AutoCAD drawing to another Windows application. We have used Microsoft Word for the example, but the procedure is very simple and will work with any Windows application that supports Windows OLE (Object Embedding and Linking).

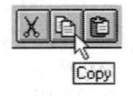

Figure 10-8

> To begin this task you should be in an AutoCAD drawing with some objects on your screen. We will use the computer workstation from the last task, but any objects will do.

> Select the Copy tool from the Standard toolbar, as shown in *Figure 10-8*.

Note that this is different from the Copy tool on the Modify toolbar. This tool is used to copy objects on the Windows clipboard for the purpose of copying them to other applications.

AutoCAD prompts:

Select objects

> Using a window selection, select all of the objects in the computer workstation assembled in the last task.

> Press Enter to end object selection.

AutoCAD will save the selected objects to the clipboard. Nothing will happen on your screen but the selected objects are stored as a block entity and could be pasted back into this drawing or another AutoCAD drawing. Most important, they can now be pasted into another Windows application. The following steps assume that a word processing applications is open in the background.

> Hold down the Alt key and hit the Tab key once without letting go of Alt.

You will see a box across the middle of the screen with the name of another Windows application as shown in *Figure 10-9*.

> Keep holding down Alt and hit the Tab key repeatedly.

Each time you hit Tab, the application named in the box will change. It will include the current AutoCAD drawing, the Word Processing Program, and the AutoCAD Text Window, at least. If there are other applications running, they will be named as well.

> Use Alt and Tab to cycle through the options and then stop on the Word Processing Program.

> Release the Alt key.

When you release Alt, the named application will come to the foreground and other applications will be hidden in the background.

> Double click on the application you want to run. In our case, we double click the Microsoft Word icon.

Figure 10-9

This will open your application.
> Move the cursor wherever you wish in the new application.
> Type Ctrl-V or select "Paste" from the Edit menu in your application.

Voila!... We hope. This will work very smoothly if your application accepts AutoCAD drawing formats, and very poorly otherwise.

Now that you have pasted AutoCAD objects into your application, any further manipulation will require you to learn about that application.

> When you are ready to return to AutoCAD, use Alt and Tab again to cycle through to the current AutoCAD drawing. You may want to close the other application before returning to AutoCAD.

That's all there is to it. It is equally simple to paste text and images from other compatible Windows applications into AutoCAD. Just reverse the process, cutting or copying from the other application and pasting into AutoCAD.

Task 5: Defining Attributes with DDATTDEF

Procedure

1. Type "ddattdef" or select the Define Attribute tool from the Attribute toolbar.
2. Specify attribute modes.
3. Type an attribute tag.
4. Type an attribute prompt.
5. If desired, type a default attribute value.
6. Include the attribute in a block definition.

Discussion. Attributes can be confusing and you should not spend too much time worrying over their details unless you are currently involved in an application that requires their use. On the other hand, they are a powerful tool, and if you have a basic understanding of what they can do, you could be the one in your work setting to recognize when to use them.

One of the difficulties of learning about attributes is that you have to define them before you see them in action. It is therefore a little hard to comprehend what your definitions mean the first time around. Bear with us and follow instructions closely; it will be worth your effort.

In this task we will define attributes that will hold information about CAD workstations. The attributes will be defined in a flexible manner so that the workstation block can represent any number of hardware configurations.

When we have defined our attributes, we will create a block called "ws" that includes the whole workstation assembly and its attributes.

> To begin this task, you should have the assembled workstation from Task 2 on your screen.

First we will define an attribute that will allow us to specify the type of computer in any individual occurrence of the "ws" block. As is often the case in Release 13, you have a choice between a command sequence and a dialogue box. We will show you the DDATTDEF dialogue box. The older ATTDEF command covers exactly the same specifications, but works in a step-by-step sequence of commands.

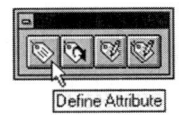

Figure 10-10

> Type "ddattdef" or select the Define Attribute tool from the Attribute toolbar, as shown in *Figure 10-10*.

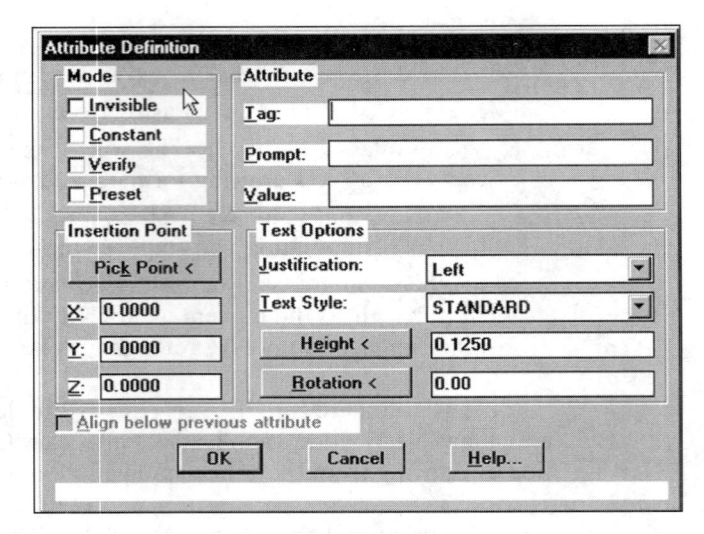

Figure 10-11

This will open the Attribute Definition dialogue box shown in *Figure 10-11*.

Look first at the check boxes at the left under "Mode". We will be using all the default modes in this first attribute definition. This means that when our workstation block is inserted, the computer attribute value will be visible in the drawing (because "Invisible" is not checked), variable with each insertion of the block (because "Constant" is not checked), verified only once ("Verify" is not checked), and not preset to a value ("Preset" is not checked).

Next look at the box under "Attribute". The cursor should be blinking in the Tag edit box. Like a field name in a database file, a tag identifies the kind of information this particular attribute is meant to hold. The tag appears in the block definition as a field name. In occurrences of the block, the tag is replaced by a specific value. "Computer," for example, could be replaced by "IBM."

> Type "Computer" in the Tag edit box.

> Move the cursor to the "Prompt" edit box.

As with the tag, the key to understanding the attribute prompt is to be clear about the difference between block definitions and actual occurrences of blocks in a drawing. Right now we are defining an attribute. The attribute definition will become part of the definition of the ws block and will be used whenever ws is inserted. Attribute definitions function as containers for information. Each time we insert ws we can specify some or all of the information that its attributes hold. This is what will allow us to use our ws block to represent different hardware configurations. With the definition we are creating, there will be a prompt whenever we insert ws that asks us to enter information about the computer in a given configuration.

> Type "Enter computer type:".

We also have the opportunity to specify a default attribute value, if we wish, by typing in the Value edit box. This time, we will use no default in our attribute definition.

The box labelled "Text Options" allows you to specify text parameters as you would in TEXT or in DTEXT. Visible attributes appear as text on the screen. Therefore, the appearance of the text needs to be specified. The only change we will make is to specify a height.

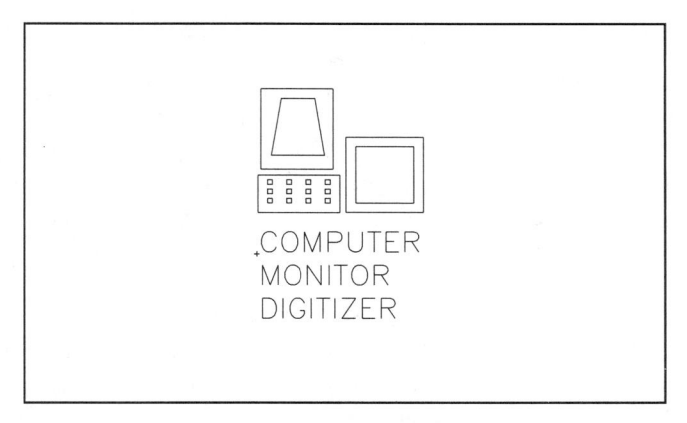

Figure 10-12

> Click in the edit box to the right of "Height <" and then type "4". If you click on the "Height <" box itself, the dialogue box will disappear so that you can indicate a height by pointing.

Finally, AutoCAD needs to know where to place the visible attribute information in the drawing. You can type in *x*, *y*, and *z* coordinate values, but you are much more likely to show a point.

> Click on "Pick Point <".

The dialogue box will disappear temporarily to allow access to the screen. You will also see a "Start point:" prompt in the command area.

We will place our attributes 8 inches below the keyboard, as shown in *Figure 10-12*.

> Pick a start point 8 inches below the left side of the keyboard, as shown.

The dialogue box will reappear.

> Click on "OK" to complete the dialogue.

The dialogue box will disappear and the attribute tag "Computer" will be drawn as shown. Remember, this is an attribute definition, not an occurrence of the attribute. "Computer" is our attribute tag. After we define the workstation as a block and the block is inserted, you will answer the "Enter computer type:" prompt with the name of a computer, and the name itself will be in the drawing rather than this tag.

Now we will proceed to define three more attributes, using some different options.

> Repeat DDATTDEF.

We will use all the default modes again, but we will provide a default monitor value in this attribute definition.

> Type "Monitor" for the attribute tag.
> Type "Enter monitor type:" for the attribute prompt.
> Type "NEC Multisync" for the default attribute value.

Now when AutoCAD shows the prompt for a monitor type, it will also show NEC Multisync as the default.

You can align a series of attributes by checking the Align below previous attribute box at the lower right of the dialogue box.

> Click in the check box labeled "Align below previous attribute".
> Click on "OK" to complete the dialogue.

The attribute tag "Monitor" should be added to the workstation below the "Computer" tag.

Next, we will add an "invisible, preset" attribute for the digitizer. Invisible means that the attribute text will not be visible when the block is inserted, although the information will be in the database and can be extracted. Preset means that the attribute has a default value and does not issue a prompt to change it. However, unlike "constant" attributes, you can change preset attributes using the DDATTE command, which we will explore in Task 5.

> Repeat DDATTDEF.
> Click in the check box next to "Invisible".
NOTE: If you use the ATTDEF command instead of the dialogue box, you must change modes by typing the first letter of the mode. To change a mode from N (no) to Y (yes), you will type the first letter of the mode, as shown in the parentheses in the prompt (ICVP).
> Click in the check box next to "Preset".
> Type "Digitizer" for the attribute tag.

You will not need a prompt, since the preset attribute is automatically set to the default value.

> Type "SummaSketch II" for the default attribute value.
> Click in the Align below previous attribute check box to position the attribute below "Monitor" in the drawing.
> Click on "OK" to complete the dialogue.

The "Digitizer" attribute tag should be added to your screen, as shown. Once again, remember that this is the attribute definition. When ws is inserted the attribute value "SummaSketch II" will be written into the database, but nothing will appear on the screen since the attribute is defined as invisible.

Finally, the most important step of all: We must define the workstation as a block that includes all our attribute definitions.

> Type "block" or select the Block tool from the Block flyout on the Draw toolbar.
> Type "ws" for the block name.
> Pick an insertion point at the midpoint of the bottom of the keyboard.
> Window the workstation assembly and all three attribute tags.
> Press Enter to end object selection.

As usual, the newly defined block will disappear from the screen. In the next task we will insert several workstations back into your drawing and use DDATTE to change an attribute value.

Task 6: Editing Attributes with DDATTE and ATTEDIT

Procedure (for ATTEDIT)

1. Type "ddatte" or select the Edit Attribute tool from the Attribute toolbar.
2. Specify one-by-one or global editing.
3. Specify blocks and attributes to include in the editing process.
4. In one-by-one editing, specify property to be edited and edit it.
5. In global editing, specify string to change and new string.

Discussion. The DDATTE and ATTEDIT commands provide the capacity to change values and text properties of attributes in blocks that have been inserted. They do not allow you to edit attribute definitions. Block definitions and attribute definitions can be changed only by recreating them.

There are two ways to use ATTEDIT. One-by-one editing allows you to change individual attribute values, text position, height, angle, style, layer, and color. Global editing allows you to change values only. DDATTE can only be used to change individual attribute values and cannot be used to change any text specifications.

> To begin this task, you should have a clear screen, but the ws block with its attributes as defined in the previous task must be stored in your current drawing.

> Insert three workstations, using the following procedure (note the attribute prompts):

1. Type "Insert" or select the Insert Block tool from the Block flyout on the Draw toolbar.
2. Type or select "ws" for the block name.
3. Pick an insertion point.
4. Press Enter for X and Y scale factors and rotation angle.
5. Answer the attribute prompts for monitors and computers.

We specified two Zenith computers and one IBM computer for this exercise and retained all the monitor defaults (NEC Multisync). Your hardware information may be entirely different, but this exercise will be simpler if you use ours. Notice that you are not prompted for digitizers because that attribute is preset.

When you are done, your screen should resemble *Figure 10-13*.

The first thing we will do with the inserted blocks is use ATTDISP ("attribute display") to turn invisible attributes on.

Displaying Invisible Attributes

The ATTDISP command allows control of the visibility of all attribute values, regardless of their defined visibility mode.

> Type "Attdisp" or select "Display" and then "Attribute Display" from the Options menu.

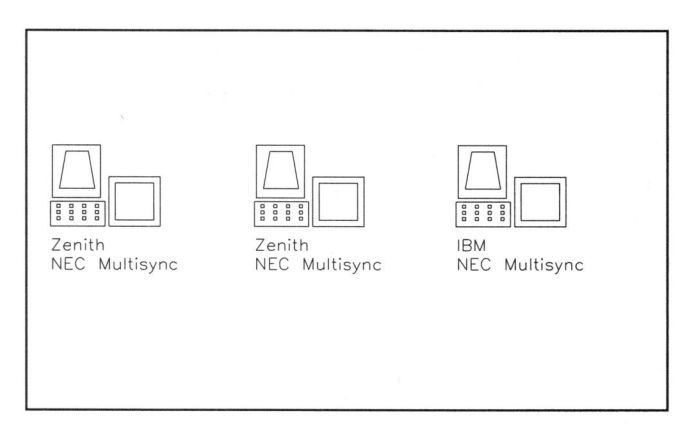

Figure 10-13

328 Part II Text, Dimensions, and Other Complex Entities

```
┌─────────────────────────────────────────────────────┐
│                                                     │
│      ┌──┐ ┌─┐      ┌──┐ ┌─┐      ┌──┐ ┌─┐           │
│      │  │ │ │      │  │ │ │      │  │ │ │           │
│      └──┘ └─┘      └──┘ └─┘      └──┘ └─┘           │
│      Zenith        Zenith        IBM                │
│      NEC Multisync NEC Multisync NEC Multisync      │
│      SummaSketch II SummaSketch II SummaSketch II   │
│                                                     │
└─────────────────────────────────────────────────────┘
```

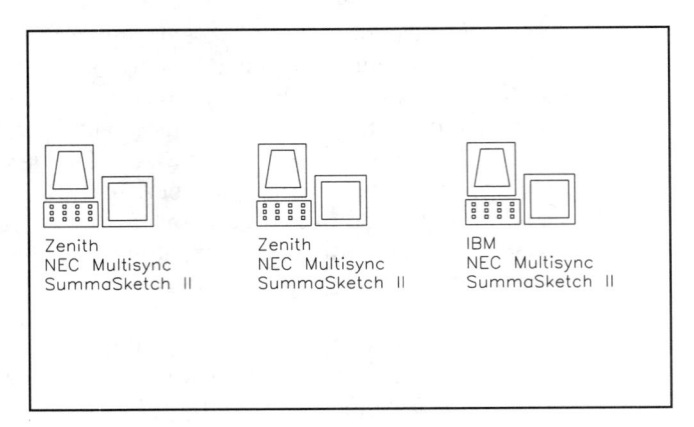

Figure 10-14

The prompt or the submenu shows you three options:

Normal/On/Off <Normal>:

"Normal" means that visible attributes are visible and invisible attributes are invisible. "On" turns all attributes on. "Off" turns all attributes off.

> Type or select "on".

Your screen will be regenerated with invisible attributes on, as shown in *Figure 10-14*.

You can leave ATTDISP on in this exercise or turn it back to "normal".

Now we will do an edit. Imagine that these three workstations represent part of a small worksite and that we just purchased a new Multisync 4FG monitor. We could erase one of the workstations and reinsert it with new attribute information, but it will be simpler to edit just the one attribute that needs to change.

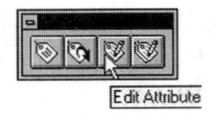

Figure 10-15

> Type "ddatte" or select the Edit Attribute tool from the Attribute toolbar, as shown in *Figure 10-15*.

This type of editing, in which we only want to change the values of attributes in a single block, is most efficiently handled with the DDATTE dialogue box.

When the command is entered, AutoCAD will prompt you to select a block.

> Select the middle workstation.

You will see the Edit Attributes dialogue box shown in *Figure 10-16*. Notice that all defined attributes are available, including the preset digitizer attribute.

Chap. 10   **329**

[Edit Attributes dialog box]
Block Name: WS
SummaSketch II
Enter monitor type: NEC Multisync
Enter computer type: Zenith

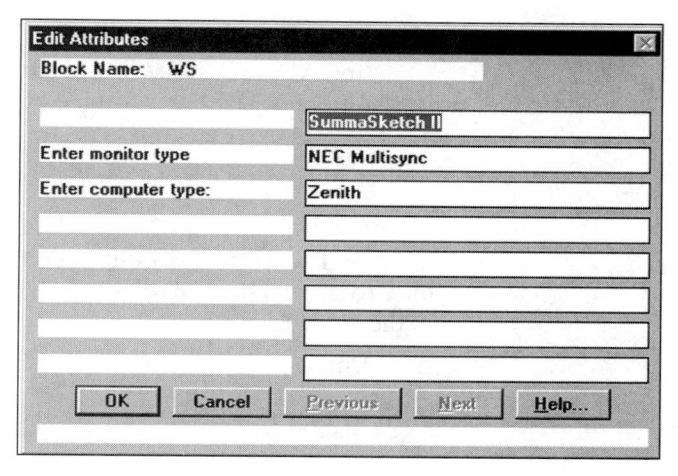

OK | Cancel | Previous | Next | Help...

Figure 10-16

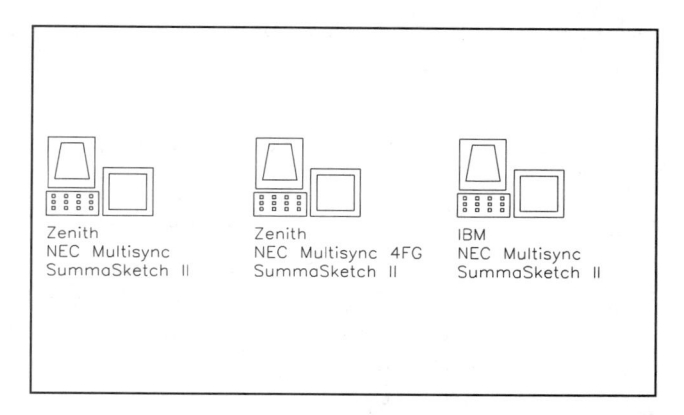

[Three workstation icons with labels:]
Zenith / NEC Multisync / SummaSketch II
Zenith / NEC Multisync 4FG / SummaSketch II
IBM / NEC Multisync / SummaSketch II

Figure 10-17

> Click in the Monitor edit box and add "4FG".
> Click on "OK" to end the dialogue.

The attribute text will be changed as shown in *Figure 10-17*.
Now let's use ATTEDIT to perform a global edit.
> Type "Attedit" or select the Edit Attribute Globally tool from the Attribute pull down menu.

The first prompt allows you to choose between global and individual editing:

Edit attributes one at a time? <Y>:

> Type "n" for global editing.
AutoCAD prompts:

Edit only attributes visible on the screen? <Y>

Since we set ATTDISP to "on" and because we have not zoomed away from any of our inserted blocks, all of our attributes are visible.

> Press Enter to edit only visible attributes.

AutoCAD issues a series of three prompts that allow you to narrow down the field of attributes to be edited.

Block name specification <*>:

If we had more than one type of block on the screen, we could limit editing to occurrences of whatever block we wished to name. But we have only the ws block.

> Press Enter.

AutoCAD prompts:

Attribute tag specification <*>:

This allows us to narrow the field to a single tag—all the digitizers, for example.

> Type "digitizer".

AutoCAD now prompts for an attribute value:

Attribute value specification <*>:

This would allow us to specify only digitizers with the value "SummaSketch II", for example. Since all of our workstations have the same value at this point, this would be useless.

> Press Enter.

Now AutoCAD asks us to select attributes by pointing or windowing:

Select Attributes:

> Select two of the three digitizer attributes.

Now AutoCAD knows which attributes to edit. It will allow you to change the entire text of the two attributes, or only part. It does this by requesting a string:

String to change:

A string is simply a text sequence. It may be part or all of the text.

> Type "II".

Now AutoCAD prompts:

New string:

> Type "III".

The two selected attributes will be changed, as shown in *Figure 10-18*.

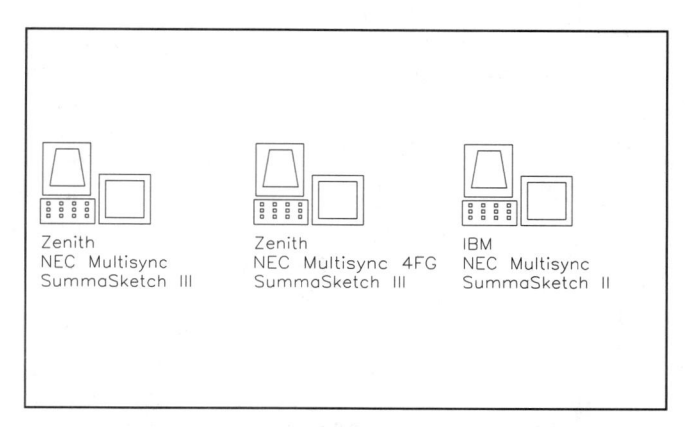

Figure 10-18

The ATTEDIT command gives you a lot of power, but it can be tricky. See the *AutoCAD User's Guide* if you need additional information.

Extracting Attribute Information from Drawings

Although there are many good reasons to use attributes, the most impressive is the ability to create extract files (the ATTEXT and DDATTEXT commands), which can be processed by other programs to generate reports, bills of materials, inventories, parts lists, and quotations. This means, for example, that with a well-managed CAD system you can do a drawing of a construction project and get a complete price breakdown and supply list directly from the drawing database, all processed by computer. In order to accomplish this, you need a complete library of parts with carefully defined attributes and a program such as dBASE III or LOTUS 1-2-3 that is capable of receiving the extract information and formatting it into a useful report.

Unfortunately, since we have no way of knowing what programs are available to you and since we want to keep the focus of this book on drawing rather than programming, it is beyond our scope to create the files and formats necessary for extracting attributes. With a little imagination, however, you should be able to see the possibilities. With dBASE III, for example, we could match the computer, monitor, and digitizer names in our block references to a price list contained in a database file, calculate totals and subtotals, and format an elaborate report. This is a matter worthy of a whole book of its own, and we have only scratched the surface here. If you want additional information, see the *AutoCAD User's Guide*.

Task 7: EXPLODEing Blocks

Procedure

1. Type "Explode" or select the Explode tool from the Modify toolbar.
2. Select objects.
3. Press Enter to carry out the command.

Discussion. The EXPLODE command undoes the work of the BLOCK or GROUP command. It takes a set of objects that have been defined as a block or group and recreates them as independent entities. EXPLODE works on dimensions and hatch patterns as well as on blocks created in the BLOCK command. It does not work on XREF drawings until they have been attached permanently through the bind option.

> To begin this task, you should have at least one ws block on your screen.
> To see why you need this command, select a ws block by pointing.

You will see grips at the insertion point of the block and at the start point of the two visible attributes.

> Try selecting the monitor independently.

You will be unable to do this. Since the monitor, computer, keyboard, and digitizer are all part of a single entity, the ws block, they cannot be selected or edited except as a unit. The attributes are an exception. They can be edited with DDATTE and ATTEDIT, and can be moved independently using the stretch feature of grip editing, if they have been defined as visible. However, in most applications you will not want to explode block references that contain attribute information, because EXPLODE replaces the information with attribute tags.

Let's try exploding a workstation.

> Type "Explode" or select the Explode tool from the Modify toolbar.

You will be prompted to select objects.

> Select a ws block.
> Press Enter to carry out the command.

Notice that the attribute information is replaced by tags, as shown in *Figure 10-19*.

> Now try selecting the monitor again.
> Try selecting other parts of the workstation.

All of the component parts of the previously blocked workstation can now be edited separately. However, notice that there are still blocks within this configuration. Try selecting one of the buttons on the keyboard, for example. You will see that the keyboard is still considered a single entity. This is an example of a nested block. The keyboard block is one component of the former workstation block. Since EXPLODE moves through levels of nesting one at a time, blocks that were included in the definition of the ws block are still blocks when it is exploded.

Before going on, take a look at the following chart, Other Commands to Use with Blocks. It is a list and description of other commands that are frequently used in conjunction with blocks.

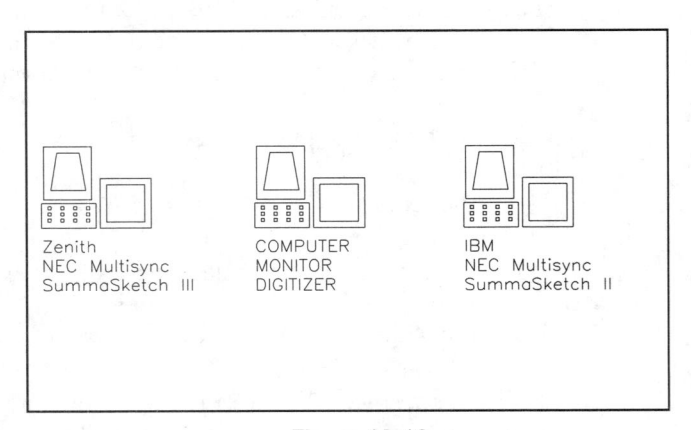

Figure 10-19

OTHER COMMANDS TO USE WITH BLOCKS

Command	Usage
BASE	Allows you to specify a base insertion point for an entire drawing. The base point will be used when the drawing is inserted in other drawings.
DBLIST	Displays information for all entities in the current drawing database. Information includes type of entity and layer. Additional information depends on the type of entity. For blocks, it includes insertion point, X scale, Y scale, rotation, and attribute values. Due to length, a database list usually must be printed using printer echo (Ctrl-Q) or viewed with scroll pause (Ctrl-S to pause, any key to resume scrolling). See "LIST", following.
LIST	Lists information about a single block or entity. Information listed is the same as that in DBLIST, but for the selected entity only.
MINSERT	Multiple Insert. Allows you to insert arrays of blocks. MINSERT arrays take up less memory than ARRAYs of INSERTed blocks. This command is initiated when you select "Insert" and then "Multiple Blocks" from the Draw menu.
PURGE	Deletes unused blocks, layers, linetypes, shapes, or text styles from a drawing. PURGE must be the first command executed when you enter the drawing editor; otherwise it will not work.
WBLOCK	Saves a block to a separate file so that it can be inserted in other drawings. Does not save unused blocks or layers, and therefore can be used to reduce drawing file size.

Tasks 8, 9, 10, and 11

The first drawing exercise focuses on the use of attributes, while the other three are purely assembly drawings. We will be making some suggestions on how to manage drawing files and blocks in assembly drawings. Such techniques will be useful and necessary in any industrial application, but they may not be required to complete the drawings as classroom exercises. Remember to create objects to be BLOCKed on layer 0, unless you have a specific reason for doing otherwise.

DRAWING 10-1: CAD ROOM

This architectural drawing is primarily an exercise in using blocks and attributes. Use your ws block and its attributes to fill in the workstations and text after you draw the walls and countertop. New blocks should be created for the plotters and printers, as described following. The drawing setup is the same as that used in the chapter.

DRAWING SUGGESTIONS

$$\begin{aligned}&\text{UNITS} = \text{Architectural, smallest fraction} = 1\\&\text{GRID} = 1'\\&\text{SNAP} = 1''\\&\text{LIMITS} = (0',0')\ (48',36')\end{aligned}$$

> The "plotter" block is a 1 × 3 rectangle, with two visible, variable attributes (all the default attribute modes). The first attribute is for a manufacturer and the second for a model. The "printers" are 2 × 2.5 with the same type of attributes. Draw the rectangles, define their attributes 8 inches below them, create the BLOCK definitions, and then INSERT plotters and printers as shown. NOTE: Do not include the labels "plotter" or "laser printer" in the block, because text in a block will be rotated with the block. This would give you inverted text on the front countertop. Insert the blocks and add the text afterward. The attribute text can be handled differently, as described following.

> The "8 pen plotter" was inserted with a Y scale factor of 1.25.

The MIRRTEXT System Variable

The two workstations on the front counter could be inserted with a rotation angle of 180 degrees, but then the attribute text would be inverted also and would have to be turned around using ATTEDIT. Instead, we have reset the "mirrtext" system variable so that we could mirror blocks without attribute text being inverted:

1. Type "mirrtext".
2. Type "0".

Now you can mirror objects on the back counter to create those on the front. With the "mirrtext" system variable set to "0", text included in a MIRROR procedure is not inverted as it would be with mirrtext set to "1" (the default). This applies to attribute text as well as ordinary text. However, it does not apply to ordinary text included in a block definition.

Chap. 10

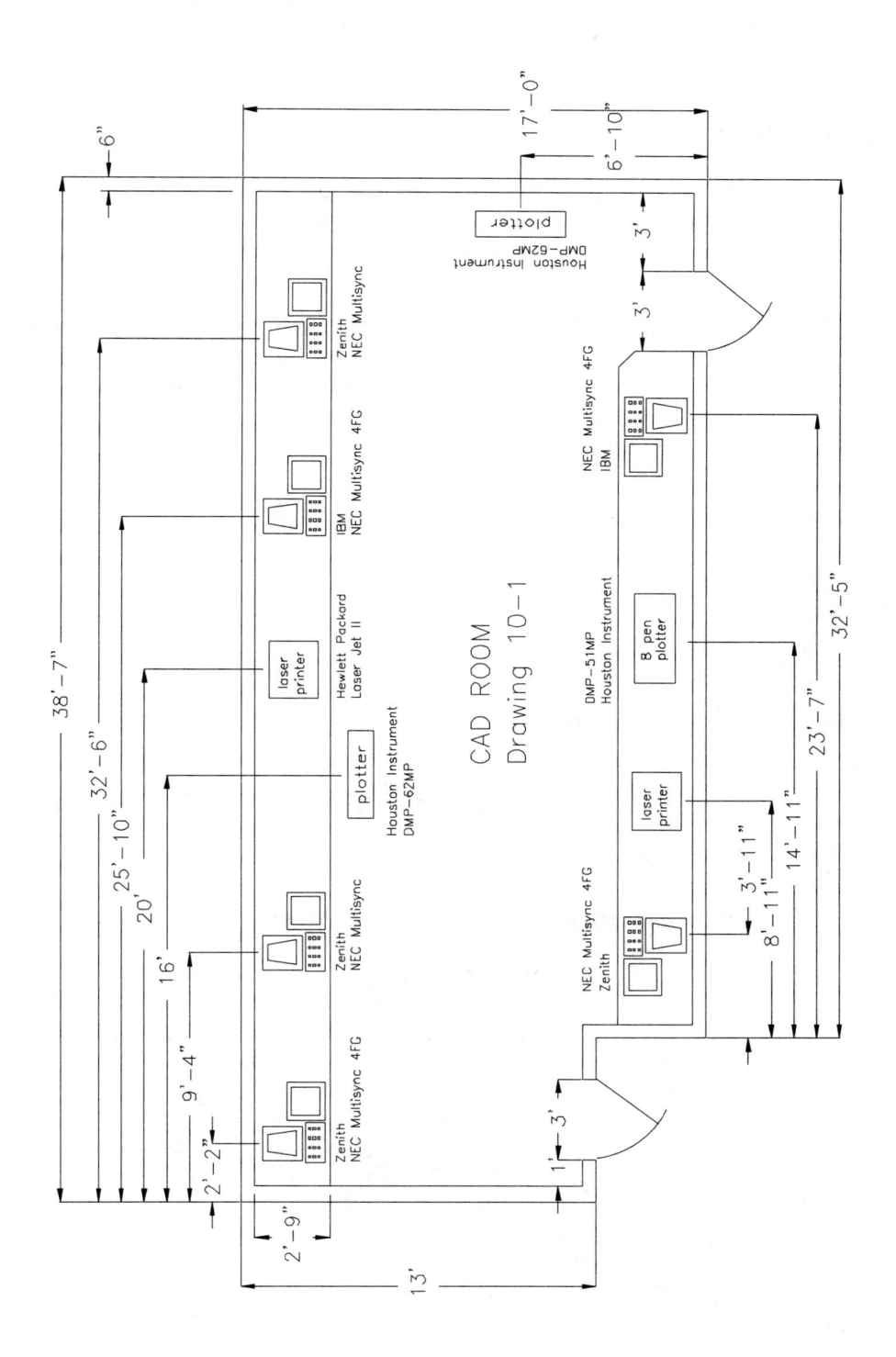

CAD ROOM
Drawing 10-1

DRAWING 10-2: BASE ASSEMBLY

This is a good exercise in assembly drawing procedures. You will be drawing each of the numbered part details and then assembling them into the "Base Assembly."

DRAWING SUGGESTIONS

We will no longer provide you with units, grid, snap, and limit settings. You can determine what you need by looking over the drawing and its dimensions. Remember that you can always change a setting later if it becomes necessary.

> You can create your own title block from scratch or develop one from "Title Block," Drawing 7-1, if you have saved it. Once created and SAVEd or WBLOCKed, a title block can be inserted and scaled to fit any drawing. Also, Release 13 includes an AutoLISP program, MVSETUP, which draws title blocks and borders, among other things.

Using MINSERT to Create a Table

The parts list should also be defined as a block. Since many drawings include parts lists, you will want to be able to quickly create a table with any given number of rows. Try this:

1. Define a block that represents one row of the parts list.
2. WBLOCK it so it can be used in any drawing.
3. When you insert it, use either ARRAY or MINSERT to create the number of rows in the table (MINSERT creates an array of a block as part of the insertion process).

Managing Parts Blocks for Multiple Use

You will be drawing each of the numbered parts (B101-1, B101-2, etc.) and then assembling them. In an industrial application the individual part details would be sent to different manufacturers or manufacturing departments, so they must exist as separate, completely dimensioned drawings as well as blocks that can be used in creating the assembly. An efficient method is to create three separate blocks for each part detail: one for dimensions and one for each view in the assembly. The dimensioned part drawings will include both views. The blocks of the two views will have dimensions, hidden lines, and centerlines erased.

Think carefully about the way you name blocks. You might want to adopt a naming system like this: "B101-1D" for the dimensioned drawing, "B101-1T" for a top view without dimensions, and "B101-1F" for a front view without dimensions. Such a system will make it easy to call out all the top view parts for the top view assembly, for example. A more detailed procedure is outlined for Drawings 10-3 and 10-4.

> Notice that the assembly requires you to do a considerable amount of trimming away of lines from the blocks you insert. This can be done easily, but you must remember to EXPLODE the inserted blocks first.

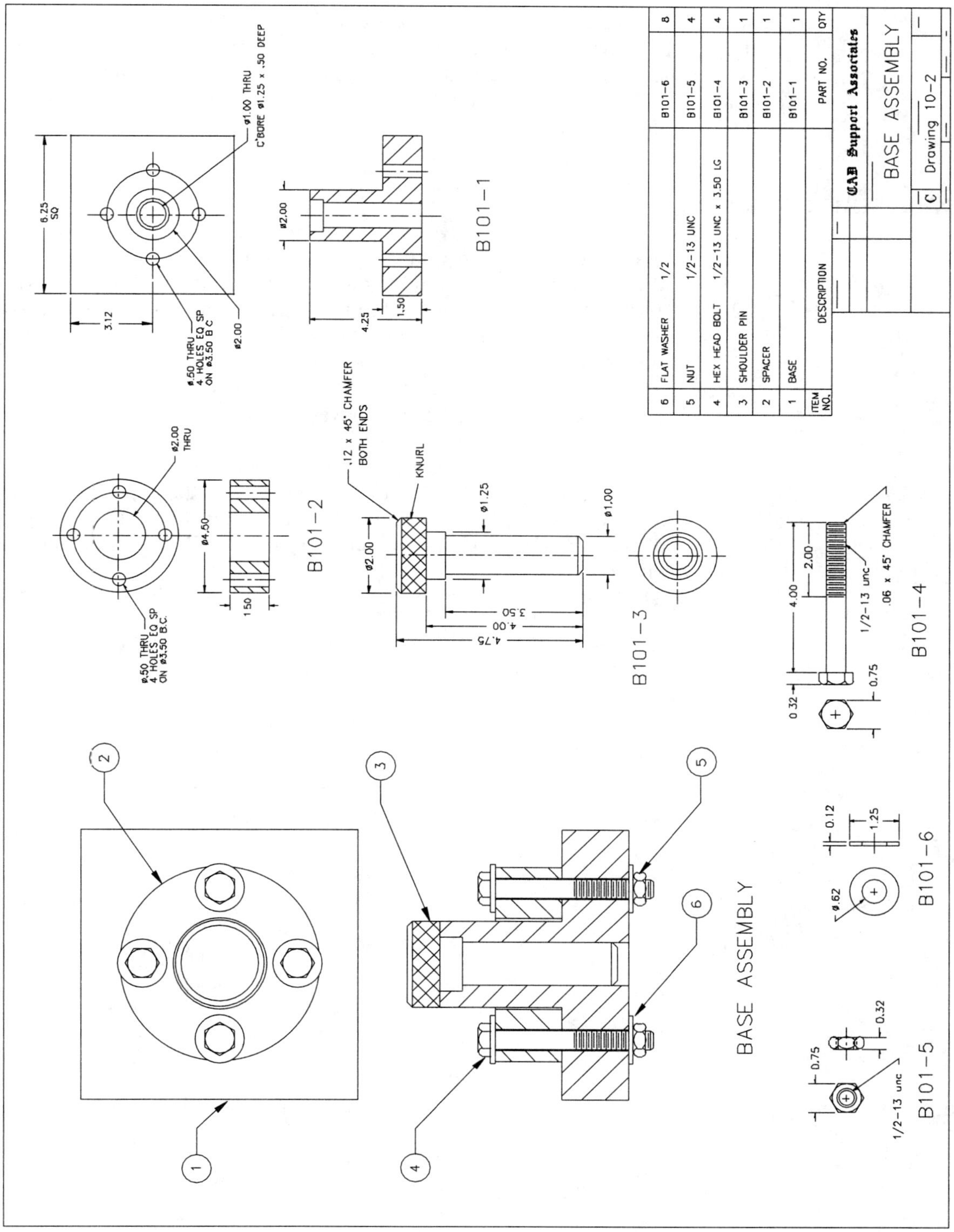
6 FLAT WASHER 1/2 B101-6 8
5 NUT 1/2-13 UNC B101-5 4
4 HEX HEAD BOLT 1/2-13 UNC x 3.50 LG B101-4 4
3 SHOULDER PIN B101-3 1
2 SPACER B101-2 1
1 BASE B101-1 1
ITEM NO. DESCRIPTION PART NO. QTY
CAD Support Associates
BASE ASSEMBLY
C Drawing 10-2
6.25 SQ
3.12
ø1.00 THRU
C'BORE ø1.25 x .50 DEEP
ø.50 THRU
4 HOLES EQ SP
ON ø3.50 B C
ø2.00
4.25
1.50
B101-1
ø2.00 THRU
ø4.50
ø.50 THRU
4 HOLES EQ SP
ON ø3.50 B.C.
1.50
B101-2
.12 x 45° CHAMFER
BOTH ENDS
KNURL
ø1.25
ø2.00
ø1.00
3.50
4.00
4.75
B101-3
4.00
2.00
1/2-13 unc
.06 x 45° CHAMFER
0.32
0.75
B101-4
BASE ASSEMBLY
0.12
1.25
ø.62
B101-6
0.75
0.32
1/2-13 unc
B101-5

DRAWINGS 10-3 AND 10-4: DOUBLE BEARING ASSEMBLY AND SCOOTER ASSEMBLY

All of the specific drawing techniques required to do the individual part details in these two drawings are ones that you have encountered in previous chapters. What is new is the blocking and assembly process. The procedure outlined below is a step-by-step elaboration of the kind of block management system we introduced in the last drawing.

DRAWING SUGGESTIONS

1. Draw each part detail in whatever two- or three-view form is given. Make the drawing complete with hidden lines, centerlines, and dimensions.
2. WBLOCK the part, giving it a file name that identifies it as a complete, dimensioned drawing. For example: "CAPD".
3. Use OOPS to return the part to the display.
4. ERASE dimensions, hidden lines, and centerlines. If you have kept your layers separated, you can turn off layer 0 and then erase everything left using a window or crossing box. Then turn 0 on again.
5. BLOCK the views separately, giving each a name that will identify it with its view. For example: "CAPT" for the top view of the cap, "CAPF" for cap front, and "CAPR" for cap right. It is essential that your naming system keep these BLOCKed views distinct from the WBLOCKed dimensioned drawing of step 2.
6. Insert blocks from step 5 to create the assembly. EXPLODE and TRIM where necessary.

Chap. 10

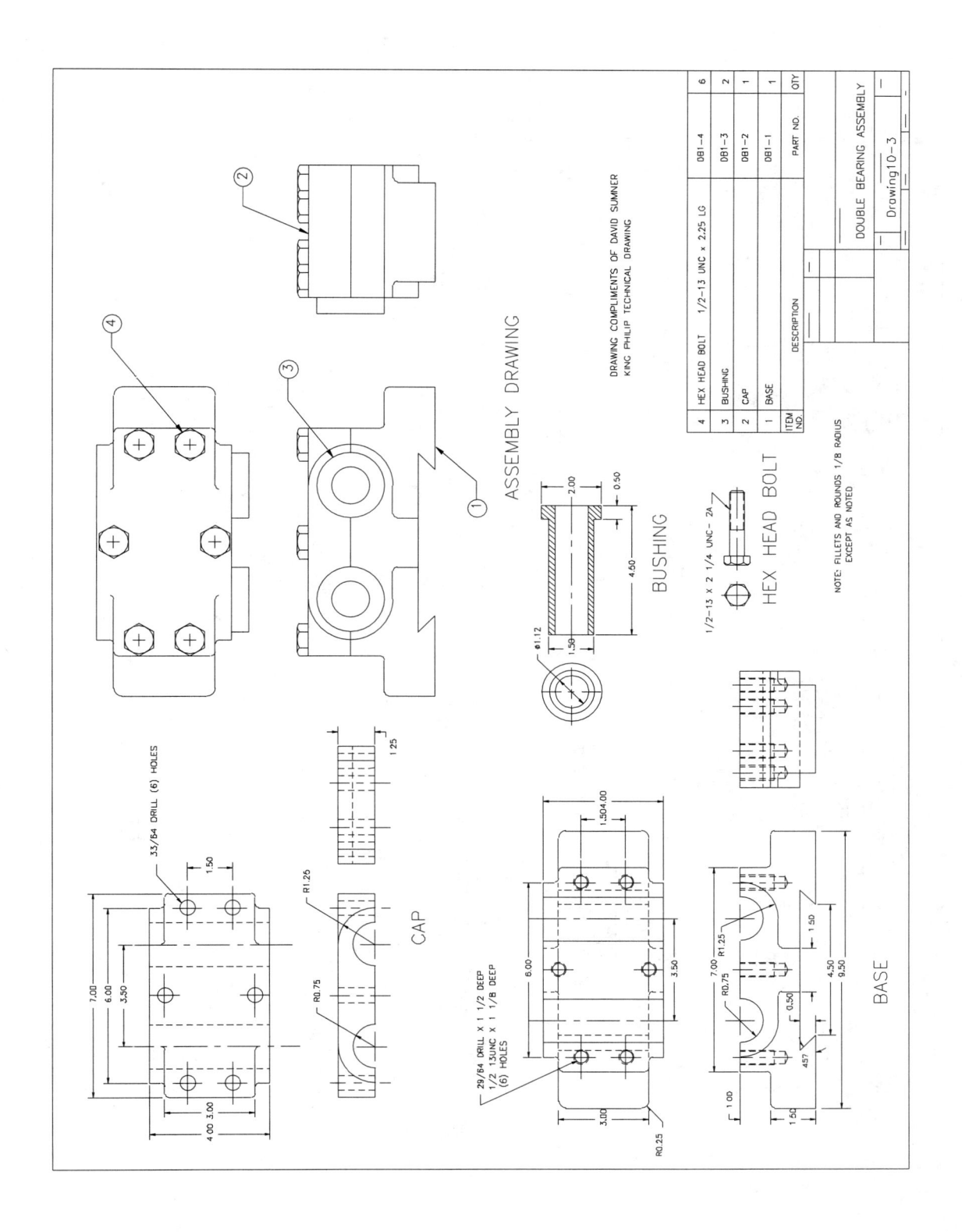

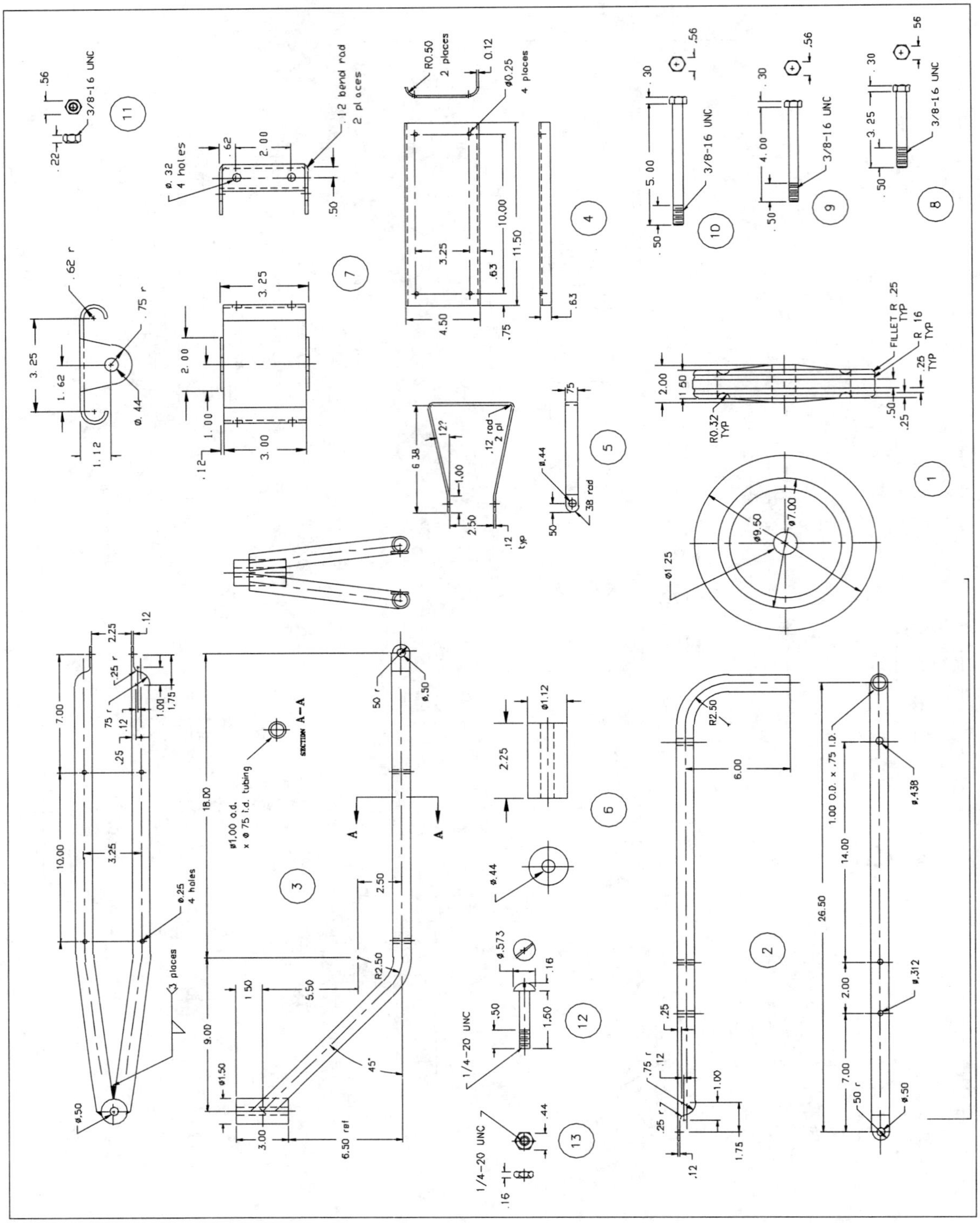
SECTION A–A
ø1.00 o.d. x ø.75 i.d. tubing
3/8-16 UNC
1/4-20 UNC
FILLET R .25 TYP

Chap. 10

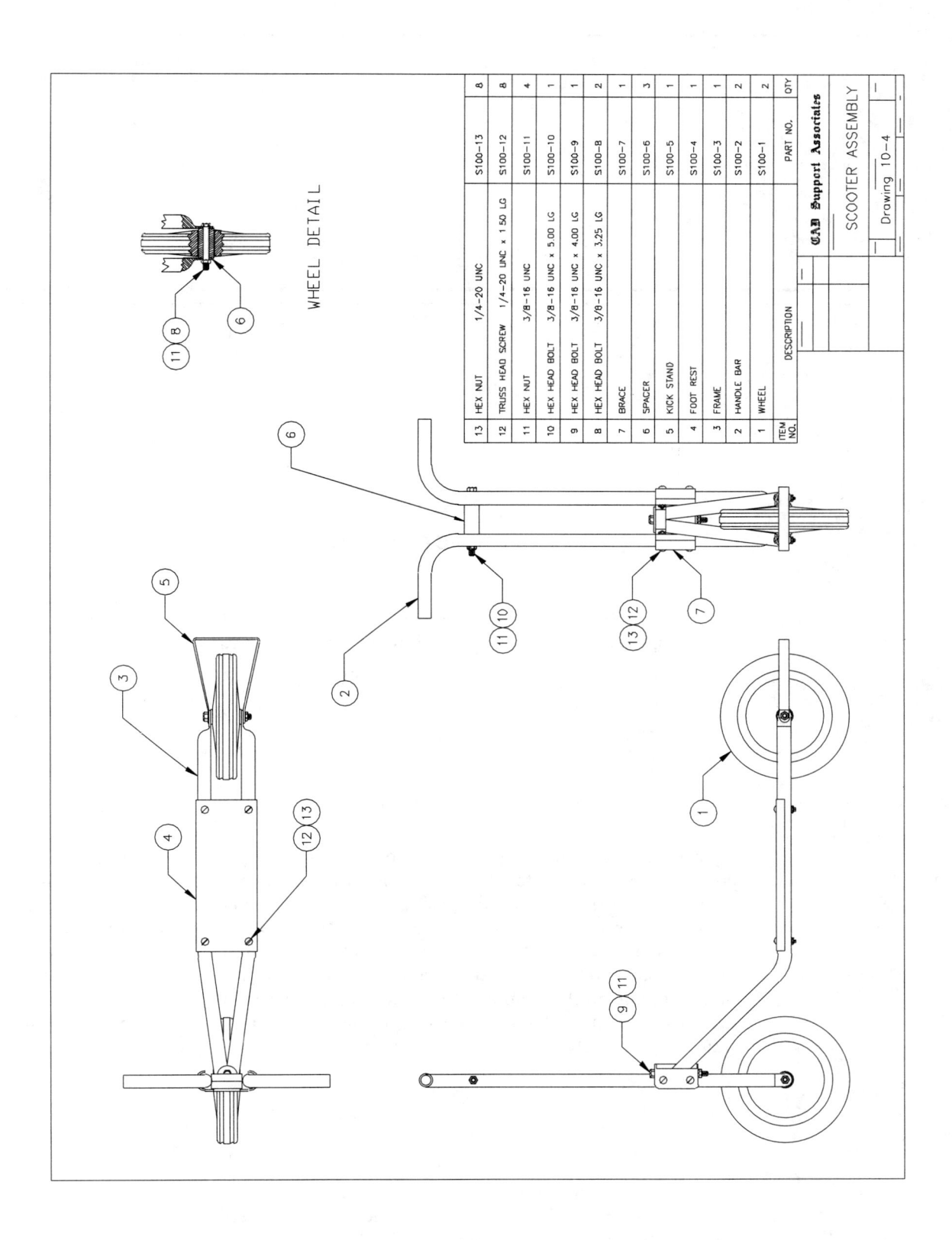

ITEM NO.	DESCRIPTION	PART NO.	QTY
13	HEX NUT 1/4-20 UNC	S100-13	8
12	TRUSS HEAD SCREW 1/4-20 UNC x 1.50 LG	S100-12	8
11	HEX NUT 3/8-16 UNC	S100-11	4
10	HEX HEAD BOLT 3/8-16 UNC x 5.00 LG	S100-10	1
9	HEX HEAD BOLT 3/8-16 UNC x 4.00 LG	S100-9	1
8	HEX HEAD BOLT 3/8-16 UNC x 3.25 LG	S100-8	2
7	BRACE	S100-7	1
6	SPACER	S100-6	3
5	KICK STAND	S100-5	1
4	FOOT REST	S100-4	1
3	FRAME	S100-3	1
2	HANDLE BAR	S100-2	2
1	WHEEL	S100-1	2

CAB Support Associates

SCOOTER ASSEMBLY

Drawing 10-4

WHEEL DETAIL

CHAPTER 11

COMMANDS

OPTIONS	DRAW	VIEW
ISOPLANE	ELLIPSE	VIEW
SNAP (isometric)		ZOOM (dynamic)

OVERVIEW

Learning to use AutoCAD's isometric drawing features should be a pleasure at this point. There are very few new commands to learn, and anything you know about manual isometric drawing will translate easily to the computer. In fact, the isometric snap, grid, and cross hairs make isometric drawing considerably easier on a CAD system than on the drafting board. Once you know how to get into the isometric mode and to change from plane to plane, you will be on your way. You will find that many of the commands you have learned previously will continue to work for you, and that using the isometric drawing planes is a good warmup for 3D wireframe drawing, which is the topic of the next chapter.

TASKS

1. Use the isometric SNAP mode.
2. Use Ctrl-E to toggle between isometric planes.
3. Use COPY and other edit commands in the isometric mode.
4. Draw isometric circles with ELLIPSE.

5. Draw ellipses in orthographic views.
6. Save views with the VIEW command.
7. Use dynamic ZOOM.
8. Do Drawing 11-1 ("Mounting Bracket").
9. Do Drawing 11-2 ("Radio").
10. Do Drawing 11-3 ("Fixture Assembly").
11. Do Drawing 11-4 ("Flanged Coupling").
12. Do Drawing 11-5 ("Garage Framing").

Task 1: Using Isometric SNAP

Procedure

1. Type "Snap" or open the Drawing Aids dialogue box from the Options menu.
2. Type "s" or select "on".
3. Type "i" or click "OK".

Discussion. To begin drawing isometrically you need to switch to the isometric snap style. When you do, you will find the grid and cross hairs behaving in ways that may seem odd at first, but you will quickly get used to them.

> Type "snap" or select "Drawing Aids..." from the Options menu.

You will see either the Drawing Aids dialogue box or the SNAP command prompt:

Snap spacing or ON/OFF/Aspect/Rotate/Style <0.25>:

> From the command line, type "s", or, in the Dialogue box click the "On" box under "Isometric Snap/Grid".

If you are typing, AutoCAD will prompt for a snap style:

Standard/Isometric <S>:

Standard refers to the orthographic grid and snap you have been using since Chapter 1.

> Type "i" or select "isometric". In the dialogue box, click on "OK".

At this point your grid and cross hairs will be reoriented so that they resemble *Figure 11-1*.

This is the isometric grid. Grid points are placed at 30, 90, and 150 degree angles from the horizontal. The cross hairs are initially turned to define the left isometric plane. The three isoplanes will be discussed in Task 2.

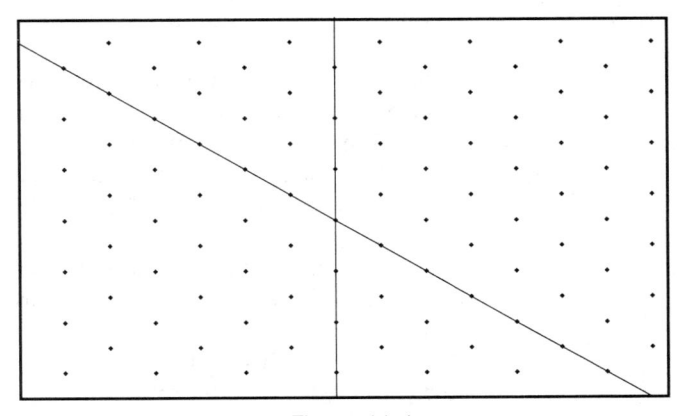

Figure 11-1

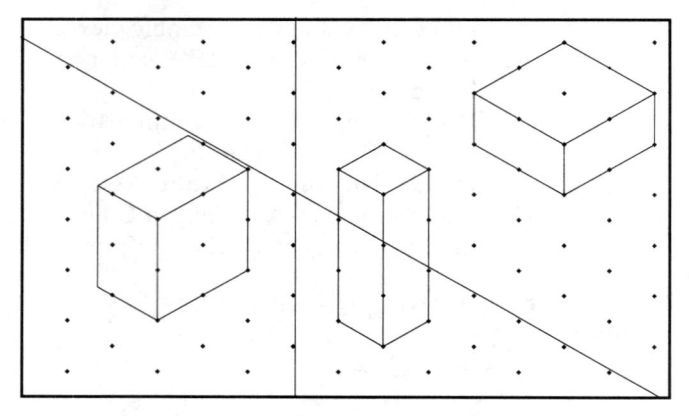

Figure 11-2

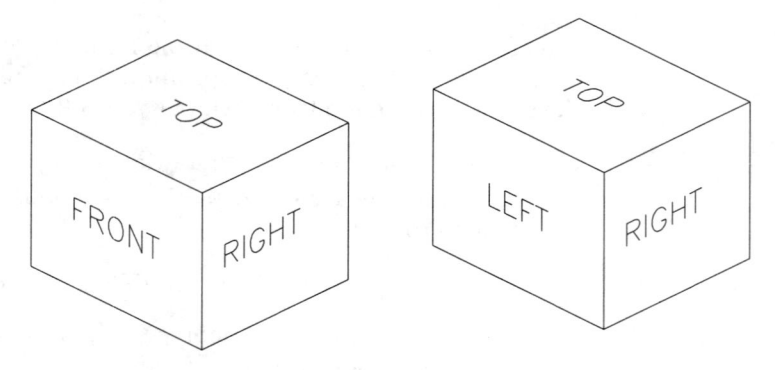

Figure 11-3

> To get a feeling for how this snap style works, enter the LINE command and draw some boxes, as shown in *Figure 11-2*. Make sure that ortho is off and snap is on, or you will be unable to draw the lines shown.

Task 2: Switching Isometric Planes

Procedure

1. Press Ctrl-E once to switch to the "top" plane.
2. Press Ctrl-E again to switch to the "right" plane.
3. Press Ctrl-E again to return to the "left" plane.

Discussion. If you tried to draw the boxes in Task 1 with ortho on, you have discovered that it is impossible. Without changing the orientation of the cross hairs you can draw in only one of the three isometric planes. We need to be able to switch planes so that we can leave ortho on for accuracy and speed. There are several ways to do this, but the simplest, quickest, and most convenient is to use Ctrl-E.

Before beginning, take a look at *Figure 11-3*. It shows the three planes of a standard isometric drawing. These planes are usually referred to as top, front, and right. However, AutoCAD's terminology is top, left, and right. We will stick with AutoCAD's labels in this chapter.

Now look at *Figure 11-4* and you will see how the isometric cross hairs are oriented to draw in each of the planes.

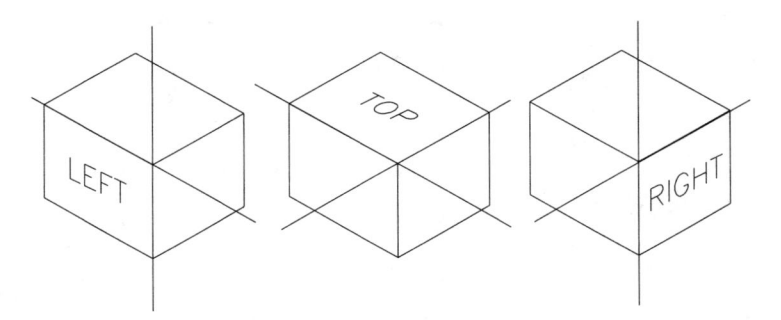

Figure 11-4

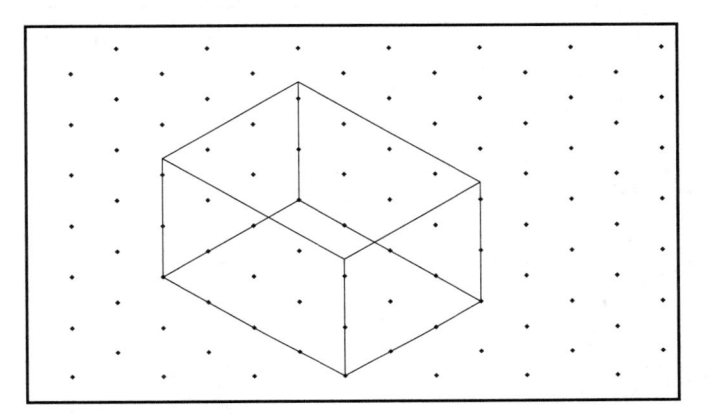

Figure 11-5

> Hold down Ctrl and press E to switch from "left" to "top."

Learn to use Ctrl-E with one hand, probably your left, so that you can keep the other hand on the mouse.

> Press Ctrl-E again to switch from "top" to "right."
> Press Ctrl-E once more to switch back to "left."
> Now turn ortho on and draw a box outline like the one in *Figure 11-5*.

You will need to switch planes several times to accomplish this. Notice that you can switch planes using Ctrl-E without interrupting the LINE command. If you find that you are in the wrong plane to construct a line, switch planes. Since every plane allows movement in two of the three directions, you will always be able to move in the direction you want with one switch. However, you may not be able to hit the snap point you want. If you cannot, switch planes again.

Task 3: Using COPY and Other Edit Commands

Discussion. Most commands work in the isometric planes just as they do in standard orthographic views. In this exercise we will construct an isometric view of a bracket using the LINE, COPY, and ERASE commands. Then we will draw angled corners using CHAMFER. In the next task we will draw a hole in the bracket with ELLIPSE, COPY, and TRIM.

> To begin this exercise, clear your screen of boxes and check to see that ortho is on.
> Draw the L-shaped surface shown in *Figure 11-6*.

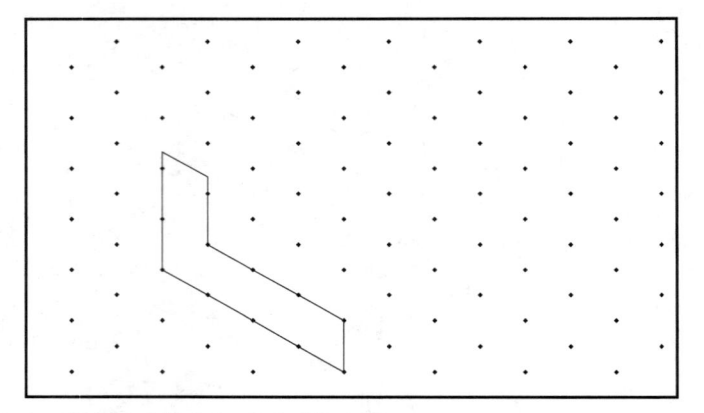

Figure 11-6

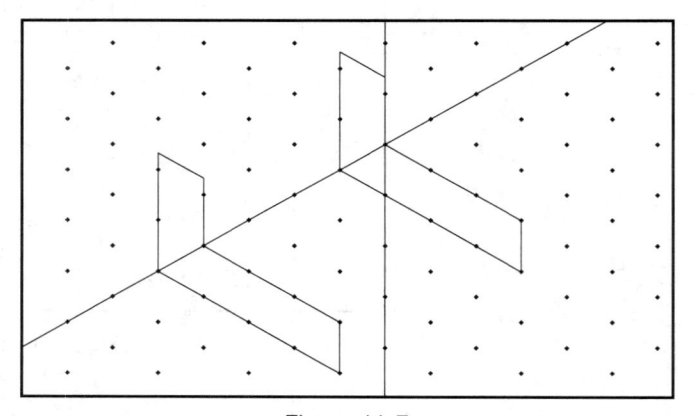

Figure 11-7

Notice that this is drawn in the left isoplane and that it is 1.00 unit wide.

Next, we will copy this object 4.00 units back to the right to create the back surface of the bracket.

> Type "Copy" or select the Copy tool from the Modify toolbar.
> Use a window or crossing box to select all the lines in the L.
> Press Enter to end object selection.
> Pick a base point at the inside corner of the L.

It is a good exercise to turn ortho on, switch planes, and move the object around in each plane. You will see that you can move in two directions in each plane and that in order to move the object back to the right as shown in *Figure 11-7*, you must be in either the top or the right plane.

> Pick a second point of displacement four units back to the right, as shown.
> Enter the LINE command and draw the connecting lines in the right plane, as shown in *Figure 11-8*.

If you wish, you can draw only one of the lines and use the COPY command with the multiple option to create the others.

Creating Chamfers in an Isometric View

Keep in mind that angular lines in an isometric view do not show true lengths. Angular lines must be drawn between end points located along paths that are vertical or horizontal in one of the three drawing planes. In our exercise we will cre-

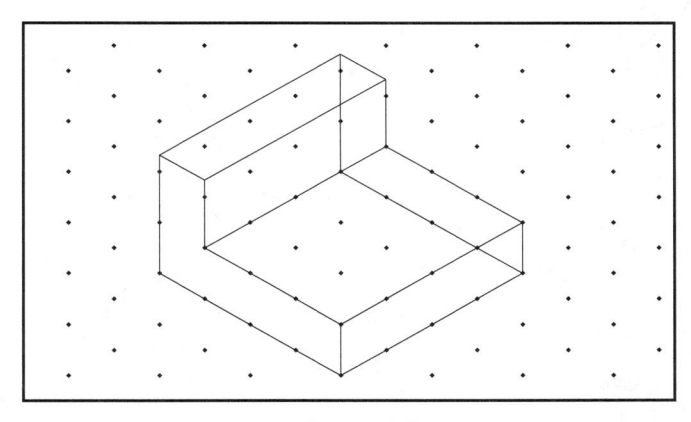

Figure 11-8

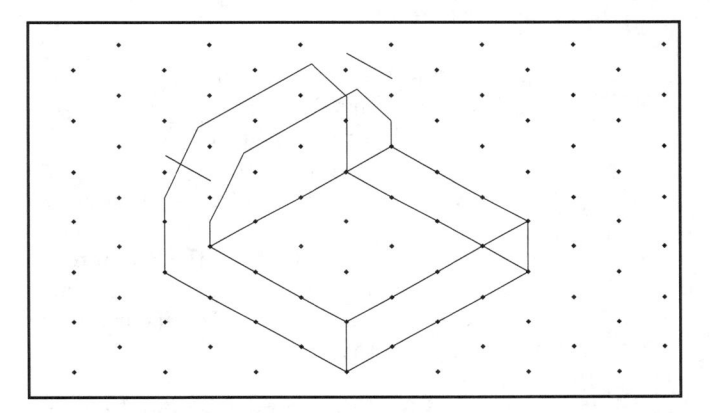

Figure 11-9

ate angled lines by using the CHAMFER command to cut the corners of the bracket. This will be no different from using CHAMFER in orthographic views.

> Type "chamfer" or select the Chamfer tool from the Modify toolbar.
> Type "D" or select "distance".
   AutoCAD will prompt for a first chamfer distance.
> Type "1".
> Press Enter to accept 1.00 as the second chamfer distance.
> Repeat the CHAMFER command.
> Pick two edges of the bracket to create a chamfer, as shown in *Figure 11-9*.
> Repeat CHAMFER.
   Chamfer the other three corners so that your drawing resembles *Figure 11-9*.
> ERASE the two small lines left hanging at the previous corners.
> To complete the bracket, enter the LINE command and draw lines between the new chamfer end points.
> Finally, ERASE the two unseen lines on the back surface to produce *Figure 11-10*.

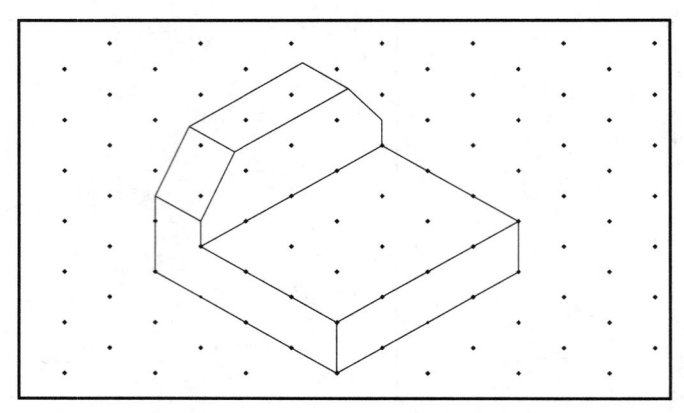

Figure 11-10

Task 4: Drawing Isometric Circles with ELLIPSE

Procedure

1. Locate the center point.
2. Type "Ellipse".
3. Type "I" or select "isocircle".
4. Pick the center point.
5. Type or show the radius or diameter.

Discussion. The ELLIPSE command can be used to draw true ellipses in orthographic views or ellipses that appear to be circles in isometric views (called "isocircles" in AutoCAD). In this task we will use the latter capability to construct a hole in the bracket.

> To begin this task you should have the bracket shown in *Figure 11-10* on your display.

The first thing you will need in order to draw an isocircle is a center point. Often it will be necessary to locate this point carefully using DIST, temporary lines, or point filters (Chapter 12). You must be sure that you can locate the center point *before* entering the ELLIPSE command.

In our case it will be easy since the center point will be on a snap point.
> Type "Ellipse".

The Ellipse tool on the Draw toolbar does not offer the isocircle option in Release 13. You can select Ellipse from the DRAW 1 screen menu if it is available.

AutoCAD will prompt:

Arc/Center/Isocircle<Axis endpoint 1>:

The option we want is "Isocircle". We will ignore the others for the time being.
> Type "i".

AutoCAD prompts:

Center of circle:

If you could not locate the center point you would have to exit the command now and start over.

Chap. 11   **349**

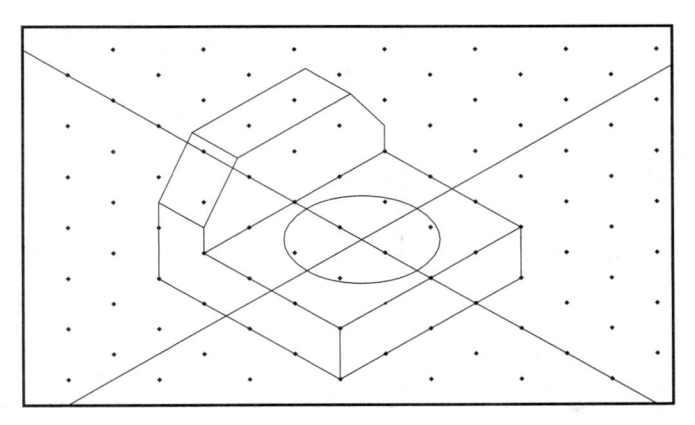

Figure 11-11

> Use the snap and grid to pick the center of the surface, as shown in *Figure 11-11*.

AutoCAD gives you an isocircle to drag, as in the CIRCLE command. The isocircle you see will depend on the isoplane you are in. To understand this try switching planes to see how the image changes.

> Stretch the isocircle image out and then press Ctrl-E to switch isoplanes. Observe the isocircle. Try this two or three times.

> Switch to the top isoplane before moving on.

AutoCAD is prompting for a radius or diameter:

<Circle radius>/Diameter:

A radius specification is the default here, as it is in the CIRCLE command.

> Type a value or pick a point so that your isocircle resembles the one in *Figure 11-11*.

Next, we use the COPY and TRIM commands to create the bottom of the hole.

> Type "Copy" or select the Copy tool from the Modify toolbar.

> Select the isocircle by pointing, or type "l" for "last".

> End object selection.

> Pick a base point.

Any point could be used as the base point. A good choice would be the top of the front corner. If you do this, then choosing the bottom of the front corner as a second point will give you the exact thickness of the bracket.

> Switch to either the right or left isoplane.

> Pick a second point 1.00 unit below the base point.

Your screen should now resemble *Figure 11-12*. The last thing we must do is TRIM the hidden portion of the bottom of the hole.

> Type "Trim" or select the Trim tool from the Modify toolbar.

> Pick the first isocircle as a cutting edge.

> Press Enter to end cutting edge selection.

> Select the hidden section of the lower isocircle.

> Press Enter to exit TRIM.

The bracket is now complete and your screen should resemble *Figure 11-13*.

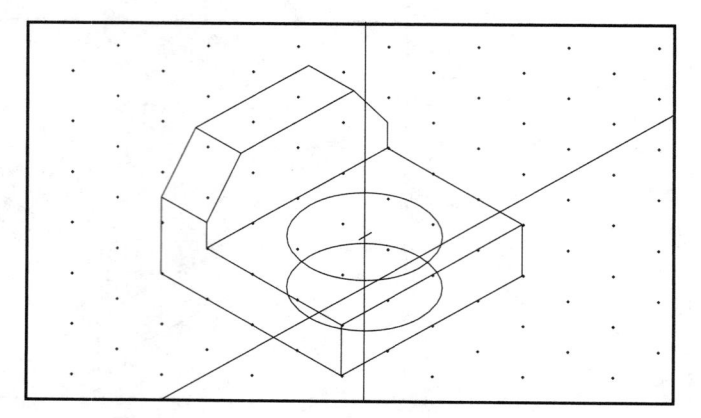

Figure 11-12

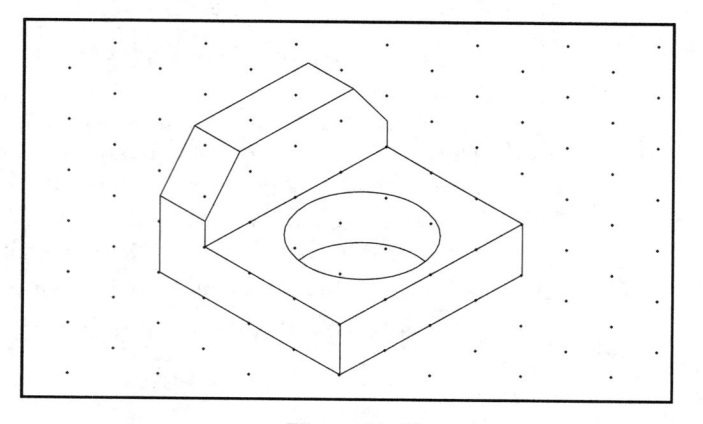

Figure 11-13

NOTE: Sometimes you will not get the results you expect when using TRIM in an isometric view. It may be necessary to use BREAK and ERASE as an alternative.

This completes the present discussion of isometric drawing. You will find more in the drawing suggestions at the end of this chapter.

Now we will go on to explore the nonisometric use of the ELLIPSE command and then to show you two new tricks for controlling your display.

Task 5: Drawing Ellipses in Orthographic Views

Procedure

1. Type "Ellipse" or select an Ellipse tool from the Ellipse flyout on the Draw toolbar.
2. Pick one end point of an axis.
3. Pick the second end point.
4. Pick a third point showing the length of the other axis.

Discussion. The ELLIPSE command is important for drawing isocircles, but also for drawing true ellipses in orthographic views. In Release 13 there is also a new option to create elliptical arcs.

An ellipse is determined by a center point and two mutually perpendicular axes. In AutoCAD, these specifications can be shown in two nearly identical

Chap. 11   351

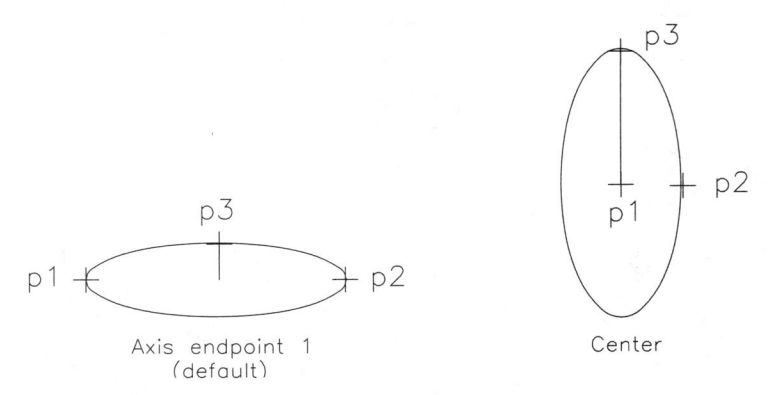

```
              p3
         p1 -+--(------+--)-+ p2
                      |
              Axis endpoint 1
                 (default)
```
```
                    + p3
                  ( | )
                  ( | )
                  (-+-+ p2
                  ( p1 )
                  (   )
                   ---
                  Center
```

Figure 11-14

ways, each requiring you to show three points (see *Figure 11-14*). In the default method you will show two end points of an axis and then show half the length of the other axis, from the midpoint of the first axis out (the midpoint of an axis is also the center of the ellipse). The other method allows you to pick the center point of the ellipse first, then the end point of one axis, followed by half the length of the other axis.

> In preparation for this exercise, return to the standard snap mode using the following procedure:
  1. Open the Drawing Aids dialogue box from the Options menu.
  2. Click the "On" box under "Isometric Snap/Grid" so that the **x** is removed.
  3. Check the Snap and Grid spacing.
  4. Press Enter or click on "OK".

You will see that your grid is returned to the standard pattern and the cross hairs are horizontal and vertical again. Notice that this does not affect the isometric bracket you have just drawn.

We will briefly explore the ELLIPSE command and draw some standard ellipses.

> Type "Ellipse" or select the Ellipse Axis End tool from the Ellipse flyout on the Draw toolbar, as shown in *Figure 11-15*.

AutoCAD prompts:

Arc/Center/<Axis endpoint 1>:

> Pick an axis end point as shown by p1 on the ellipse at the lower left of the display in *Figure 11-16*.

AutoCAD prompts for the other end point:

Axis endpoint 2:

> Pick a second end point as shown by p2.

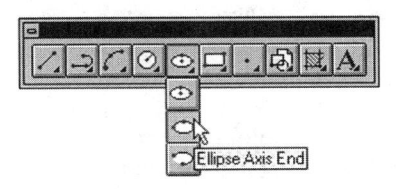

Figure 11-15

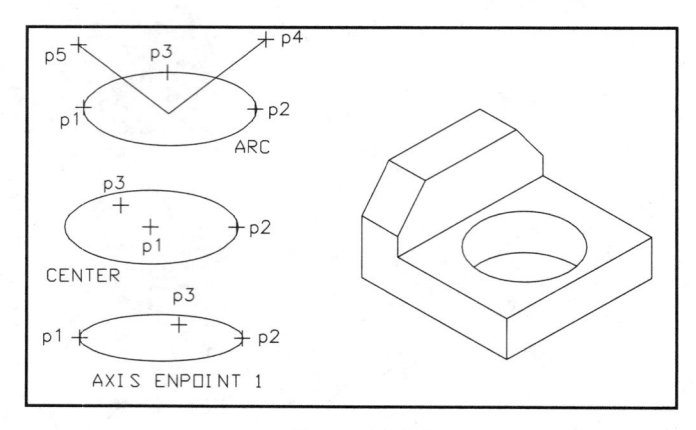

Figure 11-16

AutoCAD gives you an ellipse to drag and a rubber band so that you can show the length of the other axis. Only the length of the rubber band is significant; the angle is already determined to be perpendicular to the first axis. Because of this the third point will only fall on the ellipse if the rubber band is perpendicular to the first axis.

The prompt that follows allows you to show the second axis distance as before, or a rotation around the first axis:

<Other axis distance>/Rotation:

The rotation option is awkward to use and we will not explore it here; see the *AutoCAD Command Reference* for more information.

> Pick p3 as shown.

This point will show half the length of the other axis.

The first ellipse should now be complete.

Now we will draw one showing the center point first.

> Repeat the ELLIPSE command.

> At the "Arc/Center/<Axis endpoint 1>:" prompt, type "c" or select "center". (This step will be automated if you select Ellipse Center from the toolbar).

AutoCAD will give you a prompt for a center point:

Center of Ellipse:

> Pick a center point (p1), as shown at the middle left of *Figure 11-16*.

Now you will have a rubber band stretching from the center to the end of an axis and the following prompt:

Axis endpoint:

> Pick an end point as shown in the figure (p2).

The prompt that follows allows you to show the second axis distance as before, or a rotation around the first axis:

<Other axis distance>/Rotation:

> Pick an axis distance as shown by p3.

Here again the rubber band is significant for distance only. The point you pick will fall on the ellipse only if the rubber band is stretched perpendicular to the first axis. Notice that it is not in Figure 11-16.

Drawing Elliptical Arcs

Elliptical arcs can be drawn by trimming complete arcs or by using the arc option of the ELLIPSE command. Using the arc option, you will first construct an ellipse in one of the two methods shown previously, and then show the arc of that ellipse that you want to keep. Determining arcs can be quite complicated because of the many different parameters available. You will remember this from Chapter 4 when you learned the arc command. In this exercise we will stick to a simple procedure; you should have no difficulty pursuing the more complex options on your own.

> Select the Ellipse Arc tool from the Ellipse flyout on the Draw toolbar.
> Pick a first axis end point as shown by p1 at the upper left in *Figure 11-16*.
> Pick a second end point, p2 in the figure.
> Pick a point 3 to show the second axis distance.

AutoCAD will draw an ellipse as you have specified, but the image is only temporary. Now you need to show the arc you want drawn. The two options are "Parameter" and "start angle". Parameter will take you into more options that allow you to specify your arc in different ways, similar to the options of the ARC command. We will stick with the default option.

> Pick p4 to show the angle at which the elliptical arc will begin.

Move the cursor slowly now and you will see all the arcs that are possible starting from this angle.

> Pick p5 to indicate the end angle and complete the command.

Task 6: Saving and Restoring Displays with VIEW

Procedure

1. Type or select "View".
2. Type "s" to save or "r" to restore a view.
3. Type a view name.

Discussion. The word "view" in connection with the VIEW command has a special significance in AutoCAD. It refers to any set of display boundaries that have been named and "saved" using the VIEW command. Views that have been saved can be restored rapidly and by direct reference rather than by redefining the location and size of the area to be displayed. VIEW has a number of important applications in creating 3D drawing layouts, but it can also be useful in 2D when you know that you will be returning frequently to a certain area of a large drawing. It saves having to zoom out to look at the complete drawing and then zoom back in again on the area you want.

Imagine that we have to do some extensive detail work on the area around the hole in the bracket and also on the top corner. We can define each of these as a view and jump back and forth at will.

> To begin this exercise, you should have the bracket on your screen as shown in *Figure 11-17*.

NOTE: There is a View Control dialogue box accessible through the DDVIEW command or by selecting "Named Views..." from the View pull down menu, or "DDview" under View on the screen menu. The dialogue includes the same choices plus an option that offers information about the defining features of each saved view. This information is most useful in 3D drawings. We will not use the dialogue box in this exercise, but once you understand the VIEW command you should have no trouble using DDVIEW as well.

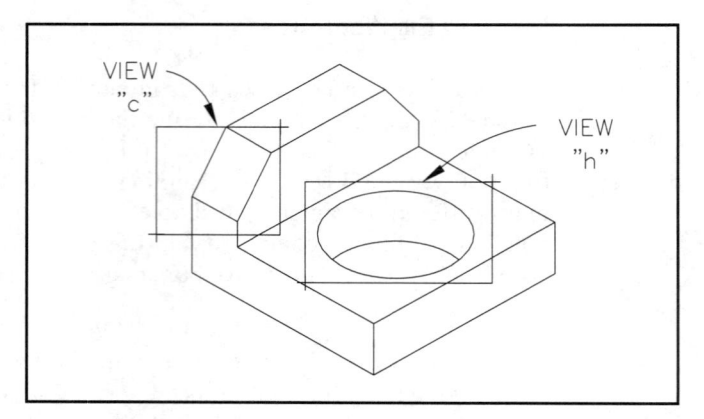

Figure 11-17

> Type "view".

AutoCAD responds:

?/Delete/Restore/Save/Window:

Notice that there is no default in this prompt. You must specify an option. In this exercise we will use "window" and "restore". The "?" is well known by now, it will get you a list of previously saved views. "Delete" erases previously saved views from the drawing database. "Restore" calls out a defined view. "Save" uses the current display window as the view definition. And "window" allows you to define a new view without actually displaying it.

> Type "w" or select "Window" from the screen menu.

AutoCAD prompts for a view name:

View name to save:

> Type "h" for "hole".

Views are designed for speed, so it makes sense to assign them short names. AutoCAD now prompts for corners as usual in a window selection process.

> Pick first and second corners to define a window around the hole in the bracket, as shown in *Figure 11-17*.

When this is done, the command sequence is complete but you will see no change in your drawing. The window you selected is now defined as a view that can be "restored," or called up, using the view name "h". But first, let's repeat the process once more to define a second view called "c" for corner.

> Repeat the VIEW command.

> Type "w" or select "window".

> Type "c" for the view name.

> Define a window, as shown in *Figure 11-17*.

You have now defined two views. To see the command in action we must restore them.

> Repeat the VIEW command.

> Type "r" or select "restore".

AutoCAD prompts:

View name to restore:

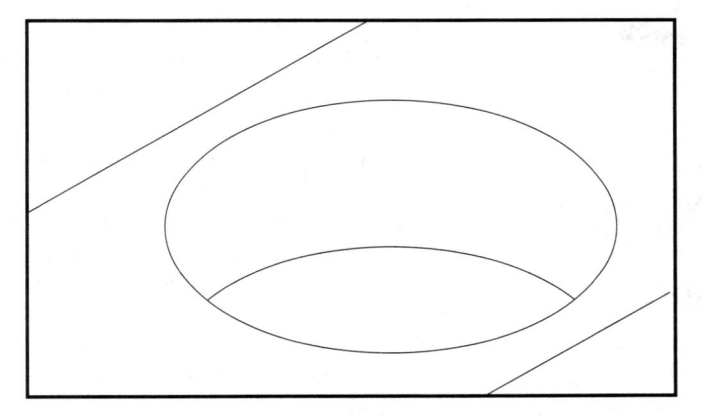

Figure 11-18

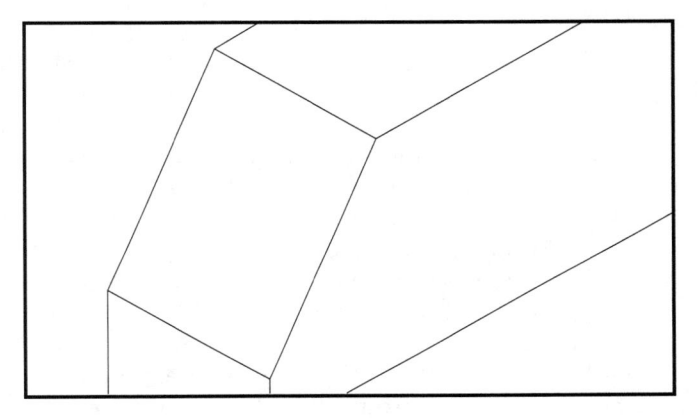

Figure 11-19

> Type "h" to switch to the view of the hole.

　　Your screen should resemble *Figure 11-18*.

Now switch to the corner view.

> Repeat the VIEW command.
> Type "r" or select "restore".
> Type "c".

Your screen should resemble *Figure 11-19*.

Task 7: Using Dynamic ZOOM

Procedure

1. Type "z" or select the Zoom Dynamic tool from the Zoom flyout on the Standard toolbar.
2. If necessary, type "d" or select "dynamic".
3. Show a pan.
4. Show a zoom.
5. Press Enter or the enter button.

Discussion. Dynamic ZOOM allows you to choose your display area while looking at the complete drawing, without having to wait for the drawing to regenerate. This can be an efficient time-saver, especially in large, slow-to-regenerate drawings.

356   Part II Text, Dimensions, and Other Complex Entities

> To begin this exercise, your screen should be showing one of the views defined in Task 6. Either will do.

> Type "z" or select the Zoom Dynamic tool from the Zoom flyout as shown in *Figure 11-20*.

> If you are typing, type "d" for the Dynamic option.

AutoCAD immediately will switch to a screen that resembles *Figure 11-21*, without the text. In order to see the view box shown, you will need to move the cursor.

This screen display can be bewildering. Take a minute to look at the text in the figure to see what each of the boxes is used for. There are three boxes. The most significant is the black view box with the **x** inside. This is the only box you can move and the one you will use to define the area you want to display.

The dotted green box frames the current view, that is, the area you were looking at before entering dynamic zoom.

The larger solid black box represents the drawing extents. Extents refer to the actual drawing area currently in use.

In larger drawings you may also see four red corner brackets. These show the boundaries of the area that is currently generated. If you zoom within these boundaries, AutoCAD will merely REDRAW the screen. If you zoom out of bounds, a regeneration will be required, causing some delay in a large drawing. AutoCAD will warn you of this by displaying an hourglass, as shown in *Figure 11-22*.

To use dynamic zoom, you must become accustomed to the two ways in which you can move the view box. It should be familiar to you from the pan and zoom box used in plot previewing. When the **x** is showing, you can move the view box anywhere on the screen to frame a new area to display. Let's try it.

> Move the view box around the screen.

Notice that the box remains the same size as you move.

> Press the *pick* button (not the enter button).

You should see an arrow at the right of the view box, instead of the **x** in the center, as shown in *Figure 11-23*. The pick button switches between panning and zooming. In other words, with the **x** showing you can reposition the box, whereas with the arrow you can change its size.

> Move the cursor to the right and left.

Notice how the box stretches and shrinks in both the horizontal and vertical directions. Unlike the usual ZOOM window, this box is always pro-

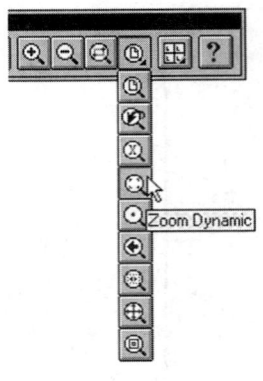

Figure 11-20

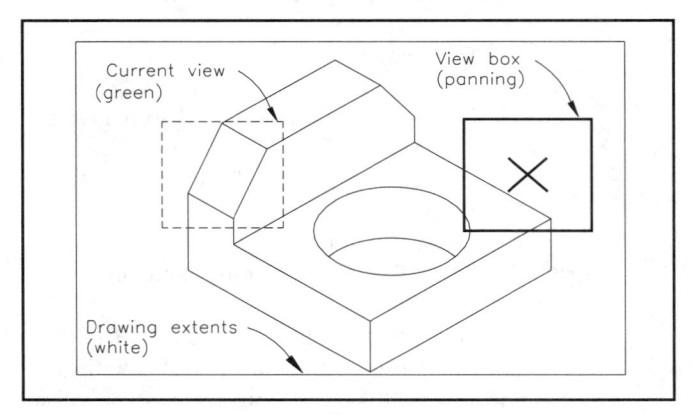

Figure 11-21

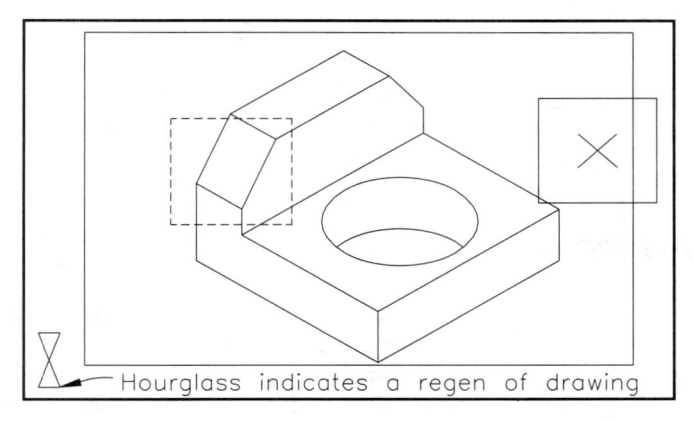

Figure 11-22

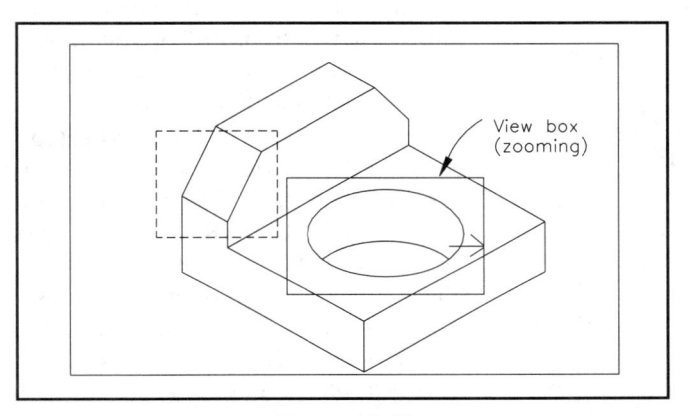

Figure 11-23

portioned to show the area that will actually be displayed. Also notice that you can pan the box vertically but not horizontally.

> Press the pick button again.

This brings back the **x** so that you can move the box in all directions again.

> Position the box as you want it and then press Enter, the space bar, or the enter button on your cursor.

This completes the dynamic ZOOM procedure and displays the area you defined with the view box.

Now that you know how to control the size and position of the box, try using dynamic ZOOM to display the area around the hole in the bracket, similar to the area you defined previously as the "h" view. Then use dynamic ZOOM to display the front corner, as in the "c" view. Remember you do not have to leave one view to zoom into another. Dynamic zoom will always show you the complete drawing.

Tasks 8, 9, 10, 11, and 12

The five drawings that follow will give you a range of experience in isometric drawing. The bracket drawing is an extension of the previous tasks, the radio drawing uses the "box method" and text on isometric angles, both the fixture and the flanged coupling drawings require you to work off an isometric centerline, and the garage drawing is an architectural drawing that introduces methods for multiple copying or using the ARRAY command in the isometric planes.

DRAWING 11-1: MOUNTING BRACKET

This drawing is a direct extension of the exercise in the chapter. It will give you practice in basic AutoCAD isometrics and in transferring dimensions from orthographic to isometric views.

DRAWING SUGGESTIONS

> When the center point of an isocircle is not on snap, as in this drawing, you will need to create a specifiable point and snap onto it. Draw intersecting lines from the midpoints of the sides so that you can snap to that intersection, or use DIST and draw a point there. Then use a "node" snap.

> Often when you try to select a group of objects to copy, there will be many crossing lines that you do not want to include in the copy. This is an ideal time to use the "remove" option in object selection. First window the objects you want along with those nearby that are unavoidable, and then remove the unwanted objects one by one.

> Frequently you will get unexpected results when you try to TRIM an object in an isometric view. AutoCAD will divide an ellipse into a series of arcs, for example, and only trim a portion. If you do not get the results you want, use the BREAK command to control how the object is broken, and then erase what you do not want.

> There is no arc option when you use ELLIPSE to draw isocircles, so semicircles like those at the top and bottom of the slots must be constructed by first drawing isocircles and then trimming or erasing unwanted portions.

> Use COPY frequently to avoid duplicating your work. Since it may take a considerable amount of editing to create holes and fillets, do not COPY until edits have been done on the original.

> The row of small arcs that show the curve in the middle of the bracket are multiple copies of the fillet at the corner.

Chap. 11

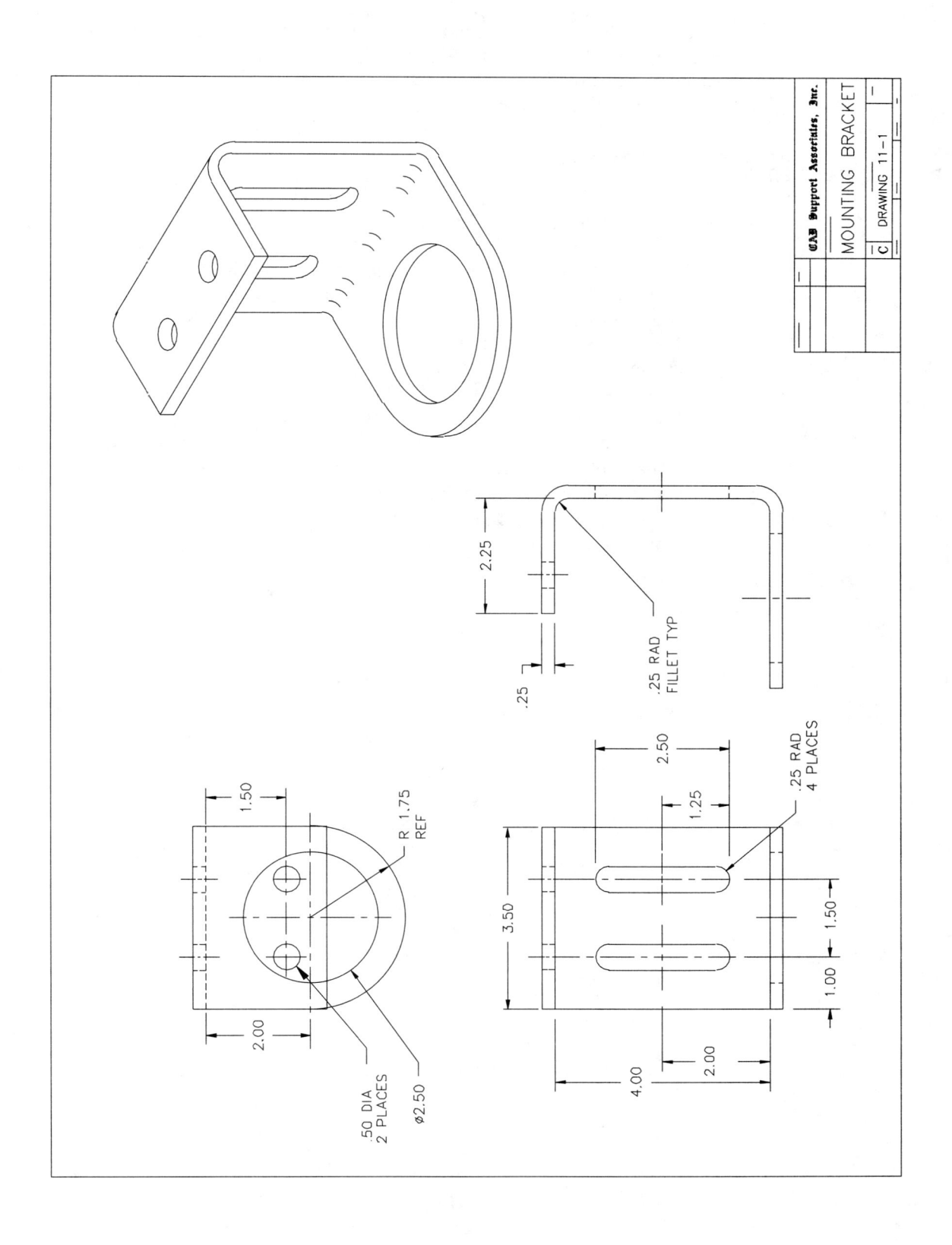

DRAWING 11-2: RADIO

This drawing introduces text and will be greatly simplified by the use of the rectangular ARRAY command. Placing objects on different layers so they can be turned on and off during TRIM, BREAK, and ERASE procedures will make things considerably less messy.

DRAWING SUGGESTIONS

> Use the "box method" to do this drawing. That is, begin with an isometric box according to the overall outside dimensions of the radio. Then go back and cut away the excess as you form the details of the drawing.

> The horizontal "grill" can be done with a rectangular array, since it runs straight on the vertical. Look carefully at the pattern to see where it repeats. Draw one set and then array it. Later you can go back and trim away the dial and speaker areas.

> Draw isocircles over the grill and break away the lines over the speaker. When you are ready to hatch the speaker, draw another trimmed isocircle to define the hatch boundary, create the hatch, and then erase the boundary.

> The knobs are isocircles with copies to show thickness. You can use tangent-to-tangent osnaps to draw the front-to-back connecting lines.

> The text is created on two different angles that line up with the left and right isoplanes. We leave it to you to discover the correct angles.

Chap. 11

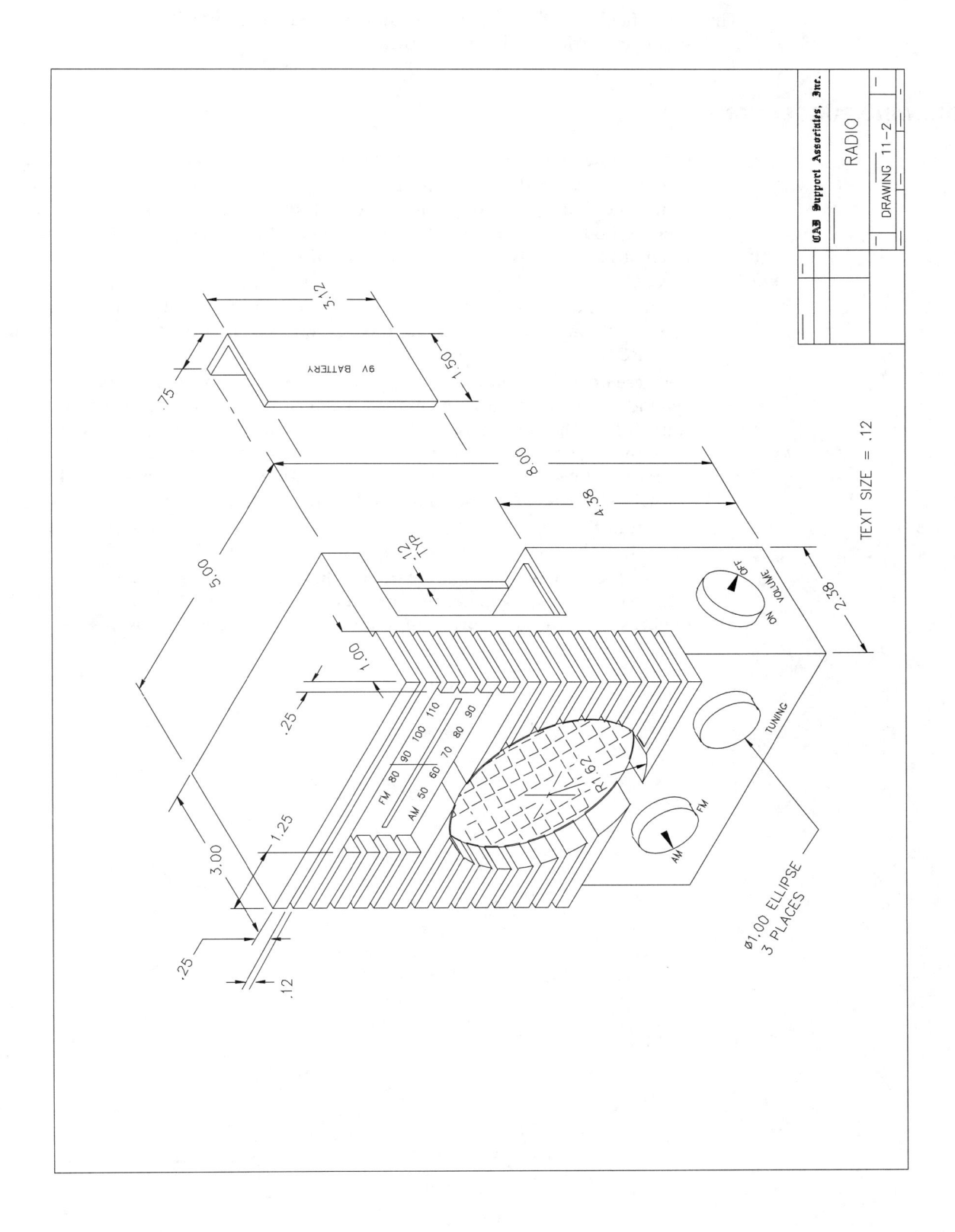

361

DRAWING 11-3: FIXTURE ASSEMBLY

This is a difficult drawing. It will take time and patience but will teach you a great deal about isometric drawing in AutoCAD.

DRAWING SUGGESTIONS

> This drawing can be done either by drawing everything in place as you see it, or by drawing the parts and moving them into place along the common centerline that runs through the middle of all the items. If you use the former method, draw the centerline first and use it to locate the center points of isocircles and as base points for other measures.

> As you go, look for pieces of objects that can be copied to form other objects. Avoid duplicating efforts by editing before copying. In particular, where one object covers part of another, be sure to copy it before you trim or erase the covered sections.

> To create the chamfered end of item 4, begin by drawing the 1.00 diameter cylinder 3.00 long with no chamfer. Then copy the isocircle at the end forward .125. The smaller isocircle is .875 (7/8), since .0625 (1/16) is cut away from the 1.00 circle all around. Draw this smaller isocircle and TRIM away everything that is hidden. Then draw the slanted chamfer lines using LINE, not CHAMFER. Use the same method for item 5.

> In both the screw and the nut you will need to create hexes around isocircles. Use the dimensions from a standard bolt chart.

> Use three-point arcs to approximate the curves on the screw bolt and the nut. You are after a representation that looks correct. It is impractical and unnecessary to achieve exact measures on these objects in the isometric view.

Chap. 11

ITEM NO	DESCRIPTION	PART NO.	QTY
7	NUT 1/4-20 UNC	F113-7	4
6	HEX HEAD BOLT 1/4-20 UNC x 3.00 LG	F113-6	4
5	CORNER PIN	F113-5	4
4	CENTER PIN	F113-4	1
3	SPACER 1.25 O.D. x 1.00 I.D. x 1.25 THK	F113-3	1
2	DISK 2.00 O.D. x 1.00 I.D. x .12 THK	F113-2	2
1	END PLATE 4.00 SQUARE x .50 THK	F113-1	2

CAD Support Associates, Inc.

FIXTURE ASSEMBLY

D DRAWING 11-3

TOLERANCE FOR HOLES AND PINS

ITEM 4   CLASS RC2 FIT
ITEM 5   CLASS LT4 FIT
ITEM 1   CLASS RC2 FIT FOR CENTER HOLE
ITEM 1   CLASS LT4 FIT FOR CORNER PIN HOLES
ITEM 2   CLASS RC2 FIT FOR CENTER HOLE
ITEM 2   CLASS RC1 FIT FOR CORNER PIN HOLES
ITEM 3   CLASS RC2 FIT FOR CENTER HOLE

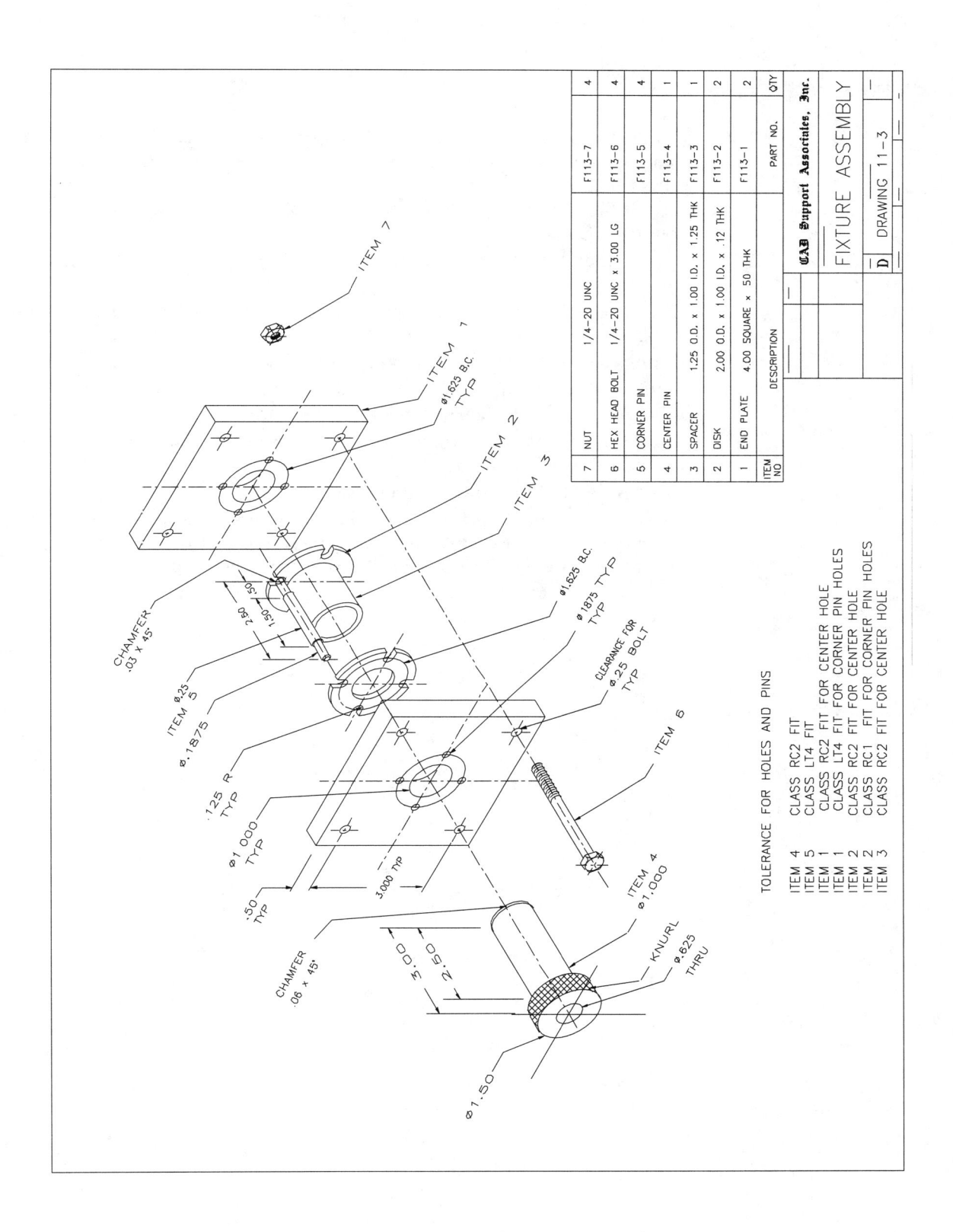

DRAWING 11–4: FLANGED COUPLING

The isometric view in this three-view drawing must be done working off the centerline.

DRAWING SUGGESTIONS

> Draw the major centerline first. Then draw vertical center lines at every point where an isocircle will be drawn. Make sure to draw these lines extra long so that they can be used to trim the isocircles in half. By starting at the back of the object and working forward, you can take dimensions directly from the right side view.

> Draw the isocircles at each centerline and then trim them to represent semicircles.

> Use end point, intersection, and tangent to tangent osnaps to draw horizontal lines.

> Trim away all obstructed lines and parts of isocircles.

> Draw the four slanted lines in the middle as vertical lines first. Then, with ortho off, CHANGE their end points, moving them in .125.

> Remember, MIRROR will not work in the isometric view, although it can be used effectively in the right side view.

> Use BHATCH to create the cross-hatching.

> If you have made a mistake in measuring along the major centerline, STRETCH can be used to correct it. Make sure that ortho is on and that you are in an isoplane that lets you move the way you want.

Chap. 11

FLANGED COUPLING
Drawing 11-4

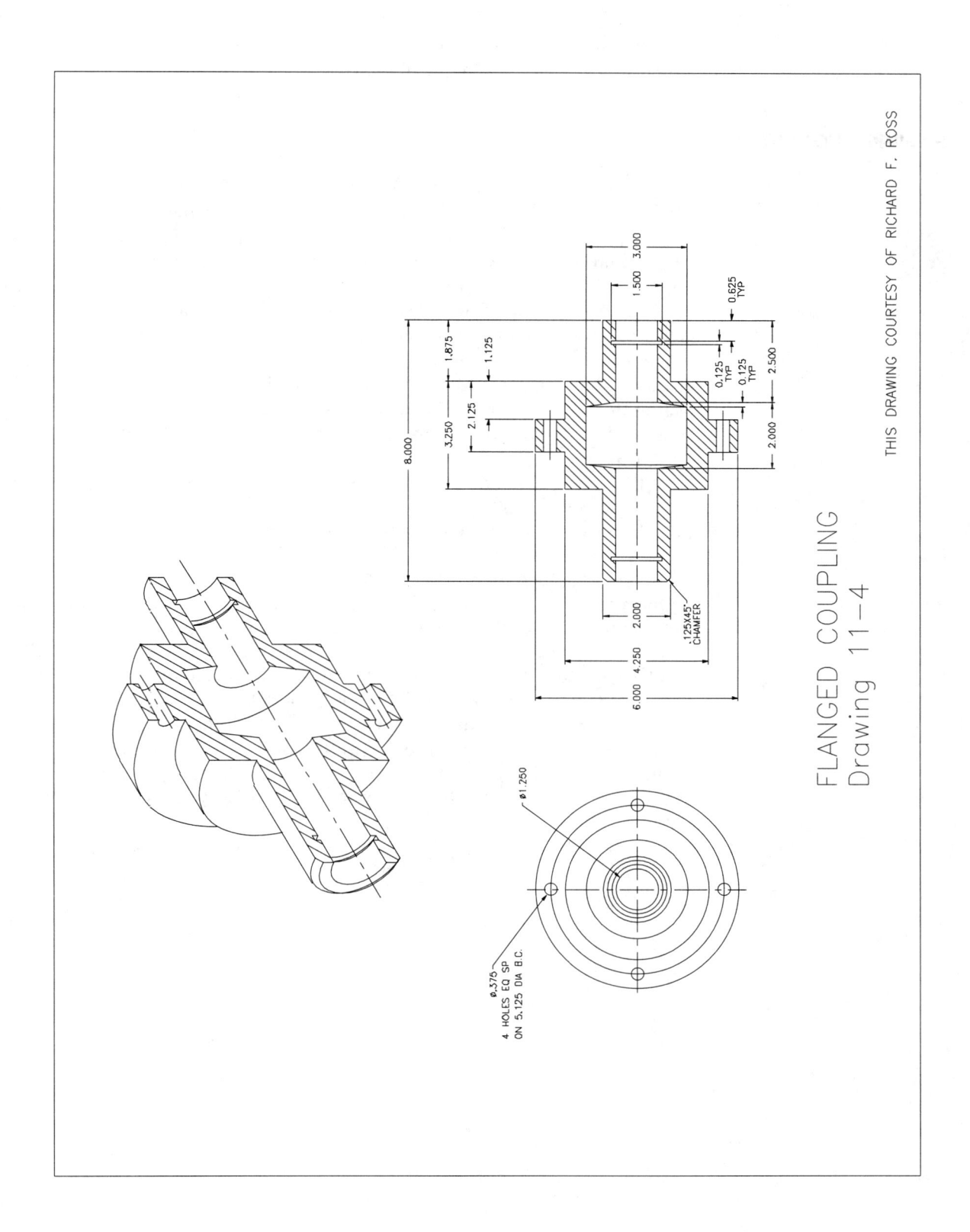

THIS DRAWING COURTESY OF RICHARD F. ROSS

DRAWING 11-5: GARAGE FRAMING

This is a fairly complex drawing that will take lots of trimming and careful work. Changing the "snapang" (snap angle) variable so that you can draw slanted arrays is a method that can be used frequently in isometric drawing.

DRAWING SUGGESTIONS

> You will find yourself using COPY, ZOOM, and TRIM a great deal. OFFSET also will work well. This is a good place to use dynamic zoom.

> You may want to create some new layers of different colors if you have a color monitor. Keeping different parts of the construction walls, rafters, and joists on different layers will allow you to have more control over them and add a lot of clarity to what you see on the screen. Turning layers on and off can considerably simplify trimming operations.

> You can cut down on repetition in this drawing by using arrays on various angles. For example, if the snapang variable is set to 150 degrees, the 22" wall in the left isoplane can be created as a rectangular array of studs with 1 row and 17 columns set 16 inches apart. To do so, follow this procedure:
1. Type "snapang".
2. Enter a new value so that rectangular arrays will be built on isometric angles (30 or 150).
3. Enter the ARRAY command and create the array. Use negative values where necessary.
4. Trim the opening for the window.

> One alternative to this array method is to set your snap to 16" temporarily and use multiple COPY to create the columns of studs, rafters, and joists. Another alternative is to use the grip edit offset snap method beginning with an offset snap of 16" (i.e., press Shift when you show the first copy displacement and continue to hold down Shift as you make other copies).

> The cutaway in the roof that shows the joists and the back door is drawn using the standard nonisometric ELLIPSE command. Then the rafters are trimmed to the ellipse and the ellipse is erased. Do this procedure before you draw the joists and the back wall. Otherwise you will be trimming these as well.

> Use CHAMFER to create the chamfered corners on the joists.

Chap. 11

GARAGE FRAMING
Drawing 11-5

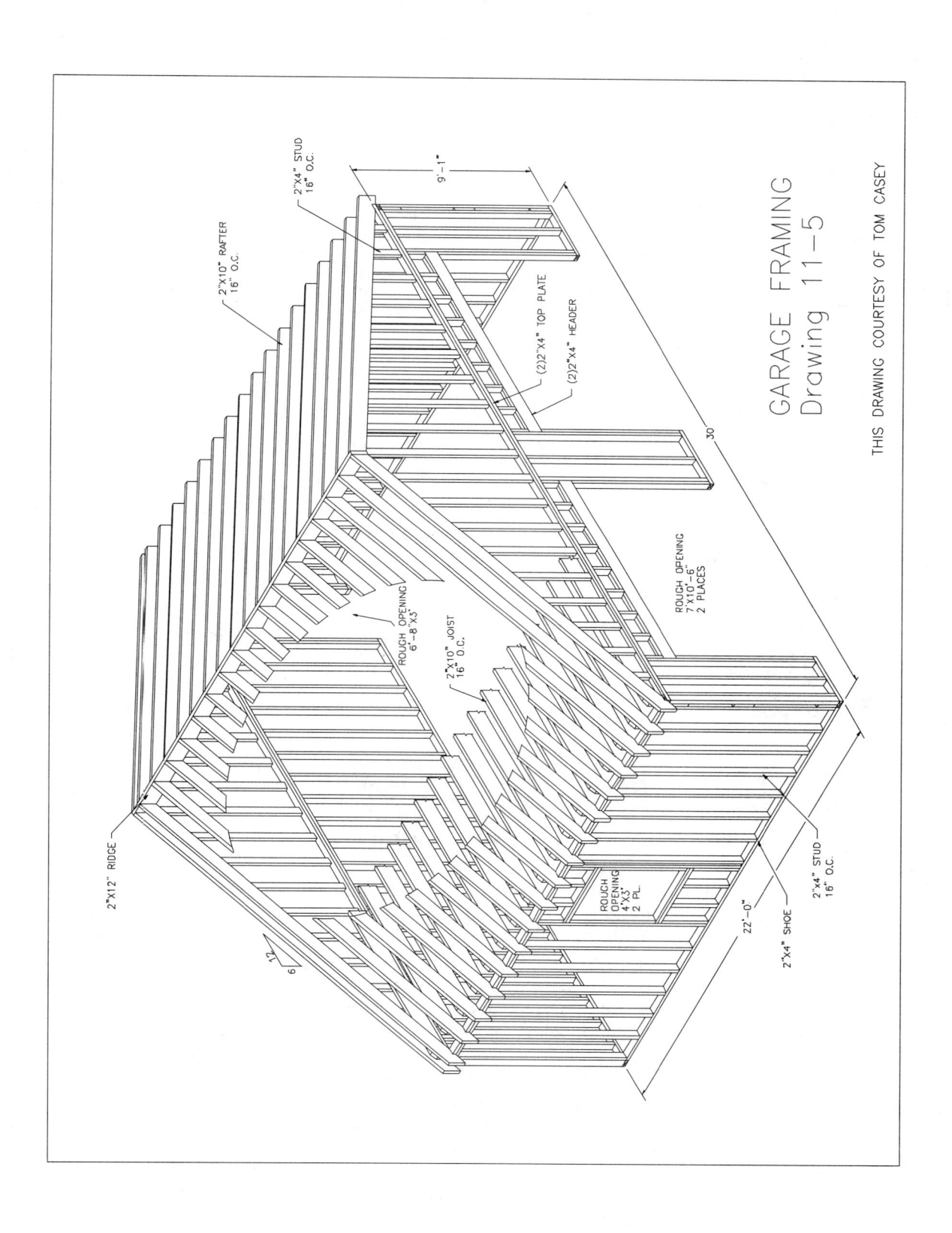

THIS DRAWING COURTESY OF TOM CASEY

PART III
Three-Dimensional Modeling

CHAPTER
12

COMMANDS

VIEW	DRAW	OPTIONS
UCS	RULESURF	UCSICON
VPOINT		
DDVPOINT		

OVERVIEW

It is now time to begin thinking in three dimensions. 3D drawing in AutoCAD is logical and efficient. You can create wireframe models, surface models, or solid models and display them from multiple points of view. In this chapter we will focus on User Coordinate Systems and 3D viewpoints. These are the primary tools you will need to understand how AutoCAD allows you to work in three dimensions on a two-dimensional screen. Tasks 1–5 will take you through a complete 3D wireframe modeling exercise using four different coordinate systems that we will define.

If you have completed Chapter 11, you will find that working on isometric drawings has prepared you well for 3D drawing. There will be a similar process of switching from plane to plane, but there are two primary differences. First, you will not be restricted to three isometric planes: You can define a User Coordinate System aligned with any specifiable plane. Second, and most important, the model you draw will have true 3D characteristics. You will be able to view it, edit it, and plot it from any definable point in space.

Chap. 12

TASKS

1. Create and view a 3D box.
2. Define and save three User Coordinate Systems.
3. Use standard edit commands in a UCS.
4. Construct a slot through an angled surface in 3D.
5. Create a 3D fillet using FILLET and RULESURF.
6. Explore other methods of using the VPOINT command.
7. Do drawing 12–1 ("Clamp").
8. Do drawing 12–2 ("Guide Block").
9. Do drawing 12–3 ("Slide Mount").
10. Do drawing 12–4 ("Stair Layout").

Task 1: Creating and Viewing a 3D Wireframe Box

Discussion. In this task we will create a simple 3D box that we can edit in later tasks to form a more complex object.

In Chapter 1 we showed how to turn the coordinate system icon (see *Figure 12-1*) off and on. For drawing in 3D you will definitely want it on. If your icon is not visible, follow this procedure to turn it on:

1. Type "Ucsicon" or select "UCS" from the Options pull down menu, shown in *Figure 12-2*.
2. Type "on" or select "Icon".

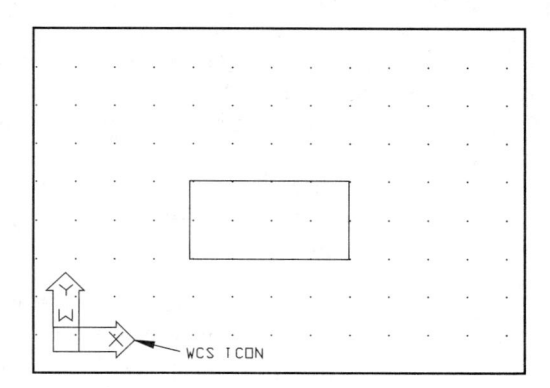

Figure 12-1

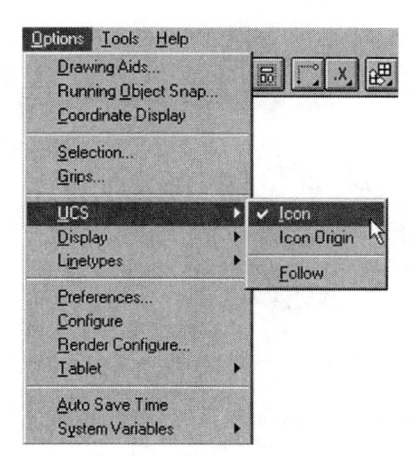

Figure 12-2

For now, simply observe the icon as you go through the process of creating the box, and be aware that you are currently working in the same coordinate system that you have always used in AutoCAD. It is called the World Coordinate System, to distinguish it from others you will create yourself beginning in Task 2.

Currently, the origin of the WCS is at the lower left of your screen. This is the point (0,0,0) when you are thinking 3D, or simply (0,0) when you are in 2D. x coordinates increase to the right horizontally across the screen, and y coordinates increase vertically up the screen as usual. The z axis, which we have ignored up until now, currently extends out of the screen towards you and perpendicular to the x and y axes. This orientation of the three planes is also called a plan view. Soon we will switch to a "front, right, top" or "southeast" view.

Let's begin.

> Draw a 2.00 by 4.00 rectangle near the middle of your screen, as shown in *Figure 12-1*. Do not use the RECTANG command to draw this figure because we will want to select individual line segments later on.

Changing Viewpoints

In order to move immediately into a 3D mode of drawing and thinking, our first step will be to change our viewpoint on this object. There are two commands that allow you to create 3D points of view, VPOINT and DVIEW. DVIEW, which is discussed at the end of Chapter 15, is complex and best suited for creating carefully adjusted presentation images, including perspective views. The VPOINT command is somewhat simpler and best used for setting up basic views during the drawing and editing process. A good understanding of all the VPOINT options will increase your understanding of AutoCAD's 3D space. For this reason we have included at the end of the chapter an optional discussion of the different options available in the VPOINT command. There are three or four different methods, developed over time as Autodesk has tried to simplify the viewpoint definition process with each new release.

In Release 13 the simplest and most efficient method is to use the 3D Viewpoints Presets submenu from the View pull down menu. For our purposes, this is the only method you will need.

> Select "View" from the pull down menu bar.
> Select "3D Viewpoint Presets" from the View menu.

This will call up a cascading submenu beginning with "Plan View", as shown in *Figure 12-3*. Using this method, AutoCAD will take you directly

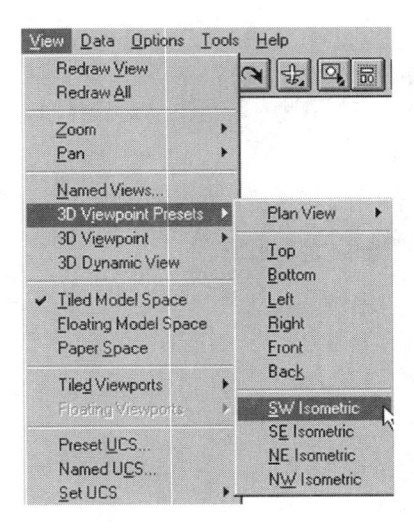

Figure 12-3

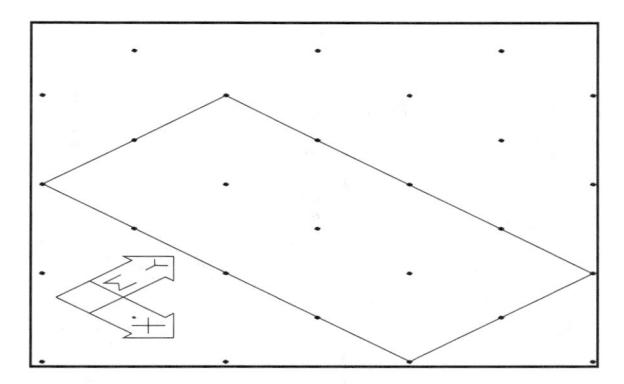

Figure 12-4

into 1 of 11 preset viewpoints. In all of the nonisometric views in the submenu (Plan View, Top, ..., Front, Back) the *x* and *y* axes will be rotated 90 degrees or not at all. You will see the drawing from directly above (Plan and Top) or directly below (Bottom), or you will look in along the *x* axis (Left and Right) or along the *y* axis (Front and Back).

We will use a Southeast Isometric view. The isometric views all rotate the *xy* axes plus or minus 45 degrees and take you up 30 degrees out of the XY plane. It is simple if you imagine a compass. The lower right quadrant is the southeast. In a southeast isometric view you will be looking in from this quadrant and down at a 30 degree angle. Try it.

> Select "SE Isometric" from the submenu.

The menu will disappear and the screen will be redrawn to show the view shown in *Figure 12-4*. Notice how the grid and the coordinate system icon have altered to show our current orientation. These visual aids are extremely helpful in viewing 3D objects on the flat screen and imagining them as if they were positioned in space.

At this point you may wish to experiment with the other views in the 3D Viewpoint Preset submenu. You will probably find the isometric views most interesting at this point. Pay attention to the grid and the icon as you switch views. Variations of the icon you may encounter here and later on are shown in *Figure 12-5*. With some views you will have to think carefully and watch the icon to understand which way the object is being presented.

When you are done experimenting, be sure to return to the southeast isometric view shown in *Figure 12-4*. We will use this view frequently throughout this chapter and the next.

Whenever you change viewpoints, AutoCAD displays the drawing extents, so that the object fills the screen and is as large as possible. Often you will need to zoom out a bit to get some space to work in. This is easily done using the "Scale(X)" option of the ZOOM command.

> Type "z" or select the Zoom Scale tool from the Zoom flyout on the Standard toolbar, as shown in *Figure 12-6*.

AutoCAD prompts:

All/Center/Dynamic/Extents/Left/Previous/Vmax/Window/<Scale(X/XP)>:

> In response to the ZOOM prompt, type ".5x".

Don't forget the "x". This tells AutoCAD to adjust and redraw the display so that objects appear half as large as before.

ICON	DESCRIPTION
	WCS (WORLD COORDINATE SYSTEM) "W" appears on "Y" arm
	UCS (USER COORDINATE SYSTEM) NO "W" appears on "Y" arm
	+ appears in box and "W" appears on "Y" arm if the current UCS is the same as the WCS
Pos. "Z"	Box appears at the base of ICON if viewing UCS from above its X-Y plane
Neg. "Z"	Box is missing if viewing UCS from below its X-Y plane
	Broken pencil ICON appears if viewing direction is "EDGE ON" or near "EDGE ON" X-Y plane of current UCS

Figure 12-5

Your screen will be redrawn with the rectangle at half its previous magnification.

Entering 3D Coordinates

Next, we will create a copy of the rectangle placed 1.25 above it. This brings up a basic 3D problem: AutoCAD interprets all pointer device point selections as being in the XY plane, so how does one indicate a point or a displacement in the Z direction? There are three possibilities: typed 3D coordinates, X/Y/Z point filters, and object snaps. Object snap requires an object already drawn above or below the XY plane, so it will be of no use right now. We will use typed coordinates first, then discuss how point filters could be used as an alternative. Later we will be using object snap as well.

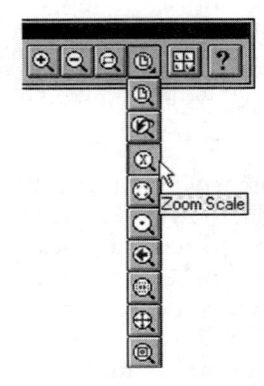

Figure 12-6

3D coordinates can be entered from the keyboard in the same manner as 2D coordinates. Often this is an impractical way to enter individual points in a drawing. However, within COPY or MOVE it provides a simple method for specifying a displacement in the Z direction.

> Type "Copy" or select the Copy tool from the Modify toolbar.

　AutoCAD will prompt for object selection.

> Select the complete rectangle.

> Press Enter, the space bar, or the enter equivalent button on your pointing device to end object selection.

　AutoCAD now prompts for the base point of a vector or a displacement value:

<Base point or displacement>/Multiple:

Typically, you would respond to this prompt and the next by showing the two end points of a vector. However, we cannot show a displacement in the Z direction by pointing. This is important for understanding AutoCAD coordinate systems. Unless an object snap is used, all points picked on the screen with the pointing device will be interpreted as being in the XY plane of the current UCS. Without an entity outside the XY plane to use in an object snap, there is no way to point to a displacement in the Z direction.
> Type "0,0,1.25".

AutoCAD now prompts:

Second point of displacement:

You can type the coordinates of another point, or press Enter to tell AutoCAD to use the first entry as a displacement from (0,0,0). In this case, pressing Enter will indicate a displacement of 1.25 in the Z direction, and no change in X or Y.
> Press Enter.

AutoCAD will create a copy of the rectangle 1.25 directly above the original. Your screen should resemble *Figure 12-7*.

X/Y/Z Point Filters (Optional)

Point filters can be very useful in 3D, although they may seem odd until you get a feel for when to use them. In a point filter we filter out coordinates from one point and use them to create a new point. Notice that in the displacement we just entered, the only thing that changes is the Z value. Note also that we could specify the same displacement using any point in the XY plane as a base point. For example, (3,6,0) to (3,6,1.25) would show the same displacement as (0,0,0) to (0,0,1.25). In fact, we don't even need to know what X and Y are as long as we know that they don't change.

That is how an ".XY" point filter works. We borrow, or "filter", the X and Y values from a point, without pausing to find out what the values actually are, and then specify a new Z value. Other types of filters are possible, of course, such as ".Z" or ".YZ".

You can use a point filter, like an object snap, any time AutoCAD asks for a point. After a point filter is specified, AutoCAD will always prompt with an "of". In our case you are being asked, "You want the X and Y values of what point?" In response, you pick a point, then AutoCAD will ask you to fill in Z. Notice that point filters can be "chained" so that, for example, you can filter the X value from one point and combine it with the filtered Y value from another point.

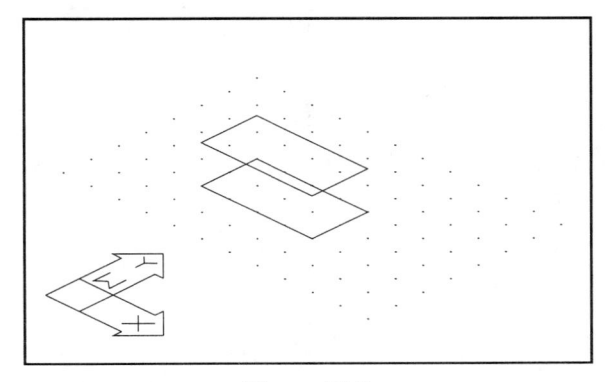

Figure 12-7

To use an .XY filter in the COPY command instead of typing coordinates, for example, you could follow this procedure:

1. Enter the COPY command.
2. Select the rectangle.
3. For the displacement base point, pick any point in the XY plane.
4. At the prompt for a second point, type ".xy" or select the .XY tool from the Point Filters flyout on the Standard toolbar.
5. At the "of" prompt, type "@" or pick the same point again.
6. At the "(need Z):" prompt, type "1.25". The result would be *Figure 12-7*, as before.

Using Object Snap

We now have two rectangles floating in space. Our next job is to connect the corners to form a wireframe box. This is done easily using "ENDpoint" object snaps. This is a good example of how object snaps allow us to construct entities not in the XY plane of the current coordinate system.

> Type "Osnap" or select "Running Object Snap..." from the Options pull down menu.

> Type "end" or select "Endpoint" in the dialogue box and then click on OK.

The running Endpoint object snap is now on and will affect all point selection. You will find that object snaps are very useful in 3D drawing and that Endpoint mode can be used frequently.

Now we will draw some lines.

> Enter the LINE command and connect the upper and lower corners of the two rectangles, as shown in *Figure 12-8*. (We have removed the grid for clarity, but you will probably want to leave yours on.)

Before going on, pause a moment to be aware of what you have drawn. The box on your screen is a true wireframe model. Unlike an isometric drawing, it is a 3D model that can be turned, viewed, and plotted from any point in space. It is not, however, a solid model or a surface model. It is only a set of lines in 3D space. Removing hidden lines or shading would have no effect on this model.

In the next task you will begin to define your own coordinate systems that will allow you to perform drawing and editing functions in any plane you choose.

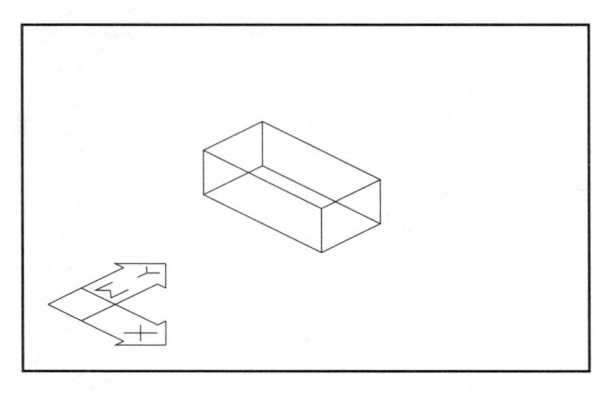

Figure 12-8

Task 2: Defining and Saving User Coordinate Systems

Procedure

1. Type "UCS" or select "Set UCS" from the View pull down menu.
2. Choose an option.
3. Specify a coordinate system.
4. Repeat the UCS command to name and save the new coordinate system.

Discussion. In this task you will begin to develop new vocabulary and techniques for working with objects in 3D space. The primary tool will be the UCS command. You will also learn to use the UCSICON command to control the placement of the coordinate system icon.

Until now we have had only one coordinate system to work with. All coordinates and displacements have been defined relative to a single point of origin. In Task 1 we changed our point of view, but the UCS icon changed along with it, so that the orientations of the *x*, *y*, and *z* axes relative to the object were retained. With the UCS command you can define new coordinate systems at any point and any angle in space. When you do, you can use the coordinate system icon and the grid to help you visualize the planes you are working in, and all commands and drawing aids will function relative to the new system.

The coordinate system we are currently using is unique. It is called the World Coordinate System and is the one we always begin with. The "W" at the base of the coordinate system icon indicates that we are working in the world system. A User Coordinate System is nothing more than a new point of origin and a new orientation for the *x*, *y*, and *z* axes.

We will begin by defining a User Coordinate System in the plane of the top of the box, as shown in *Figure 12-9*.

> Leave the Endpoint osnap mode on for this exercise.
> Type "UCS" or select "Set UCS" from the View pull down menu.

The UCS command gives you the following prompt:

Origin/ZAxis/3point/OBject/View/X/Y/Z/Prev/Restore/Save/Del/?/<World>:

On the pull down menu, you will see the same options on a submenu. In this chapter we will explore all options except "ZAxis", "OBject", and "Del". For further information see the *AutoCAD Command Reference* and the UCS icon chart, *Figure 12-5*.

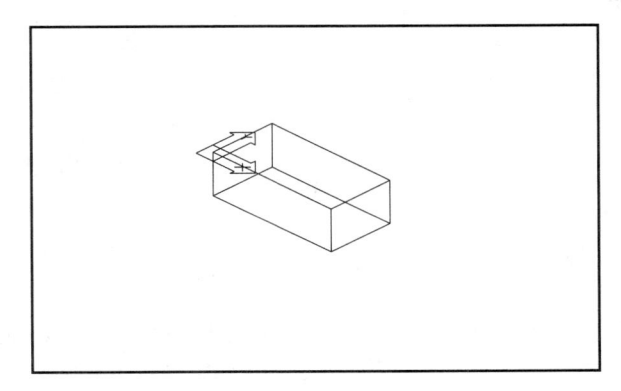

Figure 12-9

First we will use "Origin" to create a UCS that is parallel to the WCS.
> Type "o" or select "Origin" to specify the origin option.

AutoCAD will prompt for a new origin:

Origin point <0,0,0>:

This option does not change the orientation of the three axes. It simply shifts their intersection to a different point in space. We will use this simple procedure to define a UCS in the plane of the top of the box.
> Use the Endpoint object snap to select the top left front corner of the box, as shown by the location of the icon in *Figure 12-9*.

You will notice that the "W" is gone from the icon. However, the icon has not moved. It is still at the lower left of the screen. It is visually helpful to place it at the origin of the new UCS, as in the figure. In order to do this we need the UCSICON command.
> Type "Ucsicon" or select "UCS" from the Options pull down menu.

If you are typing, AutoCAD prompts:

ON/OFF/All/Noorigin/ORigin <ON>:

The first two options allow you to turn the icon on and off. The "All" option affects icons used in multiple viewports. "Noorigin" and "ORigin" allow you to specify whether you want to keep the icon in the lower left corner of the screen or place it at the origin of the current UCS. The "Follow" option on the pull down menu will cause the screen viewpoint to follow the UCS, so that you will switch to a plan view in each new UCS as you define it. This is usually not desirable.
> Type "or" or select "Icon origin".

The icon will move to the origin of the new current UCS, as in *Figure 12-9*. With UCSICON set to origin, the icon will shift to the new origin whenever we define a new UCS. The only exception would be if the origin were not on the screen or too close to an edge for the icon to fit. In these cases the icon would be displayed in the lower left corner again.

The "top" UCS we have just defined will make it easy to draw and edit entities that are in the plane of the top of the box and also to perform editing in planes that are parallel to it, such as the bottom. In the next task we will begin drawing and editing using different coordinate systems, and you will see how this works. For now, we will spend a little more time on the UCS command itself. We will define two more user coordinate systems, but first, let's save this one so that we can recall it quickly when we need it later on.

> Type "UCS" or select "Set UCS" from the View menu.

This time we will use the "Save" option.
> Type "s" or select "Save".

AutoCAD will ask you to name the current UCS so that it can be called out later:

?/Desired UCS name:

We will name our UCS "top." It will be the UCS we use to draw and edit in the top plane. This UCS would also make it easy for us to create an orthographic top view later on.
> Type "top".

Chap. 12

The top UCS is now saved and can be recalled using the "Restore" option or by making it "current" using the UCS Control dialogue box (select "Named UCS..." from the View pull down menu).

NOTE: Strictly speaking, it is not necessary to save every UCS. However, it usually saves time, since it is unlikely that you will have all your work done in any given plane or UCS the first time around. More likely, you will want to move back and forth between major planes of the object as you draw. Be aware also that you can return to the last defined UCS with the "Previous" option.

Next we will define a "front" UCS using the "3point" option of the UCS command.

> Repeat the UCS command or Set UCS on the View menu.
> Type "3" or select the "3 point" option.

AutoCAD prompts:

Origin point <0,0,0>:

In this option you will show AutoCAD a new origin point, as before, and then a new orientation for the axes as well. Notice that the default origin is the current one. If we retained this origin, we could define a UCS with the same origin and a different axis orientation.

Instead, we will define a new origin at the lower left corner of the front of the box, as shown in *Figure 12-10*.

> With the Endpoint osnap on, pick P1, as shown in the figure.

AutoCAD now prompts you to indicate the orientation of the *x* axis:

Point on positive portion of the X axis <1.00,0.00,-1.25>:

> Pick the right front corner of the box, P2, as shown.

The object snap ensures that the new *x* axis will now align with the front of the object. AutoCAD prompts for the *y* axis orientation:

Point on positive-Y portion of the UCS XY plane <0.00,1.00,-1.25>:

By definition, the *y* axis will be perpendicular to the *x* axis; therefore AutoCAD needs only a point that shows the plane of the *y* axis and its positive

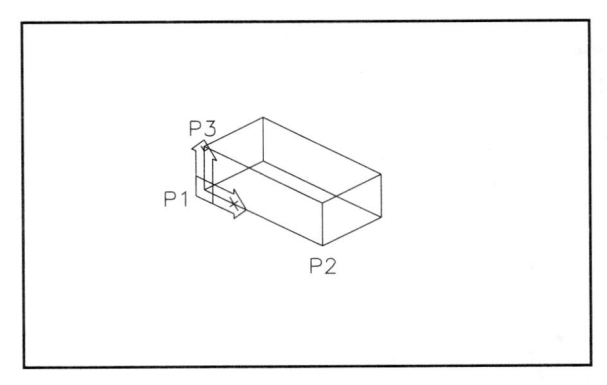

Figure 12-10

direction. Because of this, any point on the positive side of the *y* plane will specify the *y* axis correctly. We have chosen a point that is on the *y* axis itself.
> Pick P3, as shown.

When this sequence is complete, you will notice that the coordinate system icon has rotated along with the grid and moved to the new origin as well. This UCS will be convenient for drawing and editing in the front plane of the box, or editing in any plane parallel to the front, such as the back.

Now save the "front" UCS.
> Press Enter to repeat the UCS command.
> Type "s" to save.
> Type "front" to name the UCS.

Finally, we will use the "Origin" and "Y" axis rotation options together to create a right side UCS.

> Repeat the UCS command.
> Type "o" or select "Origin".
> Pick the lower front corner of the box for the origin, as shown in *Figure 12-11*.
> Repeat the UCS command.

We will rotate the UCS icon around its *y* axis to align it with the right side of the box.

In using any of the rotation options ("X", "Y", and "Z"), the first thing you have to decide is which axis is the axis of rotation. If you look at the current position of the icon and think about how it will look when it aligns with the right side of the box, you will see that the *y* axis retains its position and orientation while the *x* axis turns through 90 degrees. In other words, since *x* rotates around *y*, *y* is the axis of rotation.
> Type "y".

Now AutoCAD prompts for a rotation:

Rotation angle around Y axis <0.0>:

It takes some practice to differentiate positive and negative rotation in 3D. If you like, you can use AutoCAD's "right hand" rule, which can be stated as follows: If you are hitchhiking (pointing your thumb) in a positive direction along the axis of rotation, your fingers will curl in the direction of positive rotation for the other axis. In our case, align your right thumb with

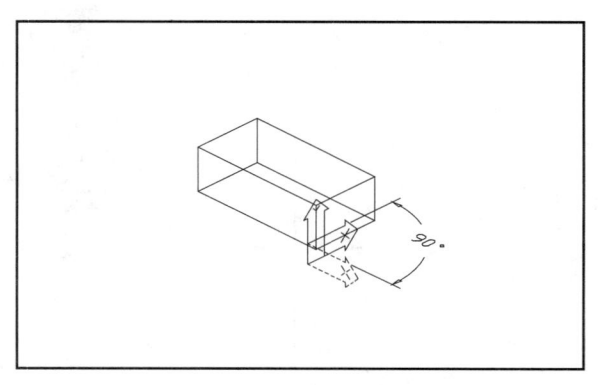

Figure 12-11

Chap. 12

the positive *y* axis, and you will see that your fingers curl in the direction we want the *x* axis to rotate. Therefore, the rotation of *x* around *y* is positive.
> Type "90".

You should now have the UCS icon aligned with the right side of the box, as shown in *Figure 12-11*. Save this UCS before going on to Task 3.

> Repeat the UCS command.
> Type "s".
> Type "right".

Task 3: Using Draw and Edit Commands in a UCS

Discussion. Now the fun begins. Using our three new coordinate systems and one more we will define later, we will give the box a more interesting "slotted wedge" shape. In this task we will cut away a slanted surface on the right side of the box. Since the planes we will be working in are parallel to the front of the box, we will begin by making the "front" UCS current. All our work in this task will be done in this UCS.

> Select "Named UCS..." from the View menu. Now that we have three new coordinate systems defined, you will find the dialogue box a simple way to switch between them.
> Highlight "Front" in the dialogue box and click on "Current".
> Click on "OK" in the dialogue box.
   The UCS icon should return to the front plane.
NOTE: In this case we also could have used the "Previous" option since "front" was the previous UCS.

Before going on, we need to turn off the running Endpoint osnap.

> Type "osnap" or select "Running Object Snap..." from the Options menu.
> Press Enter at the prompt for object snap modes or select "Clear All" and "OK" from the dialogue box.
   Now there will be no running object snap modes in effect.

Look at *Figure 12-12*. We will draw a line down the middle of the front (Line 1) and use it to trim another line coming in at an angle from the right (Line 2).

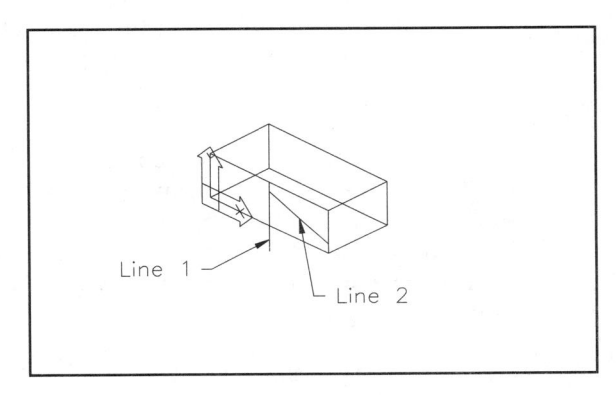

Figure 12-12

> Type "l" or select the Line tool from the Draw toolbar.
> At the "From point:" prompt, type "mid" or select the Snap to Midpoint tool from the Object Snap flyout on the Standard toolbar.
> Point to the top front edge of the box.
  AutoCAD will snap to the midpoint of the line.
> Make sure that ortho is on (F8).
  Notice how ortho works as usual, but relative to the current UCS.
> Pick a second point anywhere below the box and exit the LINE command.
  This line will be trimmed later, so the exact length does not matter.

Next we will draw Line 2 on an angle across the front. This line will become one edge of a slanted surface. Your snap setting will need to be at .25 or smaller, and ortho will need to be off. The grid, snap, and coordinate display all work relative to the current UCS, so it is a simple matter to draw in this plane.

> Check your snap setting and change it if necessary.
> Turn ortho off (F8).
> Repeat the LINE command.
> With snap on (F9), pick a point .25 down from the top edge of the box on line 1, as shown in *Figure 12-12*.
> Pick a second point .25 up along the right front edge of the box.
> Exit the LINE command.
Now trim line 1.
> Type "trim" or select the Trim tool from the Modify toolbar.
  Press F2 and you will see the following message in the command area:

  View is not plan to UCS. Command results may not be obvious.

In the language of AutoCAD 3D, a view is plan to the current UCS if the XY plane is in the plane of the monitor display and its axes are parallel to the sides of the screen. This is the usual 2D view in which the *y* axis aligns with the left side of the display and the *x* axis aligns with the bottom of the display. In previous chapters we always worked in plan view. In this chapter we have not been in plan view since the beginning of Task 1.

With this message, AutoCAD is warning us that boundaries, edges, and intersections may not be obvious as we look at a 3D view of an object. For example, lines that appear to cross may be in different planes.

Having read the warning, we continue.
> Select Line 2 as a cutting edge.
> Press Enter to end cutting edge selection.
> Point to the lower end of Line 1.
> Press Enter to exit TRIM.

Your screen should resemble *Figure 12-13*.
Now we will copy our two lines to the back of the box. Since we will be moving out of the front plane, which is also the XY plane in the current UCS, we will require the use of Endpoint object snaps to specify the displacement vector. We will also be using the Endpoint osnap in the next sequence, so let's turn on the running mode again.

> Type "osnap" or select "Running Object Snap…" from the Options menu.
> Type "end" or select "Endpoint" and press enter or click in the "OK" box.

Chap. 12   **381**

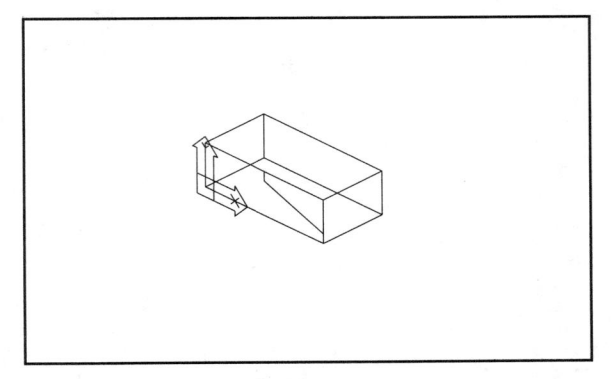

Figure 12-13

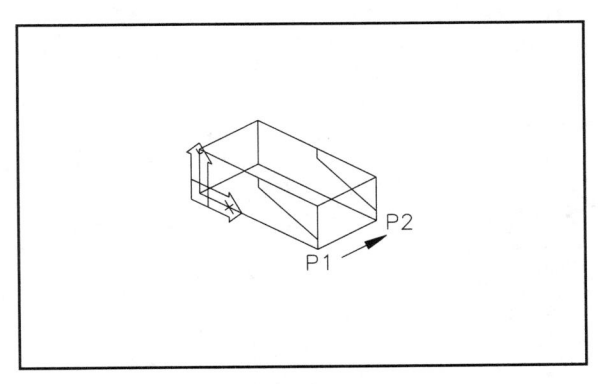

Figure 12-14

> Type "copy" or select the Copy tool from the Modify toolbar.
> Pick lines 1 and 2. (You may need to zoom in on the box at this point to pick Line 1.)
> Press Enter to end object selection.
> Use the Endpoint osnap to pick the lower front corner of the box, P1 as shown in *Figure 12-14*.
> At the prompt for a second point of displacement, use the ENDpoint osnap to pick the lower right back corner of the box, P2 as shown.

Your screen should now resemble *Figure 12-14*.

What remains is to connect the front and back of the surfaces we have just outlined and then trim away the top of the box. We will continue to work in the front UCS and to use Endpoint osnaps.

We will use a multiple COPY to copy one of the front-to-back edges in three places.

> Enter the COPY command.
> Pick any of the front-to-back edges for copying.
> Press Enter to end object selection.
> Type "m" or select "Multiple".
> Pick the front ENDpoint of the selected edge to serve as a base point of displacement.
> Pick the top end point of Line 1 (P1 in *Figure 12-15*).
> Pick the lower end point of Line 1 (P2) as another second point.

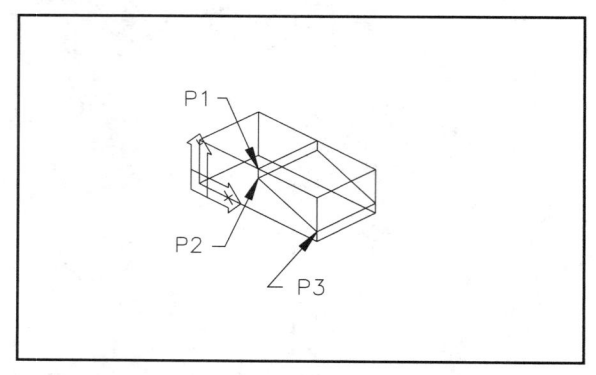

Figure 12-15

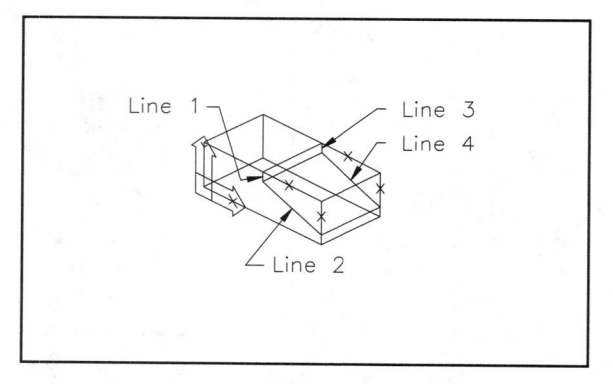

Figure 12-16

> Pick the right end point of Line 2 (P3) as another second point.
> Press Enter to exit the COPY command.
Finally, we need to do some trimming.
> Type "osnap" or select "Running Object Snap..." from the Options menu and turn off the running "ENDpoint" snap.
> Type "Trim" or select the Trim tool from the Modify toolbar.

For cutting edges, we want to select lines 1 and 2 and their copies in the back plane (lines 3 and 4 in *Figure 12-16*). Since this can be difficult, a quick alternative to selecting these four separate lines is to use a crossing box to select the whole area. As long as your selection includes the four lines, it will be effective.
> Select the area around lines 1 and 2.
NOTE: Trimming in 3D can be tricky. Remember where you are. Edges that do not run parallel to the current UCS may not be recognized at all.
> Press Enter to end cutting edge selection.
> One by one, pick the top front and top back edges to the right of the cut, and the right front and right back edges above the cut, as shown by the x's in *Figure 12-16*.
> Press Enter to exit the TRIM command.
> Enter the ERASE command and erase the top edge that is left hanging in space. We must use ERASE here because this line does not intersect any edges.

Your screen should now resemble *Figure 12-17*.

Chap. 12
383

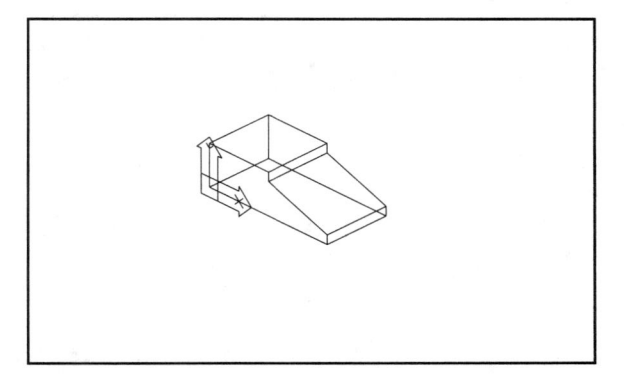

Figure 12-17

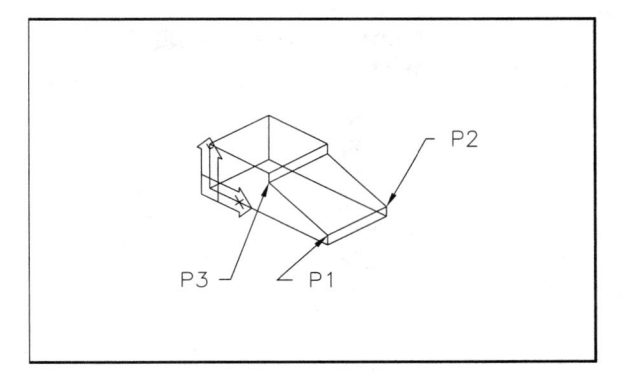

Figure 12-18

Task 4: Working on an Angled Surface

Discussion. In this task we will take our 3D drawing a step further by constructing a slot through the new slanted surface and the bottom of the object. This will require the creation of a new UCS. In completing this task, you will also use the OFFSET command and continue to develop a feel for working with multiple coordinate systems.

Begin by defining a UCS along the angled surface.

> Type "UCS" or select "Set UCS" from the View pull down menu.
> Type "3" or select "3 point".
> Using the Endpoint osnap, pick P1, as shown in *Figure 12-18*.
> Using an Endpoint osnap, pick P2, as shown.
> Using an Endpoint osnap, pick P3, as shown.
> Press Enter to repeat the UCS command.
> Type "s" or select "Save".
> Type "angle" for the name of the UCS.

Now we are ready to work in the plane of the angled surface.

NOTE: From here on, we have moved our UCS icon back to the lower left of the screen for the sake of clarity in our illustrations. You may leave it at its origin on your screen, if you like, or move it by entering the UCSICON command again and typing "no" or selecting UCS from the Options menu and then deselecting "Icon Origin".

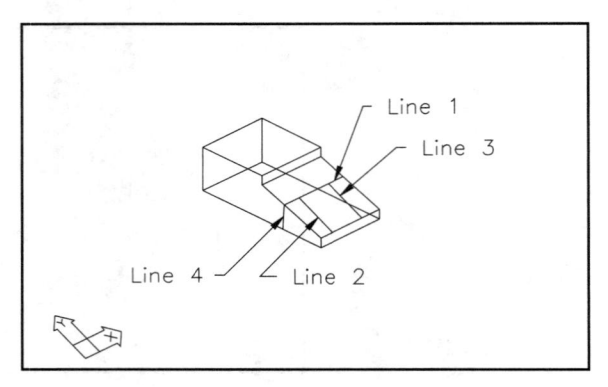

Figure 12-19

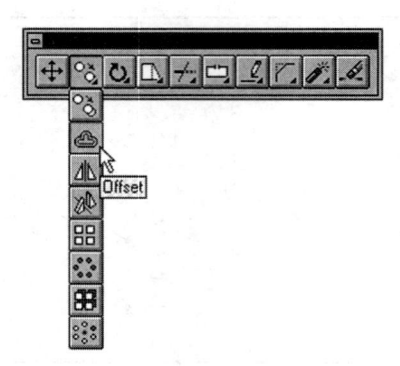

Figure 12-20

> Turn off the running Endpoint object snap.
> If ortho is off, turn it on (F8).

We will create line 1 across the angled surface, as shown in *Figure 12-19*, by offsetting the right front edge of the wedge.

> Type "Offset" or select the Offset tool from the Copy flyout on the Modify toolbar, as shown in *Figure 12-20*.
> Type or show a distance of 1.50.
> Pick the right front edge.
> Point anywhere above and to the left of the edge.
> Exit the OFFSET command.
> Draw lines 2 and 3 perpendicular to the first, as shown. They will be over .50 and 1.50 from the current *y* axis.

Watch the coordinate display and notice how the coordinates work in this UCS as in any other.

> Turn ortho off.
> Using snap for the top point and a Perpendicular object snap (single point override) for the lower point, drop Line 4 down to the bottom front edge.

Notice again how object snap modes work for you, especially to locate points that are not in the XY plane of the current UCS.

> Create lines 5 and 6, as shown in *Figure 12-21*, by making two copies of Line 4, extending down from the ends of lines 2 and 3, as shown.
> ERASE Line 4 from the front plane.
> Using Endpoint osnaps, connect lines 5 and 6 to each other in the plane of the bottom of the object.

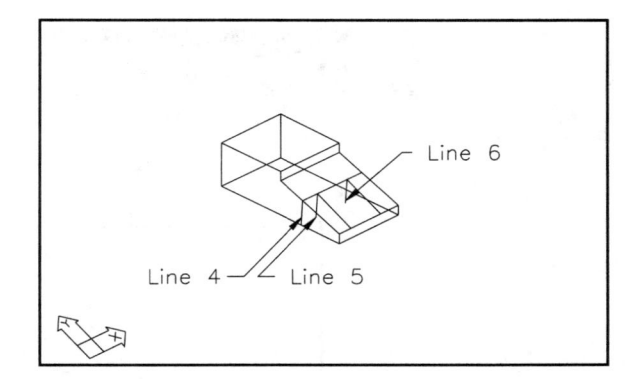

Figure 12-21

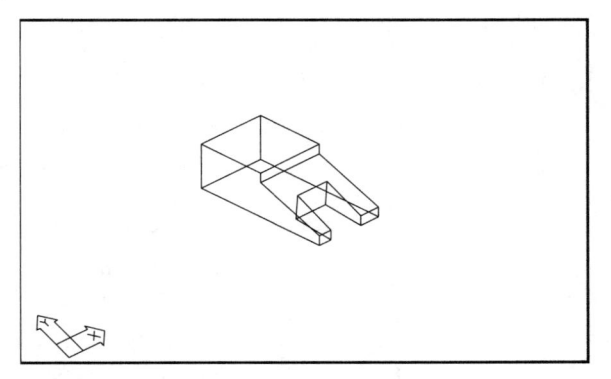

Figure 12-22

> Using Endpoint and Perpendicular osnaps, connect lines 5 and 6 to the bottom edge of the right side.

> Using Endpoint osnaps, draw two short vertical lines on the right side, connecting to lines 2 and 3.

> TRIM Line 1 and the two lines on the right side across the opening of the slot to create *Figure 12-22*.

Task 5: Using RULESURF to Create 3D Fillets

Procedure

1. Create fillets in two planes.
2. Type "Rulesurf" or select the Ruled Surface tool from the Surfaces toolbar.
3. Pick a fillet.
4. Pick the corresponding side of the fillet in the other plane.

Discussion. There are two parts to completing this task. First, we will fillet the top and bottom corners of the slot drawn in Task 4. Then we will use the RULESURF command to create filleted surfaces between the top and bottom of the slot.

> To begin this task you should be in the angle UCS, as in Task 4, and your screen should resemble *Figure 12-22*.

> Type "Fillet" or select the Fillet tool from the Feature flyout on the Modify toolbar, as shown in *Figure 12-23*.

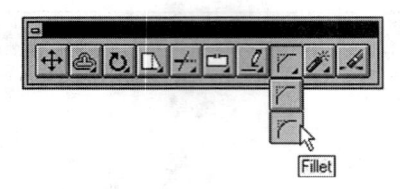

Figure 12-23

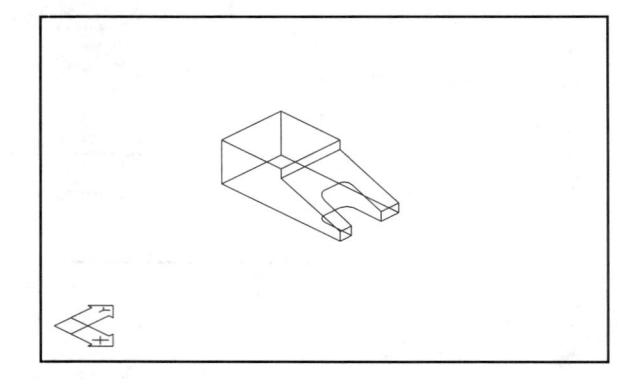

Figure 12-24

AutoCAD will prompt as usual:

(TRIM mode) Current fillet radius = 0.00
Polyline/Radius/<Select first object>:

> Type "r" or select "Radius" from the screen menu.
> Type ".25" for the radius value.
> Press Enter to repeat the FILLET command.
> Pick two lines that meet at one of the upper corners of the slot.
   Look at *Figure 12-24* to see where we are headed.
> Press Enter to repeat the FILLET command.
> Pick two lines that meet at the other upper corner of the slot.
> Repeat FILLET.

NOTE: In Release 13 you will be able to fillet the corners in the bottom of the object even though they are not in the XY plane of the current UCS. In earlier releases you would need to switch to a UCS that is parallel to the bottom of the box.

> Pick two lines that meet at one of the lower corners of the slot.
> Press Enter to repeat the FILLET command.
> Pick two lines that meet at the other lower corner of the slot.
> Erase the two vertical lines left outside the fillets.

Your screen should resemble *Figure 12-24*.

Now we will use a new command to connect the upper and lower fillets with 3D surfaces. RULESURF is one of several commands that create 3D surfaces. These commands create entities called "3D polygon meshes," which are discussed in detail in Chapter 13. This will serve as a quick introduction and will allow you to create 3D fillets in the drawings at the end of this chapter.

The RULESURF command creates a 3D surface between two lines or curves in 3D space. Our two curves will be the upper and lower fillets at each of the two corners.

> Type "rulesurf" or select the Ruled Surface tool from the Surfaces toolbar, as illustrated in *Figure 12-25*.

Chap. 12 387

Figure 12-25

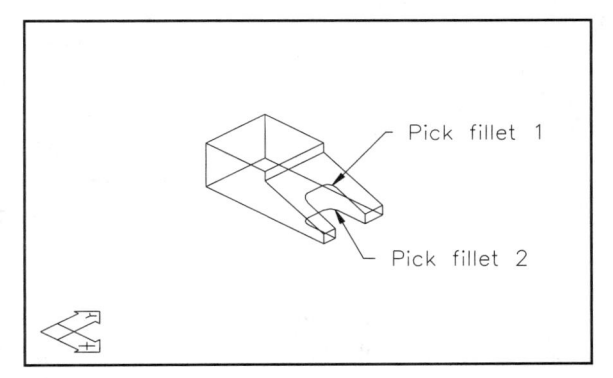

Figure 12-26

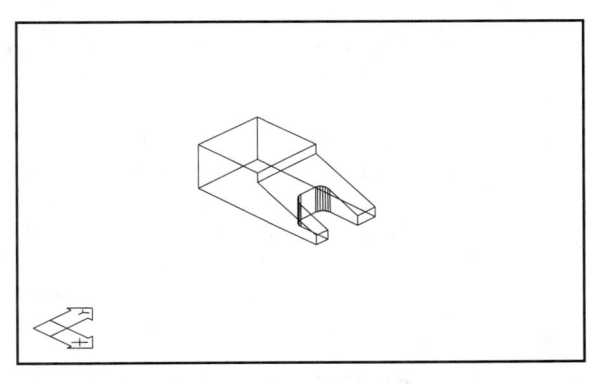

Figure 12-27

AutoCAD will prompt:

Select first defining curve:

> Pick one of the top fillets, as shown by Pick 1 in *Figure 12-26*.

AutoCAD will prompt for a second curve:

Select second defining curve:

> Pick the corresponding fillet in the bottom plane, with a pick point on the corresponding side, as shown by Pick 2 in *Figure 12-26*.

AutoCAD will draw a set of faces to represent the surface curving around the fillet radius, as shown in *Figure 12-27*.

The trick in using RULESURF is to be sure that you show a pick point toward one side of the curve, and that you pick the next curve with a point on the corresponding side. Otherwise you will get an hourglass effect, as shown in *Figure 12-28*.

We'll work more with 3D surfaces in the next chapter.

> To complete this task, repeat the RULESURF command and draw the fillet at the other corner of the groove.

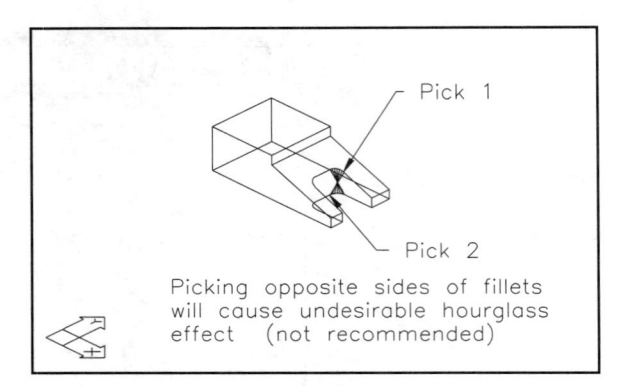

Figure 12-28

When you are done, your screen should resemble *Figure 12-27*. This completes the introduction to drawing 3D wireframe models and using user coordinate systems. What follows is a more detailed examination of the VPOINT command.

Task 6: Other Methods of Using the VPOINT Command (Optional)

Discussion. This discussion of other methods of using VPOINT is intended as a reference. The information presented here is not necessary to complete the drawings in this chapter, and no specific exercise is intended. However, if you are interested in gaining a full understanding of the VPOINT command and its options, try creating the views described and outlined in the charts and figures. In Chapter 13 you will also find a complete discussion of the DVIEW command for fine tuning and creating perspective and cutaway views.

Entering 3D Coordinates of a Viewpoint (Vector)

From the initial "Rotate/<View point>" prompt of the VPOINT command, the default method is to type in 3D coordinates. This is the same as the Vector option on the pull down menu (select "3D Viewpoint" and then "Vector" from the View menu). When you first enter the VPOINT command from the WCS plan view, the default viewpoint is given as (0,0,1). This means that you are viewing the object from a point somewhere along the positive z axis. You are at 0 in the x and y directions and at +1 in the z direction. In other words, you are directly above the XY plane looking straight down, a plan view. Think of the x coordinate as controlling right–left orientation, the y coordinate as controlling back–front, and the z coordinate as controlling up–down.

By changing the x coordinate to 1 (right), leaving y at 0 (neither front nor back), and z at 1 (above), you can create a viewpoint above and to the right of the object (1,0,1). Similarly, (1,−1,1) would move you to the right ($x = 1$), back you up a bit ($y = -1$) so that you are in front of the object, and raise your point of view ($z = 1$) so that you are above the object looking down. This common (1,−1,1) viewpoint is the same as the southeast isometric or right, front, top viewpoint used throughout this chapter.

We will explore other methods of specifying viewpoints in a moment, but first look at the following chart. It summarizes the effects of the x, y, and z coordinates and gives you coordinates for some standard views. You should have a good understanding of why each view appears as it does.

x Right–Left	y Back–Front	z Up–Down	View Description
0	0	1	Plan
0	0	−1	"Worm's eye"
1	0	0	Right side
−1	0	0	Left side
0	1	0	Back
0	−1	0	Front
1	1	1	Northeast Isometric
1	−1	1	Southeast Isometric
	etc.	etc.	

We suggest that you try some of these viewpoints and experiment with others not listed. Your goal should be to get a feel for how different coordinate combinations move your point of view in relation to objects on the screen. You can use numbers other than one, but precise distance relationships are difficult to follow in viewpoint definition.

Rotation

The other option shown in the prompt is "Rotation". This option is used with a dialogue box when you choose "3D Viewpoint" and then "Rotate..." from the View pull down menu. Rotation can also be adjusted by typing "r" or selecting "Rotation" at the "Rotate/<View point>" prompt. Then AutoCAD will prompt for two angles. The first is an angle in the XY plane. It is measured from the *x* axis, with 0 being straight out to the right, as usual.

The second angle goes up or down from the XY plane, with 0 being ground level. Thus an angle of 90 degrees from the XY plane would define the plan view.

The following chart will give you the rotation versions of some of the same major views shown on the pull down menu and the previous chart.

From X	From XY	View Description
0	0	Right side
0	90	Plan
90	0	Back side
180	0	Left side
270	0	Front
45	30	Northeast Isometric
−45 (or +315)	30	Southeast Isometric
45	−30	Back, Right, Bottom
	etc.	etc.

Rotated views are accessible through the DDVPOINT command, which calls the Viewpoint Presets dialogue box ("3D Viewpoint" and then "Rotate..." on the View pull down menu). This Viewpoint Presets dialogue box is shown in *Figure 12-29*. We will use this method to create a Northeast isometric or back, right, top view.

> Select "View" from the pull down menu bar.
> Select "3D Viewpoint".
> Select "Rotate...".

This will call up the Viewpoint Presets dialogue box, as shown in *Figure 12-29*.

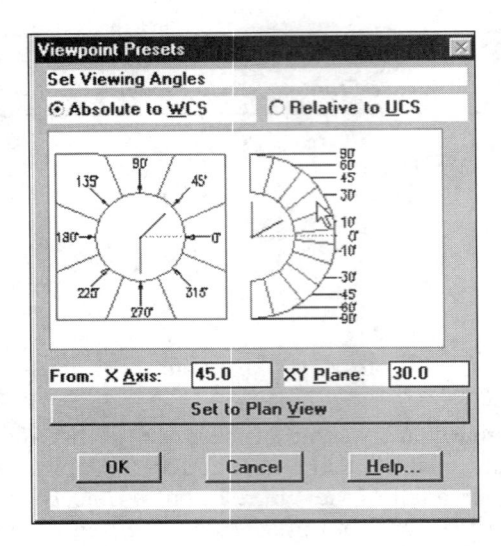

Figure 12-29

Using this method, AutoCAD lets you choose the two angles it needs to create a new viewpoint from the two "dials" on the left and right. The angle from the x axis can be specified by selecting a point in the circle on the right or by typing a number in the edit box at the bottom. The angle from the XY plane can be typed or shown using the semicircle at the right of the dialogue box. As you make selections by pointing in the circle or semicircle, the white "needle" will move and the angle value will be entered in the edit box.

> Set the angle from the x axis by picking the top right box, "45" as shown in the figure.

Notice that selecting this box enters the value 45.0 in the From: X Axis edit box and moves the white pointer to 45. The angle of 45 moves us into the "back, right" viewpoint area, the northeast quadrant.

The second angle specification (the angle from the XY plane) can be shown in a similar manner by picking a point on the semicircle at the right, or by typing a value in the edit box at the bottom. The angle you specify will be the z dimension viewing position, a viewing height above or below the object. We will choose to look down at an angle of 30 degrees.

> Pick the area labelled +30.

This will move the white pointer and enter the value 30 in the XY Plane edit box.

> When your dialogue box shows 45.0 and 30.0 as the two viewing angles, pick OK to create the new viewpoint.

Your screen should be redrawn to show a back, right, top view.

Using the two angles in the dialogue box to set rotation in the XY plane and the viewing height, you can create a large variety of points of view. We encourage you to experiment with these. Try changing the first angle to 225 to create a left, front, top view. What two angles will give you a front view at ground level? What will a view from below the object look like? As you experiment, pay attention to the UCS icon. With some views you will have to think carefully and watch the icon to understand which way the object is being presented.

The Compass and Axes System

If you enter the VPOINT command and then press Enter in response to the "Rotate/<View point>" prompt, you will see a display that resembles *Figure 12-30*.

Chap. 12   **391**

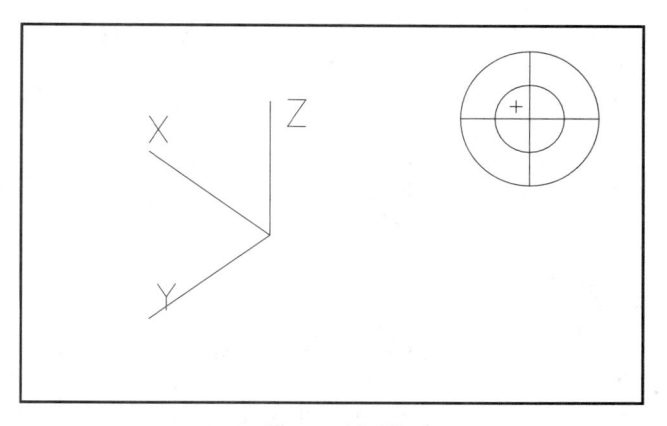

Figure 12-30

The triple axes represent the orientation of the object. When you move your cursor, you will see these rotating. Some users may find this visualization easier to comprehend because it represents the object itself rather than your point of view in relation to the object. However, this effect is much more clearly realized in the DVIEW command, discussed in Chapter 13.

The other part of the display is a rather unusual representation of a globe. The horizontal and vertical axes show the X and Y dimensions as you would expect, and the circles show the Z dimension. This actually shows a globe transformed into a cone and then flattened. The "north pole" of the globe has become a point at the center of the compass, while the "south pole" has been widened into a circle at the outside of the compass. In between is another circle representing the "equator," or ground 0 region.

This simply means that anywhere inside the first circle will give you a top-down view; outside the first circle will give you a bottom-up view. Anywhere on the middle circle will give you a ground-level view.

Notice the small cross that moves as you move your cursor. This represents your point of view in the coordinate system.

Figure 12-31 gives you a good summary of the compass points and how they relate to standard views. Try them out if you like.

Tasks 7, 8, 9, and 10

The drawings that follow are all 3D wireframe models that use the techniques and procedures introduced in this chapter. Drawing 12–1 also introduces 3D dimensioning technique. Drawing 12–4 is a 3D architectural detail. Your primary objective in completing these drawings should be to gain facility with User Coordinate Systems and 3D space.

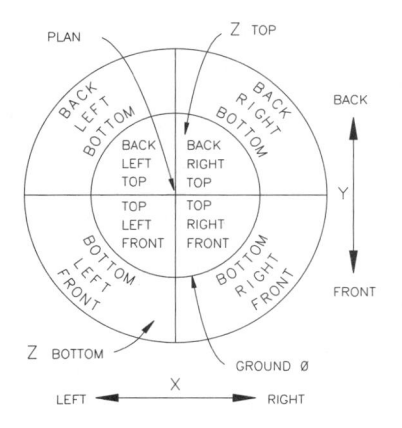

Figure 12-31

DRAWING 12-1: CLAMP

This drawing is similar to the one you did in the chapter. Two major differences are that it is drawn from a different viewpoint and that it includes dimensions in the 3D view. This will give you additional practice in defining and using User Coordinate Systems. Your drawing should include dimensions, border, and title.

DRAWING SUGGESTIONS

> We drew the outline of the clamp in a horizontal position and then worked from a southeast isometric or front, left, top point of view.
> Begin in WCS plan view drawing the horseshoe-shaped

outline of the clamp. This will include fillets on the inside and outside of the clamp. The more you can do in plan view before copying to the top plane, the less duplicate editing you will need to do later.
> When the outline is drawn, switch to a southeast isometric view.
> COPY the clamp outline up 1.50.
> Define User Coordinate Systems as needed, and save them whenever you are ready to switch to another UCS. You will need to use them in your dimensioning.
> The angled face, the slots, and the filleted surfaces can be drawn just as in the chapter.

Dimensioning in 3D

The trick to dimensioning a 3D object is that you will need to restore the appropriate UCS for each set of dimensions. Think about how you want the text to appear. If text is to be aligned with the top of the clamp (i.e., the 5.75 overall length), you will need to draw that dimension in a "top" UCS; if it is to align with the front of the object (the 17 degree angle and the 1.50 height), draw it in a "front" UCS, and so forth.

> Define a UCS with the "View" option in order to add the border and title. Type "UCS", then "v". This creates a UCS aligned with your current viewing angle.

Setting Surftab1

Notice that there are 16 lines defining the RULESURF fillets in this drawing, compared to 6 in the chapter. This is controlled by the setting of the variable Surftab1, which is discussed in Chapter 13. You can change it by typing "Surftab1" and entering "16" for the new value.

Chap. 12

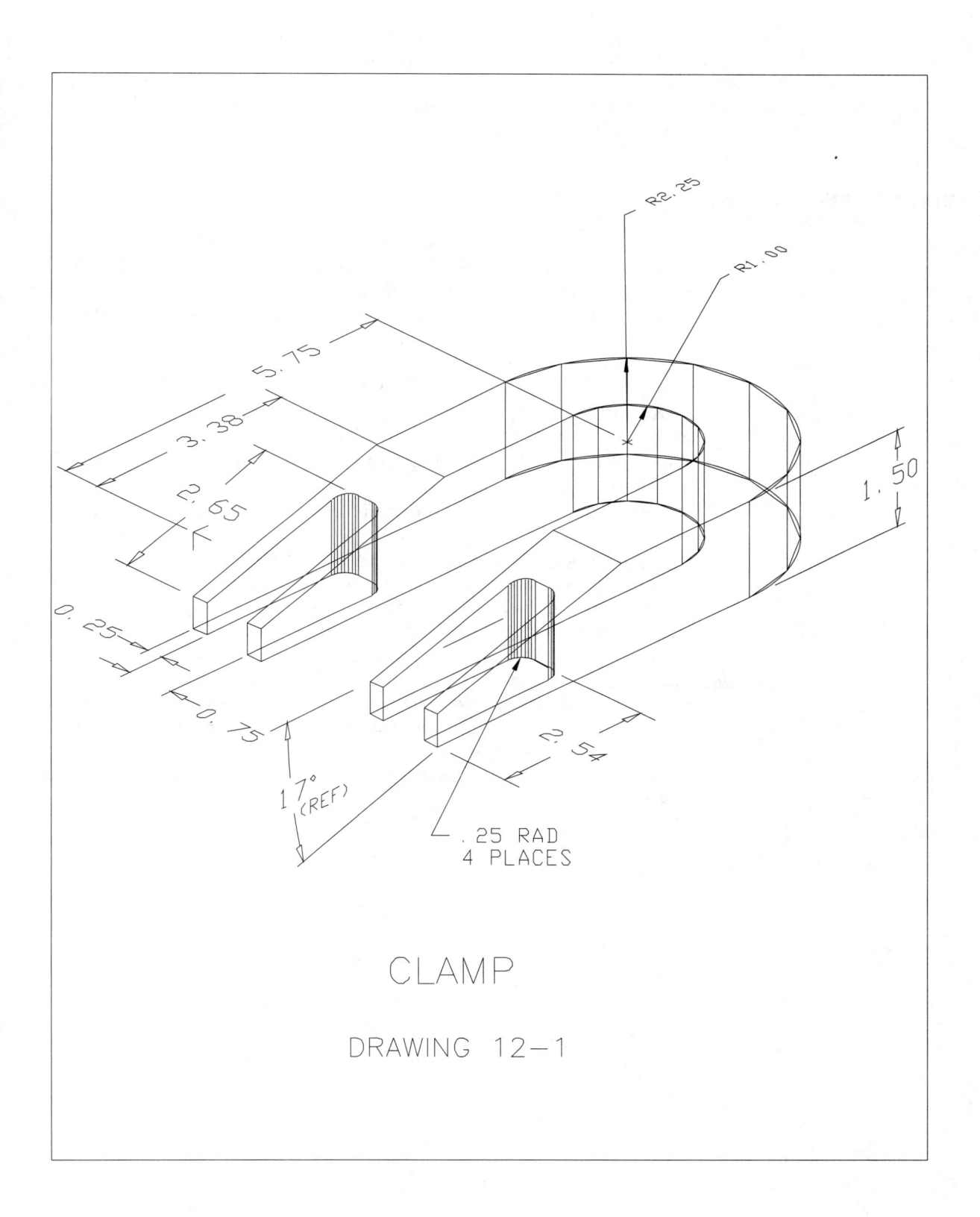

CLAMP

DRAWING 12-1

DRAWING 12–2: GUIDE BLOCK

In this drawing you will be working from dimensioned views to create a wireframe model. This brings up some new questions. Which view should you start with? How do you translate the views into the 3D image? A good general rule is this: Draw the top or bottom in the XY plane of the WCS, otherwise you will have trouble using the VPOINT command.

DRAWING SUGGESTIONS

> In this drawing it is tempting to draw the right side in WCS plan view first, because that is where most of the detail is. If you do this, however, you will have difficulty creating the view as shown. Instead, we suggest that you keep the bottom of the object in the WCS XY plane and work up from there, as has been the practice throughout this chapter. The reason for this is that the VPOINT command works relative to the WCS. Therefore, front–back, left–right, and top–bottom orientations will make sense only if the top and bottom are drawn plan to the WCS.

> Draw the 12.50 × 8.00 rectangle shown in the top view, and then copy it up 4.38 to form the top of the guide's base.

> Change over to the same southeast isometric or front, right, left 3D viewpoint we used in the chapter.

> Connect the four corners to create a block outline of the base of the object.

> Now you can define a new UCS on the right side and do most of your work in that coordinate system, since that is where the detail is. Once you have defined the right side UCS, you may want to go into its plan view to draw the right side outline, including the arc and circle of the guide. Then come back to the 3D view to copy back to the left side.

NOTE: You can save some time switching viewpoints by using the save and restore options of the VIEW command. When a view is saved, it includes the 3D orientation along with the zoom factor that was current at the time of the save. Also, ZOOM previous can be used to restore a previous 3D point of view. It will not, however, restore a UCS.

> Use RULESURF with Surftab1 set to 16 to fill in surfaces between the arcs and circles.

Chap. 12

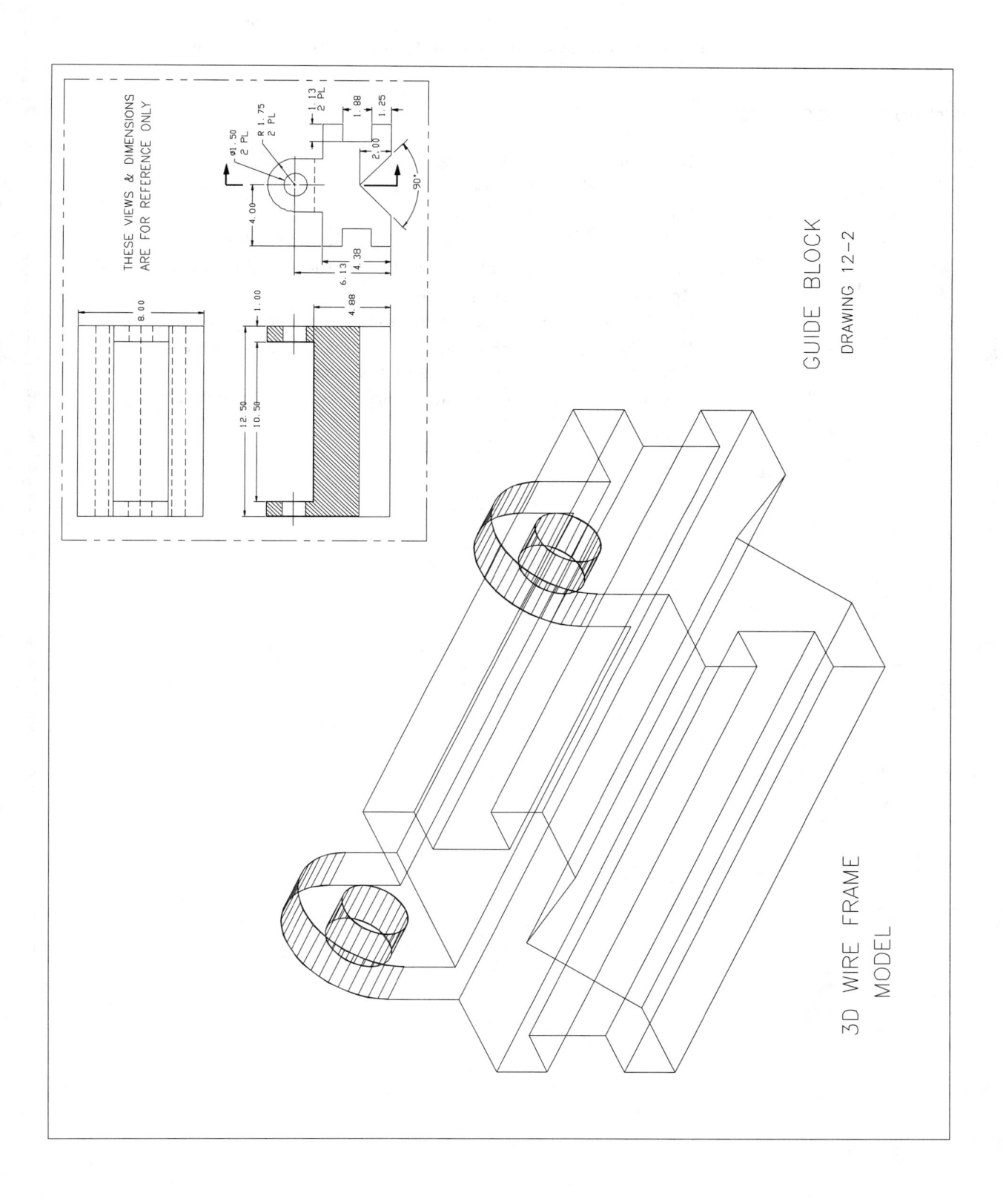

395

GUIDE BLOCK
DRAWING 12-2

3D WIRE FRAME MODEL

DRAWING 12-3: SLIDE MOUNT

This drawing continues to use the same views, coordinate systems, and techniques as the previous drawings, but it has more detail and is a bit trickier.

DRAWING SUGGESTIONS

> Draw the H-shaped outline of the top view in WCS plan.
> Copy up in the z direction.
> Connect the corners to create a 3D shape.
> Define a right side view, and create the slot and holes.
> Copy back to the left side, connect the corners, and trim inside the slot.
> Return to WCS (bottom plane).
> Use RULESURF between circles to create mounting holes.
> Draw filleted cutout and countersunk holes. Each countersunk hole will require three circles, two small and one larger.
> Use RULESURF to create inner surfaces of countersunk holes.

Chap. 12

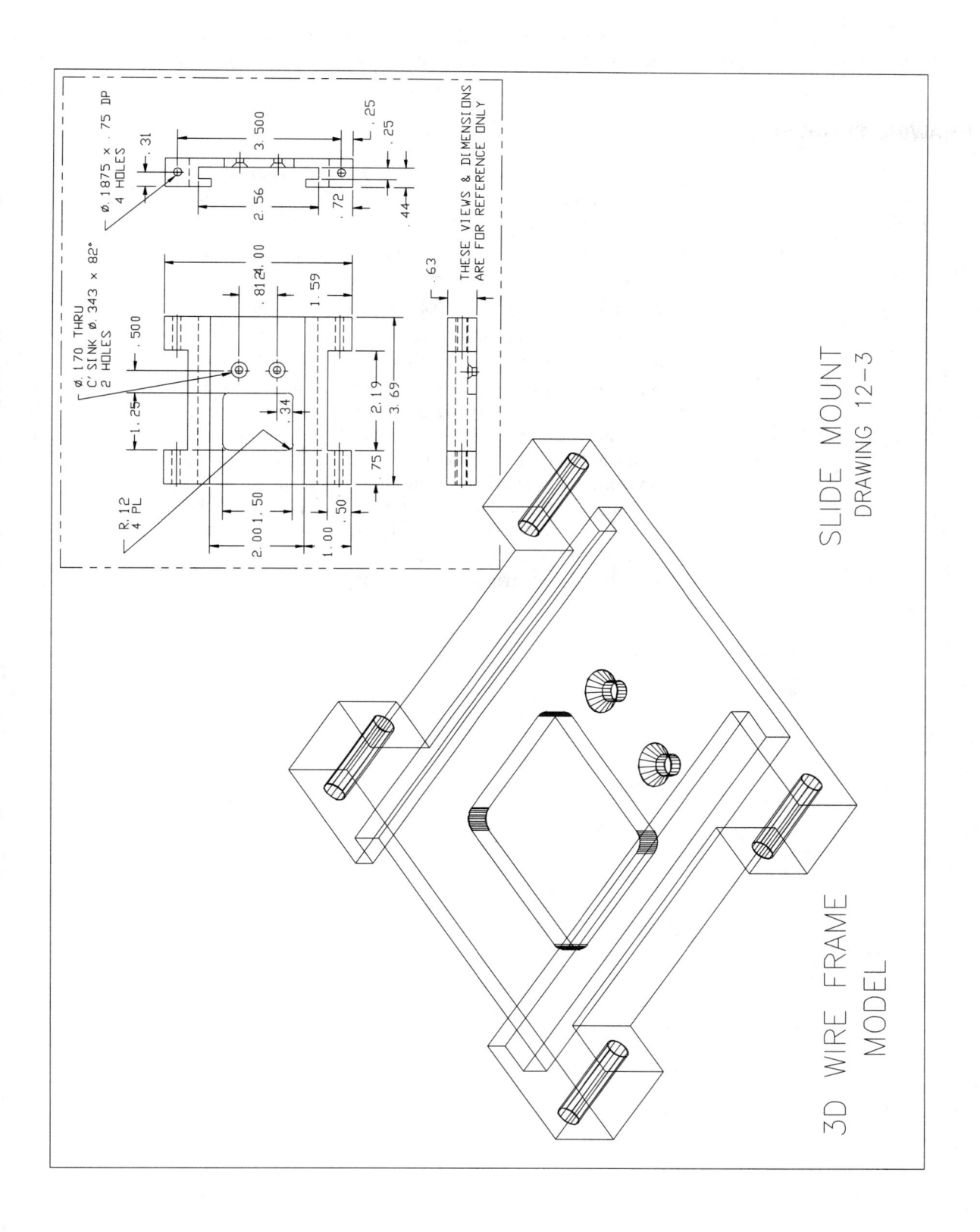

SLIDE MOUNT
DRAWING 12-3

3D WIRE FRAME MODEL

DRAWING 12-4: STAIR LAYOUT

This wireframe architectural detail will give you a chance to use architectural units and limits in 3D. It will require the use of a variety of edit commands.

DRAWING SUGGESTIONS

> In the WCS plan view, begin with a 2" × 12' rectangle that will become the bottom of a floor joist. This will keep the bottom floor in the plan view, consistent with our practice in this chapter.
> COPY the rectangle up 8" and connect lines to form the complete joist.
> ARRAY 16" on center to form the first floor.
> COPY all joists up 9'-6" to form the second floor.
> Create the stairwell opening in the second floor with double headers at each end.
> Add the 3/4" subfloor to the first floor.
> The outline of the stair stringers can be constructed in a number of ways. One possibility is as follows: Draw a guideline down from the front of the left double header and then another over 10'-10" to locate the end of the run; from the right end of the run, draw one 7 1/2" riser and one 9 1/2" tread, beginning from the top surface of the subflooring; use a multiple copy and ENDpoint osnaps to create the other steps; when you get to the top, you will find you need to TRIM the top tread slightly to bring it flush with the header.
> We leave it to you to construct the back line of the stringer. It needs to be parallel with the stringer line and down 1' from the top tread, as shown.

Chap. 12

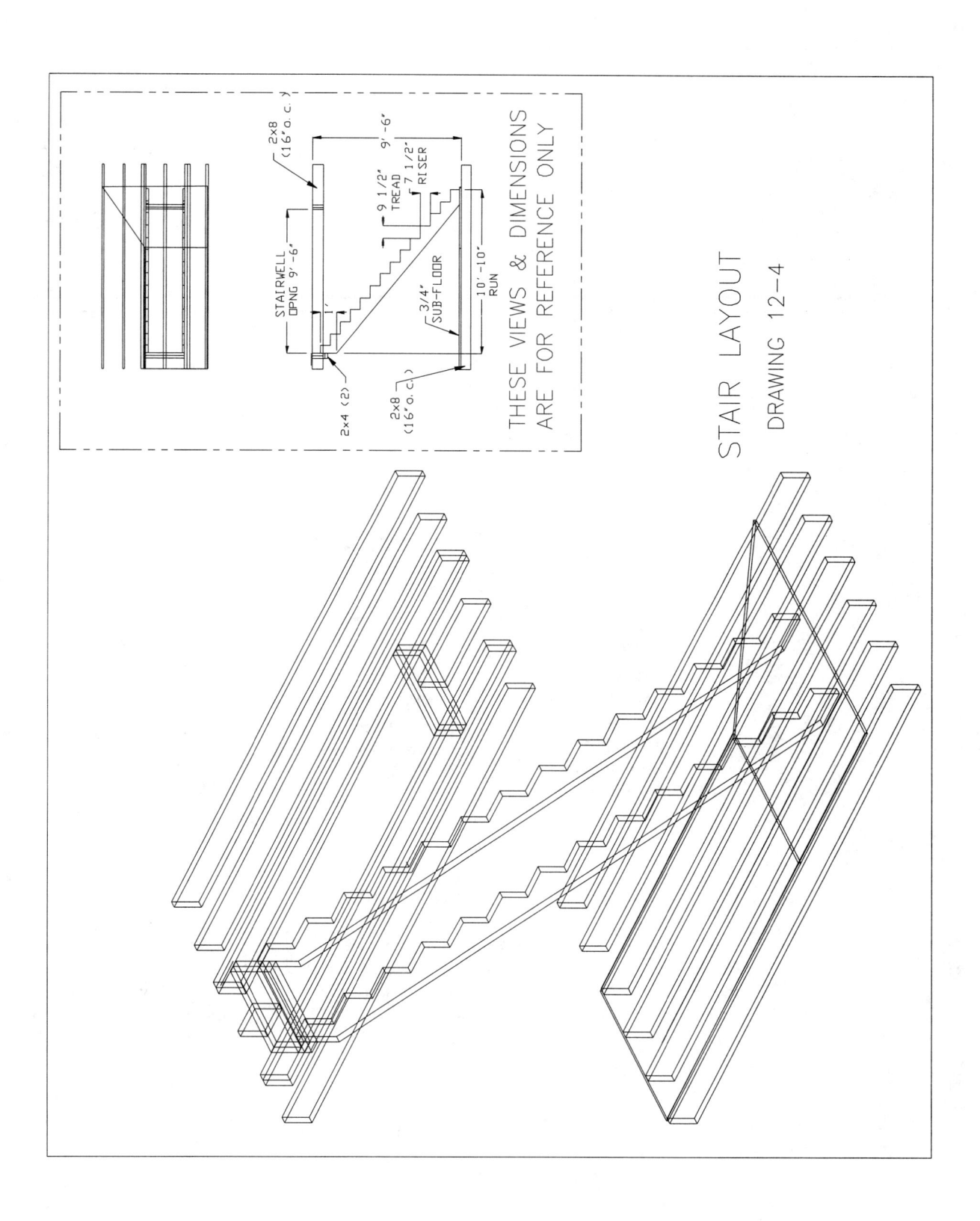

STAIR LAYOUT
DRAWING 12-4

THESE VIEWS & DIMENSIONS ARE FOR REFERENCE ONLY

2×8 (16" o.c.)
STAIRWELL OPNG 9'-6"
9'-6"
9 1/2" TREAD
7 1/2" RISER
3/4" SUB-FLOOR
10'-10" RUN
2×4 (2)
2×8 (16" o.c.)

CHAPTER 13

COMMANDS

SURFACES	VIEW	RENDER
3DFACE	DVIEW	HIDE
3DMESH	MVSETUP	
EDGESURF	REDRAWALL	**VARIABLES**
REVSURF	REGENALL	Surftab1
RULESURF	VPORTS	Surftab2
TABSURF		

OVERVIEW

In this chapter we will continue to explore Release 13 3D drawing features, with a focus on surface modeling. The VPORTS (or VIEWPORTS) command will allow the creation of multiple tiled viewports so that an object may be viewed from several points of view simultaneously. The 3DFACE command will be introduced to draw three- and four-sided surfaces. In addition, you will create "polygon meshes" to represent complex three-dimensional surfaces.

TASKS

1. Use VPORTS to create multiple tiled viewports.
2. Create surfaces with 3DFACE.
3. Remove hidden lines with HIDE.

4. Create 3D polygon meshes with TABSURF, RULESURF, EDGESURF, and REVSURF.
5. Create surface models using the "3D Objects" AutoLISP routines.
6. Create approximated surfaces using PEDIT (optional).
7. Use MVSETUP to create a 4–view layout with title block.
8. Create perspective and clipped 3D views with DVIEW.
9. Do Drawing 13–1 ("REVSURF Designs").
10. Do Drawing 13–2 ("Picnic Table").
11. Do Drawing 13–3 ("Globe").
12. Do Drawing 13–4 ("Nozzle").

Task 1: Using Multiple Tiled Viewports

Procedure

1. Type "Vports" or select "Tiled Viewports" from the View menu.
2. Enter number of viewports desired.
3. Enter orientation of viewports.
4. Define views in each viewport.

Discussion. A major feature needed to draw effectively in 3D is the ability to view an object from several different points of view simultaneously as you work on it. The VPORTS, or VIEWPORTS, command is easy to use and can save you from having to jump back and forth between different views of an object. Viewports can be used in 2D to place several zoom magnifications on the screen at once, as shown in Chapter 3. More important, viewports can be used to place several 3D viewpoints on the screen at once. This can be a significant drawing aid. If you do not continually view an object from different points of view, it is easy to create entities that appear correct in the current view, but that are clearly incorrect from other points of view.

In this task we will divide your screen in half and define two views, so that you can visualize an object in plan view and a 3D view at the same time. As you work, remember that this is only a display command. The viewports we use in this chapter will be simple "tiled" viewports. Tiled viewports cover the complete drawing area, do not overlap, and cannot be plotted. Plotting multiple viewports can also be accomplished, but only in paper space with nontiled viewports.

> Type "Vports" or select "Tiled Viewports" from the View menu.

If you are typing the command, AutoCAD will show you the following prompt (if you are on the pull down menu, you will see the same options listed on a submenu):

Save/Restore/Delete/Join/SIngle/?/2/<3>/4:

The first three options allow you to save, restore, and delete viewport configurations. "Join" allows you to reduce the number of windows so that you move from, say, four windows to three. "SIngle" is the option that returns you to a single window. "?" will get you a list of previously saved viewport configurations. The numbers 2, 3, and 4 will establish the number of different viewports you want to put on the screen.

From the pull down menu, the "Layout..." option will call the Tiled Viewport Layout dialogue box shown in *Figure 13-1*. Notice that the list on the left simply names the twelve layout options on the right. Any of these could also be specified by typing and following the sequence of command prompts.

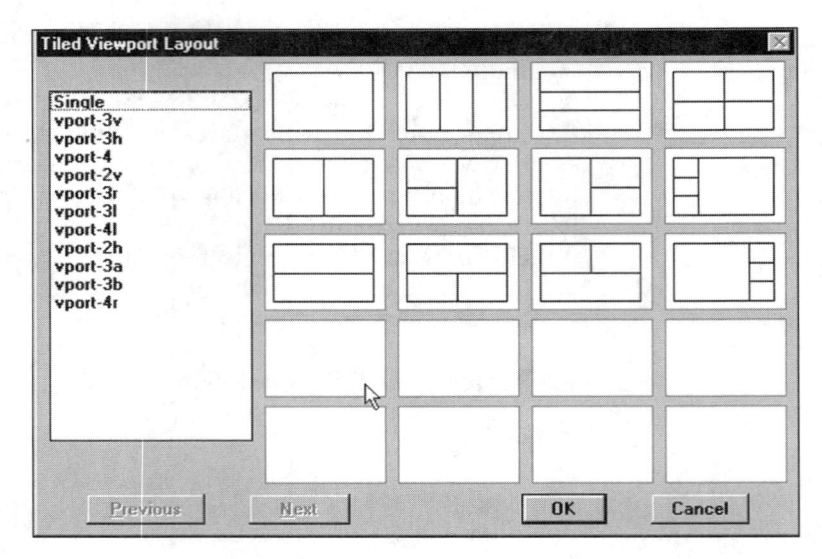

Figure 13-1

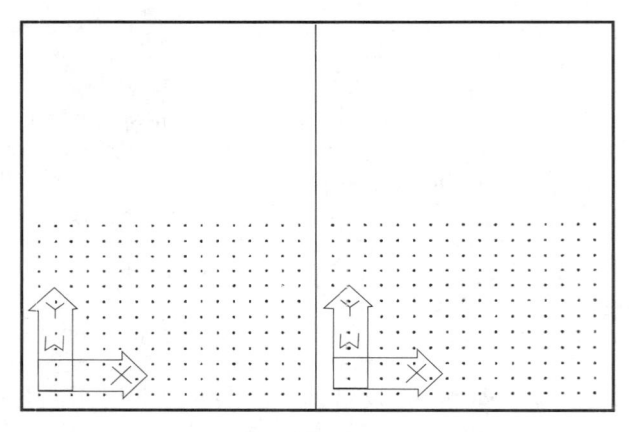

Figure 13-2

From the command line, the default is three windows with a full pane on the right and a horizontal split on the left. This is called "vport-3r" in the dialogue box.

For our purposes we will create a simple two-way vertical split, the "vport-2v" option in the dialogue box.

> Type "2" or select the box on the left end of the second row on the icon menu.

If you type the number, AutoCAD will prompt for the direction of the split:

Horizontal/<Vertical>:

> Press Enter to accept the default vertical split, or click on "OK" to complete the dialogue.

Your screen will be regenerated to resemble *Figure 13-2*.

You will notice that the grid is rather small and confined to the lower part of the window and that the grid may be off in the left viewport. The shape of the viewports necessitates the reduction in drawing area. You can enlarge details as usual using the ZOOM command. Zooming and panning in one viewport will have no effect on other viewports. However, you can have only one UCS in effect at any time, so a change in the coordinate system in one viewport will be reflected in all viewports.

If you move your pointing device back and forth between the windows, you will see an arrow when you are on the left and the cross hairs when you are on the right. This indicates that the right window is currently active. Drawing and editing can be done only in the active window. To work in another window, you need to make it current by picking it with your pointing device. Often this can be done while a command is in progress.

> Move the cursor into the left window and press the pick button on your pointing device.

Now the cross hairs will appear in the left viewport, and you will see the arrow when you move into the right viewport.

> If the grid is off in your left viewport, you may want to turn it on at this point.

> Move the cursor back to the right and press the pick button again.

This will make the right window active again.

There is no value in having two viewports if each is showing the same thing, so our next job will be to change the viewpoint in one of the windows. We will leave the window on the left in plan view and switch the right window to a 3D view. For consistency, we will use the familiar southeast isometric view used in the last chapter.

> From the View menu select "3D Viewpoint Presets", and then "SE Isometric".

Your screen should now be redrawn with a southeast isometric view in the right viewport as shown in *Figure 13-3*.

Once you have defined viewports, any drawing or editing done in the active viewport will appear in all the viewports. As you draw, watch what happens in both viewports.

Task 2: Creating Surfaces with 3DFACE

Procedure

1. Type "3DFace" or select the 3D Face tool from the Surfaces toolbar.
2. Pick three or four points going around the face.
3. Continue defining edges or press Enter to exit the command.

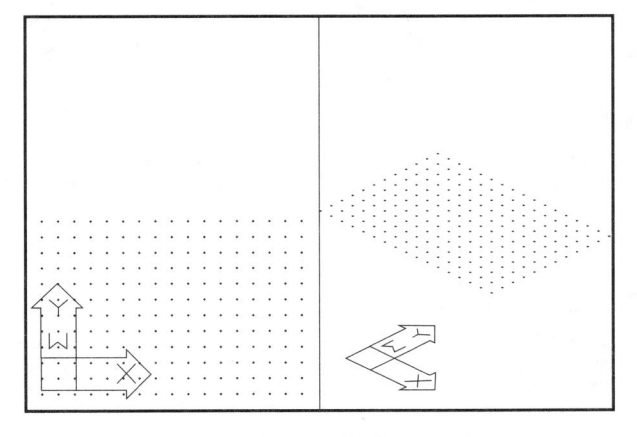

Figure 13-3

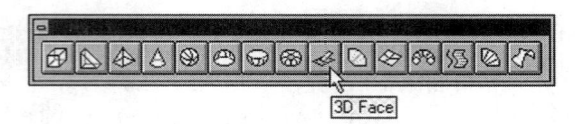

Figure 13-4

Discussion. 3DFACE creates triangular and quadrilateral surfaces. 3D faces are built by entering points in groups of three or four to define the outlines of triangles or quadrilaterals, similar to objects formed by the 2D SOLID command. The surface of a 3D face is not shown on the screen, but it is recognized by the HIDE command and by the RENDER command and other rendering programs, such as RenderMan or 3D Studio.

Layering is critical in surface modeling. Surfaces quickly complicate a drawing so that object selection and object snap become difficult or impossible. Also, you may want to be able to turn layers off or freeze them to achieve the results you want from the HIDE command. You may eventually want a number of layers specifically defined for faces and surfaces, but this will not be necessary for the current exercise.

> Type "3DFace" or select the 3D Face tool from the Surfaces toolbar, as shown in *Figure 13-4*.

AutoCAD will prompt:

First point:

You can define points in either of the two viewports. In fact, you can even switch viewports in the middle of the command.
> Pick a point similar to P1, as shown in *Figure 13-5*.

AutoCAD prompts:

Second point:

> Pick a second point, moving around the perimeter of the face, as shown.

Be aware that the correct order for defining 3D faces is different from the 2D SOLID command (Chapter 9). It is important to pick points in order around the face, otherwise you will get a bow tie or hourglass effect.

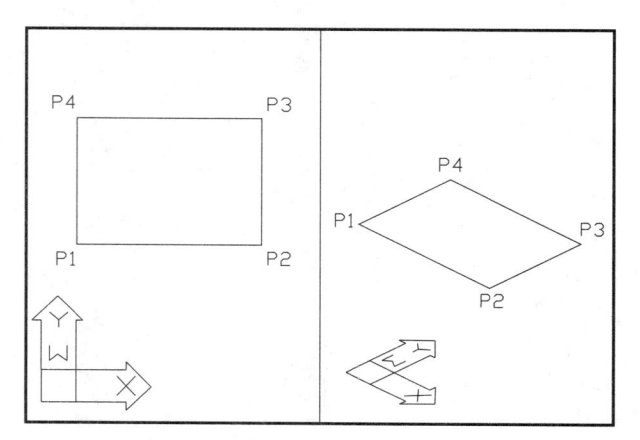

Figure 13-5

AutoCAD prompts:

Third point:

> Pick a third point, as shown.
AutoCAD prompts:

Fourth point:

NOTE: If you pressed Enter now, AutoCAD would draw the outline of a triangular face, using the three points already given.
> Pick the fourth point of the face.

AutoCAD draws the fourth edge of the face automatically when four points have been given, so it is not necessary to complete or close the rectangle.

AutoCAD will continue to prompt for third and fourth points so that you can draw a series of surfaces to cover an area with more than four edges. Keep in mind, however, that drawing faces in series is only a convenience. The result is a collection of independent three- and four-sided faces.

> Press Enter to exit the 3DFACE command.

In the next task we will copy this face in order to demonstrate the HIDE command. But first, a word about invisible edges.

Invisible Edges in 3Dfaces

The edges of a 3Dface can be visible or invisible as desired. To define an invisible edge, type "i" before entering the first point of the edge. You can even define "phantom" 3D faces in which no edges are visible.

Take a look at *Figure 13-6*. This figure illustrates the need for invisible edges in 3Dfaces. Since 3DFACE only draws triangles or quadrilaterals, objects with more than four edges must be drawn as combinations of three- and four-sided shapes. An octagon, for example, can be drawn as two trapezoids and a rectangle, as shown. However, you would not want the two horizontal edges across the middle showing, so the command allows you to make them invisible by typing "i" or selecting "Invisible" from the screen menu before picking the point that begins the invisible edge. This takes forethought and planning. You must remember

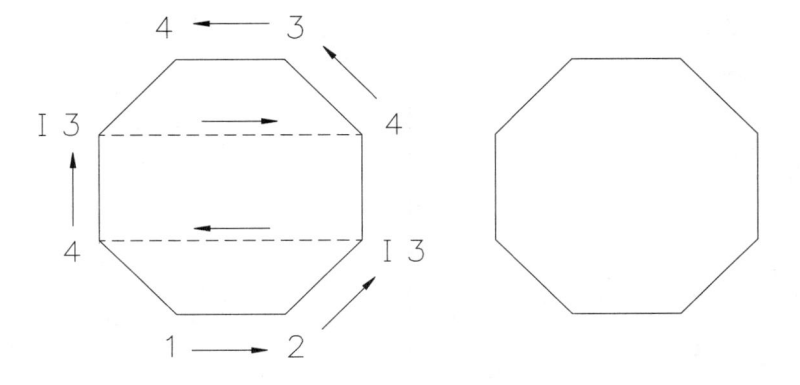

Figure 13-6

that the end point of a visible edge also may be the starting point of the next invisible edge.

> NOTE: Invisible edges will be hidden if the "Splframe" system variable is set to 0, the default setting. If the variable is set to 1, invisible edges will be displayed. This setting can be changed in the usual manner (Type "Splframe" and then "1") or by selecting "Showedge" from the screen menu.

Task 3: Removing Hidden Lines with HIDE

Procedure

1. Type HIDE.
2. Wait....

Discussion. The HIDE command is easy to execute. However, execution may be slow in large drawings, and careful work may be required to create a drawing that hides the way you want it to. This is a primary objective of surface modeling. When you've got everything right, HIDE will temporarily remove all lines and objects that would be obstructed in the current view, resulting in a more realistic representation of the object in space. A correctly surfaced model can also be used to create a shaded rendering. Hiding has no effect on wireframe drawings, since there are no surfaces to obstruct lines behind them.

> To begin this exercise, you should have the 3Dface from the previous task on your screen.
> COPY the face up 2 units in the *z* direction, using the following procedure.
  1. Type or select "Copy".
  2. Select the face.
  3. Press Enter to end object selection.
  4. Type and enter "0,0,2".
  5. Press Enter at the prompt for a second point.

You now have two 3Dfaces in your drawing. Since the second is directly over the first, you cannot see both in the plan view. From the viewpoint in the right viewport, however, the second face only partially covers the first. Since these are surfaces, rather than wireframes, the top face should hide part of the lower face.

> Make the right viewport active.
> Type "hide" (there is a Hide tool on the Render toolbar, but it is not worth opening the toolbar for this one command).

Your screen should be regenerated to resemble *Figure 13-7*.

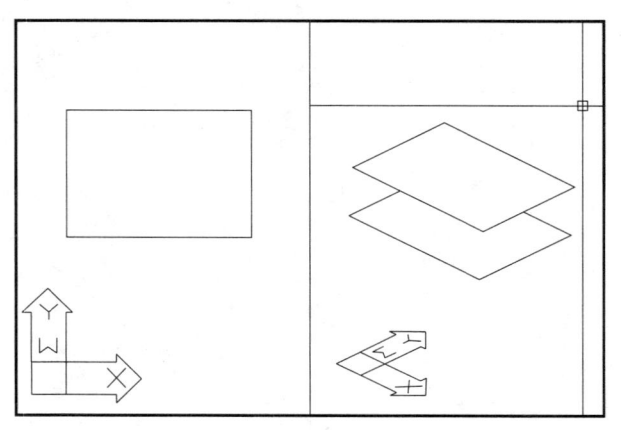

Figure 13-7

In the command area (press F2) AutoCAD gives you a message that says:

Regenerating drawing.
Hidden lines: done 100%

In this case the hiding and regeneration will happen very quickly. In a larger drawing you will have to wait.

Following are some important points about hidden line removal which you should read before continuing:

1. Hidden line removal can be done from the plot configuration dialogue box. However, due to the time involved and the difficulty of getting a hidden view just right, it is usually better to experiment on the screen first, then plot with hidden lines removed when you know you will get the image you want.
2. Whenever the screen is regenerated, hidden lines are returned to the screen.
3. The image created through hidden line removal is *not* retained in BLOCKing, WBLOCKing, GROUPing, or saving VIEWs.
4. Hidden line removal can be captured in slides (the MSLIDE and VSLIDE commands, Chapter 9). But remember, slides cannot be plotted.
5. Layer control is important in hidden line removal. Layers that are frozen are ignored by the HIDE command, but layers that are off are treated like layers that are visible. This can, for example, create peculiar blank spaces in your display if you have left surfaces or solids on a layer that is off at the time of hidden line removal.

Task 4: Using 3D Polygon Mesh Commands

Procedure

1. Create geometry to be used in defining the surface.
2. If necessary, set Surftab1 and Surftab2.
3. Enter a 3D polygon mesh command.
4. Use existing geometry to define the surface.

Discussion. 3DFACE can be used to create simple surfaces. However, most surface models require large numbers of faces to approximate the surfaces of real objects. Consider the number of faces in *Figure 13-8*, the globe you will be creating when you do Drawing 13–3. Obviously you would not want to draw such an image one face at a time.

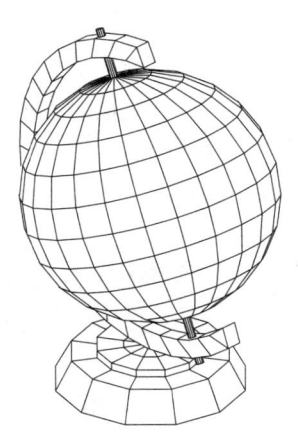

Figure 13-8

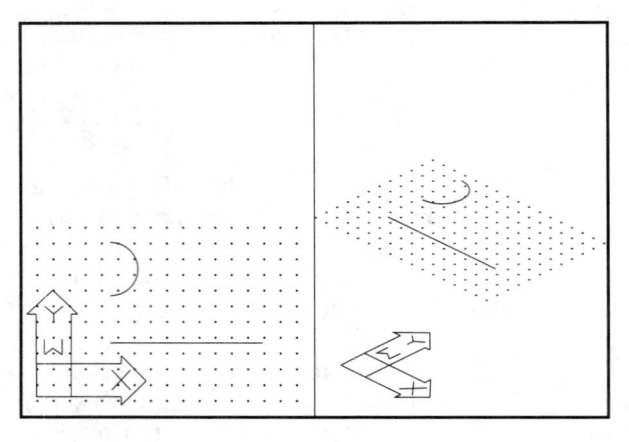

Figure 13-9

AutoCAD includes a number of commands that make the creation of some types of surfaces very easy. These powerful commands create 3D polygon meshes. Polygon meshes are made up of 3D faces and are defined by a matrix of vertices. They can be treated as single entities and edited with the PEDIT command, or exploded into individual 3D faces.

> To begin this task, ERASE the two faces from the last task and draw an arc and a line below it as shown in *Figure 13-9*. Exact sizes and locations are not important.

The entities may be drawn in either viewport.

Now we will define some 3D surfaces using the arc and line you have just drawn.

Tabsurf

The first surface we will draw is called a "tabulated surface." In order to use the TABSURF command, you need a line or curve to define the shape of the surface and a vector to show its size and direction. The result is a surface generated by repeating the shape of the original curve at every point along the path specified by the vector.

> Type "Tabsurf" or select the Extruded Surface tool from the Surfaces toolbar, as shown in *Figure 13-10*.

AutoCAD will prompt:

Select path curve:

The path curve is the line or curve that will determine the shape of the surface. In our case it will be the arc.

> Pick the arc.

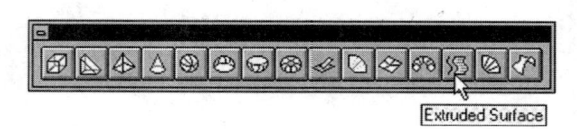

Figure 13-10

Chap. 13   **409**

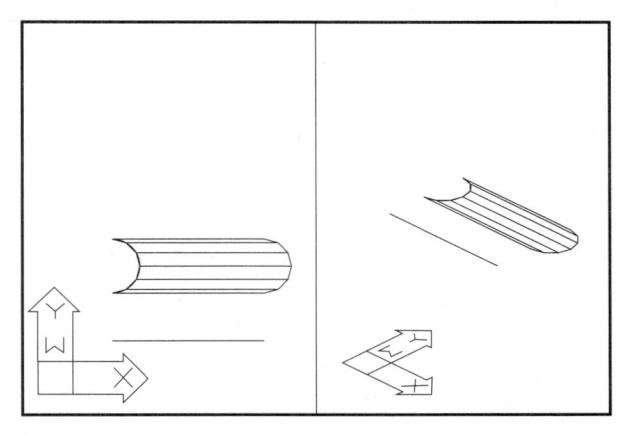

Figure 13-11

AutoCAD will prompt for a vector:

Select direction vector:

We will use the line. Notice that the vector does not need to be connected to the path curve. Its location is not significant, only its direction and length.

There is an oddity here to watch out for as you pick the vector. If you pick a point near the left end of the line, AutoCAD will interpret the vector as extending from left to right. Accordingly, the surface will be drawn to the right. By the same token, if your point is near the right end of the line, the surface will be drawn to the left. Most of the time you will avoid confusion by picking a point on the side of the vector nearest the curve itself.

> Pick a point on the left side of the line.

Your screen will be redrawn to resemble *Figure 13-11*.

Notice that this is a flat surface even though it looks 3D. This may not be clear in the plan view, but is more apparent in the 3D view.

Tabulated surfaces can be fully 3D, depending on the path and vector chosen to define them. In this case we have an arc and a vector that are both entirely in the XY plane, so the resulting surface is also in that plane.

Surftab1

You will also notice that the surface is defined by long narrow faces that run parallel to the vector. If you zoom up on either end of the surface you will see that the arc is only approximated by the shorter edges of these six faces. Unlike the polygons or broken curves AutoCAD often uses to display arcs and circles in order to speed regeneration time, this mesh of quadrilateral faces is the actual current definition of this surface. In order to achieve a more accurate approximation, we can increase the number of faces. This is done by changing the setting of a variable called "Surftab1" and drawing the object again.

Let's undo the tabulated surface so that we can draw it again with a new Surftab1 setting.

> Type "u" and then type "r" to execute a REDRAW.

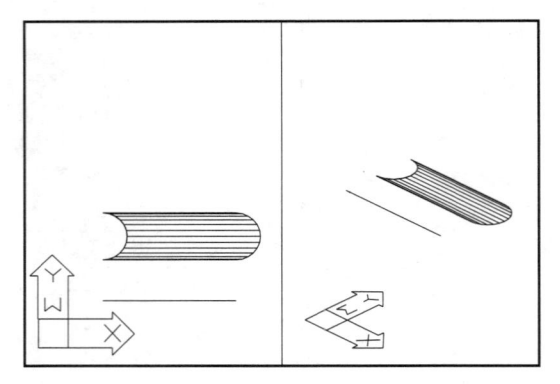

Figure 13-12

Notice that only the current viewport is redrawn. In order to redraw all viewports simultaneously, you can enter a command called REDRAWALL, located on the View menu. There is also a REGENALL command for regenerating all viewports, but it must be typed.

> Type "Surftab1".

AutoCAD prompts:

New value for SURFTAB1 <6>:

The default value shows why we see six lines in the tabulated surface. When we change the setting, we will get a different number of lines and degree of accuracy.

> Type "12".
> Type "Tabsurf" or select the Extruded Surface tool from the Surfaces toolbar.
> Pick the arc for the path curve.
> Pick the line for the direction vector.

Your screen should now resemble *Figure 13-12*.

Rulesurf

TABSURF is useful in defining surfaces that are the same on both ends, assuming you have one end and a vector. Often, however, you have no vector, or you need to draw a surface between two different paths. In these cases you will need the RULESURF command.

For example, what if we need to define a surface between the line and the arc? Let's try it.

> Type "u" to undo the last tabulated surface, then execute a REDRAW or REDRAWALL.

It is not absolutely necessary to do the REDRAW, but it makes it easier to pick the arc.

> Type "Rulesurf" or select the Ruled Surface tool from the Surfaces toolbar, as shown in *Figure 13-13*.

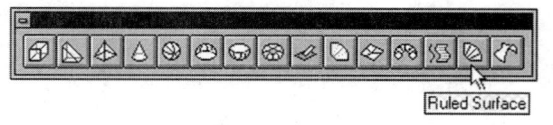

Figure 13-13

Chap. 13

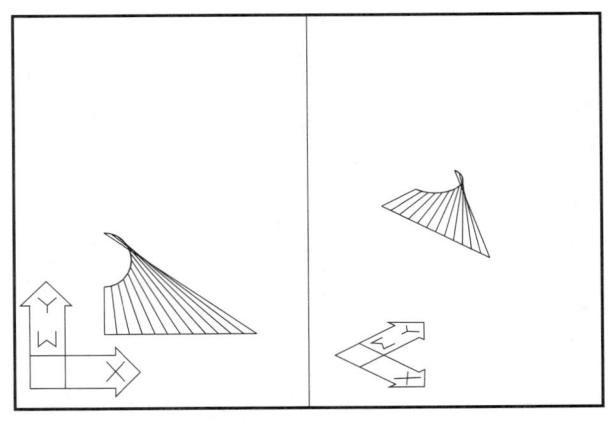

411

Figure 13-14

You are familiar with this command sequence from Chapter 12. The first prompt is:

Select first defining curve:

> Pick the arc, using a point near the bottom.

Remember that you must pick points on corresponding sides of the two defining curves in order to avoid an hourglass effect.

AutoCAD prompts:

Select second defining curve:

> Pick the line, using a point near the left end.

Your screen should resemble *Figure 13-14*.

Again, notice that this surface is within the XY plane even though it may look 3D. Ruled surfaces may be drawn just as easily between curves that are not coplanar.

If you look closely, you will notice that this ruled surface is drawn with 12 lines, the result of our Surftab1 setting.

Some other typical examples of ruled surfaces are shown on the chart, *Figure 13-22*, at the end of this task.

Edgesurf

TABSURF creates surfaces that are the same at both ends and move along a straight line vector. RULESURF draws surfaces between any two boundaries. There is a third command, EDGESURF, which draws surfaces that are bounded by four curves. Edge-defined surfaces have a lot of geometric flexibility. The only restriction is that they must be bounded on all four sides. That is, they must have four edges that touch.

In order to create an EDGESURF, we need to undo our last ruled surface and add two more edges.

> Type "u" and execute a REDRAW or REDRAWALL.
> Add a line and an arc to your screen, as shown in *Figure 13-15*.

Remember, you can draw in either viewport.

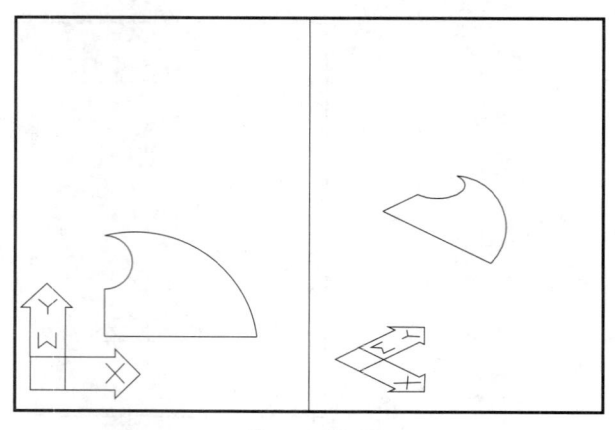

Figure 13-15

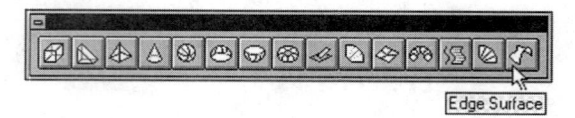

Figure 13-16

> Type "Edgesurf" or select the Edge Surface tool from the Surfaces toolbar, as shown in *Figure 13-16* (note that this is not the same as the Edge tool on the same toolbar).

AutoCAD will prompt for the four edges of the surface, one at a time:

Select edge 1:

> Pick the smaller arc.
AutoCAD prompts:

Select edge 2:

> Pick the larger arc.
AutoCAD prompts:

Select edge 3:

> Pick the longer line.
AutoCAD prompts:

Select edge 4:

> Pick the smaller line.
Your screen should now resemble *Figure 13-17*.

Surftab2

There is something new to be aware of here. With TABSURF and RULESURF, surfaces were defined by edges moving in only one direction. With EDGESURF, you have a matrix of faces and edges going two ways. You will notice that there are 12 edges going one way and 6 going the other, as shown in the figure. This

Chap. 13 413

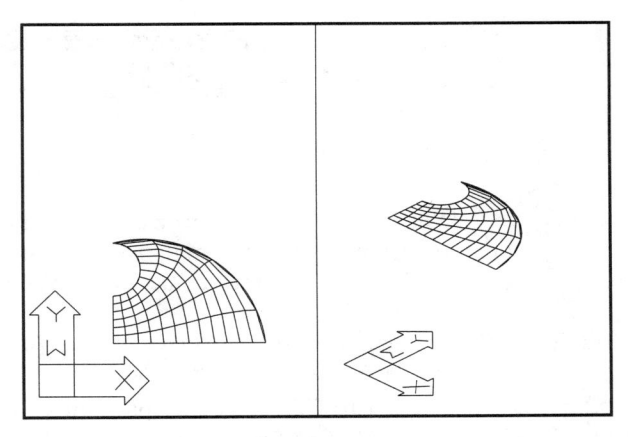

Figure 13-17

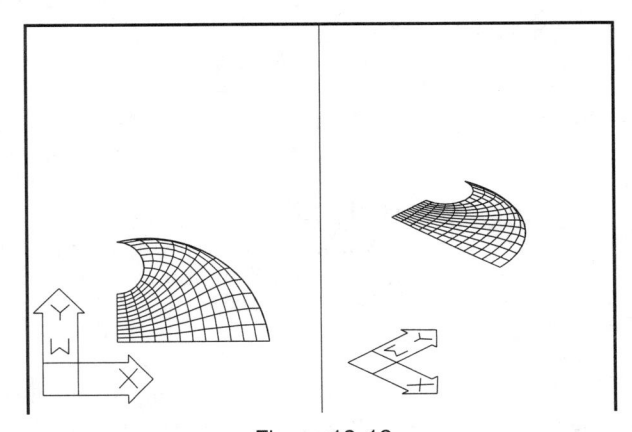

Figure 13-18

brings us to the variable Surftab2. If we change its setting to 12 also, we will see 12 edges in each direction.
Try it.

> Type "u" to undo the EDGESURF command.
> Execute a REDRAW or REDRAWALL.
> Type "Surftab2".
> Type "12".
> Enter the EDGESURF command and select the four edges again.
The result should resemble *Figure 13-18*.

Revsurf

We have one more 3D polygon mesh command to explore, and this one is probably the most impressive of all. REVSURF creates surfaces by spinning a curve through a given angle around an axis of revolution. Just as tabulated surfaces are spread along a linear path, surfaces of revolution follow a circular or arc-shaped path. As a result, surfaces of revolution are always fully three-dimensional, even if their defining geometry is in a single plane, as it will be here.

> In preparation for this exercise undo the EDGESURF, and REDRAW (or REDRAWALL) your screen so that it resembles *Figure 13-15* again.

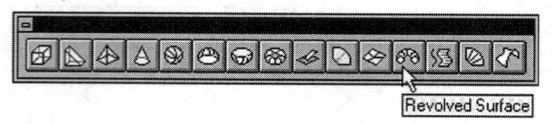

Figure 13-19

We will create two surfaces of revolution. The first will be a complete 360 degree surface using the smaller arc and the smaller line for definition. The second will be a 270 degree surface using the larger arc and the larger line.

> Type "revsurf" or select the Revolved Surface tool from the Surfaces toolbar, as shown in *Figure 13-19*.

AutoCAD needs a path curve and an axis of revolution to define the surface. The first prompt is:

Select path curve:

> Pick the smaller arc.

AutoCAD prompts:

Select axis of revolution:

> Pick the smaller line.

AutoCAD now needs to know whether you want the surface to begin at the curve itself or somewhere else around the circle of revolution:

Start angle <0>:

The default is to start at the curve.
> Press Enter to begin the surface at the curve itself.

AutoCAD prompts:

Included angle (+=ccw, -=cw) <Full circle>:

Entering a positive or negative degree measure will cause the surface to be drawn around an arc rather than a full circle. The default will give us a complete circle.
> Press Enter.

Your screen should be drawn to resemble *Figure 13-20*.

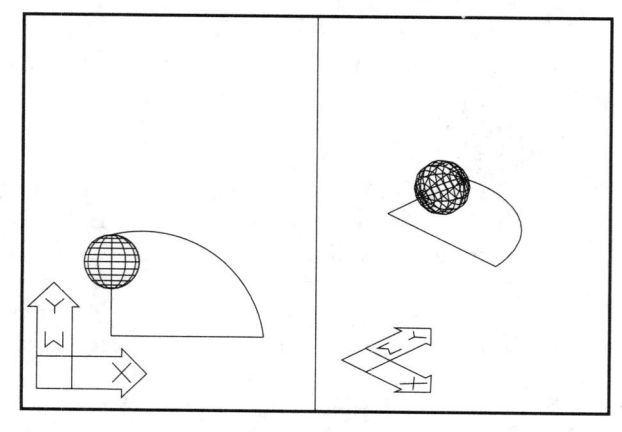

Figure 13-20

If you look closely, you will see that this globe has 12 lines in each direction. REVSURF, like EDGESURF, uses both Surftab1 and Surftab2. Also notice that this command gives us a way to create spheres. If the path curve is a true semicircle and the axis is along the diameter of the semicircle, then the result will be a sphere. There is another way to create a sphere, which we will discuss in Task 5.

Now we will create a larger surface that does not start at 0 degrees and does not include a full circle.

> Press Enter to repeat the REVSURF command.
> Pick the larger arc for the curve path.
> Pick the left end of the longer line for the axis of revolution.

If you pick the right end, the positive and negative angles will be reversed in the two steps following.

> Type "90" for the start angle.

This will cause the surface to begin 90 degrees up from the XY plane.

> Type "−270" for the included angle.

This will cause the surface to revolve 270 degrees clockwise around the axis. The result should resemble *Figure 13-21*. You may have to use PAN in one or both viewports to position the objects on the screen as we have shown them.

Next, we will demonstrate the use of the 3D Objects dialogue box, which contains AutoLISP routines to create nine more basic surface models. Take a look at the polygon mesh examples in *Figure 13-22* before proceeding.

Task 5: Creating Surface Models Using the "3D Objects" AutoLISP Routines

Procedure

1. Type "3D" or select a 3D surface object tool from the Surfaces toolbar.
2. Follow the prompts.

Discussion. Release 13 includes nine AutoLISP routines that create three-dimensional surface models of basic shapes. AutoLISP routines act just like commands, except that they take a moment to load before they execute. Also note that these routines will only work if AutoLISP is loaded with appropriate memory allocation. If you have a problem, see the *AutoCAD Installation Guide*.

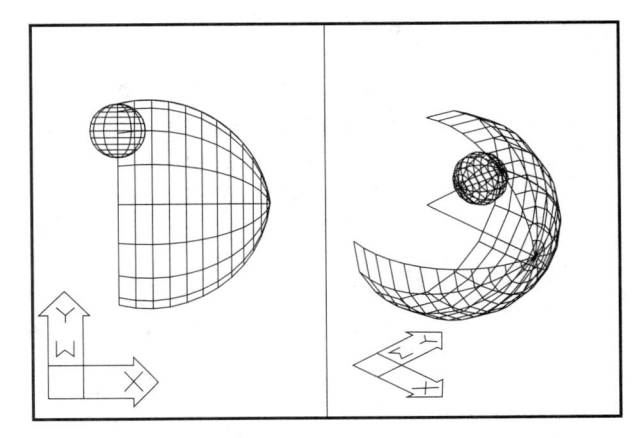

Figure 13-21

POLYGON MESH COMMANDS			
COMMAND	BEFORE	SETVAR SETTINGS	AFTER
TABSURF		SURFTAB1 = 6	
		SURFTAB1 = 12	
RULESURF		SURFTAB1 = 6	
		SURFTAB1 = 6	
		SURFTAB1 = 6	
EDGESURF		SURFTAB1 = 6 SURFTAB2 = 8	
		SURFTAB1 = 6 SURFTAB2 = 8	
		SURFTAB1 = 6 SURFTAB2 = 8	
		SURFTAB1 = 12 SURFTAB2 = 10	
REVSURF		SURFTAB1 = 16 SURFTAB2 = 8	

Figure 13-22

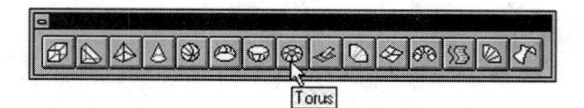

Figure 13-23

Like the 3D meshes explored in Task 4, the 3D surface models created this way can be treated as single entities or EXPLODEd and edited as collections of 3D faces. Each of the objects has its own set of prompts, depending on its geometry. We will demonstrate one object in this task and leave the rest for you to explore on your own.

> To begin this task, clear your screen of objects left from Task 3.
> Type "3D" or select the Torus tool from the Surfaces toolbar, as shown in *Figure 13-23*.

NOTE: In order to create 3D surface models you must use the 3D command or the Surfaces toolbar. Typing "sphere", "cone", "torus", etc. directly at the command line will create solid models instead of surface models.

> If you are typing, type "t" for the Torus option.

Either method will bring you to the first Torus prompt:

Center of torus:

> Pick a center point as shown by P1 in *Figure 13-24*.

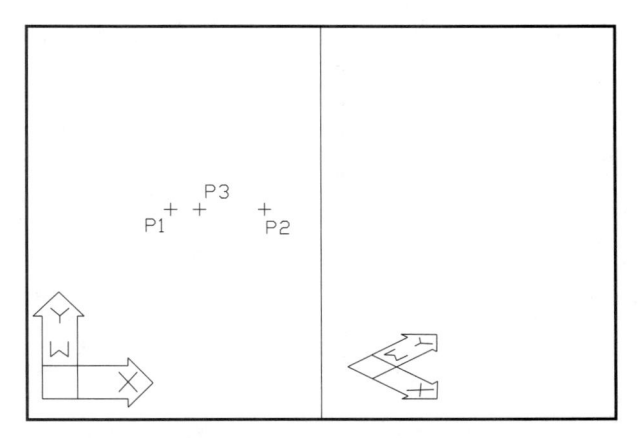

Figure 13-24

AutoCAD prompts:

Diameter/<radius> of torus:

The next point we pick will show the overall radius of the torus.
> Show a radius distance of about 6.00 units, as shown by P2 in the figure.
AutoCAD prompts:

Diameter/<radius> of tube:

This will be the diameter or radius of the torus tube. If you specify the tube size by pointing, remember that the distance is being shown from the center point of the torus, at P1, to P3, though the tube actually will be constructed from its own centerline at P2.
> Show a radius of about 2.00 units, as shown by P3 in the figure.
AutoCAD prompts:

Segments around tube circumference <16>:

You will be prompted for segment numbers around the tube and around the torus. These specify mesh density just like Surftab1 and Surftab2.
> Press Enter to accept the default of 16 segments.
AutoCAD prompts:

Segments around torus circumference <16>:

> Press Enter to accept the default of 16 segments.

Your screen should resemble *Figure 13-25*. As in the case of the 3D polygon mesh commands, notice how much surface modeling this AutoLISP routine accomplishes through a few simple prompts.

To appreciate the nature of surface models once again, we recommend that you make the right viewport active at this point and execute the HIDE command. You will see an image of the torus with hidden lines removed.

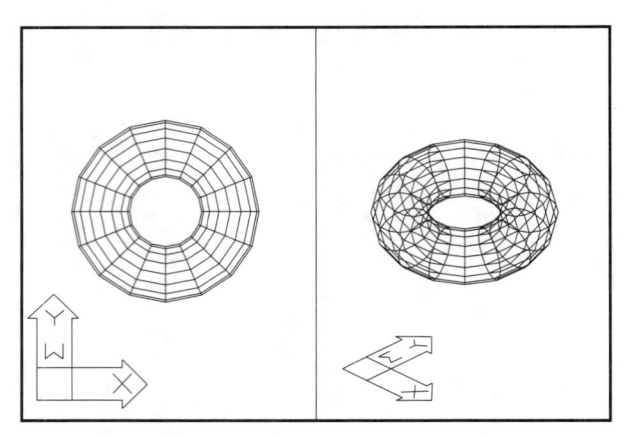

Figure 13-25

Task 6: Creating Approximated Surfaces Using PEDIT (Optional)

Procedure

1. Draw a 3DMESH in three dimensions.
2. Type "pedit" or select the Pedit tool from the Special Edit flyout on the Modify toolbar.
3. Select the mesh.
4. Specify a surface type.
5. Type "s" or select "smooth".
6. Exit PEDIT.

Discussion. Within the PEDIT command there are some very impressive design features, which we introduce in this task and the next as optional exercises. These techniques will not be needed in the drawings that follow, but your knowledge of AutoCAD and surface modeling will be incomplete without them.

The techniques of curve and surface approximation are most useful when you have a curved object in mind but have not yet derived exact specifications for it, or when an irregular curved object passes through many different planes and would be very hard to draw face by face. You may be able to draw an outline and specify some key points, but beyond that, what you conceive may be simply a smooth curve that follows the basic shape of your outline. AutoCAD provides mathematical algorithms that can translate outlines into smooth curves. This can be accomplished with 2D and 3D polylines and with 3D meshes.

3D meshes can be curved according to three different formulas, controlled by the variable "Surftype" (not to be confused with Surftab1 and Surftab2). Surftype can be set to 5 for a quadratic approximation, 6 for cubic approximation, and 8 for bezier.

In this exercise we will create a simple rectangular 3D mesh in one plane, move two of its vertices to make it three-dimensional, and then use the Smooth option of the PEDIT command to create approximated surfaces.

> To begin this task, clear your screen of all objects left from the last task, and return to a single viewport using the following procedure:
1. Make the right viewport active.
2. Type "Vports" or select "Tiled Viewports" from the View menu.
3. Type "si" (for single) or select "1 Viewport".
4. Press F7 if your grid is not showing.

Chap. 13   419

The screen will be redrawn with a single viewport resembling the currently active viewport.

3DMESH

The 3DMESH command allows you to create 3D polygon meshes "manually," vertex by vertex. Because of the time involved, the complete command is best used as a programmer's tool. However, there is an AutoLISP program that provides a very simple version of the 3DMESH command, which we will demonstrate here. Those interested in the full command sequence should see the *AutoCAD Command Reference*.

The AutoLISP version of the 3DMESH command is initiated through the 3D command. Do not use the 3D Mesh tool from the Surfaces toolbar, as this will initiate the full 3DMESH command.

> Zoom in so that the grid covers more of the screen.
> Type "3D".
> Type "m" to initiate the Mesh option.

AutoCAD prompts:

First corner:

We will be prompted for four corners to define the outer boundaries of the mesh, and then for two numbers to specify the number of vertices.

> Pick a corner, as shown by P1 in *Figure 13-26*.

AutoCAD will prompt for another corner:

Second corner:

> Pick a second corner 4.00 to the right of P1.
> Pick a third corner 3.00 in the *y* direction from P2.
> Pick P4 as shown.

When you have picked four corners, your mesh should be outlined and one side highlighted. (If your mesh is drawn in yellow, as ours is, this highlighting may be hard to see.) AutoCAD is asking for the number of vertices to be defined in the "M" direction:

Mesh M size:

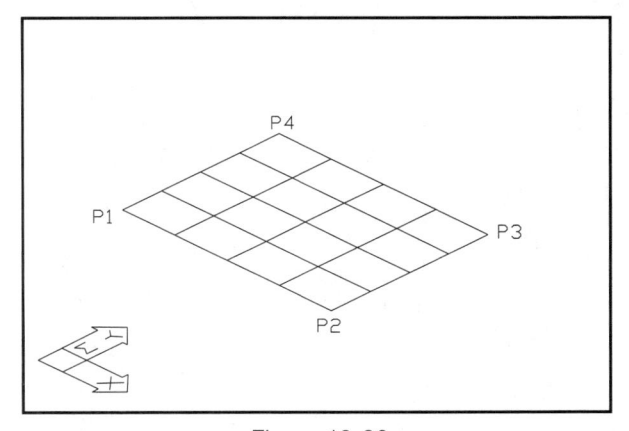

Figure 13-26

The letters M and N are used to designate the two directions in which the mesh will be defined. The highlighted side shows the M direction. The M size is equivalent to the Surftab1 setting. The highlighted side will be divided equally by the number of vertices we specify.

> Type "5".

AutoCAD highlights a side perpendicular to the first, and prompts:

Mesh N size:

Like Surftab2, the "N" specification will determine the number of vertices in this direction.

> Type "5" again.

Your screen will be redrawn to resemble *Figure 13-26*.

The mesh will be drawn with five vertices in each direction. Later we will copy it twice so that we can produce three different types of smooth surfaces, but first we need to move some vertices up and down in the *z* direction to give it three-dimensionality. This can be done using .XY filters and the grip edit stretch mode.

> Select the mesh.

The mesh will be highlighted and grips will appear at each vertex.

> Pick the grip at the back right corner of the mesh.

The stretch mode works the same as in previous chapters, except that now we will be moving vertices up and down out of the XY plane. If you have not previously used point filters, here is an opportunity to become familiar with this useful 3D tool.

> Type ".xy" or select the .XY tool from the Point Filters flyout on the Standard toolbar, as shown in *Figure 13-27*.

AutoCAD prompts:

.xy of

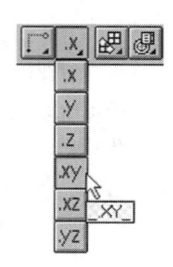

Figure 13-27

We are going to move the vertex straight up into the *z* dimension, so we want the same *x* and *y* coordinates with a new *z*. The XY filter will take the *x* and *y* values from whatever point we specify and combine them with a new *z* value. We can pick the same vertex again to show *x* and *y*, or we can type "@", indicating the last point entered. The *z* value will need to be typed since there are no objects outside of the XY plane to snap onto.

> Type "@" or pick the highlighted vertex grip again.

AutoCAD responds:

(need Z):

> Type "2".

This will move the corner vertex up 2.00, as shown in *Figure 13-28*.

Now we will move the opposite corner down −3.00.

> Pick the grip at the front left corner, opposite the corner you just edited.
> Type ".xy" or select the .XY tool from the Standard toolbar.
> Type "@" or pick the same grip again.
> Type "−3".

We are now ready to create a cubic-style smoothed surface from our 3D mesh.

Chap. 13 **421**

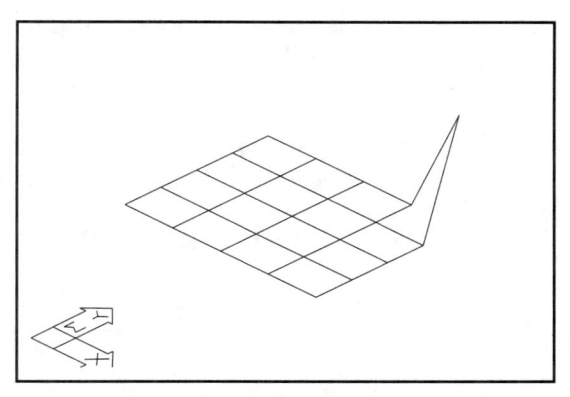

Figure 13-28

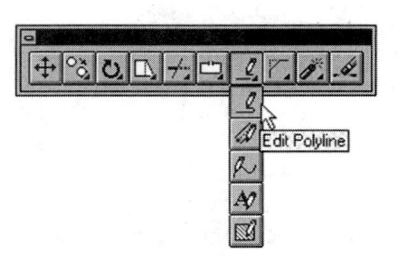

Figure 13-29

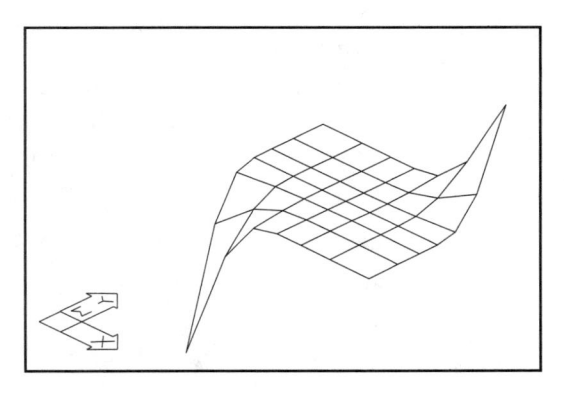

Figure 13-30

> Type "pedit" or select the Pedit tool from the Special Edit flyout on the Modify toolbar, as shown in *Figure 13-29*.

AutoCAD will prompt for a polyline, but 3D polygon meshes may also be selected.

> Pick any point on the mesh.

This will bring up a command prompt with the following options:

Edit Vertex/Smooth surface/Desmooth/Mclose/Nclose/Undo/eXit<X>:

The option we will be using is "Smooth surface".

> Type "s" or select "smooth".

Your screen will be redrawn to resemble *Figure 13-30*.

NOTE: If the variable "Splframe" is set to 1, your screen will show no change. Splframe shows the frame or outline used in defining an approximated curve. Because of the complexity of meshes, AutoCAD does not show a curved surface and its "frame" at the same time. With Splframe set to the default of 0, you will see the smoothed version with no frame. With a setting of 1 you see the original frame without the approximation.

Next we will make copies of the mesh and smooth the copies with the variable "surftype" set to create quadratic and bezier surfaces.

> Press Enter to exit the PEDIT command.
> Zoom all and make two copies of the mesh.
> Type "Surftype".
> Type "5".

    Surftype is 6 for cubic (the default), 5 for quadratic, and 8 for Bezier.

> Type "pedit" or select the Pedit tool from the Modify toolbar.
> Select the first copy of the mesh.
> Type "s" or select "Smooth".

NOTE: The differences between cubic and quadratic surfaces in this object will be slight. In fact, you will have to look hard to see them. We have indicated them with arrows in *Figure 13-31* for your convenience. In order to show a more dramatic difference, you would need to create a more dramatic 3D figure by moving more vertices up or down. If you have the time, be our guest. Also consider changing the density of surface approximation through the variables "Surfu" and Surfv". For more information see the *AutoCAD Command Reference*.

> Type "Surftype".
> Type "8" for a Bezier surface.
> Type "pedit" or select the Pedit tool from the Modify toolbar.
> Select the remaining copy of the mesh.

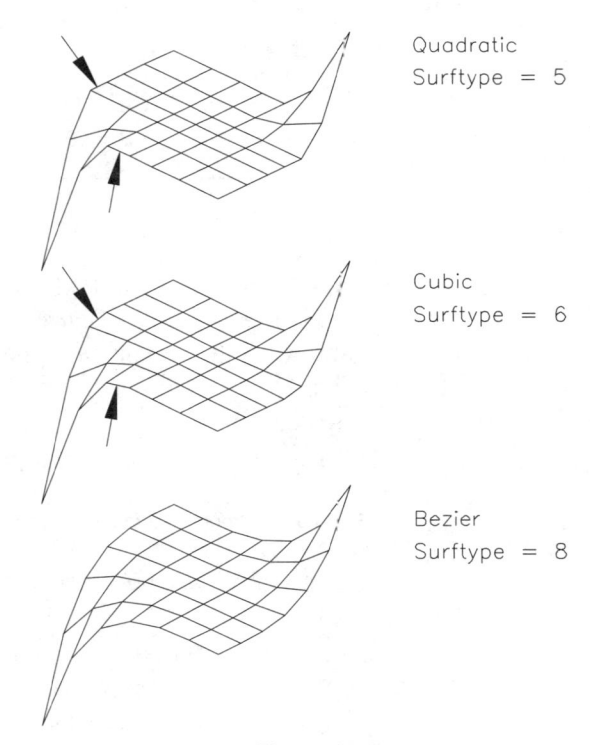

Figure 13-31

> Type "s" to smooth the mesh.

Your meshes will resemble those in *Figure 13-31*.

Now that you know how to create smoothed surfaces, creating two-dimensional curve approximations should be easy. We include the following discussion as a reference.

Curve Approximation

Creating approximated curves in two dimensions is analogous to smoothing surfaces in three dimensions. The process is the same, with a few changes in variable names. Instead of beginning with a 3D mesh, you begin with a polyline. Polyline frames can be curved through the "Fit" or "Spline" options of the PEDIT command. Fit replaces all straight segments of a polyline with pairs of arc segments. The resulting curve passes through all existing vertices, and new vertices are created to join the arcs. Spline curves follow the shape of their frames, but they do not necessarily pass through all vertices. Instead they pass through the first and last points, and tend toward the ones between according to either the quadratic or cubic formula. (There is no Bezier option for spline curves.)

If the variable "Splineframe" is set to 1 instead of the default 0, AutoCAD will display the defining frame along with the curve. Also, the degree of accuracy of curve approximation can be varied by changing the setting of the variable "Splinesegs". This variable controls the number of segments a polyline will be considered to have in the calculations of the spline formulae.

Examples of fit, cubic, and quadratic curves are shown in *Figure 13-32*.

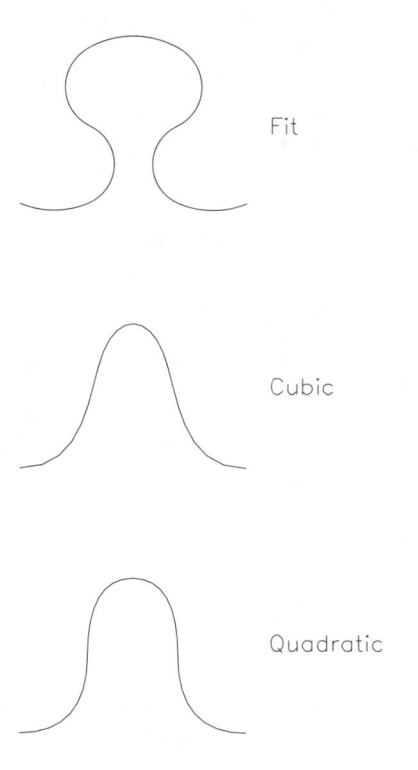

Figure 13-32

Task 7: Using the MVSETUP Program

Procedure

1. Create objects in model space.
2. Type "mvsetup" or enter paper space and then select "MV Setup" from the Floating Viewports submenu on the View pull down menu.
3. Insert a title block.
4. Create viewports.
5. Scale viewports.
6. Align viewports.
7. Set paper space limits to extents.
8. Plot.

Discussion. MVSETUP is one of a number of AutoLISP and ADS programs (see Appendix B) included with the Release 13 software. MVSETUP has a number of useful features, as evidenced by items 2 through 7 on the preceding procedure list.

In this task we will create a simple 3D surface model and then go through the steps involved in using MVSETUP to plot a multiple-view layout of the object in paper space.

> To begin this task you should be in model space with a blank screen.
> For demonstration purposes, draw a 3D surface model of a wine glass, about 6.00 units high, using the following procedure.
1. Draw a 2D polyline outline and axis of revolution as shown in *Figure 13-33*.
2. Type or select "Revsurf".
3. Select the outline as the path curve.
4. Select the line segment as the axis of revolution.
5. Press Enter twice to accept the defaults and create a complete revolution.
6. ERASE the axis.

> Type "Mvsetup". You can also select "MV Setup" under "Floating Viewports" on the View menu, but you will have to go into paper space before this option is available on the pull down menu.

If you type the command and tilemode is set to on, AutoCAD will prompt:

Enable Paperspace? (No/Yes):

You must be in paperspace to create multiple nontiled viewports.

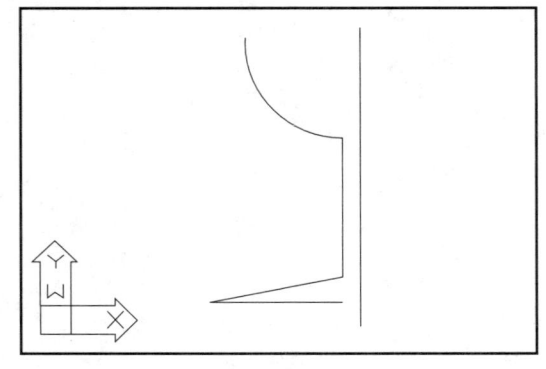

Figure 13-33

Chap. 13

> Press Enter to enable paper space.

Your screen will go blank and the paper space icon will appear, as in the MVIEW command. You will see the following prompt:

Align/Create/Scale viewports/Options/Title block/Undo:

We will be using all of these options together to create a drawing layout of the wine glass, but keep in mind that many of the options work just as well independently with any multiple-view drawing. You do not, for example, have to use the MVSETUP title block feature in order to use the alignment feature.

First, we will insert a title block and set up paper space to reflect a B-size drawing sheet.

> Type "t", for the "Title block" option.

MVSETUP prompts:

Delete objects/Origin/Undo/<Insert title block>:

> Press Enter to insert a title block at the current origin.

MVSETUP switches to the text window and shows a list of paper sizes. An ANSI-B sheet is designated by the number 8.

> Type "8".

In a moment your screen will resemble *Figure 13-34* and MVSETUP will prompt:

Create a drawing named ansi-b.dwg? <Y>:

This prompt is encountered the first time you load a given sheet-size title block. Once the title block is created it will remain on file and you will not be prompted the next time.

> Press Enter to create the B-size title block and border.

Now we need to create some viewports.

> Type "c" for the "Create" option.

MVSETUP prompts:

Delete objects/Undo/<Create Viewports>:

> Press Enter to create viewports.

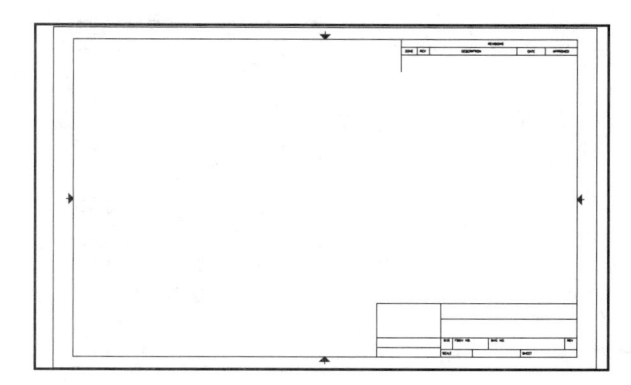

Figure 13-34

The text window returns again, showing a list of available viewport layout options. We will use a standard four-view engineering layout.
> Type "2".

The text window disappears and MVSETUP prompts with two options for specifying the boundary area of the viewports:

Bounding area for viewports. Default/<First point>:

The first point option will allow you to create a window within which the four viewports will be drawn. The default option will choose an area based on your title block. In some cases you will not be offered a default. If this happens, window the area where you want the viewports to be drawn.
> Type "d" for the "Default" option.

MVSETUP prompts for a distance between viewports in the *x* direction. This is similar to defining an array.
> Type "1".
> Press Enter to create the same distance in the *y* direction.

Be prepared for some fireworks. MVSETUP will draw four viewports and then create three 2D projections and a 3D view within them. When this is done your screen should resemble *Figure 13-35*, though the size of objects may be different.

MVSETUP also has its own scaling option, which sets zoom scale factors between paper space and viewports. We will use this feature to scale down the three orthographic views and leave the 3D view as is.
> Type "s" for the "Scale viewports" option.

MVSETUP puts you into paper space, regardless of where you were before, so that you can select viewports.
> Select the three projections (top left, bottom left, and bottom right viewports) one at a time, by pointing to the borders.
> Press Enter to end object selection.

MVSETUP prompts:

Set zoom scale factors for viewports. Interactively/<Uniform>:

The interactive mode lets you establish different zoom factors in each selected viewport independently. The Uniform option will set them all to the same factor.
> Press Enter for a uniform zoom factor.

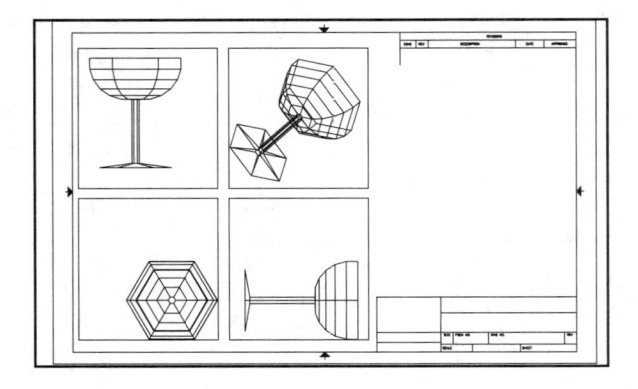

Figure 13-35

The next options will allow you to specify a ratio of paper space units to model space units. We will use a ratio of one paper space unit to two model space units.

> Press Enter to specify one paper space unit.
> Type "2" to specify two model space units.

Your screen will be redrawn as shown in *Figure 13-35*.

We have one more layout operation to perform before we are ready to plot. You may notice that the three projections are not lined up with each other. This can be readily fixed using the Align option.

> If the image in your lower left viewport does not appear to be centered, first exit the MVSETUP program, go into model space, and PAN in this viewport to center the image.
> If necessary, reenter the MVSETUP program.
> Type "a" for the "Align" option.

MVSETUP prompts:

Angled/Horizontal/Vertical alignment/Rotate view/Undo:

> Type "h" to perform a horizontal alignment.

MVSETUP prompts for a base point. This should be a point of alignment in the viewport that will remain unchanged by the alignment.

> Pick the center of the glass in the lower left viewport.

MVSETUP prompts for another point. This should be the corresponding point in another viewport. When the operation is complete this point will align with the base point selected in the first viewport.

> Pick any point along the centerline of the glass in the bottom right viewport.

The command will bring the two views in line, as shown in *Figure 13-36*.

Now do a vertical alignment on the remaining view.

> Type "v".
> Pick the same base point at the center of the glass in the lower left viewport.
> Pick any point along the center line of the glass in the top left viewport for the other point.

At this point the three views should align and your drawing should resemble *Figure 13-36*.

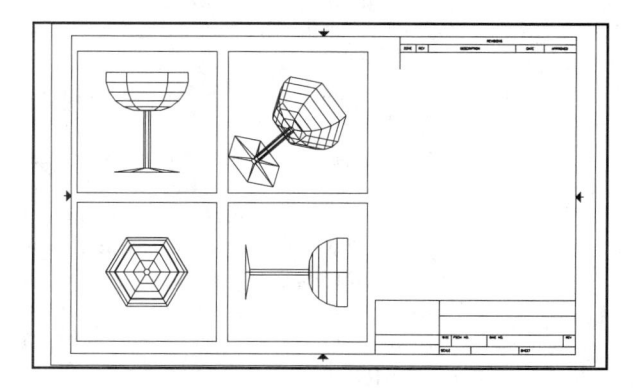

Figure 13-36

Before you proceed to a plot preview, set limits equal to extents in your drawing. This will make the plot configuration easier to manage.

> Press Enter to return to the first MVSETUP prompt.
> Type "o" for the "Options" option.

MVSETUP prompts:

Set Layer/LImits/Units/Xref:

> Type "Li" for "Limits".
> Type "y" to set drawing limits equal to drawing extents.
> Press Enter twice to exit the MVSETUP program.
> Check to be sure that you are in paper space (look for the paper space icon). If not, type "ps".
> Type or select "Plot".

We are, of course, ignoring the step of adding documentation to the title block.

> Select either "Extents" or "Limits" from "Additional Parameters".
> Assuming you are actually using B-size paper, make this selection from the Size subdialogue box.
> If "Scaled to Fit" is not checked, click in the box to check it.
> Click on "Full" and then "Preview".

If you like what you see, then you are ready to plot.

Task 8: Creating Perspective and Clipped 3D Views with DVIEW

Procedure

1. Type "Dview" or select "3D Dynamic View" from the View menu.
2. Select objects to view.
3. Specify a DVIEW option.
4. Specify a view.
5. Specify another option or exit the command.
6. Use VIEW to save 3D views.

Discussion. For most drawing purposes, using the VPOINT command or preset views from the pull down menu is adequate and efficient for creating 3D views of objects. However, the DVIEW ("Dynamic View") command has several capabilities that do not exist in VPOINT. DVIEW allows you to "drag" the object or portions of it as you define the view. In addition, it has the capability of creating perspective views and allows you to "clip" the object at specified planes to temporarily remove all objects in front of or behind a specified plane.

Within the DVIEW command there are also options to zoom, pan, and rotate ("Twist") to achieve the exact display you want, and to remove hidden lines to better visualize the view you are creating. As a general rule, DVIEW is best used when your drawing is complete and you want to create a plot or display that shows it to best advantage. Perspective views, for example, are strictly for presentation. Many draw and edit commands will not work at all in a perspective view.

In this task we will test some of the DVIEW options on a simple mesh in one plane. In particular, this mesh will demonstrate clearly the effect of the perspective view feature.

Chap. 13   **429**

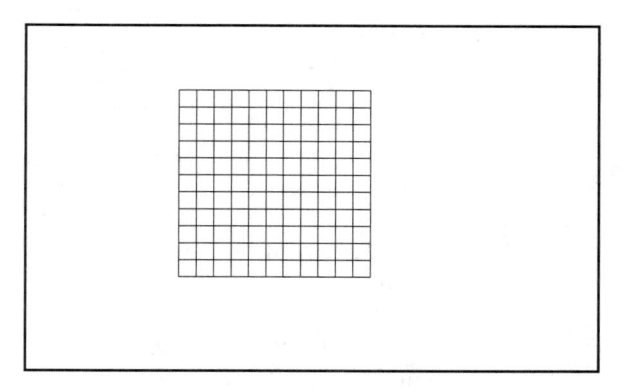

Figure 13-37

> To begin this task, you should be in model space with a blank screen.

First, create a 3D mesh using the 3D surfaces program. If you need assistance beyond the instructions that follow, see Task 5 in this chapter.
> Type "3D".
> Type "m" for the "Mesh" option.
> Pick the four corners of a square, approximately 6.00 × 6.00, as illustrated in *Figure 13-37*. Exact size and location are insignificant.
> Type "12" for the "M size".
> Type "12" for the "N size".

These two prompts establish the number of vertices in each direction of the mesh.

Before entering DVIEW it will be useful to have a smaller snap increment. This will become apparent when
we use the "Camera" option to establish a viewpoint dynamically.
> Set your Snap to .05.
> Type "dview" or select "3D Dynamic View" from the View pull down menu.

AutoCAD prompts for object selection:

Select objects:

One of the advantages of DVIEW is that it lets you adjust your view of objects in 3D space dynamically. In order to do this effectively, however, the number of objects on the screen may need to be limited. If you have ever tried to drag a complex object across the screen, you are familiar with the problem. The object is drawn and redrawn so slowly as you move your pointing device that the dragging process becomes too cumbersome to be useful. In the DVIEW command, you select a portion of your drawing to serve as a "preview image" for the process of dynamic view adjustment. The rest of the drawing is temporarily invisible and ignored. When you have defined the view you want by manipulating the preview image, exit DVIEW and the complete drawing will be restored in the newly defined view.

For our purposes, there is only the mesh to select.

NOTE: AutoCAD also provides a default preview image. If you press Enter at the "Select objects:" prompt, DVIEW will show a simple wireframe house for your preview image. Or if you prefer, you can even create your own default image. (See the *AutoCAD Command Reference*.) For most purposes, however, you will want to see at least a portion of the drawing you are working on.

> Select the mesh.
> Press Enter to end object selection.

AutoCAD will prompt with the following DVIEW options:

CAmera/TArget/Distance/POints/PAn/Zoom/TWist/CLip/Hide/Off/Undo/<eXit>:

These options vary considerably in their effect and ease of use. We will begin with a "Zoom".

NOTE: To avoid confusion, AutoCAD switches to the WCS whenever you enter DVIEW. DVIEW proceeds with the WCS in effect and then returns you to your UCS when you exit the command. We are working in the WCS in this exercise anyway, so this will not be noticeable.

"Pan" and "Zoom"

Panning in the DVIEW command is easy. After specifying a base point, you can drag objects around the screen in any direction.

> Type "Pa" or select "Pan".
> Pick a point near the middle of the mesh for a base point.
> Move the cursor slowly and observe the preview image moving along with it.
> Center the image on the display.

Zooming in DVIEW is a little different from the regular ZOOM command.

> Type "z" or select "Zoom".

AutoCAD places a "slider bar" at the top of the screen, as shown in *Figure 13-38*, and prompts:

Adjust zoom scale factor <1>:

The slider bar consists of a scale with numbered divisions (0x,1x,4x,9x,16x), a diamond-shaped "cursor" that is controlled by your pointing device, and two rubber bands that connect you to a short line marking the current magnification. The current value is always "1x." If you move the cursor to the right, objects on the screen will be enlarged by the factors shown on the scale; if you move to the left, they will be reduced by fractional factors.
> Move the cursor so that the diamond is on the short vertical line at the "1x."

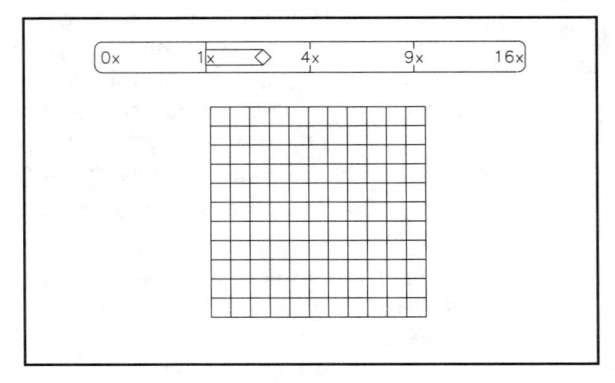

Figure 13-38

"1x" is the current magnification, so the preview image will appear as it did before you entered the zoom option, except that any color will be gone.
> Now stretch the rubber bands to the right and left and watch the mesh expand and shrink.

Notice that it doesn't take much movement to produce a significant change. Also, pay close attention to the coordinate display. It will show you your zoom scale factor to three decimal places.

If snap is on you may want to turn it off to see the full range of magnification.
> Pick a zoom factor of about 2.00.

Your mesh will be enlarged by the scale factor shown, and AutoCAD will return to the DVIEW options prompt:

CAmera/TArget/Distance/POints/PAn/Zoom/TWist/CLip/Hide/Off/ Undo/<eXit>:

> If necessary, use the PAn option to center the mesh on the screen.

"Camera" and "Target"

Next we will change our view of the image using the "CAmera" option. "Camera" and "Target" refer to two aspects of a point of view relative to a 3D object. ("Distance" is a third we will discuss shortly.)

The photographic metaphor is used extensively in AutoCAD rendering procedures as well as in DVIEW. When you sight through an actual camera, what you see is dependent on the location of the camera and the direction its lens is pointed. In the metaphor, "Camera" refers to your point of view in space, and "Target" refers to the point at which the camera is aimed. In the DVIEW command you change views by moving the point of view (Camera), by aiming it toward a new point (Target), or both.

In practice, setting the "Camera" placement is very similar to using the rotation option of the VPOINT command. If you recall, in using "VPOINT Rotate" you define an angle of rotation within the XY plane and a viewing angle above or below the plane. Viewpoints we have used typically in this book are 315 degrees in the plane and 30 or 45 degrees up from the plane.

To demonstrate the perspective feature, we are going to use a longer, flatter viewing angle. Notice that this view would be impractical for drawing purposes, but will create a dramatic perspective effect.

> Type "ca" or select "Camera".

The appearance of your preview image will depend on the placement of your pointing device. The prompt will be:

Toggle angle in/Enter angle from XY plane <90.0000>:

You can enter angles by typing or by picking a point on the screen. Picking may seem easier and has the advantage of allowing you to drag the preview image into place. However, it is difficult to conceptualize exactly what the cursor and image are doing.
> Move the cursor slowly and watch how the preview image and the coordinate display react.

The behavior of the cursor, image, and coordinate display will be unfamiliar. In effect, vertical movement of the cursor controls the angle from the

XY plane, while horizontal movement controls the angle in the XY plane. If you move the cursor freely, you are seeing both angles adjusted simultaneously. The coordinate display, on the other hand, can only show one angle at a time. You can toggle from one to the other by typing "t" and pressing Enter. The prompt line refers to these as "angle in" and "angle from".

You will have a better sense of how it all works if snap is on. This is where a small snap increment is useful in this exercise.

> If snap is off, turn it on.

> Move several snap points horizontally, and then several vertically.

If you watch the coordinate display you will see that it changes only when you move vertically.

> Type "t" and press Enter.

> Now move horizontally and watch the angle display change. There will be no change when you move vertically.

Continue moving horizontally and vertically to get a feel for the camera position system. As the camera moves up and down from the plane, the preview image appears to tip forward and back. It may be difficult to visualize what is happening as you pass below 0 degrees. As you pass zero, the front of the object begins to tip away from you so that you are looking up from underneath.

If you move the camera back and forth in the plane, the image will appear to turn.

Also notice that with snap on the angle moves in 9 degree increments from the XY plane (vertical cursor movement). This is a translation of the .05 snap increment into a degree measure. The range of angles from the XY plane is -90 to 90, a total of 180 degrees, and $.05 \times 180$ is 9.

For a good perspective view, we want an angle of about 9 degrees from the XY plane, and 0 degrees in the XY plane. To ensure that you get the results presented here, we suggest that you type in the angles.

> Type "9" for the angle from XY and then "0" for the angle in XY.

Your screen will resemble *Figure 13-39*. Though it appears that your mesh has been flattened, in fact this is a three-dimensional parallel projection. The flattening is a result of foreshortening. When we switch to a perspective view, the appearance will be quite different. Notice that it would be extremely difficult to draw in this foreshortened image.

NOTE: If you find that your mesh has turned into a horizontal line on the screen it is because you have reversed angles. With 0 as the angle from the XY plane, you will be looking edge on and the mesh will appear as a line regardless of what angle in the XY plane is specified.

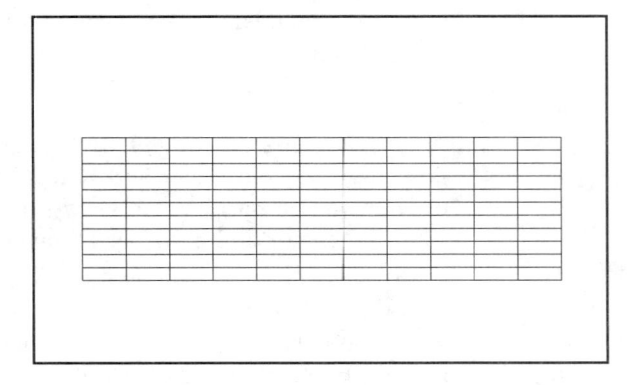

Figure 13-39

We will not use the TArget option in this exercise. The process is exactly the same. Vertical and horizontal motion controls the rotation of the target point from and in the XY plane. The camera location does not change. Instead, we change the direction in which the camera is aimed. It is like panning with a movie camera. The camera pans up and down with the vertical motion of the cursor, left and right with horizontal motion. You will notice that the image on the screen shifts more radically than in the Camera option and that it is easy to "pan" away from the image so that it flies off the screen entirely.

"Distance" and Perspective

Another aspect of any camera-to-target relationship is the distance between the two. The "Distance" option moves the camera position in or out along the line of sight. It differs from "Zoom" in that it automatically creates a perspective view.

> Type "d" or select "Distance".

The distance option uses a slider bar just like the zoom option. However, since "Distance" turns perspective on and distances are interpreted differently in perspective viewing, your preview image may look very different from the way it appeared before you entered the option.

> Move the cursor back and forth and watch the image move along the lines of perspective.

> Move the slider to about 1.5x and press the pick button.

Your screen will resemble *Figure 13-40*. Notice the perspective effect and the perspective icon that replaces the UCS icon.

NOTE: If you enter the "Zoom" option while in a perspective view, you will see AutoCAD prompt for a "Lens length" rather than a zoom factor. In perspective, "DVIEW Zoom" operates like changing lenses on a camera to enlarge or reduce the field of vision. This is consistent with the photographic metaphor. We suggest you try it.

Saving 3D Views with VIEW

Once you are in perspective, you will find that your drawing capabilities are severely limited. Many commands will not work at all. Perspective is a presentation feature, not an editing or drawing feature. If you wish to do more drawing and editing, you will need to leave the perspective view and go back to the usual parallel projection. However, by using the VIEW command you can save all the

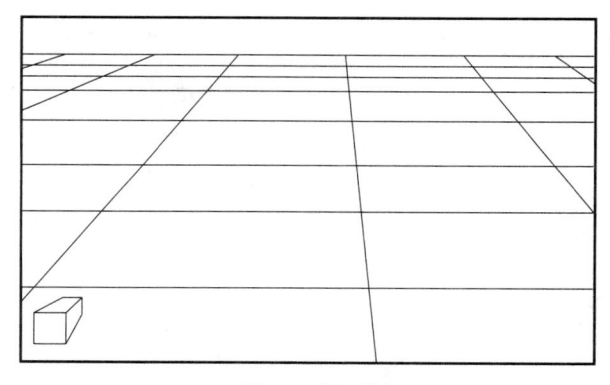

Figure 13-40

view adjustment work you have done so that you can come back to it at any time without going through DVIEW again. When you do, any editing or drawing done in the meantime will be included and adjusted to the defined view. For reference, here is the procedure for saving a view:

1. Type "view".
2. Type "s" or select "Save".
3. Type a name for the view.

Clipping Planes

We will explore one last feature of the DVIEW command. By using a "clipping" plane, we will temporarily remove part of the drawing.

> Type "cl" or select "CLip".

This option allows you to temporarily remove everything in front of or behind a specified plane. In a full 3D model of a house, for example, you can use this option to remove a wall and display the inside of a room.

AutoCAD prompts:

Back/Front/<Off>:

If "back" is chosen, everything behind the specified plane will be removed; if "front" is chosen, objects in front will be removed. We will use a front clipping plane.

> Type "f" or select "front".

AutoCAD places a horizontal slider bar at the top of the screen.

> Move the cursor all the way to the right.

This places the clipping plane completely behind the mesh, so that the entire image is clipped, leaving nothing but the horizon.

> Move the cursor slowly to the left.

Watch the image gradually appear as the clipping plane covers up less and less. Keep moving to the left until the whole image is visible. Notice that the clipping plane is perpendicular to the line of sight, parallel to the plane of the screen.

> Now move the cursor back to the right until you have an image similar to the one in *Figure 13-41*.

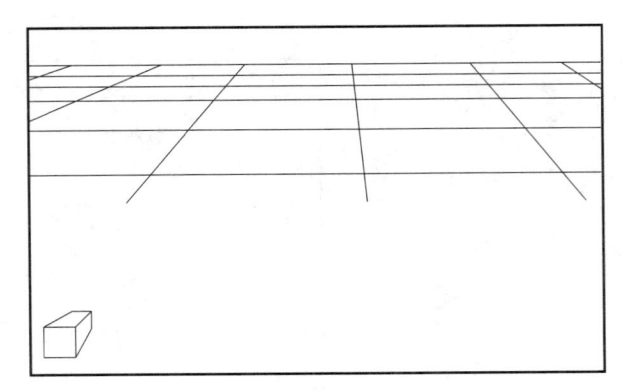

Figure 13-41

> Press the pick button to register the clipping plane position.

> Press Enter to exit the DVIEW command.

Your screen will be redrawn as shown in the figure.

Clipped images, like perspective views, can be saved using the VIEW command.

The Dview Hide Option

There is a "Hide" option within the DVIEW command that allows you to remove hidden lines from your preview image. This can help in visualizing the 3D object and as a preview of the HIDE command itself. Hidden lines are only removed temporarily. They will return as soon as you exit DVIEW.

Turning Off Perspective and Clipping Planes

It is extremely important to turn off perspective and clipping when you are through with them. With perspective on, you will be unable to execute most drawing functions. Try zooming, for example, and you will get a standard message:

** That command may not be invoked in a perspective view **

Clipping planes are somewhat less inhibiting, but remain in effect even as you change viewpoints. When you switch viewpoints the line of sight and viewing angle may change dramatically. However, the clipping plane will remain parallel to the plane of the screen and at the same "distance". This can yield some pretty strange results.

Both effects may be turned off by reentering the DVIEW command. The "Off" option of the first prompt will turn perspective off, while "CLip" has its own "Off" option. In either case, you can speed up the process by pressing Enter at the "Select objects:" prompt and ignoring AutoCAD's default preview image.

There are still quicker methods, however. For example, you usually will leave a perspective view in order to work in another 3D view or a plan view. You can go directly into these by entering the VPOINT or PLAN commands and specifying a new view.

VPOINT and PLAN will turn perspective off but not clipping planes. However, if you have saved any views you can restore them using the VIEW command. VIEW will remove clipping planes as well as perspective if they were not in effect when the view was defined.

In summary, you can use VIEW or DVIEW to remove clipping planes and perspective, VPOINT or PLAN to remove perspective only.

Tasks 9, 10, 11, and 12

The drawings that follow will give you a wide range of experience with surface models. *Drawing 13–1* is an exercise in recognizing and creating a variety of surfaces using only the REVSURF command and some simple outlines. *Drawings 13–2* and *13–3* are more difficult and make use of 3D faces and polygon meshes. *Drawing 13–4* is a very challenging 3D drawing requiring careful use of the UCS command and several polygon mesh commands.

DRAWING 13-1: REVSURF DESIGNS

The REVSURF command is fascinating and powerful. As you get familiar with it, you may find yourself identifying objects in the world that can be conceived as surfaces of revolution. To encourage this process, we have provided this page of 12 REVSURF objects and designs.

To complete the exercise, you will need only the PLINE and REVSURF commands. In the first six designs we have shown the path curves and axes of rotation used to create the design. In the other six you will be on your own.

Exact shapes and dimensions are not important in this exercise. Imagination is. When you have completed our designs, we encourage you to invent a number of your own.

Chap. 13

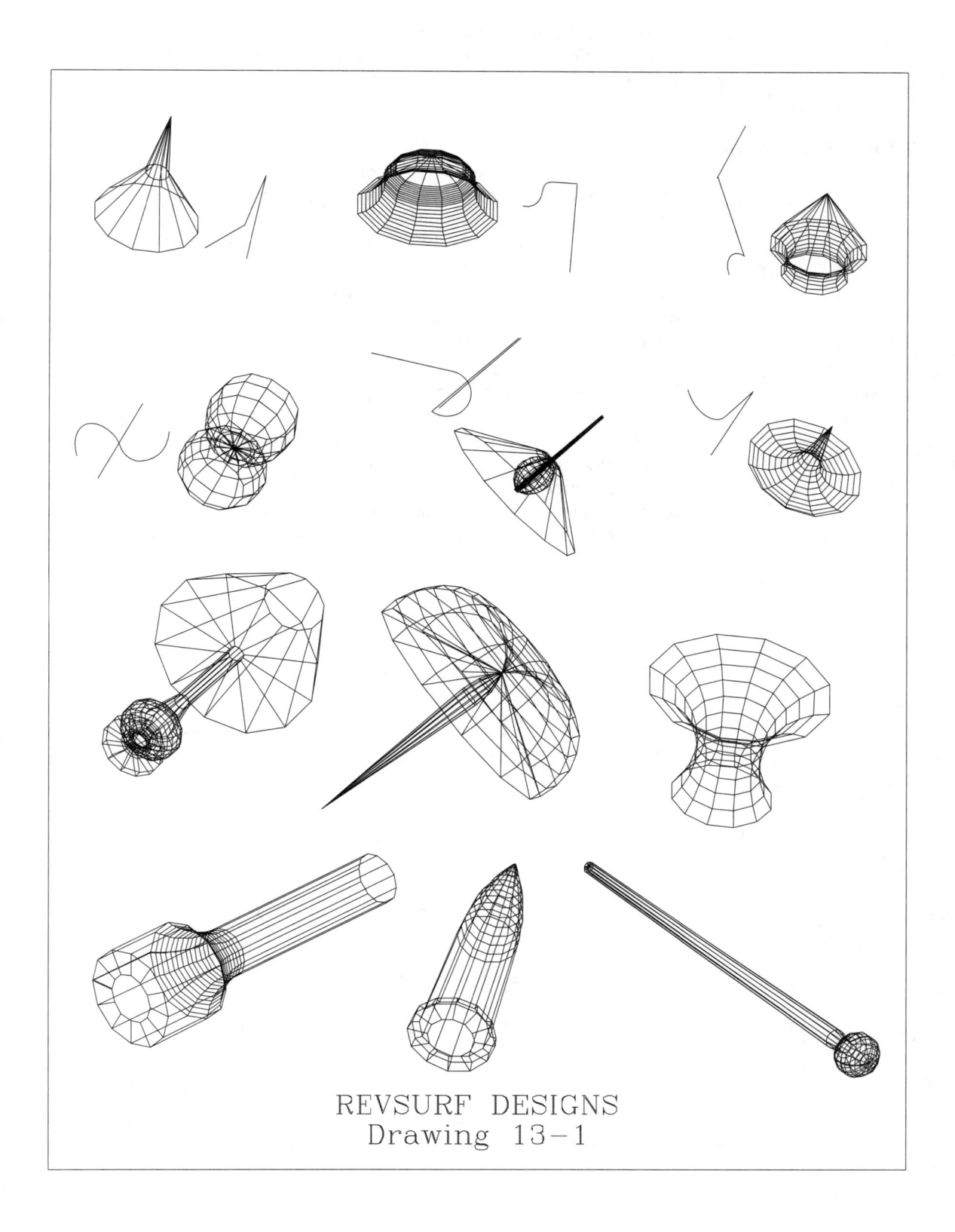

REVSURF DESIGNS
Drawing 13-1

DRAWING 13-2: PICNIC TABLE

This is a tricky drawing that must be done carefully. It requires efficient use of the UCS command along with a number of edit commands. In order to create an image that hides as shown in the reference, you must cover all surfaces with 3D faces.

DRAWING SUGGESTIONS

> Use a three-viewport configuration, with top (plan) and front views on the left and a 3D view on the right. Be sure to keep an eye on all viewports as you go, since it is quite likely that you will create some lines that look correct in one view but not in others.

> Use a separate layer for 3D faces, and add the faces as you go. This will save you from retracing your steps. Notice that the faces on the chamfered braces are drawn with one invisible line across the middle.

> We recommend that you start with the top of the table and work down. Placing the legs directly behind the chamfered braces can be tricky. One way to do this is to draw the legs even with the side of the table first (in a UCS with its XY plane flush with a side of the table), and then MOVE them back 1'-2".

> Save the angled braces for last. Once the leg braces are drawn, you can locate the angled braces by drawing a line from the midpoint of the small brace in the middle of the table top to the midpoint of the bottom of a leg brace. Then OFFSET this line 1" each way to create the two lower edges of one angled brace.

Chap. 13 **439**

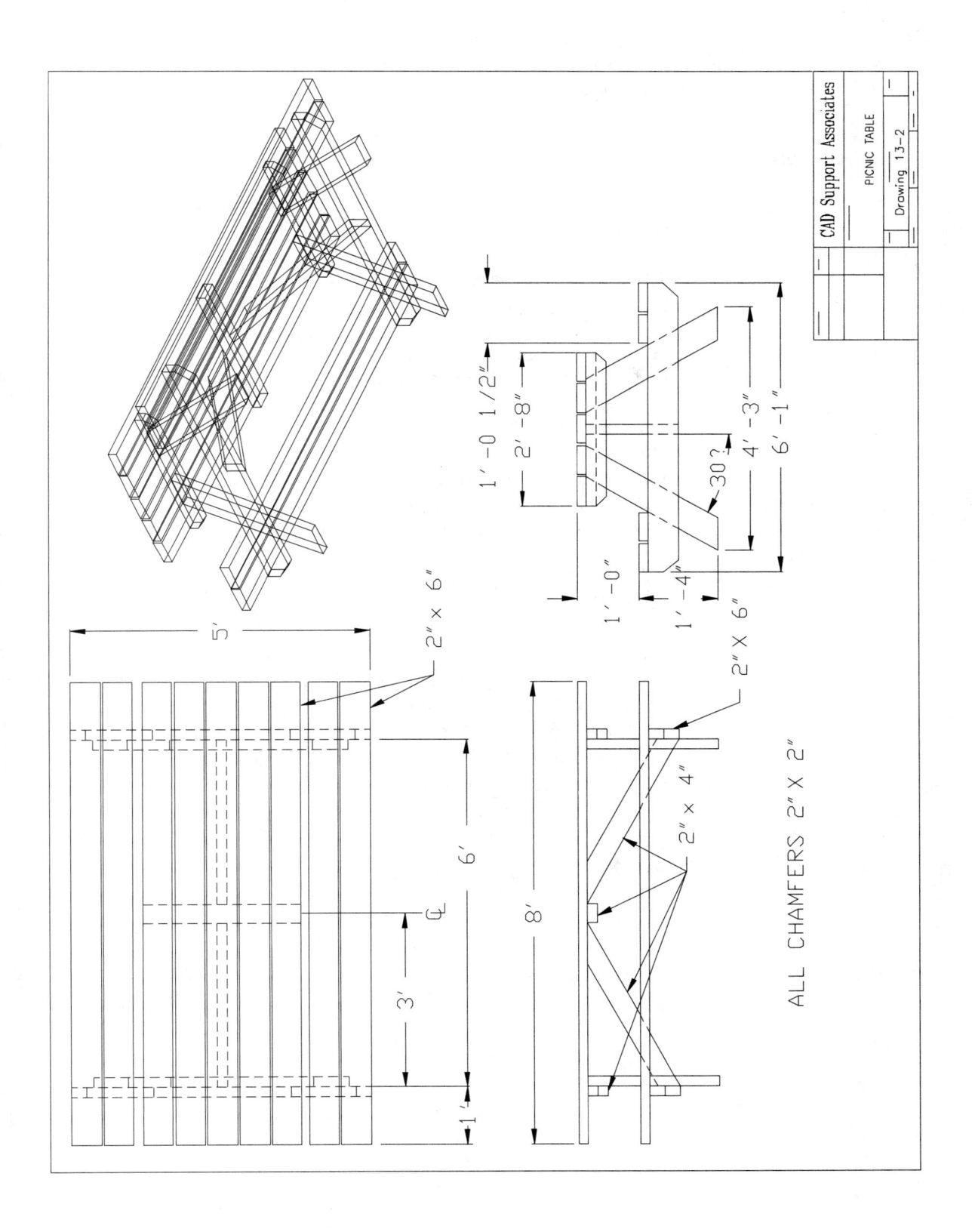

DRAWING 13-3: GLOBE

This drawing uses several of the 3D mesh commands. Some of the 3D construction is a little tricky, but you may be pleasantly surprised. Follow the suggestions and you will find that this one is easier than it looks.

DRAWING SUGGESTIONS

> Use a three-viewport configuration with top and front views on the left and a 3D view on the right.

> Begin with the base circles, drawing in the plan (top) view, then MOVE the circles into place along the z axis.

> MOVE the small inner circle up 12.25 to locate the top of the shaft. Draw the center line from the center of this circle to the top center of the base. Then COPY this line on itself and ROTATE the line and circle 23.5 degrees around the midpoint of the line to position the center of the shaft.

> OFFSET the shaft centerline .125. Later, you will TRIM a 4.00 diameter circle to this line. Then using the centerline of the shaft as the axis of rotation for a REVSURF will leave a hole in the middle of the globe for the shaft.

> Draw the 4.00, 4.75, and 5.38 circles and TRIM them to the vertical, 23.5 degree, and 46 degree lines as shown.

> With your UCS parallel to the front view, COPY the 4.75 and 5.38 circles +.25 and −.25 in the z direction to form the two sides of the globe support. ERASE the original circles.

> TABSURF the shaft.

> RULESURF the base circles. There will be three ruled surfaces to complete the base.

> REVSURF the top of the base, using a single line from a quadrant to the center for a path curve and the vertical centerline for the axis.

> RULESURF the globe support. This will require four ruled surfaces.

> REVSURF the globe.

> Freeze all nonsurface lines before HIDEing.

Chap. 13

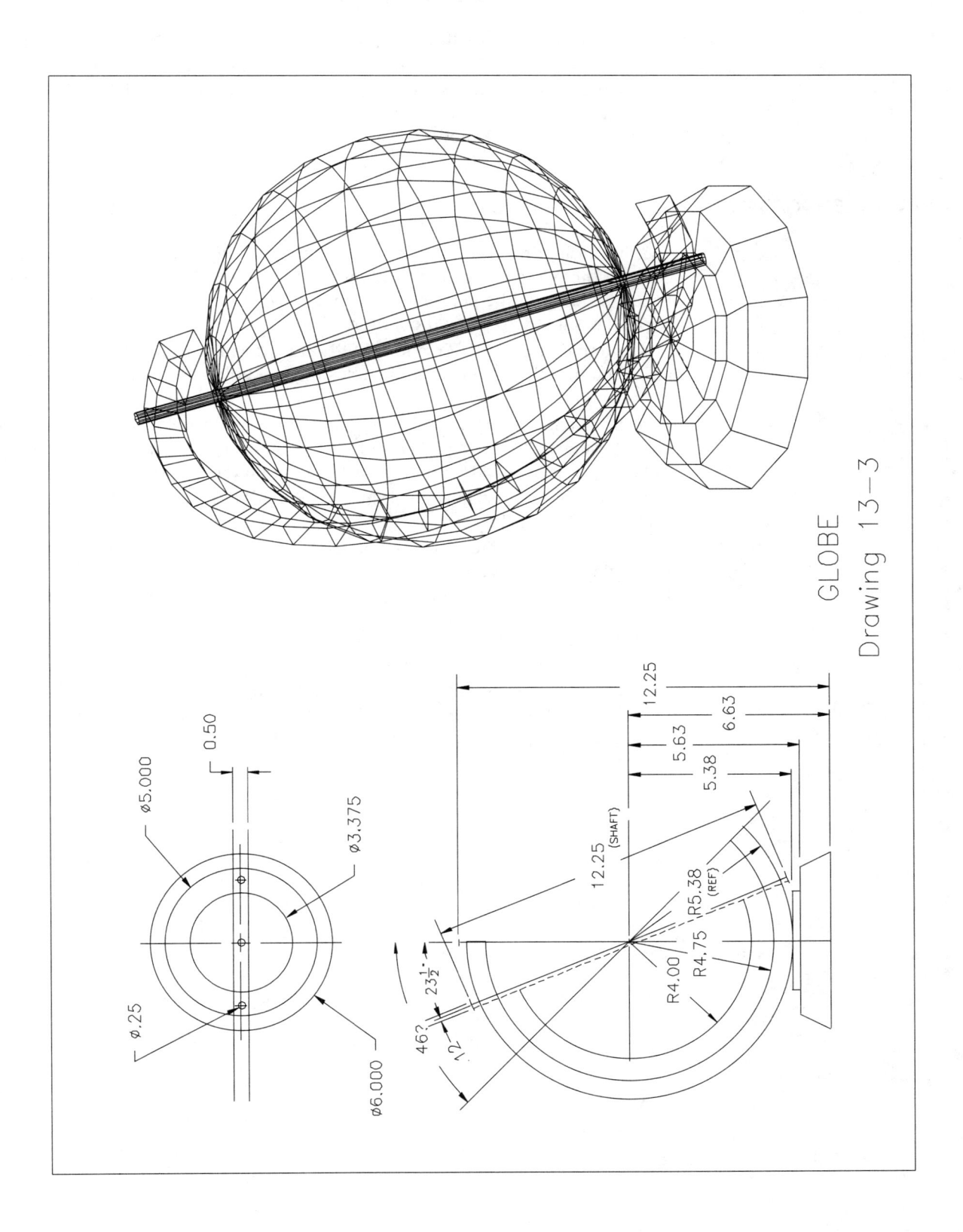

GLOBE
Drawing 13-3

DRAWING 13-4: NOZZLE

This is a tough drawing that will give you a real 3D workout. You will need to define numerous UCSs as you go. Your goal should be to create the two views A and B. Dimensioning is not part of the exercise. The dimensioned figure is not a complete wire frame, but a guide to show you the abstract relationships necessary to complete the surface model.

DRAWING SUGGESTIONS

> We began in a front, right, top view. This puts the main centerline of the nozzle in the XY plane of the WCS, while the circles that show the outlines of the nozzle would be perpendicular to it. When we were done, we rotated the objects slightly to show them more clearly.

> Make ample use of COPY and OFFSET in drawing the circles and centerlines of the nozzle, the hexes and circles of the knob, and the polyline curve path of the nozzle.

> The circle and centerline at the right end of the 45 degree angle can be constructed using a COPY and ROTATE of the circle and centerline just in front of the angle. This must be done in a UCS parallel to the WCS.

> The curve in the nozzle is a −45 degree REVSURF around the centerline 1.00 to the right of the turn.

> The two darkened lines show the path curves used with REVSURF to draw the nozzle and the knob. Construct lines first and then go over them with PLINE or 3DPOLY. 3DPOLY is similar to PLINE, but it uses 3D points instead of 2D points and has no option to draw arcs. In general, 3D polylines are more flexible and can be drawn at times when the current UCS would not allow the construction of a 2D polyline.

> The centerline through the knob (along the arrow) runs perpendicular to the polyline outline of the nozzle. Use a PERpendicular osnap to construct the centerline and then define UCSs in relation to the centerline to construct the knob.

Chap. 13

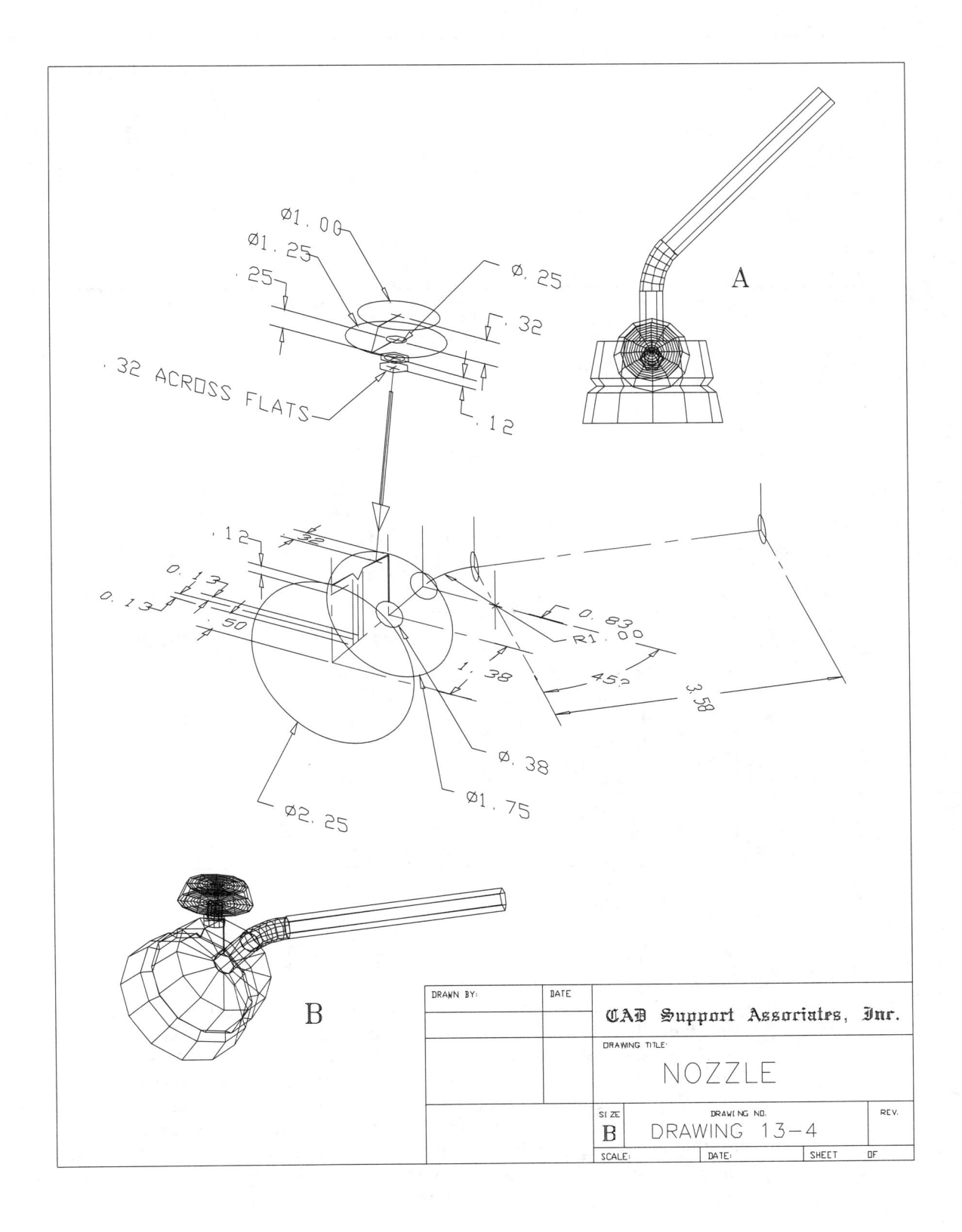

CHAPTER 14

COMMANDS

SOLIDS	MODIFY	RENDER
BOX	INTERSECT	LIGHT
CYLINDER	SUBTRACT	MATLIB
EXTRUDE	UNION	RENDER
REVOLVE		RMAT
SECTION		SCENE
SLICE		SHADE
SPHERE		
WEDGE		

OVERVIEW

In previous versions of AutoCAD, solid modeling was an extension to the standard program. It involved the add-on program AME (Advanced Modeling Extension). In Release 13 solid modeling is a built-in component of AutoCAD for the first time. Solid Modeling with Release 13 is in many ways easier than either wireframe or surface modeling. In solid modeling you can draw a complete solid object by picking a few points, in a fraction of the time it would take to draw line by line, surface by surface. Furthermore, once the object is drawn it contains far more information than a wireframe or surface model. In this chapter you will draw a simple solid model using several solid drawing and editing commands.

TASKS

1. Create a solid box using BOX and a wedge using WEDGE.
2. Create a composite solid from the UNION of the box and the wedge.
3. Create objects above the XY plane using ELEVATION.
4. Create composite solids by subtraction, using SUBTRACT.
5. Chamfer and Fillet solid objects.
6. Create solids through extrusion using EXTRUDE.
7. Create 2D region entities.
8. Create solids by revolving 2D entities using REVOLVE.
9. Create solid cutaway views with SLICE.
10. Create sections with SECTION.
11. SHADE solid models.
12. RENDER solid models.
13. Do Drawing 14–1 ("Bushing Mount").
14. Do Drawing 14–2 ("Link Mount").
15. Do Drawing 14–3 ("3D Assembly").
16. Do Drawing 14–4 ("Tapered Bushing").
17. Do Drawing 14–5 ("Pivot Mount").

Task 1: Creating Solid BOXes and WEDGEs

Procedure

1. Enter BOX or WEDGE.
2. Specify corner point and distances in the XY plane of the current UCS (or define a base plane first and then specify points).
3. Specify a height.

Discussion. Solid modeling requires a somewhat different type of thinking than any of the drawings you have done so far. Instead of focusing on lines and arcs, edges and surfaces, you will need to imagine how 3D objects might be pieced together by combining or subtracting basic solid shapes, called "primitives." This building block process is called constructive solid geometry and includes joining, subtracting, and intersecting operations. A simple washer, for example, could be made by cutting a small cylinder out of the middle of a larger cylinder. In Auto-CAD solid modeling you can begin with a flat outer cylinder, then draw an inner cylinder with a smaller radius centered at the same point, and then subtract the inner cylinder from the outer, as illustrated in *Figure 14-1*.

This operation, which uses the SUBTRACT command, is the equivalent of cutting a hole, and is one of three Boolean operations (after the mathematician George Booles) used to create composite solids. UNION joins two solids to make a new solid, and INTERSECT creates a composite solid in the space where two solids overlap (see *Figure 14-1*).

In this chapter you will create a composite solid from the union and subtraction of several solid primitives. Primitives are 3D solid building blocks—boxes, cones, cylinders, spheres, wedges, and torus. They all are regularly shaped and can be defined by specifying a few points and distances.

> To begin this task, go into a right front view (315 degrees from *x* and 45 degrees from XY). Notice that this is a slightly higher viewing angle than the southeast isometric view we used in the previous two chapters. If you are unfamiliar with the use of the 3D Viewpoint Rotate dialogue box, use the following procedure:

CYLINDER #1

CYLINDER #2

UNION

SUBTRACTION

INTERSECTION

Figure 14-1

Figure 14-2

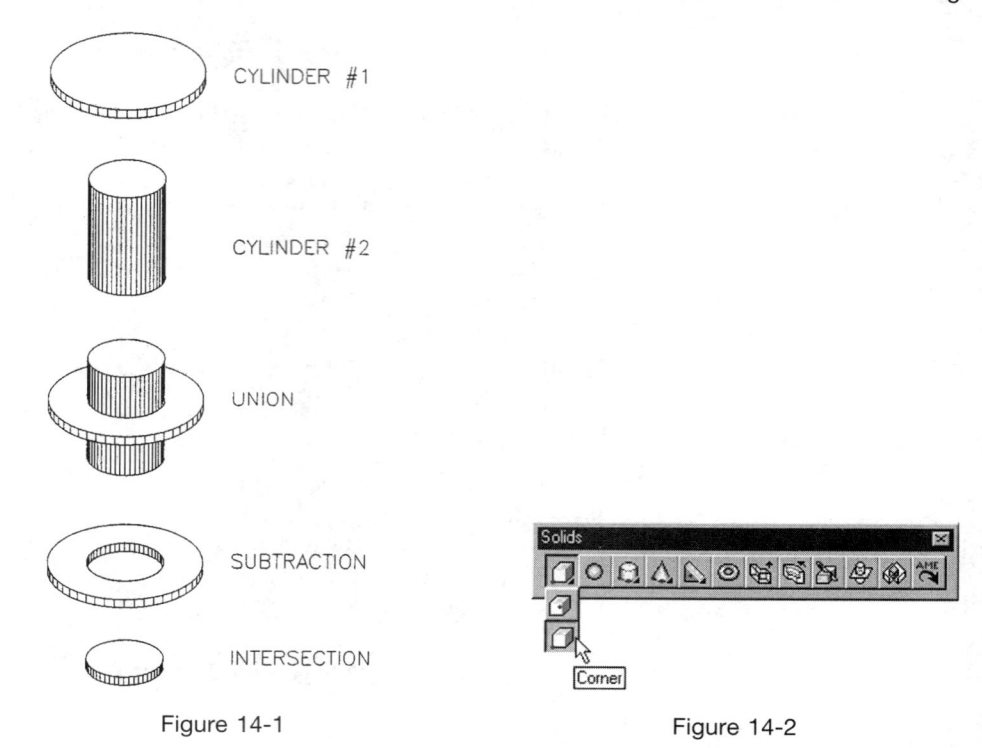

1. Type "vpoint".
2. Type "r" for "Rotate".
3. Type "315" for the angle in XY plane from *x* axis.
4. Type "45" for the angle from XY plane.

> Type "box" or select the Box Corner tool from the Box flyout on the Solid toolbar, as illustrated in *Figure 14-2*.

In the command area you will see the following prompt:

Center/<Corner of box> <0,0,0>:

"Center" allows you to begin defining a box by specifying its center point. Here we will use the "Corner of box" option to begin drawing a box in the baseplane of the current UCS. We will draw a box with a length of 4, width of 3, and height of 1.5.

> Pick a corner point similar to point 1 in *Figure 14-3*.

AutoCAD will prompt:

Cube/Length/<Other corner>:

With the "Cube" option you can draw a box with equal length, width, and height simply by specifying one distance. The "Length" option will allow you to specify length, width, and height separately. If you have simple measurements that fall on snap points, as we do, you can show the length and width at the same time by picking the other corner of the base of the box (the default method).

> Move the cross hairs over 4 in the *x* direction and up 3 in the *y* direction to point 2, as shown in the figure.

Notice that "length" is measured along the *x* axis, and "width" is measured along the *y* axis.

Chap. 14
447

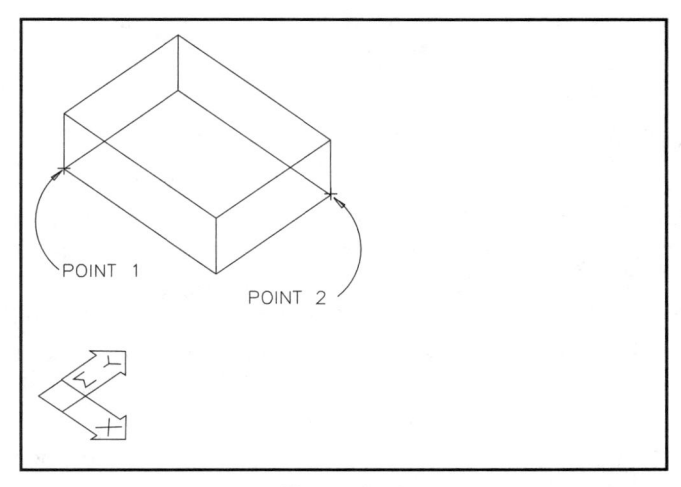

Figure 14-3

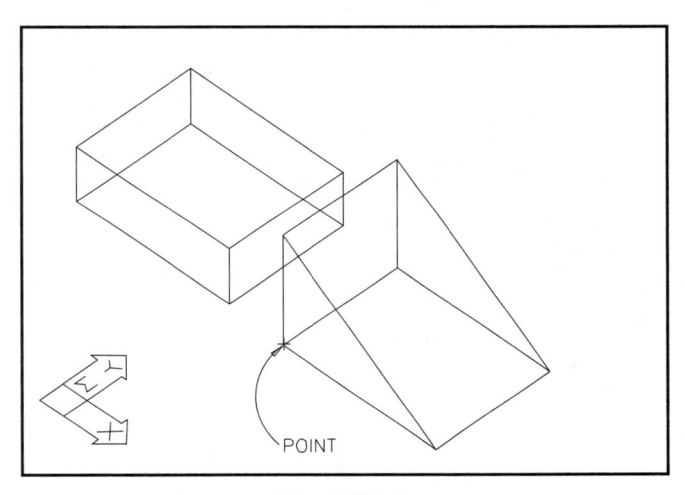

Figure 14-4

> Pick point 2 as shown.

Now AutoCAD prompts for a height. "Height" is measured along the z axis. As usual, you cannot pick points in the z direction unless you have objects to snap to. Instead, you can type a value or show a value by picking two points in the XY plane.

> Type "1.5" or pick two points 1.5 units apart.

Your screen should resemble *Figure 14-3*.

Next we will create a solid wedge. The process will be exactly the same, but there will be no "Cube" option.

> Type "Wedge" or select the Wedge Corner tool from the Wedge flyout on the Solids toolbar.

AutoCAD prompts:

Center/<Corner of wedge> <0,0,0>:

> Pick a corner point as shown in *Figure 14-4*. Precise placement is not significant.

As in the BOX command, AutoCAD prompts for a cube, length, or the other corner:

Cube/Length/<other corner>:

This time let's use the length and width option.
> Type "L".
The rubber band will disappear and AutoCAD will prompt for a length, which you can define by typing a number or showing two points.
> Type "4" or show a length of 4.00 units.
AutoCAD now prompts for a width. Remember, length is measured in the *x* direction, and width is measured in the *y* direction.
> Type "3" or show a width of 3 units.
AutoCAD prompts for a height.
> Type "3" or show a distance of 3 units.
AutoCAD will draw the wedge you have specified. Notice that a wedge is simply half a box, cut along a diagonal plane.

Your screen should resemble *Figure 14-4*. Although the box and the wedge appear as wireframe objects, they are really quite different, as you will find. In Task 2 we will join the box and the wedge to form a new composite solid.

Task 2: Creating the UNION of Two Solids

Procedure

1. Type "Union" or select the Union tool from the Explode flyout on the Modify toolbar.
2. Select solid objects to join. (Steps 1 and 2 may be reversed if noun/verb selection is enabled.)

Discussion. Unions are simple to create and usually easy to visualize. The union of two objects is an object that includes all points that are on either of the objects. Unions can be performed just as easily on more than two objects. The union of objects can be created even if the objects have no points in common (i.e., they do not touch or overlap).
Here we will move the wedge adjacent to the box before entering the UNION command.

> Select the wedge.
> Pick the lower left grip on the wedge and then the lower right corner of the box to move the wedge next to the box as shown in *Figure 14-5*.
Notice that "stretch" in grip edit works like "move" for solid objects. This is also true for the STRETCH command when used on solid objects.

There are still two distinct solids on the screen; with UNION we can join them.

> Type "Union" or select the Union tool from the Explode flyout on the Modify menu, as shown in *Figure 14-6*.
Now AutoCAD will prompt you to select objects.
> Point or use a crossing box to select both objects.
> Press Enter to end object selection.

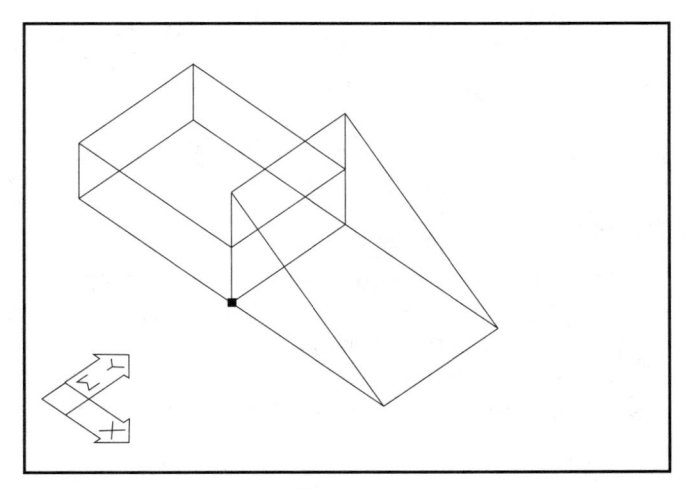

Figure 14-5

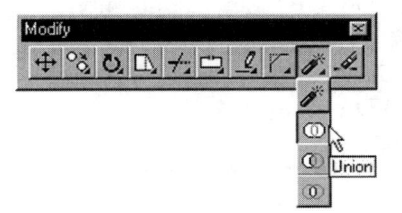

Figure 14-6

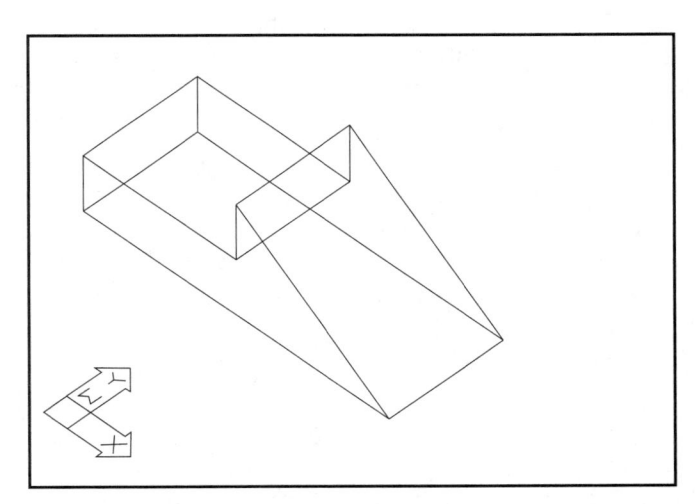

Figure 14-7

Your screen should resemble *Figure 14-7*.

NOTE: In practice it is efficient to reduce the number of union, subtraction, and intersection procedures used in creating solids. This can save time and make your solid model more memory-efficient. In this exercise, however, we are building our model in a step-by-step fashion because it makes a better learning sequence. More efficient sequencing will be suggested for the drawings at the end of the chapter.

Task 3: Working Above the XY Plane Using Elevation

Procedure

1. Type "Elev".
2. Enter elevation and thickness values.

Discussion. In this task we will draw two more solid primitives while demonstrating the use of elevation to position objects above the XY plane of the current UCS. Changing elevations simply adds a single Z value to all new objects as they are drawn and can be used as an alternative to creating a new UCS. With an elevation of 1.00, for example, new objects would be drawn 1.00 above the XY plane of the current UCS. You can also use a thickness setting to create 3D objects, but these will be created as mesh objects, not solids.

> To begin this task you should have the union of a wedge and a box on your screen, as shown previously in *Figure 14-7*.

We will begin by drawing a third box positioned on top of the first box. Later we will move it, copy it, and subtract it to form a slot in the composite object.

> Type "Elev".

AutoCAD prompts:

New current elevation <0.00>:

The elevation is always set at 0 unless you specify otherwise.
> Type "1.5"

This will bring the elevation up 1.5 out of the XY plane, putting it even with the top of the first box you drew.

AutoCAD now prompts for a new current thickness. Thickness does not apply to solid objects because they have their own thickness.
> Press Enter to retain 0.00 thickness.

This brings us back to the command prompt. If you watch closely you will see that the grid has also moved up into the new plane of elevation.
> Type "Box" or select the Box Corner tool from the Solids toolbar.
> Pick the upper left corner of the box, point 1 in *Figure 14-8*.

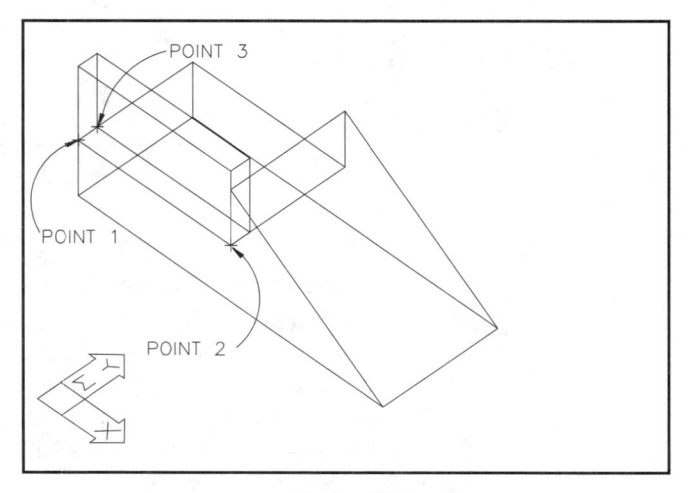

Figure 14-8

> Type "L" to initiate the "length" option.
> Type "4" or pick two points (points 1 and 2 in the figure) to show a length of 4 units.
> Type ".5" or pick two points (points 1 and 3) to show a width of 0.5 units.
> Type "2" or pick two points to show a height of 2 units.

Your screen should resemble *Figure 14-8*. Notice how you were able to pick points on top of the box because of the change in elevation just as if we had changed coordinate systems. Before going on you should return to 0.00 elevation.

> Type "elev".
> Type "0".
> Press Enter to retain 0.00 thickness.

Task 4: Creating Composite Solids with SUBTRACT

Procedure

1. Create solid objects to subtract and objects to be subtracted from.
2. Position objects relative to each other.
3. Type "Subtract" or select the Subtract tool from the Explode flyout on the Modify toolbar.
4. Select objects to be subtracted from.
5. Select objects to subtract.

Discussion. SUBTRACT is the logical opposite of UNION. In a union operation, all the points contained in one solid are added to the points contained in other solids to form a new composite solid. In a subtraction, all points in the solids to be subtracted are removed from the source solid. A new composite solid is defined by what is left.

In this exercise, we will use the objects already on your screen to create a slotted wedge. First we need to move the thin upper box into place, then we will copy it to create a longer slot, and finally we will subtract it from the union of the box and wedge.

> To begin this task, you should have the composite box and wedge solid and the thin box on your screen, as shown in *Figure 14-8*.

Before subtracting, we will move the box to the position shown in *Figure 14-9*.

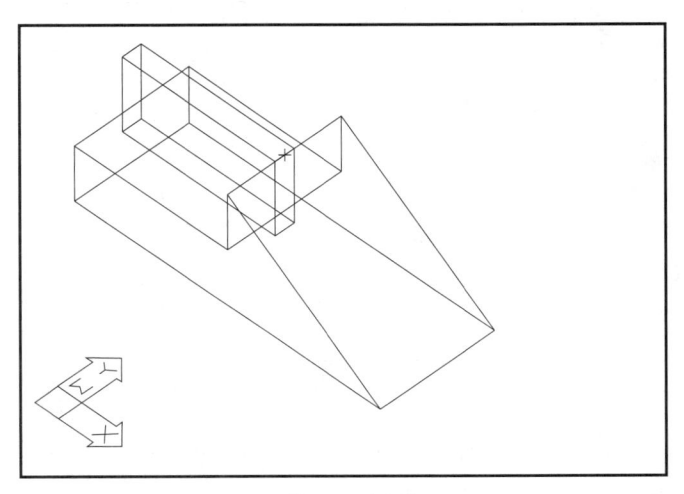

Figure 14-9

> Type "m" or select the Move tool from the Modify toolbar.

> Select the narrow box drawn in the last task.

> Press Enter to end object selection.

> At the "Base point or displacement" prompt use a midpoint object snap to pick the midpoint of the top right edge of the narrow box. (If you have trouble making this work you may need to go in to the "Running Object Snap..." dialogue box under Options and use a smaller aperture setting.)

> At the "Second point of displacement" prompt use another midpoint object snap to pick the top edge of the wedge, as shown in *Figure 14-9*.

This will move the narrow box over and down. If you were to perform the subtraction now, you would create a slot but it would only run through the box, not the wedge. We can create a longer slot by copying the narrow box over to the right using grips.

> Select the narrow box.

> Pick any of the eight grips.

> If ortho is off, turn it on (F8).

Now if you move the cursor in the *x* direction you will see a copy of the box moving with you. Solids cannot be stretched, so we must make a copy to lengthen the slot.

> Type "c" or select "Copy".

> Move the cursor between 2.00 and 4.00 units to the right and press the pick button.

If you don't go far enough the slot will be too short. If you go past 4.00, the slot will be interrupted by the space between the box and the copy.

> Press Enter to leave the grip edit mode.

Your screen will resemble *Figure 14-10*.

> Type "Subtract" or select the Subtract tool from the Explode flyout on the Modify toolbar, as shown in *Figure 14-11*.

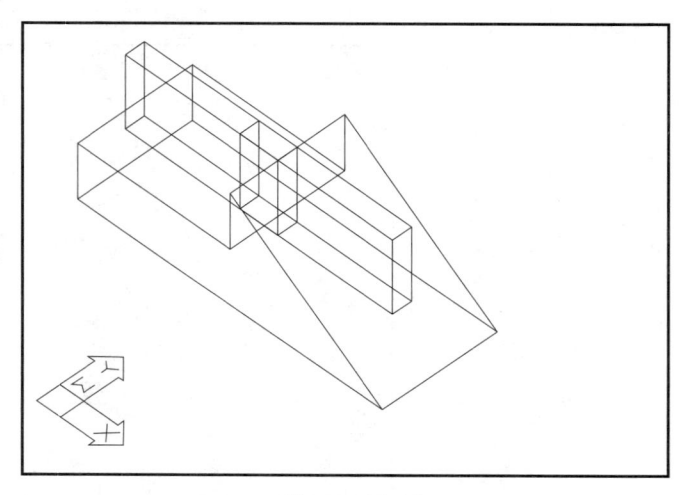

Figure 14-10

Chap. 14 **453**

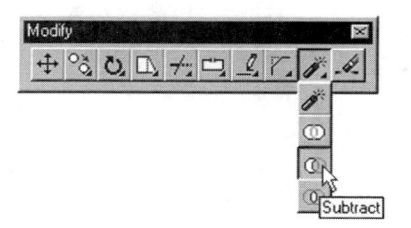

Figure 14-11

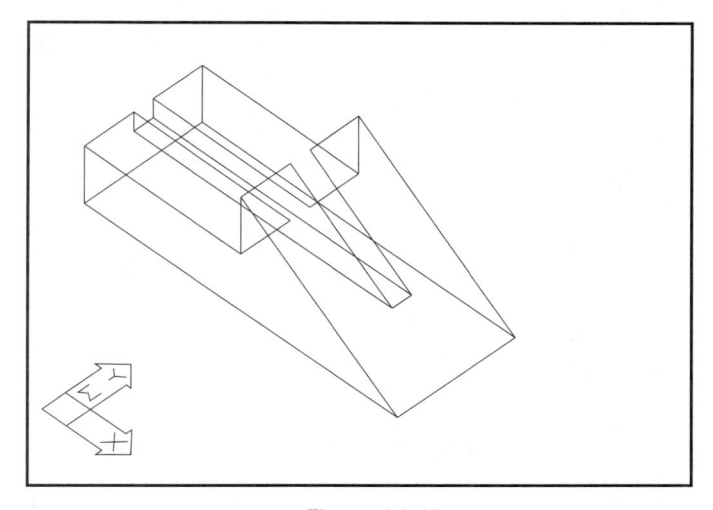

Figure 14-12

AutoCAD asks you to select objects to subtract from first (you may have to press F2 to see this in the text window):

> Select solids and regions to subtract from ...
> Select objects:

> Pick the composite of the box and the wedge.
> Press Enter to end selection of source objects.

AutoCAD prompts for objects to be subtracted:

> Select solids and regions to subtract...
> Select objects:

> Pick the two narrow boxes.
> Press Enter to end selection.

Your screen will resemble *Figure 14-12*.

Next we will draw a solid cylinder, move it into place and subtract it to form a hole at the right end of the slot.

> Type "Cylinder" or select the Center tool from the Cylinder flyout on the Solids toolbar, as shown in *Figure 14-13*.

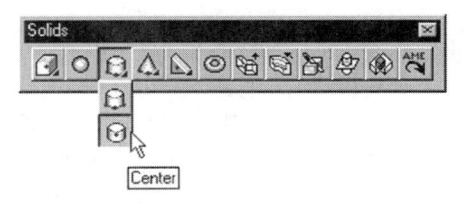

Figure 14-13

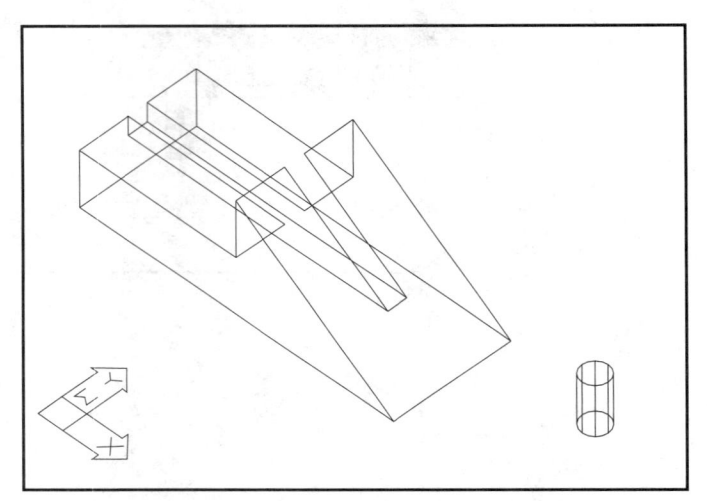

Figure 14-14

AutoCAD prompts:

Elliptical/<Center point> <0,0,0>:

> Pick any convenient center point away from the composite solid.

It does not matter where the cylinder is drawn since we are going to move it to the end of the slot using a midpoint object snap.

In order to create a hole the same width as the slot we need a diameter of 0.5, or a radius of 0.25.

> Type ".25" for the radius value.

The cylinder must be made high enough to reach through the slot. Any height over 1.00 will do.

> Type "1" for the height.

The cylinder will be drawn as shown in *Figure 14-14* except that your cylinder will probably have only four vertical lines (they will actually look like two lines because they hide each other). The density of lines displayed by AutoCAD to represent curved solid surfaces is controlled by a variable called "Isolines". We will change yours to show eight lines.

> Type "isolines".

AutoCAD prompts:

New value for ISOLINES <4>:

> Type "8".
> Type "Regen".

Next we will move the cylinder to the end of the slot using a grip edit and a midpoint object snap.

> Select the cylinder.

There will be a grip at the top and bottom centers of the cylinder. We want to move the top center to the midpoint of the end of the wedge.

> Select the top center grip on the cylinder.
> Use a midpoint object snap to move the cylinder to the end of the slot as shown in *Figure 14-15*.

Chap. 14

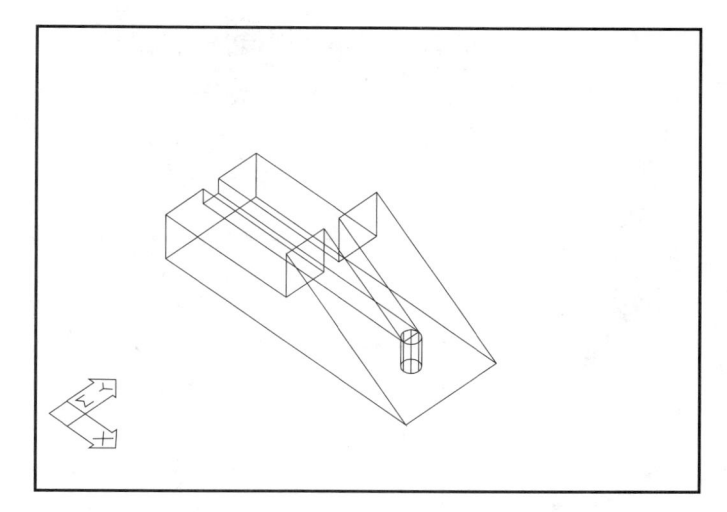

Figure 14-15

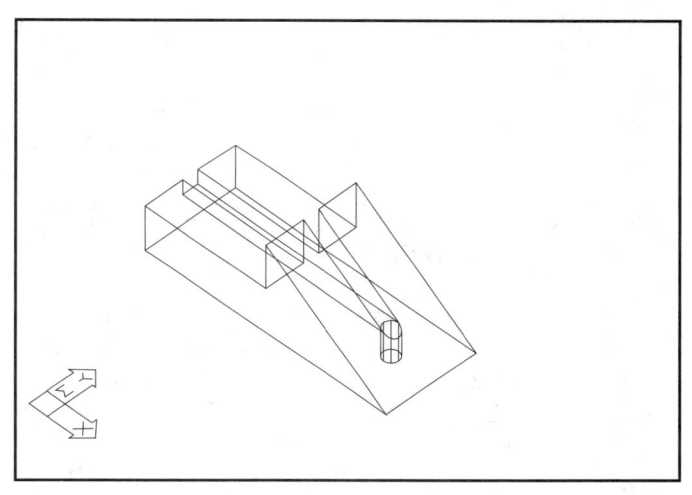

Figure 14-16

Now it's time to subtract.
> Type "Subtract" or select the Subtract tool from the Modify toolbar.
> Select the composite object.
> Press Enter to end object selection.
> Select the cylinder.
> Press Enter to end object selection.
   Your screen will resemble *Figure 14-16*.

Task 5: Creating Chamfers and Fillets on Solid Objects

Procedure

1. Type "Chamfer" or select the Chamfer tool from the Modify toolbar.
2. Pick a base surface.
3. Press Enter or type "n" to select the next surface.
4. Enter chamfer distances.

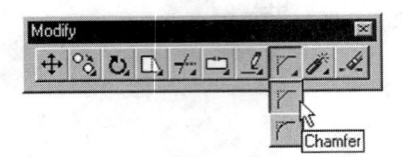

Figure 14-17

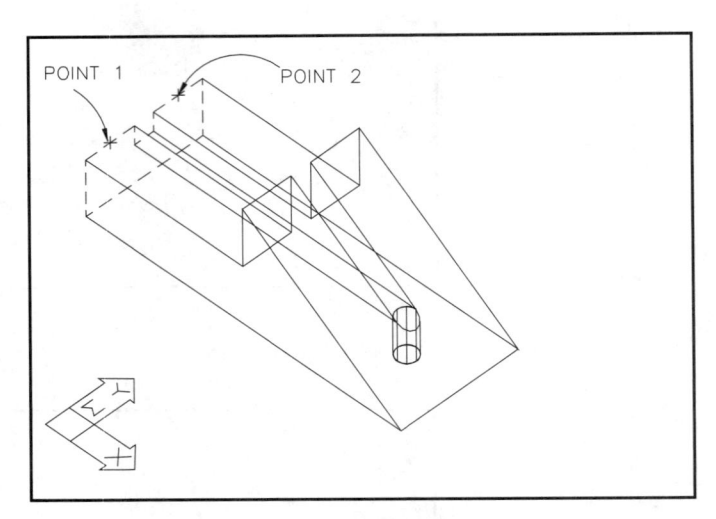

Figure 14-18

5. Pick edges to be chamfered.
6. Press Enter to end object selection.

Discussion. Constructing chamfers and fillets on solids is simple, but the language of the prompts can cause confusion. There is ambiguity in the selection of edges and surfaces to be modified, but once you catch on you will have no difficulty. We will begin by putting a chamfer on the top left of the model.

> To begin this task you should have the solid model shown in *Figure 14-16* on your screen.
> Type "Chamfer" or select the Chamfer tool from the Modify toolbar, as shown in *Figure 14-17*.

The first chamfer prompt is the same as always:

(TRIM mode) Current chamfer Dist1 = 0.00, Dist2 = 0.00
Polyline/Distance/Angel/Trim/Method/<Select first line>:

> Select point 1, as shown in *Figure 14-18*.
AutoCAD highlights the left surface and prompts:

Select base surface:
Next/<OK>:

We are constructing a chamfer on the left surface of the object. However, chamfers and fillets happen along edges that are common to two surfaces. What is a "base surface" in relation to a chamfered edge? Actually it refers to either of the two faces that meet at the edge where the chamfer will be. As long as you pick this edge you are bound to select one of these two surfaces and either will do. Which of the two surfaces is the "base surface" and which the "adjacent surface" will not matter until you enter the chamfer distances, and then only if the distances are unequal. However, AutoCAD allows you to switch to the other surface that shares this edge, by typing "n" for the "Next" option.

> Press Enter.

AutoCAD prompts:

Enter base surface distance <0.00>:

> Type ".5" for the base surface distance.

Now AutoCAD prompts:

Enter other surface distance <0.50>:

Now you can see the significance of "base surface." The chamfer will be created with the first distance on the base surface side and the second distance on the other surface side. If the chamfer is symmetrical it will not matter which is which.

> Type ".25" for the other base surface distance.

This will construct a chamfer that cuts .5 down into the left side and .25 back along the top side.

Now AutoCAD prompts for the edge or edges to be chamferred.

Loop/<Select edge>:

"Loop" will construct chamfers on all edges of the chosen base surface. Selecting edges will allow you to place them only on the selected edges. You will have no difficulty selecting edges if you pick the edge you wish to chamfer again. The only difference is that you will need to pick twice, once on each side of the slot.

> Pick the top left edge of the model, to one side of the slot (point 1 in *Figure 14-18* again).

> Pick the same edge again, but on the other side of the slot (point 2 in *Figure 14-18*).

> Press Enter to end edge selection.

Your screen will resemble *Figure 14-19*.

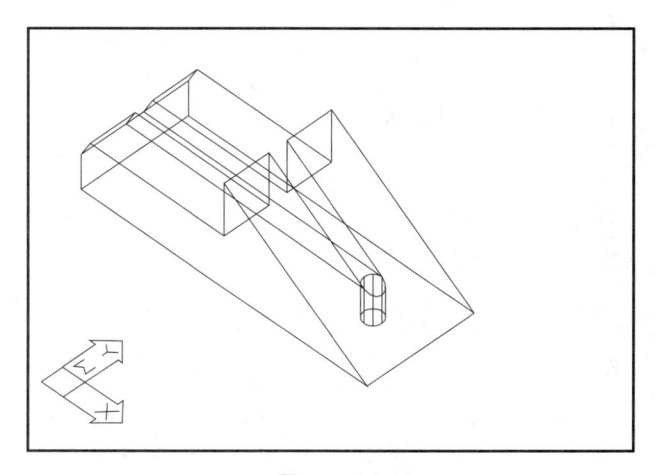

Figure 14-19

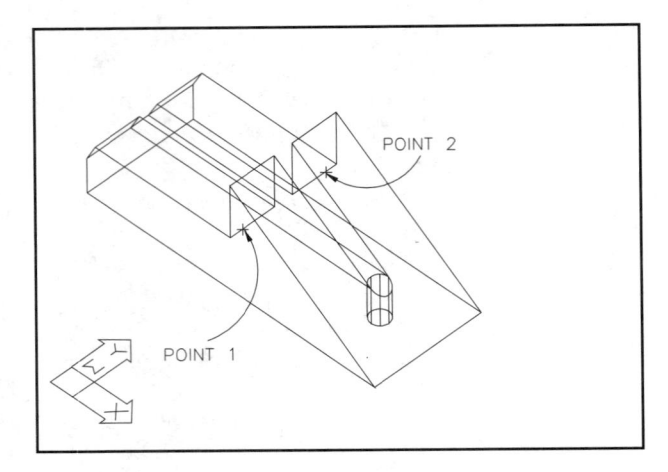

Figure 14-20

Creating Fillets

The procedure for creating solid fillets is simpler. There is one less step since there is no need to differentiate between base and other surfaces in a fillet.

> Type "Fillet" or select the Fillet tool from the Chamfer flyout on the Modify toolbar.
> Pick the edge where the box and the wedge meet, point 1 in *Figure 14-20*.

The prompt that follows is:

Chain/Radius/<Select edge>:
Enter radius:

"Chain" will allow you to fillet around all the edges of one side of a solid object at once. For our purposes we do not want a chain. Instead we want to select the two edges on either side of the slot. But first we need to enter the fillet radius for the edge we have already selected.
> Type ".5".

You will see this prompt again:

Chain/Radius/<Select edge>:

> Pick the same edge on the other side of the slot, point 2 in *Figure 14-20*.
The prompt will repeat in order to allow you to select more edges to fillet.
> Press Enter to end selection of edges.
Your screen will resemble *Figure 14-21*.

Before proceeding, save the composite wedge as a block so that you can insert it later when we use it to explore shading and rendering.

> Type "Block" or select the Block tool from the Draw toolbar.
> Select the composite wedge.
> Press Enter to end object selection.
> Select an insertion base point, any corner will do.
When the block definition is complete the wedge will disappear from the screen.

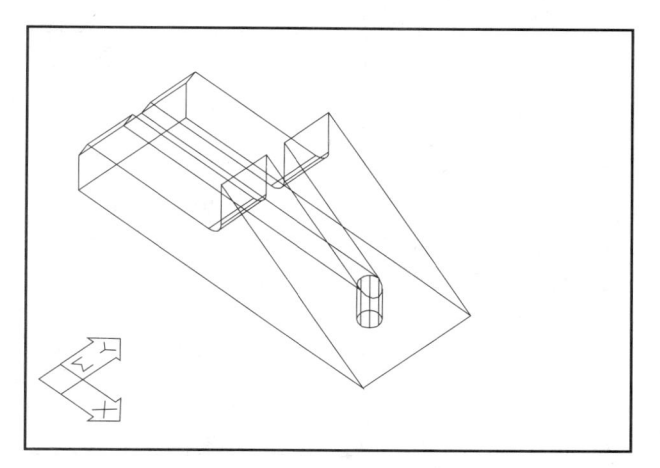

Figure 14-21

Task 6: Creating Solid Objects with EXTRUDE

Procedure

1. Create a polyline, circle, or region shape in two dimensions.
2. Type "Extrude".
3. Select objects.
4. Specify an extrusion height.
5. Specify an extrusion taper angle.

Discussion. Release 13 includes two additional ways to create solid objects. First, using the EXTRUDE command, simple 2D polylines and regions can be "extruded." That is, the 2D shape can be built up or repeated along a linear path stretching up or down from the plane in which it is drawn. Second, using REVOLVE, 2D polylines and regions can be revolved around an axis along a circular or semicircular path. The REVOLVE command is very similar to REVSURF, but it creates a solid rather than a surface model.

In this task we will draw a simple polyline shape and extrude it to create a solid. In the next task we will begin working with regions.

> To begin this task, your screen should be clear of all objects left from the previous task.
> Draw a 2.00 by 4.00 polyline rectangle as shown in *Figure 14-22*. Be sure to use PLINE to create a 2D polyline. 3DPOLY, which draws 3D polylines, will not work with EXTRUDE.
> Type "Extrude".

AutoCAD will prompt you to select objects. Only regions, polylines, and circles can be extruded.

> Select the rectangle.
> Press Enter to end object selection.

AutoCAD prompts:

Path/<Height of extrusion>:

The "Path" option is a powerful feature that allows you to create an extrusion along any pathway in the *z* direction. As in the TABSURF command, you need a line or polyline to serve as a pathway. A solid may then

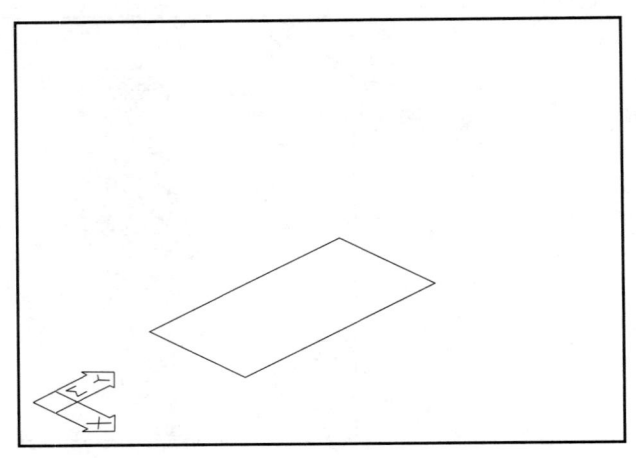

Figure 14-22

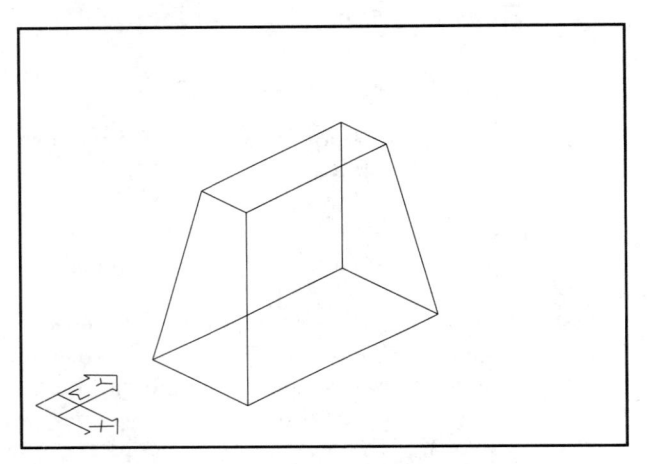

Figure 14-23

be created by essentially repeating the 2D object(s) at every point along the selected path.

If you use the default "Height of extrusion" option, the extrusion will be measured straight up into the z direction (or down if you enter a negative number).

> Type "3" or show a distance of 3.00 units (distance may be shown in the XY plane).

AutoCAD prompts:

Extrusion taper angle <0>:

This prompt gives you the opportunity to create a tapered extrusion by specifying an angle. This will be an angle between the z axis and the edge of the extruded object.

> Type "10".

Your screen should resemble *Figure 14-23*. Be aware that if your taper angle is too large, edges may meet before the specified height is reached. In the case of an extrusion with a rectangular base, this would result in a prism, with a ridge at the top rather than a smaller rectangle.

The extruded solid you have just created will function exactly like the solid objects created earlier. It can be used in union, subtraction, and intersection with other solids to create complex solid objects.

In the next task we will explore solid regions.

Task 7: Creating 2D Region Entities

Procedure

1. Draw 2D polyline shapes.
2. Type "Region" or select the Region tool from the Polygon flyout on the Draw toolbar.

Discussion. Regions are the 2D equivalent of 3D solids. They can be combined through union, subtraction, and intersection using the same commands used with solids. Regions are similar to faces in that they cover 2D spaces. Like polylines, they can be extruded to form 3D solids.

In this task we will create a simple composite region from two polyline rectangles. Individual regions are created using the REGION command on previously drawn polylines.

> To begin this task, undo the last extrusion, so that you are left with the 2.00 × 4.00 polyline rectangle shown previously in *Figure 14-22*.

> Draw a second complete polyline rectangle, 1.00 × 2.00, centered on the midpoint of the edge of the first, as shown in *Figure 14-24*.

NOTE: You must draw all four sides of this rectangle, even though you will not see the side that lies along the left side of the larger rectangle. Regions can only be constructed from closed polyline figures.

Next we will convert the two rectangles into 2D regions.

> Type "Region" or select the Region tool from the Polygon flyout on the Draw toolbar, as illustrated in *Figure 14-25*.

AutoCAD prompts you to select objects.

> Pick both rectangles with a window or crossing window.
> Press Enter to end object selection.

You will see no change, although there will be a message in the command area that says that two regions have been created (you may have to press F2 to see this in the text window).

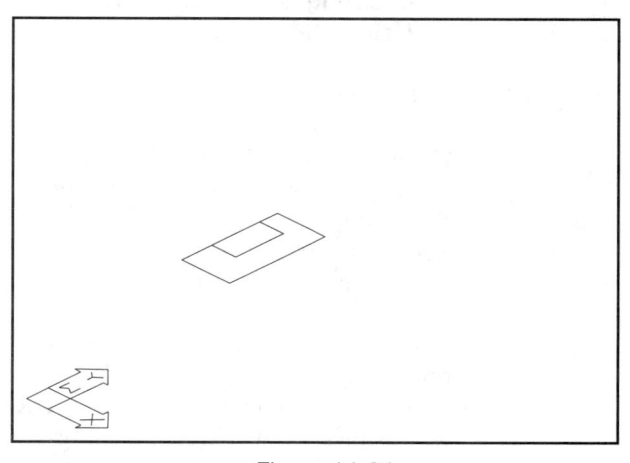

Figure 14-24

462 Part III Three-Dimensional Modeling

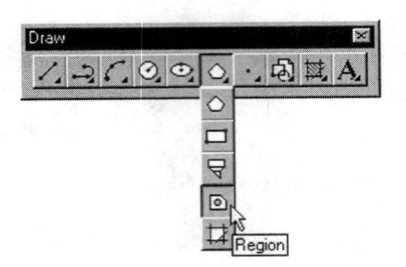

Figure 14-25

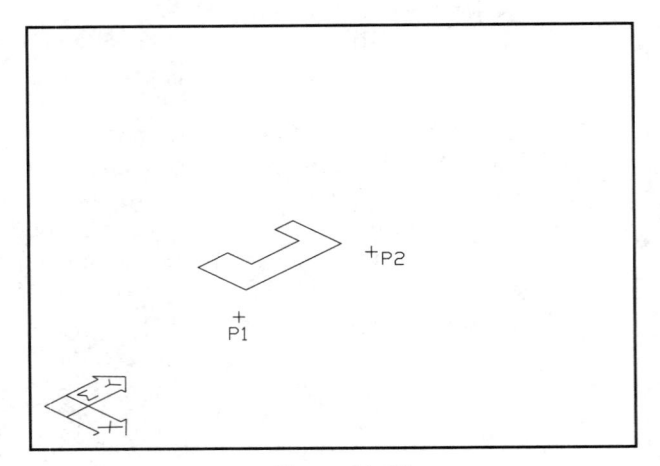

Figure 14-26

Now if you subtract the smaller rectangle from the larger, you will see that these regions behave just like 3D solids.

> Type "Subtract" or select the Subtract tool from the Explode flyout on the Modify toolbar.
> Select the larger rectangle as the region to subtract from.
> Press Enter to end object selection.
> Select the smaller rectangle as the region to subtract.
> Press Enter to end object selection.

Your screen will resemble *Figure 14-26*.

Task 8: Creating Solids by Revolving 2D Entities Using REVOLVE

Procedure

1. Draw regions or 2D polyline shapes.
2. Type "Revolve" or select the Revolve tool from the Solids toolbar.
3. Select objects.
4. Specify an axis of revolution.
5. Specify an angle of revolution.

Discussion. REVOLVE is a powerful solid modeling command that creates solid objects by revolving 2D polyline shapes and regions around an axis. It functions in ways very similar to the REVSURF surface modeling command.

In this task we will create a spool-shaped 3D solid by revolving the composite region from the last task around an axis in the XY plane.

Chap. 14   463

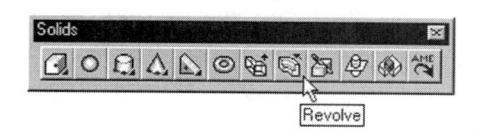

Figure 14-27

> To begin this task, you should have the composite region shown in *Figure 14-26* on your screen.
> Type "Revolve" or select the Revolve tool from the Solids toolbar, as shown in *Figure 14-27*.
> Select the composite region.
> Press Enter to end selection.

   AutoCAD prompts:

   Axis of revolution - Object/X/Y/<Start point of axis>:

"Object" allows you to select a line or a one-segment polyline as the axis of revolution. "X" and "Y" allow you to specify one of the axes of the current UCS. We will specify an axis by pointing.
> Pick a start point 1.00 unit to the right of the region, as shown in *Figure 14-26*.
   AutoCAD prompts for an end point of the axis.
> Pick an end point like P2 in the figure.
   AutoCAD prompts:

   Angle of revolution <full circle>:

Like REVSURF, REVOLVE gives you the option of creating only a portion of the circle of revolution. Unlike REVSURF, there is no option to begin the object somewhere other than in the plane of the region itself.
> Press Enter to create the full circle.

   Your screen will resemble *Figure 14-28*.

In the remaining tasks we will create a cutaway view and a section, then we will introduce shading and rendering.

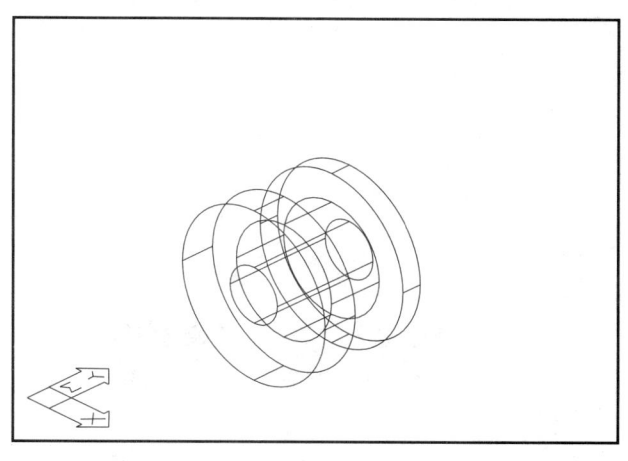

Figure 14-28

Task 9: Creating Solid Cutaway Views with SLICE

Procedure

1. Type "Slice" or select the Slice tool from the Solids toolbar.
2. Select objects.
3. Specify a cutting plane.
4. Specify a point on the plane.
5. Pick a side to retain.

Discussion. A single solid or composite solid may be sliced along its intersection with a specifiable plane. The plane is specified in terms common to several solid commands.

In this task we will cut the object created in the last task along a plane parallel to the current z and y axes, and retain the left portion so that we can view the inside of the "spool."

> Type "Slice" or select the Slice tool from the Solids toolbar, as shown in *Figure 14-29*.

AutoCAD will prompt you to select objects.

> Select the spool.

> Press Enter to end object selection.

AutoCAD now prompts for plane specification:

Slicing plane by Object/Zaxis/View/XY/YZ/ZX/<3points>:

A similar prompt is used in the SECTION command, which we will explore next. The slicing plane requested here can be determined by an object, a point on the z axis, one of the current UCS planes, or by showing three points. In this task we will use a YZ plane.

Take a look at *Figure 14-30*. It should help you visualize the XY, YZ, and ZX planes. The actual slicing plane will be parallel to a plane of origin in the current UCS. In other words, it does not have to have the same origin. Once you have determined which plane you want to use, the next step will be to specify a point on the plane.

> Type or select "YZ".

AuotCAD will prompt for a point on the YZ plane. The default point is (0,0,0), which will specify the YZ plane of the current UCS. Any other point will specify a plane parallel to the current YZ plane.

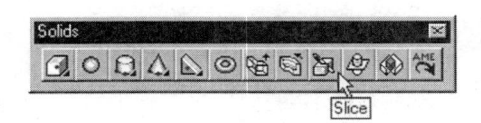

Figure 14-29

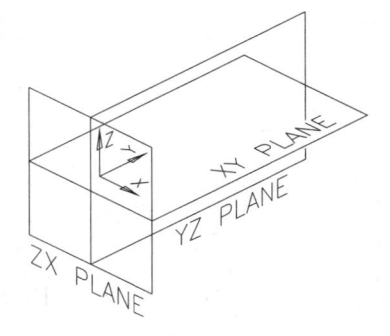

Figure 14-30

Chap. 14   465

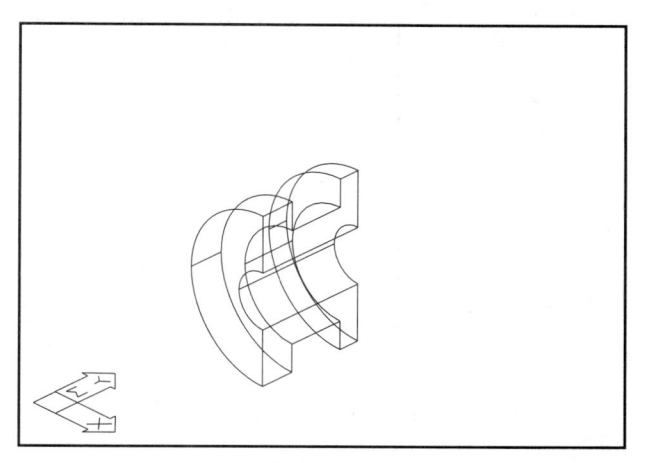

Figure 14-31

> Pick a point so that the *y* axis of the cross hairs runs through the center of the spool.

This will cause the spool to be cut along its centerline.

AutoCAD prompts:

Both sides/<Point on the desired side of the plane>:

> Pick any point to the left of the previous point (that is, left in the *x* direction).

This will show that you want to retain the portion of the spool that lies along the left side of the cutting plane.

Your screen should resemble *Figure 14-31*. Next we will create a cross section of the remaining half.

Task 10: Creating Sections with SECTION

Procedure

1. Type "Section" or select the Section tool from the Solids toolbar.
2. Select objects.
3. Specify a sectioning plane.

Discussion. Sectioning works just like slicing, but the outcome is a 2D region taken from the solid along the specified plane. In this task we will create a region section of the spool by sectioning it along the XY plane. The result will be a U-shaped block. It will look exactly like the region we used to create the revolved solid in the first place.

> Type "Section" or select the Section tool from the Solids toolbar, as shown in *Figure 14-32*.
> Select the cut spool.

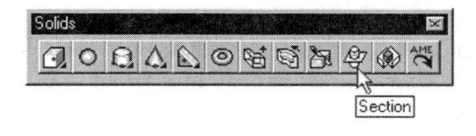

Figure 14-32

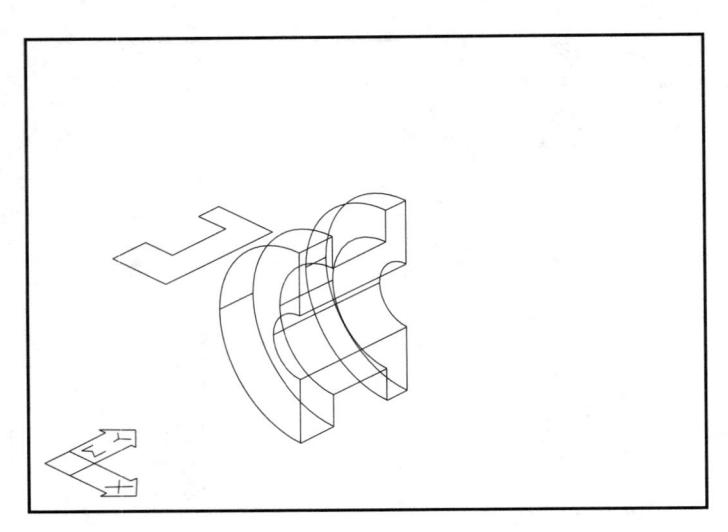

Figure 14-33

> Press Enter to end object selection.
AutoCAD prompts:

Section plane by Object/Last/Zaxis/View/XY/YZ/ZX/<3points>:

This is the same prompt as the slicing plane prompt, except for the first word. This time we will cut along the current XY plane.
> Type or select "XY".
AutoCAD will prompt for a point on the XY plane. Any point will do.
> Press Enter for the point (0,0,0) or pick any point.
AME will create the section. To see it well you will need to move it, or move the spool. When you are done your screen should resemble *Figure 14-33*.

Task 11: SHADEing Solid Models

Procedure

1. Adjust layers, colors, and variables to create desired effects.
2. Type "Shade" or select the Shade tool from the Render toolbar.

Discussion. Shaded images are simple to create. There are relatively few variables to manipulate. For more dramatic and realistic images you will need to delve into the realm of rendering, introduced in the next task. Unlike shading, rendering involves a large number of variables and will require a great deal of practice before you become proficient.

In working with shaded images your only options concern the color of objects in the image, the manner in which edges are shown, and the relative amounts of diffuse and ambient light. In this exercise we will explore a few of the possibilities. This will give you all you need to know in order to explore further on your own.

To begin, we will create a shaded image of the composite wedge from earlier in the chapter. Later we will use the same object for rendering. Since this book does not contain color illustrations, we will suggest that you move the wedge to layer 0 so that you will be working in gray and white. This way your screen images will more closely match our illustrations.

Chap. 14

> Erase all objects from your screen.
> Type "Insert" or select the Insert Block tool from the Block flyout on the Draw toolbar.
> Insert the wedge near the middle of your grid.
> Type "Explode" or select the Explode tool from the Modify toolbar.

If the wedge block is not exploded, it will not take on the color of layer 0 when you move it.

> Type "Chprop".
> Select the complete wedge with a window or crossing selection.
> Press Enter to end object selection.
> Type "la" or select "LAyer".
> Type "0".
> Press Enter to exit the CHPROP command.

Your wedge should now be on layer 0 and should be outlined in black.
> Type "Shade" or select the Shade tool from the Render toolbar, as shown in *Figure 14-34*.

That is all there is to it. Your screen should resemble *Figure 14-35*.

Besides changing layers and colors, there are two simple ways to alter the look of a shaded image. One depends on the SHADEDIF variable which can be set between 0 and 100. This variable establishes the proportion of diffuse and ambient light reflected from the object. Ambient light is light that fills space and has no specific direction. Diffuse light is directed from your viewing angle. Lighting in shaded images is not very precise, however. For real lighting effects you will have to use RENDER.

The other variable is called SHADEDGE. It controls how edges are displayed and also affects color. There are four settings (0–3): 256 Color, 256 Color Edge Highlight, 16 Color Hidden Line, and 16 Color Filled. With the default setting of 3 or 16 Color Filled, surfaces will be given their own color and edges will be drawn. Setting 2 will give a basic hidden line image, just like the HIDE command. Setting 1 will show edges and will use different colors depending on the SHADEDIF setting. Setting 0 or 256 Color will give basically the same image without edges. Try changing the settings of SHADEDGE and SHADEDIF to see the effects.

> Type "Shadedif".

You will see this prompt:

New value for SHADEDIF <70>:

The range is from 0 to 100.
> Type "100".

Figure 14-34

Figure 14-35

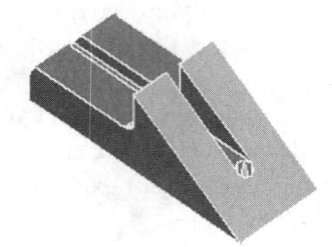

Figure 14-36

> Type "Shadedge".
> Type "1" to change the setting of SHADEDGE 256 Color Edge Highlight.
> Type "Shade" or select the Shade tool from the Render toolbar.

You will see a new shaded image that reflects these changes, resembling *Figure 14-36*. We suggest that you continue to experiment with shade settings before going on to the next task.

Task 12: RENDERing Solid Models

Procedure

1. Position lights.
2. Attach materials.
3. Adjust light intensity.
4. Render.
5. Save scene.

Discussion. Rendering goes far beyond shading by creating the effect of light falling on the various surfaces of a solid or surface model. Rendering is a complex craft that requires many hours of experimentation to master. Most of the techniques involved concern the placement and setting of lights. There are four types of lights and each light has its own set of variables and settings, which will dramatically affect the end result. Knowing the various lights, how to position them, and how to understand their respective settings is a good place to begin. But this knowledge alone will not take you very far. You will need to accumulate many hours of experience in order to know what you want and how to achieve it.

In this task we will get you started by showing you how to position lights and how to use some of the most critical settings. We will continue to use the wedge composite shaded in the last task.

> To begin this task you should have the wedge on your screen in a southeast isometric viewpoint, as in the last task.

As we proceed we will look at the different types of light, beginning with ambient light.

Ambient Light

First, we will simply render the object as is without any added lighting. What you will see will be entirely dependent on the default ambient light setting. You will recall from the last exercise that ambient light is background light that fills space and is the same everywhere. It has no direction and can only be varied as to color and intensity.

> Type "Render" or select the Render tool from the Render toolbar.

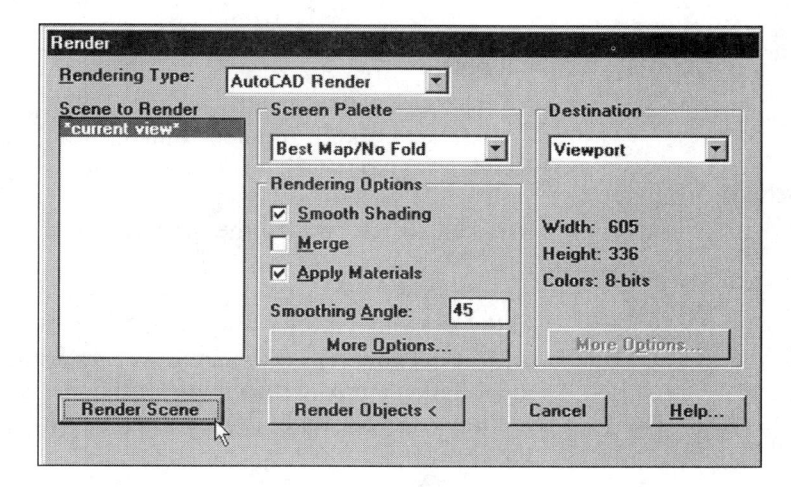

Figure 14-37

Figure 14-38

AutoCAD will initialize the Render program and then display the Render dialogue box as shown in *Figure 14-37*.

> Click on "Render Scene".

The wedge will be rendered in the current viewport and you will see an image similar to the one in *Figure 14-38*. As you can see, this image is only a slight advancement over the shaded images in the last task.

The Render Window

To get a full view of a rendered image it is often desirable to send the rendering to the full screen Render Window, rather than view the rendering within a single viewport. This will be most apparent when there are several small viewports on the screen. To use the render window you have to make one change in the Render dialogue box.

> Type "Render" or select the Render tool from the Render toolbar again.
> In the dialogue box, click the arrow to the right of the box that says "Viewport". This will be on the right in the Destination section of the dialogue box.

This will open a list that shows Viewport, Render Window, and File as Destination options. Rendering to a viewport you have already done; rendering to a file will send the rendering information directly to a file without displaying the image on your screen. Render files can be created in TGA, TIFF, GIF, PostScript, X11, PBM, PGM, PPM, BMP, PCX, SUN FITS, FAX G III, and IFF formats and may then be displayed on other systems.

To render to the Render Window, simply select this option.

> Click on Render Window.

The list will close and Render Window will be shown in the Destination box.

> Click on Render Scene.

It may take a moment but the rendered wedge will be shown in the Render Window, which is free of toolbars, command line, and status line.

You can switch back to the drawing editor using Alt-Esc, or using Alt-Tab.

> Hold down the Alt key as you press and release the Esc key. Do this until the drawing editor with your drawing is showing.

Alt-Tab works the same way, except that you will see open applications identified in a box at the middle of the screen. Release the Alt key when you see the title you want. In the steps that follow we will continue to render to the Render Window.

Before proceeding to explore a variety of light placements and types, it will be helpful to create a three-viewport configuration so that you can see what is happening from different viewpoints.

> From the View menu, select "Tiled Viewports" and then "3 Viewports".
> Press Enter to accept the default "Right" configuration.

Your screen will be redrawn with three viewports.

> Click in the top left viewport to make it active.
> Type "Plan" to create a plan view.
> Press Enter to accept the default, current UCS.
> Click the Zoom out tool from the Standard toolbar, or type "z" and then ".5x" to zoom out.
> Click in the bottom left viewport to make it active.
> From the View menu, select "3D Viewpoint Presets" and then "Front" to create a front view.
> Click the Zoom out tool from the Standard toolbar once again, or type "z" and then ".5x" to zoom out.

Your screen should now resemble *Figure 14-39*.

> Click in the right viewport to make the 3D viewport active.
> You may wish to Zoom in on the 3D image using a window selection.

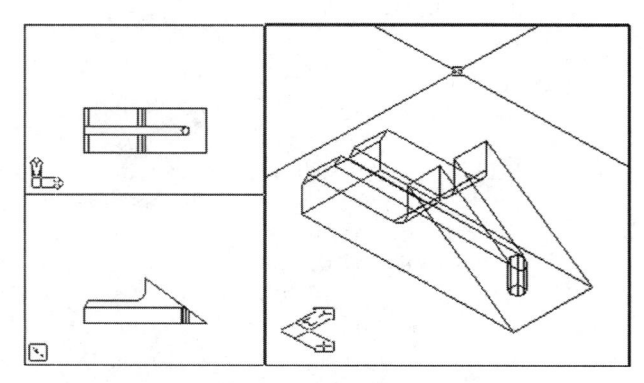

Figure 14-39

Chap. 14   471

Figure 14-40

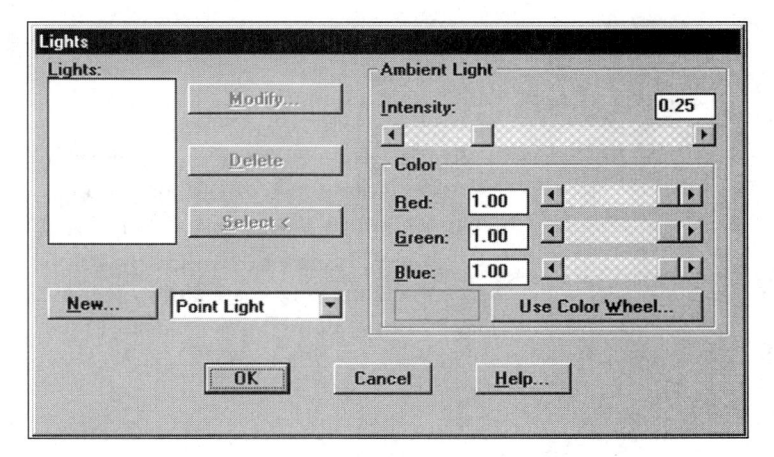

Figure 14-41

The Lights Dialogue Box

Lights are created, placed, and modified using the Lights dialogue box.

> Type "Light" or select the Lights tool from the Render toolbar, as shown in *Figure 14-40*.

This brings up the Lights dialogue box shown in *Figure 14-41*. First of all, look at the Ambient Light area on the right. Ambient light has only color and intensity. With the scroll bar at the top you can vary the intensity from 0 to 1.00. The default setting is .30. You will clearly see the effects of changing intensity. Try it if you wish, using the following procedure:
1. Using the scroll bar, change the intensity. Change it by .25 or more to see the effect clearly.
2. Click on "OK".
3. Select the Render tool from the Render toolbar.
4. Click on "Render Scene" in the Render dialogue box.
5. Use Alt-Esc or Alt-Tab to return to the drawing editor.

NOTE: The second and subsequent times you render to the Render Window, the image will appear within a box. To enlarge the image to full screen, click on the maximize arrow in the right hand corner of the box.

Also in the Ambient Light box are three scroll bars for mixing the amounts of red, green, and blue light. All types of lights have these scroll bars so that you can vary the color quality of the light coming from individual light sources as well as ambient light color. Feel free to experiment with color settings at this time. The effect of the color mix is especially clear on a gray and white object like ours. For example, if you set the green and blue on 0 and leave the red at 1.00, you will see that what remains of the ambient light is shown as small red dots on the surfaces of the object. With all three set at 1.00, the default, the effect is that of white light.

Spotlight

Next we will add a spotlight on the right side of the object, aimed in along the slot. Light placement is probably the most important consideration in rendering. If you have used point filters previously then you have already learned all you need to know in order to position lights. Keep in mind that lights will usually be positioned above the XY plane and will probably be alone in space. Point filters can be very helpful in this situation.

Before we can add a light we must designate the light type, specify that it is new, and give it a name.

> If necessary, type "lights" or click on the Lights tool on the Render toolbar to re-open the Lights dialogue box.

> Click on the arrow next to "Point Light" at the lower left of the dialogue box.

The options will be shown as Point Light, Distant Light, and Spotlight. We will begin with a spotlight because its focus and directionality make it easy to understand.

> Click on "Spotlight".

> Click on "New".

This will call up the New Spotlight dialogue box shown in *Figure 14-42*. Notice first that there is a place for a name, a scroll bar for intensity, and three scroll bars for color, just as in the ambient light box. There are also areas for position, hotspot and falloff, and attenuation. We will discuss these areas in a moment, but first let's give the light a name and a position.

> Type "Spot" in the Light Name edit box.

> Click on "Modify <" under "Position".

This closes the dialogue box temporarily and gives you access to your drawing. On the command line you will see the following prompt:

Enter light target <current>:

Spotlights have a target and a source position. As is the case with real spotlights, AutoCAD rendering spotlights are carefully placed and aimed at a particular point in the drawing. The light falls in a cone shape and dimin-

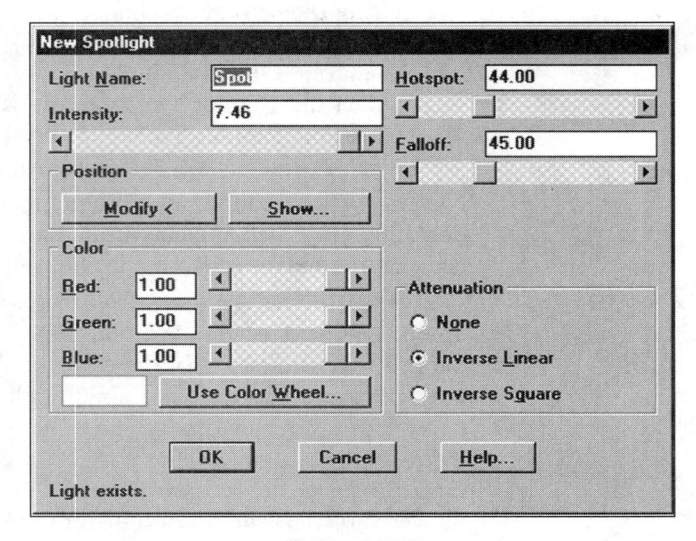

Figure 14-42

Chap. 14

ishes away from the center of the cone. You can vary the size of the focal beam using the Hotspot scroll bar, and the size of the surrounding falloff area using the Falloff scroll bar.

For this exercise we will place a light above and to the right of the wedge, aimed directly into the slot. If you look at the plan and front views in your drawing, you will see that RENDER has already placed a temporary spotlight symbol in your drawing. This is a default position, which you can ignore. We will be using point selection and XY filters to place the target and the light source where we want them.

> At the prompt for a light target, type ".xy" or select ".XY" from the Point Filters flyout on the Standard toolbar.

AutoCAD prompts ".xy of" and waits for you to choose a point in the XY plane.

> Click in the upper left window to make the plan view active.

> Pick a point about 1.0 units to the left of the cylindrical hole, as shown in *Figure 14-43*.

AutoCAD now prompts for a Z value.

(need Z):

In order to place the target point right in the slot, we will need to have a Z value of 1.00 (the bottom of the slot is 1.00 above the XY plane).

> Type "1".

AutoCAD now prompts for a light location:

Enter light location <current>:

Now we will use an .xy filter to place the light source to the right and above the wedge.

> Type ".xy" or select ".XY" from the Point Filters flyout on the Standard toolbar.

> In response to the "of" prompt, select a point about 2.00 units to the right of the wedge, as shown in *Figure 14-43*.

> In response to the "need Z" prompt, type "5" to position the spotlight 5.00 above the XY plane.

This will bring back the New Spotlight dialogue box.

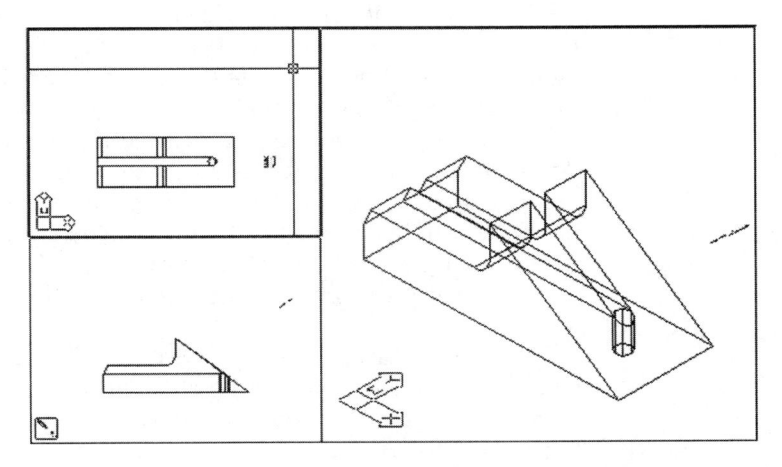

Figure 14-43

Figure 14-44

Figure 14-45

> Click on "OK" to exit the New Spotlight dialogue box.
> Click on "OK" to exit the Lights dialogue box.

You will now see a spotlight icon in your drawing. The three-view configuration will show clearly how it is positioned and directed. It is now time to render the scene again to see the spotlight in action.

> Click on the right viewport to make it active.
> Type "Render" or select the Render tool from the render toolbar.
> Select "Render Scene" from the Render dialogue box.

You will see a rendered image similar to the one in *Figure 14-44*. In this image you can clearly see how the spotlight hits the wedge just behind the hole and falls off in waves along the back on the object.

In order to achieve a more precise light cone, you can change from a Gouraud style rendering to a Phong rendering.

> Click the maximize arrow in the upper left of the render box to show the rendering in the full render window.
> Use Alt-Esc or Alt-Tab to return to the drawing editor (we will not include these reminders for the renderings that follow).
> Type "render" or select the Render tool from the Render toolbar.
> Select "More Options...".
> Click on the "Phong" radio button.
> Click on "OK".
> Click on "Render Scene".

Your new rendered image will resemble *Figure 14-45*.

Next we will be adding a point light, but before going on you may want to experiment with some of the other features of spotlighting (available in the New Spotlight or Modify Spotlight subdialogues of the Lights dialogue box). Try varying the hotspot and falloff. Notice that the hotspot must always be smaller than the falloff. You will also see significant differences when you vary the attenuation. Attenuation is the rate at which light intensity diminishes relative to distance from the light source. In the default Inverse Linear setting, light two units away from its source will appear half as bright. If you switch to Inverse Square attenuation, light at two units will be only a fourth as bright as at the source. So switching to inverse square will cause the light from a spotlight to diminish more quickly over a shorter distance.

When you are done experimenting, we suggest that you return to our settings so that your images continue to resemble ours. These include the following: ambient light is at .30 intensity and all colors are at 1.00. The spotlight is at 4.47 intensity, all colors are at 1.00, hotspot is at 44 degrees with falloff at 45 degrees, and attenuation is inverse linear.

Point Light

Point light works like a light bulb with no shade. It radiates outward equally in all directions. Like spotlighting, the light from a point light attenuates over distance.

In this exercise we will place a point light right inside the slot of the wedge. This will clearly show the light bulb effect of a small point of light radiating outward.

> Type "Light" or select the Lights tool from the Render toolbar.
> Click on the arrow to the right of "SpotLight" and switch to "Point Light".
> Click on "New...".
> Type "Point" in the Light Name edit box.
> Click on "Modify >".

For a point light you only need to specify a location, since it has no direction other than outward from the source. The prompt is:

Enter light location <current>:

We will use the same point filtering system to locate this light.
> At the prompt type ".xy" or select .XY from the Standard toolbar.
> At the "of" prompt, pick a point in the plan view at the center of the slot and about 1.00 unit behind the plane where the box and the wedge join, as shown in *Figure 14-46*.
> Type "1.25" for a Z value.

Since the slot is at 1.00 from the XY plane, this will put the point light just above the bottom of the slot.
> Click on "OK".
> Click on "OK" again to exit the Lights dialogue box.
> Click on the right viewport to make it active.
> Type "Render" or select the Render tool from the Render toolbar.
> Select "Render Scene" from the Render dialogue box.

Your rendered object will resemble *Figure 14-47*. In this image you can clearly see the effect of the point light within the slot along with the spotlight falling on the right side of the object.

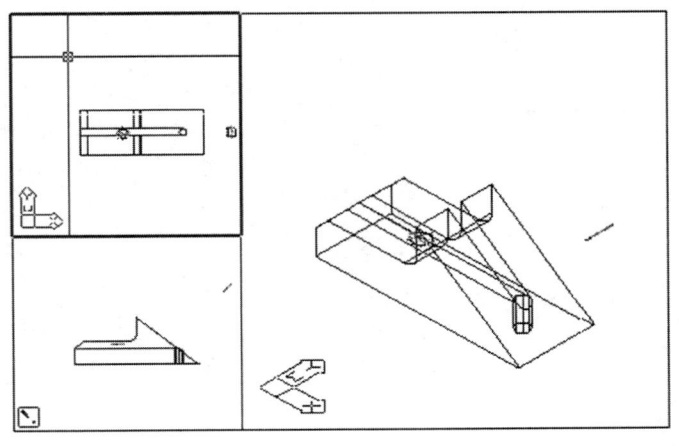

Figure 14-46

Figure 14-47

Distant Light

The last type of light is called distant light and is often used to achieve the effect of direct sunlight. In AutoCAD rendering, a distant light source emits beams of light that are parallel and travel in one direction only. Distant light does not attenuate. It is the same at any distance from the source. Distant light placement is defined by a directional vector; the command line prompt will ask for a "to" point and a "from" point. You can define this vector precisely using point filters as we have done previously. The to point will probably be on an object or in the XY plane. The from point will be above the XY plane. Most important is the angle and direction between the two points. You can also define distant light using the sunlight oriented Azimuth and Altitude dials shown in the Distant Light dialogue box. Since you have already used point filters, we will introduce the dial system here for variety.

> Type "Light" or select the Lights tool from the Render toolbar.
> Click on the arrow to the right of "Point Light" and switch to "Distant Light".
> Click on "New...".

This brings up the New Distant Light dialogue box shown in *Figure 14-48*. You will see scroll bars for intensity and color on the left. On the right you will see the Azimuth and Altitude dials and scroll bars above a light source vector modification area. By selecting "Modify <" you could proceed to place the distant light source with to and from points using points and point filters as we have done previously. The Azimuth and Altitude system may help you to think more specifically in terms of sunlight. The Azimuth setting will determine the position of sunlight relative to the east–west hori-

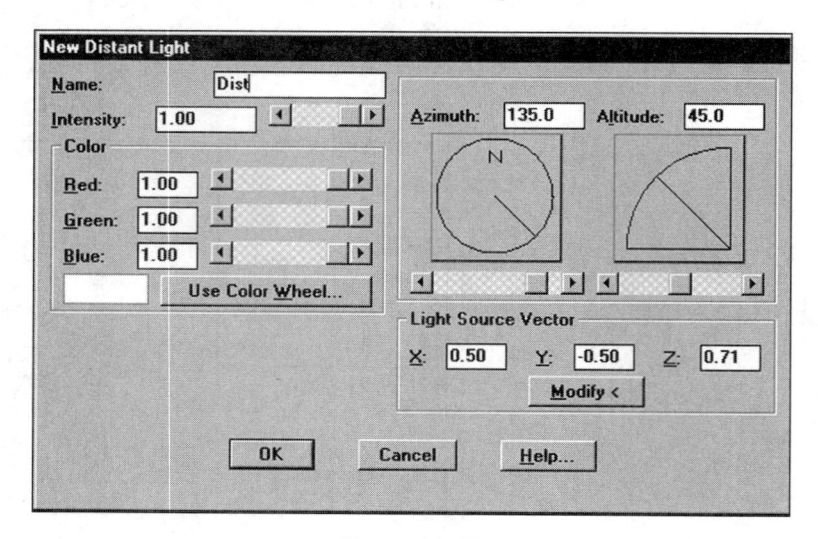

Figure 14-48

Chap. 14

zon. In other words, it will simulate the variations of sunlight depending on your position on the planet and the time of year. The Altitude setting will simulate time of day variations. In the northern hemisphere in late morning, for example, the sun is coming from the south (180 degrees on the azimuth dial) from an altitude of, let's say, 65 degrees. You can use the scroll bars, points on the dials, or typing in the edit boxes to achieve these settings.

> Type "Dist" in the Light Name edit box.

> Using the scroll bar, move the Azimuth setting all the way to the right so that the edit box reads 180 degrees.

> Using the scroll bar, move the Altitude setting partway to the right so that the edit box shows 65 degrees.

Changes in these settings will also cause changes in the Light Source Vector box.

> Click on "OK".

> Click on "OK" in the Lights dialogue box.

> Type "Render" or select the Render tool from the Render toolbar.

> Select "Render Scene" from the Render dialogue box.

Your image will resemble the rendering in *Figure 14-49*. By comparing this image with the one in *Figure 14-47*, you can see the effect of adding distant "sunlight" to this rendering.

Scenes

A rendering scene is made up of a view and a set of lights. Once you have positioned lights, you may want to present the image from different points of view and use different configurations of lights. Once scenes are defined you can save them and switch from one to another easily. For example, let's create a scene without the spotlight to see the effect of the distant light and the point light together.

> Type "Scene" or select the Scenes tool from the Render toolbar, as shown in *Figure 14-50*.

This will bring up the Scenes dialogue box shown in *Figure 14-51*.

Figure 14-49

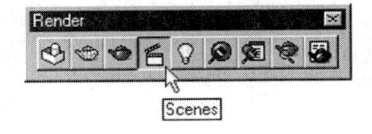

Figure 14-50

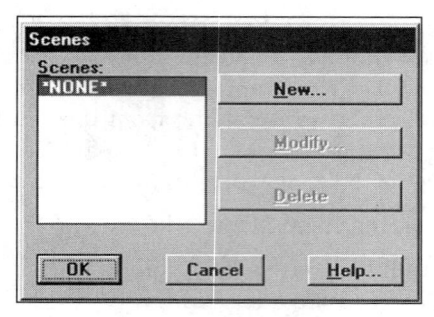

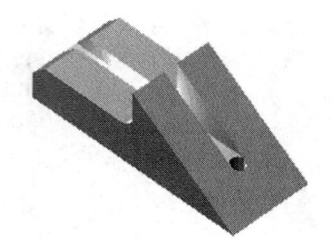

Figure 14-51

Figure 14-52

> Select "New...".
> Type "NoSpot" for a scene name (spaces not allowed in names).
> Highlight "Point" and "Dist" in the Lights area. Make sure that "Spot" is not highlighted.
> Click on "OK".
> In the Scenes dialogue box make sure that "NOSPOT" is highlighted and then click on "OK".

Now that the new scene is defined, you can create a new rendering.

> Type "render" or select the Render tool from the Render toolbar.
> In the Render dialogue box, make sure that "NOSPOT" is highlighted under "Scene to Render".
> Click on "Render Scene".

Your "Nospot" scene will resemble *Figure 14-52*.

Attaching Materials

Materials can be created or selected from AutoCAD's materials library. Each material definition has its own characteristic color, ambient light color, reflection color, and roughness value. Changing an object's material will dramatically affect the way it is rendered, so it will usually make sense to attach materials before adjusting light intensity and color. In this exercise we will simply take you through the procedure of loading materials from the AutoCAD library and attaching them to an object. When you experiment on your own you will see color effects which we cannot show you in this book.

> Type "matlib" or select the Materials Library tool from the Render toolbar, as shown in *Figure 14-53*.

Notice that there is a Materials tool as well as a Materials Library tool on the Render toolbar. Be sure to pick the Materials Library tool at this step. The Materials Library tool brings up the Materials Library dialogue box, shown in *Figure 14-54*. Before we can select and attach a material we must load at least one from the list on the right. To use this box, select a material or materials on the right and then select Import to bring them into your drawing.

> Run down the Library List on the right and select "Stainless-Steel".
> While "Stainless-Steel" is highlighted, select "<-Import".

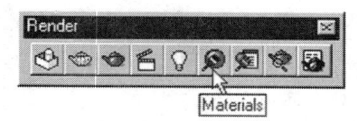

Figure 14-53

Chap. 14   **479**

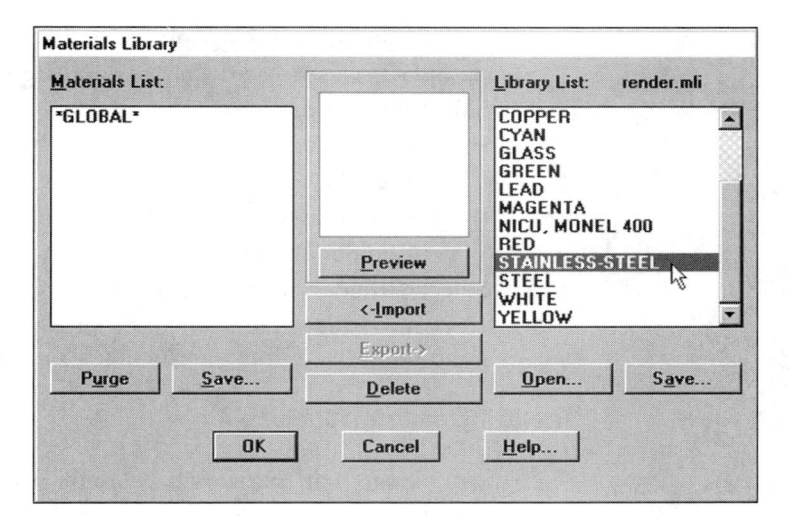

Figure 14-54

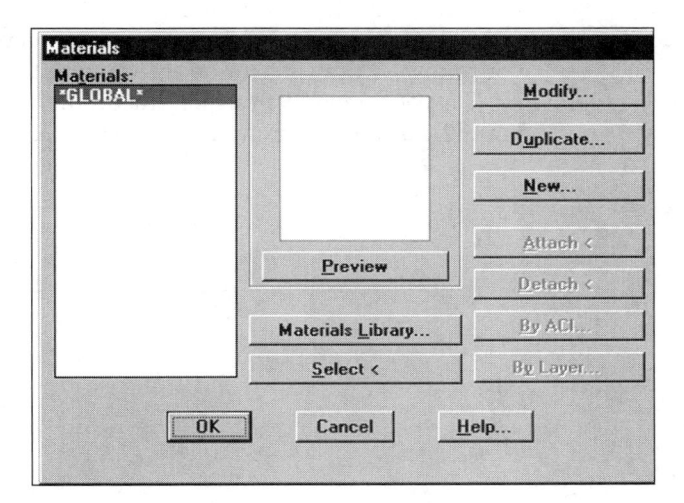

Figure 14-55

    The Stainless-Steel material definition will be loaded and you will see Stainless-Steel on the Materials List at the left.

> Click on "OK".

    Now you must attach the material to the object you are rendering. When there is more than one object you can attach different materials to different objects.

> Type "rmat" or select the Materials tool, just to the left of the Materials library tool on the Render toolbar.

    This calls the Materials dialogue box, illustrated in *Figure 14-55*. Notice that MATLIB and the Materials Library tool call the Materials Library dialogue box used in loading materials, while RMAT and the Materials tool call the Materials dialogue box used in the actual manipulation of materials in a drawing.

> Click on "Attach <"

The dialogue box disappears and you will see this prompt:

Select objects to attach "STAINLESS-STEEL" to:

> Select the wedge.

> Press Enter to end object selection.

> Click on "OK."

You are now ready to render.

> Type "Render" or select the Render tool from the Render toolbar.

> Select "Render Scene" from the Render dialogue box.

Your rendered image will be similar to the last image, but you will see some blue in the lighting, particularly on the right side.

Tasks 13, 14, 15, 16, and 17

The five drawings that follow will give you practice in the solid modeling techniques introduced in this chapter. The first is given with detailed drawing instructions, while the rest are left for you to explore on your own. As you look at the objects you will begin to view them as composites made from solid building blocks. Look for opportunities to use REVOLVE as well as union, subtraction, and intersection operations. In all cases, we encourage you to create rendered images of your finished drawings using the lighting techniques introduced in this chapter.

If you would like further practice in solid modeling, any of the drawings in this book, 2D as well as wireframe and surface models, can be turned into full solid models.

DRAWING 14-1: BUSHING MOUNT

It is important to use an efficient sequence in the construction of composite solids. In general this will mean saving union, subtraction, and intersection operations until most of the solid objects have been drawn and positioned. This approach has two advantages. It takes up less memory and it allows you to continue to use the geometry of the parts for snap points as you position other parts.

DRAWING SUGGESTIONS

We offer the following suggestions for Drawing 14–1. The principles demonstrated here will carry over into the other drawings, and we feel you should be quite capable of handling them on your own at this point.

> Use at least two views, one plan and one 3D, as you work.
> Begin with the bottom of the mount in the XY plane. This will mean drawing a 6.00 × 4.00 × .50 solid box sitting on the XY plane.
> Draw a second box, 1.50 × 4.00 × 3.50, in the XY plane. This will become the upright section at the middle of the mount. Move it so that its own midpoint is at the midpoint of the base.
> Draw a third box, 1.75 × .75 × .50, in the XY plane. This will be copied and become one of the two slots in the base. Move it so that the midpoint of its long side is at the midpoint of the short side of the base. Then MOVE it 1.125 along the *x* axis.
> Add a .375 radius cylinder with .50 height at each end of the slot.
> Copy the box and cylinders 3.75 to the other side of the base to form the other slot.
> Create a new UCS 2.00 up in the *z* direction. You can use the origin option and give (0,0,2) as the new origin. This puts the XY plane of the UCS directly at the middle of the upright block, where you can easily draw the bushing.
> Move out to the right of the mount and draw the polyline outline of the bushing as shown in the drawing. Use REVOLVE to create the solid bushing.
> Create a cylinder in the center of the mount, where it can be subtracted to create the hole in the mount upright.
> Union the first and second boxes.
> Subtract the boxes and cylinders to form the slots in the base and the bushing-sized cylinder to form the hole in the mount.

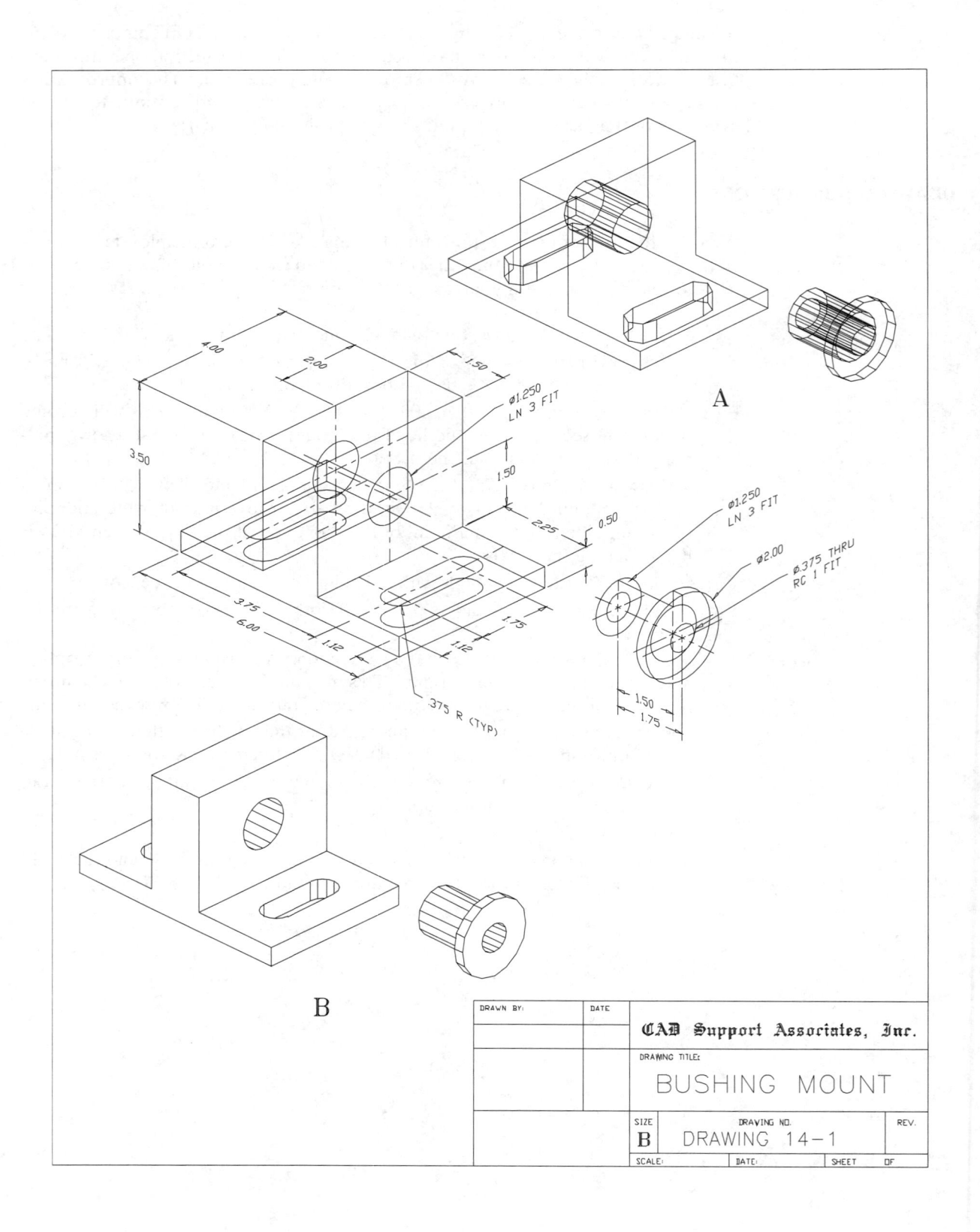

Part III Three-Dimensional Modeling

BUSHING MOUNT

DRAWING 14-1

Chap. 14

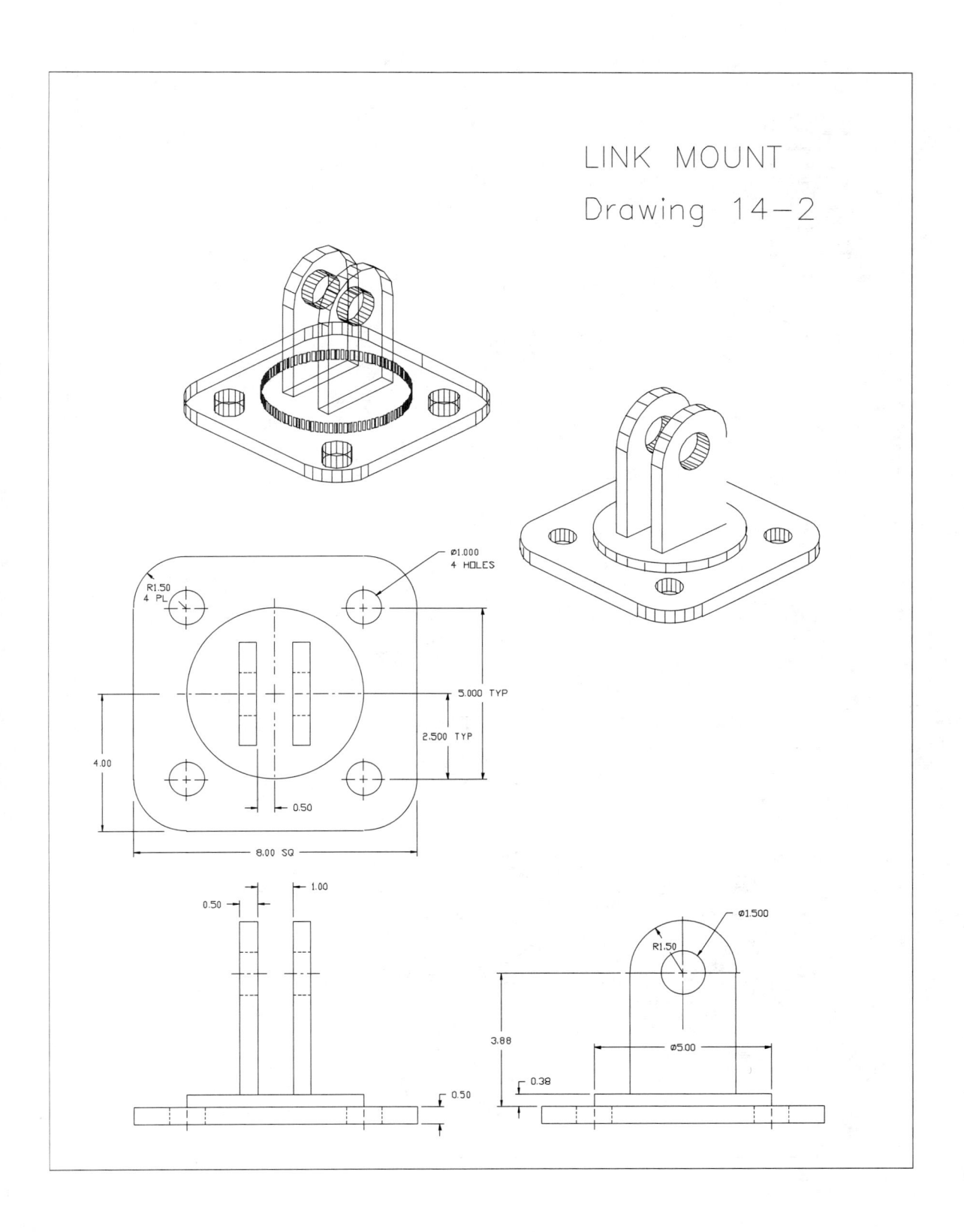

LINK MOUNT
Drawing 14-2

484   Part III Three-Dimensional Modeling

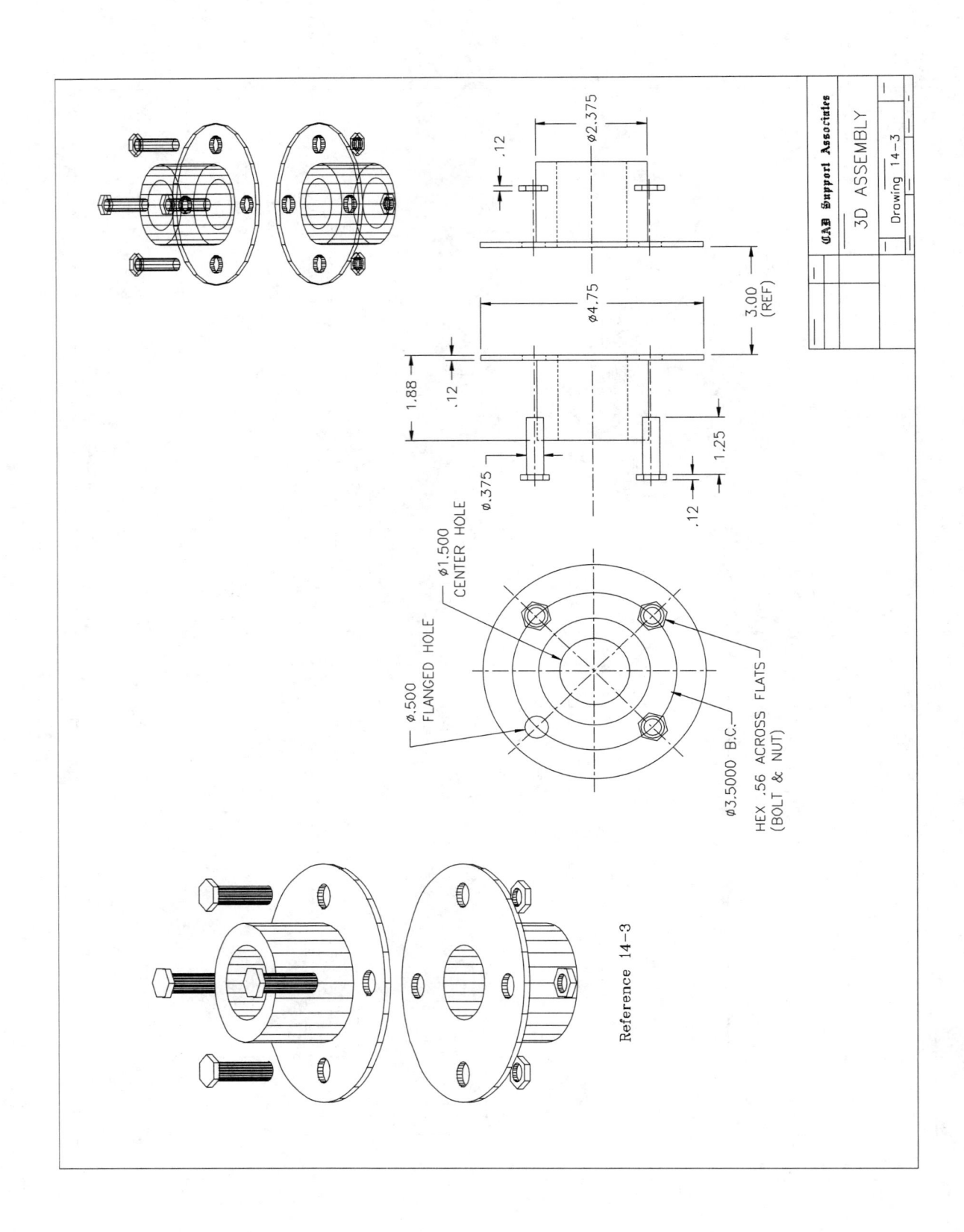

Ø2.375
.12
Ø4.75
3.00 (REF)
1.88
.12
Ø.375
1.25
.12

Ø1.500 CENTER HOLE
Ø.500 FLANGED HOLE
Ø3.5000 B.C.
HEX .56 ACROSS FLATS (BOLT & NUT)

Reference 14-3

CAD Support Associates
3D ASSEMBLY
Drawing 14-3

Chap. 14

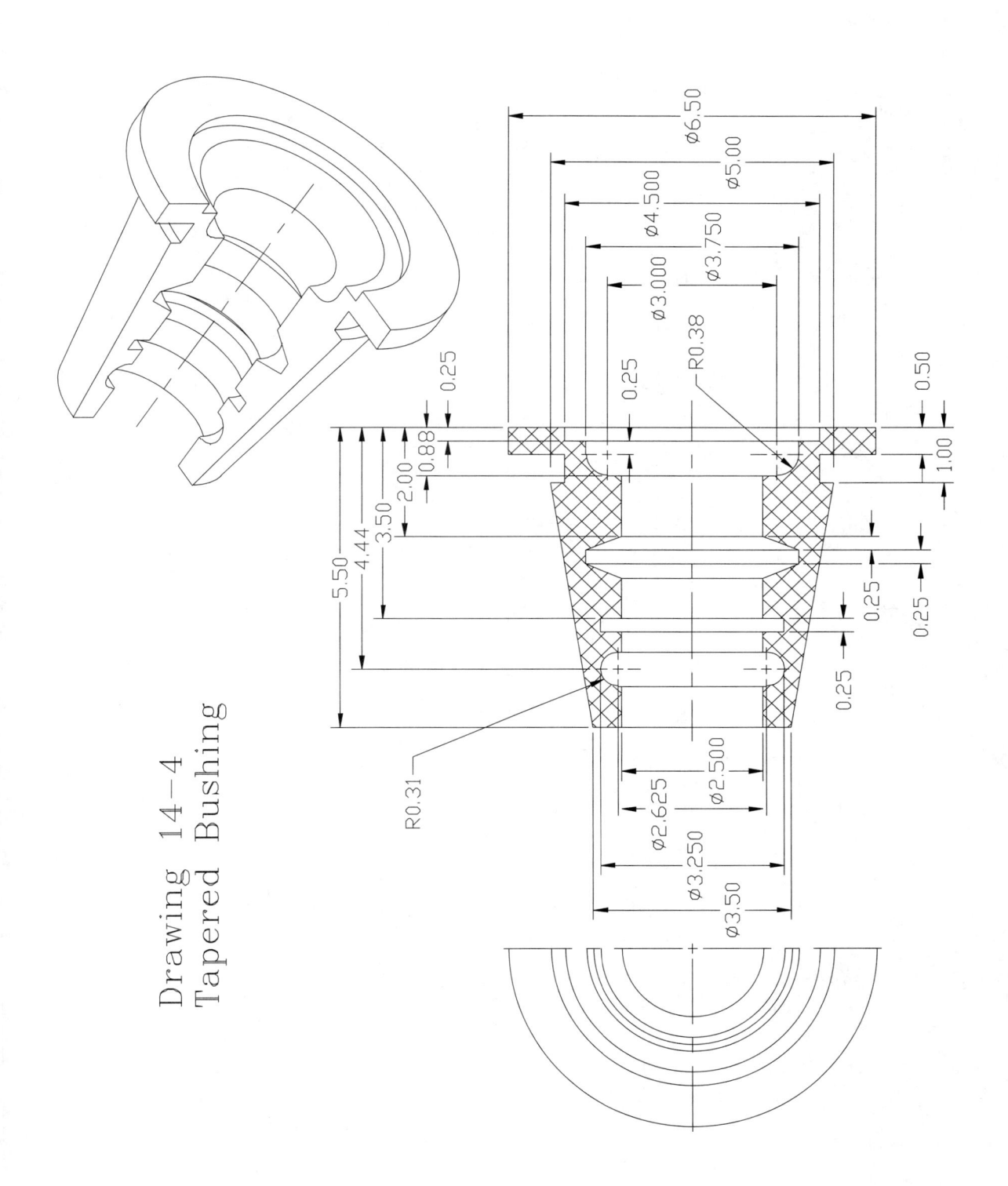

Drawing 14-4
Tapered Bushing

Drawing 14-5
Pivot Mount

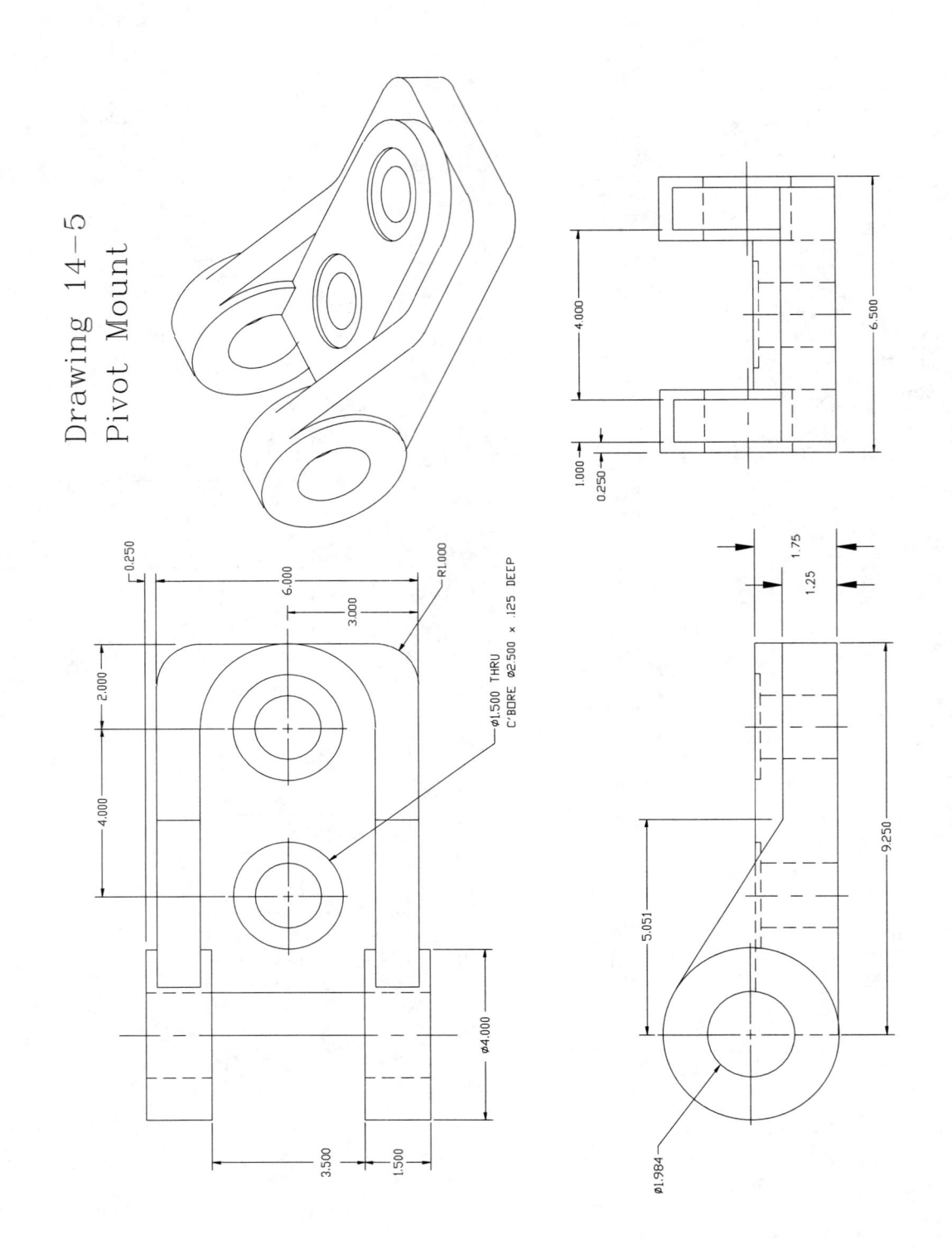

APPENDIX A

Drawing Projects

The drawings on the following pages are offered as additional challenges and are presented without suggestions. They may be drawn in two or three dimensions and may be presented as multiple view drawings, hidden line drawings, or rendered drawings. In short, you are on your own to further explore and master everything you have learned in this book.

Appendix A

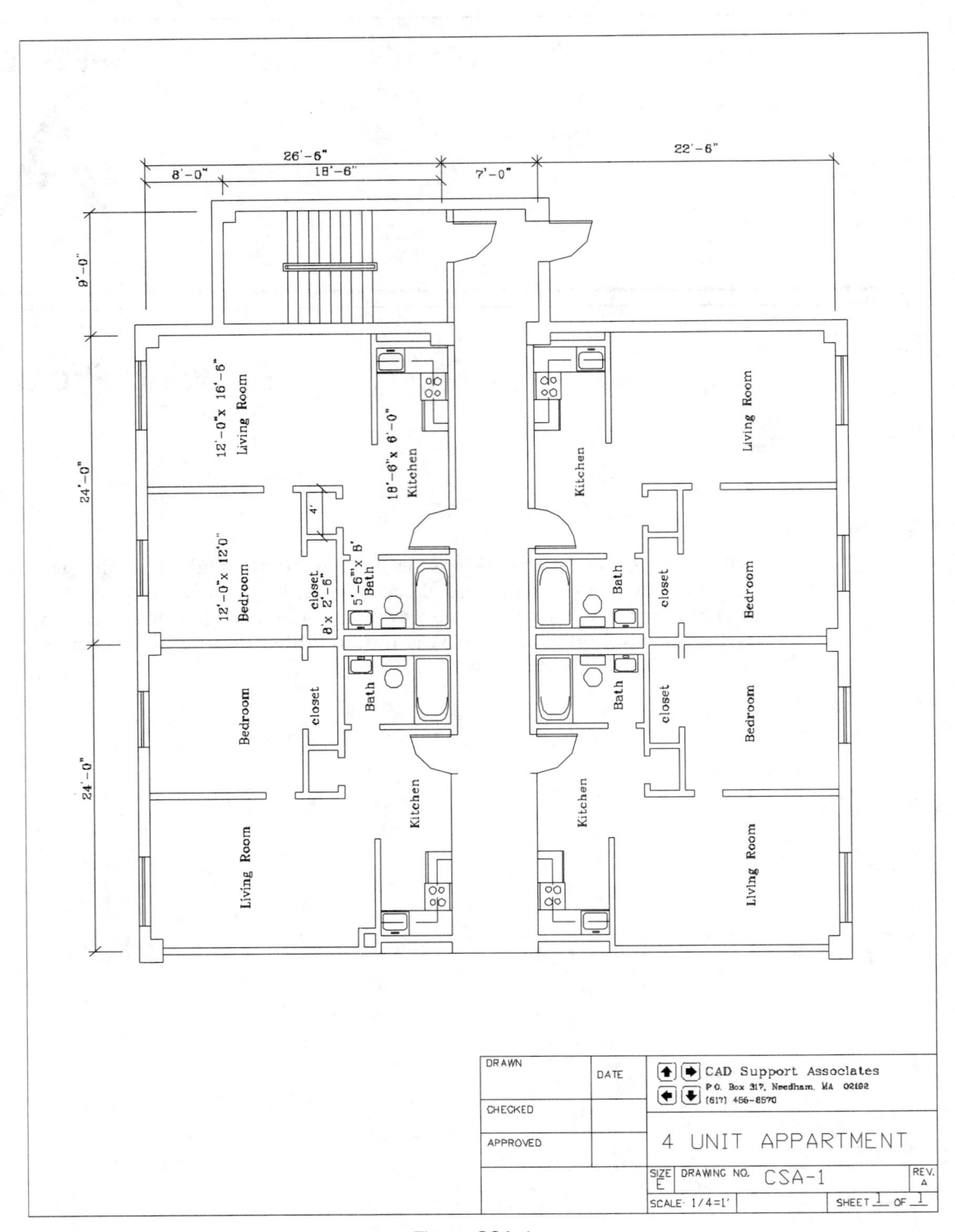

Figure CSA-1

Appendix A

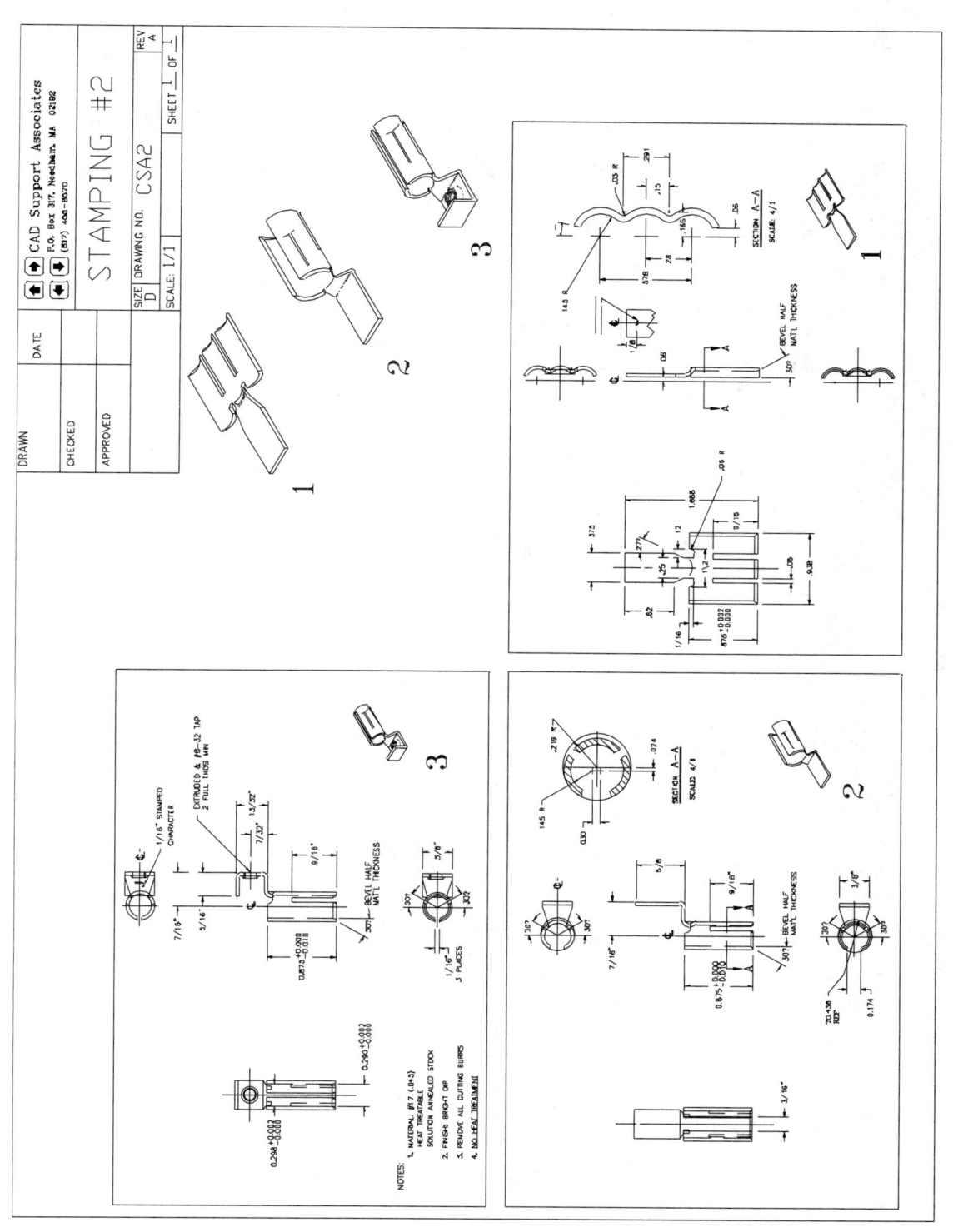

Figure CSA-2

490

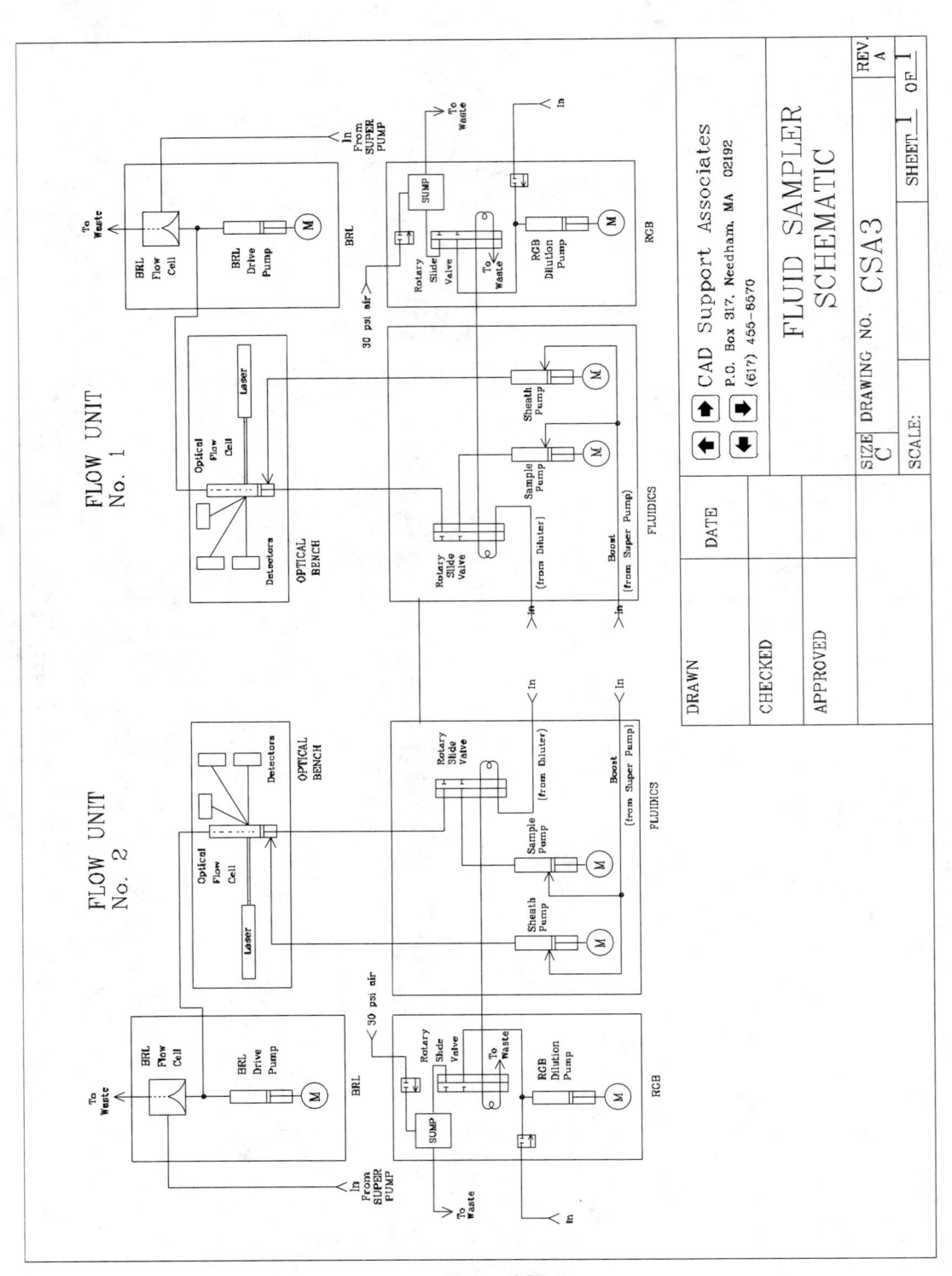

Appendix A

Figure CSA-3

Appendix A

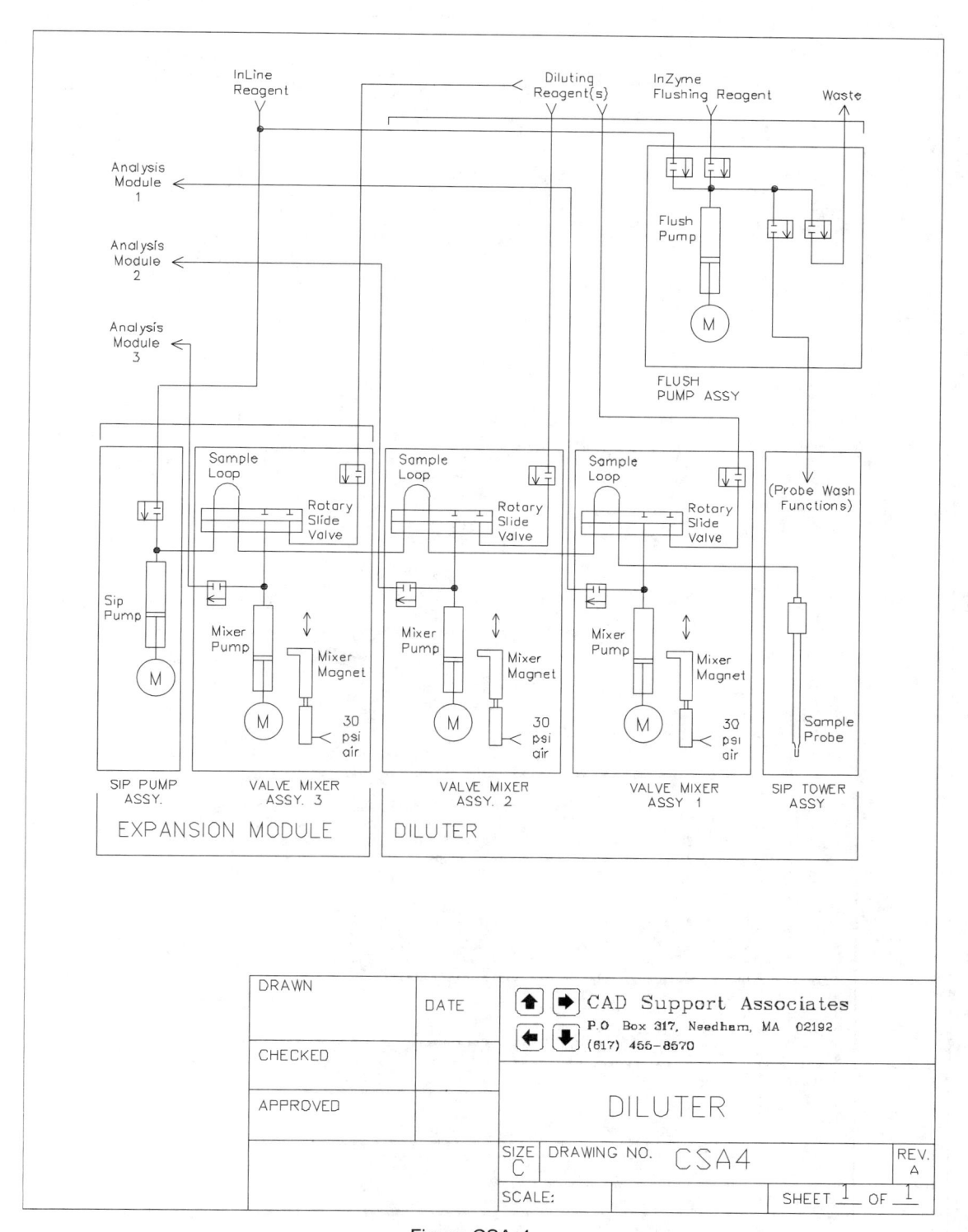

Figure CSA-4

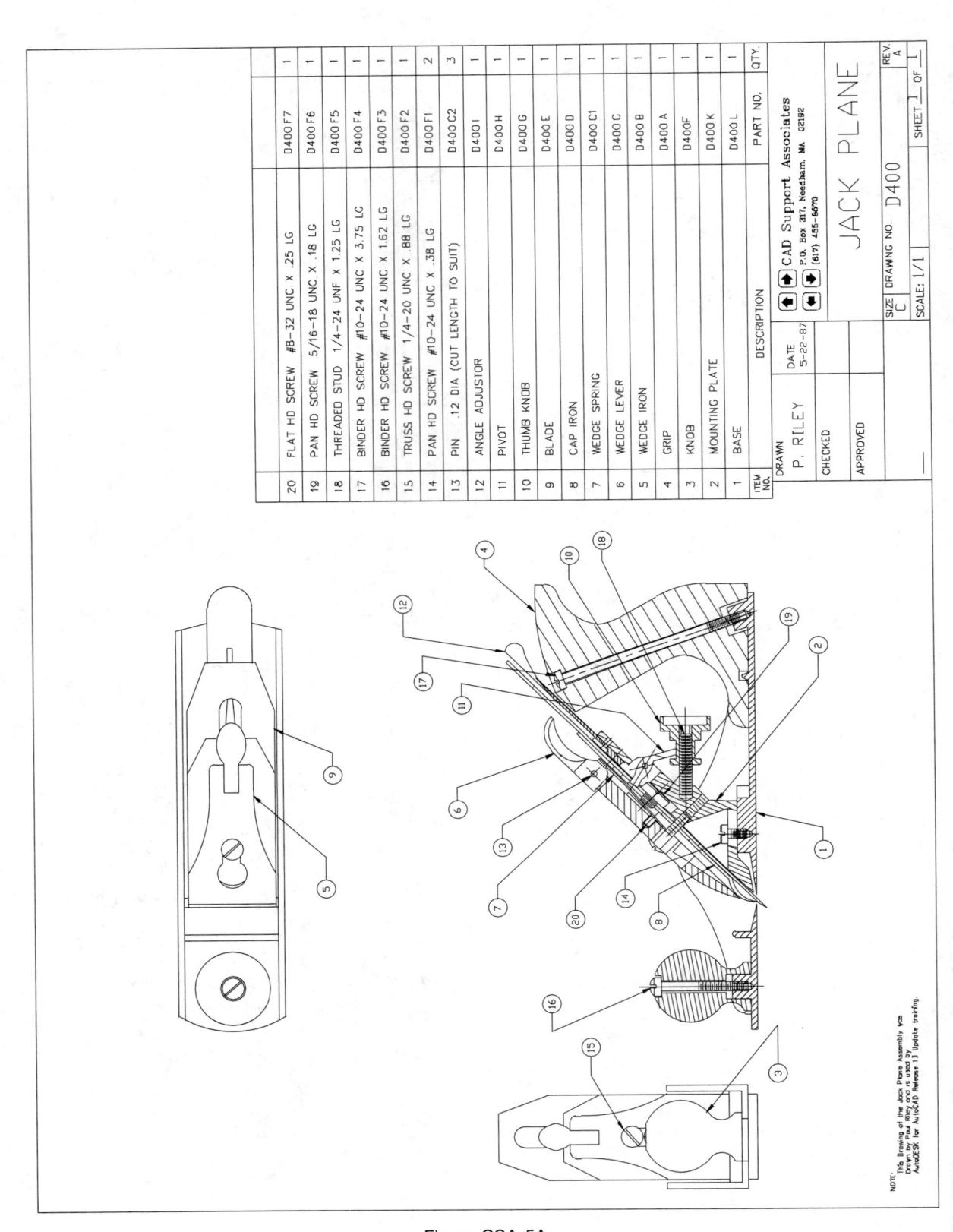

Figure CSA-5A

Appendix A

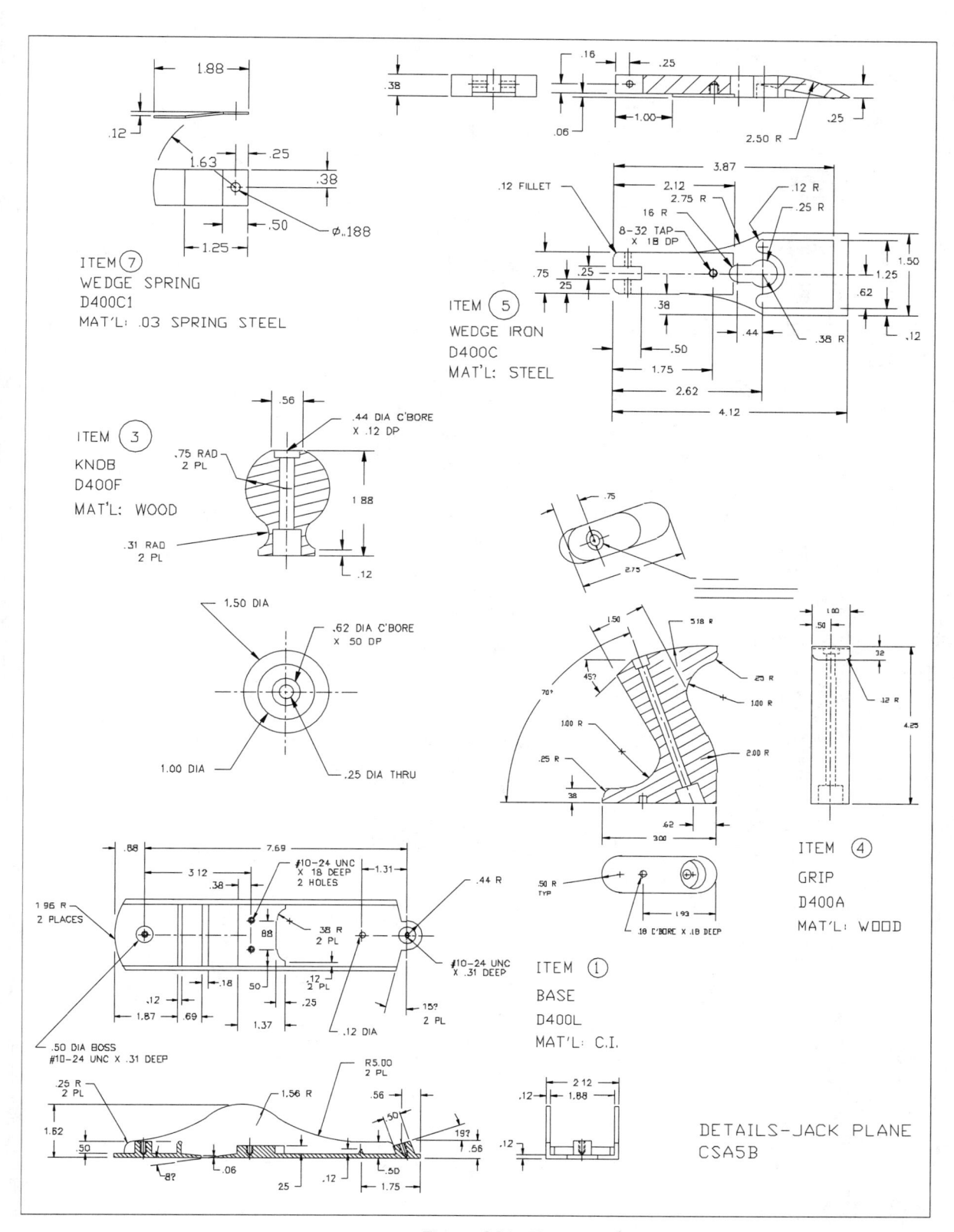

Figure CSA-5B

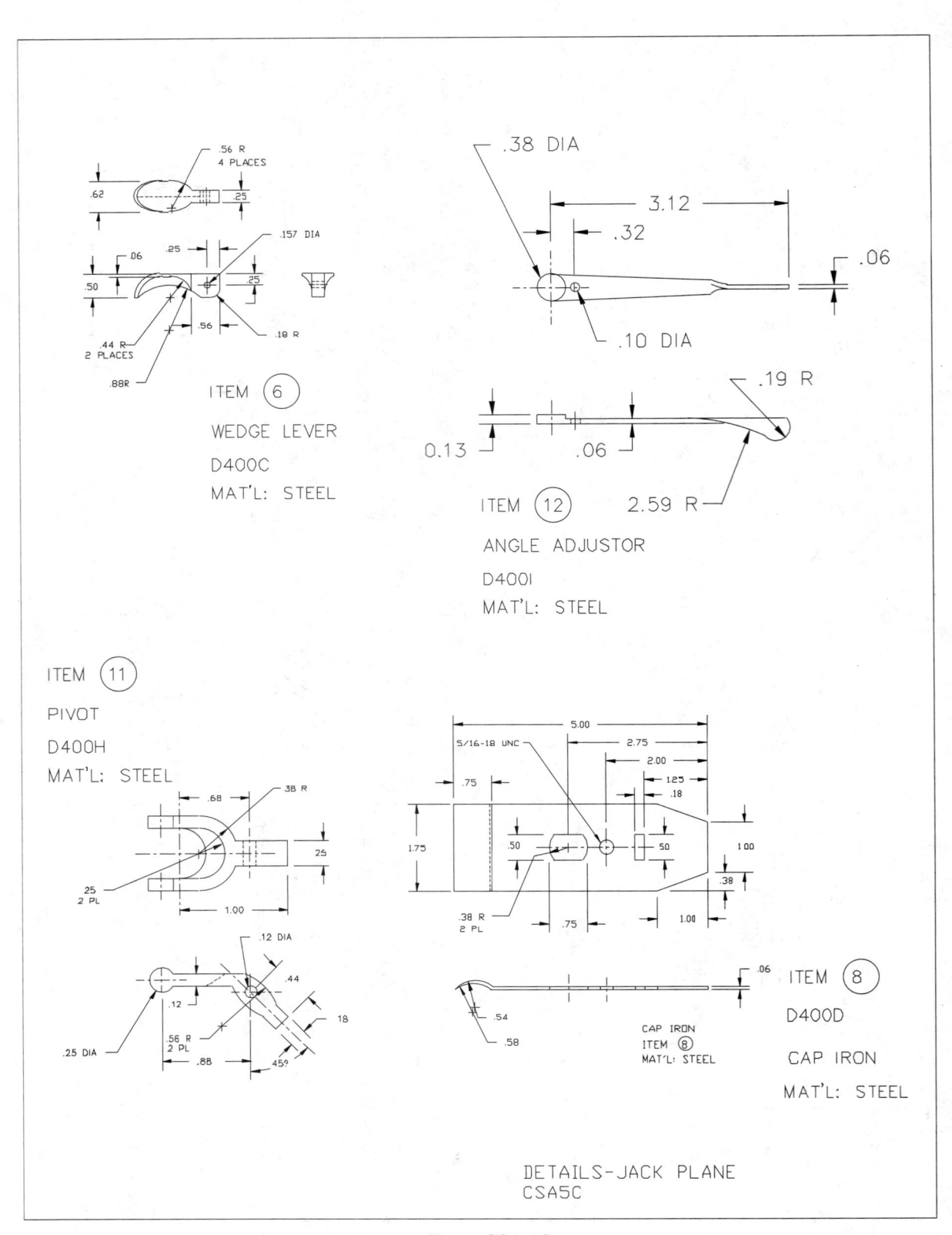

Figure CSA-5C

Appendix A

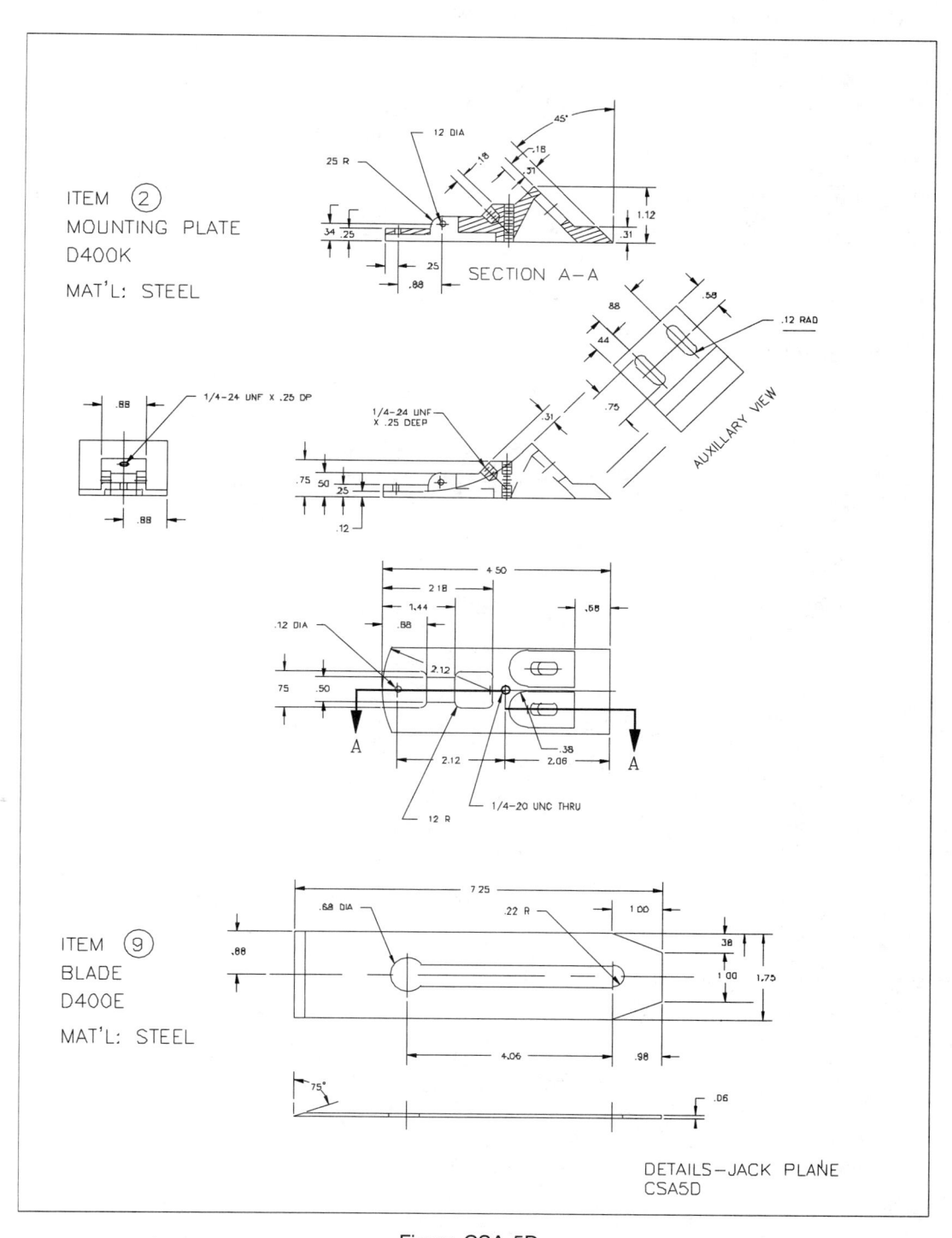

Figure CSA-5D

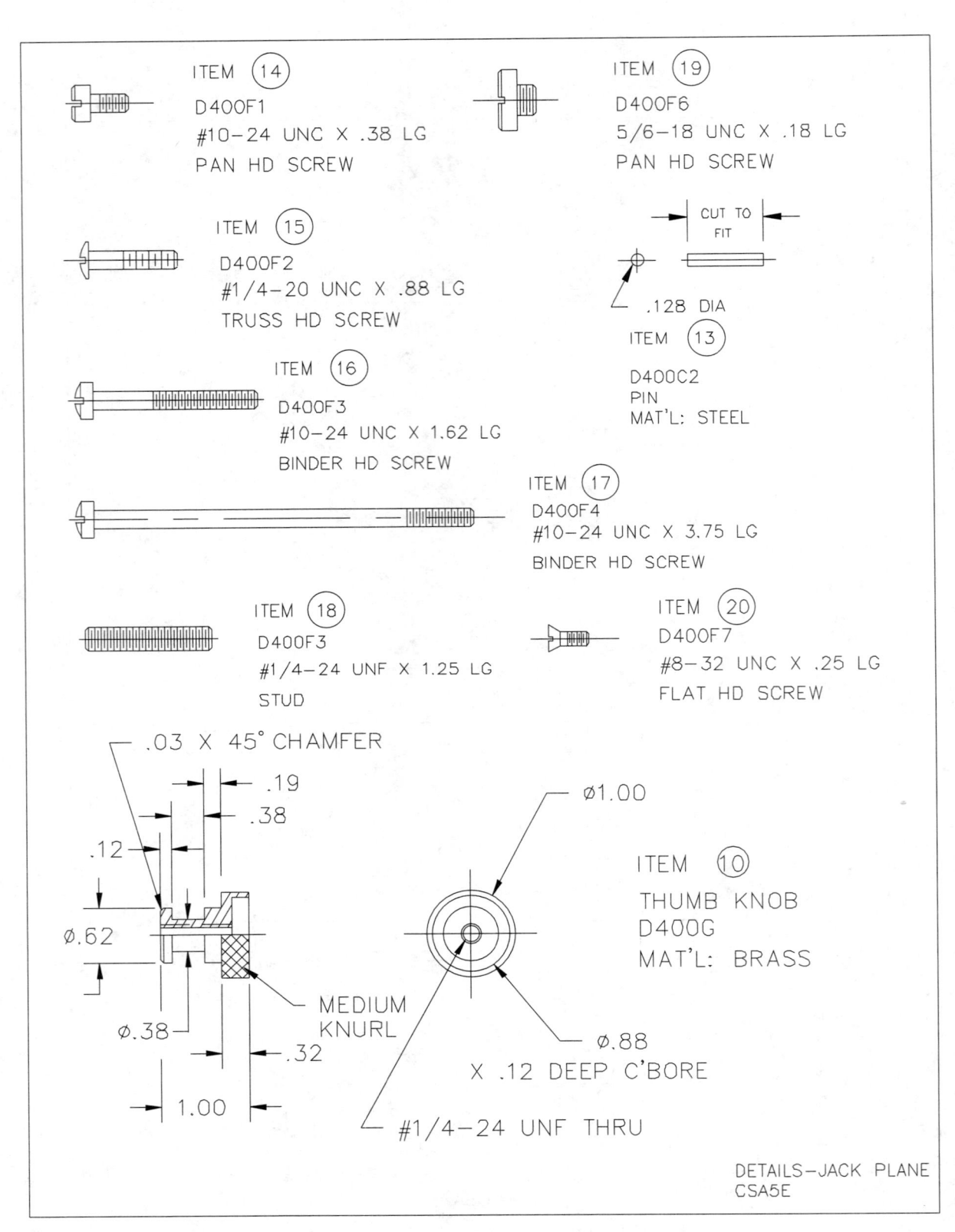

Figure CSA-5E

Appendix A

Figure CSA-6A

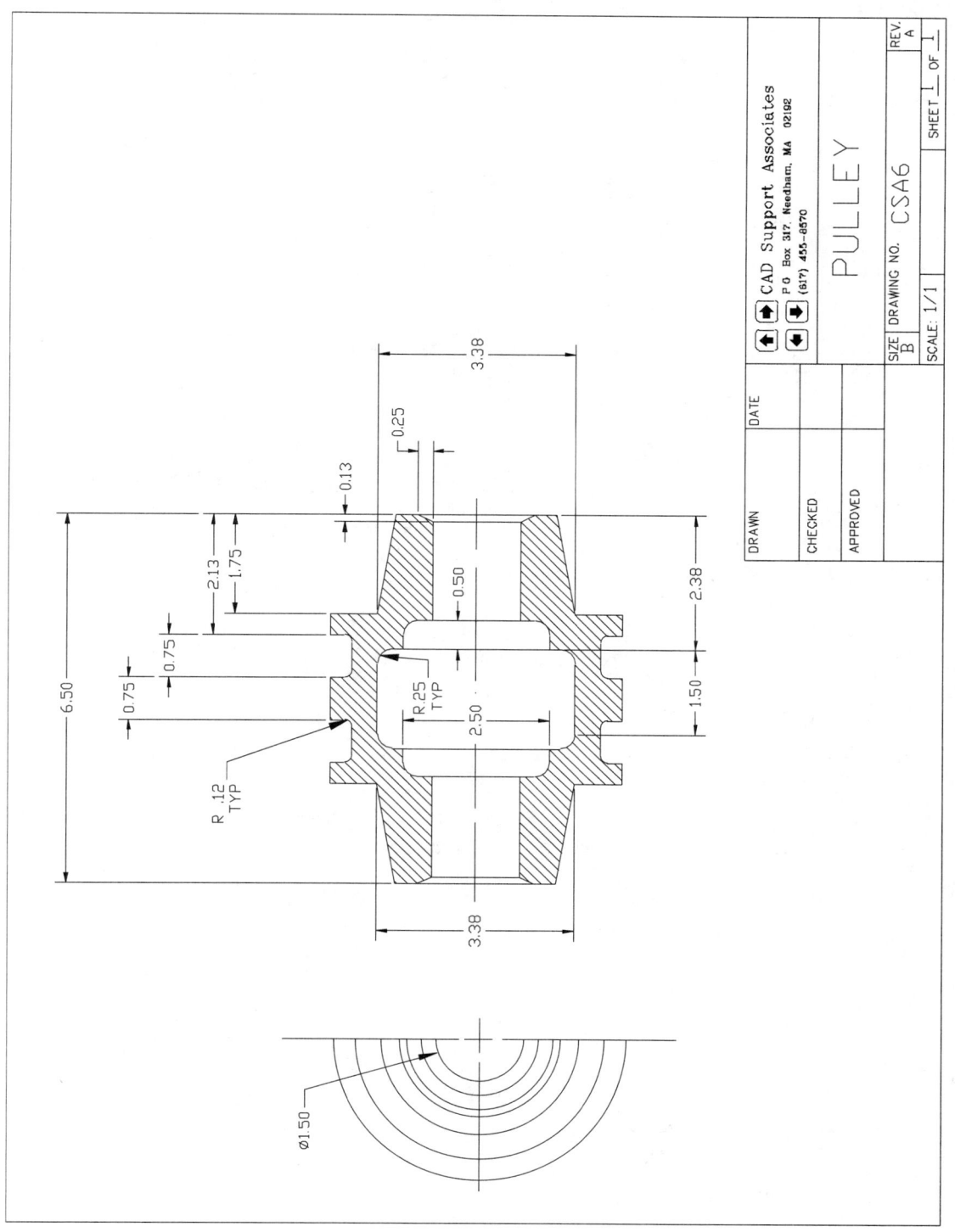

Figure CSA-6

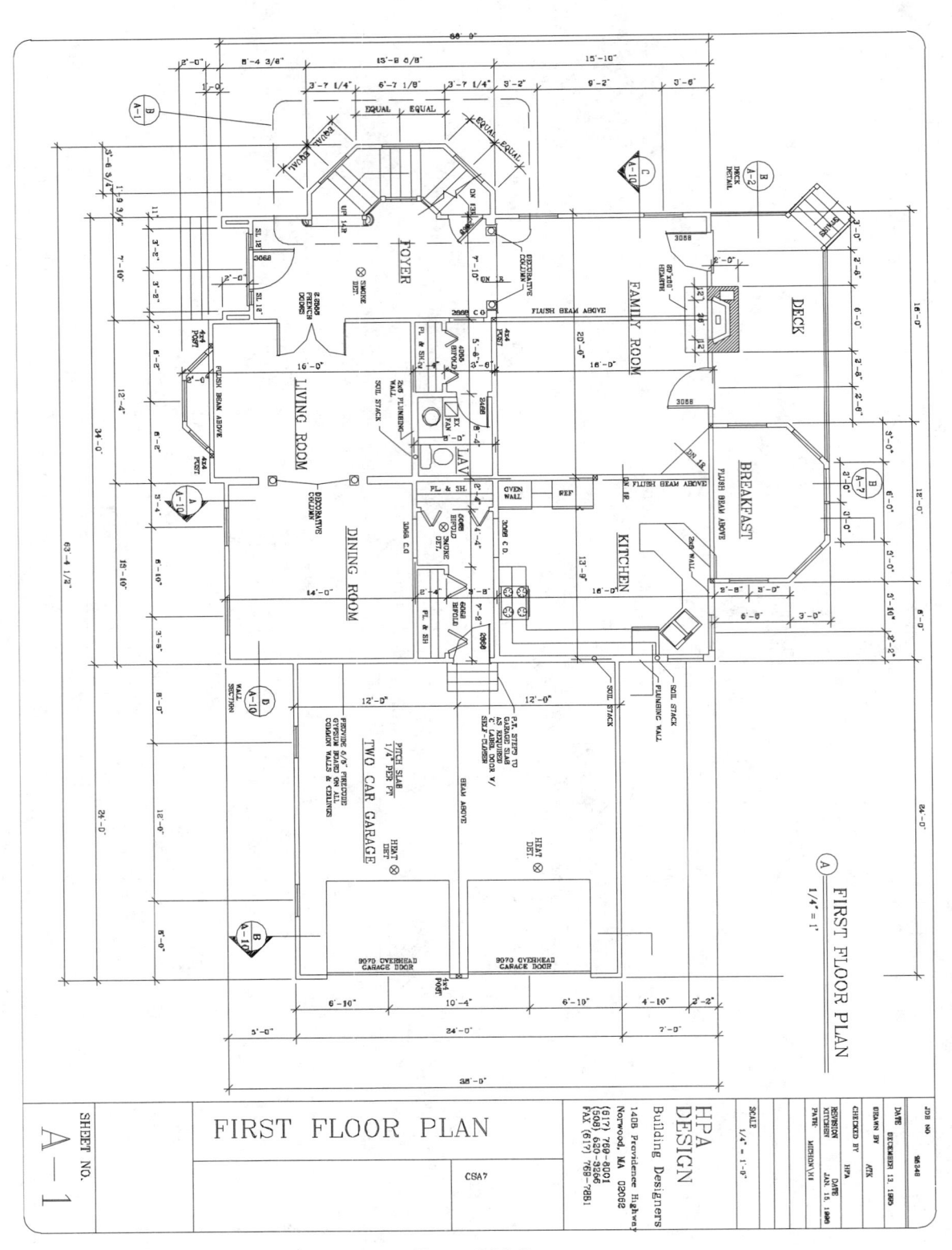

Figure CSA-7

Appendix A

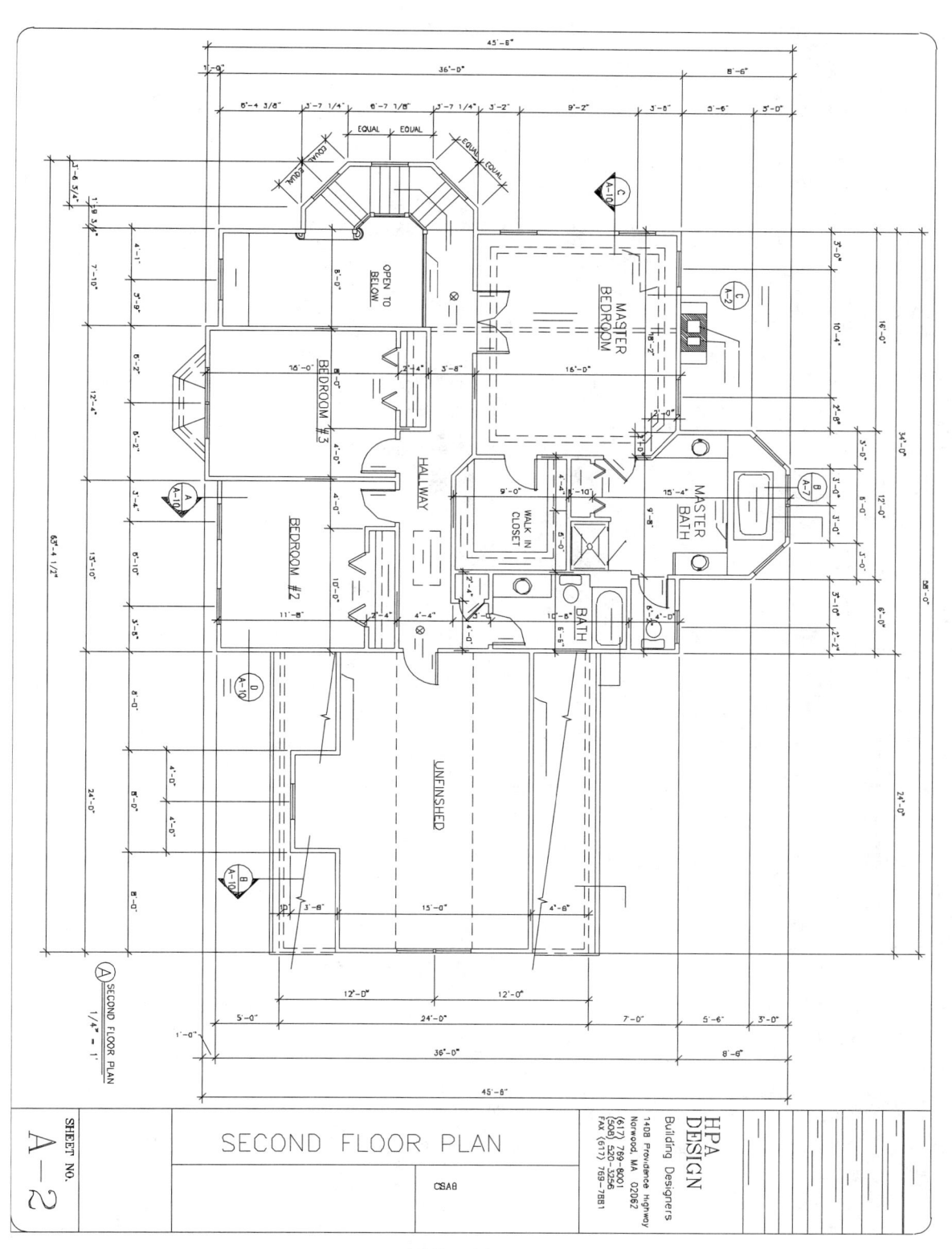

Figure CSA-8

Figure CSA-9

Appendix A

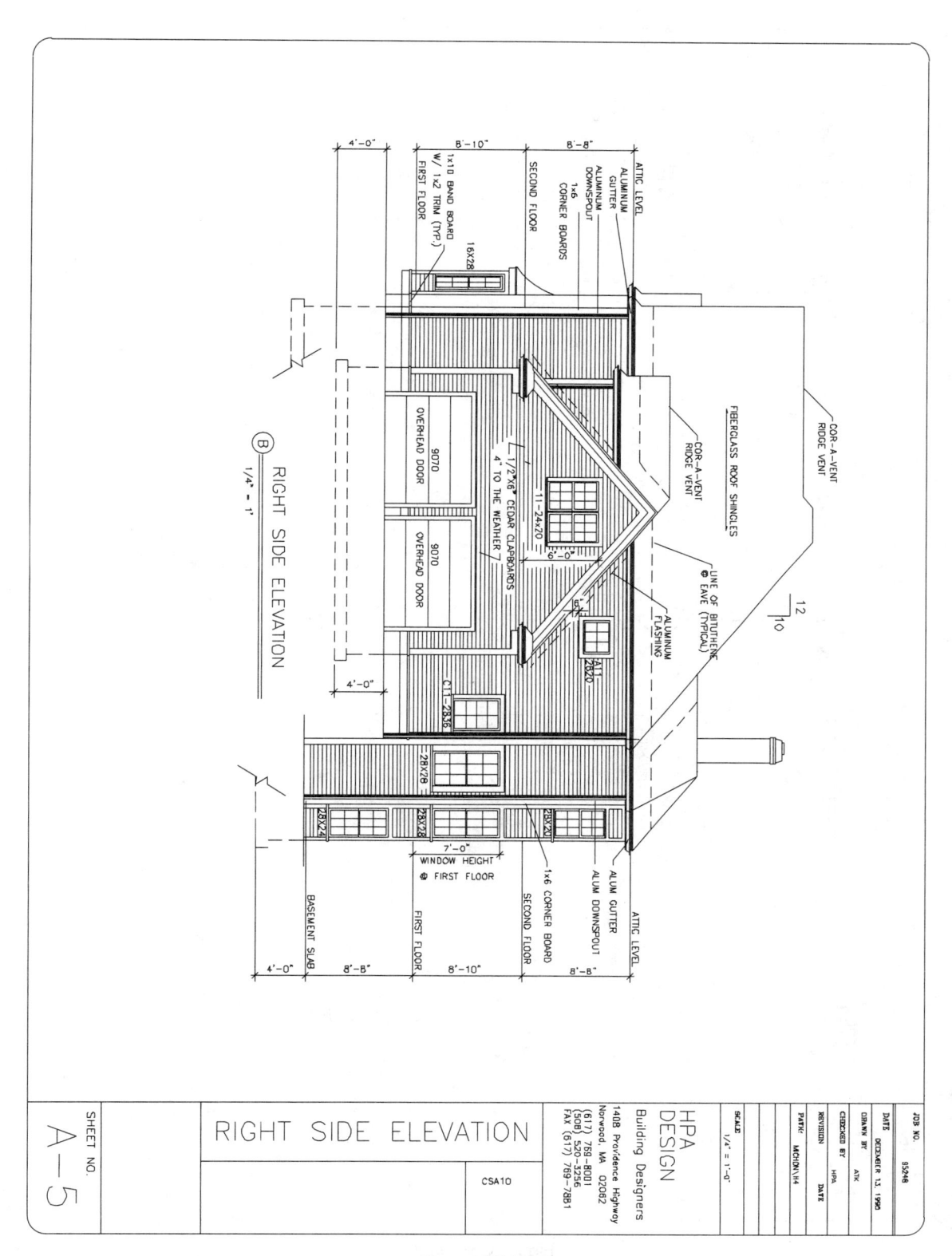

Figure CSA-10

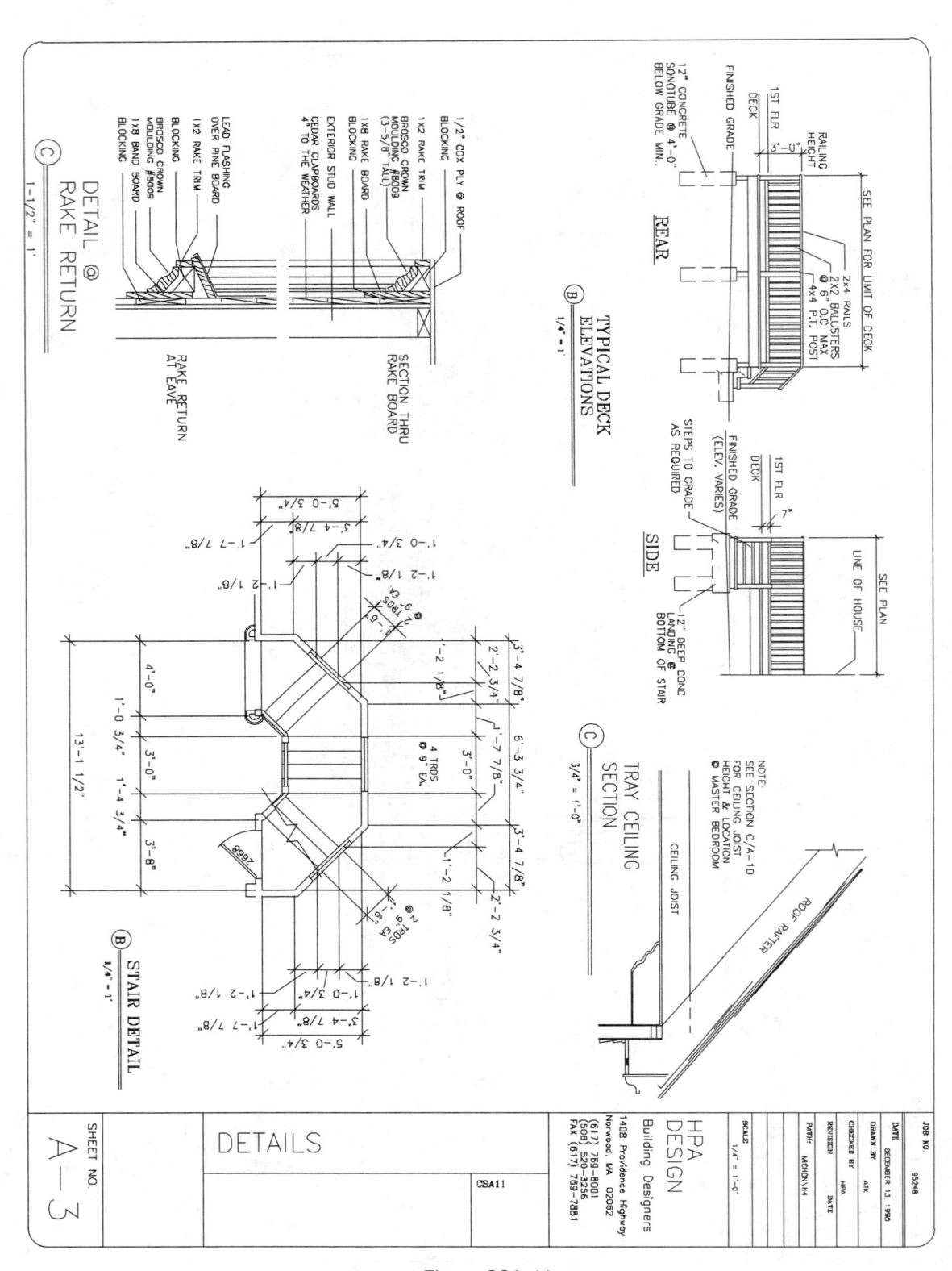

Figure CSA-11

Appendix A

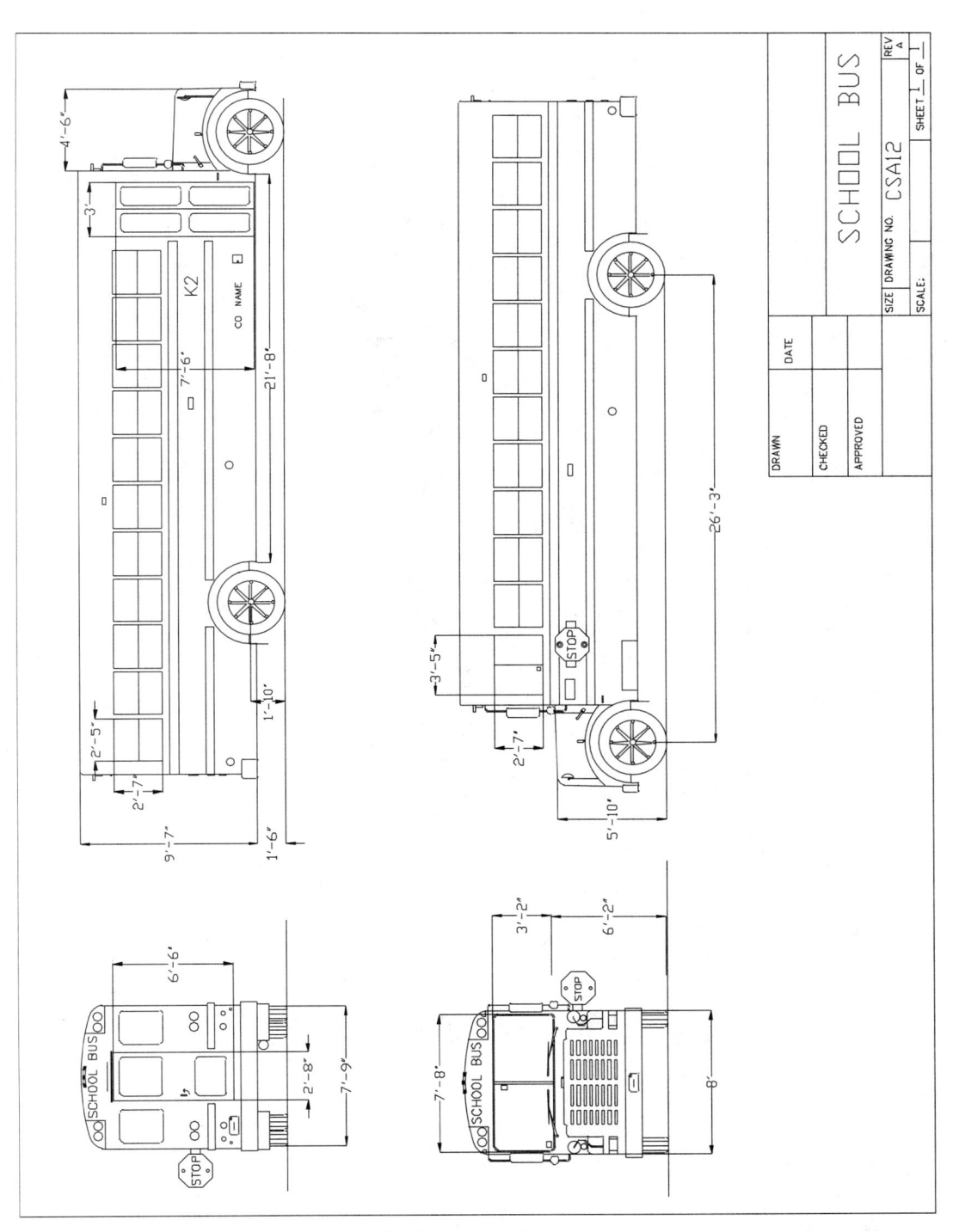

Figure CSA-12

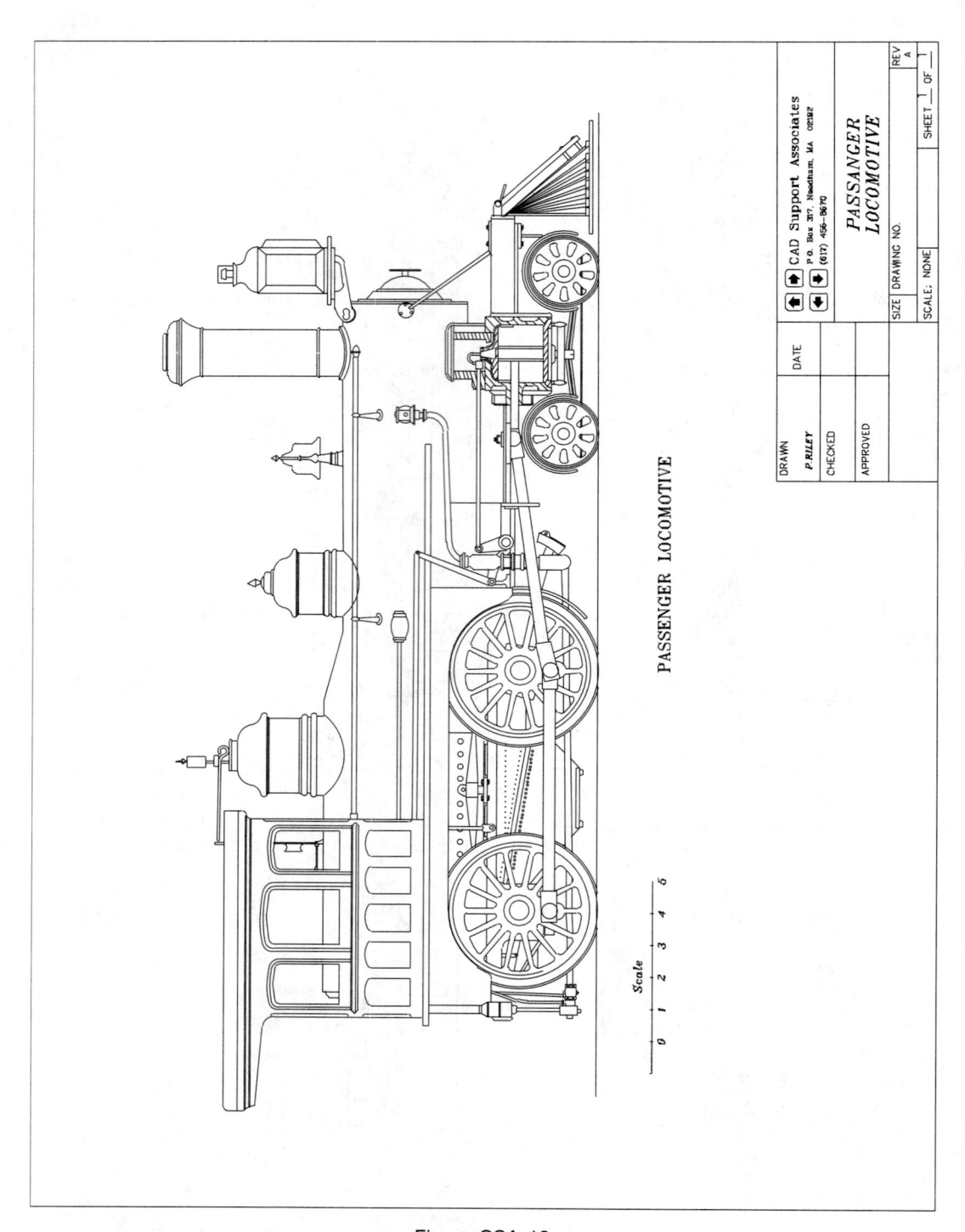

Figure CSA-13

APPENDIX B

Menus and Macros

When you begin to look below the surface of AutoCAD as it is configured straight out of the box, you will find a whole world of customization possibilities. This "open architecture," which allows you to create your own menus, commands, and automated routines, is one of the reasons for AutoCAD's success. It is characteristic of all AutoCAD releases and has made room for a vast network of third-party developers to create custom software products tailoring AutoCAD to the particular needs of various industries.

Over time, the options for customizing AutoCAD have grown and become more powerful. Many of the basics of menu structure, however, have not changed. The intention of this discussion is not to make you an AutoCAD developer, but to give you a taste of what is going on in the menu system. After reading this, you should have a sense of what an AutoCAD menu is and how it works. You should also understand that menu development is a complex subject. Before you attempt any menu development of your own you should make a thorough study of the *AutoCAD Customization Guide*.

True to form, AutoCAD provides several different ways to accomplish most customization tasks. A customized command sequence, for example, may result from a simple keyboard macro, an AutoLISP routine, a line of DIESEL string expression language, or a C language program connected to AutoCAD through ADS (AutoCAD Development System). We will confine our discussion to the organization of a menu file and the language of macros. These are easy to learn and require little programming background. AutoLISP, DIESEL, and C, on the other hand, are topics requiring a good deal of explanation and a knowledge of programming.

WHAT IS AN AUTOCAD MENU?

Most likely, every time you have begun a drawing in AutoCAD you have used either the AutoCAD standard menu or some other menu that is available on your system. This menu is what makes it possible for you to select commands off of a menu, tablet, or toolbar. Without a menu you are limited to typing commands.

Menu files have a standard format that AutoCAD can read, and standard extensions so that AutoCAD can recognize them. In the Windows version of Release 13, menu file extensions include .mnc, .mnl, .mnr, .mns, and .mnu files. For example, the AutoCAD standard menu is contained in a file called ACAD.mnc. This file is loaded when you begin a new drawing using the ACAD.dwg prototype or any other prototype drawing that was created using ACAD.mnc. The .mnc file is an executable file compiled in machine language. But there is also an ASCII version of ACAD.mnc called ACAD.mnu. ACAD.mnc was created by compiling ACAD.mnu into machine code. The importance of ACAD.mnu is that you can look at it with a word processor and revise it if you wish. Then, using the MENU command, you can compile it again with your changes included. .mnu files can be created in any word processing program or text editor and are easy to read and understand once you know the syntax.

As you know, you also make frequent changes in menu items directly in the drawing editor; hiding, showing, or moving toolbars, for example. These changes are retained in a new ASCII file with the same name as the .mnc and .mnu files, but with an .mns extension. Once an .mns file is created, it is continually updated and used in lieu of the .mnc file. To return to the original menu configuration, you must use the MENU command to compile a new .mnc from the original .mnu file.

There are also two files that are loaded along with the .mnc file. The .mnl file contains AutoLISP expressions that are referred to in the menu. The .mnr file contains bitmaps that are used in the menu.

Once you know the language you can create your own menu by modifying the ACAD files and giving the modified files a new name. You would make the changes to ACAD.mnu in any word processor or text editor with an ASCII format and give it a new name with a .mnu extension. To then load it into a drawing you would follow this procedure:

1. At the "Command:" prompt, type "menu".
2. Type your menu's name with no extension.
3. Wait...

AutoCAD will create the new .mnc, .mnl, .mnr, and .mns files and load them.

WHAT DOES A MENU LOOK LIKE?

If you go into whatever word processor or text editor you have available on your system and load the file ACAD.mnu (it usually will be located in a directory called \Acad\Win\Support) you will see the first page of the menu. Menu files are quite large and you will see only a small portion on your screen. The complete menu will be well over 100 pages long. A good way to learn about menus is to print out a few pages and study them, using the list of characters at the end of this appendix and the *AutoCAD Customization Guide*. Comparing menu lines with menu items in the drawing editor is also an essential exercise, as we will demonstrate in the next section.

Appendix B   **507**

HOW IS A MENU ORGANIZED?

Menus consist of sections for button menus, pull down menus, toolbars, tablets, the screen menu, and image tile menus. Each section type uses slightly different syntax, but there are certain generalizations that can be made. Take a look at this section from the Release 13 for Windows ACAD.mnu. It creates the File pull down menu, shown in *Figure A-1*.

```
***POP1
ID_File         [&File]
ID_New          [&New...\tCtrl+N]^C^C_new
ID_Open         [&Open...\tCtrl+O]^C^C_open
ID_Save         [&Save\tCtrl+S]^C^C_qsave
ID_Saveas       [Save &As...]^C^C_saveas
ID_SavR12       [Save R12 DW&G...]^C^C_saveasr12
                [--]
ID_Print        [&Print...\tCtrl+P]^C^C_plot
                [--]
ID_Import       [&Import...]^C^C^P_ai_3dsFiles;^P_import
ID_Export       [&Export...]^C^C_export
ID_Ioopts       [->Op&tions]
ID_Wmfopt       [WMF Op&tions...]^C^C_wmfopts
ID_Psqual       [PostScript &Quality]'_psquality
ID_Psdisp       [PostScript &Display]'_psdrag
                [--]
ID_Psprol       [<-&PostScript Prolog]'_psprolog
                [--]
ID_Mngt         [->&Management]
ID_Files        [&Utilities...]^C^C_files
ID_Audit        [&Audit]^C^C_audit
ID_Recov        [<-&Recover...]^C^C_recover
                [--]
ID_MRU          [Drawing History]
                [--]
ID_Exit         [E&xit]^C^C_quit
```

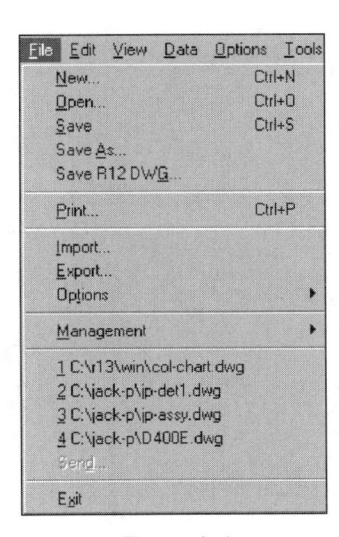

Figure A-1

Using this as an example we can make the following points about menu organization, and pull down menus in particular:

1. Menus are organized into lines. Each line is associated with a single item on a screen menu, an item on a pull down menu, a tool on a toolbar, or a box on a tablet menu. There are also single lines for helpstrings, cursor buttons, image tile menus, and user-defined accelerator key sequences.
2. The only lines that are not associated with specific menu items and functions are those added for organizational purposes. These include lines with asterisks, called section headers, and lines with double slashes (//), which are comment lines. In the POP1 menu section, for example, "***POP1" is a section header.

- 3-star headers like this one identify major sections including the button functions, the pull down menus, the screen menu, toolbars, image tile menus, and the four tablet areas. The pull down menus are identified as POP1-POP16. The standard menu only uses POP1-POP7. POP0 is the cursor menu, which contains Object Snap options.

- 2-star headers identify individual toolbars and submenus of the screen menu.

3. In Windows, menu items have name tags. In this example all of the labels beginning with ID are name tags. These name tags can be referenced elsewhere in the menu. One common use of the name tag is to call out "Helpstrings", the short phrases on the status line that describe what a particular menu selection will do. These phrases are defined in the ***HELPSTRING section of the menu.
4. For screen and pull down menu sections, the words written in brackets, such as [&File], control the labels that actually appear in the drawing editor.

    - For the pull down menus, the "&" character is placed before a letter that can be used as a keyboard alternative to selecting the item with the pointing device.
    - For the pull down menus, "\t" is the tab character. Observe, for example, the space between "New" and "Ctrl+N" in the figure in relation to the third line of the POP1 menu section.

5. The action taken by selecting the menu item is controlled by the macro that comes after the brackets. In the third line of this section, "^C^C_new" is the macro. This macro is discussed following.
6. The [--] lines create the line dividers in the pull down menu.
7. The lines between ID_Export and ID_Mgnt are the Options submenu. The line that calls the submenu is indicated by the characters "->", in this case, " [->Op&tions]". The last line of the submenu is indicated by "<-", in this case, "[<-&Postscript Prolog]".

WHAT IS A "MACRO"?

The ability to define macros is available in many software packages. Macros have the function of storing lengthy and frequently used sequences of keystrokes in a shorthand form. Much of AutoCAD's menu system depends on macros. In order to understand and create simple macros in this system there are a few items of syntax that you need to know. In the example above "^C^C_new" is the macro in the third line. Look at the line again:

    ID_New [&New...\tCtrl+N]^C^C_new

ID_New [&New...\tCtrl+N] These are the item name tag and the label that appears on the menu, as discussed previously.

^C^C This appears frequently in all menus. The "^" character is read by AutoCAD as the equivalent of the CTRL key on your keyboard. So, what you see here is the menu equivalent of typing CTRL-C (Cancel) twice. This ensures that any command in process is cancelled before another one is entered. Often two cancels are required to bring you all the way out of one command before you enter another.

_new This is the NEW command. Commands on the menu are typed exactly as they would be on the keyboard except that the _ is added as a flag identifying this as the English language command. This allows foreign language versions of AutoCAD to use menus developed in English.

Taken as a whole, then, this line does four things. First, it identifies the item and associates it with other related items. Second, it writes the lablel on the pull down menu, identifying Alt+N and Ctrl+N as keystroke alternatives to making the menu selection. Third, it cancels any command in progress. And fourth, it initiates the new command.

With this basic understanding, you should be able to make use of the list of macro characters included at the end of this appendix.

WHAT OTHER LANGUAGES CAN BE USED IN MENU DEVELOPMENT?

AutoCAD Release 13 allows you to create customized routines in three other languages in addition to the macro language presented here. AutoLISP is a programming language based on LISP. LISP is a "list processing" language. You will see AutoLISP statements in ACAD.mnu enclosed in parentheses.

DIESEL (Direct Interpretatively Evaluated String Expression Language) is a language that evaluates strings and returns string results. DIESEL borrows many of its terms from AutoLISP, and DIESEL expressions are also enclosed in parentheses. DIESEL expressions, however, are always proceeded by $. DIESEL is useful for such simple procedures as toggling the values of AutoCAD variables.

C language programs can be written and linked to AutoCAD through ADS, the AutoCAD Development System. ADS programs are read by the AutoLISP interpreter and then passed to AutoCAD as if they were AutoLISP. C is a high-level programming language. It has more power and is also significantly faster than AutoLISP. Programs written in C and run through ADS will run faster than AutoLISP programs.

In addition to these three languages, AutoCAD also includes a language for interface with database programs such as PARADOX or dBASE IV. This is called the AutoCAD SQL Extension (ASE). SQL stands for Structured Query Language.

HOW IS A TABLET CONFIGURED TO MATCH A MENU?

AutoCAD reads the tablet sections of a menu file in a particular way that must correspond to the configuration of the physical tablet overlay that is attached to the digitizer. In ACAD.mnu there are four tablet sections, each corresponding to an area on the tablet overlay. Each line of the menu file corresponds to a box on the overlay, and boxes are read from left to right, top to bottom, area by area. This means that there must be a way to tell AutoCAD how many rows and columns are contained in each tablet area. This is done using the TABLET command and the following procedure (the tablet overlay must be securely in place on your digitizer before you begin):

1. Type or select "TABLET".
2. Type or select "CFG" (configure).
3. Enter the number of tablet areas on your overlay.
4. Type "y" to indicate that you want to realign the tablet menu areas.
5. In response to AutoCAD's prompts, point to the upper left, lower right, and lower left corners of each tablet menu area. Be sure that you do this in the same order as the tablets are named in the .mnu file.
6. After the outline of each area is specified, also specify the number of columns and rows in that area.

510   Appendix B

For additional information on tablets see the *AutoCAD Customization Guide*.

The following table lists some macro characters you will find in any AutoCAD menu, along with their functions.

MOST COMMON AUTOCAD MACRO CHARACTERS
(IN ORDER OF APPEARANCE IN RELEASE 13 ACAD.MNU)

***	Major section header.
;	Same as pressing Enter while typing.
$	Begins any screen or pull down menu call, or a Diesel expression.
$pn=*	Pulls down the menu called for pull down area n.
^	CTRL
^C	CTRL-C
^C^C	Double cancel, cancels any command, ensures a return to the "Command:" prompt before a new command is issued.
***POPn	Section header, where n is a number between 1 and 16, identifying one of the 16 possible pull down menu areas, POP0 refers to the cursor menu.
[ ]	Brackets enclose text to be written directly to the screen or pull down menu area. Eight characters are printed on the screen menu. The size of menu items on the pull down menu varies.
[--]	Writes a blank line on a pull down menu.
_	English language flag.
'	Transparent command modifier.
->	Indicates the first item in a cascading menu.
<-	Indicates the last item in a cascading menu.
^P	Toggles menu echo off and on so that macro characters do not appear on the command line as they are being entered via the menu.
( )	Parentheses enclose AutoLISP and DIESEL expressions.
$S=	Calls a menu. If there is no menu name following the equal sign, the previous menu is called.
$M=	Introduces a DIESEL expression.
\	Pause for user input. Allows for keyboard entry, point selection, and object selection. Terminated by press of Enter or pick button.
~	Begins a pull down menu label that is "grayed out." May be used to indicate a function not presently in use.
*^C^C	This set of characters will cause the menu item to repeat.
space	A single blank space in the middle of a line is treated as a press of the Enter key.
$i=name	Calls an icon menu.
$i=*	Displays an icon menu.
+	Used at the end of a line to indicate that the menu item continues on the next line.

[handwritten annotation: Programming of ACAD Macro's]

APPENDIX C

Additional AutoCAD Commands

In order to make this text as clear, concise, and useful as possible, we have had to set some priorities about what to include. The following is a glossary of commands we have not discussed. Some are obsolete or seldom used, while some are very useful but only for a limited range of applications.

All commands that are marked with an apostrophe (') can be used transparently. That is, they can be executed while other commands are in process.

'ABOUT. Displays a dialogue box with the version of AutoCAD, the serial number, and other information.

AREA. Computes the area of a polygon, circle, or closed polyline entity.

AUDIT. Locates and diagnoses errors in the current drawing.

'BASE. Allows specification of a base insertion point for a complete drawing. If a base point has not been specified, (0,0,0) will be used.

BLIPMODE. When set to "off," blips are not shown.

COLOR. Sets color for subsequently drawn objects. Setting may be BYBLOCK or BYLAYER.

COMPILE. Compiles shape and font files so that they will load faster.

CONFIG. Allows configuration of video display, digitizer, plotter, and operating parameters.

COPYHIST. Copies text of command line history to the Windows clipboard.

COPYLINK. Copies the current view to the Windows clipboard so that it may be linked to other Windows applications using OLE (object linking and embedding).

CUTCLIP. Copies objects to the Windows clipboard, while removing them from the current drawing.

'DDGRIPS. Displays a dialogue box for enabling or disabling grips, and setting their colors.

'DDEMODES. When "on," makes a dialogue box available for setting current layer, color, linetype, elevation, and thickness (Release 9 or higher).

'DDLMODES. When "on," makes a dialogue box available for defining properties of individual layers.

DDRENAME. Displays a dialogue box for renaming text styles, layers, linetypes, blocks, views, User Coordinate Systems, viewport configurations, and dimension styles.

'DDRMODES. When "on," makes a dialogue box available for setting snap, grid, and axis.

'DDSELECT. Displays a dialogue box for setting entity selection modes, pickbox size, and entity sorting method.

DDUCS. Displays a dialogue box for defining, saving, and selecting User Coordinate Systems.

'DELAY. Used in script files, pauses for a specified period of time.

DIVIDE. Draws marker points at evenly spaced intervals along an object, dividing it into a specified number of parts. These points can be used as "nodes" for object snap.

DRAGMODE. When set to "A," allows dragging to occur automatically, without request, whenever possible. When "on," allows dragging by request only. When "off" inhibits all dragging.

DXBIN. Inserts a DXB format, binary coded, file into a drawing.

DXFIN. Loads a "DXF" format, drawing interchange file, into a drawing. DXF files are standard ASCII text files that can easily be processed by other programs.

DXFOUT. Creates a drawing file in DXF format.

ELEV. Sets elevation and thickness for subsequently drawn objects.

FILES. Allows access to the "File utility" menu from within the drawing editor.

'GRAPHSCR. Switches to the graphics screen. Used in script files in conjunction with TEXTSCR to switch between text and graphics.

HANDLES. Assigns a unique identification number to every entity in a drawing.

HATCHEDIT. Allows modification of associative hatching.

'ID. Displays *x*, *y*, and *z* coordinates of a selected point in the command area.

INTERFERE. Creates a composite solid from the interference of two or more solids.

LENGTHEN. Lengthens an object.

LOAD. Loads a file of shapes to be used by the SHAPE command.

MEASURE. Draws marker points at specified intervals along an object. These points can be used as "nodes" for object snap.

MENULOAD. In Windows, loads partial menu files to be used in conjunction with a base file, such as ACAD.mnu.

MENUUNLOAD. In Windows, unloads partial menu files.

MTPROP. Changes properties of MTEXT paragraph text.

OPEN. Displays a standard dialogue box file list of existing drawings. Selected drawing will be opened.

QTEXT. When "on," allows text to be written without displaying actual characters on the screen. Instead, the text area is outlined for faster regeneration. When desired, turn QTEXT "off" and perform a REGEN to replace outlined areas with actual text.

PFACE. Allows vertex-by-vertex construction of a 3D polygon mesh.

PSDRAG. When set to 0, shows only the bounding box of a postscript image file being brought into AutoCAD using the PSIN command. When set to 1 the actual image is visible for dragging into place.

PSFILL. Fills 2D polyline outlines with patterns contained in the postscript support file ACAD.psf.

Appendix C 513

PSIN. Allows importation of Encapsulated Postscript Files (.eps extension).

PSOUT. Allows exportation of the current drawing and view as an Encapsulated Postscript File.

PURGE. Deletes unused blocks, layers, text styles, linetypes, and dimension styles from the current drawing. Must be the first command executed when a drawing is opened.

RAY. Creates a theoretically infinite line beginning at a point and moving in one direction.

RECOVER. Attempts to recover damaged drawings.

REINIT. Allows reinitializing of ports, digitizer, display, plotter, and PCP file.

REDEFINE. Restores the definition of built-in AutoCAD commands that have been temporarily deleted using UNDEFINE.

REGENAUTO. When "off," inhibits automatic regenerations that occur as the result of certain commands.

RENAME. Allows user to change the names of layers, linetypes, blocks, views, text styles, User Coordinate Systems, viewport configurations, and dimension styles.

'RESUME. Used in script files, resumes execution of a script that has been interrupted.

RSCRIPT. Used in script files, repeats the script. Allows for continuous running of slide show presentations.

SCRIPT. Loads and executes a script file.

SELECT. Allows object selection to occur before entering other commands. Options are the same as those in most edit commands.

SH. Allows access to MS-DOS/PC-DOS commands while running AutoCAD. Requires less memory than SHELL.

SHAPE. Draws shapes that have been defined in the drawing database using the LOAD command.

SHELL. Allows access to operating system and utility programs while running AutoCAD. Available memory may restrict what programs can be run. Requires more memory than SH.

SPLINE. Creates a quadratic of cubic spline curve from the command prompt (instead of through the PLINE command).

'STATUS. Displays statistics and information about the current drawing on the text screen.

TABLET. Aligns tablet with paper for digitizing a drawing. Also allows tablet to be configured correctly for a tablet menu overlay.

'TEXTSCR. Switches to the text screen. Used in script files in conjunction with GRAPHSCR to switch between text and graphics.

'TIME. Displays current time and date, time and date current drawing was created, time and date of last update, time of current session in drawing editor, and elapsed time. Elapsed time is a timer function. To begin timing, it must first be set to "on."

TOLERANCE. Creates geometric tolerancing symbols and formats.

UNDEFINE. Temporarily deletes the definition of a built-in AutoCAD command. This allows the command name to be used for an alternate function defined in an AutoLISP program. *See* REDEFINE.

UNDO. Undoes multiple commands. UNDO is similar to "U", but it contains options to define a series of commands as a "group" that can be undone at once.

VIEWRES. Controls the precision with which arcs and circles are displayed prior to regeneration. The higher the resolution, the longer it takes to display objects. Resolution is based on the number of sides displayed in a "circle".

3D. Allows command line creation of 3D polygon mesh objects.

3DPOLY. Creates a 3D polyline with straight line segments only. There are no arc options in the 3DPOLY command.

XLINE. Creates a theoretically infinite straight line.

Index

2DPOLY, 459, 465
2D region, 461–62, 465
3D, 514
3D coordinates, 372–73
3D faces, 403–6
 invisible edges, 405–6, 408
3D objects, 415–17
3D polygon mesh, 386, 407–23
3DFACE, 405–7
3DMESH, 407, 419–23
3DPOLY, 459, 514

'ABOUT, 511
ACAD.cfg, 107–8
ACAD.dwg, 94, 506
ACAD.exe, 2, 95
ACAD.mnu, 506
ACAD.mnl, 506
ACAD.mnx, 506
ADS, 509
Alias, 11
AME, 444
APERTURE, 155
Apostrophe, 74, 511
ARC, 126–30
 chart, 127
AREA, 511
ARRAY, 104–7, 123–26, 366
 isometric, 366
 polar, 104, 123–26
 rectangular, 104–7
Arrow keys, 16
Ascii files, 506
ASE, 509
Assembly drawing, 336, 338
ATTDEF, 323

ATTDISP, 327–31
ATTEDIT, 326–32
ATTEXT, 331
Attributes, 312, 323–32
AUDIT, 511
AutoCAD
 customizing, 505–10
 foreign language versions, 508,
AutoCAD Command Reference, 36, 44, 70, 124, 419, 422
AutoCAD Customization Guide, 505–6, 510
AutoCAD Installation Guide for Windows, 4, 106
AutoCAD menu, 505–10
AutoCAD standard screen menu, 4, 8,
AutoCAD User's Guide, 257, 292
Autoediting, 39, 98–9
 See also grip editing
AutoLISP, 505, 509

'BASE, 333, 511
BHATCH, 252–57, 272
 advanced options, 256
 apply, 256
 boundaries, 252–57
 escher, 255–56
 ignore style, 254
 normal style, 254
 outer style, 254
 predefined, 255
 preview, 256
 user-defined, 255
Blip, 18–19, 30
BLIPMODE, 511
BLOCK, 315–21
Blocks, 315–21, 323–25, 331–33, 407,
 editing, 331–32

515

Blocks *(cont.)*
   insertion base points, 319
   insertion points, 317–20
Boolean operations, 445
   intersection, 445
   subtraction, 451–55
   union, 455, 448–49
Booles, George, 445
Box method, 360
BPOLY, 256
BREAK, 129, 157–60, 350, 358

C, 509
Cascading submenus, 5
Center Mark, 116, 239–40
CHAMFER, 65, 68–69, 283, 345–47, 455–58
CHANGE, 199, 202, 211–14
   change point, 213–14
   properties, 212, 216–18
Check Boxes, 30
CHPROP, 203, 206
CIRCLE, 34–37
   diameter, 34–36
   radius, 34
   2P, 37
   3P, 37
   TTR, 37
Clipboard, 321–23
Close, 18
COLOR, 511
Colors, 59–60
COMPILE, 511
CONFIG, 106, 511
Constuctive Solid Geometry, 445
Coordinate display, 8
Coordinates, 8, 15–16
   absolute, 15–16
   polar, 15–16
   relative, 16
      @, 16, 159
   3D, 372–74
COPY, 96, 99–102, 345–46, 372
   multiple, 100
COPYCLIP, 321–23
Cross hairs, 4–5, 14, 343–45
CTRL-E, 343–45
CTRL-G, 6
Cursor, 4
Curve approximation, 423
Cutaway view, 464–65
CUTCLIP, 322–23

dBASE IV, 509
DBLIST, 333
DDATTDEF, 323–26
DDATTE, 326–31
DDATTEXT, 331
DDCHPROP, 199, 202
DDEDIT, 199–202
DDEMODES, 210, 511
DDGRIPS, 511
DDIM, 227–30
DDINSERT, 317–20
DDLMODES, 511
DDMODIFY, 201–5

DDOSNAP, 154
DDPTYPE, 299
DDRENAME, 511
DDRMODES, 30–31, 512
DDSELECT, 512
DDUCS, 512
DDUNITS, 32
DDVIEW, 353
DELAY, 292, 512
Dialogue boxes, 3, 11, 30–34
   check boxes, 30
   edit boxes, 31
   ellipsis, 30
   help, 30
   lists, 33
   moving, 34
   radio buttons, 33
DIESEL, 509
DIMALIGNED, 231, 233–34
DIMANGULAR, 231, 236–39
DIMBASELINE, 234–36
DIMCONTINUE, 234, 236
DIMEDIT, 232, 251
Dimension variables, 247–51
   chart, 250
   dimaso, 250
   dimasz, 250
   dimcen, 116, 250
   dimexo, 250
   dimscale, 249, 250
   dimsho, 250
   dimtix, 250
   dimtxt, 250, 260
Dimensions, 26, 57, 227–51
   aligned, 231
   angular, 236–39
   annotation, 228–29
   arcs, 239–41
   baseline, 234–36
   center marks, 116, 250
   circles, 234–36
   continued, 234, 36
   diameter, 240–41
   editing, 241–42, 251
   horizontal, 230–34
   leaders, 242–45
   linear, 230–34
   moving text, 241–42
   ordinate, 245–47
   radius, 240–41
   scaling, 257–60
   status, 249
   styles, 227–30
   3D, 392
   variables, 247–51
   vertical, 230–34
Dimension Style dialogue box, 228, 249
DIMOVERRIDE, 247–51
DIMSTYLE, 227–30, 247–48
Directories, 95
DIST, 44–45, 54
DIVIDE, 512
DIMLINEAR, 230–34
DIMTEDIT, 230–34
DONUT, 279–80

Index

DRAGMODE, 512
Drawing aids, 30–31,
Drawing editor, 2–10
Drives, 20, 95
DTEXT, 189–97
DVIEW, 388, 428–35
   camera, 431–33
   clip, 434–35
   distance, 433
   hide, 435
   pan, 430–31
   perspective, 433
   target, 431–33
   zoom, 430–31
DXBIN, 5120
DXFIN, 512
DXFOUT, 512

EDGESURF, 411–13
ELEVATION (ELEV), 450–51, 512
ELLIPSE, 348–53
   isocircles, 348–50
   orthographic, 350–53
Enter key, 16, 24
ERASE, 37–44, 350
EXPLODE, 331–32, 336, 416
EXTEND, 163–65
Extents, 108, 428
External references, 320–21
Extract files, 331
EXTRUDE, 459–61

F-keys, 3–10
   F2, 4
   F6, 8
   F7, 8
   F8, 9, 16–17
   F9, 9
FILES, 512
FILL, 280–81
FILLET, 65–68, 283, 385–88
   3D, 385–88, 458
   trim mode, 68
FILMROLL, 511
Floating Viewports, 173
Floating Model Space, 171–72
Floppy disk, 20
Fonts, 206–211
   roman duplex, 209
   txt, 207

GRAPHSCR, 512
GRID, 8, 31
   isometric, 343
Grip editing, 39, 4548, 452, 454
   base point, 132
   copy, 101–2, 222
   mirror, 135–36
   move, 98–99
   offset snap, 222
   rotate, 131–32, 180
   scale, 216–17
   stretch, 167–68
GROUP, 178, 313–15

HANDLES, 512
HATCH, 252
HATCHEDIT, 512
Hatching, 252–57, 272
   see also BHATCH
HELP, 30
HIDE, 108, 406–7, 417
Highlight, 30

ID, 512
INSERT, 321–25
INTERFERE, 512
Isocircles, 348
Isolines, 454
Isometric drawing, 343–353
ISOPLANE, 343–45

Keyboard, 10–11

Layer 0, 58
Layer Control dialogue box, 57–64, 260–61
Layers, 57–64, 260–61, 404, 407
   colors, 59–60
   current layer, 62–63
   freeze, 63, 261
   linetypes, 60–62
   in multiple viewports, 260–61
   lock, 63
   new freeze, 261
   off, 63
   on, 63
   reset, 261
   thaw, 63, 261
   unlock, 63
LAYER, 63
LENGTHEN, 512
LIMITS, 8, 91–93, 428
LINE, 10–18
Linetypes, 60–62
   loading, 61
LISP, 509
LIST, 333
LOAD, 512
Lotus 1–2–3, 331
LTSCALE, 80

Macros, 505–10
   characters, 510
MEASURE, 512
Menus, 505–10
MINSERT, 333, 336
MIRROR, 132–35, 334
MIRRTEXT, 334
MLEDIT, 298–99
MLINE, 292–99
MLSTYLE, 294–98
mnl files, 505
mnu files, 505
mnx files, 505
Model space, 9, 91, 258–62
MOVE, 95–98, 372
MS-DOS, 513
MSLIDE, 291–92
MTEXT, 189, 197–99, 201–4, 244
   attach options, 204

MTPROP, 512
Multiline styles, 294–98
Multiple viewports, 74–77, 168–74, 257–62
    aligning, 426–28
    plotting, 168–74
MULTIPLE, 69
MVIEW, 168–74
MVSETUP, 426–28, 336
    align option, 426

Named objects, 321
NEW, 2–3, 94
Non-tiled viewports, 74
Noun/verb selection method, 38–40

Object selection, 18, 38–44
    add, 43
    all, 41, 43
    chart, 41
    cpolygon, 41, 43
    crossing, 41, 165–66
    fence, 41, 43
    group, 41, 43
    last, 41, 42
    previous, 41, 42–43
    remove, 41, 43
    window, 18, 40–41
    wpolygon, 41, 43
Object snap, 151–57, 299, 374
    chart, 156
    running mode, 154–57, 374,
    single point, 151–53
Offset snap, 374, 379, 380, 382
OFFSET, 287–89
OOPS, 40
OPEN, 20–21, 512
Ortho, 9, 16–17
OSNAP, 154–57
    chart, 156

Page down key, 18
Page up key, 18
PAN, 72–74
Paper orientation, 136–39,
Paper size, 91–93, 137–38
    chart, 92
Paper space, 9, 91, 169–74, 257–60
Paper space icon, 170
Paradox, 509
PC-DOS, 513
Pcp files, 106
PEDIT, 282, 286–287, 408, 421–23
    chart, 288
Pen parameters, 107
Perspective views, 433
PFACE, 512
Pickbox, 152
PICKSTYLE, 315
Pixels, 155
PLAN, 435
Plan view, 380
PLINE, 281–87, 459
    arcs, 284–86
    chart, 288
    close, 282–83
    direction, 285
    halfwidth, 285
    straight lines, 281–84
    width, 285
PLOT, 45–47
Plot configuration, 45–47, 77–79, 105–8, 136–39
Plot preview, 71–79
Plotters, 106–7
Plotting, 45–49, 77–79, 105–8, 136–39,
    scale, 138–39
    to a file, 108
Plt files, 108
POINT, 299–300
Point filters, 373–74
POLYGON, 277–79
Polylines, 277–87, 423
    chart, 288
    editing, 286–87
Pop down lists, 33–34
Preferences, 64
Preset viewpoints, 370–72
Printers, 106–7
Prototype, 3, 94–95
PSDRAG, 5120
PSFILL, 512
PSIN, 512
PSOUT, 512
Pull down menu, 5–6, 11
PURGE, 64, 333, 512

QTEXT, 512

Radio Buttons, 33
RAY, 512
RECOVER, 512
RECTANG, 54, 277
REDEFINE, 513
REDO, 16, 22
REDRAW, 18–19
REDRAWALL, 410
REGEN, 86
REGENALL, 173
REGENAUTO, 513
Regeneration, 86
Region, 461–62
REINIT, 511
RENAME, 513
RENDER, 467–80
    LIGHT, 471–77
    material, 478–80
    MATLIB, 478–80
    RMAT, 478–80
    SCENE, 477–78
Render window, 469–70
RESUME, 292, 513
REVOLVE, 459, 462–63
REVSURF, 413–15, 436, 459, 462–63
ROTATE, 129–32, 180
RSCRIPT, 292, 513
Rubber band, 14, 128–29
RULESURF, 385–88, 392, 410–11, 416, 422

SAVE, 19
SAVEAS, 19
SCALE, 214–17
    reference, 216
Screen, 3–10

Index

text window, 4
Screen menu, 12, 64–65
SCRIPT, 292, 513
SECTION, 464–66
SELECT, 513
SH, 513
SHADE, 466–68
   SHADEDGE, 467–68
   SHADEDIF, 467–68
SHAPE, 513
Sheet size, 91–93
   chart, 92
SHELL, 513
Shift key, 222
SKETCH, 300–301
SLICE, 464–65
Slides, 291–92
SNAP, 9, 29–31, 343–44
   isometric, 343
Solid modeling, 445–66
   BOX, 446–47, 450
   CYLINDER, 453,
   EXTRUDE, 459–61
   INTERSECT, 445–46
   REVOLVE, 459, 462–63
   SECTION, 465–66
   SLICE, 464–65
   SUBTRTACT, 445–46, 451–55
   UNION, 445, 448–49
   WEDGE, 447–48
SOLID, 289–91
Space bar, 16
SPELL, 205–6
Splframe, 406, 423
Spline, 423, 513
Spline curve, 423
Splinesegs, 423
SQL, 509
Status bar, 4
STATUS, 513
STRETCH, 165–68, 448
STYLE, 206–11
Surface approximation, 418–23
   bezier, 422
   cubic, 422
   quadratic, 422
Surface modeling, 401–23
System variables,
   aperture, 157
   mirrtext, 334
   pickbox, 152
   snapang, 366
   splframe, 423
   splinesegs, 423
   surftab1, 392, 409–10
   surftab2, 4112–13
   surftype, 418
   surfu, 422
   surfv, 422

Tablet menu, 13, 509
TABLET, 513
TABSURF, 408–10
TEXT, 189. *See also* DTEXT, Fonts, STYLE
   angled, 196–97
   chart, 195
   editing, 198–204
   fixed height, 207
   fonts, 206–11
   justification options, 192–204
   special characters, 196–97
   styles, 206–11
Text Window, 4
TEXTSCR, 513
Thickness, 450–51
Tiled viewports, 74–77, 401–3, 418, 470
Tilemode, 168–70
TIME, 513
TOLERANCE, 513
Toolbars, 4–7, 11–12, 36
TORUS, 416–17
Transparent commands, 73–74, 511
TRIM, 129, 161–63, 349–50, 380, 382

U, 16, 22, 104–5
UCS, 9–10, 224, 369–85
   chart, 372
   origin, 224, 378
   rotation, 378–82
   3 point, 377–78
   view, 392
UCSICON, 9–10, 369, 375–76, 383
UNDEFINE, 513
Underline character, 74, 511
UNDO, 16, 513
Unit cell, 103
UNITS, 8, 32–34, 230
Units control dialogue box, 33–34, 230
User coordinate system icon, 9–10, 375–76, 372
User coordinate systems, 9–10, 369–85

Verb/Noun selection method, 38–39
VIEW, 353–55, 433, 435
Viewports, 74–77, 260–262
   borders, 262
VIEWRES, 513
VPLAYER, 260–62
   vpvisdflt, 261
   newfrz, 261
VPOINT, 370–72, 388–91, 428, 435
   compass and axes, 390–91
   rotation, 389–90
   3D coordinate, 388–89
VPORTS, 74–77, 401–3, 418, 470
VSLIDE, 291–92

WBLOCK, 317, 333, 407
Wire frame modeling, 369–88
World coordinate system (WCS), 370, 372, 375, 430

XBIND, 321
XLINE, 513
XREF, 320–21

ZOOM, 70–72
   all, 71–72,
   center, 172
   dynamic, 355–57
   previous, 71
   scale (x), 371
   window, 70–71
   XP, 172, 257